THE GREAT TRANSFORMATION

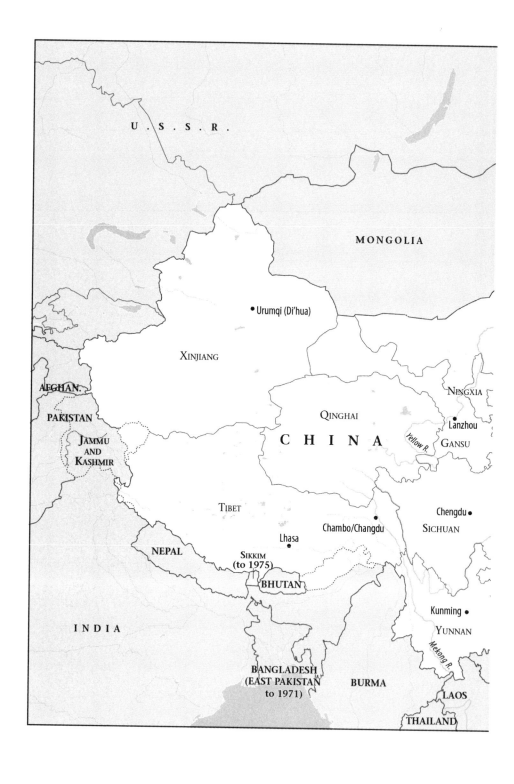

U . S . S . R .

MONGOLIA

• Urumqi (Di'hua)

XINJIANG

NINGXIA

AFGHAN.

PAKISTAN

QINGHAI

Lanzhou •

JAMMU
AND
KASHMIR

C H I N A

Yellow R.

GANSU

Chengdu •

TIBET

Chambo/Changdu •

SICHUAN

Lhasa •

NEPAL

SIKKIM
(to 1975)

BHUTAN

Kunming •

YUNNAN

INDIA

BANGLADESH
(EAST PAKISTAN
to 1971)

BURMA

Mekong R.

LAOS

THAILAND

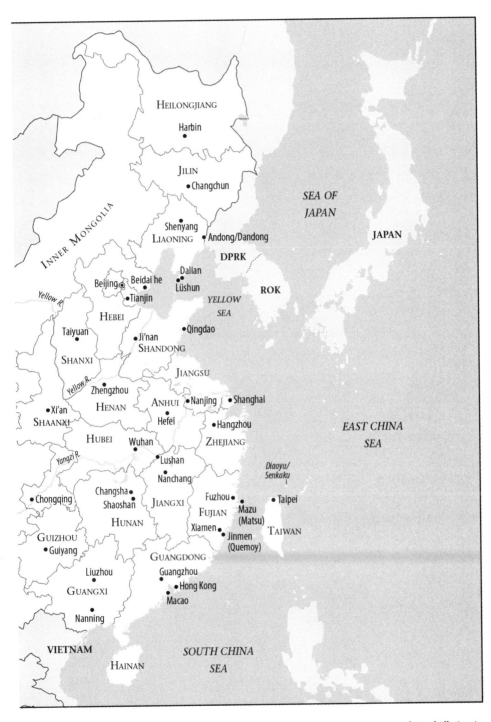

People's Republic of China. Drawn by Isabelle Lewis.

ODD ARNE WESTAD AND CHEN JIAN

The Great Transformation

CHINA'S ROAD FROM REVOLUTION TO REFORM

Yale

UNIVERSITY PRESS

NEW HAVEN AND LONDON

Published with assistance from the Kingsley Trust Association Publication
Fund established by the Scroll and Key Society of Yale College and with
assistance from the foundation established in memory of James Wesley
Cooper of the Class of 1865, Yale College.

Yale University Press books may be purchased in quantity for
educational, business, or promotional use. For information, please e-mail
sales.press@yale.edu (U.S. office) or sales@yaleup.co.uk (U.K. office).

Set in Scala type by Westchester Publishing Services.

Printed in the United States of America.

Library of Congress Control Number: 2024932150

ISBN 978-0-300-26708-2 (hardcover: alk. paper)

A catalogue record for this book is available from the British Library.

This paper meets the requirements of ANSI/NISO Z39.48-1992
(Permanence of Paper).

10 9 8 7 6 5 4 3 2 1

CONTENTS

CONTENTS

ACKNOWLEDGMENTS

OUR TITLE, AS WILL BE RECOGNIZED BY MANY, is borrowed from the work of the great Austro-Hungarian social philosopher Karl Polanyi. In *The Great Transformation: The Political and Economic Origins of Our Time*, published in 1944, Polanyi argues that all economic systems are shaped by society, culture, and politics. This is also true for markets and capital. They did not appear by themselves in Europe in the nineteenth century, as a result of some form of unavoidable economic logic, but were products of a set of historical contingencies. Therefore, Polanyi says, markets are neither necessary nor inevitable, and to understand them we have to understand the specific conditions under which they were created.

This book is an attempt to understand the way in which politics and society combined with markets and capital to produce China's great transformation, the journey from Maoist socialism in the 1960s to incipient capitalism in the 1980s. A great number of scholars, officials, journalists, businesspeople, and ordinary Chinese have helped us better understand this journey, through sharing sources and through public and private discussions. We cannot thank all of them here, in part because China's new turn toward authoritarianism sometimes makes it risky to identify sources who live or work in the PRC. When we began conceptualizing this book in the early 2010s, when China had a more liberal political climate, we hoped to include more archival research, including in private collections, and more quotes from conversations and interviews. That is not possible today. It is therefore a different book from what we first envisaged, but still one, we hope, that will be of use both to ordinary readers and to China scholars.

We would specifically like to thank Jovan Cavoski, Frank Dikötter, Chen Donglin, Niall Ferguson, Han Gang, Nancy Hearst, Denise Ho, Paul Kennedy, William Kirby, Li Danhui, Michael Meng, Niu Dayong, Niu Jun, Niu Ke, Rana Mitter, Sergey Radchenko, Tony Saich, Shen Zhihua, Michael Szonyi, Joseph Torigian, Wang Haiguang, Xiao Donglian, and Zhang Baijia. These scholars all helped at various stages of the writing of this book. So did the late, great, and much missed Harvard scholars of China, Roderick MacFarquhar and Ezra Vogel.

We would also like to thank our research assistants, Yang Chenyue, Han Junyi, and Zhang Yike (at Yale), Noah Lachs (in London), Hu Jiayun, Wang Yiling, and Cai Lechang (at NYU-Shanghai), and the Yale administrative assistants Sarah Masotta and Enit Colon.

At the Wylie Agency, Sarah Chalfant is a literary agent extraordinaire, for this as for so many other projects. And at Yale University Press we have greatly enjoyed working with Jaya Chatterjee and Amanda Gerstenfeld.

When writing the conclusion to his book, Polanyi was preoccupied with the fallacy, in his view, of the belief that markets by themselves produce greater freedom. On the one hand, he recognized that "the individual must be free to follow his conscience without fear of the powers that happen to be entrusted with administrative tasks." On the other, he pleaded for us to see "freedom not as an appurtenance of privilege, tainted at the source, but as a prescriptive right extending far beyond the narrow confines of the political sphere into the intimate organization of society itself." China's great transformation delivered economic freedom to the strong, capable, and well connected. It is still to be determined whether it will deliver freedom as a right to all Chinese.

THE GREAT TRANSFORMATION

Introduction

ON THURSDAY, SEPTEMBER 9, 1976, shortly after midnight, Mao Zedong died. It was at the end of a fine day, bright and clear, as early autumn days in Beijing often are. The sun had beaten down on the vast expanses of Tiananmen Square, and travelers who had come to visit the heart of the capital remember the day as being quite hot, but with a sudden chill in the evening. Mao's body lay in a makeshift emergency room that had been set up in Building 202 at Zhongnanhai, the leadership compound in central Beijing, just across from the house with his beloved swimming pool where the chairman of the Chinese Communist Party (CCP) had spent his final years. His staff had interpreted him as saying that he did not want to be moved out of the high-security compound. And the chairman's words were law. Even those who worked with him daily and observed the gradual decline of his physical faculties viewed him as almost a god. He was the creator of New China and the Communist Party that ruled it. His will could not be tested, even in matters of his own life and death.[1]

Mao's physical decline had started several years before his demise at the age of 82. Already in 1971 the chairman had been diagnosed with emphysema and congestive heart disease. Three years later his progressive muscle weakness led doctors to presume that he had Lou Gehrig's disease, an incurable degenerative illness that also gradually affected Mao's speech and his ability to swallow food. During his last few months he increasingly had to be fed through a nasogastric tube and breathe with the help of oxygen.[2] Mentally alert at most times up to his final, fatal heart attack on September 2, 1976, the chairman was not optimistic about the future. After his death there would be a counter-revolutionary rebellion, he prophesied. "The world is in confusion," he told one of his last foreign visitors, and the will of the people would not prevail.[3] Knowing how all-powerful he had been in China, the chairman liked to mock his own achievements, though it is hard not to notice a tone of despair beneath the old Mao's cynicism and self-depreciation. "I have only been able to change a few places in the vicinity of Beijing," he told U.S. president Richard Nixon in February 1972.[4]

The jockeying for future power in China had begun well before the chairman's passing, although with Mao still alive, all pretenders had to move with great caution. Aspire to too much power and Mao would turn against you, even from his sickbed, sometimes with fatal results. Now, with the chairman's body pumped full of formaldehyde and locked in an airtight coffin, there were no such concerns. Everyone who descended on Mao's residence in Zhongnanhai that night knew that a power struggle was coming. They also knew that new directions were needed for a country that had come to a standstill. In the early 1970s it had seemed as if all that China was doing was to wait. Now, with the first generation of China's Communist leaders passing from the scene, it seemed as if the wait might be over—though nobody could tell which direction the new leaders would take the country in, or even who these new leaders would be.

The changes that took place during the "long 1970s" transformed China and, eventually, the world. This is a book about the first steps in that process: about how China went from being a dirt-poor, terrorized society in the late 1960s to one of hope and expectation by the mid-1980s. It is about radical political change at the top, but also about how people from all walks of life broke free from the assumptions that had governed their lives before and during Mao's Cultural Revolution. It is the story of revolutionary change, in directions that almost no foreigners and very few Chinese could imagine when it all started. And, while laying out this rapid process of change, the book also attempts to explain how the earliest era of China's reform and opening to the world laid the foundation for one of the most sustained and durable periods of economic growth we have seen in modern times.

Not all of this is a story of victorious progress. It is also a story about how the Chinese Communists kept the political dictatorship in place, and about how dreams of social equality and justice were defeated. It is a story about how women and young people were marginalized and, ultimately, about how urban areas triumphed over rural ones in the wake of what most people had seen, back in the 1930s and 1940s, as a peasant revolution. China's market revolt had losers as well as winners. Even though the vast majority of Chinese welcomed the end of Maoist hunger, terror, and chaos, some regretted the political turn to the Right, and for many others the wait to have their share of China's wealth is ongoing even today. We argue that the great transformation of the 1970s changed China for the better. But, within all the progress that has been made toward a richer and freer China, we recognize that many problems remain unresolved, not least in political terms. The Communist Party's turn toward more repressive methods in the mid-2010s is just one example of these remaining challenges.

Neither is this mainly, or even primarily, a story of change from above, about how CCP elites through reforming themselves created progress for everyone else. A key part of this book is an account of how much of China's reform and opening came from below and was carried out by ordinary people who rebelled against the earlier system in order to save themselves and their families. It is a story of economic and social revolution by Chinese who had had enough of dead-end political campaigns and lethal millenarian dreams. They themselves initiated the big changes that took place, both before and especially after political permission was given from the top. Much of China's 1970s is a tale of how social, economic, and intellectual activism interacted with high politics to remake the country in unforeseen ways.

Finally, this is a story that deals with the international as well as the domestic. As both authors have argued before, history in a country as large as China is never purely internal; it always includes people who arrive from many parts of the world as well as those who travel or relocate to other regions and continents.[5] China's road from revolution to reform is full of unlikely characters: Overseas Chinese capitalists, American engineers, Japanese professors, and German designers all played a role, together with thousands of others who arrived as China gradually opened itself to the world. Layered on top of this was China's newfound security relationship with the United States, set up by Mao Zedong in the early 1970s to protect his country and his revolution against what he considered a deadly threat from the Soviet Union. Mao never intended that working with the Americans to outplay the

Soviets strategically and diplomatically should influence China's domestic directions. On the contrary, he felt—at least for a while—that U.S. leaders were foolish to support his "real" revolution against the fake Communists in Moscow. Little did he foresee the profound influence on Chinese society that the links with the United States would have after he had departed from the scene.

It is important to note that none of these interlinked stories had one necessary or even likely outcome. Everywhere you look in late twentieth-century China there is a great deal of contingency. Given the fluidity of the overall situation, domestically and internationally, it would not have taken much for very different results to occur. The political struggle after Mao's death, for instance, could have ended very differently. There were many radically contrasting groups in play, all with their constituencies and their individual chiefs. The emergence of Deng Xiaoping as overall leader by the end of the decade was in no way given, especially since Deng had already been purged twice from the CCP leadership by Mao himself.

Even if the past did not determine outcomes in the history we are looking at (or any other history, for that matter), there is no doubt that what happened was in many ways conditioned by the past. One big question, at least to us, is why China did not return to a strictly centralized planned economy as a result of the political changes in 1976. After all, it was the quest for such state-centered collectivist economic solutions to China's ills that had inspired the very creation of the CCP in the 1920s and had driven its political priorities up to Mao's sudden detour toward more dispersed and local solutions in the 1960s. There are three possible explanations at the outset: One is the ongoing conflict with the Soviet Union, which made it harder for China to return to a system that would look much like what the Soviets had established. Another is a sense, shared by many Chinese leaders of vastly different political orientations, that strict economic planning had not delivered enough growth for China back in the 1950s, and, equally importantly, that such systems were not delivering fast growth now in other socialist countries, especially in the many postcolonial states in Asia and Africa that had adopted Soviet planning principles after independence. The third is the mix of inspiration and fear that the encounter with the West and with Japan led to among some of the very few Chinese who had access to foreigners and foreign travel after the sudden thawing of Sino-American relations in the early 1970s. Going from self-imposed isolation to trickles of contact with the outside world convinced some Chinese in the know that their country was falling further and further behind. It made them, in equal amounts, fearful and impatient about the future, and more willing to take risks to overcome the obstacles that held China back.

In all of this there are strong parallels with earlier reform periods in Chinese history. At a number of occasions in the past—from the early Tang Empire in the seventh century to the late Qing and Republican eras—China had seen many eras of intense and unexpected change, very often brought on by the realization that even well-known truths would have to be looked at again or the integrity and capacity of the state would be threatened. Not all such reform attempts have succeeded, but they do show the preoccupation with the state and its functions that has been a hallmark of Chinese history for a very long time. Even in a period of astonishing liberalization like the one this book considers, there is at the core a significant elite project of rescuing the state by finding new sources for growth and development. From an elite perspective, at least, there is a conservative and state-centered aspect to Chinese reform that one should never lose track of from the 1970s up to today.

Even though this book argues that all of China's "long 1970s," from the late 1960s to the mid-1980s, ought to be seen as one integrated era in Chinese history, it is still an era of many parts. In Chinese Communist historiography, the first eight years or so, from 1968 to 1976, belong to the Cultural Revolution, which according to the official Party verdict ran from May 1966 to October 1976 and "was responsible for the most severe setback and the heaviest losses suffered by the Party, the state and the people since the founding of the People's Republic."[6] But this chronology obscures as much as it reveals. The most intense phase of Cultural Revolution turmoil was over by 1968, and at least by 1973, if not earlier, there were many new trends and tendencies that point forward to the reform era.[7] All of this begs the question about the relationship between the Cultural Revolution (whichever way you define it) and the era that followed. It is easy to conclude that the latter was a reaction against the former (which it undoubtedly was, at least in part). But was the reform era, and the changes that led to it, also conditioned by the Cultural Revolution in different ways? A minority of historians argue that the economic and social changes of the Cultural Revolution years are underestimated or at least misrepresented.[8] They point to economic growth in some sectors, diversification, increased social and geographical mobility, and more equal conditions for women and young people. Others see the Cultural Revolution as a massive, but historically necessary, work of destruction, in which "Old China," lingering since the late nineteenth century, finally died, leaving room for a completely new direction in Chinese history—including the breakthrough of integrated markets on a grand scale and new links with global capitalism.[9] The latter position, at least if one argues for unintended consequences, may have some truth to it, though its claims do rather remind us of the old Polish joke that Communism is the longest possible road from capitalism to capitalism.

The implications of the more recent views, that China's economic transformation is intimately linked with overall global changes, is also one of the issues raised in this book. During the long 1970s the world economic order went through a dramatic reorientation. The postwar system of fixed exchange rates, capital controls, and strict banking regulations was replaced with currency fluctuations, capital flows, and internationalized finance. This transformation, which would be crucial for China's future, happened mainly because the United States had lost some of its leading position in economic terms and wanted to regain it by revising the way the global economy worked. The result was that global flows of foreign investment increased five times over the course of the 1970s and world trade more than doubled. New bank lending to developing countries increased roughly fifty times. By the end of the decade, changes that the United States had initiated to strengthen its own position had resulted in a level of economic globalization that the world had not seen since before World War I. While Americans, at least in the decades that followed, benefited from these changes, they unintentionally also provided exceptional opportunities for access to capital in countries on the periphery of the global capitalist system, in Asia and elsewhere. It seemed as if capitalism had gained a new future, while countries that had opted out of the capitalist system—the Soviets, Eastern Europeans, Chinese, and socialist countries in the Third World—were stagnating. China's new leaders in the late 1970s saw this very clearly, and they acted to make their country benefit from the new opportunities.[10]

There are many other aspects of China's long 1970s transformation: environmental, intellectual, and educational, as well as dramatic changes in the workplace, in gender relations, in the military, and in the country's overall strategic position. By the mid-1980s many Chinese already saw the contours of a different country, even though most of the sensational changes that have made China a global superpower were still in the future. The worlds of ordinary Chinese changed only incrementally, as did their material position. The average income per capita when our story starts in the 1960s was about $100. In 1985 it had reached nearly $300.[11] But, even so, by the mid-1980s large numbers of Chinese sensed that the country had set out on a new path in which there were opportunities for families that were willing to take risks and work hard in order to break through to wealth and status. It may have been just the early rumblings of a new world. But some Chinese heard them loud and clear and set out to benefit from them, for themselves, their communities, and their country. This book is first and foremost their story, in victory, in defeat, but first and foremost in never-ending transformation.

1

To the Cultural Revolution

TODAY'S WUHAN, A CITY OF TWELVE MILLION PEOPLE on the Yangzi River in central China, is a hotspot for the country's economic development.[1] It is a freewheeling hub of growth, where events sometimes spin out of control, as with the initial outburst of the COVID pandemic in 2019. But half a century before that, it was not money or public health but politics that was all the rage in Wuhan. The city was the stage for some of the most ferocious battles of the Great Proletarian Cultural Revolution, the campaign that Chairman Mao Zedong launched in the summer of 1966 to remake China and transform the Chinese people's hearts and minds. Following the chairman's slogans and instructions, students and workers organized themselves into revolutionary organizations for what they saw as promoting the Cultural Revolution and defending Mao's thinking and his supreme leadership. As the months went by into 1967, especially in the wake of the January Revolution in Shanghai—during which revolutionary rebels seized political power in that gigantic city—rivalries among these new rebel groups all over China intensified. Almost everywhere, young people were joining opposing factions. Each one accused the others of being Rightists, counter-revolutionaries, capitalist roaders, and "black hands" who hatched devilish secret plans to oppose Chairman Mao and destroy Communism in China.[2]

In Wuhan most of these groups gradually coalesced into two rival blocs: One Million Heroes, composed mainly of junior Communist cadre, skilled factory workers, and student activists; and Wuhan Workers General Headquarters, led by younger and more radical students and militants from workers' rebel organizations who opposed the Party and trade union bosses. Each paraded up and down the main streets calling for blood to clean the city of revisionists and denouncing both local and central Communist leaders by name. Both outfits got access to light weapons, first, and then to machine guns, flame-throwers, and, on some occasions, artillery, which they used to attack strongholds of the opposing bloc inside factories, schools, and public buildings, all the while chanting slogans from Mao's Little Red Book: "Monsters shall be destroyed"; "It is justified to rebel"; "If you do not hit it, it will not fall."[3]

The destruction was immense, and the chaos that ensued was so great that it caught the attention of Chairman Mao himself.[4] In mid-July, he secretly arrived at Wuhan to observe and prepare for a grand entry, personally declaring the great unity of revolutionary forces in the city. But Mao's scheme ended abruptly a few days later, with the chairman having to be whisked out of Wuhan on a military aircraft, one of the few times in his life when he went anywhere by air. Mao wanted to rescue himself from danger as members of One Million Heroes invaded the plush guesthouses where he was staying.[5] Violent fighting in Wuhan continued. Thousands were killed, and almost ten times as many were injured before some semblance of order was restored by the brutal intervention, approved by the chairman, of regular units from the People's Liberation Army (PLA).

The Cultural Revolution—or at least its peak years between 1966 and 1968—was a period of enormous devastation and violence. The memory of those times has been used by all leaders in China after Mao to symbolize the epitome of chaos and political futility. "We shall never allow such mistakes to be repeated," said Deng Xiaoping when he was in power.[6] Xi Zhongxun, the father of China's later president Xi Jinping and himself a victim of persecution, put it even more starkly. In rebutting Mao's claim of the Cultural Revolution being "seventy percent good and thirty percent bad," the senior Xi said: "No, not a single percentage of it was good."[7] China's early reform period, which we depict in this book, is often construed as the antithesis of the Cultural Revolution: Where the Cultural Revolution brought stagnation, the new era brought progress. Where Cultural Revolution brought turmoil, the new era brought stability. Where the Cultural Revolution brought uncertainty, the new era brought confidence.

Reality was of course much more complicated than that. The Cultural Revolution created both the political and social dysfunction that those who succeeded Mao tried to move away from *and* the jolt that enabled them to take actions so radical and profound for Communists that they turned most former beliefs upside down. The campaigns of the 1960s symbolized transformation as well as defeat. But their upheavals also had deeper and more lasting social effects in China than what any of today's Communist leaders would be willing to admit. And the disruption of the late 1960s had deeper roots, both in the Communist period and in what had gone before it.

In the context of China's dramatic struggles with modernity, it is not surprising at all that the Cultural Revolution is regarded by so many as a nadir of the country's troubles. But all of China's history since the mid-nineteenth century has been a tumultuous one. First, there were almost two generations of foreign wars and civil wars. Then, in 1911, came the collapse of the Qing Empire and the beginning of a Chinese republic, though it was a republic with several competing centers of power and continuously burdened by crises, wars, and revolutions. In the 1930s the Japanese imperial army invaded China, ending in an all-out war that the young Chinese republic barely survived. After 1945 China rapidly descended into another civil war, from which the Communists emerged victorious in 1949. This Communist victory on the battlefields brought about the birth of a new China, or, as the Communists have named it, China's "liberation."

But China's tempestuous times did not end there. When the chairman of the Chinese Communist Party, Mao Zedong, in 1949 announced the establishment of the People's Republic of China (PRC), he declared that "We, the Chinese, have stood up."[8] Over the decades to come, Mao tried to substantiate that statement by establishing two fundamental missions for what he called a continuous revolution: to change China into a land of universal justice, equality, and prosperity, and, by destroying what had gone before, to revive China's central position in international affairs. Indeed, the PRC under Mao's rule constantly challenged the legitimacy of the existing international order, which Mao and his comrades believed to be the result of Western domination and thus inherently inimical to revolutionary China. In Mao's view, 1949 was therefore not the end of the Chinese revolution but the beginning of its new and higher phase of social and political transformation and the restructuring of international power.

Shortly after the founding of the new People's Republic, China's Communist masters took the country to war against the United States in Korea. They were concerned that the Americans posed an immediate threat to the survival of their revolution. But Mao, who pushed the decision through against considerable doubts within his own Party, also had a broader aim with the war. He wanted to use it to enhance Communist control of China's state and society while restoring China's central position in East Asia.[9] During the war, by blending revolutionary ideas and patriotism, Mao and the CCP launched a series of brutal domestic political and social campaigns, aiming at exterminating capitalism and the old social order, and at building a socialist society in the overall image of the Soviet Union, the country that they regarded as China's foremost model, ally, and friend.

These campaigns, and their murderous results, created a level of tension in Chinese society that it had never known before. At least 1.2 million Chinese were killed, mostly wealthy farmers, business owners, religious leaders, and those suspected of political disloyalty to the Communists. Close to fifteen million ended up in labor camps, patterned on Soviet gulags.[10] Even so, and in spite of tough times for most people in the 1950s, many Chinese thought that the Communists' "New China" provided an opportunity for the country to regain its national pride, as well as for recharging its society and economy. They were willing to give the experiments with socialist central planning and collective or state-owned enterprises at least some limited backing. Indeed, in spite of the immense violence it had introduced, the new People's Republic of the 1950s did provide some legitimacy to Mao's proclamation that the Chinese had "stood up" through its noticeable social and economic achievements.

Along with its towering brutality, which quashed any opposition, the regime increased its support by confiscating land and promising it to poor farmers and agricultural laborers. The regime also fueled social change through new marriage laws, which prohibited concubinage and child marriage, and emphasized free choice of partners, monogamy, and equal rights of both sexes, including the right to work.[11] By the end of the 1950s the number of women workers had increased more than five times over the course of the decade.[12] The Communists had also initiated widespread campaigns to end illiteracy and improve public health, especially in rural areas. All of this contributed to the legitimacy of Communist rule—except, of course, among those who were at the receiving end of the Party's violent attempts at overthrowing the old social order.

Most appealing to everyday Chinese was that the economy started growing fast by any standards, and certainly by those of a country that had only seen sporadic growth since the early twentieth century. The estimates for annual economic increases vary, but the most recent ones point to some economic recovery even when China was fighting the Korean War and, then, year-on-year annual growth rates during the first Five-Year Plan (1953 to 1957) of a little more than 11 percent.[13] This was an outstanding result compared with almost anywhere else; economic growth in the United States then averaged 3.5 percent, and in France and the Soviet Union it was about 5 percent. Some of the growth in the PRC, economists are quick to point out, came from starting out with a lot of catching up to do after the country had been devastated by generations of wars and civil wars. It is also, of course, impossible to say what the growth rate would have been if China had seen a different economic system and less violence. But from where China was in the early 1950s, the socialist pooling of resources to create growth made sense. Although the Chinese Communists used much more brutal means to achieve their aims, many countries, including in Western Europe, experimented with state-led economic development in the early post–World War II era and reaped benefits from it. The psychological effect was almost as important as the economic one: people, especially young people, were given a sense of their countries going somewhere, of achieving common purposes together, which had been in short supply, especially in China, in the early twentieth century.

China's socialist economic growth was achieved with the support of its main ally, the Soviet Union. Acting from both ideological and strategic motives, Moscow's post-Stalin leadership provided China with substantial and comprehensive economic, technological, and military support during the 1950s.[14] The total amount of what the USSR gave to China was enormous, equaling 7 percent of Soviet national income between 1954 and 1959 in one recent estimate.[15] In addition, the Soviets provided technology, experts, and stipends free of charge.[16] All in all, it was the largest assistance program ever carried out from one country to another, and it contributed significantly to the industrialization of China.

All this produced a sense of steady progress among many ordinary Chinese. The completion of the first Five-Year Plan witnessed a more than 40 percent increase of average wages among urban workers, about a 20 percent increase in the income of farmers, and more than a 30 percent increase in per capita consumption.[17] Not surprisingly, even those who for political reasons were skeptical of Communist rule began to believe that the Party's development model could create a better future.[18]

By the end of the first Five-Year Plan in 1957, China's industry had been taken over by the government, either as fully state-owned or, ostensibly, jointly run with previous owners, but everywhere with Party representatives in full control. Almost 70 percent of industry was directly owned by the state, which included all of China's most modern plants and all its energy production. Foreign companies, with their numbers decreasing rapidly after 1949, were forced to operate under conditions that made them unprofitable, which led to their factories being transferred to the Chinese government at low cost.[19]

In agriculture, after having confiscated land from wealthy farmers, the Communists first divided it up among poor people, as they had promised, giving them the ownership of land and tools. Then, beginning in 1953, the CCP on Mao's insistence took China in brief stages toward a full-fledged collectivization of agriculture, informed to a great extent by Soviet models. Farmers were first organized into groups of mutual production assistance, which was followed by their being brought into elementary, and then advanced, co-operatives. By 1956, close to 90 percent of all farmers worked in some form of collective.[20]

The agricultural collectivization created the basic condition for the Communist state to place greater burdens on farmers in support of the country's ambitious industrialization drive. In October 1953 the CCP leadership implemented a new system for state grain purchases throughout the country. From then on, farmers had to sell their grain to the state at a fixed, low price, for the grain to be resold to urban residents at fixed quotas.[21] This, in essence, was the government taking advantage of the price differences between industrial and agricultural products to extract value from agriculture and create a domestic capital accumulation in order to facilitate ambitious industrial and urban development. The system also effectively locked every citizen in place within the country through a household registration system, the *hukou*, which prevented farmers from leaving the land without express permission by the authorities.[22]

Many farmers demurred. Having just been given their own land, they did not like the idea of sharing it with anyone—their neighbors or the state. They were even more offended by the grain purchasing regulations, and the Party often had to use force to get farmers to sell their output for low prices. Yet farmers had no choice. Party emissaries inspected every village. "My house was also searched, causing panic," recalled Hou Yonglu, a farmer in Shaanxi. "There are villages that refuse to sell their grain, some is hidden in cellars, some is hidden in outhouses, and some is hidden in the attics."[23] The inspections could be violent. One of Hou's neighbors committed suicide after surplus grain was discovered at his house. Even so, by 1957 promises of a bright future with government support had mitigated parts of the farmers' frustration and even won some of them over. The combination of Communist prestige, relentless state control, and intense propaganda efforts meant that threats of new massive violence could be avoided even in areas where the Party had expected resistance.

At the end of the 1950s China looked more and more like a somewhat primitive version of the Soviet Union, based on collectivized agriculture, massive investments in heavy industry, and a planned economy run by the state according to output targets set centrally for the whole country. The close political alliance with Moscow secured Soviet advisers for most aspects of China's development, even below the provincial level. Education and basic health care improved across the country, especially for groups that had had no access to such services before the revolution. The literacy rate more than doubled between 1950 and 1970—a massive percentage in a country of more than 600 million people. The number of college students nearly quintupled between 1949 and 1965. Infant mortality was cut in half.[24] For many Soviet observers, China was the star pupil in the socialist class: more dedication to Communist ideals, more collectivism, and fewer bourgeois fixations than in Eastern Europe and other socialist countries.

But, inside China itself, some Communist leaders—and Mao Zedong in particular—were becoming impatient that their country was not developing fast enough along the socialist path. After the success of the collectivization campaign in agriculture, Mao seemed inspired by those who were dissatisfied. The chairman began wondering why China was not making even faster progress. By early 1956 Mao had begun to suspect that some of his senior Party colleagues did not want to advance quickly toward Communism. According to the chairman, they were too preoccupied with material limitations, balanced development, and the challenges of building socialism in China, and too enamored with the recommendations for planned, steady growth that came from their Soviet comrades.[25]

The chairman was particularly upset with Premier Zhou Enlai, who argued for stability in the development of various sectors of the economy and opposed too many bold advances, in line with what Soviet experts recommended. Mao disagreed with the premier. At a preparatory meeting for the CCP's Eighth Congress, held in September 1956, Mao harangued the Party on the need to speed up China's transformation:

> The United States has a population of only 170 million. Since we have a population several times larger, are similarly rich in resources and are favored by more or less the same kind of climate, it should be possible for us to catch up with the United States. Ought we not to catch up? We definitely ought to. What are our 600 million people doing? Dozing? Which is right, dozing or working? If working is the answer, why can't you with your 600 million people produce 200 or 300 million tons of steel when they with their population of 170 million can produce 100 million tons. If you fail to catch up, you cannot justify yourselves and you will not be so glorious or great. . . . We have such a big population, such a vast territory and such rich resources, and what is more, we are said to be building socialism, which is supposed to be superior; if after working at it for fifty or sixty years we are still unable to overtake the United States, what a sorry figure we will cut![26]

Mao was a dreamer. The CCP, he believed, had to set the creativity of the Chinese people free in order to catch up with and overtake the capitalist world. After the new Soviet leader, Nikita Khrushchev, had openly criticized much of the Soviet past, including Stalin's policies, at the Twentieth Congress of the Communist Party in February 1956, Mao felt that he finally was at liberty to set more ambitious aims for his revolution. In early 1957, as part of the process of intensifying socialist growth, Mao declared that the Communists should "let a hundred flowers bloom, and a hundred schools of thought contend."[27] Mao never intended the contention to include criticism of the Party leadership, and especially not of himself. But some Chinese, especially intellectuals and writers, took the chairman on his word and reported their unhappiness both with the dictatorship and with the bureaucracy and conformity that the Communists had introduced. The liberal intellectual Chu Anping even had an article published in the CCP's main newspaper, *Renmin Ribao*, where he criticized the Party's rule: "The relationship between the Party and the masses has not been good over the past few years, and it has become a problem in my country's political life that needs to be adjusted urgently. What is the key to this problem? In my opinion, the key lies in the ideological issue of the 'Party world.' I think that the Party leading the country does not mean that the country is owned by the Party; everyone supports the Party, but they have not forgotten that they are also the masters of the country."[28]

Mao would have nothing of it. He wanted nonconformity, but only the kind that meshed with his own visions of China's future. His response to unwanted criticism was what the Party called an Anti-Rightist Campaign, a vicious political operation that targeted those who had spoken out against one-party rule and, especially, those who had criticized policies directly associated with the chairman himself. More than four million were punished in one form or another, and thousands were executed.[29] Artists, scientists, engineers, and literary figures were particularly badly hit. The poet Ai Qing, father of renowned Chinese artist Ai Weiwei, was sent to a reeducation camp and then on to live in a village in Xinjiang, where his task was to clean the local toilets.[30]

For Ai Qing and many Chinese who had supported the revolution, the Anti-Rightist Campaign was the first time they imagined that the Party could turn on them. When the Communists had executed and imprisoned their real and perceived enemies in the early 1950s there had been very little protest. Far too many Chinese had looked the other way when these atrocities were going on, justifying or at least explaining them by the need to cleanse the country after civil war and foreign occupation and defend it against the Americans during the war in Korea. But the campaigns at the end of the decade were different. They seemed to target anyone who were suspected of not heeding whichever slogans were in vogue in Beijing at that point. The Anti-Rightist Campaign signaled a new, unforgiving, and unpredictable approach to politics and social change in China for almost everyone.

In 1958 Mao Zedong was 65 years old. He had been the leader of the CCP for almost a quarter century. Since the founding of the People's Republic, Mao had been the ultimate authority on all things. The Party leadership might discuss matters collectively, but Mao's views were decisive whenever he chose to intervene. His personalized power grew, as did the size of his portrait on the ancient Gate of Heavenly Peace, looking down on central Beijing. Most homes across China had a replica of that portrait prominently displayed. Mao was lauded in songs that all Chinese learned by heart.

The east is red, the sun is rising.
From China comes Mao Zedong.
He strives for the people's happiness,
Hurrah, he is the people's great savior!
Chairman Mao loves the people,
He is our guide
to building a new China
Hurrah, lead us forward!

Like most public figures, Mao must have enjoyed seeing his person being lauded by those he imagined himself to represent. He was also intensely jealous of his personal power and influence, believing that he himself had set the course of the Chinese revolution toward victory and that no other Communist leader could be fully trusted with sharing the breadth of his vision. But it would be wrong to think of Mao simply as a power-hungry dictator who saw personal domination as his only aim. Ever since his early youth, Mao had detested what he saw as Old China's weakness and feebleness, which had led to social and economic underdevelopment and foreign control. His aim was to make China rich and strong, and in his twenties he had found the tools that could help him to do so: Marxism and the Leninist vanguard, the Communist Party. Although there is no evidence that Mao ever undertook a detailed study of Marxism as a political theory, he found in it approaches that appealed to him. Mao liked the emphasis on constant struggle and on radical social equality. He also latched on to Marxist ideas of unstoppable progress and stages of material development. But first and foremost, he liked the idea of a centralized, skillful, and agile Communist Party, of the kind that Lenin and Stalin had created in the Soviet Union, an elitist band of brothers that could conquer China and right the wrongs of the past. Out of the struggle and the sacrifice would come a new Soviet-style country, which would be highly modern and dedicated to economic progress and social justice through the Communist Party's building of a strong and capable state.

Though Mao felt that he himself had not been treated with sufficient respect by the Soviet leader Joseph Stalin on the one occasion when they had actually met, in December 1949–February 1950, Mao still greatly admired what Stalin had been able to do with the Soviet Union. In Mao's view, Stalin had, in little more than a decade, transformed Russia from a backward, belittled country to an international superpower, almost the equal of the world's most powerful country, the United States. Stalin had proven the transformative powers of Communism for underdeveloped countries. Mao therefore did not agree with criticizing most of Stalin's actions, as happened in the Soviet Union after the Twentieth Congress of their Communist Party in 1956. It was wrong, Mao thought, to discard "Stalin's sword."[31] The Chinese leader also worried about the criticism because what Mao wanted to do with China was similar to what Stalin had done north of the border. But Mao also felt that some of the criticism of Stalin, especially when voiced within China, was a veiled criticism of Mao himself as the leader of the Chinese revolution, if not of his policies then of his position of primacy. When an enthusiastic Politburo member, Ke Qingshi, gushed that "it is all right to worship Chairman Mao to the extent of having a blind faith in him," Mao agreed, saying that he favored distinguishing "correct" from "incorrect" personality cults. And the chairman's response to the de-Stalinization challenge, as to other challenges, was to push for more radical change; the reason, Mao argued, why socialism had been attacked in Poland and Hungary in 1956 and that Stalin was criticized in the Soviet Union was that the social and economic transformation that the Communists had promised had not progressed fast enough. China should not make the same mistake.[32]

Gradually, in the two years after 1956, Mao started preparing for a great leap into socialism in China. He repeatedly criticized the CCP's economic planners, whom he compared to women with bound feet, hobbling along the path to socialism, when China should really be sprinting youthfully. At a Central Committee plenary session in October 1957, Mao announced that "the contradiction between proletariat and bourgeoisie, and the contradiction between socialist and capitalist paths, are undoubtedly now the main contradictions in the society of our country."[33] To Mao, class struggle was ongoing and real, even after almost ten years of Communist rule. At the time, his colleagues seemed to miss the importance of Mao's position, which would come to underpin his politics for the next two decades.

Early the next month, the chairman visited Moscow for the anniversary celebrations of Lenin's 1917 October Revolution. He gave a long, rambling speech in which he compared Khrushchev to a beautiful lotus-flower and predicted that even an all-out nuclear war would not hinder but advance the world's march toward Communism. "Material might is not the only thing that counts," Mao said.

> People and systems are of primary importance. . . . [I]n 15 years, within our camp, the Soviet Union will have overtaken the United States and China will have overtaken Great Britain [in steel production]. . . . [A]ll imperialists are like the sun at six o'clock in the afternoon and we are like the sun at six o'clock in the morning. Hence a turning-point has been reached, that is to say the Western countries have been left behind and we now clearly have the upper hand. It is definitely not the west wind that prevails over the east wind, so weak is the west wind. It is definitely the east wind that prevails over the west wind, because we are the stronger ones.[34]

When he returned to China, Mao chaired a series of conferences for the top CCP leadership. His comrades certainly noticed, and fell in line with, his critique of Right-leaning attitudes that in Mao's view had led some leaders to oppose bold advances in social transformation. Such leaders had, he said, emptied a bucket of cold water on the masses, dampening their socialist fervor.[35]

Mao's alternative was what he called "continuous revolution." In a note from January 1958 he outlined his thinking:

> Continuous revolution. Our revolutions come one after another. The seizure of political power in the whole country in 1949 was soon followed by the antifeudal land reform. As soon as the land reform was completed, the agricultural cooperativization followed. Then the socialist transformation of private-owned industry and commerce and handicraft occurred. The three socialist transformations, that is, the socialist revolution in the field of the ownership of means of production, will be completed by 1958, and will be followed by the socialist revolution on the political and ideological fronts. . . . [We are] now preparing to make a revolution in the technological field, so that [we may] overtake Britain in fifteen or more years.[36]

Even if all other Party leaders had rushed to bring their views into accordance with those of the chairman, Mao was still not happy with their performance. He again chose the ever-loyal Zhou Enlai as his main target. At a series of Party leadership meetings in early 1958, the chairman claimed that the State Council under Zhou's leadership had gone in the wrong direction for the past two years. Zhou's caution had cost China dearly, Mao claimed, and had "damaged the revolutionary vigor of 600 million people." He attacked the CCP economists, the planners, and the government ministers in charge of finance, industry, and resources. "I do have a method," Mao shouted, "and that is passive resistance. I will not read it [the budget]. For two years I have not read your documents and I do not expect to read them this year either." Instead of holding people back, the Party should set them free to pursue rapid progress. Merging his new plan for a great leap forward with the Anti-Rightist Campaign, the chairman accused some of his closest collaborators, such as Premier Zhou Enlai, of being "just fifty meters away from the Rightists."[37] The premier offered abundant self-criticism for his "conservative and Rightist attitude toward socialist reconstruction," which had violated Mao's "grand design for socialism."[38]

Zhou had been premier of the PRC since 1949, meaning that he chaired its State Council, a kind of prime-ministerial position under Mao. He was the Communist Party's main diplomat as well as the main organizer of its government. The suave, soft-spoken Zhou had been a Communist since the early 1920s, when he joined a Party cell in France. In the late 1920s, he rose in the ranks to become one of the party's main leaders. For a while, he was even ranked number one in the Party's hierarchy. However, he always regarded Mao Zedong as his superior, even at times when he, in name, was Mao's boss. This constant relationship between the rambunctious, free-wheeling Mao and the quiet, efficient, and hard-working Zhou has been a mystery to historians and biographers alike. In personal terms they were never very close, but Zhou fervently believed that Mao, and only Mao, would save the CCP and China, while Mao believed that Zhou was simply the best organizer the Party had. Mao was an instinctive radical, while Zhou, when given a chance, preferred practical and realistic processes over utopias. But the premier would always follow the chairman whenever Mao's wishes were clearly shown.[39]

By the summer of 1958, the set of plans that became known as the Great Leap Forward were in full swing. In Mao's vision of the future, the Great Leap should be furthered by a dramatic increase of China's steel production, so that Chinese industry as a whole would rapidly climb to new heights.[40] In early summer, cheered on by Mao, the CCP leadership decided that China's steel output should reach 10.7 million tons in 1958, doubling the level of

1957.[41] "We must turn our country into a great industrial power in three, five, or seven years," the chairman proclaimed.[42]

The Great Leap's fire also burned throughout China's vast countryside, with excessive production aims everywhere and with farmers ordered to build dams, roads, mines, and factories. From late spring to summer 1958, things increasingly got out of control. Some summer harvests were reported to be one hundred times bigger than those of previous years. So many "victorious briefings" poured into Beijing that a delighted Mao registered his concern for what should happen to all the excess grain produced.[43] Large-scale production units were the solutions to China's ills, the chairman proclaimed. Small agricultural cooperatives should be merged into big communes, he said, "with many people, much land, large production, other large businesses, combining government administrating with society, providing public dining services, and abolishing of private plots." Mao asked rhetorically: "We fought a war for twenty-two years and won. Why can we not be successful in building socialism?"[44]

Although much of the impatience and the willfulness that created the disasters of the Great Leap Forward originated with Mao Zedong, the outrages were a collective responsibility of the Communist Party's leadership. It was not only the obsequious Zhou Enlai who threw caution as well as compassion to the wind. So did the 60-year old Liu Shaoqi, Mao's designated successor, who in the 1950s had been the main political voice for planning, gradualism, and taking over models from the Soviet Union. Achieving Communism, in Liu's view, was based on maximum industrial growth and the development of socialist practices through the expansion of the working class. Liu was better versed in Marxist theory than almost anyone else in the CCP leadership and the author of foundational texts, such as *How to Be a Good Communist, On the Party,* and *Internationalism and Nationalism.* He was personally unassuming, almost ascetic, and somewhat humorless, but intensely committed to the Party and to the idea that Communism would transform China into a strong country. His position as the number-two leader in the CCP and, after 1959, PRC president, was earned by hard work and dedication. Many young party cadre admired Liu almost as much as they did the chairman himself, because of his reputation for cold, unquestioning, single-minded service to the CCP and his reputation for political rectitude. The voluntarism of the Great Leap was out of style with all of Liu's career, but he still chose to go along out of loyalty to Mao and faith in Mao's vision for the CCP.[45]

Another leader who at first had qualms about the unrealistic aims of the Leap was Deng Xiaoping, vice premier and head of the CCP's central secretariat. Deng was a gradualist in approach, but hot tempered and restless.[46] Like Zhou Enlai, he had joined the Communist cause when working in Europe and quickly become a key Party coordinator and henchman for Mao's wishes, much respected both among other leaders and in the army for his quick-wittedness and can-do attitude. In spite of his initial hesitation, Deng became Mao's main troubleshooter for the Great Leap campaign, relentlessly going after those within the Party who expressed any kind of doubt about inflated production targets or the social dislocation that went with them. "We have not caught up with the chairman's thought, and lag behind it by a very long distance," Deng declared, as he lauded Mao's plans for increasing steel production through makeshift furnaces set up in people's backyards. The idolization of steel was something Deng shared with his boss; steel output equated modernity for both Mao and Deng, and production levels were a gauge for China's position in the world and within the socialist camp. But Party leaders such as Deng also pushed for massive increases in the cultivation of grain, both for domestic and export purposes. Deng believed that more than doubling the quotas for grain within a year was "pragmatic" and "based on real conditions in all aspects." "The [grain] target is very high, but it is not frightening," Deng declared. "If we take active measures, we can exceed the target. Moreover, with much more enthusiasm, we can exceed it even more." Mao chimed in: "Even falling short of 650 million tons of grain by just one grain will not be tolerated."[47] "I am the commander [of the Great Leap]," the chairman declared, "and Deng is my second-in-command."[48]

By the late 1950s, China was not the only Communist country where the leadership believed in great leaps into the future. In Eastern Europe and in the Soviet Union there were also experiments with sharp and massive advances toward higher production levels. But Mao's imagined leap far surpassed any other Communist excesses in the extremism of its vision and its actual scope. And the outcome was much worse in China, because it was poorer and the lack of realism in targets set was even greater than elsewhere. Since the farmers who had to bear the burdens of the work that went into fulfilling the plans had less to fall back on in terms of survival, the result was starvation and death in high numbers. At least thirty million people died as a consequence of the Great Leap between 1958 and 1961, which makes it the worst man-made famine in human history.[49]

People had started dying of hunger already in late 1958, but it was the winter of 1959–1960 that was the worst, especially in the poorer provinces. A daughter of Anhui farmers recounted her family's story:

> The youngest daughter of third brother died first. This child, born in January 1959, was starving from when she was born. Her mother has no milk for her and got no extra food for the baby. . . . Then it was the death of second brother's eldest daughter. Because of hunger, the 15-year-old girl was skinny and ill all the time. Then she got pneumonia. She had no medicine or food. She was coughing and wheezing, and choked and died before the Spring Festival in 1960. . . . In mid-February 1960, second brother's 11-year-old third daughter died. . . . We suspected that the corpse, thrown in the mass grave outside the village, was eaten by wild animals. . . . Fourth brother . . . bought two and a half catties of food from coupons that he had saved . . . [but] . . . the production team leader discovered it and took the red taro and the pot away, and locked up third brother for a day. Mother finally died in April [1960]. . . . Third brother made his mother's dowry cabinet into a coffin and buried her in the mountain patch that she had reclaimed [in the early 1950s] with the assistance of her family.[50]

Warning signs of impending disaster had been arriving from early in the Great Leap Forward campaign. But the central leadership refused to take note of them. When signs of hunger were reported already in the winter of 1958–1959, Communist leaders claimed the reasons to be temporary supply problems or villagers secretly squirreling away their produce. When a few courageous Party leaders, among them Marshal Peng Dehuai, who had been commander of China's forces in the Korean War, spoke out against Great Leap policies, Mao not only refused to listen but had them purged from the leadership. Marshal Peng, a genuine national hero if the PRC ever had one, was denounced as head of an "anti-Party Rightist clique."[51]

The Great Leap disaster had fatal effects for China's foreign relations, too. Advice to curtail the Great Leap from Soviet experts working in China led to Mao became increasingly critical of the alliance with the Soviet Union, claiming that Moscow's plan was to control China and stymie its rise. Being on a revolutionary high in the summer of 1958, Mao had ordered the shelling of

Guomindang-held islands close to the Chinese coast.[52] This had provoked a terse standoff with the United States, which had pledged to support Chiang Kai-shek's government on Taiwan. But it also shocked China's Soviet allies, who had not been informed in advance.[53] By late 1959 China's relationship to the Soviet Union was quickly unraveling, with Mao accusing Moscow of cowardice in dealing with the Americans, of not supporting China in its border dispute with India, and for criticizing the Great Leap. When the Soviet leader Nikita Khrushchev came to Beijing in October 1959 in an urgent attempt to rescue the alliance, the CCP Politburo accused him of opportunism and of "making the imperialists happy." Khrushchev left in a huff. "You want to subjugate us to yourselves," the Soviet leader shouted, "but nothing will come out of it, we are also a party and we have our own way, and we are not time-servers towards anybody."[54]

By the end of 1959, Chairman Mao had convinced himself that the alliance with the Soviet Union would have to go if his new, radical reinterpretation of Communism in China should be successful. Even though it was becoming clearer and clearer that the Great Leap Forward was a budding disaster, Mao refused to budge, and those who had been guilty of helping him carry out the senseless plans chose loyalty to the chairman over common sense. By shrewdly defining and provoking foreign enemies, Mao also got his associates' support on nationalist grounds. "In terms of the political road, principles and policies that our Party adopts domestically, none are accepted by Khrushchev. If we submit to him, and admit that what we have done and are doing is wrong, we will have to step down right away," Deng Xiaoping told his assistants.[55] By 1960 Mao knew that Deng and many others were having second thoughts about the content of the Great Leap Forward. He therefore selected Deng to spearhead the criticism of the Soviet Union and thereby forced him to continue to act as the defender-in-chief of Mao's political views. Between 1960 and July 1963, when Deng went to Moscow for what was to be the final substantive meetings of the Soviet and Chinese leaderships for twenty-six years, a key part of Mao's policy was that any attempt at mending relations with Moscow was revisionist, Right-deviationist, and a betrayal of China.[56]

In early 1961, after at least thirty million people had died, Mao finally allowed his Party to begin dismantling parts of the Great Leap plans. Liu and Zhou led the recovery efforts, which were hampered by the Party's (including their own) unwillingness to take any kind of public responsibility for the disaster, even though Liu admitted within the Party that the Great Famine was the result of "70% of human mistakes, and 30% of impact of natural disasters."[57] Instead CCP bosses quietly began allowing peasants to cultivate private plots and introduce markets in which produce could be sold freely. They also introduced limited material incentives to increase production, both in agriculture and in industry. First and foremost, the ongoing damage that Great Leap policies had led to was ended: production targets were reduced, exports of foodstuffs were terminated, and most of the improvised industrial plants were closed down.[58] The extreme famine stopped mainly because the CCP's central leadership no longer insisted on starvation-inducing measures. But there was no reckoning: Mao simply declared that he wanted to withdraw to the "second line" of policymaking, thinking about the way forward, leaving it to his lieutenants to clean up the mess his policies had created.

But Mao never intended to stay away from the center of power for long. The critique of the Great Leap was a huge blow to the chairman, but it only enhanced his desire to use revolutionary means to eliminate the backwardness of China's economy while, at the same time, transforming China's state and society. He wanted to retake and rebuild his role in defining the mainstream political discourse. While Liu Shaoqi, Zhou Enlai, and Deng Xiaoping discreetly began moving China back toward the planning regime that had existed prior to 1958, the chairman came along only grudgingly and, often, with express misgivings. In early 1962, at a central Party working conference attended by 7,000 cadres, several CCP leaders suggested a more permanent reduction in political campaigns and an increase in the use of market incentives in agriculture. Others proposed foreign policy issues on which China and the Soviets could cooperate, such as defending the Vietnamese revolution against the United States, and keeping some elements of a Sino-Soviet technological and intelligence partnership in place while using "diplomacy rather than inter-party struggles in dealing with Khrushchev."[59] By then Mao had had enough. In the summer of 1962 he turned on the Party moderates with a vengeance. He openly accused Liu Shaoqi, among others, of having revisionist leanings. All criticism of the Great Leap, Mao said, was a reflection of class struggle *within* the Communist Party. There was also, Mao stated, "a connection between revisionism at home and abroad."[60]

The chairman's censure did not mean an immediate end to the attempts at rescuing the Chinese economy and abating the losses suffered in the

Great Leap Forward. Throughout 1963 and 1964 Liu, Zhou, and Deng, assisted by vice premier for economic issues Chen Yun, head of the state planning commission Li Fuchun, and minister of finance Li Xiannian, worked to get things moving back to normal. They attempted to reinstate cadre who had been purged, balance economic output and raise production standards, reduce the emphasis on constant class struggle, and consolidate the Party's leadership in the provinces. They also attempted to win back the support of Overseas Chinese and non-Party members at home that had been lost in the excesses of the Great Leap. Zhou Enlai called for what he termed the "four modernizations"—in agriculture, industry, national defense, and science and technology—by the end of the decade. Some Party members went even further. Deng Zihui, one of the CCP's leading agricultural experts, argued for a responsibility system in agriculture, in which families could rent land and equipment from the People's Commune and sell their produce to the state at fixed prices, keeping the profit themselves.[61] Sun Yefang, the director of the Academy of Sciences Economic Research Institute, recommended that some enterprises, while still state-owned, should be run for profit and not just as a part of the plan.[62]

In addition to reforms at home, the PRC needed to make up for the decline in foreign trade that happened as a result of the conflict with the Soviet Union. By 1962 trade with the Soviets was almost half of the 1950s average.[63] Since China desperately needed foreign imports to offset some of the Great Leap disasters, Zhou Enlai and his assistants had to replace Soviet trade with trade with the capitalist world. From 1960 on they had imported massive amounts of grain, mainly from Canada and Australia, to remedy the hunger that was so widespread across China. These deals were orchestrated through China Resources, a PRC trade company in Hong Kong, and payment was arranged through the Bank of China's Hong Kong branch.[64] Other forms of trade followed. Between 1960 and 1963, China-Japan trade increased more than 300 percent. By 1965 more than 70 percent of China's foreign trade was with capitalist countries. Between 1962 and 1965 there were even attempts at importing large-scale factory equipment and new technology from Japan and Western Europe.[65] Ironically, the radicalization of the Chinese revolution had brought about the PRC's first substantial economic exchanges with global capitalist markets.

But by late 1962 most reforms were coming under increasing pressure, both from the chairman's displeasure and from challenges in international affairs. As Mao had hoped, relations with the Soviets deteriorated further, and by 1963 it was clear that all aspects of the Sino-Soviet alliance belonged to the past. The brief border war that China fought with India in October 1962 over territorial claims in the Himalayas contributed further to Chinese leaders' sense of isolation.[66] Even if the war was won, the Soviets had come out in support of the Indians, as had many newly independent countries in Asia and Africa. In Vietnam the U.S. intervention was widening, contributing to the feeling of containment and foreign pressure in Beijing. Mao manipulated the fear of foreign aggression into support for his domestic program. He declared that a new world war was coming, and that China had to intensify its socialist transformation in order to defend itself, just as Stalin had done in the 1930s.

In early 1963 Mao launched what came to be called the Socialist Education Movement. The chairman criticized many in the Party leadership and provincial leaders for being overly bureaucratic and not attuned enough to revolutionary politics. They did not understand, he claimed, that the Party was increasingly coming under attack from capitalist and feudal forces, even now, after the People's Republic had existed for thirteen years. The struggle among classes would not go away after a socialist regime comes to power, Mao claimed. In fact, he said, the class struggle could sometimes become sharper. The CCP had to cleanse its own ranks and educate young people to practice socialism. "Once class struggle is grasped, everything will be solved," Mao declared.[67] In addition to his new and intense campaign, with its slogans and purges, the chairman was increasingly preoccupied with China creating what he termed a true socialist culture in order to advance class struggle. Influenced by his wife, the radical former Shanghai actress Jiang Qing, Mao found that among writers and artists "there are numerous problems involving many people. Very little has been achieved in socialist transformation in many departments that are still dominated by 'the dead.' . . . Is it not strange that many Communists are keen on promoting feudal and capitalist art, instead of socialist art?"[68] Jiang Qing introduced Mao to the Shanghai Party secretary in charge of cultural and ideological matters, Zhang Chunqiao, a radical egalitarian who fueled the chairman's view that all of the PRC's cultural sphere was penetrated by conservative thinking.

As the Socialist Education Movement unfolded, Mao's criticism of those who attempted to stabilize the economy and lessen social and political tension became more vicious. In February 1964 the chairman launched a set of furious critiques of the CCP leadership, including when speaking with foreign Communists. He told Vic Wilcox, the head of the tiny Communist Party of New Zealand, that "a few in our party advocate . . . peace with imperialism, revisionism and reactionary countries, and less support for countries and parties that oppose imperialism. This is essentially revisionist thinking. There are a few of them in the Liaison Office."[69] Mao also attacked the Party's United Front Department and the Rural Work Department when speaking with foreign leaders. Even a vice premier, he indicated, practiced revisionism. Mao was probably aiming at Deng Xiaoping or Chen Yun, the former labor organizer who, as deputy premier, was in charge of economic recovery, though he may also have had in mind Xi Zhongxun, the youngest of China's vice premiers and father of China's later president Xi Jinping, who had been purged already in 1962 for his opposition to the radical Left.[70] On April 10, 1964, in a meeting with Hakamada Satomi of the Japanese Communist Party, Mao took his criticism even further. "If China should practice revisionism, you would have a hard time," he told the Japanese. "If a Khrushchev could emerge in China and pursue the capitalist line, what would you do? You should help the Marxists in China to oppose China's revisionism." The leadership in one-third of the country had already fallen out of Communist hands, Mao told some of his younger followers.[71]

The main leaders in the Communist Party reacted to Mao's criticism in the same way as they had done in the late 1950s: by coming to heel. Though some of them may have thought the chairman's broader misgivings to be little more than random apprehension, they joined the Socialist Education Movement with enthusiasm, carrying out investigations of Party committees and factory leaderships that were accused of slacking in their ideological convictions. Some of them also joined the new Cultural Revolution Group, set up in January 1965 to promote the changes that Mao sought among Chinese writers and artists. Led by the mayor of Beijing, Peng Zhen, a dour Party apparatchik with limited cultural interests, the group soon came under attack by Jiang Qing and other radicals for doing very little. Jiang got regular reports of the group's inaction from another member, the Party's former intelligence chief Kang Sheng, a somewhat sinister organizer of the secret police who had reemerged as a supporter of radical politics in the early 1960s.

In addition to their general obsequiousness, the established Party leaders had other reasons for following Mao's wishes closely. Since the late 1950s another "ghost" from the party's early years, Lin Biao, had come back into the chairman's good graces. Marshal Lin had probably been the greatest military leader on the Communist side during the Chinese civil war in the 1940s, a commander of great imagination and strategic skill, but he was also a deeply troubled man, suffering from bouts of severe depression and indolence, effects of what we today would call bipolar disorder, which had kept him out of Chinese politics for the first decade of the PRC's existence.[72] To the surprise of almost all other leaders, Mao had made the erratic Lin Biao minister of defense in 1959. At the 7,000 cadres conference in early 1962, when Mao was under pressure from implicit yet widespread criticism of the Great Leap, Lin had leaped to the chairman's defense, claiming that the disaster had been the result of "our failure to honestly follow the chairman's teachings."[73] Mao responded, predictably, that Lin's speech was the best one at the conference.[74] In 1964 Lin became first vice premier, replacing Chen Yun. Lin responded to Mao's granting of favor by becoming the main promoter of an intensified Mao cult within the Party. In mid-1964 his assistants put together the first edition of a small book, entitled *Quotations from Chairman Mao,* mainly for use among soldiers in the People's Liberation Army. It later became known around the world as "Mao's Little Red Book." "Mao Zedong Thought is the acme of Marxism-Leninism of our time," Lin declared.[75]

In spite of his sudden disappearances and many real or imagined illnesses, Lin was also essential to another key project of the mid-1960s—the transfer of many important industries to inland areas far from China's borders. Responding to Mao's dictum that war was coming soon, Lin and other military and Party leaders began calling for new industrial areas to be set up in China's less developed southwestern provinces, mainly Sichuan, Guizhou, and Yunnan, but also in parts of other nonurban areas. The so-called Third Front campaign got underway in 1964 as a top-secret program, and the process of moving existing plants and setting up new ones in Third Front areas took up more than 25 percent of the Chinese government's capital expenditure between 1965 and 1980.[76] Most of these investments were less productive than what they would have been in more developed areas, and the infrastructural challenges were severe, as was the dislocation caused by moving parts of the workforce. Even though the Third Front campaign did contribute to development in some of China's poorer regions and a few of the enterprises established later on came to thrive as economic reform took hold, the cost for China was overwhelming, especially when adding the sharp increase in the defense budget from the early 1960s onward.

One of the Maoist inventions from the Great Leap Forward that stayed in place after 1962 were the People's Communes. The original idea was to divide all of China's population into production centers, called communes, that would also be in charge of basic welfare as well as political education. While communes in urban areas were mainly short-lived, all of rural China remained organized into People's Communes up to the early 1980s. Each commune consisted of around five thousand households and was divided into around ten production brigades, which each had about ten production teams, though the relative size of all of these units varied widely, dependent on local conditions. Within the communes, all property was supposed to be owned collectively and all production carried out jointly by the production teams according to quotas set by the heads of the commune based on instructions from the government. All activities in the commune were intended to be collective rather than family based: meals, sanitation, education, health, and cultural events were all the responsibility of the commune. Party propaganda cited a statement by Karl Marx's as an ideal: "From each according to their abilities, to each according to their needs." A farmer in Shandong recorded in his diary: "Today the commune announced that nobody would have to pay for meals anymore. I was amazed! Have we really entered a Communist society? . . . Thank you, Party and Chairman Mao! [Some people] ate so much that they could hardly walk. . . . But most people did not work hard . . . today you are sick, tomorrow he has a cold. . . . In particular heavy work, tiring work. . . . Nobody likes to do that."[77]

Mao's idea was to get rid of the dependence on family agriculture while improving production, organizing ways of life "scientifically," and having free and plentiful labor for major government projects in rural areas. The People's Communes, a Jiangsu Party secretary reported, have "freed up women as a labor force, . . . through removing washing, cooking, child-minding, mending clothes, and emptying toilets. . . . About six million women in the province have been freed from the shackles of housework, which not only effectively encourages their enthusiasm for labor, [but also] increases labor attendance and labor efficiency, and improves the political and economic status of a vast number of women.[78] As could be expected, some communes thrived while others did very badly. In spite of the many collectivist traditions in the Chinese countryside, most farmers chafed under the controls and commands imposed on them from above and the lack of opportunity to make decisions for themselves.

By the end of 1964 it was clear that Mao was becoming increasingly unhappy about what he saw as intransigence within his Party, both against his aims with the Socialist Education Movement and his new initiatives for revolutionizing Chinese society and culture. In December he asked Xie Fuzhi, the minister of public security: "How many of our industrial enterprises have gone capitalist in terms of management? One third? One half? More? We will only find out after they have been checked up one by one."[79] A week later he told another official that "the [Party] leaders taking the capitalist road have become or are becoming bourgeois elements who suck the blood of workers. . . . They are the target of struggle, the target of revolution, and must never be relied on in the socialist education movement." Mao had started believing that the main problem for China's future was within his own Party, in what he called the "bureaucrat class."[80] By the end of 1964 the Central Committee, echoing Mao's views, declared that from now on the target of the campaign was "Party members in power taking the capitalist road."[81] For many within the CCP, this was the signal that great changes were afoot.

But, much as at the start of the Great Leap Forward, all leaders of the Party imagined that the individuals the chairman had in mind for his criticism could not possibly be themselves, but had to be someone else. Zhou, Liu, and Deng kept mimicking Mao's radical policy pronouncements while attempting to carry out more moderate policies within their own competencies. In this sense it is not surprising that Mao became increasingly impatient with the direction of Chinese socialism. He feared counter-revolution, war, and his own old age. By 1965 Mao's quest was for absolute power of a kind even he had not had before: the power to completely revolutionize Chinese society before it was too late. Even though he had patterned his personal rule on that of Stalin, Mao wanted total power for a reason. He wanted the complete transformation of all modes of thinking among China's youth, and he felt that he was running out of time to see it through. To Mao, the advance toward Communism was not only about making China rich and strong, which he believed the country would be as soon as his aims were reached. It was also a moral argument about how society should be organized. His hatred of economic exploitation and social discrimination came together with a deep distrust of intellectuals and of family connections to the past.[82] Not only would the economic and social revolution have to be completed, but the cultural revolution, too, for China to be a shining example to the world. Different from most of his advisers, who attempted to use Marxism as a tool for practical change, Mao had an almost mystical approach to Marx's teachings, and a belief that they contained some hard-to-get-at secret formula for how China could rise from its ashes.

At the beginning of 1965, while Premier Zhou Enlai was extolling the practical achievements of Chinese socialism since 1960 to the National People's Congress and calling for more attention to be paid to the four modernizations, Mao concentrated on the Socialist Education Movement and preparations for war. He declared that U.S. aggression against Vietnam was seriously threatening China's security and might well be a preparation for an attack on China itself, possibly jointly with the Soviets, whom he now termed "social-imperialists."[83] Third Front construction projects swung into high gear, with the Central Committee deciding that the third Five-Year Plan should put the "building of national defense in the first place, speeding up construction in the third line regions, and gradually changing the geographical distribution of industry."[84] But Mao also set off time to dismiss most of the top people in the Ministry of Culture, and appeal to everyone within the Party to learn from the Chinese armed forces, the People's Liberation Army, and put political and ideological work first. When meeting with a group of key provincial Party secretaries on October 10, the anniversary of China's 1911 revolution, Mao summed up where he stood. "We must prepare for war," he said. "Do not be afraid of mutiny or rebellion." He repeated his warnings that the real danger of revisionism might be in the Central Committee of the CCP. "In that event, you must rebel," Mao told his astonished audience. "In the past, some people had blind faith . . . in the Central Committee. Now, you must remember, whatever is said, be it in the Central Committee, its bureaus or the provincial party committees, you can refuse to implement it if it is not correct."[85]

As if Mao's recent statements were not enough of a warning to his associates, by early 1966 it was clear that the chairman intended wider changes in the Party organization. The head of Mao's personal bodyguard, Wang Dongxing, a burly man who had served the chairman slavishly for thirty years, became the new head of the Central Committee's General Office, a job he was woefully unprepared for. The man he replaced, Yang Shangkun, had been known as an enforcer of Party norms. Wang, in taking over, knew that *his* main task would be to serve chairman Mao and whatever ideals Mao propagated.

Working with Lin Biao, Mao also purged General Luo Ruiqing, the PLA's veteran chief of staff, accusing him of usurping military power and opposing the Party. Mao suspected Luo of resisting the intense politization of the PLA that the chairman championed.[86] When the general refused to confess his sins and publicly abase himself, Mao had him hauled before the full Party leadership, including Liu Shaoqi and Deng Xiaoping, who took turns flinging accusations against him. Lin Biao's wife, Ye Qun, who was in charge of the minister of defense's private office, made a ten-hour long speech to list Luo's "crimes" in front of the Party leaders.[87] Even though Luo was reputed throughout the Party for his toughness—he had served as a very hard-line minister of state security in the 1950s—eventually the general broke under pressure. On March 18, 1966, Luo tried to commit suicide by jumping out a window, though he survived, breaking both his legs in the process and injuring his spine. Nobody in the Party leadership came to his defense during this persecution. Luo could not even kill himself properly, Deng Xiaoping said callously: "He dived like an ice-lolly."[88] Luo Ruiqing spent almost ten years in prison, with scant medical attention to his injuries. In a suicide note intended for his wife, he had written: "This is the end. Tell our children to heed the Party and Chairman Mao forever. Our Party will always be glorious, right, and great. You should keep improving yourself and conducting revolution."[89]

Revolution was what Mao wanted. Revolution was what Mao wished for. Lin Biao ordered the army to treat every single word by the chairman as "supreme instructions" and told them that every sentence uttered by Mao was "truth and carries more weight than 10,000 ordinary sentences."[90] All other Party departments attempted to outdo Lin in servile and infantile praise of the chairman. The Cultural Revolution Group, set up by the Central Committee and headed by Beijing mayor Peng Zhen, came under renewed fire for not being radical enough in following Mao's instructions. Still traveling the country on his special train, Mao met with his wife Jiang Qing and with Kang Sheng, the former chief of intelligence who now worked closely with the chairman. When Kang criticized Peng's Cultural Revolution Group for not caring about politics, Mao chimed in, accusing the Beijing Party committee of shielding undesirable people and refusing to support the Left. It should be dissolved, Mao said. So should the Propaganda Department of the Central Committee, which was a "Palace of the King of Hell." It was necessary, Mao said, to "overthrow the King of Hell and set the little devils free." Local organizations should rise up and attack the Central Committee, Mao said, continuing his classical references: "More monkey kings should come up in all parts of the country to wreak havoc in Heaven."[91] Mao deputized Liu Shaoqi to convene a Politburo meeting in Beijing to criticize Peng Zhen, Luo Ruiqing, and Yang Shangkun, as well as the propaganda chief Lu Dingyi, and designate them an anti-Party gang.[92]

In May 1966, from his lakeside residence in beautiful Hangzhou, where he had stayed for three months already, Mao ordered the setting up of a new Central Cultural Revolution Group at Party headquarters in Beijing. The group's new task was to spearhead a Great Proletarian Cultural Revolution, which the chairman now felt that the country needed. Its leading members were Mao's longtime secretary Chen Boda, Jiang Qing, and Kang Sheng, but also a younger group of Shanghai radicals, including Zhang Chunqiao and Yao Wenyuan, a writer and literary critic who had become known for his furious attacks on other artists for spreading "poisonous weeds" and not being supportive enough of the chairman's political line. Mao authorized Zhou Enlai to preside over the group's meetings whenever practical, knowing that Zhou would report its dealings directly to the chairman himself.[93]

On May 16, 1966, Mao issued a notice to the whole Party, in the name of the Central Committee:

The representatives of the bourgeoisie who have sneaked into our Party, government, army, and various cultural circles are a bunch of counterrevolutionary revisionists. Once conditions are ripe, they will seize political power and turn the dictatorship of the proletariat into a dictatorship of the bourgeoisie. Some of them we have already seen through, others we have not. Some are still trusted by us and are being trained as our successors, people like Khrushchev, who are still nestling beside us. Party committees at all levels must pay full attention to this matter.[94]

It was the clearest sign yet that the chairman had a bigger purge in mind. At his house by Hangzhou's West Lake, Mao kept receiving younger Party leaders, warning them that revisionism was on the rise and that only they could save the revolution and save China. It was a new call to action by the chairman, although the extent of his cause was not yet clear.

2

Great Disorder under Heaven

ON THE EVENING OF JUNE 1, 1966, Chinese radio broadcast the text of a poster put up at Peking University, the country's foremost institution of higher learning. This "poster written in big characters"—a traditional medium of protest in China—was compiled by seven faculty members of the Philosophy Department, headed by Nie Yuanzi, the department's Party secretary. By then in her mid-forties, Nie was well-connected in the CCP and politically ambitious. One of her contacts was Kang Sheng, who had become one of Mao's closest associates in promoting a cultural revolution. Nie had complained to Kang that the work team sent by the CCP's Beijing Committee to handle factional strife at the university was doing more bad than good. The poster Nie and her comrades put up declared that

the whole nation, in a soaring revolutionary spirit that manifests boundless love for the Party and Chairman Mao, and their inveterate hatred for the sinister anti-Party, anti-socialist gang, are making a vigorous and great Cultural Revolution. . . . But, here at Peking University, the masses are being kept immobilized. The atmosphere is one of indifference and deadness. . . . The revolutionary people must be fully aroused. . . . To hold big meetings and put up big-character posters is one of the best ways for the masses to do battle. By "guiding" the masses not to hold big meetings, not to put up big-character posters, and by creating all kinds of taboos, aren't you suppressing the masses' revolution, not allowing them to make revolution and opposing their revolution? We will never permit you to do this! . . . Resolutely, thoroughly, totally and completely wipe out all ghosts and monsters and all Khrushchevian

36

counter-revolutionary revisionists—and carry the socialist revolution through to the end. Defend the Party's Central Committee! Defend Mao Zedong's Thought! Defend the dictatorship of the proletariat![1]

Nie and her colleagues may have written the poster, but it was Mao who made sure that the whole country got to hear about the philosophers' complaint. Later, he even called it "the first Marxist-Leninist document in the whole country."[2]

By mid-1966 Mao had begun a large-scale purge of the leadership of the Communist Party at all levels. He spoke of the Cultural Revolution as his lasting legacy, as setting the people free to pursue revolution, and as the transfer of power from senior Communists, who had been tainted by the "old society" before the revolution, to younger revolutionaries who had been "born red" during the Civil War or after the Party took power. It was the young, and sometimes the very young, whom Mao believed would help him stand up to the counter-revolutionaries and guide the transition to Communism. "The period of schooling should be shortened, education should be revolutionized, and the domination of our schools by bourgeois intellectuals must not continue," the chairman instructed.[3]

Younger revolutionaries like Nie had a lot to build on in their protests. Many college students resented the rote learning methods used in all Chinese schools, as well as their authoritarian disciplinary system and hierarchical structure. Elsewhere in Chinese society, too, there was dissatisfaction with stratification and bureaucratization, and with Communist cadre who were sent in from the outside to run things. The older cadre, who had joined the party before 1949, were sometimes seen as a caste apart from the general population, and all power seemed to rest with them. The experience of purges, arrests, labor camps, executions, and, not least, the hunger disasters of the Great Leap Forward and the famine that followed, also created hatred against individual leaders and much fear and panic in society at large. The more Mao Zedong was held up as a god by his own Party, the more groups and individuals in a restless society started believing that they could appeal directly to him with their grievances, or that they could take action on behalf of the chairman against institutions and people they did not like, or against those who had wronged them in the past.[4] The Cultural Revolution, which Mao had declared, came at a time when Chinese society was already fraying at the seams, and when there were large amounts of resentment resting in society that could be easily mobilized for violent action.

But while the coming apart of Chinese society allowed the fire of the Cultural Revolution to spread quickly, it was Mao's fears and ambitions that had ignited it. He kept talking to his inner circle about how Stalin had run out of time to entrench socialism in the Soviet Union, in spite of all the Soviet advantages. "Mao now felt that Stalin may have been right in regard to his repression of class enemies," Kang Sheng told foreign visitors. "While theoretically it should be possible to remold landlords, in fact a landlord always remained a landlord at heart. . . . Mao now felt that Lenin's definition of classes was inadequate, and that it should be extended to include the political and psychological characteristics of classes."[5] On June 1, 1966, the same day that Nie Yuanzi's wall poster was read out on radio, *Renmin Ribao* published an editorial calling on the people to rise up and "sweep away all monsters and demons."[6] When student radicals at the main universities over summer 1966 began attacking university and municipal authorities, sometimes physically, Mao kept away from Beijing, watching as Liu Shaoqi and Deng Xiaoping sent CCP work teams to schools and colleges to promote the Cultural Revolution.

Since late February 1966, Mao had mainly been in Hangzhou, one of his favorite cities in eastern China, known for its scenic beauty. He did not mind having Liu and Deng seen as being in charge. Mao also noticed that the two were uncomfortable with their tasks. They repeatedly encouraged Mao to return to Beijing to direct the Cultural Revolution himself. The chairman refused.[7] He was waiting and watching. On June 15, Mao abruptly left Hangzhou. This time his destination was Dishuidong, the Cave of Dripping Water, a small, secure guesthouse partly built into a mountain near the chairman's hometown, Shaoshan, in Hunan. He needed a quiet place to think, he told his staff. He wanted to be in hiding in a small and remote village.[8]

Though the chairman may have craved seclusion, he did already know what his bigger aims for the Cultural Revolution were: He wanted to use China's youth as a new and radical means for transforming party, state, and society in accordance with his ideals. He wanted them to help crush old forms of thinking, old institutions such as family, village, religion, patronage, and even Party branches and army units, and replace them with new collectives in which the critique of the bourgeoisie and revisionism could be made permanent. He wanted an end to Chinese imitation of foreign models and the creation of new forms of revolutionary purity through which China would be an advanced example to the world. But he also wanted to maximize his own absolute authority in matters of policy and doctrine. Mao feared that after the Great Leap his reputation had been tarnished, and that other Party leaders acted independently of him. Since the early 1960s he had constantly complained that even his close associates treated him like an old uncle who should be revered in public but whose advice did not matter. Only his unquestioned and immediate leadership could secure the Chinese revolution for the future, Mao believed, and the Cultural Revolution was a means for regaining that leadership.

While in his Hunan cave house, the location of which must have reminded him of the cave dwelling he worked in in Yan'an during the war, Mao was first and foremost preoccupied with reviving his leadership. When meeting with the provincial Party leaders on June 26, he told them that "he had taken them on a Long March before, and now he was preparing to take them on a Long March again."[9] While in Hangzhou and Hunan, Mao had sent orders to Lin Biao in Beijing to attack any leaders who showed indecision or hesitation when faced with Mao's demands for a new revolution. There was no doubt that the chairman was preparing a new purge of the Party, even beyond what the CCP had witnessed in the past. When, at the end of June, Mao left the Cave of Dripping Water and moved on to Wuhan, he seems to have decided not only on his bigger aims but also on some of the methods he would use for achieving them. He would speak directly to the people, and to young people in particular, in order to mobilize the masses to a level never seen before in Chinese or world history.[10]

On July 16, near Wuhan, Mao sent a strictly choreographed message to the rest of the country about his determination and courage. Hundreds of thousands of people were marched to the banks of the Yangzi River to await Mao's arrival on a small boat. The chairman dove in and swam in the river for an hour or so, to tremendous cheering from the crowd. "Chairman Mao has arrived! Long live Chairman Mao!" the spectators shouted. *Peking Review* commented on "how healthy and full of spirit our beloved leader Chairman Mao was, and this made [everyone] immensely happy. The same afternoon the workers wrote stacks of pledges in their workshops, proclaiming their resolve to raise the great red banner of Mao Zedong Thought still higher, carry the Great Proletarian Cultural Revolution through to the end . . . [and] support national construction and the Vietnamese people in their struggle to defeat U.S. imperialism."[11] *Renmin Ribao* quoted Mao: "Even great storms are not to be feared. It is amid great storms that human society progresses."[12] If Chairman Mao, 73 years of age, could swim in the Yangzi River, what could he not do?

Mao returned to Beijing a few days after his swim in the Yangzi. When Liu Shaoqi heard that the chairman had returned, he immediately rushed to see him, but was abruptly turned away by Mao's guards. The chairman himself was already inside talking about the Cultural Revolution with his former secretary Chen Boda, Kang Sheng, and others. Knowing that Liu was outside, Mao told his assistant that he did not want to see the president of China, who was waiting at his door.[13] A couple of days later, the CCP Politburo met to discuss whether the work teams that Liu and Deng had sent to schools in and around Beijing should be recalled. Mao was listening and watching. After Liu and Deng had first said that the majority of work teams are good ones, and that there was no need to recall them, Mao condemned the whole procedure they had put in place to stop the violence. These work teams "had done a disservice and obstructed the movement," Mao said. "They must quit to let the revolutionary teachers and students make the revolution themselves."[14] Mao wanted a purge throughout the Party, but he wanted China's youth to help carry it out.

A few days later, the Beijing Party Committee invited student activists from all over the city to a rally inside the Great Hall of the People. Liu Shaoqi, Zhou Enlai, and Deng Xiaoping spoke, telling the youngsters that in the Cultural Revolution, they, the "veteran revolutionaries, have encountered new challenges."[15] Mao also came to the Great Hall that day, without the other leaders knowing about it. He listened from behind a curtain as Liu and the others spoke. When the students started shouting, "We want Chairman Mao, we want Chairman Mao," the chairman emerged onto the stage as if by magic, silently and grimly greeting the crowd. Mass hysteria erupted, but the chairman was quickly hurried away by his bodyguards.[16]

As violence spread throughout the country in late 1966 and early 1967, some of the perpetrators became younger and younger. In Beijing some high school students organized what they called Red Guards to protect Chairman Mao and hunt for bourgeois "ghosts and monsters." Mao sent them a message saying that "it is right to rebel against the reactionaries. . . . We support all those who have taken the same revolutionary attitude as you have in the great Cultural Revolution."[17] He attacked those Party leaders who were trying to hold the students to account, accusing them of "acts of suppression and terror from the Central Committee." Looking morosely at the Central Committee members he had assembled before him, he declared that "there are monsters and demons among people present here."[18] In August 1966 Mao wrote a note to his fellow leaders—but really intended for China's youth—that he headlined "Bombard the Headquarters—My Own Big Character Poster." Using terms in vogue among student radicals, Mao told them that "some leading cadre from the central down to the local levels have, adopting the reactionary stand of the bourgeoise, enforced a bourgeois dictatorship and struck down the surging movement of the great Cultural Revolution of the proletariat."[19] The Red Guards—now, because of Mao's praise, becoming a countrywide movement—took the chairman's instructions to mean that everyone could be criticized, except those Mao protected, such as Lin Biao and the new members of the Central Cultural Revolution group. For the first time, Lin was called Mao's "closest comrade in arms," the "deputy commander," and successor.[20]

Encouraged by what he called "a revolutionary high," the chairman did not just want to issue instructions from afar. In the fall of 1966 he invited Red Guards and students from all over the country to come to Beijing and see him in person. More than eleven million came. Local transportation was disrupted for months because trains and buses were taken out of regular service in order to freight students to Beijing. Some walked for hundreds of miles, waving revolutionary banners, shouting slogans, and singing songs about going to Beijing to see Chairman Mao and receive his orders. Mao appeared atop the Tiananmen Gate or in an open-top car eight times from mid-August to late November, waving at the crowds but saying very little.[21] On a few occasions he spontaneously made quick forays into the throngs, chatting with a few groups, exhorting them to combat revisionism or expose renegades, enemy agents, and unrepentant capitalist roaders. When they returned home, the Red Guards who had been to see the chairman had a special status among their peers, which some used to organize a wave of terror against the "four olds": old ideas, old culture, old customs, and old habits. Temples and libraries were burned; paintings and scrolls were painted over with revolutionary

Left to right: Jiang Qing, Zhou Enlai, Lin Biao, and Mao Zedong
at the Tiananmen rostrum, September 15, 1966.
Source: World History Archive/Alamy Stock Photo.

slogans. Worse, thousands of professors, teachers, and even Communist Party leaders who had been labeled as "capitalist roaders" were dragged through the streets, beaten up, tortured at so-called struggle meetings, and sometimes killed or left to die. Often, those who had family members who owned property before 1949 or had worked for the previous government, the Guomindang, were subjected to the same treatment, even if their relatives or they themselves had been punished and had their property confiscated a long time ago.

Many Red Guard leaders felt that destroying China's old culture was a particularly important part of the chairman's instructions. In November 1966 a group of Red Guards traveled from Beijing to Confucius's hometown, Qufu, in Shandong, where they set out to wreck temples and memorial halls. But toppling statues and burning books were not enough for their energetic vandalism. First, they dynamited the tomb of the ancient sage himself. Then they proceeded to dig up the coffins of the thousands of Confucius's descendants who had been buried there. On instructions from Beijing, local authorities provided digging crews who helped with the desecration (though the workmen insisted on being paid first). In the end, more than 2,000 graves were dug up, though most seem to have been opened by locals, quite a few of whom themselves claimed to be descendants of Confucius. Large amounts of antiques and valuables that were found were "confiscated by the revolutionary masses."[22] Some bodily remains were strung up and then incinerated. The Red Guards wrote to Mao: "We have rebelled! . . . We have torn down the plaque extolling the 'teacher of ten-thousand generations'; we have leveled Confucius's grave; we have smashed the stelae extolling the virtues of the feudal emperors and kings, and we have obliterated the statues in the Confucius Temple!"[23] Similar reports came to Beijing from all over the country: temples were set ablaze; books were incinerated in large, public fires; homes were ransacked; people were killed. Police and fire brigades stood aside, certain that the terror had Chairman Mao's blessing.[24]

By the late autumn of 1966, the Cultural Revolution had spread from schools and colleges to workshops and factories. In Shanghai, groups of younger workers, with the help of the radicals now ascendant in Beijing, set up their own rebel movements. Among them was a young man from the No. 17 Cotton Textile Mill, Wang Hongwen, who soon became a leader in the newly formed Headquarters of the Revolutionary Revolt of Shanghai Workers. In November this group put forward a series of demands, including recognizing them as a "revolutionary organization," to the municipal government and the Shanghai Party Committee, which were rejected.[25] Then, over a thousand workers, led by Wang, forced their way onto a train bound for Beijing, hoping to deliver their demands to the Central Cultural Revolution Group or to the chairman himself. The train was stopped at Anting, a small station about twenty-five miles from Shanghai. The workers occupied the station. When the Shanghai radical Zhang Chunqiao, by now a close associate of Mao Zedong and Jiang Qing, arrived at the station, he spoke to the workers, recognizing the Workers Headquarters as a legitimate revolutionary organization and, on behalf of the central leadership, accepted all of their demands. When told, Mao confirmed Zhang's views.[26] In the wake of the events at Anting, large numbers of workers joined the rebel groups in Shanghai and, eventually, also elsewhere in the Chinese cities. Something understood as a Cultural Revolution was taking hold all over China.

On December 26, 1966, Mao celebrated his birthday at home together with the members of the Central Cultural Revolution Group. After a few drinks, the chairman started speaking about his worries for the future of socialism in China. "It all depends upon this Cultural Revolution," he told his associates. "This time it is going to be an all-out struggle, from the top down, and from the Red Guards to factories, the countryside, and the offices, the whole country has to be involved." But the start of the campaign had not been promising, he confessed. "The students have been purged. The rebels in Party and government have been suppressed. And the rebels in factories and mines have been suppressed. . . . The hot and active mass movement has been made cold and passive."[27] Mao stood up, proposing a toast to "victory in a full-scale civil war in the whole country this coming year!"[28]

Just a few weeks later, in Shanghai, the chairman seemed to get his wish fulfilled. A coalition of radical students, young factory workers, and Leftist Party cadres mobilized to seize power from Shanghai's municipal Party committee and government agencies. They were inspired by the example of the Paris Commune of 1871, a revolutionary event much lauded by the CCP. A Shanghai People's Commune was declared, to replace both the local government and the Party organization. Mao applauded what he called the Shanghai January Revolution. "I support all rebellions," the chairman proclaimed. "The Left ought to seize political power; it is a good direction to pursue." "This was a great revolution in which one class overthrew another," he gushed. "Now that the revolutionary forces in Shanghai have risen up, there is hope for China."[29]

In spite of his professed admiration for communes, both in Paris and Shanghai, Mao stopped short of specifically endorsing the Shanghai commune. If there will be communes everywhere, he wondered, "then, do we still need the Party, the government, and the military?" Maybe "even the name of the country, and its government, will have to be changed, too—to be called The People's Commune of China?" After hesitating a bit, he decided that the Shanghai People's Commune was not a correct name. "It should rather be called a revolutionary committee," he ordered.[30]

Like Yegong of Chinese lore—an old man who loved dragon paintings but recoiled in horror when he met real dragons—Mao liked revolution in principle but not when it interfered with his own plans. The countrywide revolution that he foresaw still had a place for a Party, a government, and an army. If these institutions collapsed, his own power would vanish with them. He wanted a strict purging of the ranks, and he wanted young revolutionary leaders to help with these purges. He wanted new initiatives to help remake the institutions he had first created to run China. But he would not do away with these institutions, since he and his ideas remained their main beneficiaries. Like so many revolutionaries, Mao was in some ways a prisoner of the instruments of power that he himself had created.

By early 1967, with all of China engulfed by the effects of the Cultural Revolution, Mao seems to have decided that all of the old Party leadership would have to go, with the exception of those he had designated leaders of the new era, and, of course, the ubiquitous Zhou Enlai, whom the chairman thought indispensable for running the country. Liu Shaoqi had been kept in political limbo throughout fall 1966. In January 1967 he was allowed to see the chairman, and he used the occasion to resign from his state and Party positions, including the presidency of the People's Republic of China. Mao said little, though he patted Liu on the back and recommended he acquaint himself with the works of Julien de La Mettrie and Ernst Haeckel. The chairman himself spent a lot of time reading philosophy these days, Mao said. As Liu left, the chairman advised him to "study well and keep fit."[31] By then, Liu and his wife had already been subjected to a public struggle meeting inside Zhongnanhai, the leadership compound in Beijing, where Liu was accused of being China's main "capitalist-roader." Red Guards would be allowed to invade their house repeatedly, vandalize it, and post slogans inside, most of them directed at Liu himself.[32] Afterwards Liu, his wife Wang Guangmei, and their children were kept under house arrest in Zhongnanhai, though they were occasionally paraded in public within the compound and "struggled against." In July 1967 Jiang Qing organized a Red Guard struggle session outside the gates of Zhongnanhai, demanding that Liu be dragged out and punished.[33] But Mao kept him penned up inside, as his favorite prisoner.

Other key leaders met a similar fate, though some fared even worse. Beijing mayor Peng Zhen was repeatedly tortured by Red Guards at big public events. So was Marshal Peng Dehuai and many others; at one meeting the 69-year-old marshal "had been struck to the ground no less than seven times and suffered multiple injuries, including a chest injury, two broken ribs, and a bleeding wound on his forehead."[34] Liu Shaoqi and Deng Xiaoping—now, respectively, dubbed the number-one and number-two "capitalist-roaders"— remained off limits to the bigger crowds, even though the slogans "Down with Liu Shaoqi" and "Down with Deng Xiaoping" could be heard everywhere. For other old Party leaders, the new CCP municipal authorities in Beijing insti- tuted what could be called a rent-a-revisionist system, whereby each of the Red Guard gangs could take turns in publicly torturing former leaders. "[For- mer oil minister] Yu Qiuli will be accepting denunciations by the masses three times this week," they informed eager Red Guards—twice from the group "Struggle-Criticism-Criticism" and once from the "Struggle Bo [Yibo] Preparatory Group." Next week he would meet the "Struggle Bo Preparatory Group" twice more and "Struggle-Criticism-Criticism" once more."[35] Many of the purged Party leaders were held at the notorious Qincheng Prison out- side of Beijing, where they were routinely mistreated and tortured. "They would force-feed you a kind of drug that induced hallucinations," one of them recounted. "No matter how many times a day my execution was announced, I would always shout 'Long live Chairman Mao, long live the Communist Party' and sing the *Internationale*. Then the cancellation of my execution would be announced."[36]

Mao wanted the old Party leadership gone. But he did not want Party rule to collapse or the Chinese state to be severely weakened. The dilemmas this produced were seen every day, even at the height of the Cultural Revolution between 1966 and 1968. Red Guards could mistreat old cadre, but the Cen- tral Cultural Revolution Group regulated their access to the victims. Ordinary people could shout slogans, but Mao and his close associates decided which slogans were correct and therefore promoted and which were not. Even though new groups were in charge of at least parts of the CCP organization, all major decisions would have to come from within the Party's top leader- ship, now often referred to as the new Party Center, meaning not the Central Committee or even the Politburo, but Chairman Mao and his closest associ- ates. They regulated the all-important access to radio broadcasts (essential in a country with a high rate of illiteracy), the allocation of material resources, the deployment of police and militias, and the stationing and use of units from the People's Liberation Army. While proclaiming that chaos was good, Mao knew he needed the power that the Party represented, now and in the future. It would be a different Communist Party from the one that had come to power in 1949. But it would still be in charge, with him at the helm, just like Stalin's Soviet Communist Party had remained in charge after the purges there.

In late January and early February 1967, irritation within the PLA leadership over the conduct of the Cultural Revolution and the high-handed approach of its leaders, especially Jiang Qing and Chen Boda, boiled over during a set of meetings of the CCP Central Military Commission. The pretext was a Red Guard raid on the home of General Xiao Hua, the head of the PLA's Political Department, in which files were stolen and members of his family were roughed up. Marshal Ye Jianying was so angry during a heated debate with Jiang Qing that he injured a finger when slamming his palm against a table.[37] Even Lin Biao was furious over what had happened to some of the army commanders and confronted Jiang Qing over it.[38] When the whole affair was reported to Mao, the chairman was unhappy with his wife and with Chen Boda, accusing them of acting too independently and prematurely. In a fit of rage, he accused Chen of being an opportunist, and he admonished his wife: "You have great aspirations but not an ounce of talent, and you always look down on everyone else. . . . [Do not] attempt to block me out!"[39]

On February 16, at a meeting attended by senior political and military leaders, including most members of the Central Cultural Revolution Group, matters came to a head. The old army political commissar Tan Zhenlin and the foreign minister, Marshal Chen Yi, condemned the attacks on old cadre, accusing Chen Boda and Jiang Qing of attempting to destroy the Party. "I have followed the Chairman for more than forty years," said Tan, "and I was never against him. If things go on as they do now, I will quit. . . . I hate the thought of having lived sixty-five years just to end up in this mess."[40] Pale as a sheet, Zhou Enlai, who chaired the meeting, ordered all records destroyed.

But if the veteran officers who had criticized the violence thought that Mao was now on their side, they were badly mistaken. In their briefings to Mao after the meeting, Jiang Qing and Kang Sheng insisted that the criticism from the generals was an attempted coup d'etat against the chairman himself. After listening to Jiang Qing's report, Mao declared that she and the Leftists were in the right politically. "Ninety-nine percent of what the Cultural Revolution group has done is correct, and its errors are just one, two or three percent," shouted Mao.[41] Even Kang Sheng, longtime intelligence head of the CCP, shuddered. "I have never seen the Chairman in such a rage," he told others.[42]

Mao dubbed the criticism from the veterans "the February Adverse Current," and one by one the old members of the Central Military Commission and the State Council were politically sidelined. Many were purged from their positions. The chairman made it clear that he would not yield a single inch to any dissent against the Cultural Revolution within the Party. The Central Cultural Revolution Group increasingly became the key unit of decision-making, replacing both the Politburo and the long paralyzed CCP Secretariat.[43] Young staffers, some of whom had made their name as leaders of rebel groups in Beijing and elsewhere, flocked to assist the Cultural Revolution Group with issues such as worker's participation, art and literature, and antirevisionist investigations.

Along with the crushing of the "February Adverse Current," the chairman put forward two interrelated strategies to promote his new revolution. First, with the support of Lin Biao and the cooperation of Zhou Enlai, he ordered the People's Liberation Army to be actively involved in the Cultural Revolution, supporting the Left in seizing power from Party and government leaders.[44] Second, as political power shifted Left, revolutionary committees should be established at all levels. These were new authorities of political power, and Mao intended them to be composed of representatives from workers' organizations, reeducated CCP cadres, and, especially, army officers. In Mao's assessment in early spring 1967, the process of seizing political power would last for three to four months, and it would open the door for a victorious conclusion to the Cultural Revolution.[45]

But, once released, the spirit of rebellion was hard to cage. Beginning in spring 1967, almost everywhere in China the establishment of revolutionary committees led to increased conflict and factional infighting. In the cities, especially, tension continued to escalate through 1967 and much of 1968. By the summer of 1967, among China's twenty-nine provinces, autonomous regions, and municipalities, revolutionary committees had only been established in Shanghai, Heilongjiang, Shanxi, Shandong, Guizhou, and Beijing. But even there, with ongoing factional fights, the situation was ever more chaotic. Elsewhere, without a provincial-level revolutionary committee to at least pretend to coordinate things, matters were even worse.

All across the country, the Cultural Revolution rolled on. In some cities and towns, such as in Wuhan, Red Guard groups fought each other over minuscule differences in the interpretation of Mao Zedong Thought. Old resentments and hatreds, resulting from all the violence and endless political campaigns and purges perpetrated by the Party since 1949, broke out into the open. Revenge was an increasingly common motive for struggles and denunciations, as was, in some cases, material gain. Student Red Guard groups were particularly active, but there were also groups purporting to represent factories, villages, minority groups, or even extended family networks. In the southwestern province of Guangxi, mass unrest led to political chaos and fighting, in which in the end almost 40,000 people died—by beheading, beating, live burial, stoning, drowning, boiling, knifing, disemboweling, removing of hearts, livers, or genitals, slicing off flesh, or being blown up with dynamite.[46] In a few cases, the flesh of some of the victims was eaten by their opponents.[47] If outright cannibalism remained rare, all over China killings, sometimes by gruesome methods, proliferated as the political frenzy grew.

If life was terrifying for most people, including some of the Red Guard perpetrators who lost out to other factions, nowhere was the situation worse than in minority areas. In Tibet, Xinjiang, and Inner Mongolia, as well as in some of the minority regions of the Southwest, the Cultural Revolution amounted to a Chinese attempt at wiping out national identities, cultures, and religions. Sometimes the Chinese were joined by locals, out of fear, enthusiasm, or greed. Some of the bigger monasteries in Tibet were destroyed by groups of Chinese and Tibetan students who had set up Red Guards. Later, Red Guards from Beijing and elsewhere arrived to destroy the rest and teach Mao Zedong Thought to the population, as well as to arrest and terrorize Buddhist monks and former CCP leaders alike. For some it was just part of the fun. "I liked to be on the road," one of them reminisced. "Not too long after coming to Lhasa, I went with two friends to Shigatse. There the Tashilhunpo Monastery was already under attack. The shrines had been destroyed and there were broken statues and ripped up prayer texts piled up everywhere. Good stuff could still be found, though, such as small Buddha statues made out of gold."[48]

Even though the Cultural Revolution had horrible effects for people living at the edges of the Chinese empire, China in the late 1960s for the most part pulled inward, away from engaging with people outside of its borders.

Although there was plentiful rhetorical support for revolutionary movements elsewhere, there was little practical support, except in Vietnam, where China competed with the Soviet Union in providing assistance to North Vietnam and the liberation front in the south. Mao did not want to intervene directly in the Vietnam War, but he was prepared to do so if the United States invaded North Vietnam. Chinese forces already stationed there, as well as PLA units deployed along the border, had been told that China would defend the Communist regime in Hanoi, just like it had defended North Korea in 1950.[49] But, in political terms, relations with both Communist Vietnamese and Koreans deteriorated sharply during the Cultural Revolution. Both regimes viewed the chaos in China as madness and resented being constantly reminded by the Chinese of Mao Zedong's superior ideological insights.[50] Revolutionary Cuba, which had tried to straddle the Sino-Soviet split, opted decisively for Moscow, leading Red Guards to denounce Fidel Castro as "the little Khrushchev of the Caribbean."[51] Only tiny Albania, locked in a fierce quarrel with both the Soviets and its European neighbors, the Yugoslavs, held up Mao's China as an ideal.

There were, however, some foreign groups that embraced an idealized version of Maoism in its Cultural Revolution version. The concept of "People's War," propagated by Mao and Lin Biao based on the CCP's experience in the 1930s and 1940s, became popular among guerrilla groups from the Philippines to Peru. In some cases these groups also adopted other aspects of radical Maoism into their political thinking.[52] But the foreign effects that were most striking, at least in the 1960s, were among groups of college students in the West, who were attracted to Cultural Revolution slogans because of their own opposition to rigid and authoritarian universities and their critique of capitalism and of injustice in Western societies. Completely unaware of (or in some cases untroubled by) the suffering caused by the real Cultural Revolution or the extreme authoritarianism Mao stood for, some students and intellectuals in Western Europe and North America set up Maoist parties and shouted slogans from the Little Red Book. In West Germany, one favored rallying cry for revolutionary students was "You are old, we are young, Mao Tse-tung."[53] None of these parties ever got much electoral support in their home countries, but in China their existence was used as proof of the universal appeal of the chairman's teachings.

Even in China, in spite of the horrors many people went through and all the wanton battles, struggles, and destruction, for some young people the chaos of the Cultural Revolution felt like a liberation of sorts.[54] China had been a very hierarchical society long before the Communists took over, and this hierarchy was particularly visible in families, schools, and factories. When young people were suddenly told that criticizing their elders—even their parents, teachers, or bosses—was okay, there was a sense of liberation, which in some cases gave way to breaking from their background altogether. Millions of young people traveled the country for free and at their own initiative. They went to Beijing to see Chairman Mao, or to the countryside to help peasants with the harvest. They went to regions of faraway provinces where not many Chinese had been before. In the process they discovered much about their country and about themselves. For every Red Guard member who organized atrocities, there were many more who simply went along for the ride, learning new things, having fun with their friends, exploring their sexualities. For most, and especially for young women, it gave a sense of freedom that they had never experienced before, even though it happened within a movement based on worshipping authoritarian terror.[55]

By mid-1967 it was clear to most observers in Beijing that the Cultural Revolution had entered a stage where it was a real struggle for power within the Communist Party. The Central Cultural Revolution Group used the Red Guards to attack those perceived as their enemies. Jiang Qing and Kang Sheng continued to present the criticism from the generals, what Mao had called the "February Adverse Current," as an attempted coup d'etat, leading to ever wider purges. That summer General Yang Yong, the commander of the Beijing Military Region, was arrested by Red Guards. Lin Biao, again angry at not having been consulted, threatened to resign in a stormy meeting with Jiang Qing. In September 1967, Mao, attempting to remove himself from the day-to-day infighting, commented laconically that "there are two possible futures for the Cultural Revolution. One is to achieve another peak. The other is that the country splits up. There are irreconcilable factions in Nanjing, Wuxi, Beijing, and across China. If we fail to achieve unity, China may enter a state of turmoil and split up as it did during the chaos that followed the Revolution of 1911."[56] But by then the chairman had already made the decision to rein in the most radical elements of the Red Guards.

The pretext for turning on the extreme Left was their attack on China's foreign affairs institutions in August 1967. First a group of Red Guards outside and inside of the Foreign Ministry occupied and ransacked the ministry's political department and its Party committee. Then they took control of the ministry as a whole, requiring all officials to attend political education sessions and struggle meetings, thereby bringing communications with Chinese embassies abroad to a standstill. A few days later Wang Li and Guan Feng, the members of the Central Cultural Revolution Group who had supported the attack on the Foreign Ministry, helped organize attacks against a number of foreign embassies in Beijing. The Indonesian and Mongolian embassies were invaded by Red Guards. The Soviet embassy was attacked and besieged. The worst attack was against the British embassy on August 22: the offices of the head of the mission were burned down, his residence was raided, and diplomats and other employees were beaten.[57] At this, Zhou Enlai dared to take action. He insisted to Mao that Wang and Guan be taken into custody, along with another radical, Qi Benyu. Mao agreed. It was the first time leaders on the Left were arrested during the Cultural Revolution.[58] It would not be the last.

Over the year that followed, Mao became increasingly preoccupied with stabilizing the situation in China. He wanted to keep the Left in power, while excluding the old cadre who had been purged. But he did stress that "revolutionary alliances" were needed between different groups and that the use of violence in public should stop. "The overwhelming majority of our cadre are good and only a tiny minority are not. True, those Party persons in power taking the capitalist road are our target, but they are a mere handful," he declared.[59] The Central Cultural Revolution Group changed tack. Instead of encouraging public denunciations, it began accusing the senior leaders it targeted of "historical problems," claiming that they had defected from the CCP in the past and become agents of the Guomindang, the Americans, or the Soviets (or in some cases of all three). In the army, Lin Biao acted to strengthen his control, but he was held back by increasingly frequent bouts of mental illness, which could leave him passive, even listless, for weeks on end. In his place, his wife, Ye Qun, and son, the deputy commander of the Airforce Operations Department Lin Liguo, often spoke on Lin Biao's behalf. Not a great supporter of the Red Guards or Cultural Revolution politics in the first place, by 1968 Lin Biao was getting increasingly preoccupied with reestablishing order and keeping the PLA's command systems in place.

But even the attempts to use the PLA to reassert control succeeded only with great difficulty, at least at first. In spite of Mao's orders, by early 1968 there were still just nine provinces that were led by revolutionary committees. And the number of weapons taken over by rebel groups, nearly nineteen million guns according to one source, led to flare-ups of armed clashes in at least fifty different locations, despite attempts by PLA commanders sent from Beijing to quench them.[60] Mao repeatedly announced that "there exists no fundamental contradiction within the working class" and called for the "suppression of factionalism" in the whole country.[61] Yet the immediate effect of these calls was quite limited.

The prolonged chaos caused substantial challenges for China's industrial and agricultural output. Even though the production drops were nowhere near as bad as during the Great Leap Forward, China's industrial output dropped almost 10 percent year on year in 1967.[62] In some industries the situation was dire. About half of China's iron and steel plants produced nothing or very little. Coal mines delivered about half of what they had the year before. In the Northeast, one of China's main industrial areas, electricity output declined by a quarter, and many homes were unheated in winter because of a lack of coal and electricity. Transportation was chaotic. Less than half of all trains were operating according to schedule, since many of them had been taken over by revolutionary groups or seconded to freight Red Guards back and forth to Beijing.[63] In Shaanxi a group of young revolutionaries calling themselves the May 7 Anti-Revisionist Brigade had much fun running a train between Jiexiu and Huozhou, singing Red Guard songs and shouting slogans. The local coal freighters had to wait on the sidelines.[64]

Agricultural production decreased only by about 2 percent, since most rural areas were less affected by the Cultural Revolution. There were areas of China where the fragile recovery in farming after the Great Leap was endangered by the intensity of political campaigns, such as parts of Sichuan, Anhui, and Guangxi. But in other areas, mainly in the wealthier eastern parts of the country, the collapse of Party and state control left some tiny space for farmers to take more control themselves. Especially from mid-1967 on, a few districts saw a resurgence of household-based farming, completely in contradiction to the collectivist ideals of the Cultural Revolution. These practices were of course called by other names—"sacrifice labor for the common good," or "increase production through intense study of local conditions"—but they all amounted to the same thing: families, separately or together, agreeing on ways in which they could increase their output and benefit from the results.

Surprising as it might seem, a few young people in the cities also escaped Maoist regimentation, both physically and intellectually, through Cultural Revolution lessening of controls and procedures. In some places, students began writing what was later called "heterodox literature," exposing the increasingly more dramatic absurdities in everyday life during the Cultural Revolution. The pioneers were people such as Yu Luoke, a young man in Beijing who in 1966 had circulated texts questioning the Party's views on what constituted "good class origins."[65] There were also Liu Wozhong and Zhang Licai, two Beijing middle school students publishing under the pseudonym Yilin Dixi, who put up a big-character poster questioning Lin Biao's speeches on "revolutionary genius."[66] Over the years that followed, a few brave people persisted in critiquing official orthodoxy or asking for a cultural revolution from below. Yang Xiguang and his fellow students in Hunan wrote and circulated "Where Will China Be Going?" and "Investigation Report on the State of Educated Youth in Hunan."[67] Zhou Quanying at Tsinghua University explored the achievements and, especially, limits of the Cultural Revolution.[68] Lu Li'an and Feng Tianan, in Wuhan, argued for the need to "destroy the old state machine as well as the new bureaucratic capitalist class."[69] In April 1968, Red Guard groups at several Shanghai colleges and high schools called for young people to "bombard Zhang Chunqiao," the radical Shanghai Maoist on the rise in the CCP. Zhang, they claimed, was a bureaucratic careerist and not a suitable model for young revolutionaries.[70] Such heterodoxies were quickly suppressed, but they left a legacy of dissent for others to build on.[71]

By summer 1968 the same kind of terror that had been used by the radical Left against its opponents was increasingly used against Red Guard leaders themselves by the military. In July the Central Committee, the government, and the Central Cultural Revolution Group jointly issued a six-point directive threatening strict punishment against groups that interfered with government communications, robbed military trains, broke into PLA institutions, or killed or wounded PLA officers and soldiers.[72] In some places military police or regular military units on their own initiative arrested the leaders of radical groups or organizations. Some disappeared into the same jails or labor camps where their former victims were still held, but many more were sent off to work in remote rural areas or to serve as army conscripts. A few simply disappeared.

In late July 1968 the chairman finally decided to take action himself to stem the chaos. On July 27 he dispatched what he termed "Workers' Mao Zedong Thought Propaganda Teams," manned by workers but led by Party officials, to the main Beijing colleges to reestablish direct Party control there. At Tsinghua University, Red Guard groups opened fire on the team. Mao, enraged, declared the Red Guard movement dissolved, while, at the same time, he launched a nationwide campaign to suppress the rebel groups who had served as his vanguard in the early and most turbulent phase of the Cultural Revolution. At a meeting early on the morning of July 28, Mao met leaders of the Red Guards, including Nie Yuanzi, Mao's former hero from Peking University. The July CCP directives were valid for all of China, the chairman said. "If anyone are to continuously violate these regulations by attacking the PLA, disrupting transportation, killing people, or setting fire, . . . they are bandits; they are Guomindang. And they will be rounded up. If they are to resist, they will be wiped out."[73]

In the fall of 1968, with Mao's blessing, the army and workers militias began dissolving Red Guard organizations and removing their members from campus. Some of yesterday's "little red soldiers" became today's "subjects of reeducation." In late December *Renmin Ribao* very prominently displayed the chairman's instructions that "it is very necessary for educated young people to go to the countryside to be re-educated by the poor and lower-middle peasants."[74] About sixteen million left the cities, either of their own accord or because they were forced to do so.[75] That September, with revolutionary committees finally established in all twenty-nine provinces and municipalities, Zhou Enlai, representing Mao, announced at a celebration mass rally in Beijing that the Cultural Revolution had achieved great victories through "seizing power from the small number of capitalist roaders within the Party."[76] By early 1969 the most active phase of the Cultural Revolution was over, even if official slogans remained the same and those purged who had survived were still in jail, under house arrest, or in inner exile far from Beijing.

Mao had curbed the radicals and the Red Guards with the help of the army, but he wanted his campaigns to continue and had no plans of purging the

Left from the Party leadership. Instead he seems to have opted for some kind of balance between the Cultural Revolutionaries—people like Jiang Qing, Kang Sheng, Chen Boda, and Zhang Chunqiao—the PLA, headed by Lin Biao but with many alternative centers of power, and Zhou Enlai and the remaining central state and Party administration. Some of these arrangements were ratified at a CCP Central Committee plenum in October 1968, the first to be held in more than two years. By the Party's constitution, the whole affair was illegal, since the majority of the Central Committee elected back in 1956 were either dead, in prison, or purged. Even Zhou Enlai's best efforts could not rustle up much less than half of the members, some of whom had to be brought straight from their prison cells. Mao solved the problem by promoting ten alternative members on the spot, thereby pretending to make the plenum legal.[77]

At the plenum, Liu Shaoqi was formally expelled from the Party. He was, said the report on him, "just the type of plotter and schemer Chairman Mao referred to. Once he gets an opportunity, he will seize control of the party and government, and will turn the proletarian dictatorship into a bourgeois dictatorship. . . . After the basic completion of the socialist reconstruction of ownership of production materials, he advocated ending class struggle, reconciliation among classes, and individual management of land, free markets, individual responsibility for profits and losses, and the fixing of farm output quotas at the household level."[78] In other words, Liu was exactly the kind of revisionist Mao feared most, or, as Jiang Qing put it more trenchantly, "a renegade, hidden traitor, and scab." Deng Xiaoping was designated the "Number Two Capitalist Roader in the Party," formally purged from all his positions, but, remarkably, allowed to keep his Party membership on Mao's orders.[79] Other old leaders, such as the marshals Chen Yi, Ye Jianying, Nie Rongzhen, and Xu Xiangqian, even kept their Central Committee membership, but they were excluded from all key decision-making. Even Marshal Zhu De, the first commander in chief of the PLA and the most legendary military figure in China, was criticized for "persistent Right deviation."[80]

One key reason why Mao had pulled back from the brink of internal chaos and begun stressing the need for unity was his increasing fear of war. By 1969 he had concluded that the United States was mired in Vietnam and did not wish to expand the war there. But the Soviet Union seemed ever more aggressive, according to the chairman. Mao saw the Soviet intervention in Czechoslovakia in 1968 as a prelude for what could happen to China. The Soviets were the most active imperialists, Mao said. He termed them "social-imperialist," borrowing—probably inadvertently—a term Leo Trotsky first employed against German Social Democrats in 1914.[81] Mao kept telling his associates that the United States was the declining superpower, while the Soviet Union was on the rise. And he wanted to signal to the Soviets that China, despite its inner turmoil, was ready to take them on. To his own countrymen he wanted to prove that his analysis of the international situation was correct, and that the Chinese "revisionists"—those he accused of taking the Soviet road—were not only traitors to the Party but traitors to China as well. By the end of 1968, Mao had started increasing the military pressure on the Soviets in their border areas, especially in the eastern sector along the Amur and Ussuri Rivers, where Chinese troops had started patrolling river islands that had previously been under Soviet control.

All evidence points to Mao having had a preconceived plan for a limited military conflict with the Soviets in Manchuria. But after a Chinese ambush of Soviet border guards at Zhenbao (Damanskii) island on March 2, 1969, in which more than fifty Soviets were killed and almost a hundred wounded, the Soviet leader Leonid Brezhnev decided to strike back in style. Using BM-21 "Grad" mobile rocket launchers, Soviet Red Army units destroyed the Chinese positions on the island, killing more than 200 regular PLA soldiers.[82] China and the Soviet Union seemed headed for war. The Soviet premier, Aleksei Kosygin, tried to call the Chinese leaders to discuss a cease-fire. The Chinese telephone operator shouted antirevisionist slogans at him and hung up.[83] Both sides showed some restraint in the aftermath of the battle; Mao ordered the PLA "that [it] is enough, no more fighting," and Zhou told the Soviets that China was ready for a diplomatic initiative.[84] But there were more clashes along both sectors of the Sino-Soviet border in the summer of 1969. By that fall Mao had become convinced that the Soviets were planning a nuclear first strike against China. In October he ordered the leadership (and his most prominent political prisoners) evacuated from Beijing to various parts of the interior. He himself went to Wuhan, and Lin Biao to Suzhou. Liu Shaoqi was flown to Kaifeng, naked and shackled to a stretcher. There he died a few days later from lack of medical attention. Deng Xiaoping was taken to rural Jiangxi Province, where he was to remain for the next four years. Of the top leaders, only Zhou Enlai and Jiang Qing were left in the capital, to watch the Soviets and each other.[85]

But there was no Soviet attack, at least not this time. Mao was left seriously shaken by the crisis that he himself had set in motion. Already in 1968 he had begun contemplating the dangers that China's strategic isolation could entail for his revolution. He had concluded that the Third World alliance that China had hoped to build and lead had come to nothing. Obsessing with the threat of a world war coming soon, Mao explained that China's situation was similar to what it had been prior to World War II, with the Soviets now in the role of Japan. China needed to draw nearer to all those countries that opposed the Soviet Union. Leaders in Moscow suspected that Mao had engineered the border clashes in order to approach the Americans and their allies. But the chairman still held back from contacting the United States directly, probably for ideological reasons. He did, however, authorize the foreign minister, Chen Yi, and a number of other military leaders—all of whom had been in the political doghouse during the Cultural Revolution—to think through the international situation and provide him with confidential advice, "not to be restricted by the old frame of thinking."[86] After new border clashes with the Soviets in August 1969, Chen and the other marshals—probably sensing the chairman's wishes—summoned their courage to recommend that China very carefully reach out to the Americans. Even so, it was the new U.S. administration of President Richard Nixon that first began signaling a wish for improved relations with Beijing by offering to restart secret diplomatic contacts through the U.S. embassy in Warsaw. China accepted in December 1969.

By 1969 Mao was also ready to "consolidate the gains of the Cultural Revolution" by holding another Party congress—the first since 1956. Obviously aging, but unwilling to give up any form of control, the chairman wanted to have the question of his successor formally established by a Party congress. Many of those close to Mao wondered why he had chosen Lin Biao, a man never known for his attention to political detail and now undoubtedly in failing health. One reason was probably the need for someone with military prestige to keep the country united after the chairman's passing. Another was Lin's always lavish praise of Mao and what he stood for. But the chairman also apparently felt that Lin was manipulable and could be removed if necessary, unlike younger and more energetic leaders who could have built the number-two position into an alternative focus of power within the Party. Always suspicious of the power of others, by 1969 Mao's suspiciousness was nearing paranoia; he assumed that every other leader in the Party wanted, eventually, to replace him or change his political legacy. Lin Biao seemed a dependable, pliable, disposable choice as number two, at least for now.

At the Ninth CCP Congress Lin Biao gave the main political report, as Mao's previous successor, Liu Shaoqi, had done back in 1956. The report was almost entirely composed of political slogans against domestic revisionism, U.S. imperialism, and Soviet "social-imperialism" and its "fascist" aggression against China. "The entire history of our Party has borne out this truth," Lin said solemnly. "Departing from the leadership of Chairman Mao and Mao Zedong Thought, our Party will suffer setbacks and defeats; following Chairman Mao closely and acting on Mao Zedong Thought, our Party will advance and triumph. We must forever remember this lesson. Whoever opposes Chairman Mao, whoever opposes Mao Zedong Thought, at any time or under any circumstances, will be condemned and punished by the whole Party and the whole country."[87] In the lead-up to the congress, Lin—acting in consort with Premier Zhou Enlai—had spoken of giving some weight to issues of production and industrial development. Chen Boda, who had drafted one version of the main report, had inserted some references to production, but Mao had them deleted, accusing Chen of not concentrating enough on revolution.[88] The chairman had the ever-ready Zhang Chunqiao submit revised drafts to him, and Mao liked them very much, feeling that Zhang had caught the essence of Maoist thought on "continuous revolution." It was Zhang's version Lin Biao presented and which was adopted as the Congress's political report. In the aftermath, Mao criticized Chen Boda for having "served other masters behind my back."[89] Mao's suspicions were boundless, and nobody could feel safe.

The Cultural Revolution had been a disaster for all of China, but first and foremost it had been a calamity for the Chinese Communist Party itself. In his search for absolute political supremacy and radical social transformation, Mao Zedong had unleashed forces well beyond his or anyone's ability to control. In the chaos that followed, many people suffered, and even more people suffered as Mao's state, party, and army fought to regain control. Among those who suffered most were the groups who should have led China forward: teachers, scientists, administrators, and young enthusiasts who had joined

Mao Zedong posting his vote, followed by Lin Biao, Zhou Enlai,
Chen Boda, Kang Sheng, Jiang Qing, Zhang Chunqiao, and Yao Wenyuan,
at the CCP's Ninth Congress, April 1969.
Source: World History Archive/Alamy Stock Photo.

the revolution for no other reason than that they wanted to make their country rich and strong. In the aftermath Mao's own prestige was still robust—to
most, he was a godlike figure who symbolized the new China, and he could
do no wrong. But people did not forget the atrocities carried out in his name.
Nor did the Party officials who had been paraded through the streets wearing dunce caps, been spat on, and had their limbs broken, forget who had
tormented them. Even though the active phase of the Cultural Revolution was
over, China was set for another period of political shocks and rapid change.

3

A Successor Dies

AFTER LIN BIAO BECAME MAO ZEDONG'S designated successor at the 1969 Communist Party Congress, the 62-year-old Lin spent much time trying to figure out which direction China should move in over the next decade. Lin had come a very long way in Communist politics after first joining China's Red Army as a teenager in the 1920s. During the 1940s, as a general, he had commanded some of the most spectacular CCP military operations, and it was his strategic acumen that had allowed the Communists to turn the tables on their enemies in Manchuria, setting the stage for the victories that brought Mao Zedong to power in 1949. Lin had always had a complicated relationship with Mao. As a field commander, he had often ignored the chairman's instructions and gone his own way to triumph. He had declined the offer of leading China's forces in the Korean War, believing that directly engaging the Americans there was a fool's errand.[1] In the 1950s he had mainly stayed out of politics, and had seemed to be in steep decline, battling depression and a variety of real or imagined physical illnesses. He had accepted the position as minister of defense in 1959 because it allowed him to outshine Peng De-huai, the marshal who had accepted the command in Korea and who had now fallen into political disfavor for his criticism of the disastrous consequences from Great Leap Forward. After his return to power, Lin was punctilious in his service to Mao and to the image of the chairman as China's great savior and helmsman. Nobody was more alert to the chairman's wishes and to his increasingly changing moods. In the cult of Mao, Lin Biao simultaneously took on the roles of high priest and supreme servant.[2]

But there were other sides to Lin Biao that started coming to the fore as his position was secured. He took revenge on the many among his military colleagues who had regarded him as a bit of an oddball and who had ignored him during the 1950s. Excessively vain and easy to take offense, Lin sought to put officers in command in the PLA who admired him and were beholden to him. In spite of his lip service to Mao's new revolutionary ideals, Lin regarded much of the Cultural Revolution as excessive and chaotic, and he deplored the way the PLA was dragged into factional clashes at the local level.[3] Lin was more of a traditional Stalinist in his political approach: he liked the idea of using the Cultural Revolution to purge those who were unworthy and pick new and younger leaders. But he also believed that out of the Cultural Revolution scourge should come a new order, a purified and stronger party and state, that could move China faster toward the goals of international power and fortune. The new order that Lin foresaw was strictly hierarchical and based on intense dedication to the teachings of the CCP, in a setting where peasants were quickly transformed into highly productive industrial workers. A bit like the chairman, Lin had an almost mystical devotion to Marxism, believing it to be the culmination of China's long history.

Lin's biggest enemy in making use of his new and exalted position was in his own head. By late 1969 the successor was increasingly unwell, with a number of episodes indicating severe bipolar disorder. Sometimes he did not sleep for days at an end, or he sat, entirely mute, in his study, staring at the ceiling. He suffered from hallucinations and paranoid rages. When these moods hit, Lin Biao would hide away in his Beijing residence, an old princely compound called Maojiawan, or in one of the grand houses he had taken over in the provinces. Sometimes he would not be heard from for weeks. On such occasions it was increasingly his wife, Ye Qun, and his son, the air force officer Lin Liguo, who communicated on his behalf, or Lin's longtime associates who were now appointed to some of the PLA's most important positions: Huang Yongsheng as chief of staff, Wu Faxian as commander of the air force, Li Zuopeng as political commissar of the navy, and Qiu Huizuo as deputy chief of staff and commander of the PLA General Logistics Department. The military leaders Lin had put in charge around the country were sometimes able to see him, though not as often as they wanted. Most of them were satisfied with biding their time, hoping for greater rewards—or at least greater safety—after Mao Zedong passed from the scene.

Lin Biao's many illnesses were perhaps metaphoric for China in the early 1970s, a time when street violence had died down but political infighting intensified. Maybe it was China's frenzied politics that caused the vice chairman's ailments. Mao's frame of mind seemed to change with increasing frequency, and his megalomania and distrust grew. At times it appeared to other leaders as if the chairman was simply playing with them for his own amusement, setting one group against another, noting his displeasure with someone only to laud the very same person to the skies the next day. Mao often had a bit of fun terrifying others. But his restlessness may also have been a result of him being uncertain about where to move next politically. He saw the Cultural Revolution as positive and would stand no criticism of its results. He spoke of the need to intensify class struggle and announced that more Cultural Revolutions would be necessary in the future.[4] But Mao also became increasingly preoccupied with remedying China's weakness vis-à-vis the outside world. The next Five-Year Plan, the aims of which were set in early 1970, aimed at "taking class struggle as the key link, firmly grasping preparations against war, and bringing about a new leap forward in the economy."[5] Politics were still in command, but the threat of war made China's economic development more important than in the previous decade.

During 1970 Mao was getting increasingly demanding and impatient with some of his followers on the Left. He accused them of staking out positions for themselves and of not being honest in their reporting to him. It is hard to figure out whether there were real policy differences, or whether the chairman had simply started to worry that some of the leading figures of the Cultural Revolution were getting too much power, so much that they might be tempted to work around him or, in his ultimate nightmare, do without him. At the Ninth Party Congress in 1969, Mao had agreed to the elevation of his wife, Jiang Qing, and Lin Biao's wife, Ye Qun, to the Politburo, but he had blocked Jiang from joining the Politburo's Standing Committee.[6] At times he turned furiously on Jiang Qing. On one occasion, in circulated remarks, he called his wife "a person with undeserved reputation" who "has shown gross incompetence."[7] But he also started to worry about his successor Lin Biao. Mao was unhappy that Lin had issued orders in his own name, the so-called Order Number One, for a general mobilization during the Soviet war scare in the autumn of 1969.[8] By early 1970 Lin was sometimes included in Mao's grumbles about being treated like "an old boot" by his associates.[9]

The start of the falling-out between Mao and parts of the Left could almost be written as a comedy, if it had not had such tragic outcomes for those involved. The script centers on an old man who was increasingly suspicious of his surroundings and for whom excessive flattery set off alarm bells about treacherous intent. It was not surprising, perhaps, that Ye Qun began reading Shakespeare's tragedies as the story unfolded.[10] The starting point was Lin Biao and Zhou Enlai worrying in the spring of 1970 that China no longer had a head of state after Liu Shaoqi, still nominally China's president until his death in 1969, had been eliminated. Lin and Zhou had had a long history of cooperation, respected each other, and often worked together and supported each other during the Cultural Revolution. They felt that only Mao himself could fill such an important post, even though the chairman had already indicated that he was not interested, and had suggested Lin Biao himself take the position, if it was necessary to have a president.[11] In spite of Mao's views, Lin brought the issue back to a Central Committee plenum at the mountain resort of Lushan in August 1970. In a rambling speech, Lin Biao extolled Mao's supreme genius and said that only the chairman could fill the state presidency.[12] Chen Boda, the head of the Central Cultural Revolution Group and Mao's former chief secretary, had documents supporting Lin's views disseminated at the meeting, and circulated further shortly thereafter. Chen himself spoke in support of Lin Biao, lauding Lin's qualities and insights. He attacked others, implied to be Zhang Chunqiao, a key member of Jiang Qing's group, for not having supported Lin's views strongly enough, accusing him of being an "ambitious schemer and a conspirator, an extreme reactionary, a counterrevolutionary, an agent of Liu Shaoqi's reactionary line without Liu Shaoqi, a running dog of imperialism, revisionism and reactionaryism, and a bad man. Therefore, he should be exposed and displayed to the public, expelled from the Party, fought and knocked down with odious reputation, hacked in pieces, and punished by the entire party and entire people."[13]

There is no evidence that Lin or Chen intended anything else than the further glorification of Mao and an opportunity for one-upmanship over their sometime rivals Jiang Qing and her younger associates. But the chairman reacted furiously. In his rage, he claimed, without naming Lin, that Chen wanted to elevate him into oblivion by forcing him to become president—a largely ceremonial post—while they took over the Party and the army. On other occasions, he cursed Lin for secretly plotting to become president himself, aiming to outshine Mao. The fact that the two charges contradicted each other did not bother the chairman much. He called a Politburo meeting denouncing his old associate Chen Boda, accusing him of sophistry and rumor-mongering, but sparing Lin Biao from direct criticism.[14] Zhou, Lin, and others backpedaled furiously, and the proposal to make Mao president was quietly dropped. But it was too late to save Chen Boda. The man who for almost forty years had done more than anyone else to develop Maoism as a political theory was himself denounced as an anti-Party element, a traitor, and a spy, who had been an anti-Communist reactionary since his youth and a secret member of the Guomindang.[15] The powerful Chen, who a fortnight earlier had been ranked as number four in the Party leadership, disappeared into the regime's interrogation centers and, eventually, to house arrest and prison.

Chen Boda's fate showed that the newly emerged Party leadership, in its post–Cultural Revolution form, was inherently unstable and entirely dependent on Mao's mood swings. The chairman did not want one single faction to get too powerful, but his heavy-handed approach meant that groups and individuals would fight others for position and status almost constantly, out of fear of being turned on next. It did not help, of course, that two of the other key leaders, Lin Biao and Jiang Qing, were almost as emotionally unstable as the chairman. Jiang had never come to terms with Lin Biao as Mao's successor and imagined herself in that role. Lin, in his more lucid moments, increasingly soured on the chairman's political projects and longed for some peace and stability to be restored to Chinese politics and society. He was convinced that only the army would be able to deliver such solidity and worked to strengthen the influence of the PLA, both at the central and local levels.[16] Mao, at his end, did not want to see too much of Jiang Qing. Even as he sided with her politically, he could stand her personal presence less and less. Though Jiang was still technically his wife, Mao disagreed with her on family matters, and she resented the steady stream of girlfriends who attended his house in Zhongnanhai (though she knew well enough to keep her mouth shut in public).[17]

If street violence had abated by 1970, political campaigns rolled on. The last big purge of the Cultural Revolution, the campaign against the so-called May 16th Anti-Revolutionary Clique, reached its peak that year. The campaign itself made no sense at all—there is no evidence that this "clique" ever existed. The starting point was the investigation of a small Leftist student group that back in 1967 had distributed leaflets in Beijing critical of Premier Zhou Enlai. With his usual sense of irony and dialectics, Mao had appointed the Left-winger Chen Boda as head of the commission investigating the "clique." After at first discovering very little, in early 1970 the investigation was widened to include a number of groups that had, at some point during the Cultural Revolution, fallen afoul of official policy, including Leftist organizations.[18] By the fall of 1970 Chen Boda himself had become a target of investigation within his own commission. By then, ever-widening "conspiracies" were uncovered all over the country, in ways reminiscent of revolutionary panics at other times, such as the Great Fear of the French revolution or the Stalin-era Soviet purges. Anyone could be drawn in, irrespective of their background and viewpoints. Groups that individual Party and military leaders wanted to get rid of figured prominently among them. One city targeted the following: Christians, people with "bad" class backgrounds, those who had been arrested earlier, relatives of the purged, people denounced by neighborhood committees, people who knew foreign languages or had traveled abroad, poets, thieves, peddlers, and those who since 1966 had written wall posters with political mistakes.[19] Countrywide, 3.5 million people were investigated. Tens of thousands were executed. Hundreds of thousands were sent to prison or to labor camps.[20] All those found guilty of belonging to an organization that never existed had to confess to their crimes.[21] One female prisoner wrote: "I admit to being guilty of crimes and to being, myself, an active counter-revolutionary guilty of May 16th counter-revolutionary activities. I admit these things to the Party and to the broad revolutionary masses and ask of them to punish me. I am determined to sincerely mend my ways, forsake evil and do good, thoroughly remold myself, and become a new person."[22]

Wang Tongzhu, from Xiangyang in Hubei Province, could serve as an example of what happened to many ordinary people during the last great Maoist campaigns. Wang was a poet, author of short stories, and a translator from Russian. He was arrested after the Hundred Flowers Campaign in 1957 and labeled an "ultra-Rightist" for having criticized the party's political campaigns and policies. Wang was sent to the Qingde Labor Camp in Hebei Province for "re-education through labor." In 1966, when the Party had to empty all labor camps near Beijing to make room for massive numbers of new prisoners, Wang was moved to Xinjiang as a forced laborer. Three years later he fled from the camp with two comrades, making it to Jiangsu Province, where they worked odd jobs and sold cigarettes on the street. In 1970 they were arrested, charged with being members of the "May 16th Anti-Revolutionary Clique," and, on July 30, publicly executed along with twenty-one other prisoners. After having spent twelve years in prison for no reason, Wang Tongzhu was killed for belonging to an organization that never existed.[23]

In minority areas the campaigns also continued. In and around Inner Mongolia, Party investigators had "discovered" a nonexistent Inner Mongolia People's Revolutionary Party, said to be a separatist and nationalist group, which ostensibly aimed at unification with the Soviet-sponsored Mongolian People's Republic next door.[24] Inner Mongolia's long-serving CCP leader Ulanhu, a Politburo member, was arrested and tortured, and a number of separate campaigns—against the "Ulanhu Anti-Party Treason Clique," the "February Counter-Current in Inner Mongolia," and the "Inner Mongolia People's Revolutionary Party"—dragged on into 1970, with roughly 800,000 arrested and nearly 100,000 killed. By the end of the Cultural Revolution, between 30 and 35 percent of the Mongol population in Inner Mongolia had been imprisoned in some form by the authorities. Massive numbers of Chinese were moved into the province, reducing the Mongols to a small minority within their own "autonomous region."[25]

In 1970 the Chinese system of forced labor camps, the so-called Laogai, was at its peak in terms of numbers. A conservative estimate is that almost nine million people served time in more than 1,400 camps of various kinds. Many of the camps were built to assist with Third Front construction projects in the interior, but there were also agricultural camps, mines, and lumber camps. Some of the sites seem to have been set up as pure extermination camps, where the purpose was to kill prisoners through malnourishment and physical mistreatment. But most of them were based on getting as much advantage as possible out of the inmates through backbreaking work and minimal sustenance. The camp system saw systematic mistreatment of prisoners, and in addition there were constant self-criticisms, endless hours of shouting slogans, and executions for real or imagined infringements. Sexual violence was rife in the camps, as were disease and starvation. Any reason why a prisoner had ended up in the camps seemed lost from the moment they entered; inside it was all about survival or passing into oblivion.[26]

As the country suffered, political infighting at the top intensified. The main trend in 1970–1971 was still the increased role of the army, with Lin Biao as its leader. Many of the new provincial Party secretaries were army people, as were many of those who staffed the central Party institutions that were slowly reemerging after the chaos of the late 1960s. Though some leading officers were skeptical of Lin's leadership skills, or fell afoul of his inconsistencies, the overall feeling among the generals was that Lin Biao was a better alternative than the Cultural Revolution leadership, which most of them despised intensely.[27] Lin Biao's personal following in the PLA was limited, although officers close to him were now constantly being promoted, and he was generally respected for his legendary military exploits in the past. The main problem for those who wished Lin to counter-balance Jiang Qing and the younger radicals in the Party was Lin's own persona: his lethargy and his many inexplicable absences.

Those charged with bringing Party and state institutions back to life after the chaos, such as Premier Zhou Enlai, were often caught in the middle of the infighting. During the Cultural Revolution, Zhou had always gone out of his way to praise Jiang Qing, both out of respect for the chairman and because he knew that she was a dangerous and unpredictable opponent. In the summer of 1968, at the same Central Committee plenum that denounced Liu Shaoqi as "a traitor, renegade, and spy," Zhou had publicly called Jiang "a strong Communist Party member and a proletarian fighter. Not [only] from today or from the beginning of the Great Proletarian Cultural Revolution, but [from] the 1930s she was already a firm Communist, a brave woman warrior fighting with traitors, fake Communists, secret agents, and anti-revolutionaries."[28] Sometimes Zhou overdid his obeisance; in late 1968, after Jiang had harangued a group of Lin Biao's leading generals, Mao's chief bodyguard Wang Dongxing had, on behalf of the chairman, put her in her place, criticizing the premier, too. "Comrade Jiang Qing has an appetite for cursing and insulting comrades, which is really bad," Wang told them. "The Premier is much too accommodating of Jiang Qing."[29]

With Lin Biao still in the political doghouse after the Lushan plenum, Jiang Qing, Zhang Chunqiao, and their associates saw opportunities of improving their standing with the chairman. They fed Mao bits of information that were intended to increase his suspicion of Lin. In the fall of 1970 Mao called for Lin Biao's closest military associates, and Lin's wife Ye Qun, to undertake self-criticism for their support of Chen Boda.[30] Although the chairman did not call for Lin himself to engage in the ritual, it was clear that he expected some form of apology from the marshal. Lin Biao apologized to Mao in person, but did not write a more extensive mea culpa, even after Zhou Enlai had implied that he should do so.[31] Lin's associates had to write lengthy self-criticisms, which Mao personally commented on.[32] If the chairman was not entirely happy, he had them write another version in which they abased themselves a bit more. At the same time Mao reassured them that even if they "had stopped listening to him" before Lushan, "the Party's policy is to cure the sick, which can be applied to all, except Chen Boda."[33] Even so, Mao had Zhou Enlai intervene to demote or remove several of Lin Biao's appointments as heads of China's military regions, most of whom had not in any way been involved in the Lushan intermezzo.[34]

The wave of attacks on his close associates left Lin Biao even more silent and depressed than usual. In the spring of 1971 he spent most of his time in his house at the Party leadership's summer resort in Beidaihe on the Gulf of Bohai, about 170 miles east of Beijing. His only communication with Mao was through occasional short notes by mail. As Mao launched another Party rectification campaign, now aimed at Chen Boda and Lin Biao's associates, Lin kept out of view. He told others that he felt he would sign his own death warrant if he engaged in public self-criticism.[35] Lin knew that he had many enemies, including in the military, who would pounce on him if given a chance. When Mao in April 1971 invited some of the old marshals whom Lin had helped purge during the Cultural Revolution to a meeting at which Lin's subordinates presented their self-criticism, Lin must have seen the writing on the wall.[36] Still, he did nothing: when Zhou Enlai was able to convince him to appear on the rostrum at Tiananmen for the celebration of May 1, Lin arrived late, was ignored by the chairman, and left without spending much time with Mao or other leaders present.[37] By then it was clear to the rest of the leadership that Lin Biao's position was in serious trouble.

In June, Lin Biao and his household returned to Beidahe. Encouraged by the chairman, Lin kept sending plans for defensive war against a foreign attack back to the Party Center in Beijing, but they elicited little response. Associates who came to see him reported that the vice-chairman was deeply depressed and spent much time in bed. He could not touch pens, he said. They made him nervous and sweaty. Lin told several of his staff that he expected to die soon, and that he would not leave Beidahe.[38] Lin's son, Lin Liguo, remained behind in Beijing. He had been talking to a number of other disgruntled younger officers, some of whom were afraid of what Lin's fall would mean for them and the PLA, and some who were simply exasperated with the direction things were taking under Mao's leadership. In March 1971 one of these officers, Yu Xinye, a staff member in the air force central Party committee, had put together a note based on conversations with Lin Liguo and others. "For more than a decade, the national economy has stalled," the note said.

> The actual living standard of masses and the lower-level cadres has declined, and there is growing discontent. People are angry. . . . The upper part of the ruling clique is corrupt and incompetent, and their followers are leaving them. . . . The essence of their socialism is fascism. They made the state ma- chine of China a meat grinder. . . . They made the political life of the party and the state a feudal autocratic dictatorship. [Mao Zedong] has become a contemporary Qin Shi-huang . . . a dictator with less and less popular sup- port. The Red Guards were deceived, and served as cannon fodder in the early days of the Cultural Revolution.[39]

Lin Liguo and his youthful associates talked bravely about staging an armed uprising, getting rid of Mao, and setting things right in the country.[40] Liguo also had a son's preoccupation with protecting his father. But they had no power, and their dreams of conspiracy and valor—inspired, it seems, from secretly watching too many forbidden American and Japanese movies—came to nothing.

Instead it was the chairman who was touring the country, speaking openly about his plan to get rid of Lin Biao and concentrate more power in his own hands. In the South, in the summer of 1971, Mao made no secret of Lin no longer being the successor. Instead he spoke of bringing "old comrades" back to the center of power to assist him. He mentioned Li Xiannian and Ye Jian- ying, and sometimes also Deng Xiaoping.[41] In Wuhan, Mao met with many provincial leaders, among them the new Party secretary of Mao's own home province Hunan, Hua Guofeng, discussing how younger cadre could join the top leadership. Hua went back to Hunan with the chairman on Mao's special train. While on board, Mao told the 49-year-old Hua that he wanted to take personal control of the PLA.[42] "How can they say that I created the PLA and that Lin Biao commands it? Why cannot the one who created the army command it? The army was created by me. Now, I will be in charge of the army. I do not believe that the army will rebel. They cannot mobilize the army to do bad things."[43]

Very soon messages about Mao's talks in the South started to spread in Beijing. Zhou Enlai, especially, was worried about the increasing attacks on Lin Biao, fearing that they could lead to new splits in the Party. Lin Liguo and his small group fantasized about ways to assassinate the chairman and the heads of the Party Left.[44] Nobody knew what would happen when Mao returned to Beijing. Lin Biao had dictated a letter to the chairman that he never got to send. In the rambling text, he gave his full support to the political campaigns going on but suggested lenience at the top level after the campaigns were concluded: "no arrest, no detention, no killing, no removal." He recommended increasing security in and around the leadership compounds. "Some comrades are worried about security issues, and their mood is anxious, so it is worthy of attention and reflection." "I really want to talk to the Chairman," Lin said, in desperation. "If the Chairman has time, please let me talk to you."[45]

Mao continued his travels. He arrived in Shanghai on September 10 but did not leave his special train.[46] The next day he abruptly ordered the train to leave for Beijing, arriving there around noon on September 12. Nobody in Beijing knew about his return—not even Zhou Enlai. While still on the train at Fengtai railway station in southwest Beijing, Mao summoned some of his leading generals in the capital to meet him in his carriage, where he casually repeated the criticism of Lin Biao. At 4:00 P.M. Mao arrived back at his house in Zhongnanhai.[47] Three hours later Lin Liguo flew from Beijing to Shanhaiguan, an airport close to his father's residence at Beidaihe. When he arrived at Lin Biao's house, he and his mother went into his father's bedroom. An hour later, the three of them emerged, ready to leave. Their destination was unclear.[48]

In the meantime, Lin Liguo's sudden and unauthorized flight to the coast had set off alarm bells in Beijing. Around 10:00 P.M., Wang Dongxing called Zhou Enlai with the news.[49] Zhou called the commander of the air force, General Wu Faxian, to check. Wu, who was close to Lin Biao, first denied it. Then, after he had checked, he called back to confirm that the aircraft had indeed landed at Shanhaiguan. Zhou ordered it to return immediately to Beijing, but the officer in charge claimed that the aircraft had an engine fault that had to be repaired. It should return to Beijing once it had been repaired, Zhou instructed, with no passengers.[50]

In Beidaihe, Lin Biao's wife Ye Qun had been tipped off that Beijing was starting to ask questions. She called Premier Zhou and told him that Lin had decided to go on an urgent inspection tour of Dalian in the Northeast. They would fly there as soon as an aircraft was ready. Zhou offered to meet Lin and Ye in Beidaihe first. Ye was noncommittal.[51] Immediately after finishing her conversation with the premier, Ye Qun and Lin Liguo helped Lin Biao to a waiting car and drove to the airport. The vice chairman's chief bodyguard, who was in the car, heard Lin Biao ask his son, "How far is it to Irkutsk? How long does it take to fly?" "Not very far," responded Lin Liguo. At the checkpoint out of the Beidaihe leadership compound, the car slowed down. Lin's bodyguard, acting on impulse after what he had heard, jumped from the car. Shots were fired. The car sped off toward Shanhaiguan Airport.[52]

The biggest mystery of Lin Biao's escape plans is why the leadership guard unit, at least one team of which was now in hot pursuit, allowed the marshal and his companions to board the plane and take off at 12:30 A.M. on September 13. Premier Zhou had personally ordered the plane grounded, and the ground staff at the airport were aware of the order. Even so, the plane was in the air, at first flying erratically, and then setting its course northwest. As it approached Chifeng Air Force Base in Inner Mongolia, Zhou Enlai notified Chairman Mao, asking whether Lin Biao's plane should be intercepted. Mao thought for a while, and then responded with an old saying: "Clouds want to rain and girls want to marry. Let him go."[53] At 1:50 A.M. the Trident carrying Lin Biao, Ye Qun, and Lin Liguo crossed into the People's Republic of Mongolia, then a close ally of the Soviet Union. Forty minutes later it crashed near Öndörkhaan in the eastern part of the country, killing everyone onboard.

The flight and death of Marshal Lin Biao, still Mao's official successor at the time, was a shock to the Chinese political system even beyond the purges and killings of the Cultural Revolution. As always, Mao ordered Zhou Enlai to clear up the mess. Zhou verified Lin's death, and then spearheaded the removal of the vice chairman's closest associates from the PLA, and the arrest of those who had conspired with Lin Liguo, or even worked close to him in the air force.[54] Zhou plugged away with the Cultural Revolutionaries Zhang Chunqiao and Yao Wenyuan to prepare a report on Lin's "historical crimes," to show—in true Cultural Revolution style—that the marshal had been a traitor and a fake Marxist ever since the 1930s. Mao did not participate, though he approved the report. Those who saw him in the weeks after Lin's death reported a changed man; Mao said very little and did not want to meet with anyone. His only substantial meetings were with Zhou Enlai.[55] The chairman's radical associates Zhang, Yao, and Jiang Qing tried to see Mao but were sent away. Mao's doctor reported that "his physical decline after the Lin Biao affair was dramatic. . . . He took to his bed and lay there all day . . . and developed a chronic cold and cough."[56] Others said that he had aged noticeably in just a few weeks. Mao may have provoked his deputy's flight, but the outcome still unsettled him.

Only gradually did information on Lin Biao's fate leak out. On September 18 the premier sent a short text, drafted by Zhang and Yao and endorsed by Mao, to the provincial top leaders, declaring Lin a traitor and conspirator, who had attempted to assassinate the chairman and carry out a counter-revolutionary coup d'etat. Some of the same text was later used for the Central Committee and top military commanders.[57] Wang Dongxing led the investigations at the Lin family residences and the houses of their close associates. It was during one of these raids that Yu Xinye's text talking about an armed uprising was found, making it much easier for Party leaders to prove their point about an anti-Mao conspiracy on Lin's part.[58] What had begun as Mao's conspiracy against Lin Biao ended, as far as the CCP was concerned, with Lin being condemned as the biggest traitor in the Party's history. But, even for those who had known Lin and disliked his Cultural Revolution activities, this was a version of the truth that was hard to swallow.

As it became known inside and outside of China that the chairman's chosen successor had died fleeing to the Soviet Union, even fervent supporters of Mao and China's Cultural Revolution had to ask themselves some hard questions. Across China, many young people who had dedicated their lives to Mao's campaigns remember the moment they first heard about Lin Biao's treason as when they first started having doubts about the aims they had in their own lives.[59] It was hard to uphold the idea of the chairman's infallibility when the man he had personally selected to be his successor turned out to be another long-standing agent of imperialism and reaction. Many wondered how Lin could have gotten away with it for so long, and then almost succeeded in escaping to the Soviets. Zhou Enlai, always sensitive to people's doubts, assured a group of senior officers that Lin had been a traitor and that he, Zhou, had had nothing to do with Lin's death: "Let me repeat, I did not order Lin Biao's plane shot down; the plane went straight down and crashed, it was suicide. . . . Can I order the army to kill the Vice-Chairman of the Party Central Committee and the Deputy Commander-in-Chief of the army? He is the successor according to the party constitution adopted at the Ninth Congress! . . . The Chairman was generous with Lin Biao. Why should I kill Lin Biao?"[60]

Zhou might have had reason to think that people in the know suspected him of being somehow implicated in the vice chairman's death. At least in the moment, the premier was a major political beneficiary of Lin's sudden demise. The affair had reminded Mao Zedong of how dependent he was on Zhou for running the country and assisting in times of crisis. But it had also left the premier as, by far, the most senior leader of the Party besides the chairman himself. As Zhou knew full well, this position entailed both dangers and opportunities. But with Mao at times scathing in his assessment of the Party radicals—not to mention of the maladroit Jiang Qing—Zhou felt that he could begin to move, very carefully, with implementing a new agenda, emphasizing industrial development and administrative competence. Ironically, Lin Biao and Zhou Enlai had agreed on some of these needs, but it was Lin's fall that enabled Zhou to get going, with Mao's at least temporary blessing. Mao was grateful, for as long as it lasted. The chairman quoted Du Mu, a poet from China's Tang era:

> The broken halberd buried in sand, its iron not yet rusted,
> I wash it, discover it is from ancient times.
> If the East Wind had not assisted Master Zhou,
> The brass bird would have locked up the two Qiaos.[61]

After the fall of Lin Biao, the first task was to fully rearrange leadership in the military. Following the purge of anyone suspected of having been personally close to Lin (which was a great number, given that Lin Biao had been minister of defense for twelve years), new leaders had to be brought in. Zhou recommended, and Mao agreed, to bring back Marshal Ye Jianying, an old associate of the premier's, as the new deputy head of the Central Military Commission, in reality the top military position under Mao himself.[62] The feisty Guangdong native, married six times and known for his opposition to what he called empty theorizing within the Party, had been one of the great survivors of the Cultural Revolution. He had been publicly attacked, forced to undertake self-criticism, and sidelined from his Party and military positions, but he had not been arrested or thrown out of the army. Now he was back as Mao's military deputy. In 1975 he was formally confirmed as minister of defense.[63]

Zhou's main deputy in the government was Li Xiannian, a former officer who had been minister of finance before the Cultural Revolution. Like Ye, Li had never been purged, even though he too had been politically sidelined and sometimes ridiculed by Chairman Mao for his caution and preoccupation with gradual and planned economic growth. To balance Zhou and Li, Mao had brought in Hua Guofeng, the Party secretary from his home province of Hunan, where Hua had become known as a prime promoter of the Mao cult but also as a competent administrator. After 1971 Hua was promoted several times within the central government while keeping close ties to Hunan Province. In 1973 Hua was made a member of the CCP Politburo. It was clear that Mao increasingly regarded him as a key member of the "successor generation." Hua responded by enthusiastically singing the chairman's praises whenever there was an opportunity. Otherwise he moved very carefully, hiding most of his own thoughts about politics behind an inscrutable but always friendly face.

Gradually a number of top leaders who had been criticized during the Cultural Revolution started coming back to new positions in Beijing or in the provinces. The process was sometimes very random; the premier's office or other government or Party officials would suggest names, and Mao would pick and choose who should be rehabilitated and who should remain in limbo. Leaders like Peng Zhen, the former mayor of Beijing, the propaganda chief Lu Dingyi, or Bo Yibo, the former chair of the State Economic Commission, could not be rehabilitated, according to Mao, because they had opposed the Cultural Revolution. Others, like Deng Xiaoping or the former chief of staff General Luo Ruiqing, could possibly be brought back in the future, if they repented and accepted correction by "the masses." A third category included leaders such as the foreign minister, Marshal Chen Yi, and the head of China's nuclear program, Marshal Nie Rongzhen, who were in a kind of political void, never cleared of the charges against them but also never formally purged from their positions. A fourth group was rehabilitated soon after the fall of Lin Biao, mainly on Zhou Enlai's initiative. These included planning commission chair Li Fuchun and the chief of the agricultural commission, Tan Zhenlin. These leaders were on record as having clashed with Lin Biao in the past, which helped them after 1971 irrespective of what these conflicts had been about.

One reason why the processes of government ran more smoothly than before was Mao's increasingly poor health. In the autumn and winter of 1971 he had constant chest infections, always coughing, and spending his time mostly in bed at his house by the swimming pool in Zhongnanhai, smoking and reading. His doctors tried to treat him, but the chairman refused most treatments, except some traditional Chinese remedies and pills that he seems to have chosen almost at random from his closets. His appearance deteriorated and he lost weight. At some point in early winter his doctors diagnosed congestive heart failure, but Mao still refused treatment.[64] In January, after foreign minister Chen Yi died, still in political no man's land, Mao on the spur of the moment decided to attend the memorial service at Babaoshan, the cemetery for CCP heroes in Beijing's western suburbs. The chairman left the house with just an overcoat over his pajamas. It was only the second time he had left Zhongnanhai after Lin Biao's death, and it was a bitterly cold day. Mao joined the mourners in crying at the service, telling the widow repeatedly that Chen Yi had been a good man and a good Communist.[65] A few weeks later, on February 12, Mao himself suddenly collapsed.[66] He lost consciousness and had to be resuscitated by his medical staff. It was the first of many such episodes in the final years of the chairman's life.

While the chairman ailed, China seemed to recover. After the economic shocks of the politically induced chaos between 1966 and 1968, the Chinese economy began improving from 1969 on. By 1970 the country saw substantial rates of growth in most sectors, even though the growth was imbalanced both in terms of location and output. The preoccupation with industrial development that many leaders at the center began to give voice to, as an accompaniment to Mao's insistence on revolution and class struggle, did produce results in terms of new projects being started and increased capital allocations from Beijing for infrastructure and construction in the provinces. But much of the money was spent on repairs of equipment that had deteriorated to such an extent that it was beyond rescue, on huge infrastructural projects that were primarily intended for strategic purposes in the coming war, or on moving or building new plants in the interior for the same strategic purpose. Even though the economic disaster of the Cultural Revolution was much less severe than that of the Great Leap Forward, it did show a China that was not making meaningful economic progress.

One reason why the negative effects were much less marked than in the last round of Maoist excess was that agricultural production was mostly sheltered from the chaos. There were of course exceptions: in minority areas or Chinese areas where there was substantial infighting between factions or military groups, planting and harvesting was disrupted, and people starved. But in most areas the communes were able to protect peasants and their fields from the disruption seen in cities and towns. Most peasants had a very clear memory of the consequences of the Great Leap and were willing to do whatever it took to protect themselves and their families. In a curious way the breakdown of the Party's command system as a result of the Cultural Revolution helped peasants survive. Compared to ten years before, there were fewer emissaries from the center running around ordering farmers to do things that they knew would be economically ruinous. Most Party cadre had enough with just protecting themselves.

In some of China's richest agricultural areas, such as Zhejiang, Jiangsu, lower Guangdong, and parts of Sichuan, communes in the early 1970s began experimenting with incentives to work units in order to increase production. Not all of these were material incentives. Very often high praise from the commune leaders, medals, citations to higher institutions, or just the admiration of their peers could be enough. Production teams were sometimes allowed to keep part of any surplus, which they could sell or barter inside the commune or outside, and divide the proceeds among team members. Crucially, the stigma for rewarding productive output—often being called a "capitalist roader"—gradually went away in some places. In parts of China, at least, the hindrances against production were lessened, if not lifted.[67]

All these initiatives for increasing agricultural output seem to have come from below, or at least from communes or production brigades. And although incentives helped, it was the farmers' own concern with the disasters of the past and hope for a better life in the future that pushed production to the fore. The Great Leap and the years from 1966 to 1968 had shown how little stood between the farming population, even in rich provinces, and catastrophic hunger. As long as farmers believed that part of their harvest could benefit themselves in times of need, they were willing to work. That the Party had now began emphasizing the overall need for development of agriculture, but without the shock methods of the past, also helped, as did military control in many provinces. The military wanted to feed its soldiers and was less concerned about the means by which the food was produced.

The situation in industry was not altogether different. Although a much smaller part of China's output—in 1970 the country was still 75 percent agricultural in terms of employment—industry had suffered during the initial phase of the Cultural Revolution.[68] There were many problems. The constant political campaigns and factional battles took workers' and managements' attention away from production. Some factories had almost come to a standstill by 1968. Production was also disrupted by moving whole plants, and their workers, to the interior as part of the Third Front initiatives. Shirking had been rampant, as had "confiscation" of tools and products by revolutionary organizations (some of which later showed up for sale). Incentives to spend much time in the factories were very limited, since revolutionary activities were appreciated more by the authorities. At one factory in Wuhan, for instance, "factional struggle among the workers caused a suspension of operations in 1968, and the workers typically 'arrived at 7 A.M., went off duty at 8 A.M., and disappeared completely by 9 A.M.'"[69]

One key aspect of the worker experience of the Cultural Revolution was the receding of any form of effective centralized planning. Even during the Great Leap Forward, the state planning system that the Chinese Communists had imported from the Soviet Union held up reasonably well; in fact, it could be argued that one of the reasons why the Great Leap had become such an unmitigated catastrophe was that inflated and sometimes entirely unhinged production aims were enforced by the planning system. In the Cultural Revolution this was no longer the case in many places. Communist cadre were under attack everywhere and had little time to compel output. But the signals from the Party Center also changed. Mao, especially, had begun to emphasize decentralization and decisions being made closer to the production units. He repeatedly praised workers taking control of their own factories and electing their management, rather than having managers imposed on them by local Party units.[70] Many workers felt a sense of empowerment, which some of them would later expand as they got more of a say over the production process.

The first turn for industry after the chaos of the Cultural Revolution was, however, a more regimented regime under military control. From 1969 on, more of the state-owned enterprises and some of the smaller ones controlled by cities or urban districts saw some form of military presence. In a few cases a military-led committee was stationed in the factory to oversee production. In others, inspection commissions from the city or province, mostly led by military personnel, visited regularly in order to ensure that the factory produced the quota assigned to it. "Arriving late and leaving early were impossible," recalled one worker. "The factory's management was in the hands of the military. . . . If you were late, they'd look for ideological reasons and be mean to you, saying that you didn't understand Mao Zedong Thought. . . . Everyone thus came under high pressure because of this. No freedom. . . . Come late or leave early? You didn't dare do it."[71]

Even though the big state-owned plants still offered the best conditions and pay for workers, and were therefore more prestigious to work in, much of the expansion in Chinese industry in the 1970s took place in smaller enterprises in nonurban areas. From 1970 on, People's Communes were encouraged to set up their own machinery repair factories, tool workshops, and small fertilizer and cement plants. In many areas, such enterprises were developed in addition to the handicraft industries that already existed. At the same time, the Party decided that all smaller enterprises and institutions hitherto managed by the departments of the State Council should be transferred to local governments. The result was an upswing in industrial activity in rural areas, especially those that were close to major population centers and therefore already relatively wealthy and well-connected.[72]

The Party Center never intended that these enterprises should do more than produce necessary goods for the local communes. The CCP's objective was to save money and avoid the responsibility of coordinating the supply of essential articles and tools, which was difficult to do given the state of disrepair in central planning after the Cultural Revolution. The aim was faster mechanization of agriculture and higher output. The Party leadership was even willing to organize limited credit for such purposes through rural credit cooperatives. By 1973 there were 91,000 such institutions spread across China, but with the vast majority in the richer provinces along the coast.[73] The government dutifully emphasized that priority funding should be given to less well-off farmers to set up workshops and small collective enterprises. In reality, local authorities and managers quickly found impeccably poor peasants who could issue such requests, while the higher-ups took control of any funds delivered.

As these forms of rural industrialization from below got going in the early 1970s, the result was not only a rapid expansion of the facilities the government had in mind. It was also, in some areas, increasing diversification and, somewhat later, surpluses. By 1973 at the latest, a few enterprises were bartering or even selling parts of their surplus, even if such activities remained strictly illegal. One example is the Xu Hang People's Commune of Jiading County, now a part of Shanghai. At the end of 1973, the commune's income from industry was more than twice that from agriculture. The commune set up twelve enterprises, producing everything from farm tools to towels and light bulbs. Other units dealt with farm machinery repair, grain and feed processing, and fish farming. There was a small chemical factory and a large workshop for weaving yellow grass handbaskets and sandals.[74] The commune easily paid for the mechanization of agriculture itself, but production rose only sporadically, perhaps because it was hard to get any surplus from agriculture as long as the state bought almost all the harvest at fixed prices. Even though the Xu Hang experience in industry is at the forefront of what was happening in the rest of China's most advanced provinces, its agricultural experience is pretty typical; there was little increase in agricultural output countrywide between 1970 and 1978.[75]

Much further south along the coast, in Guangdong Province near Hong Kong, others had similar ideas even earlier. In Shunde, at the end of the long Hongqi canal leading into the Pearl River estuary, 26-year-old He Xiangjian helped pool his village's resources to set up what he called, somewhat pretentiously, the North Sidestreet Plastics Production Group. It was 1968, the Cultural Revolution was at its peak, and the inhabitants of Shunde were fearful that hard times, like during the Great Leap, were coming their way again. They thought that making money was one way of preparing against the worst. The people of this district had been rich before, or at least moderately wealthy, back when trade with Hong Kong and Macau was possible. The Communist takeover had forced them back into local agriculture. But they knew what business was—many had relatives abroad who told them what was happening elsewhere. And young He had a good reputation locally; he was known as a bookish young man who was fond of quoting Mao Zedong and Communist slogans.

He Xiangjian and his twenty-three fellow residents of Shunde had raised 5,000 yuan, a vast sum in 1968. About half of it came from the participants, and the rest from the commune administrative office, which, in turn, borrowed money from the local credit cooperative. The factory was set up as a collective enterprise, and at first it produced plastic bottle caps. A couple of technicians from a neighboring state-owned sugar factory helped finesse the product, which became known throughout the province for its high quality. Other factories began requesting bottle caps from Shunde. In 1973, when imported machinery deployed elsewhere threatened to make their product uncompetitive, the workers at North Sidestreet Plastics switched to producing medicinal glass tubes, which also turned out to be a successful product.[76] Three years later the enterprise reinvented itself again, now becoming the Shunde Auto Parts Factory, producing trailer brakes for tractors and trucks. By 1977 its annual profit topped 26,000 yuan.[77] In the reform era after 1980 it was transformed into an industrial company producing electric appliances. Today, under the name of Midea, it is one of the world's biggest appliance makers, employing more than 150,000 people globally.[78]

Some of this reorientation in Jiading and Shunde and a few other places came out of extraordinary circumstances as well as personal courage and inventiveness. It is even possible that some of the contributors to these experiments did not see them as grossly out of tune with the official message of heroic labor, thrift, and dedication to a common cause. In Dazhai, the district in Shanxi that during the Cultural Revolution became the core of one of Mao's most famous slogans, "Learn from Dazhai," stories of almost superhuman efforts to exceed cultivation targets for corn and sorghum abounded.[79] But it was also widely known that the commune added substantially to its income through mining and small-scale industry. One way of understanding the "Dazhai miracle," according to leaders like He Xiangjian and his counterparts in the Xu Hang commune, was that the constant struggle that the chairman so lauded could also be a struggle for the creativity that produced success and its rewards.

As these changes began to be dimly visible in some of the richer parts of the Chinese countryside, state-led construction of Third Front industries intensified for a second wave. Mao's message—that war was coming and China had to be prepared—was as strong as ever in the early 1970s. All put together, building Third Front factories in inland provinces far from major population centers was the biggest industrialization program of Maoist China, at least in terms of investments; bigger than the plans of the 1950s and regular investment in industry for the rest of the period up to 1980 combined. Between 1965 and 1980, the CCP spent more than 20.5 billion yuan on Third Front projects.[80] For comparison, that equals the value of close to two complete yearly national budgets at the time, or almost as much as China spent on education for the whole decade of the 1960s.

The Third Front campaign oversaw the construction of close to 2,000 industrial projects, in addition to multiple mines, dams, roads, railways, and power plants. A bit less than half of the plants were geared toward military production, though some of these were dual-use. Construction was made more costly by the need to hide these projects from enemy view. In a number of cases costs were nearly doubled by the Party's insistence that the whole plant had to be built inside a cave in a remote mountainous area. Few of the Third Front projects reached the same level of productivity as similar plants in urban areas. They suffered from enormous problems with missing supplies, shoddy engineering, and transportation difficulties. The emphasis on heavy industry led to an overproduction of steel, for instance, the effects of which were made worse by breakdowns in the planning system, so that large amounts of the finished product never reached their intended destination.[81]

In addition to the uncounted labor camp population, more than sixteen million nonincarcerated people were directly engaged in building the Third Front.[82] They came from all over China to remote areas of Yunnan, Guizhou, Hubei, Hunan, Shaanxi, and Sichuan. From Shanghai they were sent to Anhui or Jiangxi, sometimes called the "Little Third Front." Some were students and graduates sent from the cities, some had worked in factories that were moved to Third Front areas, some were recruited locally, and some came from other parts of China, especially from rural areas. Many of the latter felt lucky to join. They received stable wages and were assigned more prestigious tasks, and they could learn a trade in the process. For others, especially those from the cities, boredom and regimentation soon outwore any enthusiasm they may have felt for the project at the beginning. They missed friends and family, and disliked political mass indoctrination, uniform clothing styles, and lack of entertainment. Workers at the giant steel plant in Panzhihua in southern Sichuan complained about the only movies available being versions of revolutionary operas much promoted by Jiang Qing. They wanted more North Korean films, which at least had good love stories.[83]

While it is clear that the short-term economic implications of the Third Front campaign were pretty dismal, the long-term effects are more uncertain. The campaign did introduce industrial production to areas of China that had seen none of it before, and it helped the economy in some of the country's poorer areas. It also contributed massively to Chinese infrastructure and energy production. Peasants who had lived at subsistence level saw new futures and met new kinds of people. Although about half of the industrial plants failed and were later closed down and dismantled, some reinvented themselves and thrived under reform. The Panzhihua steel mill, for instance, is now the largest steel producer in western China. It is also the world's second-largest producer of vanadium, a metal used in jet engines and surgical instruments. Still state-owned, it has three subsidiaries listed on the Shenzhen stock exchange.[84]

Among those who participated in the Third Front campaign, the "sent down youth"—young people from the cities who were sent to the countryside to work and learn from the farmers—were among the most conspicuous. The campaign to get young people to leave urban areas was an old one for the Chinese Communists. In many ways this was how most of the leaders themselves had learned their trade: they had moved from the cities to the countryside to lead an army of peasants. After 1949 the CCP had repeatedly encouraged educated, urban youth to choose the "mass line" and relocate to the villages in order to learn about the 80 percent of the population who constituted the real China. During the Cultural Revolution this message became a doctrine and, after a while, a vade mecum for the Party's problems in urban areas. Of the almost twenty million who moved from the cities to the countryside during the late 1960s and the 1970s, the initial groups, in 1966–1968, consisted mostly of enthusiasts who heeded the Party's message. Later, the Party used force, sending away, first, victims of the Cultural Revolution, then many among the Red Guard perpetrators, and finally anyone suspected of making trouble for the reimposition of order by the military. From being a social experiment for making China whole, the "To the Countryside!" campaign became a dumping process for urban undesirables.[85]

The chances of being "sent down" depended very much on where you grew up and which year you were born. In the cities of Liaoning Province in Manchuria, 35 percent of those born between 1942 and 1952 were sent down. In the rich coastal province of Jiangsu only 17 percent of the same age cohorts were. If you were born in a bigger city in 1950–1951, you stood almost 50 percent chance of getting sent down at some point during the campaign, but if you were younger or older than that, the chances decreased. Children with a "bad" class background were intensively targeted, while those from military families stood a much better chance of avoiding the campaign altogether, often serving for a while in the army instead. Of those who were sent down, most found their way back to the cities within three years. But many stayed, making a life for themselves in the region they were sent to, marrying into peasant families if they were lucky enough to be accepted by the locals.[86]

For those who did stay, many suffered intense hardship because of a lifestyle they were not used to. They knew nothing about farming—and farmers, understandably, regarded them as an unnecessary burden and wanted them gone. The villages had too many mouths to feed already. Between 1970 and 1973, there were almost 600 reported cases of sexual assault against female new arrivals in Shaanxi Province alone.[87] Most of the rusticated youth suffered the consequences of lack of education, and few of them did well later in life, even if they chose to return to the cities. Though there were of course exceptions, particularly among those who used their in-between position to become middlemen for trade and exchanges between the cities where they had grown up and the areas where they lived. Because the cities that the youth came from were expected to assist with the resettlement process, some young people could become intermediaries between town and country, helping manage the assistance that "their" city provided, and getting a privileged position in the process. Some became experts at bringing in consumer goods that the peasants had never seen before and therefore valued highly, including in monetary terms.

Those who made it back to the cities did not fare much better. With most high schools and colleges closed between 1966 and 1972, they could not return to education, and most of them were in the cities illegally, meaning that they had no access to government services: no jobs, no health care, no rationing coupons. These policies created a vast floating population of young people who had been thrown out of society. Many of them made do peddling wares on the street or through petty crime. They learned to fend for themselves, to be cynical, and to be forever careful and watchful. But they also learned to fear political leaders, because they could do terrible things to you, and to trust nobody.

4

Americans

IN 1970, CHINA WAS AS ISOLATED INTERNATIONALLY as it was rudderless domestically. Having provoked clashes with most of China's neighbors and with all of the world's major powers, Mao Zedong—hailed by his party as the Great Helmsman—seemed to have no certain sense of where to steer. His main foreign preoccupation was with the threat of a Soviet sneak attack on China, which he regarded as a very high probability within the next five years. He also believed, as a matter of doctrine, that there would be a new world war soon, though he wavered on how it would begin. Would the Soviet Union attack China first? Would it be an imperialist war between the Americans and the Soviets? If the latter, could China stay out of it? In his ambivalence, Mao was drawn to the interwar era, when he had first become leader of his party. Back then, Stalin had attempted, at least temporarily, to work with the West against Hitler. Later, during World War II, Mao himself had tried to get support from the Americans against Japan. Maybe China needed such temporary respite now?

While Soviet leaders, in their cynicism and world-weariness, believed that Mao had orchestrated the whole conflict with Moscow just in order to reach out to the Americans, there is little evidence of such ideas prior to 1969. On the contrary, Mao, in his Cultural Revolution mode, regarded the two superpowers as equally inimical to China, because he believed that they hated and feared Chinese Communism and his own position as the leader of the world's downtrodden people. There is little doubt that his worries about a coordinated Soviet-American attack on China were genuinely held, although he of course registered the divergent global interests of the two powers. What changed Mao's mind was the Soviet military intervention in Czechoslovakia in 1968 and the Sino-Soviet border clashes that followed.[1] By 1969 the chairman set out, as an article of faith, that Soviet "social-imperialism" was the more aggressive of the two global imperialisms. He also feared the strategic consequences of China's material weakness, although he of course paid no attention to his own role in creating that weakness. Mao believed that China's struggle for Communism, combined with the CCP being the focal point of world revolution, made China a likely target for a sudden strike by Moscow. The false Communists in the USSR, the chairman argued, might undertake such an attack in order to improve the Soviet global position and remove China's revolutionary leadership. Beginning a conversation with the Americans could therefore be a way to help save the Chinese revolution, Mao thought in late 1969.[2]

It was at this point that the chairman got lucky in his strategic ruminations. The newly elected president of the United States, Richard Nixon, also worried about his country's position in the Cold War against the Soviet Union. Nixon was concerned about the relative weakening of the U.S. economic position and about the willingness of Americans to make the sacrifices, personal and material, that were needed to prevail in a worldwide competition with the Soviet Union. The domestic opposition against the U.S. war in Vietnam had convinced Nixon that the United States was weak and divided at home, and he was less and less certain that the traditional Cold War allies of the United States, Western Europe and Japan, would support American attempts at containing Soviet power on a global scale. Even before his campaign for president had started, Nixon had pointed to Asia as one area in which the United States ought to reduce tension.[3] After the election, working with his national security adviser, the German-born Harvard professor Henry Kissinger, he had begun exploring how talking directly to the Chinese could help end the war in Vietnam. But Nixon also, from early 1969 on, had a bigger aim in mind: how engaging with Beijing might help the overall American position vis-à-vis the Soviets in terms of global strategy. If the Chinese, in spite of their Communism, were in fact deadly enemies of the Soviet Union, could there be a potential for not just detente with Beijing, but some form of anti-Soviet cooperation? Nixon did not care much how China was ruled. "We should give every encouragement to the attitude that this Administration is 'exploring possibilities of rapprochement with the Chinese,'" Nixon instructed Kissinger two weeks after his inauguration.[4]

Sino-American advances proceeded very cautiously at first, especially from the Chinese side. Given the political climate in Beijing, it is in many ways remarkable that they got going at all. Mao had strong ideological and nationalist reservations against being seen courting the Americans too openly, and his ploy with engaging senior military leaders, who were already in limbo politically, to review China's strategic position was part of his caution. It gave him someone else to blame if things went wrong, but also an occasion to proceed with caution. When the old marshals in late July 1969 had proposed that China not be too eager to seek contact with the United States, this was probably exactly what the chairman wanted to hear. "The Americans are anxious to be in touch with us," they reported, "and therefore we should remain aloof for a while."[5] Mao also worried that any links with the United States could increase the likelihood of a Soviet attack. This is probably the reason why he gave the go-ahead for an impromptu meeting between Zhou Enlai and Soviet premier Aleksei Kosygin at Beijing Airport in mid-September, even if Mao believed that the USSR was moving ever closer to bombing strategic targets in China.[6] As the Soviet war scare proceeded, the marshals pointed to China's "American card," and Foreign Minister Chen Yi—always courageous in spite of the accusations the Cultural Revolutionaries were hurling at him—noted, as his own opinion, that the Sino-American talks in Warsaw, which had proceeded fruitlessly for fourteen years, could be elevated to a higher level.[7]

In mid-October 1969, just as the Soviet war scare was at its peak, Mao received a message from Pakistan's president Yahya Khan, saying that President Nixon wanted to establish direct contact with the Chinese leadership.[8] Again, the chairman hesitated. He was afraid of provoking the Soviets, and of appearing weak to the Americans. No message came back to Washington. Exasperated at the lack of reaction from the Chinese side, Nixon instructed his ambassador to Poland, Walter Stoessel, to contact his Chinese counterpart directly. But the Chinese kept avoiding him. Finally, on December 3, when he spotted a second secretary from the Chinese embassy at a diplomatic reception, Stoessel ran up to the Chinese interpreter and declared, in poor Polish, that President Nixon wanted to have important, concrete talks with China.[9] When he received the message in Beijing, Zhou Enlai, showing unusual bravery, told Mao that this might be a good opportunity to test the Americans.[10] Mao first hesitated, then agreed. The following day he ordered the release of two Americans who had been arrested in Guangdong, and Zhou made sure the news was brought first to the U.S. embassy in Warsaw.[11] Mao seemed ready to move to the next stage.

The Warsaw talks were restarted in January and moved to the Chinese and U.S. embassies, presumed to be out of earshot to Polish (and thereby Soviet) ears. On February 12, Zhou Enlai got Mao and the Politburo to accept the principle of a Sino-American summit: "If the U.S. government is willing to send a ministerial representative or a special envoy of the U.S. president to Beijing to further explore the fundamental issues in China-U.S. relations, the Chinese government is ready to receive [them]."[12] A week later, Nixon suggested that the Chinese meet Kissinger secretly in Paris, during the Vietnam peace talks that were taking place there.[13] The flirtation seemed to move to a more serious stage. But then events in other connected arenas intervened.

Since before setting up its government in Beijing in 1949, the CCP had been involved in what its leadership saw as Vietnam's struggle for national liberation under the leadership of Ho Chi Minh and the Vietnamese Communists. The PRC had provided weapons and military advisers, as well as financial aid. Mao regarded the Communists in Vietnam as the foreign party most closely associated with China. Ho Chi Minh crossed the border regularly and held meetings with China's top leaders, including the chairman himself. By early 1966 Mao reviewed the military situation in Vietnam almost daily and offered advice on strategy to the North Vietnamese and the South Vietnamese National Liberation Front (NLF). Thousands of Vietnamese were trained in China, and more than 100,000 Chinese support troops served in North Vietnam.[14] Mao's advice was always to fight harder and not compromise; as late as April 1968 Zhou Enlai had lambasted the North Vietnamese for finding "it easy to compromise. . . . That you changed your positions has increased the number of expected votes for [U.S. president Lyndon] Johnson, increased the price of stocks in New York, and decreased the gold price." Vietnam's willingness to negotiate had even contributed to the murder of Dr. Martin Luther King Jr., Zhou claimed. "With your statement, it has been seen that your position is now weaker, not stronger." "It is for the sake of our two parties' relations," added Zhou somewhat condescendingly, "that we take every opportunity to remind you of this matter."[15]

But after Nixon's election, the Chinese advice to North Vietnam changed. Mao seems to have believed that Nixon was so eager to get out of Indochina that negotiations would now be for the good. He was also concerned that as the war dragged on, the Vietnamese were becoming increasingly dependent on Soviet aid, which the Chinese could not match. And he was probably thinking about using the prospect of peace in Vietnam as a way of enticing the new American administration to speak to Beijing. When meeting a Vietnamese Communist delegation right after Nixon had won the presidency, Mao suddenly concurred with his guests: "We agree with your slogan of fighting while negotiating," the chairman said. "Some comrades worry that the US will deceive you. But I tell them not to [worry]. Negotiations are just like fighting. You have drawn experience, understood the rules."[16] Mao still promised to support the North Vietnamese militarily until they had won a full victory and reunified their country.

Very soon after Nixon became president, he had—on Kissinger's advice—ordered the bombing of NLF bases in Cambodia. This expansion of the war angered Beijing, but not enough to prevent the CCP leadership from engaging with the Americans or moving toward supporting negotiations. When Cambodia's prime minister Lon Nol, assisted by U.S.-backed military officers, overthrew the head of state, Prince Sihanouk, in March 1970, the Chinese reaction was much stronger. The coup took place when Sihanouk was on his way to visit Beijing, and Mao immediately decided to back a Cambodian government in exile, headed by the prince but with several Cambodian Communists in key positions. Unlike their Vietnamese comrades, the Cambodian Communists, known as Khmer Rouge, had taken a decidedly pro-China position against the Soviets. Their leader, a man known as Pol Pot—"Brother Number One"—had spent much time in China and was there when the 1970 coup took place.[17] The Chinese regarded the coup as American overreach, which in the end would facilitate a Communist revolution in Cambodia. The incursion of 50,000 U.S. ground troops across the border from South Vietnam into Cambodia in May 1970 did not change the Chinese view, even though it destroyed much of the infrastructure for the NLF, which had operated in Cambodia for several years. In the meantime, Sihanouk's presence in Beijing at the head of a Chinese-backed Cambodian government in exile was a signal that Mao wanted to restore China's regional position after the interruptions of the Cultural Revolution.

The coup in Phnom Penh and the U.S. invasion meant that Beijing put its U.S. courtship on hold.[18] Even a secret message from Nixon, this time directly to the CCP leaders, had no effect. "The United States has no aggressive intentions concerning Communist China," Kissinger wrote on Nixon's behalf. "On the contrary, we would like to establish regular relations with her, recognizing our differences in ideology. We have no interest in establishing military bases in Vietnam, and we believe that a peace that takes into account everyone's interests in that area can be achieved." He added, hopefully, that "Dr. Kissinger is prepared to talk to a person of stature on the Communist Chinese side if this can be done secretly."[19]

Mao's public response was quick and angry. On May 20, 1970, he released a message to a rally in Beijing protesting the U.S. invasion. "A new upsurge in the struggle against United States imperialism is now emerging throughout the world," the chairman said. "While massacring the people in other countries, United States imperialism is slaughtering the white and black people in its own country. . . . It is not the Vietnamese people, the Laotian people, the Cambodian people, the Palestinian people, the Arab people or the people of other countries who fear United States imperialism; it is United States imperialism that fears the people of the world. . . . Unite and defeat the United States aggressors and all their running dogs!"[20] The Chinese canceled all diplomatic contacts. In July, two Chinese jet-fighters tried to intercept a U.S. spy plane flying more than a hundred miles off the Chinese coast. Mao obviously wanted to make his displeasure known, loud and clear.

It took more than eight months before the CCP leaders again responded to U.S. overtures.[21] In November 1970, after Nixon had restated his willingness to send an envoy to open talks with China, Zhou Enlai responded through the Pakistanis that if the United States would be willing to resolve the Taiwan issue, the Chinese government would be willing to "receive representatives of President Nixon in Beijing."[22] Operating through the Pakistanis suited Zhou, both because he saw them as friends of China who also had a long-standing relationship with the United States and because of the chaos that still reigned in the Chinese Foreign Ministry in the wake of the Cultural Revolution. Rebel factions had taken control of several Foreign Ministry offices and Chinese embassies abroad. Chinese ambassadors, who were slowly sent back to their embassies after long sessions of struggle and self-criticism at home, were in no position to carry out secret missions. With most of its senior

officials still sidelined, the ministry was to a great extent controlled by younger diplomats, including one of Mao's relatives, Wang Hairong, and the U.S.-
born Tang Wensheng (Nancy Tang), who hitherto had mainly served as an
interpreter. These two young female diplomats had participated as rebels in
the Cultural Revolution and had the chairman's ear.

On December 18, 1970, the chairman met with the Left-wing U.S. journal-
ist Edgar Snow, who had first interviewed Mao in northern Shaanxi back in
1936. Snow had been in China for more than two months at the invitation of
the Chinese government. Mao wanted to send a signal to the Americans, but
he did not realize that Snow, who had been a victim of the McCarthy era and
now lived in self-imposed exile in Switzerland, might be an unlikely conduit
for his message to a Republican U.S. president. Mao saw Snow for breakfast
at the swimming pool house in Zhongnanhai, and they spoke for almost five
hours. Mao, as usual, was rambling but clear in terms of direction. "I do not
like the Democrats, I prefer the Republican Party," he told the incredulous
Snow. "I welcomed Nixon's victory. Why is that? He, too, is deceptive, but a
bit less so. . . . If he wants to come to Beijing, you send him a letter, tell him
to come in secret, do not go public, just get on a plane and come. . . . If Nixon
is willing to come, I am willing to talk to him; we can talk or not talk, quarrel
or not quarrel, he can come as a visitor or as president. . . . I do not like revisionists. . . . Tell him from me [that he] is a good man. He is the number one
good man in the world. That Brezhnev is no good, [West German Chancellor
Willy] Brandt is no good."[23]

Even if he had not chosen the most suitable messenger, Mao's message
reached the White House soon after he met with Snow.[24] Nixon and Kissinger
began the process of figuring out what the United States could actually offer
the PRC at this stage, beyond a promise of talks. Nixon already knew that the
PRC would call for a withdrawal of U.S. military personnel from Taiwan, and
he was willing to grant that, given the small number of Americans who were
on the island. In addition, the White House was ready to relax the strict export
controls that had been in place for U.S. trade with China, remove currency
controls, and allow visits to take place between the two countries, including by
U.S.-owned ships sailing under foreign flags.[25] While this process went on in
Washington, both Mao and Zhou grew impatient. In April 1971 they tried to
send a more visible signal of Chinese intentions by inviting the U.S. national
table tennis team, which had been competing at the World Championship in

Japan, to visit China to play against Chinese teams. Both Zhou and the Foreign Ministry radicals had originally recommended against extending such an invitation after it was reported that one of the U.S. players had casually mentioned at a reception to the Chinese players that he would like to play in China.[26] But, one evening after having gone to bed, Mao suddenly ordered Wu Xujun, his head nurse, to call the Foreign Ministry and tell its officers to invite the whole U.S. team to China.[27] When the Americans arrived, Zhou Enlai met with them and U.S. journalists in the Great Hall of the People. "In the past," Zhou said, "a lot of American friends have been in China. You have made a start here in bringing more friends."[28]

Zhou followed up with a direct message to Nixon through President Khan a week later. "The Chinese Government," the premier said, "reaffirms its willingness to receive publicly in Peking a special envoy of the President of the U.S. (for instance, Mr. Kissinger) or the U.S. Secretary of State or even the President of the U.S. himself for direct meeting and discussions."[29] President Nixon toyed with the idea of sending a personal representative, such as UN ambassador George Bush, but in the end took Kissinger's advice that Bush was "too soft and not sophisticated enough."[30] Having convinced the president that he was the only one up to the task, Kissinger got the go-ahead. The U.S. national security adviser would pay a secret visit to China, Nixon told the Chinese, in preparation for his own visit later. On July 8, while visiting Pakistan, Kissinger feigned illness at an official banquet and went to a waiting Pakistani plane to meet a small Chinese delegation, headed by Zhang Wenjin, the head of the Foreign Ministry's U.S. Department and an old associate of the Chinese Premier. The "two ladies," Wang Hairong and Tang Wensheng, were also on board, probably to keep an eye on things for the chairman. They flew through the night to Beijing, where Kissinger met Zhou Enlai the next day.[31]

Kissinger's secret visit to Beijing was a momentous occasion: the first time a high-ranking U.S. official and PRC leaders had ever sat down to talk. The "visit was a very moving experience," Kissinger reported to Nixon. "The historic aspects of the occasion; the warmth and dignity of the Chinese; the splendor of the Forbidden City, Chinese history and culture; the heroic stature of Chou En-lai; and the intensity and sweep of our talks combined to make an indelible impression on me. . . . My assessment of these people is that they are deeply ideological, close to fanatic in the intensity of their beliefs. At the same time they display an inward security that allows them, within the framework of their principles, to be meticulous and reliable in dealing with others."[32] In spite of its orientalism, and its ignorance of the intense political infighting that was going on in Beijing, Kissinger's view was not altogether wrong. Mao and Zhou were out to make a deal that would protect their Party's rule against its main opponents, abroad and at home. And in Nixon and Kissinger they believed that they had found the best vehicles ever for making a security bargain with most powerful country in the world.

In the seventeen hours of conversations that Zhou and Kissinger had over two days, Kissinger at first came across as awestruck by the moment and by the personality of the premier. The visitor then found his ground, playing on Chinese concerns about Soviet power and Japan's resurgence. Zhou still wanted to reduce Kissinger to some form of supplicant, knowing that the records would be pored over by Mao and Jiang Qing's associates, and that he could easily be criticized if he did not stick closely to the script. The premier pressed on two main points: a U.S. withdrawal from Taiwan, with no U.S. support for Taiwan independence, and a quick U.S. withdrawal from Indochina. Zhou also presented a laundry list of U.S. withdrawals from elsewhere in Asia, but these were presented pro forma, and not really subject to much discussion.[33]

Both on Taiwan and on Indochina the Chinese side got more than it expected. Kissinger indicated a gradual U.S. withdrawal from Taiwan and, crucially, acceptance of the basic point for Beijing that Taiwan was part of China. On Indochina, Kissinger went further. Reflecting the current mood in Washington, he stressed that the United States was "prepared to withdraw completely from Indochina and to give a fixed date." He also added— very significantly for the Chinese—that, after a ceasefire, Nixon would "permit the political solution of South Vietnam to evolve and to leave it to the Vietnamese alone." "We will not re-enter Vietnam," Kissinger added.[34]

Kissinger's first visit moved U.S.-China relations in the direction Mao wanted to see. When Zhou reported to him, Mao underlined his belief in evolution: "Monkeys still have their tails," said the chairman. But the Taiwan issue had evolved. It was no longer a monkey but an ape. "Apes can evolve into human beings." The conflict over Taiwan could be resolved slowly. Vietnam, Mao stressed, might then be more important.[35] He sent Zhou to North Vietnam and to North Korea, straight from the talks with Kissinger. The

Vietnamese were, understandably, horrified, and, even if they treated Zhou Enlai with respect, their party newspaper made sure to fire off an editorial about the "bankruptcy of Nixonism" just after the Chinese Premier left Hanoi.[36] North Korean leader Kim Il-sung was less openly critical, but told Zhou that he now expected China to facilitate direct talks between himself and Nixon.[37] The North Koreans, who had been staunch critics of the Cultural Revolution—"a great madness, having nothing in common with either culture or a revolution," one of them called it—must have been taken aback by the latest twist in Chinese foreign policy.[38]

The global effects of the sudden Sino-American rapprochement were staggering. The Soviets saw it as a major setback; even if they had already lost China politically, the fear of Americans and Chinese joining in an intensifying containment of the USSR led Moscow to an increased emphasis on its own role as a global superpower. Soviet leader Leonid Brezhnev wanted the Americans to recognize his country as an equal, and he sped up support for socialist regimes and revolutionary movements elsewhere in the world in an attempt to show that the Soviet Union was truly a country with worldwide interests and obligations. Soviet support for North Vietnam increased, as did its aid to Cuba and to anticolonial movements in Africa. In South Asia, India became a major Soviet partner, as did radical Arab regimes in the Middle East. When China's commitment to global anticapitalism faded, the Soviets were happy to step into the breach.

If Soviet leaders were horrified, Japan's prime minister, Sato Eisaku, was in shock. Those who saw him watching Nixon's live broadcast on July 15, when the U.S. president announced that he would be visiting the PRC in 1972, reported that he went pale as a sheet of paper. Having no inkling of Kissinger's China visit destroyed Sato's position in Japan and contributed to his resignation. While the ruling Liberal Democratic Party tried to find his successor, contenders scrambled to be in a position to negotiate with Beijing. Miki Takeo, who hoped to become the new Japanese prime minister, visited China in April 1972. Zhou Enlai made it clear to Miki that the CCP, too, wanted to normalize relations with Japan. The Chinese Premier said that he did not want any territorial issues to stand in the way; the Diaoyu Islands dispute could "wait for the future to be ripe through consultation and negotiation, by the two countries, to find a reasonable, mutually acceptable solution. At present, the urgent issue we face together is not to debate who owns this East China

Sea island, but how to overcome difficulties, remove resistance, and restore diplomatic relations between our two countries as soon as possible."[39]

The flamboyant, personable, but also very corrupt Tanaka Kakuei, who took over from Sato as prime minister, visited China in September 1972 and initiated the normalization of relations. Tanaka had served in China as a Japanese soldier during the war. But to the Chinese side it was more important that he was known as a Japanese nationalist, who stood up for national interests, even against the United States. Tanaka had a warm meeting with Mao, where they compared events from their childhoods. "With your visit to Beijing, the whole world is trembling in fear, mainly one Soviet Union and one United States, the two big powers," Mao told Tanaka. "They are fairly uneasy, and wondering what you are up to. . . . [We] can go without an agreement for decades and centuries and yet resolve the issue in a matter of days." "Yes, it can be resolved so long as the timing is right," responded Tanaka. "Indeed," the chairman said, undoubtedly thinking about how remarkable it was that the leader of Japan had come to him, in Beijing, to ask for an improvement of relations.[40]

Mao might also have been thinking about how the world had changed in the early 1970s, allowing for the change in China's international circumstances. The unique economic and strategic predominance of the United States, which had been in place since the end of World War II, was receding. Japan and Western Europe had mainly recovered from wartime destruction and had become serious competitors for the United States in economic terms. The Soviet Union had, at least in terms of strategic nuclear weapons, matched U.S. capabilities. Meanwhile, the United States was bogged down in deeply unpopular and seemingly unwinnable wars in Indochina that also did great damage to its international reputation. Mao was convinced that it was this shift in fortunes that had brought the U.S. president to Beijing.

But Mao also needed a foreign policy victory, as the presidential visit would give him. Lin Biao's flight and death had severely challenged the legitimacy of the Cultural Revolution and of Mao's revolutionary enterprise in general. However unlikely it seemed, the Americans would come to his rescue in terms of prestige. They would also, or so Mao hoped, help defend the real Communists—his Chinese Communist Party—against the false Communists in Moscow. Lin, Mao believed, had been a Soviet stooge, if not a Soviet agent. Zhou Enlai, who was now, for the first time since 1949, the real CCP number two, was perfectly suited to help Mao work with the Americans, as

Zhou Enlai and Richard Nixon at Beijing's airport, February 21, 1972.
Source: AFP via Getty Images.

he had so often served the chairman in diplomatic or other delicate ventures in the past. Other old leaders, whom Mao had suspected of being rightists in the past, could also be brought back, at least for a while, to serve the same purpose, Mao thought.

Nixon's arrival in Beijing, on a cold day in late February 1972, was a spectacle to behold. As Air Force One landed, Zhou Enlai was waiting at a bit of distance from the runway, so that the president's plane could come to him. It was the tiniest revenge, choreographed by the premier himself, in return for the times in the past when he had been snubbed by U.S. diplomats. Otherwise, the Chinese went along with every protocol point raised by the camera-conscious Americans, including timing key events to fit with prime-time television in the United States, not easy to do given a twelve-hour time difference. To the U.S. delegation, including the president himself, China seemed perplexing and strange, almost like another planet. But Kissinger kept reminding Nixon about the momentousness of the occasion and how it enhanced the president's stature. And for the Chinese side, the historic nature of the visit was obvious: it was the first time a top Western leader had come to China to seek a settlement of international disputes. Mao was ecstatic. In spite of having been at death's door just nine days earlier, he readied himself to see the U.S. president. He even washed and brushed his teeth, his doctor reported.[41]

Nixon met Mao in the afternoon of February 21, at Mao's swimming pool house in Zhongnanhai. The chairman had trouble breathing and was guided and partially held up by Wang Hairong and Tang Wensheng so he should not stumble. He would only talk about philosophy, he told Nixon, not politics. But he did reference his old statement that he had voted for the president in the elections, and that he "liked rightists." When Nixon gushed that "the Chairman's writings moved a nation and have changed the world," Mao replied in usual style that he had "only been able to change a few places in the vicinity of Peking." The only conversation of substance was when Mao stressed that "the question of aggression from the United States or aggression from China is relatively small; that is, it could be said that this is not a major issue, because the present situation is one in which a state of war does not exist between our two countries." China does not "threaten Japan or South Korea," Mao said, and noted, with obvious pleasure, that "you want to withdraw some of your troops back on your soil."[42]

The key, to Mao, was that cooperation against the Soviet Union was possible even if all big questions had not been resolved. China was determined to proceed. The chairman could not resist slandering the departed Lin Biao, whom, he claimed to Nixon, belonged to "a reactionary group which is opposed to our contact with you. The result was that they got on an airplane and fled abroad." "The situation between our two countries," Mao said, "is strange because during the past 22 years our ideas have never met in talks. Now the time is less than 10 months since we began playing table tennis. . . . You wanted some exchange of persons on a personal level, things like that; also trade. But rather than deciding that we stuck with our stand that without settling major issues there is nothing that can be done with smaller issues. I myself persisted in that position. Later on I saw you were right, and we played table tennis."[43] Obviously weakened, Mao grabbed Nixon's outstretched hand in both of his when the Americans were leaving. The camera caught a beaming Zhou Enlai, giddy with relief that the meeting had gone well. Mao's doctors, assembled outside the door, must have felt equally relieved.

But Zhou Enlai's challenges in managing the Nixon visit were far from over. As the U.S. president toured the country, Zhou and Kissinger tried to put together some kind of joint statement about relations between the two governments, to be released at the end of the visit. This process had started already during a preparatory visit by Kissinger in the autumn of 1971 and was far from simple. Mao, who restricted himself to the one meeting with Nixon, was watching every step closely from in-depth reports, sometimes several times per day, and he wanted China to state its revolutionary principles loudly and clearly. Kissinger, understandably, recoiled at having the U.S. president associated with anticapitalist and anti-imperialist slogans. Zhou was able to hide some of the most blatant Maoist phrases in what became the Shanghai Communique, released by the two sides on February 27, 1972, but what really broke the deadlock was the agreement on Taiwan. "The United States," stated the Shanghai Communique, "acknowledges that all Chinese on either side of the Taiwan Strait maintain there is but one China and that Taiwan is a part of China. The United States Government does not challenge that position. It reaffirms its interest in a peaceful settlement of the Taiwan question by the Chinese themselves. With this prospect in mind, it affirms the ultimate objective of the withdrawal of all U.S. forces and military installations from Taiwan. In the meantime, it will progressively reduce its forces and military installations on Taiwan as the tension in the area diminishes."[44]

Zhou, under increasing pressure from Mao and the radicals, held an awkward last meeting with Nixon and Kissinger in Shanghai. "If the war in Vietnam and the other two countries of Indochina does not stop," Zhou said, "it will be impossible to relax tensions in the Far East. And we will be forced to continue aid to their just struggles. . . . We have no right to negotiate for them." Under direct instruction from Mao, Zhou told Nixon that "we would rather let the question of Taiwan wait a little while, while we would rather have the war in Vietnam and the whole of Indochina come to a stop because we feel this is a more urgent issue." "Because during the struggles against others, whether in Korea or Vietnam, our three countries have participated in each other's struggle. . . . As Chairman Mao has pointed out, we who have been victorious have only an obligation to assist them, but not the right to interfere in their sovereignty." Zhou deplored the continued U.S. bombing of North Vietnam during the visit, which, he said, had given "the Soviet

Union a chance to say that the music played in Peking to welcome President Nixon has been together with the sounds of the bombs exploding in North Vietnam."[45] The visit ended on less of a high note than the U.S. guests had hoped for.

With the United States now fully in play to assist China's security needs, a group of hastily reassembled diplomats in Beijing turned their attention to Japan, as we have seen, and to Western Europe. Britain and the PRC set up full diplomatic relations in March 1972, and, more remarkably, Beijing normalized relations with West Germany in September 1972, breaking the embargo that socialist countries had had against relations with the Federal Republic. France had established diplomatic relations with the PRC already in 1964, under President Charles de Gaulle, but links were significantly expanded after the Nixon visit. Most Western European countries had voted with the majority when the PRC had finally been able to take over China's seat at the United Nations from the government in Taibei in October 1971.

China's international position had therefore changed dramatically in the early 1970s, in spite of the political chaos inside the country. Much of this success should be ascribed to Zhou Enlai, who—after Lin Biao's death—was not only the number-two leader in the Party, but its chief diplomat. Zhou had no aspirations to lead the CCP. On the contrary, the fact that he was now number two seemed to terrify him at times; maybe this was not surprising, given the sorry fate of Mao's most recent chief lieutenants. In the fall of 1971, after Lin Biao's death, Ji Dengkui, the political commissar of the Beijing military region and a rising star in the Party, came across the premier sitting alone in his office, crying. Ji tried to cheer him up, saying that with Lin Biao gone, the premier could push for his own economic plans to be realized. "You do not understand," Zhou said through tears. "Things are not so simple. It is not over yet."[46]

In spite of his occasional despair over the direction of Chinese politics, Zhou did try to link China's more favorable international position to advancing its productive capacity. Ever since the early 1960s, the premier and some of his associates had hoped to acquire new technology from the West and Japan for China's run-down factories. Even during the height of the Cultural Revolution, a trickle of such new investments had continued, but at a scale that did little to mend China's backwardness.[47] After 1971 the requests for modern technology swung into high gear, after Mao had given his blessing.

The purpose of such modernization, the chairman stressed, was not to change the structure of China's socialist economy, but to make it more effective and easier to control from the center. Mao had promoted some forms of economic decentralization, but he believed firmly that the central government should control the overall economy and that modern technologies would help in that purpose.

The scale of the plans for industrial modernization were staggering. In January 1972 the government signed off on a scheme to import machinery for producing synthetic fibers and chemical fertilizers for a total sum of up to $400 million.[48] Six months later it cleared a request for $200 million for new steel production equipment.[49] And in January 1973 Zhou and the State Council agreed to a more comprehensive plan for importing a vast array of machinery for petrochemical plants, mining, electricity, engines, cement, food processing, pharmaceuticals, refrigeration, and ship-building with a total value of US$4.3 billion.[50] It was China's most ambitious technology import program since the Soviet era in the 1950s, and, the planners noted, China could get advantageous prices given the economic crisis in the West. But, first and foremost, they knew that China would now have access to the most advanced technology their money could buy, since politically motivated embargoes would no longer stand in their way. The diplomatic outreach of the early 1970s enabled China's state-owned companies to begin their modernization process. Some of the imported machinery eventually found its way to smaller, collective-owned companies in the more advanced provinces.

One key element of the "4.3 Plan," as China's new attempts at acquiring foreign technology was called, was to prepare some production for export. If the CCP's new emphasis on modernization were to continue, the country needed foreign currency—meaning mainly U.S. dollars—in much larger amounts than before. And the best way of getting dollars was through exports, especially since borrowing overseas was against Mao's slogans of self-reliance. By the end of 1973 China had set up an investment fund for export goods, where companies could get assistance to gear some of their production toward overseas sales. And, in order to arrange for the bigger state-owned factories to get necessary machinery or parts, there was a set of foreign exchange loan programs, through which these units could get direct access to foreign currency. Increasingly, the government began to facilitate foreign travel for Chinese trade officials, down to the factory level, and commercial sections within the embassies were ordered to be on the lookout for opportunities for Chinese exports.[51] In most cases they were disappointed: the quality of Chinese goods was so atrocious that their market opportunities were limited.[52] But the Communist salesmen began to get an impression of what opportunities existed, and in the process they learned much about how markets worked.

Most of China's foreign trade was facilitated through Hong Kong, where the local Bank of China branch acted as the PRC's main economic representative (and much else besides). The lack of currency controls in the British Crown colony fitted China's purposes to a T and made it possible to move vast amounts of money and Chinese products through Hong Kong. Chinese-owned companies based in Hong Kong also delivered handsome profits for the PRC. By the early 1970s more than half of the country's foreign currency earnings moved through Hong Kong, and the 1973/1974 stock market crash, which wiped out two-thirds of local share values, allowed mainland companies to buy into Hong Kong business at a fraction of their real worth. In 1974 Chinese border controls with Hong Kong were also substantially relaxed, allowing an explosion in immigrants to the colony. At times, more than a thousand individuals crossed over in a day. Those caught by the British at the border were generally sent back, while those who made it to the city were often allowed to remain.[53]

In addition to the "official" trade (often carried out in a very unofficial manner), there were many attempts by the newly empowered collective enterprises in Guangdong and other nearby provinces to make use of access to the Hong Kong market. Since these businesses in most cases could not trade legally with Hong Kong, the most ingenious of them resorted to sizable smuggling and black market operations, sending their own products or products they had acquired in China down the Pearl River or across to harbors on the eastern side of Hong Kong's new territories. By 1973 a few of these enterprises had their own bank accounts in the colony and access to credit. A couple of years later at least nine of them ran full-scale commercial operations in Hong Kong, with salespeople, lists of goods, and guaranteed delivery times. Military and border guard units sometimes shared in the profits. All of this was of course strictly illegal in the PRC, and the organizers would probably have received death sentences if they were caught. But the attraction of economic gain in a world dominated by poverty was such that at least some Chinese were willing to take the risk.

Smuggling of goods to and from Hong Kong in the early 1970s shows both an increasing Chinese supply of desirable products and an appetite within China for foreign merchandise. Among the key products smuggled from China were antiques, silks and furs, live animals, gold and silver, jewelry, steel, guns, and Chinese medicine. To China went video cameras and cassette recorders, cosmetics, glasses, nylon stockings, refrigerators and air conditioners, pornographic movies, engines, and watches. Drugs and alcohol went in both directions. In some of these cases criminal organizations in Hong Kong were involved in the operation, but not always. The trade went on in a gray zone between established organized crime in the colony, often referred to as the Triads, and mainland initiatives. Triad leaders knew well enough not to get in the way of powerful PRC interests. And there were enough hidden harbors in Hong Kong through which smugglers could ply their trade and enough fishing boats at sea.[54] By 1975 the smugglers had their own fleets of small motorized boats and a system of paid lookouts all the way from the origin to the destination.[55]

With the new relationship to the Americans came new thinking in Beijing on how to approach the Taiwan issue. To the leaders of the CCP, dealing with Taiwan was a matter of national reunification. For more than twenty years they had accused the United States of illegally occupying the island and preventing its return to the motherland. But in their hearts they knew the situation was not that simple. A part of the population on the island wanted independence from China. These groups opposed both the dictatorial regime of Chiang Kai-shek, who had arrived from the mainland in 1949, and the prospect of unification under the CCP. Beijing's greatest fear, as expressed in the talks with Nixon, was that the independence movement would get U.S. support, and that Taiwan thereby could be lost to China forever.

With the Shanghai Communique in hand, Mao Zedong believed that he had forestalled the possibility of Taiwanese independence, at least for now. He hoped for some kind of grand reconciliation with Chiang Kai-shek in his own lifetime, and he often pointed out to visitors that Chiang was a genuine Chinese patriot who was welcome to join the motherland, as so many of his former associates had done in the past. One reason why the chairman instructed Zhou Enlai to go easy on the Taiwan issue in his talks with the Americans was his hope that Chiang, abandoned by Washington and under pressure from Taiwanese nationalists, would seek to settle with his old enemies in

Beijing. But for Chiang the Cultural Revolution was the confirmation of what he had always thought about the Communists: not only were his old comrades who had returned to the mainland persecuted all over the country, but his own ancestral tombs in Zhejiang were damaged by Red Guards. "Harbor the hatred forever" and "avenge the insult and wipe out the humiliation," the Generalissimo exhorted his sons and grandchildren.[56]

But in the Taiwan case, too, informal commercial contacts were undermining official enmity. In the early 1970s smuggling operations between the Guomindang-held islands and the mainland increased dramatically. Most of the exchange of goods took place at sea, where fishermen from both sides soon concentrated on products other than fish. In spite of the heavily militarized zones in the region, locals always found a way through.[57] Some of the smaller towns in Fujian, on the mainland coast opposite Taiwan, became quite wealthy in the process, when privately operated stores for selling smuggled goods attached themselves to local collective enterprises. Shishi, a harbor township near the ancient trading port of Quanzhou, had shown an instinct for enterprise throughout the Maoist era. At the height of the Cultural Revolution the township specialized in producing Mao badges, bigger and shinier than anywhere else. In the early 1970s the surplus from Mao badge production was transferred on to cross-straits smuggling. By 1974 there were almost a thousand shops in and around Shishi selling products from Taiwan.[58] There were periodical crackdowns—in 1975 Vice Premier Chen Yonggui (the one of Dazhai model-collective fame) accused the people of Shishi of selling everything from Taiwan except the Guomindang flag—but overall everyone got by through local police, military, and party officials profiting handsomely from the trade.[59]

Trade with more faraway places increased, too, through official means. In 1971 there had been no direct trade between the United States and the PRC. Four years later China imported almost $400 million worth of U.S. goods per year. By 1981 it would be more than $4.3 billion.[60] And while this growth in direct trade was significant from a Chinese point of view, even more significant was the removal of most U.S. obstacles for China's trade with third countries. On the contrary, by the mid-1970s the Americans were pushing other nations to remove trade barriers with China. As U.S. leaders realized just how weak China was economically, they wanted to promote trade as one way of making the PRC a credible partner in dealing with the Soviets. Given the state of the Chinese economy, neither Nixon nor Kissinger believed that Sino-American trade would be significant for the United States, at least not in the short run. But they knew its importance for the Chinese, and Nixon and his successors in the White House hoped that it would also help them politically with a U.S. business community that was eager to trade with China.

Between 1950 and 1970, on average, only about seventy-five Americans had visited China each year.[61] It was an extraordinary example of noncontact between two of the world's biggest countries. But, by the mid-1970s, the situation had changed significantly. U.S. businesspeople and Chinese economic representatives led the way. Beginning in 1973, the National Council for United States–China Trade and its journal, the *U.S. China Business Review*, helped U.S. companies find contacts in the PRC. The council was peppered with representatives of important U.S. firms: Honeywell, McDonnell Douglas, Cargill, IBM, Caterpillar, Ford, and Exxon. American businesspeople, who knew even less about China than Chinese Communists knew about the United States, were surprised that all trade was "official" trade, channeled through the PRC government. Even so, some of them started coming to China repeatedly, mostly as members of large government-sponsored trade delegations. The Chinese wanted as many business contacts as they could get, even with lesser known firms. The group inside the Ministry of Foreign Trade that specialized in building commercial links with the United States had done their homework.[62]

Even if links with the United States were important for China's new attempts at importing technology, we should not exaggerate their significance in terms of direct trade. Because the two countries did not yet have full diplomatic relations, the PRC could not get the most-favored-nation status necessary to full regularize bilateral trade. And even if Chinese trade representatives were impressed by the singular abundance of consumer goods and all forms of technology they found in the United States, their political masters were careful not to put all their eggs in one basket. Other countries sometimes had technology that was less expensive and more appropriate for China. In some cases they could even offer equipment that the Americans were reluctant to sell to China for strategic or commercial reasons. The important thing was that the United States no longer attempted to prevent such deals from going ahead.[63]

Trade with Japan was especially important. Unlike with the United States, Sino-Japanese trade had never been entirely cut off after 1949, but with diplomatic relations restored in 1972 it increased significantly.[64] Given that Japan was in the middle of its globalized export-led growth strategy, China had to be fitted into more general Japanese aims. What China could provide was oil and coal, which were the most important import products into Japan in the 1970s. It could also sell textile fibers and fabrics, as well as fish and vegetables. In addition to machinery, China imported steel and fertilizer from its neighbor. By 1978 almost two-thirds of China's import of manufacturing equipment came from Japan, within a total trade of more than $5 billion.[65] In spite of the historical friction between the two countries, Japan played a major role in the early modernization of Chinese industry, not least in terms of ideas about development and investment patterns.

Chinese trade officials also followed up on the opportunities offered by the diplomatic normalization with countries in Western Europe. Britain was particularly important to begin with, both because of existing trade connections and connections through Hong Kong. Already in 1972 Britain's direct trade with China was significant, and new agreements were signed that year that included cooperation in science and technology and student exchanges. Britain was also willing, with U.S. blessing, to sell China jet engines and aircraft. France got less out of its early normalization with the PRC in terms of trade.[66] Even so, China did acquire civilian nuclear technology, helicopters, and advanced radars from France, and, for a long while, Air France was the only Western airline serving Beijing.

In trade terms, by far the most important European link for China was with West Germany. Not only did the Germans have the kind of technology that Chinese experts wanted to import, but their products were good quality at decent prices, with stable and dependable contracts. By 1979 bilateral trade had reached more than $2 billion, and it kept expanding. The Chinese, and especially Mao himself, were aware of West Germany's increased political significance in Europe, and deeply skeptical of Willy Brandt's detente policies toward the Soviet Union.

In January 1975 Mao made a point of meeting the conservative leader of Bavaria, Franz Josef Strauss, when he visited China. The chairman had noted Strauss saying that "the troops on the other side of the Elbe are not Chinese, but Soviet." When the visitor opined that countries that aim at hegemony always start with phrases about peace, Mao wholeheartedly agreed. "Every day," said the chairman, "the Soviet Union speaks about peace and prepares for war. We do not think much of it when a state just trumpets words of peace, relaxation and friendship." Europe had to be alert to Moscow's plans, said Mao, even after he was gone. "My body is breaking down . . . [and] I can no longer speak clearly." But his brain still worked, he said, and he knew who the enemy was.[67]

In general, the significance that Chinese leaders attached to Germany was strategic as well as economic. Mao's obsession with the risk of a Soviet attack on China meant that any European accommodation with the Soviets was dangerous for Beijing, because it would allow the Soviets to move their forces eastward. Both Mao and Zhou believed West Germany to be the emerging European power, and they wanted to get their message across loudly. When West German chancellor Helmut Schmidt, who had replaced Willy Brandt in 1974, visited Beijing the following year, Mao told him that "there will be war." "Europe is too soft and divided, and also full of deadly fear about war. . . . If Europe will still remain unable during the next ten years to unite politically, economically, and militarily, it will suffer. The Europeans have to learn to rely on themselves. Would it not be possible that the sixty million of West Germans can achieve the same as the North Vietnamese?"[68]

In spite of its obsession with security and with the Soviet Union, it was the dramatic global economic changes in the 1970s that would have the most impact on the future of China. As the world moved on from the era of post–World War reconstruction, the role of the state receded in Western economies. Capital controls were abolished and fixed exchange rates dropped. Instead, capital flowed increasingly freely and currencies floated relative to each other. The result was a strengthening of international banks and corporations, and through them global trade and investment. For the United States, it meant an internationalization of its economy both through foreign capital coming in and U.S-based companies investing and lending abroad. As a result, the financial conditions for global trade improved to an extent that had not been seen since before World War One. Trade was also helped by transport getting less expensive, just like markets and foreign investing were assisted by a beginning revolution in communications and information technology. Altogether the changing global economic circumstances of the 1970s thoroughly suited China's wish for technology imports and increased foreign trade, especially since many large corporations liked dealing with authoritarian regimes or at least with those such that had a US stamp of approval.

By the mid-1970s, therefore, China's international position was beginning a transformation. From isolation and disengagement in the 1960s, the strategic rapprochement with the United States had given China opportunities to engage the capitalist world in search of trade and technology. And the timing of China's strategic and economic reengagement was propitious. It came just as global capitalism was entering its most liberal phase for several generations, with much easier access to hard currency, technology, and trade than had been the case before. The international expansion of markets and capital suited the CCP's purposes in the late Maoist era, as long as the Chinese state could make use of new opportunities to modernize while keeping capitalist practices at bay at home. The PRC had benefitted diplomatically from the most recent turns in the Cold War. Now some CCP leaders also hoped to make use of the twists in modern capitalism to help rebuild their country and strengthen their government.

None of these changes came about through superb strategic insights, certainly not on Mao's part. They were caused by a combination of fear and luck. By the end of the Cultural Revolution CCP leaders feared their country's weakness and the enfeeblement of their own regime. Following Mao's thinking, they thought that war was coming and that China was ill-prepared for it. They also feared that the CCP dictatorship could be in real trouble because of the domestic upheavals of the previous decade. Engaging with the United States that, for its own purposes, wanted to enhance China's strategic position and improve its economy was, for these leaders, both a supreme irony and a stroke of luck. Having the leader of world capitalism rooting for them did not get the CCP to abolish its revolutionary agenda. But it made some of its leaders believe that they could be more successful in fulfilling their aims for Chinese Communism than they had been only a few years earlier.

5

The Fall and Rise and Fall
of Deng Xiaoping

THE MOST PROMINENT COMMUNIST LEADER who had been purged in the Cultural Revolution but still survived was Deng Xiaoping. Deng had been publicly denounced as "the number-two capitalist roader" after Liu Shaoqi and excluded from his state and Party positions. His brother was publicly tortured and died by suicide, his eldest son was paralyzed from the chest down after jumping from a window when terrorized by Red Guards at Peking University, and a brother-in-law died while being persecuted. After two years under house arrest, Deng and his wife were sent to work near Nanchang in Jiangxi, a poor province inland from Fujian and Guangdong. But he was spared public humiliation sessions, even though he had been beaten by Red Guards in his Zhongnanhai residence.[1] And, most crucially of all, he kept his Party membership—whenever he was listed by the radicals for expulsion, Mao laid down the law: there were substantial differences between Deng and Liu Shaoqi, the chairman said. Deng could possibly be redeemed at some point in the future.

The reason why Mao saved Deng's life has been the subject of much speculation among the Chinese elite in the 1970s and since. In reality, it is not so difficult to understand. Deng had been a Mao loyalist all of his political life. He had dedicated his immense capacity for hard work to promoting the chairman's ideas. In the early 1930s, when Mao was in political trouble, Deng had lost his CCP positions twice because of his close association with him. In the 1940s he had been a guard dog against anyone suspected of deviating from Mao's political line. In the 1950s, as mayor of Chongqing in his home province

of Sichuan, Deng had helped consolidate the new regime there while carrying out the CCP's initial purges. Then, as Party general secretary beginning
in the mid-1950s, he had been a key supporter of the Anti-Rightist Campaign, the Great Leap Forward, and the break with the Soviets. After the
Leap, Deng had joined with Liu Shaoqi and Zhou Enlai to clean up the economic mess and strengthen production.[2] Deng's forthright style and disdain
for dogma had led to clashes with the CCP Left, though he had always been
respectful of the chairman's position. But when Mao turned decisively against
the economic consolidation measures of the early 1960s, Deng had not been
quick enough to change tack. Mao deemed Deng's early support for the Cultural Revolution to be insincere, and supported the radicals in attacking and
purging him in the fall of 1966.

But there were also other reasons for sparing Deng Xiaoping's life. Deng
had always been close to a number of senior military leaders, and he was admired within the army for his contributions both during the anti-Japanese
war and the civil war that followed. And, crucially, Deng's self-criticism—a
seventy-page document written while he was under house arrest in Beijing—
was to the chairman's liking, especially the part where Deng praised the
achievements of the Cultural Revolution. The depth of Deng's despair seems
also to have pleased Mao. "I am truly at a loss what to do," Deng wrote to the
chairman after the Red Guards had broken into his house. "I sincerely hope
for a chance to seek your instructions personally. I know this request may
not be appropriate, but I have no other way to express the feelings in my
heart."[3]

In October 1968, at a plenary meeting of the CCP Central Committee,
Jiang Qing, supported by Lin Biao, again attempted to remove Deng's Party
membership, something which, in effect, would have been a death sentence.
Mao, who had already signaled very clearly that he did not want that to happen, got annoyed. "As for this person Deng Xiaoping," Mao said at the plenum, "I always say a few words in his defense. This is because during the
anti-Japanese and liberation wars he beat up on the enemy. Moreover, no other
problems were uncovered about his past. . . . Now all of you want to expel him,
but I still have some reservations about this. I always think that we should
distinguish him from Liu Shaoqi; in fact, there are some differences between
them. I'm afraid my views are somewhat conservative and do not fit your taste,
but still I would like to say some good words about Deng Xiaoping."[4]

In spite of Mao's piecemeal protection, it is very likely that it was Deng's removal to rural Jiangxi during the Soviet war scare in 1969 that saved his life. Out of reach of the Red Guards and his radical enemies in the Party leadership, Deng and his wife spent three-and-a-half years in Xinjian County, where both worked in the local tractor repair factory set up by the county. Deng was employed as a fitter, just as he had been in a Renault factory in France almost fifty years earlier. The area where Deng lived was under the control of the Fuzhou Military Region, headed by General Han Xianchu, an old acquaintance of Deng's who survived the Cultural Revolution by gingerly finding a balance between Lin Biao and Lin's military opponents.

While in Xinjian, Deng kept informed about local concerns and got news from Beijing by listening to the radio. He sometimes spoke with officers from the local regiment, and it was from them he learned about Lin Biao's death. Afterwards Deng wrote directly to Mao, for the first time in a while. "I have no requests for myself, only that someday I may be able to do a little work for the Party," Deng said. "Naturally, it would be some sort of technical work. My health is pretty good. I can put in a few more years before retirement. . . . I am longing for a chance to pay back by hard work a bit of what I owe. . . . I sincerely wish you long life. Your long and healthy life ensures the greatest happiness for the whole Party and all our people!"[5] He got no reply. But Mao did read the letter and wrote on the envelope to "print and issue to the Politburo." The chairman also instructed Wang Dongxing to help Deng's son get medical attention.[6]

After Nixon's visit in February 1972, Mao was pleased with the political outcome but was upset that Zhou Enlai got so much of the praise for bringing the two countries together, not least in the foreign press. In a series of top-level Party rectification meetings in the summer of 1972 the premier had to go through several rounds of self-criticism on many aspects of his past behavior as part of a general house-cleaning after the Lin Biao affair. Mao seemed almost to have forgotten Zhou's crucial role in steadying the ship only a few months earlier. Chairing meetings in which many people came forward to self-criticize, Zhou offered up mistakes from his own past to the participants so that, in his own words to Mao, "they can criticize me, supervise me, reform me, and learn from my case . . . and know how the Chairman saved and educated me."[7] To everyone present it seemed a routine exercise, but it also made it clear that Mao wanted to take Zhou down a peg or two. That the premier had been diagnosed with bladder cancer a few weeks before did not affect the proceedings.

By mid-1972 Deng had picked up the changing circumstances in Beijing. With Zhou Enlai's role hanging in the balance, and the military more influential than ever, Deng deemed the moment opportune for writing to Mao again, underlining how he had reformed throughout his exile from power. Deng knew, of course, about Mao's positive reference to him at Chen Yi's funeral, and he aimed at convincing the chairman that he could be used to further Mao's designs.[8] "Chairman," he began cautiously, "you know that Lin Biao and Chen Boda wanted to kill me off.

> I do not know what it would have been like if I was not protected by the Chairman. . . . I had not held up the great red flag of Mao Zedong Thought for a long time. The Great Proletarian Cultural Revolution revealed and criticized me, which is totally and completely necessary, and it also saved me. I fully support the Chairman's saying that "the Great Proletarian Cultural Revolution is absolutely necessary and very timely." . . . I fully understand that a man like me, who made a lot of mistakes and misdeeds, and has a bad smell in the community, cannot get the trust of the masses any more, and it is impossible to work at any important position. However, I think my health is okay and, although sixty-eight years old already, [I] can do a work of some technical nature (such as investigation and research work) for seven or eight more years for the Party and the people, so that I can subtract from my mistakes. I have no other requests and will wait for the instructions from the Chairman and the Center. I sincerely wish the Chairman a long life![9]

This time Mao read Deng's letter and told Zhou Enlai that he viewed it positively. What caught the chairman's attention was one statement that Deng made in it: "In the autobiography that I wrote in June and July of 1968, I made self-criticism of myself and the mistakes and crimes that I had committed. I do not know what it would have been like if I were not protected by the chairman. Today, I stand by everything that I said in the self-criticism. I once again confirm the promise that I made to the Party Center, which is that I will never attempt to reverse the verdict on myself."[10]

"The mistakes committed by Comrade Deng Xiaoping are serious," Mao said. "However, he is different from Liu Shaoqi." He then highlighted several of Deng's major contributions in the history of the Party—as a Maoist in the early 1930s, a wise and accomplished military commander in the civil war, and an unyielding fighter against the Soviet revisionists in the 1960s.[11]

Zhou Enlai almost immediately began looking for a way to get Deng back to Beijing, but he knew he had to be careful. Jiang Qing and Zhang Chunqiao were already accusing the premier and his associates of misinterpreting the Lin Biao affair. They contended that Lin's political position had not been ultra-Leftism, as Zhou had claimed, but ultra-Rightism.[12] The implication was that the turn toward economic issues and increasing production, which Zhou Enlai had spearheaded since Lin's death, was an attack on the Left. But Zhou was also cautious because he did not know exactly which political attitude Deng would take were he to return. Deng was without doubt hated by the Left. But he also had a history—almost as much as Zhou himself—of following the chairman slavishly in whatever political turn Mao took. Could this instinct be turned against the premier?

Deciding on Deng's return in the fall of 1972 became a kind of intricate political dance, in which Zhou sought a decision but did not want to propose one himself. In the end, in December, when the Politburo were discussing the possible rehabilitation of several other veteran leaders, Zhou, after summarizing those cases in a letter to Ji Dengkui and Wang Dongxing, mentioned that "Comrade Deng Xiaoping has requested to come back to do some work. Please consider his request. The Chairman has also mentioned this several times."[13] Wang Dongxing, almost certainly on Mao's orders, wrote back to Zhou and recommended that Deng Xiaoping be brought back to Beijing and given a government post.[14] Wang had been among those suspected of seeking to delay Deng's return, which was perhaps not surprising given that Wang now held positions controlling the Party organization similar to those Deng had had before he was purged. But by December 1972 Mao had made up his mind. He wanted Deng back, though he was still uncertain how to employ him. With Mao's own health in doubt, and with his suspicions about Zhou Enlai's political loyalty growing, Mao may have thought about Deng as an alternative to Zhou, should he ever need one. Someone had to run the country while the chairman himself carried out the new stages of a cultural revolution.

By the winter of 1972 there were increasing signs that Mao had had enough of the implicit rejection of his Cultural Revolution aims that the new policies driven by Zhou, Li Xiannian, and Ye Jianying seemed to entail. The chairman made it clear that he sided with Jiang Qing's and Zhang Chunqiao's views of Lin Biao as an ultra-Rightist, signaling that the main threat against the Party now came from those who wanted to restore markets and material incentives.[15] In typical fashion, just at the same time as Deng Xiaoping returned to Beijing, Mao ordered Zhou Enlai to lead a nationwide campaign denouncing Lin Biao's ultra-Right views. Later in 1973 the campaign was widened into the unlikely combination of a "Criticize Lin, Criticize Confucius" movement. Mao had never liked the ancient sage. But the fact that a number of Confucian texts were found in Lin Biao's house and that the note from Lin Liguo's group compared Mao to the anti-Confucian first emperor of Qin (Qin Shi Huang)—a second-century-B.C. tyrant who had buried Confucian scholars alive—grated on the chairman. "Lin Biao accused me of being the first emperor," Mao confided to a perplexed Egyptian vice president who visited in September 1973. "I am in favor of emperor Qin, not Confucius. Emperor Qin Shi Huang unified China for the first time. . . . He centralized power into his own hands and that of the central government."[16] So the recently dead Lin and the long dead Confucius became subjects of the same denunciation campaign. Some among the Party leaders wondered from the very beginning whether the real target of the campaign was neither a dead marshal nor a dead philosopher, but a living Premier.

Deng Xiaoping returned to Beijing on February 20, 1973. A month later he was appointed a vice premier of the State Council, with the right to attend the Politburo when required.[17] Deng's specific duties were unclear, but Mao seemed inclined to have him assist Zhou Enlai on foreign affairs. The chairman probably remembered the dogged loyalty Deng had shown when attacking the Soviets back in the early 1960s, and he may have wanted Deng's nationalist instincts to balance Zhou's internationalism in dealing with the Americans. But Mao, always suspicious, also wanted to balance Deng's economic pragmatism. He allowed three other leaders—Wang Hongwen, the former rebel leader in Shanghai; Hua Guofeng, the former Hunan provincial chief; and the Beijing Party chief Wu De—to sit in on Politburo meetings, too. Mao also accelerated the preparations for a new CCP Party congress and put Wang Hongwen in charge of it. For many observers, this decision meant that the 38-year-old Wang was now being groomed as a prospective successor. It elated the Left wing of the Party, who regarded Wang as one of their own.

The Tenth Congress of the CCP in late August 1973 was a rushed affair, convened because Mao wanted to get Lin Biao's name out of the Party constitution, and because he wanted to bring new people into the Party leadership. When the congress opened, Mao sat in the middle of the central podium, flanked by Zhou Enlai and Wang Hongwen. Wang reported on the amendment of the Party constitution, and Zhou delivered the main political report, although most of his text had been written by the Left-wing leaders Zhang Chunqiao and Yao Wenyuan. In the new Central Committee, Zhou was first vice chairman and Wang Hongwen was second vice chairman. Zhang Chunqiao was elected a member of the Standing Committee of the Politburo. Jiang Qing and Yao Wenyuan were elected to the Politburo, where the Left and their sympathizers now had a majority. Eight of the twenty-five Politburo members were military officers. Deng was not elected to the Politburo but would be elevated into it two years later.

As the battle for control of the Party Center intensified, a crisis—well hidden from the public—engulfed the Ministry of Public Security. The longtime minister and head of China's secret police, General Xie Fuzhi—a close ally of Kang Sheng and Jiang Qing—had died in March 1972. In spite of a record of stomach cancer, the Left deemed his death suspicious. Then, in October 1973, Xie's successor, General Li Zhen, was found hanged in the basement boiler room of a building in the ministry compound. Jiang Qing intimated that Zhou Enlai's henchmen had played a role. The chairman, through Zhou Enlai, immediately put Hua Guofeng in charge of the delicate investigation, but when Hua arrived at the ministry, Wang Hongwen was already there, claiming that Li had been murdered by class enemies. Studying the knot of the rope, Wang declared that Li could not possibly have tied it himself. Hua, in usual style, said little, but it was clear that Wang's behavior annoyed him. After a few days, with more than a hundred witnesses interrogated and intense study of the forensic evidence, Hua concluded that Li's death had been a suicide, caused by fear of having his previously close relations with Lin Biao discovered. Speaking at a meeting of all ranking members of the ministry, Hua insisted that secret policemen had to work together to protect the CCP, irrespective of their political opinions in the past. In private, Hua called Wang Hongwen's behavior "really childish."[18]

After the Tenth Congress, the CCP leadership was as split as it had been ever since the Cultural Revolution started. The general sense was that the Left,

with Mao's backing, was again in ascendance and that its leaders had the upper hand against Zhou Enlai and the moderates. Zhou had been criticized in
1972 and again in the summer of 1973 for his "misreading of Mao's three-
worlds thesis."[19] But the accusations leveled against him in the fall of 1973
were more serious. The pretext was his negotiations with Henry Kissinger
in November 1973, during which the American had proposed closer surveillance and intelligence cooperation between the United States and China.[20]
Zhou had been cautious during the talks, and had gone to see Mao for instructions right after they ended. But, finding the chairman asleep, Zhou had
not waited patiently for him to wake up. Instead, probably weakened by the
recurrence of his cancer, he had returned home. When Mao was told of the
content of the talks the next day, he was incensed.[21] He ordered a series of
Politburo and extended leadership meetings in late November and early December 1973 for the express purpose of criticizing the premier.[22]

   As soon as the meetings opened, it was clear that this was one of the biggest challenges Zhou Enlai had faced in his long and remarkable political
career. Zhou had survived politically by following two principles: always try
to stay closer to Mao's overall political direction than anyone else, and always
know more about other leaders' foibles than anyone else. When attacked, the
premier was a master of conducting self-criticism until Mao let him off the
hook. This time, however, Zhou acted differently. Nancy Tang, the 30-year-old
Foreign Ministry interpreter, gave the opening remarks—which lasted for
almost three hours—on behalf of the chairman, detailing the premier's
"Rightist deviations" in his meetings with Kissinger. "If the Soviet Union
comes in, Zhou Enlai would be the emperor. If imperialism comes in, Zhou
Enlai would surrender," Mao told his acolytes.[23] But this time Zhou refused
to admit wrongdoing and debase himself. With some of the participants calling Zhou a traitor, his political career seemed to be over.[24]

   What in the end rescued the premier and the meetings was the intervention
of Deng Xiaoping. Deng had been asked by Mao to sit at the proceedings. He
kept silent at first, but, with the meetings stalled over how to proceed, Nancy
Tang and Wang Hairong told Deng that Mao wanted him to say something.
Deng sensed that the chairman wanted Zhou chastised, but not totally com-
promised. Besides, he knew how dependent government operations were on
the premier, in spite of Zhou's now much reduced capacity for work. Deng's
speech was a masterly blend of Mao sycophancy, nationalist bravado, and

reminders of how the chairman had warned against open splits in the Party. The superpowers were not yet fully ready for war, Deng said, and China, under the chairman's leadership, was strong enough to defend itself. Zhou had made many mistakes, but his biggest mistake was not understanding the chairman's line and replacing the chairman's views with his own. Avoiding terms like "traitor" and "capitulationist," Deng stressed the premier's failure to report to Mao before concluding the talks with Kissinger. "Your standpoint is just one step below the Chairman's," Deng said to Zhou. "For others, the Chairman's standpoint is within sight but beyond reach. For you, however, it is within sight and within reach. This is the essence of your problem."[25] Mao was quite satisfied with Deng's presentation. After Zhou finally made "profound self-criticism" along the lines of Deng's critique, Mao abruptly decided to end the meetings held to criticize Zhou. This meant that Zhou's mistakes were organizational problems rather than a full-blown political struggle. Zhou, still PRC premier, was allowed to resume his medical treatment.

The main Leftist members of the Politburo were irate at Zhou's political, and personal, survival. This had been their best chance so far to get him removed and secure the succession for one of their own. With the "Criticize Lin, Criticize Confucius" campaign reaching a new and more intense stage, it had been clear for months that the real target, for the Left, of that campaign was Zhou Enlai and his associates. At the Politburo meetings, Jiang Qing had accused Zhou of complete surrender to imperialism as a matter of principle and referred to the criticism of the premier as the "eleventh line struggle in the Party," every inch as serious as the ninth, against Liu Shaoqi, and the tenth, against Lin Biao. Yao Wenyuan claimed that Zhou represented everything that was wrong within the CCP.[26] That it was Deng Xiaoping, whom they were absolutely convinced was a political renegade, who got the final word infuriated the Left even more.

But, even with Zhou remaining—however shakily—in place, the Left felt that it had the upper hand. Increasingly, across China, it was slogans set up by the Left that were seen most often, and most people seemed to realize which direction the wind was blowing. Enterprising collectives and secretive traders everywhere were quick to help stage revolutionary operas recommended by Jiang Qing or rename brigades or work units according to Cultural Revolution battles against revisionism. Practices may have remained, but names changed, and there were many more crackdowns on units that went too far in commercial transactions. In Beijing and, especially, in Shanghai the Left prepared new plans for political education and for intensified class struggle. With Jiang Qing's blessing, Yao Wenyuan prepared proposals for autonomous worker-led factories, in which the criteria for material rewards were not production, but levels of political consciousness and adherence to Mao Zedong Thought. After the criticism of Zhou, Mao warned the Politburo in a special meeting on December 12, accusing them of not taking politics seriously. "If you do not change . . . I can fight a few more. Do you want to fight? The world is in chaos, including China! I can eat and sleep, so, if you want to fight, you are most welcome. Get ready for war! Inside and abroad. I can fight a few more battles. . . . It will [be made] clear who is really willing to fight, [and] who wants to make use of foreigners to become emperor. If there is revisionism in China, we should root it out!"[27]

Mao's view was echoed by leaders on the Left. In a report to the Central Committee in January 1974, Wang Hongwen made it clear that "the theories of Marxism can be boiled down to one sentence: Rebellion is justified, and Marx taught us to rebel. Some dismissed us as grabbing power through rebellion. The Communist Party of China rebelled against imperialism, feudalism, and bureaucratic capitalism under the leadership of Chairman Mao, and it won the revolutionary wars and seized power. What's wrong with that? In the Cultural Revolution, we rebelled against the capitalist class and all exploitative classes, and we consolidated the dictatorship of the proletariat. What's so wrong with that?"[28]

Increasingly during 1974, Shanghai—the most industrialized city in China, and the biggest—was made into a stronghold of the CCP Left. Working-class organizations had played an outsized role in Shanghai during all of the Cultural Revolution. Many of the national Left's most prominent leaders came from the city, and their local adherents were still in control of most factories, trade unions, and city organizations. The "Criticize Lin, Criticize Confucius" movement was taken as a signal to increase trade union power and for more radicals to take over top Party positions. Some even spoke of a "second power seizure," similar to what had happened at the peak of the Cultural Revolution. There were even public struggle meetings against senior Party figures whom the radicals found wanting, though not widespread violence as in 1966–1968.[29]

In many places across China, the CCP Left used the "Criticize Lin, Criticize Confucius" campaign to counterattack against what they saw as attempts by the moderates to curtail or even control them in the wake of the Lin Biao affair. Wang Xiuzhen, the female trade unionist who became Wang Hongwen's top deputy in Shanghai, summed their position well in a speech in the spring of 1974: "There is a group of old cadres who were criticized at the outset of the Cultural Revolution who harbor revenge which they want to vent. They want to reverse verdicts on the Cultural Revolution and settle accounts. They want to restore things to the pre-Cultural Revolution situation. . . . This sort of attack is an indication of line struggle. Actually, this sort of attack is not only directed against Shanghai, but even more is directed at the three leading comrades in the center."[30]

The upsurge in radical activity in the spring of 1974 was not just directed against moderates within the Party, though this was the main essence of the "Criticize Lin, Criticize Confucius" campaign in cities such as Shanghai, Wuhan, and Hangzhou. In Nanjing, the capital of Jiangsu Province and the headquarters of the powerful Nanjing Military Region, the brunt of Left-wing ire was turned against the PLA, which had dominated provincial politics since 1970. The formidable General Xu Shiyou, who had served as commander of the military region for twenty years, was no friend of the radicals; they had attacked him viciously in 1967, burned his house down, and—even worse for someone known as "the warrior monk"—had foisted the loquacious radical Zhang Chunqiao on him as his political commissar.[31] General Xu's doggerel on Zhang went: "Wearing glasses, clutching a briefcase, writing verdicts, you can move up; talking ideology, complete nonsense; when the battle begins, flee to the rear."[32]

One of Mao's many worries after the Lin Biao affair was the loyalty of the army. He wondered aloud that he had "persecuted many people; will these people still protect me after that?"[33] In one of the many reshuffles of the top brass, General Xu was moved from Nanjing to Guangzhou in early 1974, with the result that massive demonstrations erupted against the much weaker leadership that he left behind in Jiangsu Province. Most of the protesters were young people who had been sent to the countryside and now wanted their urban residence permits back. Some were former Red Guards who had been unceremoniously deported by the army after 1969. But much of Nanjing seemed against the PLA in politics. Some of the protesters threatened to go to Beijing by commandeering train carriages, leading the Center to purge some of the leading officers in the Nanjing region—having suddenly found that they were supporters of Lin Biao—and putting new Left-leaning civilian party bosses in charge.[34]

In Beijing, at the Party Center, the Leftist leaders were caught in a quandary, in spite of the resurgence of Left-wing activity across the country that they had—at least in part—instigated. They hoped to make use of the unrest to strengthen their own positions and those of their political views. But they also knew that the chairman himself did not want a new campaign to be a repeat of the 1966–1968 experience. In spite of generally siding with the Left, he also kept emphasizing unity and stability.[35] Therefore, consistently supporting regional radicals was too dangerous for the Shanghai three—Zhang Chunqiao, Yao Wenyuan, and Wang Hongwen—or even for Jiang Qing. Any direct attacks on the army were particularly dangerous for them, except when officers could be linked to Lin Biao's treacherous activities. In the summer of 1974, when their political strength was probably at its peak, they therefore exhorted their adherents to be careful and cautious, and only carry out struggles for power when expressly sanctioned by the Party Center.

After the Tenth Party Congress, which he sometimes referred to as "the congress of victory"—the same term Stalin had used for the Seventeenth Bolshevik Congress in 1934—Mao spoke more often about the need to unite the Party leadership. He wanted to see the Left in charge of the overall political line, while the moderates dealt with production and modernization. Perhaps as a result of China's new position in world politics, Mao wanted more of an emphasis on economic development, even though such processes had to be completely subservient to political rectitude. The Cultural Revolution was a success and had to be repeated in the future, Mao thought. The leaders of the Left would defend its achievements, even after he was gone. But he sometimes felt that they were not practical enough to lead the revolution on their own. People such as Deng Xiaoping were needed to keep the state moving forward and to consolidate and solidify the results of the shake-up.

The duality of political power in China in the mid-1970s is nowhere better illustrated than in the simultaneous rise of Deng Xiaoping and of the Left-wing leaders. While Jiang Qing and the Shanghai Three labored to expand their power in the cities, unite the Left, and promote rebel workers, Deng strove to rehabilitate old associates, take control of foreign affairs, and develop closer connections with the PLA. The PLA links were particularly important to Deng; he defended senior officers even as they were castigated by the Left through suspicion of past links with Lin Biao. As his power grew in 1974, Deng was not beyond reminding the Leftists that they themselves had once been exceptionally close to the disgraced Marshal Lin.

Mao watched the squabbling from afar. He cracked down on the Left when he thought they overstepped, as when they organized a meeting of Central Committee and State Council officials in January 1974 implicitly to criticize Zhou Enlai and explicitly to attack Ye Jianying.[36] After a scolding by Mao, a tearful Jiang Qing wrote a long letter of self-criticism. "I did something stupid. I am sorry, Chairman!," she told her husband. "In the future, [I will] study hard [and] overcome metaphysics and one-sidedness."[37] But Mao also warned the moderates not to exceed the political limits, cautioning Zhou, Deng, Ye Jianying, and Li Xiannian not to behave as a "clique" of their own well before he first used the term "Gang of Four" for the Politburo radicals Jiang Qing, Zhang Chunqiao, Yao Wenyuan, and Wang Hongwen.[38]

With Zhou Enlai increasingly weakened by illness, Deng Xiaoping soon became Mao's key assistant on foreign affairs. Mao's thinking had turned to a new, development-oriented framework for how to understand the world. Without giving up the emphasis on revolution, the chairman now postulated that it was levels of economic and technological advancement that divided the world into three parts. "I hold," he instructed Zambia's president Kenneth Kaunda in February 1974,

that the U.S. and the Soviet Union belong to the First World. The middle elements, such as Japan, Europe, Australia and Canada, belong to the Second World. We are the Third World. . . . The U.S. and the Soviet Union have a lot of atomic bombs, and they are richer. Europe, Japan, Australia and Canada, of the Second World, do not possess so many atomic bombs and are not so rich as the First World, but richer than the Third World. . . . All Asian countries, except Japan, belong to the Third World. All of Africa and also Latin America belong to the Third World.[39]

When the chairman wanted to use the UN General Assembly's special session on global development in April 1974 to propagate some of his ideas, Deng was chosen to speak for China, in spite of strong protests from Jiang

Qing and others. The speech itself was a hodgepodge of different parts, prepared by various groups in the Foreign Ministry and in the Central Committee. But the central part was dictated by Nancy Tang and Wang Hairong after
long conversations with Mao himself. What the chairman wanted to get across
was that different stages of development now divided the world more than
formal alliances and professed ideologies. "In this situation of "great disorder under heaven," he had Deng tell the meeting in New York, "all the political
forces in the world have undergone drastic division and realignment through
prolonged trials of strength and struggle."[40]

> A large number of Asian, African and Latin American countries have achieved
> independence one after another and they are playing an ever greater role in
> international affairs. As a result of the emergence of social-imperialism, the
> socialist camp which existed for a time after World War II is no longer in ex-
> istence. Owing to the law of the uneven development of capitalism, the West-
> ern imperialist bloc, too, is disintegrating. Judging from the changes in
> international relations, the world today actually consists of three parts, or three
> worlds, that are both interconnected and in contradiction to one another. The
> United States and the Soviet Union make up the First World. The developing
> countries in Asia, Africa, Latin America and other regions make up the Third
> World. The developed countries between the two make up the Second World.

"The imperialists, and the superpowers in particular, are beset with troubles and are on the decline," Deng told the assembled delegates. "Countries
want independence, nations want liberation and the people want revolution—
this is the irresistible trend of history."[41] Deng may have thought about the
perilous situation at home when he repeated the Maoist mottos on his first
foreign trip in almost a decade. But the core message on the need for development and for combating poverty and backwardness must have pleased him.
This is what Deng himself wanted to concentrate on for his own country.

In the spring of 1974 power really seemed to hang in the balance in China.
The Party radicals attempted to mobilize the working class in the cities to
intensify the "Criticize Lin, Criticize Confucius" campaign and took aim at examples of restoration of market initiatives and incentives. In these attempts,
they sought not only to promote "rebel workers" of the Cultural Revolution
generation but also to create a more united Left by allying with older trade
union leaders. The setting up of new autonomous workers organizations

spread from the bigger to medium-size cities between March and May 1974. In some cases these events took place in direct violation of provincial decrees that demanded adherence to decisions made by local Party committees. Even instructions from the Center, written by Zhou Enlai and stressing unity and moderation in workers' demands, seemed to have little effect.

In June 1974 Zhou Enlai was hospitalized for his long-postponed cancer operation. From then until his death eighteen months later, Zhou would leave the hospital only for important meetings and would play less and less of a role in directing the day-to-day work of the government. Mao was exhausted and wanted to travel to the South to recuperate. He would spend the next ten months moving between his residences in Wuhan, Changsha, and Hangzhou. But before he left in July the chairman convened an extended Politburo meeting to let everyone know that he expected them to cooperate in his absence, irrespective of past differences. Jiang Qing, who had annoyed Mao with domestic squabbles and by being widely reported to speak on the chairman's behalf, was in for another scolding. When Jiang tried to defend herself, Mao warned her against setting up "a small sect of four." Addressing the other members, the chairman made clear that "she does not speak for me; she speaks only for herself."[42] Even so, by 1974, as everyone in the room realized, Jiang Qing's words were important even when she did not speak directly for the chairman.

Mao wanted to recuperate in the South, but he also wanted time to think. Even though he was physically in better shape than a few years before, he knew he was so ill that he could die at any moment. Four attendants had to lift him onto his train when he left Beijing, and the train itself had been equipped as a field hospital, staffed by some of China's best doctors. The chairman wanted to test how cooperation in the top Party leadership would hold up without him physically present in Zhongnanhai. He had, of course, no intention of giving up power while he was still alive, but he wanted to watch and decide from afar. During Zhou's illness, Deng Xiaoping was put in charge of coordinating the work of the State Council, China's government. Wang Hongwen would chair the meetings of the Politburo in Mao's absence. In his last conversations before leaving, Mao stressed how impressed he was with the "new" leaders who had joined work at the Center, people like Hua Guofeng, soon to become minister of public security; vice premier Ji Dengkui; Beijing mayor Wu De; and General Chen Xilian, a leading member of the Central

Military Commission. They added greatly to the Party's work, the chairman thought. Undoubtedly, he also knew that they were uniquely reverent and incessantly loyal to Mao himself.

With both Mao and Zhou staying away from day-to-day policymaking, it did not take long before the battles in the Politburo reached a fever pitch. As Deng moved methodically to strengthen his position among army commanders, police, and state security officials, the Left tried to hook him on issues of policy and ideology. In the early fall they thought they had an ideal issue. Among Deng's initiatives for foreign procurement were several ships intended to increase transportation capacity along the Chinese coast. Meanwhile, a Chinese-built 10,000-ton ship, the *Fengqing*, returned from a months-long voyage to Europe, much lauded by the Left and by the workers in the Shanghai shipyard that had constructed her. In October, Yao Wenyuan circulated some of the criticism of buying foreign ships to the Politburo. Jiang Qing added that she "was full of wholehearted proletarian indignation. Is the Department of Transportation a department led by Chairman Mao? . . . A few people who are crazy about foreign things and obsequious to foreigners, and with ideas [similar to those] of a comprador class, dictate to us. . . . Can we not struggle against the slavish mentality towards all things foreign?"[43]

The matter came to a head at a Politburo meeting on October 17. With the support of Wang Hongwen, Zhang Chunqiao, and Yao Wenyuan, Jiang Qing accused Deng Xiaoping of supporting those in the Department of Transportation who worshipped foreign things. Deng first tried to avoid an open confrontation, but when Jiang, looking straight at him, asked about his "attitude towards the criticism of comprador philosophy," Deng exploded. "We are all equal in a Politburo meeting," he told her. "You should not force others to agree with you."[44] While Jiang Qing sat in stony silence, Li Xiannian maneuvered Deng out of the room. When the Leftist leaders reconvened that evening at Diaoyutai, the state guesthouse that Jiang had commandeered as a residence for herself and her supporters, Jiang said that it was now clear that Deng would fight against the Cultural Revolution and Chairman Mao to the end. They agreed that Wang Hongwen would fly to Changsha, where Mao had settled, in order to immediately report to the chairman.[45]

As they had done at the beginning of the year, the Left overreached. Mao was with his close assistants and female friends in his home province, doing very little except having extracts from Karl Marx's work or classical Chinese texts read to him. Mao had always struggled with making sense of Marx, and he drew much more often on the work of Lenin and the later writings of Friedrich Engels, which he found easier to understand. Now he needed to make an effort. He wanted time to think and plan, and was in no mood to be interrupted by the young Wang Hongwen, who arrived on his doorstep uninvited. Wang reported on Deng's misdeeds for a few minutes, before Mao waved him off. Jiang Qing should stop quarreling with everyone, the chairman told him, and Wang himself should spend more time with people like Zhou Enlai and Ye Jianying, and not only hang around Jiang Qing.[46] Then Mao looked at his bodyguards, who looked at Wang Hongwen, silently encouraging the putative successor to make a hasty retreat back to the airport.

It is possible that Wang Hongwen's unwelcome visit prodded Mao to make some immediate decisions for the future. Only a couple of days later, when talking with the two young officials from the Foreign Ministry, Nancy Tang and Wang Hairong, who had helped him receive a foreign leader, the chairman told them that he had decided to call a meeting of the National People's Congress, China's presumptive national assembly, which had not convened for almost ten years. The purpose of the meeting was to elect a new State Council and deal with development plans for the future. He told them that he intended to nominate Deng as first deputy premier, in charge of the State Council.[47] It is clear from Mao's conversations in late 1974 that he was disappointed with Wang Hongwen, who did not, the chairman complained, know Party history or international affairs, and who looked lost at a number of public occasions.[48] The matter of successor seemed again to be in doubt, and the Left began to fear the outcome.

In late December 1974, Mao made a final attempt at getting the two main factions in the Party to cooperate. He invited Zhou Enlai and Wang Hongwen to join him for several days at his residence in Changsha. The premier flew to Changsha straight from his sick bed at the 305 Hospital, though his doctors feared that he was too ill to travel. The chairman met with both of them, outlining his plans for the upcoming National People's Congress, and his reasons for relying on Deng for day-to-day work in the government. But Mao also warned against making any changes to the fundamental ideological approach: "Lenin," he warned them, "says that small-scale production constantly, daily, and spontaneously produces capitalism and capitalists in scores. It happens to some of the working class and members of the Party. The bourgeois way of life can be seen in the proletarian class and personnel in state administrative organs. Thus, if Lin Biao or people like him take power, it would be easy for a capitalist restoration to happen."[49] As he always did, Zhou made sure that all arrangements were to Mao's satisfaction, including the celebration of the chairman's eighty-first birthday on December 26. It was a warm occasion, participants remember, with many toasts and fireworks on the terrace. Mao said little but seemed in a good mood. Afterwards Mao and Zhou met for four hours, alone, to talk about the future. It was to be the last long meeting between the two. Their doctors were hovering at the door at either end of the room.[50]

By the time the National People's Congress convened in January 1975, Mao had decided to give Deng Xiaoping even longer reins of power. Not only would the 71-year-old Deng become first vice premier, he would also become vice chair of the Central Military Commission and chief-of-staff of the People's Liberation Army. This was an unusually powerful combination of appointments. Mao tried to balance Deng's power by appointing Zhang Chunqiao political commissar of the army and by making a number of prominent Leftists responsible for ideology, culture, and education. But there was no doubt that the chairman had turned to his old assistant to get things done, irrespective of his suspicions about Deng's political reliability. With Zhou Enlai in the hospital and Wang Hongwen's incompetence clearly on display, Mao may have thought that Deng—with his proven abilities—would be the right person for the moment, until the younger generation of leaders, shaped by the Cultural Revolution, were ready to take over.

Deng did not lose much time. In the government's main report to the Congress, delivered by a visibly ailing Zhou Enlai but written by Deng and his assistants, production and development were the chief items. The report concentrated on the four modernizations—in agriculture, industry, national defense, and science and technology—and on achieving them in two stages: a complete overhaul of China's capacity for industrial production by 1980, and reaching a level similar to that of the West by the early 2000s. Given the pitiful state of the Chinese economy, this may have seemed entirely as wishful thinking. But Zhou stressed to his colleagues that China had to get started, building, as he put it with a wry smile, "on the achievements of the Cultural Revolution."[51] The representatives of the Left did not smile back. They suspected that all the talk about "improvements" were hidden attempts at taking power away from the workers and neglecting the need for a continuous revolution in patterns of thinking and behavior.

Most of the provincial representatives at the Congress knew how dire China's economic situation was in 1975. All areas of the Chinese economy seemed stagnant, except imports and government expenditure, which together created a significant budget deficit. Transportation and communications had suffered particularly badly in the Cultural Revolution. On the railways, departures and arrivals were unpredictable, and there was a constant lack of functioning locomotives and rolling stock. In some areas, trains were held up by armed bands and parts of their cargo stolen.[52] These challenges were highlighted to the Party Center as Mao continued his impromptu journey through the South. In February 1975, when the chairman decided to leave Changsha to celebrate Chinese New Year in Hangzhou, the capital of the normally wealthy and stable Zhejiang Province, the local railway administration was concerned about his safety, because there had been so many robberies and factional battles along the tracks where his personal train was supposed to proceed. Upon reaching Hangzhou, after special units of the PLA had been deployed along the length of the track, the supply and security situation was so bad that the chairman's bodyguard units worried whether the visit should go ahead. Not only were there acute shortages of pork, vegetables, salt, bread, and even matches, but the factional infighting had again reached a fever pitch: when the provincial CCP secretary of Zhejiang, Tan Qilong, convened a meeting in the Hangzhou Hotel to report on the National People's Congress, a rebel faction attacked the building and attempted to kidnap the secretary and his staff. The units that guarded the chairman were desperately trying to shield him from these events; they also worked to prevent him from seeing the long lines that formed outside any store that sold food for the holidays.[53]

The group that Deng Xiaoping assembled in Beijing to help him carry out the rescue operation for the Chinese economy was very diverse. Even so, they all had been purged in the late 1960s and only recently returned to the Party Center. Hu Yaobang had been head of the Communist Youth League for more than a decade and was appointed Party secretary of Shaanxi Province in 1965. The following year he was removed and sent to herd cattle in the countryside. Hu was an impatient reformer, who had been waiting for years—even before 1966—to remove the most oppressive aspects of Communist Party rule. When he was assigned a leading position at the Chinese Academy of Science, he immediately tried to introduce a series of reform measures to correct the wrongdoings of the Cultural Revolution.[54] In Deng's think tank, the State Council's newly formed Policy Research Office, Mao's one-time secretary Hu Qiaomu was joined by officials like Liu Shaoqi's former personal assistant Deng Liqun. Both of them believed that China's problems were mainly caused by Cultural Revolution chaos and deviations from planning principles. Also on the staff of the Policy Research Office were the reformist economist Yu Guangyuan; Wu Lengxi and Xiong Fu, the pre–Cultural Revolution editors of *Renmin Ribao* and Xinhua News Agency; and the Marxist theoretician and historian Hu Sheng.[55] These Party officials and intellectuals may not have agreed on much, but all of them saw a desperate need to move China's economy forward through reform.

From February 1975 on, the reformers convened a series of conferences to discuss production and economic regeneration. They were assisted by some of Deng's military allies, such as the new minister of defense Marshal Ye Jianying and General Wang Zhen, a much-feared PLA fighter who Deng had helped make a vice premier. Among their first targets were the railways. The new regulations made the provinces responsible to the State Council for train services improving according to set aims. Attempts at disrupting rail transportation were made punishable by death.[56] There were similar conferences and targets set for industry, banking, and the army. Deng and Ye issued orders, through the State Council, that removed or sidelined Leftist commanders and warned the generals only to obey orders issued by the Central Military Commission. All was done in the name of efficiency and economy. Ye Jianying attacked what he claimed were problems of overstaffing, undisciplined troops, wasteful practices, and weak commanders. When speaking with the heads of the military regions, Ye hinted that there were conspiracies afoot at the Center, while quoting Mao's occasional criticism of the "Shanghai Gang."[57] He and Deng knew full well that Shanghai, China's most Westernized city, was not popular among senior generals with strong nationalist instincts.

The Left seemed unable to respond to the sudden avalanche of reformist initiatives. With the chairman out of town and local Leftist groups again under attack in the provinces, the Politburo Left concentrated on political sniping against Deng and his associates rather than preparing new initiatives of their own. This may have been a fatal mistake. In mid-1975, many activists and organizations still looked to the Left for leadership, and in some cities and provinces Leftist Party bosses seemed to have solidified their positions during the "Criticize Lin, Criticize Confucius" campaign. But without Mao leading them and with Deng pushing his initiatives hard, the Politburo Left seemed lost. Wang Hongwen decided to decamp for Shanghai, where he did little but drink with old buddies and complain about the situation in Beijing. "There is no date set for when I should report to the Chairman," he complained, "and I do not want to go back anyway. . . . Now, what rights do I have? The Party Central Committee and the State Council are Deng's, the Army is also his; I can only organize study groups among workers, peasants and soldiers. . . . I am most worried that the Army is not in our hands, there are no people in the army. . . . This is the Chairman's order, what can I do?"[58]

The one person who had not given up the struggle against the Party moderates was Jiang Qing. As Deng's reform plans moved into high gear in the summer and early fall of 1975, Jiang began attending an increasing number of high-level meetings in which these plans were discussed, and she gave voice to the Left's dissenting views. In September she clashed with Deng after his criticism of the Party's past policies in an opening speech at a major conference on agriculture. "For twenty-five years," Deng began, "our agriculture has produced just enough for us to eat. . . . We are still very poor and backward." After outlining the emphasis the State Council put on increasing agricultural production through mechanization and improved fertilization and irrigation, he went on to criticize the imbalances that existed in how agriculture had advanced. Citing his home province, Sichuan, he said that "the country also has some counties and regions where grain production is not as good as right after Liberation." "You cannot say that!" Jiang Qing interrupted. "Those are exceptions!" Deng retorted: "They are worth paying attention to, even if they are exceptions!" He then went on to list endless statistics to prove his point, while Jiang Qing sat stone-faced.[59]

Chairman Mao had finally returned to Beijing in mid-April 1975, after having been away for almost ten months. Soon after he was back in Zhongnanhai, he called an extended Politburo meeting to convey his instructions. Mao shuffled into the room after everyone else had arrived. Everyone at the meeting was struck by how feeble the chairman seemed. It was clear that he did not recognize some of those present—even people he had known for a long time. His remarks, when he finally got to them, were rambling. He wanted to send "young proletarian girls" to Peking University, he claimed, but even his "bourgeois legal rights" had now been taken away from him.[60] After complaining about having been treated for high levels of cholesterol, he summed the treatment up as a Soviet plot. Deng Xiaoping was helping him now, he declared loudly. When Jiang Qing brought up a question of Marxist theory, Mao seemed at first not to recognize his wife. He then responded with a tirade: "Do not be spontaneous, be disciplined, be careful, do not make your own claims, discuss with the Politburo . . . do not issue anything in my name. . . . I ran away for ten months, [I] did not say anything. . . . I was sick, while listening to documents, every day they sent a plane. Now, God has not asked me to go [yet], I can still think, I can listen, I can talk, I cannot write. I can eat, I can sleep." He looked angrily at Jiang Qing. "I do not have much to say, only three sentences. I had three sentences to say at the Ninth and at the Tenth Congress. We want Marxism-Leninism, not revisionism; solidarity, not division; and openness and honesty, not conspiracies or tricks."[61] He looked at them in silence for a few minutes. Then his favorite assistant, Zhang Yufeng, helped him out of the room. It was the last time Mao Zedong chaired the Politburo.

Mao met with Deng Xiaoping several times during the summer and early fall of 1975. In these conversations the chairman gave his support to Deng's reform plans, and instructed him to proceed in carrying them out.[62] But Mao's mind drifted increasingly toward cultural and educational issues. While away from Beijing, he had approved major articles by Zhang Chunqiao and Yao Wenyuan that called for speeding up the Cultural Revolution in the universities. Mao had also been reading—or had read to him—classical Chinese literature, and he noted his dislike for much of it. After returning to Beijing, he commented on the classical novel *The Water Margin* that it only taught people how to surrender. "Do the opposite," he instructed his attendants, "so that the people know [which is] the surrender faction."[63] When administrators of major Beijing universities, with Deng's support, tried to reinstitute regular educational curricula in August, Mao sided with the "rebel factions" who wanted to emphasize the teaching of class struggle and antirevisionism. In late September the chairman expressed dissatisfaction with Deng's assistant Hu Qiaomu's draft report on the Academy of Science, which quoted Mao in saying that "science and technology are productive forces." "I cannot remember saying that," said the chairman, obviously suspecting that Deng's people were playing fast and loose with his own quotations in order to prioritize technical expertise over political correctness.[64]

Deng probably sensed the subtle change in the chairman's thinking in the fall of 1975, but he refused to change tack. To Deng, setting things right the way he saw them was more important than constantly nodding to the views of the Party Left. Maybe he still did not quite understand how important Mao viewed the Cultural Revolution to be for his own legacy. Or he believed that Mao's critique was limited to the culture and education fields. Or maybe Deng thought that at that stage the ailing Chairman was too dependent on him to turn against him. Others did pick up on the turning of the tide. Zhou Enlai, as he was being sedated for his final surgery on September 20, cried out, "I am loyal to the Party and the people! I am not a capitulationist!"[65] And Mao's nephew, the radical Mao Yuanxin, who by now had replaced Wang and Tang as the liaison between the chairman and other members of the Politburo, spent hours with his uncle explaining how he thought Deng was undermining the chairman's achievements.[66] Still Deng pressed on, with new development plans being presented to Mao almost every week, even though by October fewer and fewer of them were returned with the chairman's stamp of approval.

Around mid-October 1975, Mao decided to make his dissatisfaction with some of Deng's actions public. He ordered the vice premier to attend a meeting with other leaders and one of the heads of the Tsinghua University Revolutionary Committee. The plans of the university administrators were, Mao claimed, "a spearhead directed against me."[67] When the first meetings produced few concrete results on university policy, Mao asked his nephew to intercede directly with Deng. "You can talk to Xiaoping, [Wang] Dongxing, and [Chen] Xilian about all of your views. Be straightforward. Do not be hesitant. You have to help him."[68] When the four met, Mao Yuanxin criticized Deng's views on Party rectification. Deng defended himself vigorously. "Practice," he said, "will be the only proof."[69] After several more meetings in November, Mao got the impression that Deng was repentant. The chairman laid down the law on the Cultural Revolution: it was "basically correct, with some shortcomings. What we need to study now are the shortcomings. It should be seventy percent versus thirty percent. Seventy percent are achievements. Thirty percent are mistakes." Deng Xiaoping, Mao told other leaders, "wants to make a turn, he has started to turn, and . . . has a good attitude. Let us . . . discuss it a bit. It does not matter if it is noisy. . . . The discussion is limited to the issue of the Cultural Revolution and [we will] make a resolution."[70]

With Deng increasingly under attack by his Left-wing opponents, university radicals, and even the chairman himself, some of the vice premier's associates urged him to abase himself before the chairman in order to rescue the reform agenda. Leaders such as Li Xiannian thought that Deng had moved too fast and wanted him to conduct self-criticism and abandon some of his younger assistants. Deng refused. He would self-criticize on points where he thought he had been wrong, if other leaders would do the same. In late November, Deng chaired several expanded Politburo meetings of a hundred leaders or more, in which he offered limited self-criticism, including admitting that he had never understood the Cultural Revolution, but stuck to his guns on drawing lessons from experience and on the main part of his proposed reforms. When Mao asked him to chair a meeting specifically to draft a resolution on the Great Proletarian Cultural Revolution, Deng at first tried to excuse himself, indicating that he could not do so, since he had not been at the Party Center during much of the Cultural Revolution. The Politburo decision, which Deng signed off on, concluded that the Cultural Revolution was 70 percent successful, and set three principles, according to Mao's instructions: that the debate about policy mistakes at the universities should continue; that these mistakes "were not isolated, but reflect the current struggle between two levels, two roads, and two directions. There is a Right-leaning wind in these cases. . . . Some people are always dissatisfied with the Cultural Revolution, always try to hold the Cultural Revolution to account, always want to overturn cases." And third, that Chairman Mao had instructed that "some comrades" should be helped to prevent them from making further mistakes in the future.[71]

During the last two months of 1975, Deng Xiaoping was gradually pushed aside from the supreme position he had held for almost a year. With the Politburo Left at first holding back at openly criticizing Deng, out of fear that the chairman would later again empower the vice premier to act against them, Mao pushed Zhang Chunqiao and Yao Wenyuan to participate more actively in the sessions. Even the demoralized Wang Hongwen, still officially number three in the Party leadership, returned from his most recent excursions to attack Deng's associates. Through all of this, Deng himself tried to steer a middle course: bend to Mao's will, while keeping a modicum of self-respect and, most importantly, not admitting to mistakes that would further endanger him and strengthen the Left in the all-out battle for power he saw approaching.[72] But it was clear to everyone in the leadership that Deng's time was running out. In December, after meeting with U.S. president Gerald Ford, the chairman, who had barely managed to speak at the meeting, held the Chinese leadership group back for a moment. With Zhang Yufeng interpreting his slow mumbling, Mao launched another appeal for everyone to work together, old cadre and rebels. But, he ended by saying, "some people have been attacked and feel unhappy. They are angry [and] that can be forgiven. But their anger cannot be directed at the majority, or at the masses, censuring them and denouncing them."[73] Some of those present believed the chairman tried to lift his head and look straight at Deng. Deng looked away. It was to be the last time the two met.

According to his nephew's reports, Mao's thinking in the winter of 1975–1976 was about the future of China and of the revolution. "Is there class struggle in socialist society?" Mao Yuanxin quotes his uncle as saying.

Stalin made a big mistake on this issue. Lenin did not; he [foresaw the] establishment of bourgeois countries without capitalists. . . . We ourselves have built such a country . . . [we] take money to buy rice, buy coal, buy oil, buy vegetables. What did the Cultural Revolution do? It is class struggle. Liu Shaoqi said that class struggle was extinguished, [but] he himself was not extinguished, he wanted to protect his pile of traitors, to kill the Party. Lin Biao wanted to knock down the proletariat and stage a coup. Why do some people not see the contradictions in socialist society clearly? . . . The impact of small production, corruption, speculation, is it not everywhere? . . . Some party members do not want to move forward, some people are afraid of the revolution. Why is that? They have been made big officials, [so they] protect the interests of big officials. They have good houses, cars, high salaries, and waiters, better than capitalists. There is always going to be revolution. Always some people will feel pressured, small officials, students, workers, farmers, soldiers, they do not like big people pressure them, so they want revolution. Ten thousand years from now, you think these contradictions will not be visible?[74]

When China launched its first recoverable space satellite in November 1975, the Central Committee, in line with Mao's thinking, hailed it as a victory of the line of class struggle.

While Chinese technology was racing for the skies, old revolutionaries were drawing their last breath of earth. Kang Sheng died in December and was lauded as a great proletarian fighter and a great Marxist-Leninist in a eulogy read by Ye Jianying. Zhou Enlai was fading quickly. In his last meetings with Deng Xiaoping, Zhou had pleaded with his deputy to avoid antagonizing Mao and concede in order to keep his position.[75] The premier's final recorded meeting was on December 20 with Luo Qingchang, the head of the Central Investigation Department, China's main intelligence organization.[76] After that, the 77-year-old Zhou slipped in and out of consciousness. He died in the morning of January 8, 1976. On hearing the news, Chairman Mao closed his eyes and cried. But he said nothing, and nobody among his attendants dared say a word about Zhou in his presence.

6

1976

AS NEWS OF ZHOU ENLAI'S DEATH SPREAD, people in China started to grieve. The dignified, always charming premier was widely admired and even loved as a political figure. In the public image, Mao Zedong was the volatile super-genius who had created the Chinese revolution and imagined a new China. He was admired, but at a distance, as emperors used to be. Zhou was his warmhearted, approachable sidekick, someone who worked day and night to look after the people, someone who cared. Mao was faraway; Zhou had been close. It was an image that the premier, when he was alive, had done much to cultivate. Now his death led to an avalanche of mourning that the Party found hard to control.

In the midst of the political crisis over Deng Xiaoping's political future, the Left was determined that the funeral of Zhou should not be turned into a manifestation of support for Deng. When the Politburo met on January 12 to decide how an eulogy for Zhou should be finalized, a heated quarrel followed. Zhang Chunqiao proposed that it should be read by Marshal Ye Jianying. Ye immediately refused and said that it should be delivered by Deng, who was still first vice premier and, officially, the person in charge of the work of the State Council. After much wrangling, the Politburo majority supported Ye's proposal. More importantly, Mao, after quite a bit of hesitation, signed off on Deng giving the speech.[1]

But while accepting the Politburo recommendation, Mao had no intention of letting Deng off the hook. While granting Deng the right to read Premier Zhou's eulogy, the chairman also ordered the Politburo to discuss Deng's self-criticism, which he had been forced to make in late December and early January. In these presentations, Deng acknowledged that the "most important and most fundamental reasons" for his serious mistakes lay in his "attitude toward the Cultural Revolution."[2] Deng made these admissions on the advice of Marshal Ye, who had argued in private that Deng might yet avoid being purged if he was seen as bending to Mao's will.[3]

But the Politburo Left understood the chairman's intentions better than the old cadre. Although the vice premier would be allowed to deliver the official eulogy, they made sure that the text of the obituary as agreed by the Politburo reflected Mao's views. There was no mention of the deceased premier being "a great Marxist-Leninist." Moreover, the chairman decided not to attend the memorial service himself, saying that he was "too frail to go."[4] Yet, many in Zhongnanhai noted, less than a month later the frail Mao would take time to meet with former U.S. president Richard Nixon for more than an hour. "The Premier opposed me over launching the Cultural Revolution," Mao commented privately later. "And not a small batch of veterans all listened to him [although] on the surface they supported me . . . because there was nothing they could do about it. I understood clearly that there was no way to bridge the gap between me and the Premier."[5]

Jiang Qing and Yao Wenyuan also got the Politburo to agree to strict limits on the numbers of mourners who could attend Zhou's lying in state, funeral, and memorial meetings. However, their plans went wrong from the very beginning. Even though Zhou's body could only be viewed in a small hall at Beijing Hospital, the number of official mourners who insisted on attending was more than four times what had been agreed. As ordinary folks watched the proceedings on TV, resentment against Zhou's presumed opponents boiled over. In one assembly hall, people turned away with loud groans when Zhang Chunqiao hugged the widow. In another, seeing Jiang Qing appear in a black coat and hat led to loud shouting: "Take off your hat!" "Take that damned hat off!"[6] When the body was transported the dozen miles to Babaoshan Cemetery in a bus converted into a makeshift hearse, more than a million people braved the icy streets in a spontaneous show of grief. At the cemetery there were chaotic scenes when the glass coffin was brought in and mourners wanted to get as close as possible. Some slammed their hands on the coffin, crying out for the premier to help them in their misery.

In central Beijing, at Tiananmen Square, ordinary people brought wreaths and flowers for Zhou that they placed at the Monument to the People's Heroes. Some were inscribed with poems or texts in memory of the premier, a few of which caught the attention of the Politburo radicals as politically erroneous. Probably as a result, Zhou's memorial service, held on January 15, would now end the public rituals of mourning for him, the CCP Center suddenly announced. "In all the organizations, units, factories, schools and others, forbid setting up a mourning hall or hold a memorial service. Do not allow wearing black armbands and white flowers; do not hold commemorative activities in streets or in Tiananmen Square. Newspapers and radio stations must not interview or organize any funeral activities, nor issue commemorative articles."[7] Instead, the Left, now in full control of the media, ordered the newspapers to concentrate on "repulsing the Right-deviation wind" that they claimed was engulfing the country.[8]

The conflict between Deng Xiaoping and the Left came to a head at a Politburo meeting on January 20. At the start of the meeting, which he chaired, Deng again undertook a brief self-criticism, and then moved on to other matters. Jiang Qing would have none of it. She and her allies began leveling a long list of accusations against the much-weakened vice premier, especially his attempt to reverse the verdict about his attitude toward the Cultural Revolution. Deng looked at them quizzingly, saying that he adhered to all the self-criticism that he had made in the past.[9] That evening, Deng wrote a letter to the chairman, offering to resign.

> I have twice requested to see the Chairman, [and] in addition to describing my own mistakes and hearing the Chairman's teachings, I truly hope to talk about my own work. . . . After much consideration, I still would like to see the Chairman for a face-to-face discussion of these issues. . . . The first thing that I would like to raise with the Chairman is to resign my responsibility of leading the daily work at the Center, and I earnestly hope that my request will be approved. . . . If I did not put forward this request now, I would be failing my own conscience. . . . As for myself, I will obey any decision by the Chairman and the Party Center.[10]

When they learned about Deng's letter, the leaders of the Left celebrated the outcome. This was exactly what they wanted to see: the mighty vice premier chastened and removed from office. When Mao Yuanxin briefed his uncle on the Politburo meeting the following day, the chairman mulled it over. He would approve Deng's resignation, he told his nephew. But, Mao said, Deng's problems "are still contradictions among the people. If properly guided, he will not necessarily go to the other side (as Liu Shaoqi and Lin Biao did). . . . Deng's responsibilities can be cut back, but he should not be removed—he should not be killed with one blow."[11]

Mao Yuanxin also had something else on his mind when he met with the chairman. On January 21, he brought a note signed by three of the vice premiers—Hua Guofeng, Ji Dengkui, and Chen Xilian—requesting that the chairman name a new person to lead in overseeing the work of the State Council, in effect replacing Deng and—at least temporarily—taking Premier Zhou's old position.[12] The request, and the list of those who made it, seemed odd. Why was Zhang Chunqiao, next in line as vice premier after Deng, not one of the signatures? Zhang may have believed that he was the natural choice, so it would be better for him to not sign. But Mao thought otherwise. "Hua Guofeng," muttered the chairman, to Mao Yuanxin's surprise. "Let Hua Guofeng take the lead, for all that he thinks of himself as someone without much political sophistication. And [Deng] can be put in charge of foreign affairs."[13]

Surprised as he was, Mao Yuanxin did not immediately report to the Politburo what Mao had said. Hua Guofeng, the nondescript former head of Hunan Province, had proven himself a loyal and effective leader in Beijing, but he was not widely known, and so he was an unlikely choice to replace Premier Zhou Enlai, who had led the government for twenty-seven years. It took another week before the chairman made a dictation to his nephew saying that it would indeed be Hua, and that General Chen Xilian would be in charge of the Central Military Commission, replacing Ye Jianying, who was placed on "sick leave" although Ye himself stated that he was "in good health."[14] In a telling sign of how far Party decision-making had declined during the mid-1970s, it was left to the young Mao Yuanxin, acting alone and with no other authority than the word of his uncle, to seek out Hua and Chen in the Great Hall of the People to tell them about their appointments to lead the state. Wearing a shiny new military uniform, Yuanxin let each of the men know that they had been selected; Hua at first tried to decline, possibly out of modesty, but certainly because he knew the fate that had befallen all of the chairman's designated successors, as he now would become. Three days later, though, Mao approved a Central Committee document, prepared by Mao Yuanxin in consultation with Wang Hongwen and Zhang Chunqiao, formalizing these arrangements.[15]

The Left, who had wanted Zhang Chunqiao to be premier, were horrified at Mao's choice, and Jiang Qing soon went out of her way to stress Hua's lack of knowledge and experience. But others were surprised, too. Most generals tried to circumvent Chen Xilian and go directly to General Yang Chengwu, the deputy chief of staff. And Party old-timers asked themselves what qualifications Hua had for the job, except having served as head of Mao's home province. With his quiet manner and jovial but expressionless face, Hua Guofeng was easy to underestimate, but by 1976 he had got a good overview of central politics, and he was determined to follow the chairman's policy of emphasizing class struggle while increasing production. He wanted reform, but only in line with Mao's wishes. At the extended Politburo meeting at which his appointment was confirmed, he spoke very briefly, saying only that he did not see himself as qualified for the post but would accept the chairman's instruction.[16] As those assembled exited, the minister of health, Liu Xiangping, Xie Fuzhi's wife and an ally of the Left, was heard saying loudly that "Hua Guofeng is Premier for now, Zhang Chunqiao is the Premier of the future." Hua looked at her but said nothing.[17]

From Mao's perspective, the choice of Hua as China's number-two leader and putative successor to himself was no irrational move. Mao had known the taciturn but amiable Hua for a long time, and even though there is no sign that he had regarded Hua as a significant Party figure, he knew him to be capable enough. Besides, there were not many other good choices. Mao probably knew that if he had chosen a representative of the Left, he risked blowing the Party to pieces when he himself was incapacitated or dead. And the chairman refused to turn to anyone suspected of Rightism. He wanted Deng gone, and regarded his 1973 rehabilitation as a mistake.[18] After Deng's fall, Mao hoped that Hua would be the right person to glue the Party leadership together around a continuation of Cultural Revolution policies, with the chairman's blessing and under his watchful eye.

Mao's naming of General Chen Xilian to lead China's military had been even more unexpected than his choice of Hua as premier. One of Chen's key qualifications was his friendship with Mao Yuanxin and other members of

the Mao household. General Chen had also been a regional commander during the border war with the Soviet Union in 1969, a set of clashes that Mao
still regarded as a great victory for his revolutionary line, and the chairman
remembered his name from then. But within the Party and especially within
the military, Chen's seniority was low. During the revolution prior to 1949,
he had only been a corps-level commander. After 1949 he had not been involved in any other of China's wars. He had not even participated in the Korean War. In the PLA, even (or maybe especially) after the upheavals of the
Cultural Revolution, seniority was of critical importance. And as soon as Chen
took up the huge responsibility that Mao had assigned him, he was constantly
facing a real dilemma: he knew that the chairman would like him to stand
on the side of the Leftists on all important matters, but Chen's room for ma-
neuver was limited: He did not have the personal prestige and authority to
stand up to the PLA's senior commanders, never mind the old marshals, who,
though no longer in their posts, increasingly held decisive sway over China's
military through their former subordinates and old comrades in arms, and
who for the most part detested the Left.

On February 6, just four days after the CCP Center had formally announced
that "Chen Xilian will be in charge of the work at the Central Military Commission [CMC]," the standing committee of the Commission met to discuss
the "mistakes that Ye Jianying has committed."[19] In the CMC's report to the
Party Center, it claimed that the speeches by Deng and Ye at an enlarged meeting of the CMC in July 1975 had been filled with grave political mistakes, and
that the speeches "should no longer be studied or . . . implemented."[20] From
that moment, it was clear that Mao also wanted Ye Jianying gone, just as he
did with Deng Xiaoping. It was a critical point in the struggles for power. Many
senior commanders watched in disbelief. They had supported Deng Xiaoping,
but they revered Marshal Ye. Now, some of them feared that China was sliding
back into Cultural Revolution chaos. Throughout spring and summer 1976,
there are clear signs that orders from the Center about new study materials for
the troops or even movements of troops within China were not carried out. It
is also clear that there were secret networks among senior PLA officers who
consulted with each other about what the future might bring. To these, Chen
Xilian's appointment was bad enough. But the criticism of Ye was even worse.

The Leftists, however, celebrated Ye's demise with almost as much fervor
as they had Deng's—though, in spite of Chen Xilian's appointment, they

struggled with making much political headway within the PLA. Marshal Ye was gone from the Center, but many of his friends and former subordinates had remained in their positions in the PLA. Zhang Chunqiao, thanks to Mao now in the unlikely role of director of the PLA's Department of Political Affairs, liked to complain that he was just a "rubber stamp," and that his orders stopped to work "five meters beyond my office."[21] Zhang and other Leftists in the Politburo sometimes despaired at Chen Xilian's inability or unwillingness to stand up to their enemies, complaining that the person Mao had named to be in charge of the Central Military Commission was far from the ally that the Leftists would like to see. Zhang Chunqiao and Jiang Qing saw Chen as weak, while Chen tried to keep his distance from the Politburo Leftists, even after Mao repeated his order for Chen to work with them. According to some sources, Chen feared for his life if he was seen as an agent of the Left, since he had to work in buildings that were filled with Ye Jianying's appointees. On one occasion, Chen had to suffer the indignity of meeting with senior commanders in a room where Marshal Ye's picture was still prominently displayed.

The response of the Leftists, especially Zhang Chunqiao and Jiang Qing, to Hua Guofeng's dramatic ascendance was fierce. Zhang was particularly frustrated with Hua's appointment at the personal level. This had been his big opportunity to become, as premier, the leader of the government, and set out some of the principles for how a radical state enacting continuous revolution would actually operate. On February 3, just before Chinese New Year, Zhang confided to his diary: "This is another document number one, after the one last year. When they gain, they become rampant. But the quicker they rise, the faster they will fall. The wrong line will eventually fail. . . . This is just like:

A year has come to an end amid the boom of firecrackers,
And the spring wind has wafted warm breath to the wine.
While the rising sun shines over every household,
All strive to put up new peachwood charms for the old.[22]

Jiang Qing shared Zhang's frustration. She was close to Zhang, probably now more than ever, and had long regarded him as a confidante and trustworthy ally. During the peak of the Cultural Revolution in the late 1960s, she had admired him intensely. Zhang was the kind of revolutionary intellectual she aspired to be, in spite of the many aspersions of her by her husband and some of his comrades in power. By 1976 the admiration and idealization had turned into a real friendship. With Deng's fall, she had hoped that Mao would name Zhang as the person in charge of government work, possibly leading up to his becoming Mao's official successor. Like Zhang, she also looked down on Hua Guofeng as not worthy of his new position, having never before thought of Hua as a potential successor to the chairman. So, Mao's decision was a disappointment for Jiang almost as much as for Zhang Chunqiao himself. Jiang Qing tried to appeal directly to Mao but found that she had less and less access to her husband. As his health failed, Mao had withdrawn to his compound in Zhongnanhai, and on most occasions when his wife wanted to see him, she was turned away by the senior members of his bodyguard.

Mainly confined to his bedroom, which doubled as a study, Mao did not see many people outside his immediate household. Even the two young women, Wang Hairong and Tang Wensheng, who used to visit in the past were no ·longer welcome. In addition to his chief bodyguards, access to Mao was regulated by Zhang Yufeng, a former lover who now acted as head of the household staff, and Meng Jinyun, a dancer Mao had known in the 1960s who was now his chief nurse. The chairman often had trouble breathing and was bedridden at times. His mind stayed reasonably clear. Since his eyesight was poor, he arranged to have the guards and nurses read to him from all the books he was attracted to: foreign philosophy and history, as well as Chinese history and classics. He poked fun of them when they stumbled on names and concepts, though in general he spoke less and less.

As Mao withdrew further, it dawned on the Chinese political elite that Hua Guofeng may turn out to be the final successor, the one who would end up inhering the mantle. In the spring of 1976 posters of Hua's ever smiling face started to appear across the country, always placed respectfully below and in a smaller frame than those of the chairman. Party officials and military leaders started to show some deference to Hua, even if they remained unconvinced about his qualifications for the job. The Politburo Left remained openly contemptuous. Instead of trying to develop at least a good working relationship with Hua, who was, after all, their idol Mao Zedong's appointee, they showed the acting premier scant respect. Even after Hua was confirmed as premier in April, they seemed to be waiting for the chairman to appoint one of them to an even higher position. Wang Hongwen and Yao Wenyuan privately made fun of Hua as a country bumpkin who sometimes got Party slogans and aspects of Maoist theory badly bungled up. Some of these stories got back to Hua and undoubtedly wounded his pride. By the summer of 1976, relations between the new premier and his Leftists colleagues on the Politburo were increasingly awkward.

Given the tense political situation, it was hard even for seasoned leaders to know where to turn. One example of those who got into trouble was Qiao Guanhua, a senior Party diplomat who had served as foreign minister since 1974. In that role he became Hua Guofeng's main tutor on foreign affairs, a topic on which the new premier, by his own admission, knew very little. Qiao could not help making humorous remarks to his young wife Zhang Hanzhi, a fellow diplomat, about the premier's lack of facility in geography and general knowledge, and she, in turn, provided these stories to her Leftist friends in the Party inner circle.[23] Hua never forgave Qiao, and he suspected the foreign minister of being part of a Left-wing clique who was out to denigrate him to other Party leaders and possibly to the chairman himself. Hua knew that Zhang, Qiao's wife, had been Mao's English teacher in the past, and that she, at least for a while, had enjoyed privileged access to the chairman.

From February 25 to early March 1976, Hua convened a conference of provincial leaders and PLA regional commanders. The main purpose was to convey Mao's criticism of Deng Xiaoping and the Rightist deviations he was supposed to symbolize.[24] In his own comments at the conference, Hua stressed that the primary task facing the whole Party was to make sure that the campaign to criticize Deng would be effective, well-organized, and peaceful.[25] Deng should not be criticized by name in public, and wall posters attacking him would not be allowed. His supporters would be criticized but not purged. But internally, Party leaders had to make clear that Deng had committed "revisionist line errors," a very serious accusation within a Party where revisionism was the ultimate sin. Meanwhile Deng remained at liberty, but under strict surveillance by CCP security headed by Wang Dongxing.

Deng's supporters, understandably, fled for the hills. A few were removed, such as the minister of railways, Wan Li, and the minister of education, Zhou Rongxin. Zhou was subjected to a set of Cultural Revolution–style struggle meetings, and, after one of these, he died from a heart attack.[26] Deng Liqun, who had been one of Deng's key staffers, refused to cooperate with his accusers. Others close to Deng, such as Hu Yaobang, chose to agree with the accusations at a general level but refused to engage in specific criticism of their former boss. Some broke under pressure. Hu Qiaomu, perhaps Deng's closest assistant in many matters, wrote a lengthy self-criticism in which he attacked Deng Xiaoping and offered his services to the Leftists.[27]

Meanwhile, those who had opposed Deng while he was in office saw the campaign as a cause of joy and celebration. Jiang Qing in particular was jubilant, and decided to offer her own take on how to conduct the campaign most effectively. She called a meeting in Beijing of representatives from twelve provinces to provide her instructions. Deng, she said, was the most dangerous enemy the Party had ever faced. He was "an agent of international capitalism," a fascist, and a "two-faced counter-revolutionary." Jiang held up a dossier she and her associates had compiled of Deng's wrongdoings over the years and suggested it be disseminated to all leading cadre with a copy of her speech.[28] When he heard about it, Hua Guofeng complained to the chairman, who got so angry that he sat up in bed and dictated: "Should not be printed and distributed. Doing so is inappropriate. Jiang Qing interferes too much. [It is wrong] to summon [representatives of] twelve provinces without permission."[29]

But the chairman's anger did little to dampen the Left's enthusiasm. Across the country, and especially in the cities where supporters of the Cultural Revolution Left were strong, there were anti-Deng rallies and marches. On a number of occasions Leftist leaders got their revenge on their opponents, who had gradually replaced them in office over the past two years. Some were dragged before "antirevisionist" tribunals not unlike the ones from the late 1960s, and a few were mistreated physically. When the police tried to intervene, Leftist groups laid siege to police stations and shouted slogans about understanding "the Chairman's mass line." In a few provinces, such as Sichuan, Henan, and Yunnan, there was large-scale violence against "capitalist roaders." The Politburo Left, sensing that the political winds fanned their sails, cheered the anti-Deng rallies, in spite of the attempts by Hua Guofeng and others to limit the campaign. Yao Wenyuan called Deng's reform programs from the year before "a general outline for the restoration of capitalism." Jiang Qing believed, as she put it, that the masses still "preferred socialist grass to capitalist flowers."[30]

The advance of the Left, though, was not the only piece in the Chinese political puzzle. At the same time as the Leftists celebrated Deng's downfall, others were still in mourning over Zhou Enlai. There was a deep feeling, even among some who had previously sympathized with the Left, that the premier had been snubbed in death by careerists and bureaucrats who did not live up to his perceived high moral standards. Very few paused to consider Chairman Mao's role in the insults to Zhou Enlai's memory. Instead, all kinds of rumors circulated, completely contrary to reality, about how the aged chairman sincerely wanted to commemorate his old comrade in arms but was prevented from doing so by a coterie of evil advisers. In a number of counties there were spontaneous commemorations on what would have been Zhou's birthday, March 5, where ordinary women and men brought out wreaths and fruit, festooned with bands extolling the premier.

In a rumor-infested environment, fake documents flourished. Among these was a purported "Last Will of Premier Zhou," which first started circulating in February. The forgery was put together by a young worker in Hangzhou and seemed authentic, convincing many of the those who read it that these were indeed the premier's final words. "Comrade [Deng] Xiaoping has done a very good job in various aspects of his work in the past year," Zhou's fake will stated. "[He] will be facing heavier pressure in the future. Yet, so long as the political line is correct, any difficulty can be overcome." The Politburo did its best to suppress the forged document, but the more the CCP tried to squelch it, the more widespread it became. More than 7,000 individuals were interrogated and the author was discovered, but nothing seemed able to convince ordinary people that it was not genuine and represented Zhou's endorsement of Deng from beyond the grave.[31]

The spontaneous local commemorations of the dead premier were of course not just about Zhou and his memory. They symbolized a form of protest against a China in obvious stagnation and against the harsh living conditions for ordinary people. The winter of 1975–1976 had been severe in many parts of the country, and in the spring both food and fuel were scarce. The new Party slogans about increasing production through raising the people's political consciousness were not taken very seriously by anyone, with families and production units just too preoccupied with simply getting through the next few months. The chairman had not been seen in public since the

Tenth Party Congress in 1973, and the photos that appeared of him meeting foreign leaders at the swimming pool house in Zhongnanhai looked bad in spite of maximum retouching—an old man slouched in a chair, unable to hold his head steady, drooling heavily. There were rumors that Mao only had weeks to live and that he was a virtual prisoner of his Leftist allies in the Politburo. Anger was rising among people who felt ignored and left behind.

On March 25, *Wenhui Bao,* a Shanghai-based newspaper, published an article on the importance of "repulsing the Rightist trend of negating the Cultural Revolution." Its aim was obviously to attack Deng Xiaoping and his followers, but a couple of sentences sounded as if they extended that attack to Zhou Enlai and others who had promoted Deng in the past. In the old capital Nanjing, hundreds of students went to the streets to protest an attack on Zhou. "Defend Zhou Enlai," they shouted. "Down with those who oppose Premier Zhou." The police, bewildered, took some time in dispersing them.[32] In Beijing and other cities, leaflets denouncing the Leftists had already appeared several times. "Zhang, Jiang, and Yao are a small fleet of Linbiaoists, Chen Boda–style political liars who want to put a large number of old comrades to death and usurp the party's power," said one. Another called on "the people of the whole country to take urgent action to resolutely fight against the aims of traitors, careerists, and conspirators [such as] Zhang Chunqiao, Jiang Qing, and Yao Wenyuan."[33]

The burgeoning unrest was stimulated by all kinds of rumors that spread across the country, mainly by word of mouth. Since official news sources were so deeply mistrusted by many Chinese, rumors were often believed much more than anything that came from the mouths of Party cadre, as both authors of this volume can personally testify to through their experiences. Many of the rumors involved Jiang Qing. All kinds of scandalous stories about her were passed from mouth to mouth and jumped from one work unit or living quarters to another. In Shanghai, accounts of her as a sexually promiscuous movie actress in the 1930s already abounded. As they made their way through the country, these rumors were embellished with tales of Jiang's current love affairs, all of which were probably untrue, with people such as Hao Liang, a famous Peking Opera star, Liu Qingtang, a dancer of revolutionary ballets, and even Zhuang Zedong, a ping-pong world champion suddenly promoted to minister of sports. Jiang Qing was certainly targeted not only for her politics but also because, as a woman, she would be more exposed to these kinds of sinful stories than her male comrades. But the rumors were also a sign of the similarities that ordinary people now noticed between politics at Mao's court and those at imperial courts of old.

During the week after the first student protest in Nanjing, the Politburo Left used the event to claim that more counter-revolutionary upheaval should be expected and that Deng Xiaoping and his followers were behind it all. They again asked for permission to criticize Deng by name, but could not get a majority in the Politburo for the proposal, in part because Mao had already made his position known. However, Politburo members started calling provincial leaders and military commanders, warning them that there could be counter-revolutionary threats ahead.[34] But when receiving reports that major unrest could occur at the upcoming Qing Ming festival, the traditional Chinese commemoration of the dead, the Leftists and their Beijing allies themselves did very little. Yao Wenyuan noted in his diary that there was no need to be afraid of a ghost festival. But he also celebrated the increasing "sharpness of the class struggle."[35] In Yao's mind there was little doubt who would come out on top.

On March 30, even before the eve of the festival on April 5, wreaths commemorating Zhou Enlai and other revolutionary heroes had started appearing at the monument at the center of Tiananmen Square in Beijing. Expecting trouble, the Beijing Party head, Wu De, set up a joint command post for police, militia, and Central Committee security personnel in a building at the southwest corner of the square. They had a force of at least 3,000 ready to act. In the early morning of April 3, Wang Hongwen decided to visit the square. What he found enraged him. Not only were there unofficial wreaths and banners commemorating the late premier in politically dubious ways, there were also other subversive posters exhorting him and other Party leaders to listen to the voice of the people. To top it all, there was a memorial wreath to Yang Kaihui, Mao Zedong's second wife, whom he left in 1928 and who was later executed by the Guomindang. Furious, the third-ranked Party leader called the command post directly and ordered the officers to arrest the ring leaders and photograph what happened in the square, so that others could be dealt with later.

But it was too little and already too late. On April 4, in spite of orders to all work units not to send people to Tiananmen, hundreds of thousands arrived at the square. They carried wreaths, declaimed poems, and sang songs in

Tens of thousands of Chinese gather at Tiananmen Square
in early April 1976 to mourn the late premier Zhou Enlai.
Source: Top Photo Corporation/Alamy Stock Photo.

memory of Zhou but also deploring their lot or recounting grievances. Slogans against members of the Politburo Left, including Jiang Qing, appeared
openly. Among the hundreds of poems that were posted on walls or circulated in leaflets or by word of mouth, one had the refrain: "The era of Qin
Shihuang's dictatorship has passed away forever, and the people are no longer so easy to fool!"[36] One banner said, simply, "Hello, Xiaoping!" And in
the streets around the square and in the vast workers' quarters to the south
of it, people had put out little bottles. In Chinese, "little bottle" sounds like
Xiaoping.

The Leftists reported to Mao, through Mao Yuanxin, that this was a counter-
revolutionary rebellion organized by Deng. There were rumors, later proven
untrue, that Deng himself had been seen in the square among the protesters. At an extended Politburo meeting that evening, there was panic in the
air. Jiang Qing pushed for the square to be cleared by force. Hua Guofeng
acknowledged the seriousness of the situation, but tried to distinguish between counter-revolutionary elements and the masses that had been misled
by them.

He suggested more time was needed to do "mass-work," even though "a batch of bad people has come up with writings, some directly attacking Chairman Mao." But the Left won the day. The meeting reported to the chairman that "the disturbances were stirred up by counter-revolutionaries in an attempt to oppose the Chairman and the Central Committee and to interfere with and undermine the struggle against Deng Xiaoping." Mao Yuanxin reported to his uncle that the Politburo had concluded that "the incident was a counter-revolutionary offensive against the revolution and that there seem to be a Petöfi Club engaged in premeditated activities underground. The Politburo decided to clear the square of the wreaths and posters and round up the counter-revolutionaries on the night of the 4th."[37]

Mao agreed. The reference to Petöfi Clubs and the Hungarian uprising of 1956 was a whistle the chairman understood. The militia cleared the square of most of the banners and garlands overnight. The next morning, April 5, Qing Ming day, both police and militia patrolled the square while plainclothes security people watched from the perimeter. As the police tried to prevent protesters from entering Tiananmen Square, the protesters noticed that their wreaths had been removed. The mood turned ugly. Police cars were attacked and set on fire. Demonstrators pushed down fences and entered Party buildings around the square, including the Great Hall of the People. Hundreds of protesters were injured in the melee, but no shots were fired. Some of the Left seem almost to have regretted the absence of lethal force. "In China there is so much fierce struggle, but [we] always fail to fully resolve contradictions," Yao Wenyuan noted in his diary. "Why can't we shoot a bunch of counter-revolutionaries? Dictatorship is not embroidery."[38]

The Politburo met again in the afternoon of April 5. Mao had ordered Deng Xiaoping to join the meeting. Deng arrived, sat down, and did not say a word. "You are Nagy!," Zhang Chunqiao shouted as Deng entered.[39] Yao Wenyuan said that there was no need for discussion. "This is a counter-revolutionary coup attempt," and the Politburo had to clear the square immediately and arrest the perpetrators. Then further measures had to be taken against the ones responsible inside and outside of the Party. The Left was in total control at the meeting. The Party boss in Beijing, Wu De, and the head of the security forces, Wang Dongxing, wanted to avoid excessive bloodshed, but they were under pressure from Jiang Qing and others. Jiang pointed at Wu De and asked, "Why do you want to preserve a pulpit for counter-revolutionaries? . . .

The Qing Ming festival is over, the memorials should be ended, and you have every reason to explain that to the masses. Let us do it now, and you must send all the wreaths to [the national cemetery] Babaoshan before dawn."[40] During the meeting, Mao Yuanxin came running in with the chairman's orders. The square should be cleared and the counter-revolutionary leaders should be arrested. The whole Party should go on the offensive against counter-revolutionary subversion.[41]

In the evening, an order from Wu De for the remaining protesters to immediately vacate the square or face severe consequences was broadcast at Tiananmen. At 9.30 P.M., thousands of policemen and militia poured into the square, using clubs and sticks to beat and drive away hundreds who still stayed there. Many were arrested. By midnight, the square had been fully cleared. Then the whole square was sealed off, occupied by large numbers of armed police. Small-scale protests continued in Beijing and Nanjing over the next couple of days, though the security forces seemed to have the situation on the streets under control. But stories about what had happened at Tiananmen spread fast within the capital and to the rest of the country. The damage to what remained of the Party's credibility was acute. Even officials drew comparisons with the peak of the Cultural Revolution. But, back then, the millions at Tiananmen had shouted the chairman's name. Now, they seemed to revile him and his regime.

On the morning of April 7, Mao summoned Mao Yuanxin for a briefing about what had happened at the square. Listening to his nephew's account, the chairman commented: "This is reactionary behavior." Mao then approved a series of decisions. Deng would be named as the "black hand" behind the unrest and would be deprived of all of his official titles, but, for now, allowed to keep his Party membership. Hua Guofeng would be confirmed as premier and named first vice chairman of the CCP.[42] For decades, Mao had used the strategies of mobilizing the masses to stir up, promote, and sustain his continuous revolution. Now, even as his body was failing him, he drew on his tremendous willpower to contain mass protest and move the Party toward a compromise in terms of succession. Hua and the Left would have to share power after he was gone, but Deng and the reformers would be altogether excluded.

While the chairman worried, the Politburo Left was jubilant. For them, completing the purge of Deng was a big victory. And their insistence, following Mao's earlier views, that class struggle also existed within the Party had, they believed, just been demonstrated at Tiananmen Square. In their speeches, they dwelled further on the comparison with Hungary in 1956 and claimed that the clearing of the square had been a great victory against an anti-Communist rebellion in the capital. Radio and newspapers flowed with accounts of happy farmers and workers working twice as hard as before to prove their dedication to the Party and their disgust at Deng and "the Right-deviationist wind" he represented. An April 18 editorial in *Renmin Ribao* represented the Left's summing up of where they stood:

> Under the leadership of the Party Central Committee headed by our great leader Chairman Mao, the heroic people in the capital crushed at one stroke the counter-revolutionary political incident that took place at Tiananmen Square. . . . The hearts of the people, the Party and the Party members all turn to Chairman Mao and the Party Central Committee as sunflowers do to the sun. The revolutionary current or hundreds of millions of army-men and people determined to continue the revolution and oppose restoration and retrogression is irresistible. The class enemies tremble with fear. The small number of people who were duped have come to a quick awakening. The situation is excellent.[43]

To the Left, the Tiananmen protests presented opportunities as well as dangers, even after they had dealt with their enemies:

> Poisonous weeds can be transformed into fertilizer. The counter-revolutionary political incident at Tiananmen Square is a bad thing, but it is a good thing as well. It exposed the enemy and educated the cadres and masses. We must conscientiously study Chairman Mao's theory on classes, class contradictions and class struggle in the period of socialism. We must raise our consciousness of class struggle and the struggle between the two lines and our awareness of the need to continue the revolution under the dictatorship of the proletariat. It is imperative to suppress the handful of counter-revolutionaries who attack Chairman Mao, try to split the Party Central Committee and undermine the struggle against the Right deviationist attempt to reverse correct verdicts, put up counterrevolutionary slogans, distribute counter-revolutionary leaflets, fabricate counter-revolutionary political rumors, mail counter-revolutionary anonymous letters and organize counter-revolutionary groups.[44]

Many people wondered, on reading the editorial and the Leftist propaganda over the next few months, why there could be so many counter-revolutionaries in China after a decade of Cultural Revolution. As more and more campaigns against Deng and the "Right-deviationist wind" were launched in early summer 1976, most people kept their heads down. They came out for the rallies and marches, but there was far too little enthusiasm for the taste of the Politburo Left. Having declared to the top Party leadership that China faced a unique revolutionary moment, Jiang Qing took to the road, visiting communes and factories and giving speeches where she stressed the need to defend the chairman against the vicious attacks by reactionaries. Her dramatic delivery, in which she insisted that she was reporting to them on the chairman's behalf and exhorted them to come to her aid, politically if not physically, had an effect on her audience. That effect, however, was less about revolutionary mobilization than about wondering what was going on inside Zhongnanhai, the CCP leadership compound in Beijing.

The purge of real or suspected followers of Deng Xiaoping continued, but in most places it seemed a rather cursory affair. Officials were ordered to attend meetings at which they were criticized and instructed to stay away from their offices while engaging in the study of Mao Zedong Thought and the most recent Party instructions. There was little violence and few public struggle sessions were held except in areas where Cultural Revolution factionalism was still rumbling on. Even Deng himself was kept out of harm's way. In the aftermath of the Tiananmen protests he and his family were whisked away to a safe house by Wang Dongxing's security guards, possibly on Mao's orders.[45] The incessant shouting of Leftist slogans, now back in favor as a public ritual, gave visitors the impression that China was heading back toward the situation of a decade prior, in spite of Hua Guofeng's insistence that revolution and production still went hand-in-hand and that workers should show their revolutionary spirit by working harder.

After Hua's appointment as premier, Mao summoned him several times to the swimming pool house to issue political instructions in person, even though most communication still went through Mao Yuanxin. On April 30, after meeting with New Zealand prime minister Robert Muldoon, Mao asked Hua to stay and tried to whisper something to Hua. However, even Zhang Yufeng, who was among the few who could still understand the chairman's inarticulate words, was unable to catch the chairman's meaning. Mao then wrote three notes for Hua: "Take your time. Do not hurry"; "Follow past guide-

Mao Zedong shaking hands with Hua Guofeng, 1976.
Source: World History Archive/Alamy Stock Photo.

line"; "I am relying on you to do the job, and my heart is at rest."[46] When Mao's words were circulated around Zhongnanhai, Party leaders read them as meaning that he had chosen his successor. On June 5 Mao had a near-fatal heart attack, but he recovered enough to summon Hua and the Leftists in the Politburo two weeks later and inform them that the class struggle was now so intense that a peaceful succession may not be possible after his death. If so, Mao said, "then let power be transferred in turmoil. . . . Blood may flow."[47]

It seemed as if the Left were preparing for such an eventuality, even though their preparation, as usual, was mainly through declarations. Zhang Chunqiao told a large group of central Party cadre hastily assembled on June 28 that "class struggle still exists, and capitalist roaders maintain their capitalist course.

All revolutionaries should cast away their innocent illusions that the world
has become peaceful. . . . The reason Deng Xiaoping dared to put up such
resistance is that he has many followers. Some speak up publicly for him;
some stay hidden and yet release poisonous arrows. . . . We should carry on
the political struggle against the Rightist whitewashing activities, and mostly
against Deng Xiaoping, to the end. . . . [We] should launch more, larger-scale
actions against the counter-revolutionaries in our country. If we do not
achieve it this year, we will continue next year. If one year is not enough, we
will take two years, three years, and if necessary five or ten years.[48]

Then, suddenly, in midsummer, the Party leaders' attention was thrown
in another direction, away from class struggle. In the middle of the night on
July 28, 1976, a magnitude 7.8 earthquake struck Tangshan, a city just ninety
miles east of Beijing. It was a shallow quake, and buildings started collaps-
ing immediately. In Beijing and Tianjin the earth shook and walls and ceil-
ings caved in, but nearer the epicenter the devastation was almost total.
Tangshan itself was flattened, and mines, bridges, and railways collapsed. In
the villages families were buried in landslides or simply, one eyewitness
reported, swallowed up by the earth. According to official figures, 240,000
people died and 160,000 were seriously injured.[49] Estimates from outside the
PRC indicate numbers almost twice as large. A huge area of coastal northern
China was left in ruins, and emergency assistance was badly needed.

In Zhongnanhai, leaders were also startled out of their beds. Their first priority, as always, was to look after the chairman's welfare. Mao was wheeled
in his bed out of the house and across the street to Building 202, a newer
and bigger edifice constructed to withstand earthquakes. Medical facilities
were already set up there, in case the chairman for any reason had to be evacuated.[50] With Mao assumed to be safe, Hua Guofeng assembled a small
group of leaders to deal with the effects of the earthquake. For Hua, this was
his first test as a top leader, and the outcome was at best mixed. He did
organize the relief effort at the central level quite ably, making sure that the
PLA, the only institution in China capable of handling such a disaster, sent
its best units to help with the rescue operations. But his decision to not pub-
licize the extent of the catastrophe, while not visiting the stricken region for
more than a week, further undermined people's faith in the government ever
telling the truth. And his reluctance in accepting foreign assistance, undertaken after pressure from the Left, who claimed that foreign powers wanted

to use their aid to send in spies, hampered the relief efforts for millions who had been left destitute, homeless, or injured. When Hua told Mao about the extent of the disaster, the chairman cried.[51] Mao may have been mourning the victims. But he may also have been thinking that in Chinese history earthquakes are often regarded as omens of great change or even of a turnover in the Mandate of Heaven.

During August, the chairman's condition deteriorated rapidly. It seems that Mao himself had finally realized that he was dying. In mid-June, when he had met with Hua and the Leftists, he had proposed a political verdict on himself. "In China," Mao told them, "we speak of 'the conclusion of the coffin.'"

Although the coffin has not yet been closed on me, I am nearing the conclusion! I did two things in my life: Fighting Chiang Kai-shek for decades and driving him away to the islands [and] sending the Japanese back home after eight years of the Anti-Japanese War. Most people would agree with this, though there are some who whisper that I should take those islands back as soon as possible. Another thing [I did] that you all know about is the launch of the Cultural Revolution. Not many people support me in this matter, and many oppose it. [But] these two things are not over yet; they are my legacy to the next generation. . . . How to deal with them? Only heaven knows.[52]

The chairman told his nurses that he wanted to go to Shaoshan in Hunan, his birthplace, to see it one last time.[53] Even if they knew it would not happen, the Politburo started making preparations. Then, in the evening of September 2, Mao had another heart attack. He seemed to rally after being treated, but on September 8 he told his nurses that he felt very weak. That evening, as Mao's life was slipping away, the members of the Politburo gathered in Building 202 of the Zhongnanhai compound. Jiang Qing, who had been out of town reporting to the workers at Dazhai, rushed back to Beijing. Mao's breathing got shallower in spite of oxygen and various treatments. Ten minutes past midnight on September 9, his heart stopped. Jiang Qing wailed: "Do not leave us, Chairman, do not leave us." She soon left the room to—as it later became known—take possession of documents kept at Building 202 and over at the swimming pool house. Hua Guofeng was ashen faced, realizing the terrible burden that had now fallen upon him. Outside the door to the room where the dead chairman lay, with tubes protruding from his body and with documents that had been read to him as late as that afternoon spread by his bed, Wang Dongxing could be heard barking orders to the security guards.[54]

Even though it had been clear for months that the 82-year-old Mao was in poor health, his death came as a shock to people inside Zhongnanhai. Some officials refused to believe it. Others threatened to kill themselves now that Mao Zedong was no more—a sign of how cult-like Maoism had become in its final years. At the Party Center, only Wang Dongxing seemed to have his head about him. As long-time commander of the chairman's bodyguards, Wang knew where the secrets were hidden inside Zhongnanhai. He gave orders to prevent the news of Mao's death from leaking before the Politburo could meet to decide what to do next. Wang also took control of Mao's papers and asked Jiang Qing to return those she had taken to her own house. Jiang indignantly refused. With the chairman gone, she regarded herself as the guardian of Mao's legacy. On her own authority, she asked Wang Hongwen to set up a "revolutionary headquarters" within Zhongnanhai, with seventeen telephone lines in case of need. They took control of the Hall of Purple Light, a Ming-era palace that the emperors had used to receive foreign delegations and where Mao had set up parties and dancing during his first decade among the old imperial mansions. Hua Guofeng was angry when he found out and complained to Wang Dongxing. But they could do little about it.[55]

When the Politburo met only hours after Mao's death, the atmosphere was tense. Jiang Qing, unwisely, concentrated on the issue of Deng Xiaoping, insisting that he should be expelled from the Party, or he would attempt to grab power by force. Hua Guofeng tried to steer the discussion back to the announcement of the chairman's death, and the funeral arrangements. It was agreed that the Party would announce Mao's death in a broadcast in the afternoon, at 4:00 P.M. Beijing time. Mao's body should be injected with formaldehyde and kept at a low temperature until the Politburo could decide what to do with it. While Mao himself had asked to be cremated, it was clear that a majority in the leadership wanted his body preserved, like Lenin's was in Moscow. The publication of volume five of the chairman's selected works should be sped up. Jiang Qing offered, as the chairman's closest comrade in arms, to lead the editorial process, but it was agreed to postpone that decision to later. Toward the end of the meeting, Marshal Ye Jianying, who, to the surprise of many, had been called to Zhongnanhai in spite of being under political attack, spoke about how the Party needed to unite around the Central Committee, headed by Hua Guofeng. Hua said nothing. Jiang Qing slowly shook her head.[56]

Toward morning and early the next day, those who had been close to Mao started to show up to say goodbye. His household staff, nurses, doctors, and bodyguards were first. There was much wailing and tears. Members of the Politburo remained in the room, keeping watch over the body and on each other. Some of Mao's old generals started arriving, invited and uninvited. To them, the chairman was first and foremost theirs, their commander in war, the leader of their revolution. General Xu Shiyou, the commander of the Guangzhou military region who had known Mao since the late 1920s, embraced the body, saluted, and, in leaving the room glanced darkly in the direction of Jiang Qing, whom he did not acknowledge with one word. Xu was later heard muttering that maybe the chairman had been murdered, since his body looked blue. If so, there was no doubt of whom he suspected of the deed.[57] When the Politburo, after some discussion, agreed on the funeral committee, the four principals in ranking order were Hua Guofeng, Wang Hongwen, Ye Jianying, and Zhang Chunqiao. That Marshal Ye was among the heads of the committee indicated a shift. Given the mood of the generals, even the Politburo Left, who had been gearing up to criticize Ye in public, may not have dared to leave him out.

When the news announcers the following afternoon started intoning the ritual "The Central Committee of the Communist Party of China, the Standing Committee of the National People's Congress of the People's Republic of China, the State Council of the People's Republic of China, and the Military Commission of the Central Committee of the Communist Party of China announce with deepest grief to the whole party, the whole army and the people of all nationalities throughout the country," many Chinese understood what had happened even before Mao's name was mentioned. One of the authors of this book, Chen Jian, remembers walking home from the morning shift at his local production unit, through the golden autumnal sunshine in Shanghai, when he heard the loudspeakers. His first thought was that he would never have to shout "Long Live Chairman Mao" again.

There was widespread grief everywhere in the country. Mao had led China for twenty-seven years and the CCP for more than forty. Most Chinese had never known another leader, and many had looked up to him almost as a god.

But the grief was less spontaneous and unfeigned than it had been when Zhou Enlai died. And, after having mourned in public, people went back home and asked themselves what the future would bring. One local CCP leader remembered wondering first how the Party would manage without its chairman, and then, later in the evening, about just how much China needed change, and whether Mao's death could be the beginning of better things. But, of course, as all Chinese, she kept her thinking strictly to herself.[58]

As preparations for Mao's memorial service, set for September 18, got underway, the struggle for power at the Party Center intensified. Premier Hua Guofeng, the man most of the other leaders considered Mao's hand-picked successor, feared that his constant appeals for Party unity would be wrecked by the Left. Just two days after Mao's death, Hua and Wang Dongxing, the Party's security chief, began discussing the need to "resolve" what Hua called "the Gang of Four problem."[59] The same day Hua, on the pretext of an urgent medical checkup, went to see Zhou Enlai's old deputy, Li Xiannian, and asked Li to secretly canvas opinion within the leadership about how "contradictions" with the four Politburo members could be resolved. Hua was especially eager to get Marshal Ye Jianying's opinion. Although Hua Guofeng was generally seen as a main beneficiary of the Cultural Revolution and an ideological ally of the Left, it was becoming clear that he did not intend to share power with Jiang Qing and her associates. Neither did Hua believe that his much-vaunted "unity" could be achieved while he was constantly challenged from the Left within the Politburo.

Three days after his secret conversation with the premier, on September 14, Li asked his driver to take him for a walk to the botanical garden at Xiangshan. But he did not go to smell the flowers. Instead Li drove straight to Marshal Ye's residence just outside the city, toward the Western Hills. Their conversation was difficult. Ye was cautious. He questioned Li about the position of other military leaders, first and foremost General Chen Xilian, who was in charge of the CCP's powerful Central Military Commission. When Li assured him that Chen was "absolutely trustworthy," the old marshal agreed to further conversations later.[60] At some point around this conversation, Wang Dongxing sent his associate Li Xin, Kang Sheng's old secretary and a top security official, to visit Premier Hua at his private residence outside Zhongnanhai, on Dongjiaomin Lane to the east of Tiananmen Square, in the old Legation Quarter. Li straightforwardly proposed to Hua that "resolute measures" should be taken to remove the so-called Gang of Four from power.[61] Hua's concern had, if anything, grown since Mao's death, with the Left supplying much of the eulogy for the late chairman that Premier Hua would give on September 18.

On September 16 Hua took another important step by calling a meeting attended by Li Xiannian, Wu De, Chen Xilian, and Chen Yonggui, all of whom were politburo members. He intentionally excluded Zhang Chunqiao. After stating that "the Chairman has raised the issue of settling the problem of the Gang of Four," he straightforwardly asked them for opinions and suggestions about "how this could be done."[62] This was a smart move on Hua's part. By asking these leaders directly, he was able not only to identify the support he could expect from his Politburo colleagues but also, and more importantly, to legitimize any radical action that he would take against the Left by claiming that he did so to fulfill the chairman's wish.

On September 18, the day of the memorial service, more than half a million selected representatives from all over China trouped into Tiananmen Square. Wang Hongwen chaired the proceedings. Hua's eulogy was vintage Cultural Revolution: Never forget class struggle. Capitalist roaders are still on the capitalist road. Politics decides everything. Deepen the struggle to criticize Deng Xiaoping and repulse the Right deviationist attempts to reverse correct verdicts. Consolidate and develop the victories of the Great Proletarian Cultural Revolution.[63] Watching Hua's moon-face droning on about Maoist rectitude, some of the audience seemed to struggle to keep awake. Then, when the tones of "The East Is Red" sounded from the loudspeakers, the spectators seemed to come alive.

> The east is red, the sun is rising.
> From China comes Mao Zedong.
> He strives for the people's happiness,
> Hurrah, he is the people's great savior!

The night before the memorial service, the remains of the great savior were moved from the Great Hall of the People, where he had lain in state, to the secret underground bunker that connected the Great Hall, Zhongnanhai, and the PLA's 305 Hospital on the shore of Beihai. Wang Dongxing worried that Jiang Qing and her associate, Mao's nephew Mao Yuanxin, would take control of the body. Now the PLA was in charge of the chairman's corpse, as well as his documents. Jiang Qing's attempt during the memorial service to send some of her assistants to the swimming pool house in Zhongnanhai to retrieve batches of papers had been rebuffed by Wang Dongxing's guards.[64]

On September 25, Marshal Ye visited Hua Guofeng at his house in Dongjiaomin Lane. The premier outlined his plan to arrest the Gang of Four and investigate their crimes. We do not know what Ye said, but he must have concurred. Soon afterward, Hua shared his plans with Li Xiannian and Beijing Party chief Wu De, while swearing them to absolute secrecy.[65] Hua knew that power hung in the balance. If the Left could put their case for leadership to a Central Committee plenum, they might well command a majority.

Hua's uncharacteristic sense of urgency came in part from a sense of responsibility. He felt that the late chairman had left him in charge of, somehow, moving China forward, and that he could not fulfill that supreme duty as long as the Politburo kept fighting over minor matters. When Hua met with Wang Dongxing on September 23, he showed him the note by Mao saying, "I am relying on you to do the job, and my heart is at rest." Hua saw himself as the chosen successor, even if parts of that position terrified him. But he was also personally exasperated with Jiang Qing and her claim to a principal position within the Party. He complained to one of his security bosses that "every night, Jiang Qing calls me, yelling and shouting so loudly that I cannot sleep [afterward]."[66] But some of the urgency came from rumors peddled to him by military and security officials, claiming that the Politburo Left was determined to take power for themselves. It was said that they wanted to mobilize students in Beijing, as they had done many times before, and provide heavy weapons to militias in Beijing, Shanghai, and other cities. Mao Yuanxin's Manchurian military associates were rumored to be preparing to send their tank divisions to the capital. If a Central Committee plenum were convened, Jiang Qing would have Deng Xiaoping expelled from the Party and accuse Hua himself of having been in league with the disgraced vice premier. The parallels with the late 1960s and the purge of Liu Shaoqi must have been ever present for Hua.

There is no evidence that the Left was planning to seize power at any point in the summer or fall of 1976. On the contrary, the leading Leftist Politburo members seemed to move between defeatism after the death of their leader and calls to resist a revisionist coup. Already the day after Mao's demise, the

Left's propaganda chief Yao Wenyuan told several of his associates that if he were to disappear, they should continue their work unabated.[67] On September 21, as the coup plans by their adversaries were being formed, Zhang Chunqiao wrote to one of his close supporters, the Shanghai Party boss Ma Tianshui, that "he should be particularly wary of revisionism within the party, mainly from the central government, at the top. People like Lin Biao do have a lot of helpers. I hope you are actually ready to respond."[68] A week later, Zhang added an oral message to Ma and Xu Jingxian, telling them that "Shanghai should be more vigilant and more confident. [We know] that the bourgeoisie still has power, [and] the question now is who will be in charge. Shanghai has not really been seriously tested yet. Shanghai will have a big test, [must] be ready for war!"[69]

In spite of their dire predictions, Zhang and Yao wanted to keep their peace with Hua Guofeng, both because they reluctantly accepted that he was Mao's chosen successor and because they regarded him as a centrist, different from Ye Jianying and the military, whom they saw as the biggest threat. Jiang Qing did not agree. The idea of Hua replacing the chairman was anathema to her, and much of what she did in late September and early October was intended to show that she did not accept the new order of things. Matters came to a head at an extended Politburo meeting on September 29. Jiang Qing proposed herself as editor in chief of Mao's selected works, and Mao Yuanxin as responsible for writing the political report for the upcoming Third Plenum meeting of the CCP Central Committee. Hua Guofeng, supported by a majority in the Politburo, refused both requests. Jiang Qing exploded. Weeping, she turned to Hua and told him that she had been "sure that all of you would listen to Chairman Mao and follow Chairman Mao's established guidelines.

Comrades, I have lived with the Chairman for more than forty years, and I knew him well. He had his own views of, and deep feelings for, every comrade here. He has often spoken to me about this. Therefore, it is my duty to organize the manuscripts and works that Chairman put together when he was alive. Moreover, Comrade Yuanxin [spent] a year as liaison to the Chairman, [he knew] the Chairman's thoughts and instructions for more than a year, [and has] the deepest understanding. Comrade Chunqiao and Comrade Hongwen asked him to stay and draft the report of the Third Plenum, but there was opposition. Is it not chilling that Chairman Mao has just passed away [and already you] adopt this attitude towards us?[70]

Tired of Jiang's accusations, Hua brought the meeting to a close and wanted to leave. Zhang Chunqiao intervened, telling him in the corridor that "that is just how Jiang Qing is, go have a talk with her, mollify her a little and things will be fine." But Hua refused.[71] The break between the two seemed total. A couple of days later, on the PRC national day October 1, when the Politburo had decided to cancel all events out of respect for the late chairman, Jiang Qing showed up at Qinghua University, where she addressed a large crowd of students. Her message was twofold. On the one hand, she stressed that she had proposed expelling Deng Xiaoping from the Party but had been prevented from doing so, and that she had more than enough experience to lead the CCP herself, because of her closeness to the chairman for so many years. On the other hand, she also called for unity between older and younger cadre, as the chairman himself had ordered.[72] Meanwhile, some of her associates, such as Yao Wenyuan, seemed to suggest a division of power between the Left and its opponents at the forthcoming plenum, with the Left leading on issues such as culture, education, and health.

But Hua Guofeng, Ye Jianying, and the top military and security commanders had now lost all faith in compromises.[73] Even before the Politburo meeting on September 29, Marshal Ye had told his associates that "our struggle with them [Jiang Qing's supporters] is a life-and-death struggle. Only by crushing them will we be able to live. There is no room for a compromise."[74] On October 2, alarmed by Jiang Qing's appeal to the students and following instructions from both Hua and Ye, Wang Dongxing met with his deputies in his office in Zhongnanhai. The key people present were Wu Jianhua, deputy director of the Central Security Bureau and political commissar of Unit 8341, which looked after the leaders' personal security; Zhang Yaoci, head of the Central Guard Corps; and Li Xin, the deputy director of the CCP Central Administrative Office. At the meeting, Wang told them about the plans to arrest the Gang of Four. He also said that Hua Guofeng wanted action within a week. They worked through the night and got the go-ahead from Ye Jianying on their detailed plan the next morning.[75]

The plan for the coup against the Left that Wang and his associates presented to Hua Guofeng on October 3 had three main elements to it. Hua would invite the four key members of the Politburo Left to an urgent meeting inside Zhongnanhai. On arrival they would be arrested by officers from Unit 8341. At the same time, other security officers supported by military personnel would fan out across Beijing, arrest other leading Leftists, and secure ministries, radio and television stations, railway stations, telephone exchanges, and newspaper offices. Military units inside the capital that were known to be loyal to the plotters would be placed on full alert, and other units, including two tank battalions stationed north of the city, would move closer to Beijing. Wang Dongxing did not expect much resistance, but he wanted to be prepared for it. Marshal Ye Jianying had written a statement of support from the PLA leadership to be read over the airwaves in case of need. To keep absolute secrecy, the time for the coup was set at 8:00 P.M. on October 6, ninety hours after Hua gave the go-ahead for the plans, and none of the officers involved would be allowed to leave Zhongnanhai before then.[76]

The normally placid Hua seemed to have relished his role as chief plotter. The first vice chairman even went so far as to join Wang Dongxing for an inspection tour of the holding cells beneath Zhongnanhai where the Leftists would be taken after their arrest, ironically not far from the subterranean rooms where Mao's body was stored. There was a bit of a scare on October 4, when Jiang Qing suddenly decided to leave Beijing by a special train. Based on intelligence reports Hua had received, he worried that she might go to Shanghai and set up a headquarters there, presaging a civil war between the Left and its opponents. But, seemingly irresolute, Jiang only traveled as far as Baoding, where she stopped the train and spent a couple of hours picking wild chrysanthemums before returning to Beijing.[77] The coup plotters must have drawn a sigh of relief.

In the morning of October 6, the Central Administrative Office, following Hua's order, sent a note to all members of the Politburo Standing Committee, including Wang Hongwen and Zhang Chunqiao, informing them that there was to be an urgent meeting of the committee that evening to discuss the publication of volume five of Mao's selected works.[78] Not being members of the committee, Yao Wenyuan was not invited, and neither was Jiang Qing. The plan was to arrest them elsewhere. Jiang Qing was at home in her residence, Chunlian Hall, just a few minutes' walk south of Huairen Hall, where the meeting had been called and where the conspirators were waiting. Ye Jianying arrived at the hall at 7:20 P.M., and Hua Guofeng arrived twenty minutes later. They sat at a big meeting table in the central room. Wang Dongxing and two officers stood behind a screen at the back. Over twenty selected junior officers from Unit 8341 were positioned outside the room.[79]

Wang Hongwen was the first of the targets to enter the building. When the outer door closed behind him, he was grabbed by two uniformed officers and hauled into the room where Hua and Ye waited. Hua read a brief prepared text accusing Wang of belonging to an anti-Party group planning to usurp power and said that the Central Committee had ordered him held and placed under investigation. While Hua was reading, Wang struggled to get free, shouting repeatedly, "What are you doing, what are you doing?" Another officer entered, and together the guards lifted Wang Hongwen off the floor, carrying him to the side door. When they put him down, Wang shouted, "I did not think you would be so quick!" He continued to fight the guards, who beat him quite badly as he was handcuffed and tossed into a waiting car at the back of the building.[80]

Zhang Chunqiao arrived a few minutes later. Zhang did not say a word as Hua read the accusations against him and was treated quite gently by the guards. He looked almost disinterested as he was led out the back door and driven away.[81] Yao Wenyuan, whom Hua called to invite to the "special meeting" after the two others had been arrested, was apprehended by guards when he arrived at Huairen Hall. When Yao started shouting slogans, he was handcuffed and gagged.[82] Meanwhile, Wang Dongxing's deputy Wu Jianhua and eight other officers entered Jiang Qing's apartment in Chunlian Hall. They found Jiang Qing sitting on a sofa in her living room, drinking tea and reading documents. "Why have you come?" she asked. One of the officers rushed through the text he had been given, stumbling over words as he did so. "Who speaks for the Central Committee?" Jiang asked. "Who directed you to come?" When the officers said it was Hua and Ye, she shook her head slowly. "Hurry. Get her out of here now," one of the officers shouted. But Jiang refused to leave until she had put the key to her safe in a sealed envelope marked "For Hua Guofeng." She asked an assistant to pack some clothes while she went to the bathroom. Nobody dared to handcuff her.[83] When the car driving Jiang Qing out of Zhongnanhai passed Huairen Hall, Wu Jianhua looked up and saw Hua Guofeng, Ye Jianying, and Wang Dongxing standing on the steps outside, smoking cigarettes.

7

Succession Struggles

WHEN THE COUP PLOTTERS MET at Marshal Ye Jianying's house outside Beijing in the late evening of October 6, they were still astonished at how easily their plan had worked. Some of them felt quite light-headed with a mix of relief and excitement. But all of them knew that there were challenges to come. The Left still had some of its institutional power intact, and, in some places, such as Shanghai, enough armed militias to put up a fight.[1] And then there was the relationship among the plotters themselves. It was, at best, an uneasy and fragile alliance among leaders who had very little in common except a political and personal dislike for the group they now had agreed on dubbing the "Gang of Four." Some of the coup-makers had been victims of the Cultural Revolution, and some were among its main beneficiaries. Some believed very deeply that the chairman's every word was a valuable instruction, while others were already looking beyond "old Mao" to a different kind of China in the future. All of them were struck by the enormity of what they had just done: a few weeks after the chairman's funeral, they had arrested his widow and a quarter of the last Politburo Mao had chosen. Like Soviet leaders after Stalin, they must have been wondering how they could manage without their leader, even as they acted against his family and closest associates.

The coup-makers had chosen Marshal Ye's house as a meeting place because they could not be certain beforehand that the coup would succeed. If the Left leaders had escaped and mobilized their supporters in Beijing, then a civil war could break out with clashes in the capital. But, knowing that the key targets had been taken into custody before he left Zhongnanhai, Hua Guofeng had ordered his assistants to call members of the Politburo and some military officers to a late-night meeting at Ye's house while he and Wang Dongxing were on their way there.[2] When the meeting got underway around 11:00 P.M., Hua first asked Marshal Ye to take the chair, indicating the centrality of the army in the plot, but also because Ye was the oldest member and the meeting was taking place at his residence. Ye refused. "You are the first vice chair of the Central Committee," he told Hua. "You must preside over this meeting." Hua spoke briefly and in a hushed voice. "We are meeting here," he said, "in order to keep a high degree of confidentiality, to ensure the security of the Party Center, and to make some very necessary decisions." "I would now like to announce to you that at 8 P.M. this evening, the Party Center has arrested Wang Hongwen and Zhang Chunqiao. . . . Jiang Qing was arrested at her home in Zhongnanhai. On the basis of their serious crime of usurping the power of the Party, they were informed of the decision of the Central People's Government, signed by me, to place them in isolation for a review of their activities."[3] Hua then said that other arrests had also been carried out in Beijing and that military personnel had taken control of the radio and television stations, the main newspapers, and the central Party archives.

> [When] Chairman Mao died, they thought the time has come to intensify unbridled, urgent anti-revolutionary activities to usurp the party's power. They used the propaganda tools [they] controlled to create counter-revolutionary public opinion that usurped the power of the Party. They tampered with Chairman Mao's signed instructions and falsified the so-called final instruction of Chairman Mao. They set up armed forces in Shanghai under their control and command, and distributed large quantities of guns and ammunition. All indications are that the fate of our Party and our country is at a critical juncture. In order to ensure that the leadership of the Party and the state is not usurped by them and that their criminal plot is not allowed to succeed, the Central Committee has taken resolute and decisive measures. . . . [It] quickly crushed the "Gang of Four" counter-revolutionary groups [and] achieved a major historic victory, for the Party, for the country, and the people.[4]

Many of those assembled went visibly pale, especially Ji Dengkui and Chen Yonggui, who, before the meeting, had asked rather innocently whether they should wait for "more members" to arrive. Seeing their confusion, Marshal Ye summed matters up: "Our Party and the 'Gang of Four' are not the same; [it is] 'you die, I live.'" "The army fully supports and implements this important decision of the CCP Central Committee."[5] Hua Guofeng interjected: "In this . . . struggle and victory, our Marshal Ye played the most important role." "But you cannot say that," Ye responded. "After Chairman Mao's death, you are the first vice chairman . . . and the premier of the State Council; this is a big event, if you had not made up your mind, it would have been difficult to do." Ye Jianying would not be seen as the main plotter; he needed Hua Guofeng to offer legitimacy to their enterprise, just like Hua needed Ye and Wang Dongxing to carry out the operation. Ye made plain their debt to Wang and his security forces: "In this struggle with the 'Gang of Four,' Comrade Dongxing . . . and the soldiers of Unit 8341 made great contributions to the Party [and] to the people." When Hua promptly and politely proposed Marshal Ye as the new chairman of the Central Committee, the old man demurred. "Comrade Hua Guofeng should serve as chairman. . . . He is more than twenty years younger than me, has practical work experience, is a trustworthy person with good democratic style, who can unite comrades, [who] respects the old comrades. . . . I think he is the more suitable candidate."[6] Unsurprisingly, the attendees decided unanimously on Hua before the meeting broke up around 3:00 A.M. Those present were then told by the guards there that they would have to stay at the military compound in Yuquanshan, near Marshal Ye's residence, for the duration of the emergency. They could not go back to the center of Beijing. Ye, Hua, and Wang Dongxing were not yet certain what the situation in the capital would be like.

Over the next couple of days, it became clear that there was no resistance in Beijing. Disorganized and without their leaders, Left-wing activists who found out about the coup mostly laid low. Shanghai was a different matter, as was potentially the industrial city of Wuhan and some of the cities in the northeast, where the Left had much support.[7] Even though the Politburo Left had been careful with not taking any action that would provoke an immediate crisis right after Mao's death, in Shanghai the workers militia had, with Wang Hongwen's blessing, accessed arms depots and moved its headquarters closer to key government buildings. Their leaders probably realized already in the late evening of October 6 that something was afoot, when they could not reach Wang and Zhang Chunqiao in Beijing by phone. By October 8, radical leaders in Shanghai had concluded that a military coup had taken place. The militia was mobilized, and units were stationed in the vicinity of strategic locations in the city, including local broadcasting stations and Party offices. At least parts of the Shanghai Left were planning for armed resistance.[8] Wang Xiuzhen, Wang Hongwen's deputy in the city, told a hastily arranged leadership meeting that "Chairman Mao has only just passed away and they couldn't wait to stage a palace coup. This is more Khrushchevian than Khrushchev!" Others chimed in: "If party Central goes revisionist, never fear. We'll counter it." "We can instigate a strike, organize workers' demonstrations, post slogans and manifestoes." "We can't surrender; we can't become traitors." "When the fighting begins, you must all go to the various command-posts and take charge."[9]

Meanwhile, at Yuquanshan, the new Party leadership was working overtime to coordinate their message and bring the country into line. When meeting with military leaders on October 8, Hua underlined that although he demanded absolute obedience to the new regime, extreme changes were not in the making. The Party had to show "correct treatment of the Cultural Revolution, correct treatment of the masses, correct treatment of our own." "The Gang of Four is the Gang of Four: the great majority of cadres, workers are good; in any case we cannot do too much, if someone did bad things, say something incorrect, they will not all be investigated. This is very important, do not be too quick, do not turn too fast."[10] The story now presented was that Chairman Mao himself had chosen Hua as his successor and asked him to act against the Gang of Four. The Gang had engaged in a Right-wing conspiracy to take power from the chairman's proper heirs. With the help of the army and the security forces, Chairman Hua, as he was now referred to, had uncovered their plans and acted in the nick of time to prevent them subverting the rightful succession. Hua termed it "the eleventh line-struggle" in the Party, coming right after the "conspiracies" of Liu Shaoqi and Lin Biao.[11] Even though some of the coup-makers demurred, Hua Guofeng insisted on carrying out the purge of the Left in a form identical to oustings during the Cultural Revolution. The leaders of the Left, who had worked closely with Mao for years, were presented as a Right-wing, pro-capitalist conspiracy, and Jiang Qing, now held in the basement under the Great Hall of the People, was a witch who had usurped Mao's power and hastened his death. The chairman had wanted to get rid of her, the commanders were told. Jiang Qing had been pestering him for money and interfered with his "private life." She was a female usurper in the mold of Empress Wu Zetian of the Tang Empire. She even dressed like a lesbian, Admiral Su Zhenhua said.[12]

With the key commanders of the PLA having sworn allegiance to the new regime, Marshal Ye Jianying and the others laid out the compromises on which their authority was based. Hua would be presented as the successor. "Comrade Guofeng is our leader," Ye said. People in Hunan, he added, somewhat condescendingly, said Hua Guofeng was "selfless, not stupid (in fact, very clever). We have to hold up, to support, to unite around Comrade Guofeng."[13] Other leaders, such as Chen Yonggui, who had been close to Jiang Qing, were quick to disassociate themselves from any links with those who had now been purged. Chen, in his slightly comical fashion, insisted that he had never, ever invited Jiang to his power base in Dazhai. She had invited herself, and what could he do? Li Xiannian, who had been the closest assistant of Zhou Enlai, assured them that "the great achievements of the Cultural Revolution must be affirmed; [it] knocked down Liu [and] Lin's two bourgeois headquarters, and then exposed Deng Xiaoping's Rightism." "The situation is really good, as long as we master policy [and] carry out work patiently work, the problems, I think, are not difficult to solve."[14] The message was that everyone who was willing to join in the struggle against the Left would get something, in terms of political or personal positions.

In Shanghai, the leaders of the Left-wing Revolutionary Committee and the trade unions continued to prepare an uprising, but held back from implementing it, waiting for news from Beijing. The head of the Revolutionary Committee, Ma Tianshui, had traveled to the capital on October 7, but the others had not heard back from him since he left. Some Shanghai leaders argued that the general uprising had to start immediately, antirevisionist slogans had to be issued, and workers rallies organized. The dock workers offered to sink ships outside the harbor, making it harder to land troops. Railway workers wanted to cut the railway lines between Shanghai and Nanjing, preventing the military from using them to enter the city. The talk was of a Paris Commune–style revolt. "We are going to do it," swore Zhu Yongjia from the Shanghai Writers' Group. "We're going to mobilize the militia, we're going to fight for a week. . . . We're going to let the whole world know, just like the Paris Commune."[15] But others, more familiar with their revolutionary history, remembered how much blood had been spilled when the Paris Commune was crushed by the army back in the 1870s. Even though the plans were ready, nobody wanted to take the responsibility for implementing them. Instead, after Ma Tianshui had been pressured into calling his Shanghai comrades and assure them that all was well in Beijing, they decided to send a delegation to the capital to see for themselves.[16]

Sending their main leaders to Beijing was one of the crucial mistakes that the Shanghai Left made in the aftermath of the coup. When Wang Xiuzhen and Xu Jingxian arrived at Beijing Airport, they were immediately detained, and then hauled before the new leadership group on October 12. "Shanghai has been blinded and blocked," Marshal Ye told them. "Our determination is great and our methods are correct. . . . It has been them against us, and they are sectarian anti-party elements." "Shanghai's workers, students, have made special progress since the Cultural Revolution. If you plan to join up with the Gang of Four again, that will not be good for your positions. You have worked with them in Shanghai for so long, [but] I hope you do not stand on their side now, but [rather] draw a line under their conspiracy to undermine the Party. They call people revisionists, [but] they are revisionists themselves. If we solve the problem of Shanghai well, that will have a great impact on the whole country and the whole world."[17] Wang and Xu, joined by a tearful Ma Tianshui, told Marshal Ye and his companions that before coming to Beijing, they had thought that the four comrades at the Center "were the representatives of Chairman Mao's revolutionary line . . . and that some bad guys had arrested these leaders, and they had [therefore] joined several comrades in Shanghai and in the army, and also mobilized militiamen, to prepare for a deadly war. Now we understand that these people were usurping power in the Party, and [we] feel great indignation, and express determination to draw a clear line between us and them, [and are] determined to [support] the leadership of Comrade Hua Guofeng . . . to defend Chairman Mao's revolutionary line."[18] They offered to return to Shanghai to make sure the city followed the new leaders. Hua Guofeng smiled. "When you go back, the others will scold you as traitors," he said. "If you now have decided to change your position, you must pick yourself up and do a good job."[19]

Hua could smile because he knew that the situation in Shanghai was already changing. The Center had sent its agents into the city on October 7, and they were reporting that support for an armed uprising was waning fast.[20]

When it became known that the military region around Shanghai had been put on full combat readiness, talk of a "Paris Commune" became less frequent. Some still argued that it was necessary to defend the revolution in Shanghai against the revisionist coup in Beijing. The expanded Shanghai Revolutionary Committee spent the morning of October 13 agreeing on twenty-one slogans for a mass protest to be held "soon," among them "Carry forward the glorious tradition of Shanghai working class" and "Never allow the experience of the Soviet Union to be repeated in China."[21] But when the Beijing delegation returned later that day, a majority of those present agreed not to challenge the Center. Some accepted the stories they were told about Mao having chosen Hua as his successor, and that Hua was therefore the legitimate leader of the Party. But, later that evening, Ma Tianshui told a friend about the real reason he had chosen not to fight: "The army is not in our hands, [and] the militia is in no position to fight against the army."[22] He cried, saying that the momentum for a revolutionary uprising had gone, probably forever.[23]

But if the Left-wing leaders in Shanghai were despondent, others had reason to celebrate. As it became known that Jiang Qing and her associates had been purged, many places in China saw spontaneous festivities, well before the Party's official denunciation meetings and anti-Jiang marches had got underway.[24] A few learned the news already in the days after the coup, from relatives or friends in the army or higher Party echelons. A Beijing writer got his suspicions confirmed by an acquaintance who, on seeing him, crossed the road and whispered, "It is almost dawn!" In Wuhan, the first wall posters denouncing the Gang of Four went up already in the evening of October 8. Since there were no streetlights, people brought out torches to illuminate them for reading. One man started shouting, "The day has finally come," and others joined in. By morning, there were street parties near the posters, with dancing and singing. Even in Shanghai it became clear in the week after the coup that there were probably more people saluting events in the capital than lamenting them. On October 15, tens of thousands demonstrated in front of the Revolutionary Committee's headquarters on Kangping Road, now mainly deserted, with slogans disavowing the Shanghai radicals. Over the following week, as news seeped out to the villages, people were trying to make sense of it. A group of youngsters remember hearing about the arrests from an old

Party veteran, who could barely recall the names of those purged. But on hearing Jiang Qing's name, one girl was dizzy with excitement. "This time," she said, "it is really going to change."[25]

As the new Party leadership, with the help of the army, solidified their power throughout China, it was still not clear exactly what was going to change. It was not even obvious that October 1976 would be a dividing line in the history of the CCP. Much continued as before: Cultural Revolution ideals were still upheld by the new leaders, Deng Xiaoping and many former Party leaders remained purged, and Mao Zedong's instructions in his final years were still regarded as law by many. The Party leadership had a new chairman, Chairman Hua, but it was impossible to tell what new ideas, if any, were hidden behind his benevolent visage. His insistence that those arrested were "Right-deviationists" did not bode well for new forms of thinking; the pattern of the purges seemed a bit too similar to those after the fall of Lin Biao five years earlier. The Party leadership appeared as divided as it had been back then, or, indeed, when the Cultural Revolution started. And even if many Chinese, especially those in the CCP who had been persecuted, celebrated Jiang Qing's fall, it was hard to tell which direction the country was going to move in after the coup.

What was clear was that the CCP Left had suffered a major setback both in terms of people and policies. Most of the disaster was self-inflicted. The Left, represented in the Politburo in 1976 by Jiang Qing, Wang Hongwen, Zhang Chunqiao, and Yao Wenyuan, but also supported by a large number of other leaders, had neither a strategy nor a program. As a rule, it was easier to say what they were against than what they were for. Ideologically, they seemed lost without the support of Mao Zedong, who had been the main leader of the Left in the Party since the mid-1950s. Since the early 1970s, they had attempted to develop policies that increased workers' autonomy and changed education and culture more fundamentally in the direction of collectivist values. Their critique of CCP leaders' corruption and misuse of power struck a chord with many Chinese. But, in the end, it was too easy to use them as culprits for all that had gone wrong in China over the past twenty years. That their most prominent representative was a woman did not help either, in a Party where misogyny was rife. It was simple to blame Jiang Qing for past disasters, even though the policies that led to them had been Mao's responsibility. But most of the new leaders, having learned from Soviet troubles after

Stalin, did not want to touch Mao's position. Neither did they want to admit that it was the Party's collective failure to check willfulness and authoritarianism that had led to cruelty and stagnation.

As Hua Guofeng, Ye Jianying, and the other leaders consolidated their power in Beijing, they had a host of immediate problems to deal with. Three of these stood out. The first was to carry out anti-Left purges in the central administration and in the provinces without risking further damage to the Party and its public standing. Not only did they have to rescue the position of the dead chairman, in whose cloak of authority they had dressed themselves, but they also had to find ways to avoid unnecessary bloodletting and give less prominent Leftists a chance to come to heel or fade into obscurity. Then, they had to deal with what they called "historical issues," meaning the official verdict on officials purged or killed during the Cultural Revolution and the Party's evaluation of past events, first among them the Tiananmen protests in the spring of 1976. And, inside the Party, they had to figure out what to do about Deng Xiaoping and those who were purged alongside him less than a year earlier. Deng was a big beast; all of them realized that he could not be left out in the cold for long, but some feared him as a rival and others were frightened by his unorthodox approaches. Chairman Hua wanted team players, not self-seekers who would put his own accomplishments in the shadow.

The number of arrests of Leftists in the first months after the coup was surprisingly small, probably in the tens of thousands, but the figure of those put under investigation was substantially higher. In some parts of China, where the Left had been strong, the key issue was to get new leadership in place while preventing rebellions and putting political opponents under investigation. Already in the days after the coup, Shanghai received a twelve-person leadership group from Beijing to take over power in the city. Called the Central Committee Shanghai Work Group, it consisted of a number of senior leaders, headed by Admiral Su Zhenhua, the former political commissar of the navy, who had distinguished himself in Beijing on the night of the coup by leading the takeover of the Xinhua News Agency and the broadcasting stations. Admiral Su now combined the offices of Party secretary and mayor of Shanghai. His principal deputies were Ni Zhifu, a young trade unionist originally from the city, and Peng Chong, a veteran Communist who was transferred from the job as Party secretary of neighboring Jiangsu.[26] Along with them came a number of less senior cadre, including the young bureaucrat Jiang Zemin, a Jiangsu native with good knowledge of the city.[27] Some Shanghai workers described the Shanghai Work Group's rule as the second Communist occupation after 1949, but overall it proved a good combination in terms of competencies. About a third of leading cadre in Shanghai were removed from their posts in a very gradual purge up to 1981.[28]

Similar arrangements were put in place for other regions in which the Left had been predominant, such as Liaoning in the northeast, Shaanxi in the northwest, and Yunnan in the far south. In Liaoning Province, the investigation and rectification group sent by Beijing viewed the now imprisoned Mao Yuanxin, Mao Zedong's nephew, as the root of all evil. "By virtue of his special status," they reported, "he manipulated the power of the provincial party committee . . . [and] became the emperor of Liaoning. . . . After Chairman Mao's death, Mao Yuanxin wrote to his cronies asking them to 'study the lessons of Khrushchev's rise to power,' and his cronies immediately conducted 'research,' private seminars, and talks, pointing the finger directly at Chairman Mao's personally chosen successor [Hua Guofeng]." Their slogans, the report said, claimed that people like Khrushchev and the Hungarian leader Imre Nagy had come back to power in China. According to the report, "The Gang of Four and its Party members attach great importance to Liaoning, their base for usurping the power of the Party."[29] Even after the arrests in Beijing, the investigators asserted, Mao Yuanxin's associates had helped Leftists escape or destroy evidence. But the numbers first purged in Liaoning were still small, around 500 people in all.

In Shaanxi a similar number was purged during the first few months, including three leaders of the provincial Revolutionary Committee, who were accused of having committed "extremely serious mistakes." The accusations against them were much the same as elsewhere: following the Gang of Four, they had "fanned the flames of dissent, created chaos, and undermined stability and unity." But in Shaanxi their activities had peaked, it was claimed, *after* the arrests in Beijing, when they had attacked the new authorities, comparing them with Louis XVIII of the French 1810s restoration "relying on nobles," thereby "causing serious damage."[30] In faraway Yunnan, supporters of the Left were also accused of having "conspired to plan an armed rebellion" by gathering weapons and preparing to start guerrilla warfare in the mountains. The reason why they were so certain they could get arms and supplies, was, according to the investigators, the support they had got in the past from

Jia Qiyun, a Party veteran who combined the positions as Party secretary, provincial governor, and political commissar for the military region, and who had thrown in his lot with the Left.[31] As an old Party member, Jia lost his position in the purge, but he was not arrested. The investigators "invited him to correct his mistakes and return to Chairman Mao's revolutionary line."[32]

Even though the Party leaders mandated lenience as a general principle, some of the purges got out of hand in a by now time-honored fashion. In some places, the campaign against Jiang Qing and her associates was used to settle old scores, and by late 1976 there were many of those in China. Impatient young Party bureaucrats also used it to remove their seniors and gain advancement for themselves. In addition, some of those who had been purged during the Cultural Revolution wanted to come back into official positions, and Jiang Qing's fall provided the perfect opportunity to claim that they had been set up by the now disgraced radicals and were worthy of returning. Also, there were instances—similar to during the "Criticize Lin, Criticize Confucius" campaign—where local officials understood that reporting problems with "anti-Party elements" was a sure way of attracting extra material resources from the Center. In a few cases, even Party cadre had gone through so many campaigns for and then against the same people, for and then against slogans and political formulae, that they got genuinely confused about what they were supposed to say, and thereby put themselves at risk of sanctions by Beijing. The language used to condemn suspected Gang of Four supporters came straight out of purges in the past. The prosecutor's charges against Chen Yaode, a Shanghai primary school teacher who was arrested in early 1977, are typical.

Chen is a son of a counter-revolutionary who has a deep hatred for our Party and the socialist system, has overturned the case against his father, and has been criticized by the masses, but still does not repent. When the people of the whole country warmly celebrated the great victory of the Party Central Committee headed by Chairman Hua Guofeng, who crushed the "Gang of Four" anti-Party group, Chen, because of his counter-revolutionary nature, wrote two anonymous counter-revolutionary letters to the Party in Shanghai on October 18 and 19, 1976, attacking the Party Central Committee headed by Chairman Hua and encouraging the promotion of the spirit of the Gang of Four in Shanghai. Chen's crime is very serious and the masses are very angry.[33]

The other two key issues for the new leadership, reevaluations of the April 1976 Tiananmen events and of Deng Xiaoping's case, proved to be more difficult than the campaigns against the Left, because they cut straight through the precarious alliances among the new top leaders. On Tiananmen, Hua Guofeng issued instructions soon after the coup on quietly releasing those who had been arrested, but he balked at a wholesale reevaluation of the protests. To him, and to many of the Cultural Revolution beneficiaries, Mao himself had made the verdict on those events, and Mao's decisions should not be questioned. Hua's policy, with considerable support from other leaders, was to go slow, and gradually figure out how to handle the issue. The Beijing Party secretary and Politburo member Wu De, who many held responsible for the crackdown, had later joined the conspiracy against the radicals and worked closely with Hua and Ye in the aftermath of the coup. Wu was of course very aware of how his own position was connected to the evaluation of the Tiananmen protests, and he attempted to link his actions as much as possible to the late chairman. In late November 1976, Wu tried to close the case in a speech by simply saying that "whatever Chairman Mao instructed, Chairman Mao affirmed, we must all strive to act accordingly, and strive to do it well."[34] It was the earliest form of what later became known as "the two whatevers," set out in a joint editorial in *Renmin Ribao* and the *People's Liberation Army Daily* on February 7, 1977: "We will resolutely uphold whatever policy decisions Chairman Mao made, and unswervingly follow whatever instructions Chairman Mao gave."

The problem with this position was the amount of increasingly vocal opposition to it, at least as regarded the Tiananmen events, within Beijing and elsewhere. The police reported wall posters demanding the reversal of the official verdict on those who had mourned Premier Zhou Enlai in April. Around the first anniversary of the premier's death in early 1977, Chairman Hua agreed that public commemorations would be allowed, including wall posters and wreaths put up by "the masses." But the ceremonies quickly turned into an outpouring of anger against the Beijing city authorities and the police, who responded by roughing up and arresting a number of those who protested. Wu De, the Beijing Party secretary who had been in charge the year before, declared the protests to be hooliganism, and got Hua Guofeng's grudging support. A breaking point for Hua was when protesters put up posters on the scaffolding around the mausoleum the new leaders were building to exhibit Mao Zedong's body at the far end of Tiananmen Square. The posters called for inquiries into past injustices and purges, the renewal of socialism, and the return of Deng Xiaoping. A few of the posters championed democracy or extolled the qualities of the Chinese nation. Among the protesters were a few former Red Guard leaders, including Li Dongmin, now a worker in Beijing, who were promoting very different ideals from ten years earlier. After the most outspoken protesters were charged with counter-revolutionary crimes and their wall posters at the mausoleum torn down, new posters sprang up elsewhere in the city, including at the crossroads at Xidan, the main intersection west of Tiananmen.[35]

Having failed to resolve public anger over its treatment of past protests, the leadership turned to the issue of Deng Xiaoping. Having been protected by the army after his purge at the beginning of the year, Deng was now back in Beijing and obviously awaiting word from the new leaders of his recall to power. When he learned about the arrest of the Gang of Four, he wrote to Hua Guofeng proclaiming his full support for his actions and for his elevation to be the new chairman.[36] Hua and Ye Jianying decided almost immediately after the coup that Deng should return to some position in the Party hierarchy, but Hua, especially, wanted to make sure that it happened according to Party procedures and not too suddenly. Otherwise, he felt, they would be seen as acting against Chairman Mao's expressed wishes. Ye agreed, at least initially. In late October he told a close friend that "Xiaoping is going to come back to work, but it will take a while. We do not want to upset the applecart. This matter with Xiaoping was brought up by Chairman Mao [and] the Politburo through the Party inspection mechanisms. . . . There must be a process. If not, it was just a palace coup."[37] By December 1976, with Deng conveniently in the hospital for prostate surgery, the leadership, prodded by Marshal Ye, decided in principle that the former vice premier should return to work at some point, and allowed him to again receive high-level Party briefings. But the issue of timing proved difficult. Hua wanted to fully inform the Chinese about the counter-revolutionary character of the Gang of Four before bringing Deng back in. Before then, he told the other leaders at the opening of a Central Party Work Conference in March 1977, "It would be rushed to solve Comrade Deng Xiaoping's problems. It would lead some cadres and the masses to have all kinds of doubts. . . . If we rush to get [Deng] back to work, we may be acting in the interests of the class enemies; we will mess up the struggle to expose the Gang of Four, [and this] may push us into a passive position."[38]

But by then pressure was mounting even inside the Party for a resolution to both the Tiananmen issue and Deng's situation. In discussions in and around the conference, several Party veterans voiced dissenting views. Chen Yun, a hard-nosed Party elder who had been a strong promoter of intensified central planning in the 1950s, took the lead. Chen had an impeccable CCP background: he had been in the Central Committee since 1931 and had headed the Party's organizational bureau. In a written statement, he said:

> My views on the Tiananmen incident are that the vast majority of the people wanted to memorialize Premier Zhou. . . . As for the very few bad people who were mixed in with the masses, it is necessary to check whether the Gang of Four was involved and whether there was a ruse. Because Tiananmen is a matter of public concern, [since] there were similar incidents across the country at the time. Comrade Deng Xiaoping had nothing to do with the Tiananmen incident. For the sake of the Chinese revolution and the needs of the CCP, it is absolutely right and necessary to . . . propose that Comrade Deng Xiaoping be reinstated in the leadership of the CCP Central Committee. I fully support it.[39]

Wang Zhen, a tough general known for his earthy language and total dedication to the Party, chimed in: "Deng Xiaoping has strong political ideas and rare talents. In 1975, he . . . made great achievements. He was [our] pioneer in the fight against the Gang of Four. The Gang of Four tried to frame him in a despicable manner. The Tiananmen incident was a powerful protest movement of the masses against the Gang of Four and for the pride of our nation. Whoever does not recognize the nature . . . of the Tiananmen incident, do, in fact, defend the Gang of Four."[40]

In spite of his willingness to unite the Party as much as possible, Hua Guofeng had a stubborn streak. While not attacking his critics directly, as Mao would have done, he refused to give in to pressure. In his concluding speech at the Work Conference, he did make clear that "the conditions for solving Comrade Deng Xiaoping's problems are gradually ripening." But he added that it was more appropriate to announce a decision at the forthcoming Central Committee plenum, or at a new Party congress, which he hoped to convene as soon as possible. "There should be steps; there should be a process,"

Hua said. "Our policy is to hold high Chairman Mao's great banner, work harder, and let Comrade Deng Xiaoping work at the appropriate time." He also admitted that "the vast majority of people who went to Tiananmen Square were good . . . [and] cannot be said to have participated in counter-revolutionary events." Even so, there had been a few counter-revolutionaries there, and it was therefore hard to change the Party's previous verdict on this episode. Hua warned the other leaders against "reopening such issues as the Tiananmen incident. . . . The Central Committee, in solving the problems of Comrade Deng Xiaoping and the Tiananmen Incident, is standing firm in its fundamental position [of] safeguarding Chairman Mao's great flag and adhering to Chairman Mao's line and policy. . . . The proletarian Cultural Revolution should be treated correctly. . . . [It] was a seven-point achievement and a three-point error. . . . All decisions made by Chairman Mao must be maintained; Chairman Mao's great banner must be held high [and] cannot be thrown away."[41]

After the Work Conference, therefore, many of the most immediate problems of the CCP were still left unresolved. Hua Guofeng and a group of leaders who were close to him made clear that they wanted to concentrate on economic growth and modernization, not issues of the past. Hua himself combined being Party chairman with being premier of the State Council, giving him an extraordinary powerful position. These two posts had never been combined before in the history of the People's Republic. Alongside Hua, key leaders included the former security boss Wang Dongxing, now, somewhat unlikely, in charge of ideology, culture, education, and youth work; Ji Dengkui, in charge of agriculture; and General Chen Xilian, in charge of military affairs. All of them had risen to power during the Cultural Revolution but viewed themselves as reformers who wanted rapid economic progress under a collective Party leadership. They were, however, also very aware that all of their legitimacy was connected to Mao's decisions during his final years, and they would not allow any criticism of the late chairman, real or imagined. In the spring of 1977, Wang Dongxing even blocked criticism of the Gang of Four's writings, telling other leaders that Mao had personally endorsed these views, and that they should attack those purged but not statements personally approved by Mao Zedong.[42] Wang's main project that spring was the publication of volume five of Mao's selected writings. It proved to be a tough task in terms of content as well as printing. Massive amounts of paper that had been held in storage for several years awaiting the publication were by then moldy. In several places there was not enough electricity to run the printing machines. Typographers and printers worked very carefully, terrified that something should go wrong, since they thought that any misprints or delays would mean their death.[43] And, when the book was published to great fanfare, there were fewer takers than expected, and Wang had to tell Party organizations to increase their orders.

The predicament of Mao's volume five was in a way characteristic of the overall situation in China in the year after the chairman's death. The changes at the top were not, as yet, mirrored further down in society. Even if most people found it easy to join in the campaigns against the Gang of Four, everyone was careful to stick to the script as they understood it, fearful of further changes at the top. Given how many turnarounds people in China had experienced over the past decade, this was in no way surprising. Nobody could tell what the future would bring in terms of who was up and who was down. In some villages and neighborhoods, residents organized reading groups for studying volume five of Mao's writings, where the real purpose was to learn the names of those now in power in Beijing and in their province and find out, through collective efforts, which slogans were out and which were in. Training in saying the right things was an easy manner of survival. And given the limited scope of the initial anti-Left purge—presented, of course, as an "anti-Right" campaign—some communities acted on their own, replacing bosses who had risen during the Cultural Revolution with older leaders who had more trust among the public. But in many places the new local leadership was a mix between new and old. Cultural Revolution beneficiaries sat next to those who had been arrested, purged, or beaten, with even some former Red Guards or followers of Jiang Qing mixed in—now, of course, singing to a new tune. As shown on other occasions, too, Chinese communities have a tremendous ability to put the past behind them and find ways of surviving together, even if resentment over past injustices linger. Blaming now-purged leaders in faraway Beijing for their collective misfortunes also helped start a communal healing process, though given the atrocities that had been committed by some against their workmates, neighbors, or relatives, the mending would take a long time to complete, if it ever can be completed.

In terms of power, everyone now knew that the People's Liberation Army was in charge and that military leaders made, or at least sanctioned, all key decisions. Although, as we have seen, this military preeminence had been a gradual process, which began long before the coup in October 1976, it hardened during the year that followed, and many people came to think of it as a permanent fixture in how China was led. But although public perceptions now meant that in most places people would look to local commanders for leadership, this did not mean that the military replaced the Party. It rather meant that officers and CCP leaders with strong links to the PLA now had a predominant position within the Party, as they did in the government at large. Many Chinese believed that military control indicated at least some degree of stability and predictability, compared with what had gone before. But, especially in wealthier parts of the country, there was also a sense of PLA commanders as interlopers, who were out to gain status and, if possible, enrich themselves at the expense of the local population. Local military strongmen were more tolerated than loved.

Like in government affairs, there was more continuity than change in the country at large after 1976. In most of the countryside, the People's Communes continued as before, with very varied results, as before. Where change had begun in the early 1970s, it sped up after 1976, after a go-slow period in the years before when the Left had been seen as ascendant in Beijing. Selling rice, grain, vegetables, and meat for cash became quite common in some of the richer provinces, and especially in areas closer to the cities. The same was true for other staples, such as cooking oil, coal, and firewood. Repairs of machinery and household goods was sometimes carried out for cash or through barter, outside the plan. Smuggling from Hong Kong and Taiwan increased, and new avenues of illicit imports appeared, such as from Burma to Yunnan or even from North Korea to Manchuria.[44] In the cities and in the wealthier parts of the countryside, black-market trade expanded. By late 1978, even the Party's own internal reports found that there were few things that could not be bought for cash or, worse, foreign currency, which began to reemerge in the coastal cities. Foreign consumer goods and clothes fetched high prices, since China produced so little such goods itself, and, for the little there was, there was no variety. Most important of all, people were not afraid of obtaining such merchandise, since Party officials no longer prioritized pillorying individuals for their consumer choices.

In the poorer parts of the countryside, which, in terms of numbers, held about two-thirds of China's population, life continued much as before. The battle was to get enough to eat, and the end of the most extravagant Communist campaigns was welcome, because it meant more time to work the fields or tend the livestock. The criticism of Jiang Qing and her associates was in most places quite pro forma; some paused in shock at seeing the wife of Chairman Mao attacked, but most were encouraged by the elevation of Chairman Hua, who seemed a reasonable enough fellow to most farmers. Posters with his benign countenance were soon put next to those of Chairman Mao. But, as controls and political regimentation seemed to slip, some young people tried to leave China's poverty-stricken villages for a different life in the towns and cities. There was not much for them there either. No jobs, since their presence was strictly illegal, but maybe the opportunity to get by by begging, stealing, or peddling, at least for a while. For some, it was just the opportunity to see a different world that attracted them, to experience a life that had its own predicaments, but away from the grinding poverty of the countryside.[45]

Among China's vast prison population there was hope that the changes at the Party Center could mean a reconsideration of cases and, possibly, release. But, at least to begin with, very little changed. The special case investigations that could lead to execution, even after many years in prison or labor camps, became fewer, and the hours spent on "brain washing," self-criticism, and political education reduced in number. But the reduction in politics meant more hours could be taken by mind-numbing toil in fields, mines, or factories. By the late 1970s prisons and labor camps held survivors from waves of arrests going back to the civil war era—former officials, landlords, or bourgeois, "rightists" from the 1950s campaigns, farmers who had protested the expropriation of land, Christians, people with relatives abroad, party cadre purged in the Great Leap Forward of the Cultural Revolution, former Red Guards who had lost out in the battle for political influence, or people who had just happened to be at the wrong place at the wrong time or had got their slogans mixed up. After October 1976 they were joined by Leftists who had been, at least in part, responsible for putting many of them there in the first place. The number of appeals for clemency or rehabilitation increased in 1977, but the new CCP leaders were far too busy with their infighting to have many of them considered.

If Hua Guofeng thought that he had forged a set of reasonable compromises on both ideological and practical matters at the CCP Work Conference in the spring of 1977, he turned out to be badly mistaken. Realizing the strength of his position, Deng Xiaoping simply refused to accept the outcome. Deng regarded himself first and foremost as a soldier, with some right. He had been political commissar for one of the CCP main forces, the Second Field Army, and during the civil war he had been the organizer of victory in the crucial 1948 HuaiHai campaign in central China. For the first seventeen years of the PRC's existence he had been the key liaison between the political leadership and the army, and he was still very popular among the old commanders who were now in control of the country. A number of them traveled to Beijing to meet with him, even though he was still officially in the political wilderness. When Marshal Ye Jianying celebrated his eightieth birthday that spring, Deng was among the guests, and Ye greeted him by saying, "You are the commander of us old marshals." Ye and Deng sat next to each other, holding hands and speaking intimately. Among other things, they spoke about how to handle army affairs after Deng returned to work.[46]

The visible support of leading generals for Deng Xiaoping during and after the Work Conference created a bit of panic among Chairman Hua's closest associates. Wang Dongxing tried to stiffen the chairman's resolve by pointing out that many of those who were now trying to set the political agenda had been criticized, repeatedly, by his predecessor, Chairman Mao, for Rightwing deviations. According to several witnesses, Wang argued against accommodating Marshal Ye Jianying's views too much, and warned the new chairman about the consequences of a rapid return for Deng Xiaoping. But Hua insisted that he would practice democracy within the Central Committee and listen to a wide range of views. Wang Dongxing must have been unconvinced.[47]

Instead of Hua pushing Deng to make concessions in order to return to the leadership, for a while, at least, it seemed to be the other way around. When Wang Dongxing went to see Deng in early April, in order to get him to accept that the Tiananmen demonstrations the year before had been counterrevolutionary, Deng refused point blank. "It does not matter if I can come back to work or not," Deng told him. "The 'Tiananmen Incident' is a revolutionary action."[48] On April 10, Deng sent a letter to Hua, which in form was another acceptance of Hua's elevation and of Mao's criticism of Deng himself. But part of the letter was obviously aimed at the Party leadership's position on the "two whatevers." "From generation to generation," Deng said in an authoritative tone, "we should follow Mao Zedong Thought accurately and completely to guide our whole Party, the army and the people."[49] The emphasis was on *completely*.

Remarkably, Deng urged that his letter should be circulated to all Party leaders. Even more remarkably, Hua agreed, probably because he felt that the letter confirmed Deng's support for the Party leadership as then constituted. When Deng in May assembled some of his former assistants in preparation for his return to work, he made his position and his authority entirely clear. "The 'two whatevers' are unacceptable," Deng said. "If this principle were correct, there could be no justification for my rehabilitation, nor could there be any for the statement that the activities of the masses at Tiananmen Square in 1976 were reasonable. We cannot mechanically apply what Comrade Mao Zedong said about a particular question to another question, what he said in a particular place to another place, what he said at a particular time to another time, or what he said under particular circumstances to other circumstances. . . . When we say we should hold high the banner of Mao Zedong Thought, we mean precisely that we should study and apply Mao Zedong Thought as an ideological system."[50] Deng told them not to worry. "The matter of my returning to work has been settled. As for what type of work I will do, it will certainly include managing the military, and now I am also considering managing science and technology."[51]

At the Central Committee plenary meeting in July, Deng was—as expected—brought back into the leadership, as vice chairman of the CCP Central Committee, vice chairman of the Central Military Commission, and chief of the General Staff of the People's Liberation Army.[52] It was quite a comeback for someone who had been seen as politically dead only a year earlier. But the main event at the plenum was the confirmation of Hua Guofeng as chairman of the CCP Central Committee, as well as premier and chairman of the Central Military Commission. Hua had worried quite a bit about continued support for the Left in the Central Committee, which was probably the reason why he waited nine months after the coup to call a full meeting. With his leadership now confirmed, Hua in his speeches at the plenum, and at the Eleventh Party Congress the following month, concentrated on economic growth. He told the Congress that the Cultural Revolution had been brought to a successful conclusion. Now China had to move rapidly forward with so-

Hua Guofeng, Ye Jianying, Deng Xiaoping, Li Xiannian,
and Wang Dongxing step into the venue of the Eleventh Congress of the
Chinese Communist Party, convened August 12–18, 1977.
Source: World History Archive/Alamy Stock Photo.

cialist construction. Hua's speeches echoed much of the emphasis on production from the final few years of the Mao era, and especially the initiatives
taken by Deng Xiaoping and others in 1975. The way forward, according to
Hua, was to intensify growth within the framework of a planned economy,
and his language at times reflected Great Leap—like phrases about how speed-
ily socialist transformation could be carried out with the right kind of initiative and leadership. In private, however, Hua seemed much more willing to
experiment with new incentives for economic growth, such as decentralization, material incentives, and technology imports. He also emphasized the
need to increase trade with the capitalist world, and initiated a number of
overseas visits by top members of the CCP.[53]

The Party leadership after the Eleventh Congress remained a mix of those
who had thrived during the Cultural Revolution and those who had been sidelined, with the important addition of Deng Xiaoping. In addition to Hua and
Deng, the Politburo Standing Committee consisted of Ye Jianying, Wang
Dongxing, and Li Xiannian. Eleven of the other eighteen Politburo members
were PLA generals. The army was still in charge, with Deng now formally in
charge of day-to-day military affairs. On August 1, when the People's Liberation Army celebrated its seventieth anniversary, there was an audible gasp

from the thousand of officers present when an enormous portrait of Deng, standing in front of a military flag, was carried on stage. Then riotous cheering broke out, with some climbing their chairs to applaud. There was no doubt that Deng's return was willed by the military, as was the whole idea of orderly progress that he seemed to symbolize. Nobody could tell, however, what Deng's actual plans were, or what initiatives he would take.

Neither, it seems, did Deng himself. He brought the staff and advisers he had been working with in 1975 back again, irrespective of what they had said or done in the meantime. When some of them tried to apologize for participating in the campaigns against him, he cut them off, in his usual brusque style. He would have done the same, he told them, if he had been in their position. To those who had not seen him for more than a year, his sense of desperation seemed palpable. China had lost so much time, Deng said, and "we are in a race against time."[54] Not only had China fallen behind in the international competition for production and economic development, but the threat of war was hanging over the country. Even though he did not believe that war between the superpowers was imminent, the PLA should "prepare for the possibility that some countries may want to fight a big war, and soon. For the hegemonists [the Soviets] are desperate, and no one can tell for sure when or where some small incident they create may provoke a war."[55] Deng had taken over Mao's views on the unavoidability of great-power war, making the need to accelerate China's economic development even more desperate.

Both Hua and Deng had made science, technology, and education a key part of the modernizations they sought, in addition to agriculture, industry, and defense. Already in early 1977 Hua had spoken about the need to strengthen education across the board, but especially higher education. Deng agreed with the agenda and pushed it with vigor. At a CCP conference on science and education in August 1977, chaired by Deng, a young assistant professor from Jiangsu was brave enough to suggest that the national college entry exam, the *gaokao*, should be reinstituted. The *gaokao* had been a target of much Red Guard ire during the Cultural Revolution. Deng said that he agreed with the young man and that the exam for 1977 should be prepared immediately.[56] When the ministry came back with the proposed criteria for entry a few weeks later, they emphasized admitting young people whose "political history is clear, love Chairman Mao, love Chairman Hua, support the Communist Party, study the works of Marx and Mao, understand class struggle [and] line struggle and continue our revolutionary awareness," in addition to six other political criteria. Deng wrote on the proposal, "Nonsense. Tedious and cumbersome. . . . Exams should be open to everyone. [Those] who perform well will be admitted on merit."[57]

A total of almost six million people sat the *gaokao* in the winter of 1977. It was the first such exam in more than ten years. Most of those who sat the exam had no high school education, because they had been thrown out of school during the heyday of the Cultural Revolution. And they had only about fifty days to prepare, from when the news was announced to sometime in December, when the exam was to be held in different parts of the country. Most had to study on their own, with the help of family and friends. Young people in work brigades or army detachments got help from the farmers or soldiers they worked with; having a young person succeed in the *gaokao* would reflect well on the whole unit. Sometimes the towns where the exam was to be held were hundreds of miles away and the biggest problem was how to get there. One girl remembers that her collective used its fuel allocation for a whole week to get her part of the way on their tractor.[58]

In addition, there were no textbooks to be found, except in libraries, where the numbers who tried to get in were so immense that readers could only access the building for one hour, according to surname. An enterprising Shanghai publisher began reprinting textbooks from the early 1960s, which soon were worth their weight in gold. Young people in faraway places were pleading to relatives to send the books to them. Soon there was a black market. Printers sold imperfect copies outside the printworks. Textbooks were resold at phenomenal prices.[59] In one part of the country, manuals on tractor repairs, normally in high demand, were exchanged twenty to one for physics textbooks. When the doors to the examination halls were finally opened, few prospective students were surprised that one topic set for Chinese composition was "An unforgettable day." In the end, 278,000 students were admitted for college starting in the fall of 1978.[60] One student, enrolled at Yan'an University in Shaanxi, wrote home to his family about how surprised he was that people in the city were nearly as poor as those in his village. But his admission to college opened a new world for him, with new kinds of people.

One day he even spotted a foreigner on one of the city's bridges. "Most of all," he wrote, "I am grateful to you, my brother and my sister. . . . It is my brother's urging and tutoring that helped me learn, and it is my sister who stood in for me at work, and then cooked delicious meals that gave me the strength to read constantly. . . . I will never be able to repay my brother's and sister's kindness."[61]

8

Visions of China

BY THE END OF 1977 IT WAS CLEAR that the Chinese Communist Party had been able to survive the immediate aftermath of the death of its paramount leader without disintegration or civil war. Given how badly split the Party had been only a year before, this was no mean feat. Most of the acclaim for the achievement, if we call it that, belonged to Hua Guofeng. He had led the coup against Mao's widow and her Left-wing associates, he had brought the army and the security forces on board with the new regime, and he had carried out a limited and controlled purge against the Left. Through all of this he had been able to protect the memory of Mao Zedong while bringing some of those Mao had gotten rid of back to the leadership. Hua had also set out a strict priority for improving the economy, and indicated that he wanted to see much more Party democracy in the discussions about how to achieve economic success. Hua, it seemed, was much less fearful of top-Party rivals than he was of socialist China failing in its quest for modernity.

Chairman Hua's approach was understandable. Even though there were many policy differences and personal conflicts among top CCP leaders after the coup, there was also much that united them. The first was a fear of the Cultural Revolution Left and its possible return to power. Even though Jiang Qing and the three other Politburo members were held incommunicado at the high-security Qincheng Prison just outside Beijing, and their closest adherents had been arrested or purged, it was still quite obvious that Left-wing arguments and positions had influence in the Party. A majority of Party members had, after all, joined during the Cultural Revolution. But the regime was also held together by its dedication to Party rule, and by the worry that the CCP could be challenged internally or externally. And then there was the over-all dread of war and that China could be attacked by the Soviets. All key Party leaders held fast to Mao's conviction that war was coming and that China could at any time be a victim of foreign aggression.

Even if it was fear rather than hope that held the Party leadership together, ordinary Chinese had begun to dream of a better future. By the late 1970s, the immense energy that many people had poured into the revolutionary project—all the unrewarded work, rallying, sacrifice, and faith—was being turned toward simply improving one's lot through personal or family advance-ment. This was not a sudden transformation; by 1980 there were still firm believers in Communism, just as there had been those who prioritized per-sonal gain a decade earlier. But the balance was shifting, both because of changes from below and because Party rhetoric had become less strident. Some Chinese remember the reintroduction of the gaokao—the college en-trance exam—as a turning point, after which personal improvement seemed possible.[1] But the gaokao only affected a small number of people in a country where the vast majority lived in the countryside and about half were illiter-ate. For change to be believable, it would have to extend to these parts of the country, too.

By the late 1970s China had spent two decades without any substantial pro-gress in agricultural production, and the situation was getting desperate. Output had barely kept pace with the increase in population, and in some areas not even that.[2] The Party's own reports show how precarious the situa-tion was in many parts of the countryside. Even very small changes in weather or work conditions could set off hunger disasters in many provinces.[3] All but the richest areas—Guangdong and the Yangzi delta region—were still grind-ingly poor, and in some places poorer than what they had been when the Com-munists came to power in 1949. Even though the Party leadership recognized that a food crisis was brewing if action was not taken immediately, the CCP spent less time on the direction economic reform should take than on the Party's internal problems and, especially, how to view its own past. These is-sues were of course to some extent linked, although the reform preferred by most senior cadre, at least in the immediately aftermath of the coup, seemed to be a return to the strict planning regime of the 1950s. Chen Yun, who had been at the forefront of China's economic development up to 1962, when he was sidelined by Mao, made his return to Chinese politics in 1977 with a plea for strengthening national planning as a key instrument for realizing the Four Modernizations.[4] Deng Xiaoping, who underlined China's deficiencies more than anyone in the leadership, also seemed to prefer stringent and coordinated economic planning.[5] Neither Chen nor Deng were adverse to experimentation in order to increase production, especially in agriculture. But both clearly believed that it was the disorderly damage the radicals had done to the Chinese economy that had led the country to the edge of the precipice.[6]

Given Hua Guofeng's own rural background, it is not surprising that he took the lead in attempting to kick-start China's agricultural development. Together with Ji Dengkui, who had been given the difficult post of Politburo member in charge of agriculture, Hua wanted to pick what he saw as the best practices from the Mao era, including slogans from the early Great Leap Forward, to achieve a breakthrough in the countryside. After all, the Great Leap had been about maximizing production, and fast, even though Hua saw with some clarity how the actual policies implemented back in 1958 had led to disaster. When Hua spoke about "learning from Dazhai," he sometimes implied the opposite of what had been the policy under Mao, at least as propagated by Chen Yonggui, the former head of that People's Commune who was now a vice premier. While Chen argued for ever larger units of production and distribution, Hua drew somewhat different lessons. He emphasized the autonomy of brigades and production teams and even, on occasion, increasing the size of private plots and the setting up of produce markets. In early 1978 Chairman Hua went even further. At the Fifth National People's Congress, he called for a significant increase in the price the state paid for agricultural products, reducing the negative trend in farming prices versus prices for industrial goods.[7] Hua also reduced the requisitioning of corvée labor in the countryside. No longer, he declared, could farmers be ordered to offer their labor to big state projects without their consent and proper pay.[8] Both initiatives helped improve agricultural output already in 1978, when production increased by more than 10 percent.[9]

But even if changes in policy at the Center were important for improvements in agriculture, what happened in the provinces was even more significant, especially for future directions. A number of provinces had begun, or in most cases simply allowed, new practices to increase production in rural areas. The two best known cases of early reform are Anhui and Sichuan.

These two provinces are very different. Anhui was (and still is) the poorest province in eastern China, with a long history of hunger disasters and economic underdevelopment. Sichuan, the most populous province in China, located in the fertile western basin bordering the Tibetan highlands, had been, at least in parts, a rich place, but one that seemed to have gone backwards since the Communists took over. Zhao Ziyang, the new CCP first secretary of Sichuan, who had arrived there in 1975, remembers seeing village after village living in real poverty. The following year his government had to import half a million tons of grain from other provinces to stave off starvation.[10] Zhao began allowing farmers to experiment with rice planting and pig rearing, making use of local knowledge rather than *diktat* from the Center, and allowing farmers to keep more of their income.[11] The results were immediate. Agricultural output in Sichuan increased by 6 percent in 1977.

Zhao Ziyang, a Henan native, had spent the first part of his CCP career in Guangdong, where he by 1965 had risen to become the youngest Party secretary of any Chinese province. Known in the early 1960s as an agricultural reformer with strong military links, he was purged during the Cultural Revolution, paraded by Red Guards through the streets of Guangzhou with a dunce cap on, and then dispatched to a small town in Hunan as an industrial worker. In 1971, to his own great surprise, he was called back to serve as deputy Party secretary in Inner Mongolia, a province regarded as the front line in the conflict with the Soviet Union. While in Inner Mongolia he stuck close enough to the Maoist script to be promoted in 1975, during Deng's brief comeback, to first secretary of Sichuan.[12] And, having embarked on a reformist course in his new province, Zhao's convictions and ambitions came to the fore. Picking up on Hua Guofeng's new agricultural policies, Zhao was quick to experiment with incentives and markets, expanding private plots and providing credit for irrigation and fertilization. In 1977 he reduced the burden of taxation on farmers and allowed poor counties to keep more of the food they produced. Zhao also set up a system of output allocations, where each work team was rewarded for fulfilling its production quota and allowed to keep any surplus itself.[13] As a consequence, in 1978 the results were even better than the previous year: a whopping 18 percent increase in output for food production.

If Sichuan had been a terrible case of agricultural underperformance, Anhui was a veritable disaster zone. Things had always been bad in large parts of this province, where dust-dry and poor land provided only a meager outcome for farmers during the best of times. Under the Communists things had gotten worse. In 1976 total agricultural output was below what it had been twenty years before and was not much more than it had been in 1949.[14] In parts of the province people were starving, and whole villages were depopulated because the survivors had gone begging elsewhere in the region.[15] According to one villager's account, it was common to eat grass and tree bark, and they might go months between each meal of rice.[16] When the veteran Communist Wan Li arrived as first secretary in early summer of 1977, he found it difficult to believe how bad conditions were in the countryside. Wan was 61 years old; he had joined the CCP in 1936, and during the wars he had fought in various places all over China. After 1949 he had become a Party troubleshooter, first on national construction projects and then in the Beijing city government, until he was purged and sent for reeducation through hard labor in 1967. He returned with Deng Xiaoping in 1973 and had served as minister of railways before he was sent to govern Anhui. Wan had no experience with agriculture, but he realized immediately how bad things were, and began making use of Hua Guofeng's new policy signals to think about alternative solutions.

Wan's arrival in Anhui coincided with the worst drought the province had experienced for more than twenty years. In the villages, people feared a return to the hunger disasters of the Great Leap, which had been particularly bad in Anhui. Acting on their own initiative, some farmers began dividing up collective land, animals, and tools for private production, believing that each family unit could best fend for itself in case of an immediate catastrophe. They knew well enough that the government would do little to help, and deemed the communes to be useless under these circumstances. Realizing how desperate the situation was, Wan Li decided to ignore the new practices, accepting local CCP officials' view that decollectivization should neither be publicized nor advocated, but neither should it be prohibited.[17] In de facto breaking up the collectives, farmers were inspired both by older practices and by more recent events. Some remembered the experiments with production incentives in the early 1960s, and many had heard about how collectives in other parts of the country had begun semi-private ventures from the early 1970s on. But, first and foremost, decollectivization simply meant a return to family farming, in which farmers took back land that had been theirs before the collectives were set up. Those who had reared ducks went back to rearing ducks. Those who had grown vegetables went back to growing vegetables. And rice farmers, who for generations had made their own decisions about planting and harvesting, started making these decisions again.[18] As a result, there was hunger in Anhui in 1978 and early 1979, but no widespread famine. Output increased just about enough to prevent disaster.

While spontaneous decollectivization undoubtedly saved lives in these lean years, it was far from being any kind of official policy anywhere. Even officials such as Zhao and Wan accepted it as an interim measure rather than a recipe for the future. Decollectivization from below only happened in a few places, and even in these places it did not mean that the collectives were gone. Most farmers still depended on machinery and distribution through the commune, and most of the production was still bought by the state at fixed prices. There were also all kinds of entanglements and conflicts over rights and justice. Could farmers buy tools from the collective? Who had the right to farm animals—those who had brought livestock to the production team in the first place, or those who had raised the animals prior to decollectivization? Who had the right to the use of land—those who had owned it prior to 1949, those who had owned it after land reform, or those who were working it in the 1970s? Fields cultivated by one family could be scattered all over the village, and assistance from neighbors may be needed at the peaks of the farming year, during sowing and reaping. In many places collective practices had existed before the Communists took over and, of course, some communes were both productive and popular among their members. Even though spontaneous decollectivization was occurring, it would take a long time for policies and practices to change, or at least so most people thought in 1977 and 1978.

With the countryside still barely keeping its head above water in the battle for survival, factional infighting at the top level of politics continued. Two of the old marshals, Nie Rongzhen and Xu Xiangqian, legendary figures from the civil war era, wrote articles in *Renmin ribao* right after the Eleventh Party Congress where they stressed the need for practical experience. "Stubbornly oppose [attempts at] taking a few phrases from Marxism-Leninism and Mao Zedong Thought and making them dogmas separate from time, space, and conditions," Nie wrote.[19] Chen Yun followed up on September 28, publishing an article in which he "insisted on a revolutionary style of seeking truth from facts."[20] Hua Guofeng did not see these articles as attacks on him and made clear that they should be discussed among Party members.[21] But Wang Dongxing was furious, seeing them not just as attacks on current CCP leaders but, worse, as assaults against Chairman Mao himself.[22] The powerful Wang's ire was even greater when the deputy director of the CCP's Central Party School, Hu Yaobang, a month later published an article in which he stated, as a matter of fact, that it was the Party's erroneous policies on cadre selection that had produced the Gang of Four and their adherents, and that the CCP therefore had to radically reform how it operated internally.[23] Again, Chairman Hua ordered that no action should be taken, even though the implications of Hu Yaobang's views were that the ways in which the CCP had operated in the past were fundamentally unsound.[24]

Hu Yaobang was 62 years old in 1977, a son of poor farmers in Hunan who joined the Communist movement when he was thirteen years old, and had been a child soldier in the CCP army before he became a political commissar and head of the Communist Youth League (CYL).[25] Fiercely intelligent, but with no formal education, Hu had a history of calling things as he saw them, which had gotten him into trouble on several occasions. Still, he survived all accusations up to the Cultural Revolution, in part because of the close relations he had with Deng Xiaoping, who then headed the Party organization.[26] Moreover, as head of the CYL Hu had a unique opportunity to work with younger leaders as they made their way up the Party hierarchy, and many saw him as their main leader and mentor. His politics were eclectic; he was a serious student of Marxism but also attracted by Mao's message of individual liberation and revolutionary spirit. Like Deng, he was a nationalist who worried about China's slow progress and was constantly on the lookout for methods that could help the country advance.

After a furious conflict with Leftists within the CYL in 1967, Hu was detained by Red Guards and forced to work as a janitor at CYL headquarters in Beijing. He then spent two years in prison before he was sent to herd cattle at a labor camp in Henan. Hu said that he was lucky to survive the Cultural Revolution, and given the special hatred that some of the Left's leaders reserved for him, he was undoubtedly right.[27] When Deng reemerged in central politics in 1973, he insisted on bringing Hu with him, this time to lead the work of the Chinese Academy of Sciences.[28] He spent the years up to 1975 fighting the Left and insisting that science should take priority over politics in research and education.[29] When Deng fell in early 1976, Hu was purged with him, and many thought this would have been his last foray into top politics. But his demise turned out to be brief. Already in the spring of 1977 Hu was back as a senior official, rescued by Hua Guofeng. His new job at the revived Central Party School put him in pole position to influence the training of Party cadre and also, at least in his own view, to pronounce on organizational issues within the Party. When Deng returned, he stuck by his old mentee. Not only did Deng protect Hu from attacks by Maoists of the Wang Dongxing kind; Deng also insisted on making Hu head of the CCP's Organizational Department, the office that proposes cadre for positions within the Party and deals with purges and rehabilitations. Deng's choice was a brave one given the amount of controversy Hu had created in his earlier political life. But the old leader thought that stirring things up a bit would help the Party move forward, not least in terms of dealing with issues of the past.

By spring 1978 it was clear that the tension in the Party leadership would be difficult to paper over, even in the short run. The irony was that not so much divided the top leaders in terms of policy, but in terms of status and legitimacy there were huge divides. They were also haunted by the past; those who had been purged during the Cultural Revolution wanted to be fully restituted politically, even if they had already rejoined the leadership. And those who had risen during the past ten years were fearful that their association with the Cultural Revolution would harm them politically, even if they were part of the post-coup government. Hua Guofeng was about the only top leader who believed that long-term political compromises could be worked out by extending Party democracy and by focusing on rapid economic development. In early 1978 Chairman Hua, now termed "the wise leader" in official propaganda, believed that the anti-Left purges should soon be brought to an end and that leaders who still had not been rehabilitated after the Cultural Revolution should be brought back to work. "Why is it," he asked in a note, "that some old cadres cannot be liberated? Why can there not be reciprocal forgiveness?"[30]

In spite of joining Hua in the push for economic development, Deng Xiaoping, for understandable reasons, looked differently at the past. Having been cautious after his return, making sure to stick to his military and education briefs, Deng was emboldened by the degree to which other veteran cadre looked to him for leadership. In addition to his old team, which he had brought together again right after his return, he started reaching out to reformist provincial leaders, such as Zhao Ziyang and Wan Li. In February 1978, Deng flew straight to Chengdu, the capital of Sichuan, after a visit to Burma, and had long talks with Zhao.[31] In private conversations, Deng was dismissive of the leadership qualities of those who had been brought in by Mao during the Cultural Revolution. He often accused them of not understanding how urgent China's need for development was, even though his own ideas about economic expansion were as unclear as theirs. But, in his mind, Deng had formed an opinion of his recently elevated colleagues not only as complicit in the persecution of himself and other senior cadre during the Cultural Revolution, but as laggards on the way to much-needed reform, prioritizing political correctness over practical projects. He may not have been actively conspiring against them, but he certainly did not hold them, including Chairman Hua, in great respect.

During the first part of 1978, debates within the CCP over the past and the future seemed to break in ways that accentuated antagonisms that already existed. In his haste to deal with past injustices, already in December 1977 Hu Yaobang authorized wall posters at the Central Party School attacking Kang Sheng, the Party's former spymaster, now safely dead for two years.[32] Kang, the posters said, had contributed to many people having been unjustly persecuted in the Cultural Revolution and before. Wang Dongxing prevented the criticism from being aired in public. Hua Guofeng supported Wang, saying that it was an old Chinese custom to not speak ill of the dead. Deng Xiaoping, who privately called Kang Sheng an unprincipled scoundrel, decided to hold off; he told Hu that it was more important to proceed with rehabilitating old cadre than dealing with the perpetrators, at least for now.

From late 1977 on Hu Yaobang headed a process that over the next two years would see almost all of those purged during the Cultural Revolution rehabilitated.[33] But Hu wanted to go further, as his attack on Kang Sheng showed. He wanted to deal with injustices in the Party going back to the 1930s: people who had been unjustly persecuted or excluded, false accusations, and blanket condemnations. In his view, the CCP had to deal with all the grievances coming out of the past in order to save itself after the Cultural Revolution. He instructed the CCP Organizational Department, as well as its offices in the provinces and localities, to encourage survivors to write letters seeking rehabilitation for themselves or for relatives or friends long dead. The Party, he said, would deal justly with all cases.[34] As we have seen, Hua Guofeng supported a gradual process of rehabilitation, but he instructed that it should be conducted in an orderly fashion and without blaming Mao Zedong or cadre who still held responsible positions. The latter, it turned out, would be a difficult instruction to abide by.

In the spring of 1978, Chairman Hua moved to consolidate the new leadership through holding meetings of the National People's Congress and the Chinese People's Political Consultative Conference. The People's Congress—China's putative parliament—had only met once over the past fifteen years, and most people assumed that both it and the Political Consultative Conference had become irrelevant to the governance of China. Hua thought otherwise. Calling the two meetings gave him and other leaders the opportunity to stress how the country had entered a new era of order and progress. Politically, Hua declared, the big campaigns against enemies of the revolution were now over and the union of the Party and the people had been perfected. In his usual slow and passionless delivery, he told the People's Congress that the CCP valued socialist democracy and lawfulness.[35] The new national constitution, which he introduced, promulgated annual meetings of the Congress and the strengthening of the judiciary. Building on what had been added during the Cultural Revolution, it underlined the rights for all Chinese "to speak out freely, air their views fully, hold great debates, and write big-character posters."[36] In his concluding speech, Hua spoke about getting rid of old work habits and setting people's thinking free.[37]

The new constitution also spelled out in law the resolve to make China "a great and powerful socialist country with modern agriculture, industry, national defense, and science and technology by the end of the century."[38] Most of the two meetings dealt with economic issues, with Hua presenting dramatic plans for China's industrial growth. He envisaged almost a doubling of China's production capacity within five years, with new steel mills, manufacturing plants, and oil and gas fields being constructed in different parts of the country.[39] Unmentioned at the public meetings, the CCP leadership wanted to finance much of this development by foreign credits; by summer 1978 Hua spoke of an import program that could have cost, over ten years, more than US$30 billion. Even the most development-oriented leaders among the old CCP cadres, including Chen Yun, felt that Hua wanted to move too quickly and with too much focus on heavy industry. Privately Chen warned that such massive programs would create serious imbalances in the Chinese economy.[40] But the growth plans were popular among the delegates, and Hua relished being seen as their originator.

The general sense in the leadership was that the meetings in spring 1978 had gone well for the Party, in spite of the ongoing worries among some about the evaluation of the past and the pace of the rehabilitation campaigns. Quite a number of leaders, including reform-oriented apparatchiks such as Li Xiannian, Hu Qiaomu, and Deng Liqun, believed it was best to leave well enough alone, at least for now. Hu Yaobang and his associates from the Central Party School disagreed. Their writers and journals kept publishing material on the need for quick rehabilitations and a thorough investigation of the past.[41] They also took a stand on key ideological questions. In late March 1978, *Renmin ribao* published an article underlining that practice is the only criterion for testing what is true or not. Marxism and Mao Zedong Thought are true, but they are not in themselves criteria for testing everything.[42] Hidden away inside the paper, the article had few immediate repercussions, but when the *Guangming Daily* six weeks later published a longer article arguing the same point, which was soon reprinted both in *Renmin Ribao* and the *People's Liberation Army Daily*, the main military newspaper, all hell broke loose.[43] Wang Dongxing and other Party leaders accused the editors of major errors of judgment, or worse. "Which Party center is this the opinion of?" Wang yelled. "This incident must be investigated, people must be taught a lesson, [our] thinking must be unified. This must not set a precedent."[44] On May 18 Wang told the editor of *Red Flag*, the Party's principal theoretical journal, that these articles opposed Mao Zedong and in no way reflected the thinking of the Party Center. Newspapers should be more careful, Wang said. And their editors needed more "Party spirit."[45]

There is no evidence that Deng Xiaoping knew about the plans to publish an article that so directly attacked not only the idea of the "two whatevers" but also the principle that ideology should be the yardstick for CCP policies. After reading the article, he held off for a while, while Hu Yaobang and others were attacked by Party hardliners or, in some cases, by some of Deng's own associates. Hu Qiaomu was among those warning Hu Yaobang that he had gone too far. "The debate was started by you. It is targeted against Chairman Hua. Chairman Hua is already unhappy; Wang Dongxing has already started asking which Party center you represent. If this debate continues, it will inevitably cause a new split in the Party!"[46] Hu Yaobang, however, stuck to his guns. He claimed that thousands of ordinary Party members had written to the newspapers in support, especially from military units that had read the article in the *People's Liberation Army Daily.*[47]

Deng may have noticed the same. On June 2, in what was to be a watershed in the inner Party debates, Deng spoke out forcefully in front of a PLA audience. "Many comrades in our Party are persistent in their study of Marxism-Leninism and Mao Zedong Thought," he began.

> This is very good and should certainly be encouraged. There are other comrades, however, who talk about Mao Zedong Thought every day, but who often forget, abandon, or even oppose Comrade Mao's fundamental Marxist viewpoint and his method of seeking truth from facts, of always proceeding from reality and of integrating theory with practice. Some people even go further: they maintain that those who persist in seeking truth from facts, proceeding from reality and integrating theory with practice, are guilty of a heinous crime. In essence, their view is that one need only parrot what was said by Marx, Lenin and Comrade Mao Zedong—that it is enough to reproduce their words mechanically. According to them, to do otherwise is to go against Marxism-Leninism and Mao Zedong Thought and against the guidelines of the Central Committee. This issue they have raised is no minor one, for it involves our general approach to Marxism-Leninism and Mao Zedong Thought.[48]

Deng was undoubtedly attacking some of his fellow Party leaders, including Wang Dongxing. Was he also attacking Chairman Hua? To most of those who read the speech, Hua glared mostly by his absence. Nowhere, in a fairly lengthy speech on ideology, did Deng mention the Party chairman. For most leaders, both at the center and in the provinces, Deng's speech, and the fact that it was left publicly uncontested, proved that Deng Xiaoping posed an alternative as head of the CCP. Never mind that both Hua and Deng went out of their way to heap praise on each other later that summer. The genie was out of the bottle. Together with Deng's statement to a group of visiting U.S. Communists that the 1976 Tiananmen rally "was by no means a counterrevolutionary event," his "seek truth from facts" speech underlined his position within the Party, and allowed others to step forward to criticize senior leaders.[49] In late July 1978 *Renmin Ribao* published an article openly accusing

Beijing Party boss Wu De of blocking a reversal of verdicts handed down during the Cultural Revolution including, implicitly, the Tiananmen events.[50] After Wu complained to Hua Guofeng, the chairman told the editors that the problem was not the article itself but that the authors did not request prior permission.[51] As a consequence, Wu was left politically dead. He offered to resign in September, although the Party leadership did not grant his wish until the end of the year.[52]

In the summer of 1978, the stage was set for political confrontations that would change China's political future. Other leaders soon started using Deng Xiaoping's and Hu Yaobang's formulations, without reference to Hua Guofeng. Hua was silent, while Hu and others began criticizing some of the chairman's closest associates as "whateverists," Hu's favored term for those who stood by Maoist approaches. General Luo Ruiqing, purged by Mao in 1966 but now back in the Central Military Commission, started using the same phrase. Pale and in dreadful pain after his suicide attempt, Luo haunted the halls of the Zhongnanhai until he died in August 1978, a reminder of the terrible violence of the past. Over the next few months, Party committees throughout China one by one fell in line with Hu Yaobang and Deng Xiaoping by starting to use the phrases "seeking truth from facts" and "practice is the sole criterion for truth." Defining terminologies always matters in politics, and in Chinese politics more than most. Throughout the CCP, Deng Xiaoping now presented himself as having more "practice" and therefore more "truth."[53] The new formulae confirmed his senior position, irrespective of the titles other leaders may have held.

Some of Deng's advisers made use of the new slogans to propose thorough overhauls of economic principles. The economist Yu Guangyuan, who had studied rewards systems in Yugoslavia and Hungary, wanted China to go much further than what had hitherto been proposed in terms of material incentives for workers. "The Communist Party of China," Yu argued, "seeks to maximize the material interests available to the proletariat and all working people. Distribution according to work reflects the principle of material interests which, in the socialist context, means linking socialist production to individual, collective, local, departmental, and corporate interests. Distribution according to work is essentially a matter of material interests, with more pay granted for more work."[54]

While the Party leaders squabbled, pressure for more radical change was building from below. Since early summer, more and more wall posters had gone up in the cities demanding that the CPP listen to the voice of the people. There was no unified message; some called for democracy, some for workers' autonomy, and some for a deepening of socialism. Many were concerned with personal or political grievances, the need for rehabilitations, or the right for sent-down youth to return to their place of birth. Some simply pointed out that people in parts of the country were starving, and that the Communist Party did not seem to care. There were some that warned against revisionism, and a few that lauded Jiang Qing and condemned the 1976 coup. Overall, though, officials in the provinces found it harder and harder to manage the situation without clearer orders from the Center. Some resigned; caught between the Party they served and rising popular anger, stepping down or claiming illness seemed the best way out.

In the midst of this commotion, only Hua Guofeng seemed unflappable. He ensured his associates that everything was going according to plan and that the processes of gradual change were working. His own attention was squarely on the economy, and in the fall he spent much time working on problems in agriculture. Hua decided to call another Central Committee work conference to discuss economic issues and to make sure that provincial and military leaders were fully on board with the reform plans. He also wanted to listen to advice on particular sectors of the economy, first and foremost agriculture, but also industry, infrastructure, and foreign trade.[55] The Work Conference first met on November 9, 1978. From then until March 1979 the Party leadership sat for a series of almost continuous meetings, which in fundamental ways decided the CCP's future.

From Chairman Hua's perspective, the Work Conference went wrong from the very beginning. In his optimistic opening speech, he stressed "orderly and steady" progress, the end of political campaigns, and the goal of achieving "socialist modernization, which urgently demands that we mobilize the whole Party and nation to focus their attention on it." "Capitalists in Eastern Europe, Japan and North America have seen the emerging environment of stability and unity in our country," Hua reported, "and [they] are all fighting to do business with us. Such a favorable situation is unprecedented since the founding of our state."[56] But when the participants dispersed into small groups to discuss the chairman's speech, many of the groups decided that they wanted to deal with historical issues first. As he had done in the spring, Chen Yun was at the forefront of the criticism. On November 12 Chen told his group that the Party could not move forward until the injustices of the past had been rectified.[57] Others agreed. Wang Renzhong, the former Party secretary of Hubei Province who had been purged during the Cultural Revolution, put it succinctly: "We must first solve the problems that are not conducive to stability and unity."[58]

Chen Yun listed a number of issues that should be reconsidered by the Party. A large group of Party leaders, including Bo Yibo and An Ziwen, who had been condemned as traitors during the Cultural Revolution, should be exonerated. Other leaders, including Peng Dehuai, should have their cases reevaluated. The verdict on the Tiananmen protests should be overturned. And the Party should condemn Kang Sheng's "serious mistakes."[59] All of these were issues Hua Guofeng had tried to go slow on in order to avoid splitting the Party leadership. But Chen Yun's statement opened up a barrage of criticism of his measured policy. Seeing the support the criticism had among senior leaders, Hua immediately granted some of their wishes. On November 14 the CCP Beijing city committee declared the Tiananmen protesters revolutionaries who had acted out of "infinite love" for Premier Zhou Enlai. They should all have their verdicts overturned.[60] Ten days later the chairman agreed to deal with all of Chen Yun's other issues, too. He told his associates that he did not find it difficult. For him it had been a question of timing, not substance. Hua declared to the conference that now it was time to turn to economic issues.[61]

But the floodgates had opened. On November 22, Wang Dongxing was criticized by name for his role during the Cultural Revolution. Several speakers stressed the need to return to collective leadership and spoke out against any cult of personality, including for the Party chairman. At one point, General Xu Shiyou accused Hua Guofeng's close associate Ji Dengkui of having been "promoted as a Leftist rebel, entered the Politburo with high rank, what was that all about? You basically went with the Gang of Four."[62] Military leaders demanded that several members of the Politburo conduct self-criticism. Hua remained silent until the end of the Work Conference in December, when he, encouraged by Ye Jianying and others, decided to put a brave face to the criticism in his concluding speech.[63]

At some point during the conference, Deng Xiaoping decided that Hua's paramount position would have to go. What drove him to this conclusion seems to have been a combination of personal ambition and consensus views, alongside the barrage of criticism of the Party's past. At first, after he returned from a visit to Southeast Asia on November 14, Deng had been silent about the rising tide of remonstrances, even to the point of recommending a return to Hua's planned economic agenda for the meeting. He then turned to underlining the "facts" and "practice" slogans, with the clear indication that Hua had not done enough to support these. But from late November onward, it was enough for Deng to indicate support for demands and criticism raised by others; he did not have to do much himself to reduce Hua's position. Increasingly, those who criticized the outcome of the Cultural Revolution looked to Deng as their and the Party's main leader.[64]

Hua must have felt that he was in a strange position. On the one hand, he had done more than anyone else to encourage Party democracy and free discussion. On the other, it was now clear that much of this freedom would be used to criticize him and his leadership. A bit like Mikhail Gorbachev in the Soviet Union a decade later, Hua had opened the floodgates for a wave that threatened to drown him. Moreover, there was an alternative leader, Deng Xiaoping, with much more support among senior cadre than what he himself had. The more Hua encouraged the rectification of past mistakes, the more he opened himself up to criticism for having been complicit in those mistakes. Nobody did the same for Deng, even if he was at least as guilty in encouraging Mao's megalomania and disregard for human life as Hua was. What separated them was that Deng had been part of the CCP leadership since the 1930s and purged during part of the Cultural Revolution, while Hua's rise was only connected to the final disastrous decade of Mao Zedong's life.

In his final speech to the Work Conference, which would also be his final speech as China's supreme leader, Hua said the meeting had

> fully embraced the spirit of democracy, enabled everyone to speak freely and tapped the collective wisdom. . . . Everyone was able to emancipate their minds, speak up, and voice their criticisms, including those directed at the work of the Central Committee. Like many comrades have said, this is something that we have not seen in many years of Party life. . . . I sought to defend all the policy decisions Chairman Mao had made and suppress all words and actions that tarnished his image. . . . Thinking about it now, I wished I had not proposed the "two whatevers." Although my words . . . were read, discussed,

and approved by the Politburo, I ought to shoulder the main responsibility. I should engage in self-criticism on this issue.[65]

Hua ended his speech unassumingly by encouraging participants to stop addressing their requests or reports to him personally. Instead, they should be sent to the Central Committee. Party members should no longer address him as "wise leader," just as "comrade," Hua said. At the Central Committee's Third Plenum, which started right after the Work Conference ended, the chairman's wishes were fulfilled to a greater extent than what he had bargained for. Hua was entirely brushed aside by Deng Xiaoping and his associates, who set the agenda for the meeting both on dealing with the past and with the new reform agenda. Before the Third Plenum, Deng had not argued for the immediate rehabilitation of all Cultural Revolution victims, nor had he advocated the wholesale condemnation of the Cultural Revolution itself. But, having looked at the events of the Work Conference and encouraged by Hu Yaobang and others, Deng now felt that it was time to go further than before. Presumably, Deng was also concerned that other leaders from the past, Chen Yun especially, would steal his thunder. Part of Deng's political genius was to fit himself to the times while presenting his own take on events. And the December 1978 Third Plenum was a masterpiece in this regard.

Although the Third Plenum does not deserve the place it has been given in official CCP historiography, as the starting point for all things reform, it was a remarkable meeting as a symbol of change. While economic reform, both from below and from above, had started well before December 1978, the plenum summarized the direction the Party wanted to go in better than anything that had been presented until then. In its final communique, it underlined the need for China to work with other countries to improve its economy. It stressed decentralization and individual responsibility in economic development, saying, bluntly, that "power is too concentrated, and leadership should be boldly delegated to allow local and industrial and agricultural enterprises to have more autonomy in operation and management."[66] It called for the implementation of continuous assessment, rewards and penalties, and promotion systems. In agriculture, the meeting wanted to overcome egalitarianism through distribution according to work, remuneration based on the quantity and quality of labor, and the development of private plots, family sideline jobs, and markets. None of this was new, and it reflected a reasonable degree of consensus among post-1976 Party leaders. But it was said more daringly, and—as Deng liked—in ways that people could understand.

More important than its economic message was the shift in political power from Hua to Deng. In spite of the somewhat lame conclusion to the document, calling for the Party to unite around the Central Committee headed by Hua Guofeng, it was now clear where authority lay. "In 1975," the communique said, "when Comrade Deng Xiaoping was entrusted by Comrade Mao Zedong to preside over the work of the Central Committee, great achievements were made in all aspects of work, and the whole party, the whole army and the people of the whole country were satisfied."[67] It could not be said more clearly: this may have been the past, but it was the future, too. It meant more predictability and order. But, while the communique was cautious about any future verdict on the Cultural Revolution and on Mao Zedong, it was clear on what was needed to avoid the chaos of the past: a new legal system had to be built, which safeguarded the independence of the judiciary and ensured that everyone was equal before the law. It was this part that stood out to most Chinese who read the communique. Could it be possible that the Party would give up parts of its power to impartial officials?

In addition to its political statements, the Third Plenum meant significant changes at the top. While Hua kept his position, at least in name, other Cultural Revolution beneficiaries, such as Wang Dongxing, Ji Dengkui, and Chen Xilian, saw their standing reduced. Wang lost both the command of the Center security forces and his position coordinating the Central Committee general office. None of them were purged, but they were kept in political limbo until they lost all of their political positions at the beginning of 1980. In their place, those who had been purged during the Cultural Revolution rose again. Chen Yun became head of the CCP's Central Disciplinary Commission. Hu Yaobang became secretary-general of the Central Committee. A number of reformers rejoined the Central Committee, including the formerly much-criticized Xi Zhongxun, who became Party boss in Guangdong Province. After the Third Plenum, there was never any doubt that it was the senior cadre who had ruled China prior to the Cultural Revolution who were back in charge.

But the open inner-Party discussion of the past and the future did not stop after the Third Plenum. Hu Yaobang and his associates from the Central Party School and the Academy of Social Sciences organized a central Theory Conference in early 1979, which saw much more profound criticism of the CCP and Chinese society, and much more radical reform plans, than the two Party meetings that preceded it. At the beginning of the gathering, one delegate stood up and announced that now, thirty years after the PRC was founded, "two hundred million people still do not have enough to eat. . . . Comrades, something, somewhere, must have gone terribly wrong!"[68] Delegates then attacked the Great Leap Forward and the Cultural Revolution, pointing out that Mao Zedong carried the main responsibility for both of these disastrous mistakes. In photos from the meeting, one can see delegates from all over the country, with flushed faces, speaking their minds for perhaps the first time in their life. There was little that could not be criticized or proposed. Communist delegates called for freedom of speech and for human rights. Others demanded the rule of law and the end to Party dictatorship. "Continuing the revolution under the dictatorship of the proletariat," as the Third Plenum had called for, "is a fundamental problem, which involves [the legacy of] Comrade Mao Zedong," shouted one participant.[69]

This wave of criticism did not just center on domestic affairs. The former diplomat Huan Xiang, now with the Academy of Social Sciences, took aim at the fundamentals of Maoist foreign policy. "The development of domestic Leftist ideas over the past twenty years is also related to . . . the debates in the international Communist movement," Huan began. He then proceeded to dismantle the whole edifice of China's foreign policy ideology. Defending Stalin had been wrong, as had the attacks on Yugoslavia. "Previous comments on Khrushchev's false communism and its lessons for world history were fundamentally wrong," Huan told a hushed audience, and the CCP's international positions had been based on misunderstandings of economics, ideology, and politics abroad. The Party had promoted cults of personality, and "Lin Biao, Kang Sheng, and the Gang of Four had taken advantage of this to market their intrigues. The 'two whatevers' is the continuation of such cults of personality."[70] Other delegates went even further. One accused the CCP of having created a form of "feudal fascism" and demanded not only the abolition of the dictatorship but that the Party should immediately start discussing how democracy could be introduced in China.[71]

The 1979 Theory Conference was a unique moment in the history of the CCP. As one participant put it, it was so free because it fit both with the need from above, meaning Deng's wish to attack the "two whatevers," and pressure from below, meaning the increasingly plentiful meetings and marches demanding justice and freedom. As the conference progressed in January and February 1979, assembling almost five hundred delegates, there were increasing links with the protest movements outside the Great Hall of the People, where the conference was held. Delegates organized "evening salons," where they met with people from the city or those who had traveled to the capital to inveigh against past injustices. In a few cases there was even a taste of direct democracy, when some units claimed that they did not like what their delegates had said, and replaced them with others. One evening, a few younger Party delegates organized an informal competition to find the most outrageous Mao quotes for common entertainment. It was a world so different from what anyone could have imagined only in the past summer.[72]

Meanwhile, in other parts of Beijing and elsewhere in China, a wave of protest was rising. Suddenly, it was not just one group that was protesting; it seemed to be almost everyone at the same time. People who had been persecuted during the Communist era, for whatever reason, but especially those who had been terrorized during the Cultural Revolution, staged local protests or sent petitioners to the provincial capitals or to Beijing. Sent-down youth rallied at the places they had been evicted to or returned illegally to the cities and staged protests there. Farmers protested against their land having been illegally taken away from them. Minorities—Tibetans, Mongols, Muslims, and other ethnic and religious groups—started to speak out publicly against the atrocities they had been subjected to by the CCP. People called for freedom and the rule of law, for democracy and the right to travel abroad. One poster begged U.S. president Jimmy Carter to raise the subject of human rights in China when Deng Xiaoping visited the United States in January 1979. Other posters proclaimed that "the source of all evil is the dictatorship of the proletariat" or proclaimed, "Liquidate the Communist Party" or "Overthrow socialism." A few denounced the Chinese attack on Vietnam, which started in mid-February 1979.[73]

It was a cacophony of voices in what amounted to a festival of freedom. Nobody had seen anything similar since the Communists came to power, though a few feared that the CCP was simply allowing protest in order to do what it had done in the late 1950s: find out who its enemies were and destroy them. Such fears did not seem to hold back protesters in Beijing, who since late autumn had been congregating around the busy intersection at Xidan,

Democracy Wall in Beijing in 1979 with big-character posters.
Source: Dennis Cox/Alamy Stock Photo.

where they put up wall posters and talked with passersby. Soon the drab Xidan bus station became known as "Democracy Wall," with other such centers
of protest propping up across the city, including at university campuses and
near the big factories.[74] And it was not only in Beijing; in Shanghai since late
November 1978, thousands of people had met in People's Square every
evening to discuss topics that could not be discussed in print, and in other
cities and towns public meetings were held to discuss the future of China.[75]
Many of these events were not organized by the Communist Party; it was ordinary citizens who, for the first time in their lives, dared give voice to what
was on their minds.

Not all of the protest was in favor of democratic reform. Parts of the Left
also found their voice again in the winter of 1978–1979. A group calling itself
the Marxist-Leninist Mao Zedong Thought Research Association distributed
leaflets about "the revisionist line of Hu Yaobang and Hu Qiaomu."[76] Another
society, the National Coalition against Opportunists, wrote long letters to the
newspapers identifying Deng Xiaoping as a Right-wing opportunist.[77] Both

on the Left and among the democrats there were quite a few who had their background in some form of Red Guards, where they had learned about organization, mobilization, and fighting their enemies. The reoccurrence of these figures in the protests alarmed CCP leaders even more than the content of what they said. That the majority of them had learned from their past mistakes and now clamored for more democracy and openness had little impact on the authorities. But even as the first big protest marches in Beijing took place in late November 1978, when, on one occasion, more than ten thousand people marched past the CCP leadership compound at the Zhongnanhai shouting, "Down with hunger, down with repression, we want human rights, we want democracy," Deng Xiaoping was not willing to openly criticize what was now turning into a mass movement. He told Chinese and foreign reporters that "we have no right to deny or criticize the masses' carrying out democracy and putting up big-character posters. If the masses have opinions, let them vent them."[78]

But as the Theory Conference progressed, many CCP leaders started getting cold feet. Even Hu Yaobang, who in the public mind was more associated with rehabilitations and openness than anyone else, was concerned. Already at the opening of the conference, he had warned the delegates not to take their criticism too far. "Some comrades seem to think that the more mistakes we find that Chairman Mao made, the better it is," he told participants at the conference. During the meeting, he told those present not to discuss what had been said at the Theory Conference publicly. It was too early for that. "The majority of the petitioners were wronged, and 98 or 99 percent have reasonable demands. This is the main issue. We did not do a good job, they suffered, [and] we have to help them solve the problem. But . . . our Party advocates people's democracy, democratic collectivism, or democratic centralism, and opposes democratic individualism."[79] He encouraged the delegates not to abandon Marxism, but to improve their own practice. Other leaders were far less lenient, but with Hu's position strong and Deng Xiaoping protecting him, they dared not openly attack the democracy movement.

By early spring of 1979, with the Theory Conference still in session, the popular organizations seemed to develop very fast. In Yunnan Province, a hundred thousand sent-down youth organized and went on strike, with the demand that they be allowed to return home. When their representatives arrived in Beijing they were received by Party leaders, who told them they had the right to return and promised to abolish the rustification programs.[80] In Beijing and all over the country, independent journals and magazines appeared, mimeographed or produced after hours by print workers. They had titles such as *Exploration, April 5th Forum,* and *Science-Democracy-Law.* The most famous of them was *Beijing Spring,* a monthly publication that took its name from a book the editor, Wang Juntao, had gotten hold of on the Prague Spring in Czechoslovakia in 1968. Wang was a Communist and a political celebrity. In April 1976 the 18-year-old Wang had been arrested as a ringleader of the Tiananmen protests. In 1978 he was rehabilitated and elected a Central Committee member of the Communist Youth League while still a student at Peking University. Wang's political ideal was Alexander Dubcek, the hero of the defeated Prague Spring. Like Dubcek, and like his friend Xu Wenli, the former soldier who edited the *April 5th Forum,* Wang wanted "socialism with a human face."[81]

But not all leading activists were convinced about the superiority of socialism. Among them was Wei Jingsheng, a former Red Guard member who worked as an electrician at Beijing Zoo, and who founded the journal *Exploration.* Wei was best known for the wall poster he put up at Xidan on December 5, 1978. Entitled "The Fifth Modernization: Democracy," Wei's poster attacked Deng Xiaoping, calling him an aspiring dictator and political swindler.[82]

Newspapers and television no longer assail us with deafening praise for the dictatorship of the proletariat and class struggle. This is in part because these were once the magical incantations of the now-overthrown Gang of Four. But more importantly, it's because the masses have grown absolutely sick of hearing these worn-out phrases and will never be duped by them again. . . . Now there are those who have offered us a way out: if you take the Four Modernizations as your guiding principle, forge ahead with stability and unity, and bravely serve the revolution like a faithful old ox, you will reach paradise—the glory of communism and the Four Modernizations. . . . With all due respect, let me say to such people: We want to be the masters of our own destiny. We need no gods or emperors and we don't believe in saviors of any kind. We want to be masters of our universe, not the modernizing tools of dictators with personal ambitions. We want the modernization of people's lives. Democracy, freedom, and happiness for all are our sole objectives in carrying out modernization. Without this fifth modernization, all others are nothing more than a new promise. Comrades, I appeal to you: Let us rally under the banner of democracy![83]

Already in early 1979 the Politburo agreed to the arrest of some of the most active petitioners and democracy campaigners who "disturbed the peace" or attacked socialism.[84] But the police were ordered to be careful and only arrest those who they had been ordered to pick up by the local Party committees. Things changed by March, however. Senior Party leaders were horrified at the thought that CCP reformers and the non-Party opposition could join forces, as seemed to be happening at the Theory Conference. Deng Xiaoping's views of the conference and the democracy movement had also changed upon returning from his visit to the United States in February. Besides his dislike of being attacked in increasingly personal terms by some democracy activists, Deng worried about what he saw as the potential for foreign meddling in China's political crisis. Deng had been impressed but also frightened by the wealth and productive capacity he had witnessed abroad, and he was more than ever struck by China's relative weakness. That weakness had also been brought home to Party leaders by the many failures in China's brief war against Vietnam that ended in mid-March. To Deng Xiaoping, the country needed unity and material progress, not further political dissension.

Wei Jingsheng was arrested on March 29, though neither he nor the other dissidents who were detained that spring were told what they had been put in jail for. The following day Deng Xiaoping showed up at the CCP Theory Conference and declared that the meeting was about to end. He then proceeded to deliver what was perhaps the most important speech of his political career. Socialist China, he said, was in danger from the Left and the Right. The Left had been defeated, although some remnants remained. Now the Right was rearing its ugly head. The CCP, Deng said, had to stick to four basic political principles: socialism, the dictatorship of the proletariat, the leadership of the Communist Party, and Marxism-Leninism Mao Zedong Thought. The Party had to guard these principles, insisted the Party's new number-one leader, because "a handful of people in society at large are spreading ideas which are against them or at least cast doubt on them, and because individual Party comrades, instead of recognizing the danger of such ideas, have given them a certain degree of direct or indirect support."

Capitalism already has a history of several hundred years, and we have to learn from the peoples of the capitalist countries. We must make use of the science and technology they have developed and of those elements in their accumulated knowledge and experience which can be adapted to our use. While we will import advanced technology and other things useful to us from the capitalist countries . . . we will never learn from or import the capitalist system itself, nor anything repellent or decadent. . . . We must recognize that in our socialist society there are still counter-revolutionaries, enemy agents. . . . Lin Biao and the Gang of Four, as they put it, kicked aside the Party committees to "make revolution," and it is clear to all what kind of revolution they made. If today we tried to achieve democracy by kicking aside the Party committees, isn't it equally clear what kind of democracy we would produce?[85]

The audience was silent at first, but many applauded Deng's verdict on Mao Zedong. "Comrade Mao, like any other man, had his defects and made errors. But how can these errors in his illustrious life be put on a par with his immortal contributions to the people?"[86] The new Party leader then launched a frontal attack on what he saw as deviations from the Party line.

These trouble-makers generally say they speak in the name of democracy, a claim by which people are easily misled. Taking advantage of social problems left over from the time when Lin Biao and the Gang of Four held sway, they may deceive some people who have difficulties which the government cannot help to clear up at the moment. The trouble-makers have begun to form all kinds of secret or semi-secret organizations which seek to establish contact with each other on a nationwide scale and at the same time to collaborate with political forces in Taiwan and abroad. Some of these people work hand in glove with gangster organizations and followers of the Gang of Four, trying to expand the scope of their sabotage. They do all they can to use as a pretext—or as a shield—indiscreet statements of one sort or another made by some of our comrades. . . . [This] will inevitably lead to the unchecked spread of ultra-democracy and anarchism, to the complete disruption of political stability and unity, and to the total failure of our modernization program. If this happens, the decade of struggle against Lin Biao and the Gang of Four will have been in vain, China will once again be plunged into chaos, division, retrogression and darkness, and the Chinese people will be deprived of all hope.[87]

Deng Xiaoping had made clear the limits to liberalization. Other Party leaders fell into line, though some with more misgivings than others. Hu Yaobang later regretted that he had gone along with Deng's condemnation of the democracy protesters. But Hu and other Party reformers were still satisfied that there was not an overall crackdown and that room for what was allowed was infinitely greater than before. The majority of senior leaders who had returned from political exile after the Cultural Revolution—people like Chen Yun, Peng Zhen, and the marshals and leading generals now in the Politburo—Nie Rongzhen, Xu Xiangqian, Wei Guoqing, Xu Shiyou—all applauded Deng's position.

But although Deng Xiaoping and the new Party leadership had laid down what they saw as the limits for new political thinking and criticism of the past, Chinese society continued to make use of the new freedoms that the CCP's crisis allowed for. People spoke more freely, just as newspapers and magazines were more daring and critical. In the cities, young people began to dress differently; among the ladies of Shanghai and Beijing, skirts and perms were all the rage. Music and literature changed dramatically, as did film and television. Many people started listening to foreign shortwave radio stations from Taiwan, Japan, or the United States, and often news received this way was written down and circulated. Foreigners who visited or lived in China were sources of endless curiosity for ordinary Chinese; no longer did people fear testing out their English or the foreigners' Chinese.

The newspapers were at the forefront of exploring freedom of speech. Most leading papers, including the Party's flagship publication *Renmin Ribao*, printed daily exposés of abuses of power, nepotism, corruption, and resistance to change. Party officials struggled to make journalists and editors adhere to the limitations as defined by Deng Xiaoping and the new top leadership, but in 1979 and 1980 they often failed. Even the arrests of petitioners or democracy activists were covered by Party-affiliated newspapers, in spite of strict orders not to report on such cases.

Radio and television also played an important role, both for news and for other broadcasts. In October 1978, Zong Fuxian's play "In a Land of Silence" was first performed in Shanghai, telling the story of the Tiananmen protests of 1976. The play not only hailed the protesters as revolutionaries but also questioned how the CCP could have determined otherwise, and concluded it was because of the CCP's authoritarianism and lack of respect for the people it claimed to represent. When city authorities allowed the play to continue to be performed in Shanghai, Chinese Central Television arranged for it to be broadcast live to the entire country. The play's final sentence, "People will not be silent forever," became a slogan for democracy activists all over China.[88]

Literature, as well, played a significant role in the making of a more liberal China. Writing about the Cultural Revolution, often referred to as "Scar Literature," was particularly important, since it provided an outlet for people to reflect on and mourn what had happened in the past. Scar Literature got its name from a 1978 short story, "The Scar," by the young writer Lu Xinhua. In the story, a Red Guard member denounces her mother as a traitor. When the young woman later returns home from the countryside, she finds her mother dead, with a deep scar on her forehead.[89] Similar themes of suffering, guilt, and distrust could be found among many Chinese writers—even those who still followed the Communist playbook and incorporated upright officials and expectations of a better future.

For young people all over China, the first, uncertain, contradictory years of the reform era are best remembered in song. Where young people gathered, in schools and universities, in sports clubs, on street corners, or on hikes, a new kind of song was sung. Many of them dealt with injustices of the past, or how young people in China had been betrayed by their masters, how their idealism had been trodden down and discarded, and how the older generation was not to be trusted. One song that was especially popular in the late 1970s had as its refrain:

> Everything is in pursuit of the past.
> Those who have survived
> Return to their homes.
> Separated lovers meet again.
> Go to the open room with the flowers,
> Gather the family and put on a feast.
> Celebrate the broken mirror that is still hanging.[90]

9

Imagining the World

ON JANUARY 28, 1979, Deng Xiaoping boarded a plane for his first trip to the United States. He was in very high spirits. A few weeks earlier, at its Third Plenum, the CCP Central Committee had agreed to a set of reform plans that Deng was seen as the prime promoter of. The Third Plenum had made him the most powerful leader of the Party, more powerful, even, than its chairman, Hua Guofeng. Almost at the same time, the PRC and the United States finally established diplomatic relations. Deng saw these two events as linked. The United States, Deng Xiaoping thought, could play a central role in China's reform plans and in his own political ascent. Deng was not a talkative person, especially when he was among his close advisers. Yet, during the long cross-Pacific flight, he at times spoke a lot, and spontaneously. Several of those who were on the plane with him recall him talking about the long-term relationship between the United States and China. "As we look back, we find that all those countries that were with the United States have become rich, whereas all those against the United States have remained poor. We shall be with the United States."[1]

For Deng and everyone in the CCP leadership, the years since Mao's death and the October 1976 coup had been a massive exercise in finding their own way forward, not just in domestic policy but in international affairs as well. Within China, they had not only broken with Mao's Cultural Revolution policies but also had arrested his widow and other members of his family, as well as his most valued comrades. Internationally, they had moved ahead with closer relations with the United States, as well as with Japan and western

Europe. With Mao gone, there had been CCP leaders who had argued for at least a stabilization of relations with the Soviets, just like there had been those who believed that a return to Soviet-style central planning was the solution to China's economic ills. But Deng was not among them. To a surprising degree, Deng had taken over Mao's general view of the world. In his estimation, the Soviet Union was an implacable enemy of China. It was also an imperialist superpower on the rise, with an endless appetite for territorial conquest built into its revisionist ideology. It could serve neither as foreign friend nor as an economic model for China, Deng insisted.[2]

Most CCP leaders agreed with Deng, though there had been dissenting voices, especially in the immediate aftermath of the 1976 coup. The disagreement was not so much about policy toward the Soviet Union. Almost all Chinese leaders saw returning to Sino-Soviet friendship as an impossibility. But quite a few leaders, particularly those in charge of the economy, viewed their task as reinvigorating and strengthening the planned economy after what they saw as the chaos of the Cultural Revolution. They wanted Soviet-style economic planning, but better and without direct association with the Soviets. Leaders such as Hua's key economic adviser Li Xiannian, the head of the State Planning Commission Yu Qiuli, and the Politburo member in charge of agriculture, Ji Dengkui, all recommended getting suggestions and ideas from other socialist countries such as Yugoslavia, Romania, and Hungary.

Yugoslavia was an unlikely model for Chinese socialism given how much vitriol CCP leaders had thrown at Yugoslav leader Josip Tito in the past. Tito had been seen as the epitome of revisionism and a renegade from Communism because of his country's experiments with material incentives for production and workers' control of factories.[3] But by 1977 things had changed. The former "renegade and scab" Tito was invited to visit Beijing, while Chinese support for Albania, Yugoslavia's detested neighbor and China's long-time ally, was dramatically reduced.[4] During his visit in August 1977, Tito presented his views of a decentralized and flexible form of socialism to an attentive Chinese audience. Hua Guofeng went on a return visit to Belgrade a year later, after a number of Chinese delegations had visited Yugoslavia—so many, in fact, that Chairman Hua apologized to his Yugoslav hosts not only for China's past policies but also for now sending so many delegations that it must have been exhausting for the Yugoslav comrades.[5]

What the visiting delegations found in Yugoslavia, Hungary, and Romania changed their views of socialism. The economist Yu Guangyuan, who became a key adviser to Deng Xiaoping, visited Eastern Europe in 1978 and again in 1979, and praised the use of material incentives and decentralized decisions he found there. "The ideas underpinning many of their policies really put a spell on me," Yu reported. He wanted a China more similar to Hungary, where, he found, "if a factory is profitable, workers earn more; if not, they earn less." Yu and his colleagues also collected publications by Yugoslav economists and Hungarian economists such as János Kornai, who wrote about systemic deficiencies in the planning process. They even made sure to bring back to China works by dissident economists such as the Pole Włodzimierz Brus and the Czech Ota Šik, both of whom had been forced to emigrate to the West.[6]

But contacts with socialist regimes, and the study of their economies, were only one part of China's post-1976 reorientation. In the aftermath of taking power, Hua Guofeng and his leadership group had also begun deepening relations with capitalist countries. These contacts were built on the security relationship with the United States that had developed since the early 1970s, when Mao was still alive, and on the expanding trade and technology imports from the West and Japan during that same period.[7] Although Mao had never intended China to learn from the West in terms of markets and material incentives, Hua and later Deng were keen to experiment with at least some aspects of economic development in the capitalist world. They knew how far behind China was to almost everyone else and realized that their country needed to catch up fast if the Communist Party were to stay in power and China were to be prepared for global war.

As a result of this thinking, it was not only Eastern Europe that was given priority in terms of PRC visits abroad. One of the most noteworthy missions, headed by vice premier Gu Mu, an old ally of Deng Xiaoping, visited France, Switzerland, Belgium, Denmark, and West Germany in May 1978. As a sign of his rising position within the Party, Deng met with Gu and other delegation leaders before their departure. "You should make broad contacts," Deng instructed, "and conduct thorough and deep investigations about critical issues. . . . You should observe what levels the development of these countries' modern industry has reached, and study how they manage their economic affairs. We should learn from the advanced and positive experiences of capitalist countries."[8]

While in Western Europe, Gu's delegation acted on Deng's advice. Gu and his associates toured more than twenty cities and visited over eighty factories, mines, ports, farms, and universities and research institutions. When he returned to China, Gu Mu reported to the Party leaders that the delegation had "observed the transformative changes in the societies of the five Western European countries since the Second World War," and that they had "clearly seen how China lags far behind these countries in industrial and agricultural production, transport, education, science and technology, and management of enterprises." In presenting to the Politburo on June 30, 1978, Gu stressed how the advances Western Europe had made in technology had not just improved labor productivity but also transformed people's daily lives.[9]

Gu and his colleagues also saw opportunities for China in developing contacts with Western Europe. These countries were in general quite friendly toward China, Gu said.[10] They also faced the classic capitalist dilemma of having too much surplus capital, and therefore needed to find new markets. This made them interested in general trade and technology exports to China and other developing countries. In addition to increasing trade, Gu proposed arrangements such as foreign investment in joint stock companies "so as to accelerate China's reconstruction for modernization." There was no class analysis or condemnation of imperialism in Gu's report.[11] The aim, obviously sanctioned by Deng, was to encourage Party leaders to think about the country's economy in new terms.

The overall theme for the expansion of economic relations with the capitalist world was what Premier Zhou Enlai had termed "the Four Modernizations": modernization of China's industry, agriculture, science and technology, and national defense. Hua Guofeng found it easy to promote these plans. They had had Chairman Mao's blessing, at least in principle, and they fit in with Hua's own emphasis on rapid economic development as the overall goal for his new leadership. By continuously stressing that China was a developing country, Hua also echoed the late Mao's "Three Worlds" theory. In a presumptuous appropriation of the Third World concept, in the early 1970s the late chairman had presented China as primarily a poor country, whose interests, as those of other poor countries, were in development issues. Hua agreed, not least because the stress on development and modernizations enabled him to move away from some of the thornier issues that Mao's revolutionary agendas had presented his successor with.[12]

Beginning in early 1977, at the same time as Hua's domestic mobilization efforts, the CCP leadership had launched a massive campaign to improve China's economic output through the import of foreign technology. In name, these measures were a continuation of the import programs introduced in 1973, sometimes called the "4.3 Project" because of the total cost of $4.3 billion. But they went far beyond even what had been envisaged in these expansive plans, most of which were moving toward completion in 1977. In July 1977 the State Council, with Hua as the premier, called upon the whole country to take the beginning recovery of the Chinese financial system in the first half of the year as the starting point for making "a new great leap in China's national economy."[13] Over the months that followed, ministries in charge of various aspects of heavy industries, including coal, iron, steel, and oil production, competed with each other to present their own plans for a "new leap." In early 1978 the State Economic Planning Council presented a document entitled "Main Points of Economic Planning" to the Party leadership, and Hua and the Politburo approved it on February 5. China would construct ten big oil fields, ten large iron and steel plants, nine metal processing centers, ten chemical fiber plants, and ten large petrochemical works in less than a decade.[14] What followed were great waves of demands for importation of ready-made equipment and advanced technologies from foreign countries, and from Western capitalist countries in particular. The initial budget of Hua's new endeavor was $6.5 billion, so some people started calling it the "6.5 Project." But, as expenditure increased, the estimates for the overall cost for these ventures almost tripled. Within less than a year, the total planned budget for the whole project had surpassed $18 billion. Some of the CCP planners were horrified at the expense and started referring to the plans, in private, as the "importation great leap forward."[15]

Despite its extraordinarily ambitious outlook, the 6.5 Project was similar to earlier Maoist modernization efforts in the sense that its administrators wanted to import machinery and technologies to work within a Soviet-style planned economy. Although Hua continuously called for more efficiency and more local responsibility for carrying out modernizations and increases in production, he did not imagine any deeper structural changes in the Chinese economy. His vision, and that of most other Party leaders—including Deng Xiaoping, who still waited on the sidelines—was to increase productivity and output through a combination of the reimposition of order in production and the import of massive amounts of foreign technology. The State Council and the Central Planning Commission would still be in charge of these projects and develop them according to strict aims and directives.

When criticism within the Party of the 6.5 Project began to emerge in late 1977 and early 1978, it was therefore not directed against the uses of these ventures. What Deng and others increasingly attacked was the amount of expenditure within particular sectors of the economy that the 6.5 Project entailed. They also used the spiraling cost estimates as a way of showing that Hua and his closest advisers had little economic competence. Although never voiced in public, Deng used that argument to bring back some of the key economic experts whom he had worked closely with before. Even though it had been agreed by a united Party leadership, Deng and his allies used the "importation great leap forward" as a stick to beat Hua Guofeng with, and to show that some of the chairman's plans were both irresponsible and spendthrift. After the CCP meetings in the fall of 1978 that dramatically increased Deng's power in the Party, some of the 6.5 Project plans were quietly shelved or renegotiated.[16]

Among the most important "investigation and study" delegations that the CCP sent out in 1978 was a visit to Japan in April. Led by the Shanghai chief of economic affairs Lin Hujia and the vice chairman of the Central Planning Commission Duan Yun, this delegation was the biggest overseas deputation that the Party sent out as it struggled to find new inspiration for China's flagging economy. The significance of Japan was very clear to all of those who participated in the visit. Not only was Japan the most modern and developed country in Asia, but it had also become a global economic powerhouse, ranked third in gross domestic product (GDP) after the United States and the USSR. The Chinese were impressed by the productive capacity of Japanese companies, their level of technology, and by the strength of their export schemes. The visitors spent much time studying the coordinating role of Japan's Ministry of International Trade and Industry (MITI) in the country's economic development. The Chinese understood that MITI had helped synchronize Japan's industrial policy through directing investment to companies that could succeed in terms of export. They wondered if something similar could be possible in China.[17]

The Chinese delegation to Japan met a number of high officials and discussed the progress that had been made since the early 1970s in Sino-Japanese economic relations. But the most significant part of the visit was the talks the

Chinese leaders held with representatives of the big Japanese companies, such as the New Nippon Steel Corporation and other leading firms in Tokyo, Osaka, Yokohama, and Kobe. In their report after returning home, the Chinese delegation leaders highlighted the need for the newest technology, foreign investment, and research and education. Among the readers of the report was Deng Xiaoping, who used it as background material to prepare his own visit to Japan a few months later.[18]

Duan Yun also led another "investigation and study group" to Hong Kong and Macau in April 1978. This was the first time that a PRC delegation was specifically charged with studying these regions' own economic development to find ideas that could be useful for China. While in Hong Kong, the group examined how this small British colony, with almost no land or raw materials, had been able to emerge as a trade, financial, and maritime center in less than twenty years. In the delegation's report to the Party leaders and the State Council, Duan emphasized the need for China to "take full advantage of Hong Kong and Macao through long-term planning," not only as depots for expanding trade but also as a reservoir of experience for financial and economic development and management structures.[19] The group also suggested as a possibility that areas close to these foreign-held ports in China could be developed as export processing zones, combining Chinese labor and foreign capital.[20] It was from such suggestions that the idea of Special Economic Zones inside China would later be born.

On June 1 and 3, 1978, Hua chaired a State Council meeting to hear reports by Lin Hujia and Duan Yun about their trips to Japan, Hong Kong, and Macau. Lin and Duan proposed that in addition to importing equipment, more emphasis should be placed on absorbing new technology and patents, as well as attracting foreign investments. Thus, China's system of foreign trade and, more basically, approaches toward foreign investment had to be reformed. Lin particularly mentioned that Japan was willing to provide both technology and capital support to China, especially by helping to build a gigantic steel plant, which could almost double China's annual steel output.[21]

This became the origin of the enormous Baoshan Steel plant that would be constructed in the Shanghai suburbs in the 1980s. The plans for the Baoshan plant were a perfect merger of Communist and capitalist gigantomania, in which sheer scale was supposed to overcome both investment and

Shanghai's Baoshan Iron and Steel complex.
Source: Dennis Cox/Alamy Stock Photo.

production difficulties. The project ran into problems from the very beginning, when it became clear that Japanese engineers and Chinese workers did
not see eye to eye on construction methods. But these problems were soon
overtaken by the spiraling costs of the project, which, by 1980, were projected
to equal those of the 6.5 Projects, if not exceed them. In 1981 the Politburo
pulled the plug. Most of the project was canceled, and China had to pay com-
pensation to the Japanese companies involved. The Baoshan Steel plant took
another decade to reach production capacity.[22] But the project, even when severely curtailed, did lay the foundation for China's modern steel industry.
Having expanded into other parts of China, the Baoshan Iron and Steel Company is today by far the world's largest producer of steel.

As we have seen throughout this book, ideas and debates about China's
economic modernization were crucial to its views of the outside world. In
mid-1978 some of these debates came into focus at a State Council economic
theory forum in Beijing. Li Xiannian, the vice premier now in charge of economic and financial affairs, chaired the forum, which began on July 9. Hua

Guofeng attended the forum at least thirteen times. Even so, the leader who fashioned most of the discussion, even if he did not personally attend it, was Deng Xiaoping. In a long conversation with Gu Mu, one of the most important speakers at the forum, Deng gave his views about how opening more rapidly to the outside world was a precondition for China's successful development. Deng highlighted China's relations with capitalist countries, which could supply the most advanced know-how and technology. He wanted to speed up the process of getting foreign loans and investment. Deng stressed that the Party could not hesitate on these issues, but had to act quickly.[23]

While delivering a report about his Western European tour at the forum, Gu Mu said that "Comrade Deng Xiaoping initiated the major move of stepping up technology imports and boosting exports as early as 1975. It is high time that we carry it out in a meticulous and methodical way. We have to liberate our minds to open the path in this respect. Under no circumstance should we lock ourselves up in a cage and let the opportunities to slip away."[24] Li Xiannian and Chen Yun (who was back as a key Party leader) supported these views. Hua Guofeng played a critical role by giving his blessing to the speeches by Gu Mu and Hu Qiaomu, another Deng deputy, who stressed that the Party's policies had to operate within universally accepted economic laws. In his concluding remarks, Li Xiannian emphasized that the current world situation was favorable for China to adopt a new policy of opening the country to the world. "We should have the guts and determination to boost China's development by utilizing the technology, equipment, funds, and management expertise of foreign countries."[25] A new agenda for China's development strategy as a crucial part of its foreign policy was beginning to emerge.[26]

One reason why Deng did not attend the forum was because he was focused on China's relations with Japan and with his upcoming visit to that country. After the establishment of PRC-Japan diplomatic relations in September 1972, the relationship between the two countries had moved forward, but slowly. Japan had already become a very important source of trade and technology for China, but not at the levels that the post-Mao leaders would have wanted. One barrier was the stalled negotiations over a peace and cooperation treaty between the two governments. Another was concerns on the Chinese side that Japan had not properly atoned for its attack on China in the 1930s and the brutal occupation policy that followed. And finally there was the territorial issue of control of the Senkaku/Diaoyu Islands in the ocean between the two countries, held by Japan but claimed by China.

Deng wanted these three issues resolved, at least in very general terms, before his planned visit to Tokyo in the fall of 1978. He threw himself into attempts at settling them. He explained to his associates that assistance from Japan would be crucial for China's modernization efforts. One assistant remembers Deng saying that no other country, including the United States, was more important to China than Japan.[27] He impatiently waved away concerns about the two countries' troubled past and about the language that should be used in a treaty, while mobilizing Japanese intermediaries from business and cultural institutions. In order to get the Treaty of Peace and Friendship between the two countries signed, Deng instructed the Chinese Foreign Ministry to accept several of the formulations proposed by the Japanese side. The treaty was signed in Beijing on August 12, 1978.[28]

Deng Xiaoping's visit to Japan took place in late October. It was the first time ever that a Chinese top leader had visited Japan, and Deng strove to make the most of the occasion. He decided not to bring up the burden of history, except to accentuate the positive. Despite an unfortunate period in the mid-twentieth century, Deng told his hosts on a number of occasions, the two countries had enjoyed two millennia of good relations. Instead the Chinese leader underlined his own respect for Japan, telling Emperor Hirohito that "bygones should be bygones."[29] "For years I have been looking forward to visit Japan, and finally I can realize it. I am very happy," Deng said.[30] Asked about Senkaku/Diaoyu at a press conference, in itself a rare event for Chinese leader, Deng answered that the question should be set aside, to be resolved by future generations.[31]

Deng's focus was not on territory or history. It was on China's modernization. He wanted Japan's help, and he believed that the Japanese would appreciate the commercial opportunities that China could offer, now and in the future. "Even after we have achieved the Four Modernizations, we will probably still be poor," Deng told Japanese prime minister Fukuda Takeo. "At that time, your country will probably have advanced further. Accordingly, even after achieving the Four Modernizations, we will probably need your country's cooperation. . . . [But] it is not that China will be of no use to your country. If China develops, then the areas of possible cooperation will also probably

increase further. I think that as China develops more and more, the importance of cooperation will emerge."[32]

Deng had a keen eye for Japanese companies that could invest in China.
He visited machine factories, pharmaceutical companies, and car manufac-
turers. When visiting a Nissan factory, Deng was told that it produced ninety-
four cars per worker per year. Deng said that was exactly ninety-three cars
more than in China's best automobile factory. "Now," he added, "I understand
what modernization is." "We are a backward country and we have to learn
from Japan."[33]

In spite of the important meetings going on in Beijing in the fall of 1978,
which would propel him to the position of paramount leader, Deng continued his foreign travels after visiting Japan. His next stop was Southeast Asia,
where he visited Malaysia, Singapore, and Thailand. All three countries had
difficult relations with China. They had large Chinese populations within
their borders. In Singapore the ethnic Chinese were a majority, in Malaysia
they were about 35 percent of the population, and in Thailand, though a
smaller group, they dominated trade and industry. As a result, nationalist leaders in Malaysia and Thailand were keen to curtail the political power of their
Chinese populations, while Lee Kuan Yew, the authoritarian ethnically Chinese Singaporean leader, was a staunch anti-Communist and jealous of any
PRC influence in his city-state. Worse, the CCP had for years sponsored armed
Communist rebellions in Malaysia and Thailand, providing the rebels with
training, weapons, and communications.

Deng hoped to set China's relations with Southeast Asia on a new track.
He wanted increased investment and trade from the countries to China's
south, irrespective of their political outlook. But he also wanted to learn from
their strategies of industrialization, especially in Singapore, which was the
wealthiest country in the region. The fact that all three countries worked
closely with the United States did not bother him. On the contrary, during
his first stop in Bangkok, he lauded not just the anti-Communist Thai government, which had come to power through a U.S.-supported military coup
in 1976, but also the Association of Southeast Asian Nations (ASEAN), which
China until then had often condemned as a tool of U.S. imperialism. Contrary to earlier CCP propaganda, ASEAN, Deng told his astonished audience,
had established "a zone of peace, freedom, and neutrality."[34]

At his now customary press conference before leaving, Deng dealt openly with problems in Sino-Thai relations. He underlined that people of Chinese descent living in Thailand should take Thai citizenship and work for their country. When asked about China's support for the Communist Party of Thailand, which was waging an increasingly successful guerrilla struggle against the regime in Bangkok, Deng responded, laconically, that this was a "historical problem" in relations between the two countries that could not be resolved overnight. The Chinese leader spent most of the press conference condemning Vietnamese threats against the China-supported Khmer Rouge regime in neighboring Cambodia. Vietnam, Deng said, is the "Cuba of the Orient," involved in "hooliganism" in Southeast Asia. "We are waiting to see how far they advance into Cambodia before deciding on countermeasures," Deng concluded.[35]

Malaysia, Deng's second stop on his Southeast Asia tour, had similar difficulties in its relations with China as Thailand. The ethnic dimension was even starker here, with the Malayan Communist Party (MCP) having fought an intense war against, first, British colonial authorities and then a Western-supported postcolonial regime. Most of the MCP fighters were of Chinese descent, and Malay leaders accused the MCP of being the spearhead of a CCP attempt at dominating Malaysia. Deng repeated the same position he had taken while in Thailand, even though the official reception he got in Kuala Lumpur was considerably cooler than the one he had received in Bangkok. When pressed by the Malaysian prime minister to disavow the MCP, Deng refused to do so, but he noted afterward to his staff that these problems would have to be resolved if China should benefit from its relations with Malaysia in the future.[36]

The most difficult, but also the most important, stop on Deng's tour was Singapore. Led by the blunt and authoritarian Lee Kuan Yew, whose own family, like Deng's, traced its ancestry back to southern China, Singapore was distinctly anti-Communist and deeply skeptical of the PRC mingling in its affairs. With three-quarters of Singapore's population of Chinese descent, Lee insisted that all inhabitants of the city-state should have their exclusive loyalty to Singapore and to his own model of social and economic planning for creating a high-income society. Dissent was not tolerated, and suspected Communists were imprisoned or expelled to China. The CCP and Radio Beijing

Lee Kuan Yew welcoming Vice Premier Deng Xiaoping
at the Singapore airport, 1978.
Source: Imago Alamy Stock Photo.

had for years labeled Lee and his "clique" "running dogs" of imperialism and U.S. stooges.[37]

The conditions for Deng and Lee's first meeting on November 12, 1978, were therefore not the best.[38] Deng tried to disarm Lee by saying that he had been to Singapore before, on his way to France in 1920. Now he wanted to understand how the city-state had become rich. Deng then launched a blistering attack on the Soviets and their allies, the Vietnamese, as the common enemies of China, Southeast Asia, and the rest of the world. Vietnam was Asia's Cuba, Deng repeated, out to make trouble on behalf of the Soviet Union. China had broken its ties with the Vietnamese after Hanoi's aggression against its neighbors (meaning the PRC-supported Pol Pot regime in Cambodia) and against its ethnic Chinese population. The reason for Vietnam's behavior, Deng claimed, was its leadership's plans for creating an Indochina federation under Hanoi's command. The Soviet Union was backing Vietnam, since Hanoi's schemes fit into Moscow's goals of a southern thrust, as already seen in Afghanistan, Iran, and Africa. The Soviets were warmongers and a danger to the whole world, Deng stressed to Lee Kuan Yew. Their aims were furthered by American weakness and by global disunity. Deng wanted to unite with the ASEAN countries in confronting Vietnam and its Soviet backers. He went as far as indicating that China would react in some way if Hanoi tried to take over all of Cambodia. Lee had never heard these kinds of statements from a Chinese leader before. He wondered, as did some of Deng's associates, whether Deng was really focused on the Soviet threat or whether his anti-Soviet and anti-Vietnam rhetoric while in Southeast Asia was primarily a tool for convincing his hosts that China was not the real enemy.

Deng would soon prove the sturdiness of his anti-Soviet credentials. But, in his response the following day, Lee Kuan Yew left his visitor with no illusions that Chinese leaders would not have to do more to prove their intent of friendship with the ASEAN leaders. With characteristic bluntness, Lee told Deng that he agreed with many of his assessments of the Soviets and Vietnamese. But what about China's own actions? Why did the CCP encourage and support overseas Chinese to lead Communist insurgencies in Thailand, Malaysia, and the Philippines? Singapore's neighbors were more concerned about the Chinese dragon than the Russian bear. "Because China was exporting revolution to Southeast Asia, my ASEAN neighbors wanted Singapore to rally with them, not against the Soviet Union, but against China," Lee told Deng.[39] What do you want me to do, Deng asked. A first step, Lee replied, would be to stop the radio broadcasts from China by the Southeast Asian Communist parties. Deng said that he would think about it.[40] Even though it would take twelve years before Singapore and the PRC established full diplomatic relations, Deng's visit was a breakthrough, not just in political terms but also through the insights the Chinese gained in the city-state's housing and industrialization programs.

Establishing better relations with Japan and Southeast Asia were among the new Chinese leaders' top aims. The big prize, though, was cementing relations with the United States and getting U.S. assistance for China's development goals. The new Chinese leadership knew that the United States, in spite of its recent troubles—Watergate, stagflation, and Vietnam—was still by far the most powerful country in the capitalist world. The United States and the Chinese Communists had been locked in enmity since the foundation of the CCP. The Party was, after all, founded on an anticapitalist agenda, holding up the Americans as the primary example of all that was wrong with markets and the imperialism that they produced. Mao's early 1970s turn toward an accommodation with the United States in international affairs had reduced the sense of antagonism but not the zeal for radical anticapitalism at home. The new leaders now had to figure out how best to exploit the new relationship with the Americans for the CCP's purposes.

In spite of the degree to which China and the United States had started working together, strong suspicions remained, especially on the Chinese side. Some of these suspicions were perceptual: What did the world's strongest capitalist power expect to get out of working with socialist China? How could China, as the weaker power, avoid being exploited and taken advantage of? Taiwan remained a bone of contention, irrespective of the 1972 declarations. And Deng Xiaoping and other Chinese leaders worried that American irresolution on international affairs could leave the CCP exposed. How come, for instance, that, six years after President Nixon's China trip, formal diplomatic relations between the PRC and the United States were still not established?

But these worries were significantly overshadowed by the Chinese leaders' sense that a closer relationship with the Americans would be a key part of China's security and modernization. The fear of a Soviet attack still ran high. The Soviet Union, Deng had told Japanese prime minister Fukuda in October 1978, was "expanding its armaments and making preparations for war." And, very different from Mao Zedong, the new Chinese leaders wanted America's help to reshape and improve the economy. Deng Xiaoping may have been emerging as the leading voice on the need for U.S. assistance in transforming China, but it was a perspective that almost all of the leading figures in the CCP after the 1976 coup came to share.

Everyone realized, though, that without a full normalization of diplomatic relations between the United States and China, such hopes for American aid in rescuing the Chinese economy would be far-fetched. Small countries, such as Singapore, could find provisional diplomatic solutions in dealing with the PRC. Both from the Chinese and the U.S. perspective, Washington could not. As the U.S.-Soviet détente process slid into ever-widening trouble, the new administration of President Jimmy Carter wanted to move more quickly on China in order to put pressure on the Soviets. And the CCP leaders wanted full recognition not just because of security, trade, and technology, but also because such a step would mean U.S. derecognition of the Republic of China, the rump regime on Taiwan now headed by Chiang Kai-shek's son, Chiang Ching-kuo. If the Americans dropped their links with Taiwan, CCP leaders believed, reunification with the mainland through negotiations would become a real possibility.

In August 1977 Carter's secretary of state, Cyrus Vance, had brought with him new proposals for full normalization on a visit to Beijing. Vance had suggested that Washington establish formal diplomatic relations with the PRC while keeping some official personnel in Taiwan. It was more than the Chinese side could accept. On August 24, Deng told Vance that Beijing opposed Washington's "reversal of liaison offices" plan. "If personnel of the U.S. government are allowed to stay in Taiwan under an 'informal arrangement,'" Deng said, "this will be no difference from leaving an embassy with no governmental sign on its gate or national flag hanging there." Despite his eagerness to get a solution, Deng insisted on three conditions for normalization: abolition of the U.S.-Taiwan treaty, withdrawal of U.S. troops, and cutting off U.S.-Taiwan diplomatic relations. The Chinese showed their displeasure by not even agreeing to a joint communique at the end of Vance's visit.[41] Instead of progress, Carter's initiative had produced a setback.

But the disappointment did not change the underlying conditions for progress in U.S.-China relations. In Washington, Carter's national security adviser, Zbigniew Brzezinski, pushed for a quick recognition of the PRC to counter what he saw as increasingly aggressive Soviet policies in Africa and the Middle East. Brzezinski lobbied hard for being sent to China as the president's personal envoy. In the spring of 1978 Carter had agreed, and Brzezinski arrived in Beijing in May for meetings with Deng Xiaoping and foreign minister Huang Hua. The May 21 discussion between Deng and Brzezinski proved a breakthrough. Carter's national security adviser told Deng that the United States accepted China's three conditions on Taiwan. Deng welcomed Carter's decision and told Brzezinski that the United States could say whatever it wanted to say on Taiwan as long as it accepted the "one China" principle. Brzezinski was amazed to find a leader who outdid him in anti-Soviet attitudes. Deng accused his U.S. visitor of being afraid of offending the Soviets by selling advanced technology to China. "I can assure you," Brzezinski retorted, "that my inclination to be fearful of offending the Soviet Union is rather limited." Deng persisted: "You think that your help to the Soviet Union in technology and economy will help to restrain the Soviet Union. It is impossible."[42]

Negotiations made further progress in the summer of 1978 and into fall. One sticking point was the U.S. insistence on continuing what President Carter called "the restrained sale of some very carefully selected defensive arms" to Taiwan. Deng objected very strongly, but he still emphasized at the Politburo meeting on November 2, "It seems that the Americans are hoping to accelerate the process of normalization. We should catch this opportunity." He also stressed that "in an economic sense, there is the need to push it forward, too."[43] Deng tried to the very last to push for an end to all arms sales, but he had to settle for a one-year moratorium. Still, he agreed that a joint communique announcing mutual diplomatic recognition would be issued on January 1, 1979, and that Deng himself would follow up with a visit to the United States soon afterward.

Full normalization of relations with the United States was a breakthrough for Chinese diplomacy and for Deng Xiaoping's leadership. It came just when Deng needed it most and when he had, very tentatively, begun pushing for further economic reform in the wake of the Third Plenum. But, to all of the Chinese leaders, it also came just when China's security and future economic prospects demanded it. Diplomatic normalization would open the doors to closer strategic cooperation with the United States. It would also, they hoped, give China further access to trade, capital, and technology not just from the United States but also from U.S. allies across the world—first and foremost Western Europe and Japan. Even among those leaders who did not fully trust Deng on reform at home, there was no doubt that he would be the perfect salesman for China in the United States. His visit, the first of any top CCP leader to the United States, was set for late January 1979.[44]

Deng prepared thoroughly for his U.S. visit. He read briefing books on American politics and devoured translated excerpts from U.S books, journals, and the press. He spent a lot of time studying the leaders he would meet, both in government and in business. Deng was particularly eager to know more about which U.S. corporations could contribute the most to the Chinese economy. His understanding of American society was basically Marxist, or at least crudely materialist. U.S. leaders were beholden to big business, and it was American economic interests that determined U.S. foreign policy. The ins and outs of American democracy did not concern him much, nor did recent events such as Watergate or the energy crisis. Deng's focus was squarely on what the United States could do for China in the future.

Deng's assistants were surprised at the keenness with which the Chinese leader approached his nine-day visit. In spite of spending a lot of time dealing with foreign relations, Deng was not known for enjoying travel or the company of foreigners. His intense nationalism meant that any success he observed abroad was written down as a loss for China, and his mastery of Chinese politics meant that he did not like to be away from the country, maybe especially during such a critical year as 1979. Yet, as he explained to his advisers on the flight, this mission was very important. China had to get the cooperation of the United States in international affairs and in terms of its own development. For most of the flight, as Deng sat alone in his own cabin, those traveling with him knew that he was mainly thinking about three issues: how to get U.S. support for a Chinese war against Vietnam and for Beijing's wider confrontation with the Soviets, how to enlist U.S. business in the quest for China's modernization, and how to make the U.S.-China relationship into an enduring alliance, which could weather changes in American politics and, for that matter, Chinese politics, too. For a man of supreme self-confidence, Deng's advisers thought that he looked nervous on the flight, not knowing what to expect on arrival.

Whatever concerns may have been there beforehand, Deng's nine-day visit turned out to be a stunning success. Not only did his talks with President Carter and other U.S. leaders go well, but Deng also was able to enlist the interest of leading U.S. companies in doing business in China. Most important of all, a usually gruff and exacting leader managed to come across as affable and vivacious. Deng's advisers admired the self-discipline this temporary transformation demanded, and knew that he had studied for it before leaving home. But they also thought that even Deng was somewhat carried away by the enthusiasm many Americans showed for the visit and by the energy that they all experienced in the United States. One of Deng's advisers observed that if this was a United States in crisis, as they had been told in Beijing before they left, then all China should aspire for half of the dynamism that an America in crisis could show for itself.[45]

Deng's first preoccupation was to get as close to the American leaders as possible. For that purpose, he had accepted a plan for coming straight from

Deng Xiaoping and President Jimmy Carter in the Oval Office
during the vice premier's nine-day state visit in January 1979.
Source: Everett Collection Historical/Alamy Stock Photo.

his flight to a private dinner at Zbigniew Brzezinski's home outside of Washington. The meal projected the kind of intimacy that Americans revel in, but Chinese—especially leaders of the Communist Party—usually abhor. Deng joined in the jokes and banter around the table, and smiled when waited on by Brzezinski's three young children, although they dropped food in his lap. Among the bonhomie, Deng immediately began sending political signals, telling the national security adviser that he needed a one-on-one meeting with the president the following day to discuss Vietnam.[46] When Deng and Carter met, after a formal White House reception for the vice premier in which he was treated as a visiting head of state, Deng laid out his formal agenda. War would come, he told a startled President Carter. China needed to prepare for it. If the United States and China worked together, then the Soviet war could perhaps be postponed. China's modernization plans were therefore in the U.S. interest as well.[47]

That afternoon, in a small meeting of the principals on both sides, Deng told Carter that he had decided to attack Vietnam. After the Vietnamese invasion of Cambodia, "we consider it necessary," Deng said, "to put a restraint on the wild ambitions of the Vietnamese and to give them an appropriate limited lesson."[48] The U.S. reaction was deliberately divided. On the one hand, the president told Deng, in a handwritten note, that an attack on Vietnam would be "a serious mistake," because it would be unlikely to stop the war in Cambodia and would cede some of the moral high ground to Hanoi. It could also lead to the Soviets getting more involved.[49] On the other hand, the Americans agreed to supply Beijing with intelligence on Vietnamese positions and, especially, Soviet troop movements along the Chinese border. In return, Deng agreed to U.S. intelligence installing surveillance equipment and listening stations in Xinjiang, close to the Soviet border. The spy deal was struck during a late-night visit by Deng to CIA headquarters on his final day in Washington.[50]

Deng was happy with the outcome of his Washington visit. He did not trust Carter, but he liked what he heard from Brzezinski about the Soviets, and he was convinced that the national security adviser would not speak without authorization from the president. Deng also knew that some of the most important visits on his America trip remained. The Chinese leader had asked to see more of the United States, and his hosts had arranged tours of Georgia, Texas, and Washington State. Wherever he went, Deng spoke with businesspeople, bankers, and chambers of commerce. His message was that the People's Republic of China was open for American business. In Texas Deng attended a rodeo and put on a ten-gallon Stetson. The hat looked bigger than the diminutive Chinese leader. Shown on Chinese television, the meaning was clear: Americans were no longer enemies. They could be partners in China's development. But if there was opportunity in Deng's trip, there was also a warning. When the Chinese visited a Texas supermarket, Deng was overwhelmed by what he found on offer. The next morning, he told his advisers that he could not sleep, thinking about how far behind the United States China was, and how much effort was needed to catch up. Only when China had caught up with the United States, Deng told them, would it be fully prosperous and safe.[51]

But the threat from a productive United States was for the future. The threat from an aggressive Soviet Union was for the here and now. While in the United States, Deng had spent a lot of time explaining to the Americans why China viewed the USSR as such an existential threat. Some of his harping insistence was tailored to suit his audience. Deng knew full well that many Americans found it difficult to tell Chinese Communists and Soviet Communists apart, and his anti-Soviet declarations were intended to remind his hosts of China's intense opposition to all of Moscow's foreign policy. Confronting the Soviets could help gain America's friendship, Deng thought. But his hatred of the USSR also came from the heart. While other Chinese leaders had started to wonder whether some of the Sino-Soviet conflict had come out of Mao's excesses and idiosyncrasies, Deng would hear nothing of it. To him, the Soviet Union was an enemy set on global domination, with China first on the list of countries it wanted to control. A main proof, according to Deng, was Soviet encouragement and assistance to Vietnam's policy of expansion in Indochina.

The Sino-Vietnamese conflict was one of the stranger aspects of international affairs in the late Cold War era. China had been a main sponsor of the Vietnamese Communist movement and of Communist North Vietnam since it was set up. After the split between China and the Soviet Union in the early 1960s, support for North Vietnam in its war against the United States was one of the few issues on which the two adversaries could agree. But underneath the joint support lay a great deal of suspicion and resentment. The Chinese told their Vietnamese allies that the Soviets were not real Communists and could not be trusted, and they were upset when Hanoi, for very good reasons, wanted to receive equal support from both Communist great powers. "The Soviets used their support to Vietnam to win your trust in a deceitful way," Zhou Enlai had told the North Vietnamese in 1966. "Their purpose is to cast a shadow over the relationship between Vietnam and China, to split Vietnam and China, with a view to further controlling Vietnam to improve [their] relations with the US and obstructing the struggle and revolution of the Vietnamese people."[52]

As North Vietnam moved closer to defeating the Americans and the Sino-Soviet relationship grew worse, the one-time tight alliance between Beijing and Hanoi disintegrated. The Vietnamese were deeply upset by Mao's decision to reach out to the Americans in 1971, just after President Nixon had widened the war in Indochina through his invasion of Cambodia. And Hanoi was further riled by Chinese advice to negotiate with South Vietnam's president Nguyễn Văn Thiệu, especially since the Chinese before had spent many years haranguing their Vietnamese colleagues about negotiations being of no use. Not surprisingly, Hanoi pulled closer to the Soviet Union, seen as a more trustworthy ally and less likely to intervene in Vietnam's domestic affairs. Even so, Chinese support for Vietnam continued up to North Vietnam's conquest of the South in 1975.

As soon as Vietnam was unified, Sino-Vietnamese relations went into a freefall. Deng Xiaoping, who had never got on with the Vietnamese Communists, launched a furious attack on Le Duan, Hanoi's top leader, at a meeting in September 1975, only four months after the fall of Saigon. "There have been some problems in the relations between our countries," Deng told Le Duan. "Some of them emerged when President Ho [Chi Minh] was still alive. We have to say that we are not at ease when we get to read Vietnamese newspapers. . . . In fact, you stress the threat from the North. The threat from the North for us is the existence of Soviet troops at our northern borders, but for you, it means China."[53] As the Vietnamese Communists started their campaigns against traders and businesspeople in the newly conquered areas, the situation got worse, since many of these were of Chinese origin. Between 1976 and 1980, more than 250,000 people in Vietnam who defined themselves as Chinese sought refuge in the PRC. Hostility from the Vietnamese government played a significant role in this exodus, as did rumors among ethnic Chinese from all walks of life that there would be no place for them in the new, reunified Vietnam.

However bad relations had become between China and Vietnam by 1978, it was their international affairs that led to the outbreak of war. As relations with Vietnam deteriorated, the Chinese Communists had become increasingly close to the Cambodian Communist Party, the so-called Khmer Rouge, and its leader Pol Pot. The relationship between China and the Khmer Rouge was in part based on ideology. Pol Pot's radical version of Communism appealed to many Leftists in China during the late Mao era, and the Khmer Rouge, increasingly out of step with the Vietnamese, appealed for assistance from China after it took power in Cambodia in 1975. Pol Pot's increasing xenophobia and his mass murders did not seem to much bother his Beijing sponsor—and the assistance to the Khmer Rouge continued after Deng Xiaoping returned to power. Deng viewed Cambodia as a counterweight to Vietnam, and the Beijing–Phnom Penh axis as a balance against Vietnam's increasingly close links with the Soviet Union, in spite of his knowledge of the terrible crimes the Khmer Rouge was carrying out.

After Pol Pot in a state of nationalist frenzy had launched several attacks into Vietnamese territory, Le Duan and the other leaders in Hanoi decided to strike back. Buoyed by a new treaty of friendship and cooperation with the Soviet Union, the Vietnamese chose to launch an all-out invasion in order to remove the Khmer Rouge from power. But while Le Duan argued that the aim of the war was to improve Vietnam's security and stop Pol Pot's genocide against his own people, Deng and the Chinese leaders saw the hidden hand of the Soviets and of Vietnamese expansionism. On December 25, 1978, some 150,000 battle-hardened Vietnamese troops invaded Cambodia. Phnom Penh fell on January 7, 1979. Pol Pot fled to the Thai border area, where he and the remnants of his murderous movement would be holed up for the next twenty years. Most Cambodians celebrated the collapse of the Khmer Rouge, but both China and the United States viewed the Vietnamese operation as Soviet-sponsored aggression.

China had warned Vietnam against an invasion of Cambodia. When the invasion happened, Deng immediately made himself the chief spokesman for a quick Chinese military reaction. Others in the leadership were more skeptical, including both Hua Guofeng and Marshal Ye Jianying and other military leaders, though nobody in the leadership opposed taking military action when Deng had proposed it.[54] We do not know why Deng was so intent on attacking Vietnam. It presumably was a combination of his nationalism, his poor relations with the Vietnamese in the past, and his preoccupation with the Soviet threat. It is also possible that he thought a quick action against Vietnam would prove his chops with the Americans. It is also very likely that being seen as the man in charge on such an important issue would solidify Deng's own position within the Party, as well as his control of the military.[55] What is less clear is whether Deng knew how woefully unprepared for an offensive action the Chinese People's Liberation Army was. Some Chinese historians wonder whether he made his decision fully knowing the PLA's weakness, on the expectation that exposing some of these limitations would take the powerful military down a peg or two in political terms. But there is no evidence for this view. It is more likely that Deng did not consider the possibility that a Chinese offensive could run into trouble against a much smaller Asian country.

China's war against Vietnam began on February 17, 1979. The PLA objectives for the war were limited; its officers were told that it would be a brief campaign across the border to teach the Vietnamese a lesson. China sent around 200,000 frontline troops across the border, supported by 350,000 rear troops operating on both sides of the frontier line. The frontline troops suffered heavy casualties at the hands of better trained and more mobile Vietnamese forces. In all, the PLA had around 62,000 casualties, with as many as 26,000 soldiers killed in action, during three weeks of war.[56] "We do not see big risks," Deng had told his generals before the operation began. "The strategic emphasis of the Soviet Union is in the West. The total size of Soviet military forces stationed along its borders with China is only of one quarter of its total military strength." "The Americans," Deng said, "on the one hand, hope that we will be restrained and fear that we will launch a [big] fight. On the other hand, however, they have shared military intelligence with us, informing us that there has been no change in the deployment of Soviet troops. . . . If we do well in the South, the danger of a major Soviet action against us can be excluded."[57]

Fighting turned out to be relentless within a relatively small area in northern Vietnam. Corpses piled up on the battlefield, so that the stench of dead soldiers was almost unbearable. There were many civilian casualties. Like U.S. soldiers in the past, Chinese troops could not distinguish between combatants and other Vietnamese. "Adults, children, and even women in Vietnam used different methods to sneak up on us, and when they attacked us, they were all soldiers, and when they could not attack us, they all became ordinary people, and [then] they launched sneak attacks at night. . . . The wounded and stretcher teams, especially, were the targets of their women." "In the later stages of the war," remembers another Chinese soldier, "faced with the threat to the lives of [our] officers and men caused by the Vietnamese irregulars, many officers did not care about discipline. Whether it was a Vietnamese soldier or an ordinary person, as long as he posed a threat, he would be shot. Right at the end, some soldiers opened fire as long as they saw a Vietnamese, no matter who it was."[58]

Already at the beginning of the war, the commander of the Chinese forces, General Xu Shiyou, had ordered that not a single house in the main Vietnamese border towns should be left standing. As the war progressed, the Chinese strategy became one of total destruction. Villages, fields, roads, and bridges were all razed. Livestock was killed or driven across the border. Everything that could be of value was put on trucks and sent back to China:

Chinese tanks approaching Lang Son, a Vietnamese border town,
in the 1979 Chinese-Vietnamese War.
Source: CPA Media Pte. Ltd./Alamy Stock Photo.

furniture, clothing, bicycles, sewing machines, even windows and doors. As Chinese losses mounted, destruction became ever more intense. Some soldiers regretted it afterward. "War is not a soldier's choice," commented one of them, "and future generations will blame and can only blame the politicians who led them to war."[59]

In spite of the PLA's losses, with the bulk of Vietnamese troops fighting in Cambodia, China reached its strategic aims, conquering the border cities of Lang Son and Cai Bang. Declaring that the road to Hanoi now lay open, Chinese leaders decided to withdraw all of their troops, saying that Vietnam had been taught a lesson. "We have not fought a war for almost thirty years," Deng announced at an internal conference attended by Party leaders and military commanders. "So there are people at home and abroad who are concerned whether we may fight well. . . . [Most] of our troops who fight in this war have not participated in the War to Resist America and Help Korea. We will use this rare opportunity to train our troops."[60] As the fighting died down, both sides declared victory, while, as usual, it was the civilian population that suffered the most in a Vietnam that had just emerged from thirty years of war. The Chinese attack displaced more than a million people from their homes, and the damage caused by the war added to the immense burden of reconstruction that Vietnam already faced. In the Vietnamese border areas, it left a bitterness toward China that can be felt even today.

China's Vietnam war was an unnecessary war for an uncertain purpose. In addition to the large numbers of people killed on both sides, the campaign locked the two countries in enmity for a generation. It did not produce a Vietnamese withdrawal from Cambodia, and it solidified rather than weakened the Soviet-Vietnamese alliance. If China scored a victory, it was in proving Vietnam's regional isolation and by demonstrating to leaders in Hanoi that when confronted by the United States, China, and the ASEAN countries even Vietnam's Soviet alliance was of limited value. The war also proved to the Americans that China was willing to pay with blood to contain the Soviets and their allies, which thereby helped further Sino-American relations. And it strengthened Deng's leadership. He claimed it as a victory for himself. The mistakes had all been made by others, and the losses showed why modernization was needed in military affairs as everywhere else in China.

Within the CCP, Deng Xiaoping benefited politically from the Vietnam war as well as from the closer relationship with the United States that followed normalization. Deng's ability to make decisions and to bring matters to a conclusion was admired even by those who had disagreed with him in the past. As Deng gradually replaced Hua Guofeng as the Party's top leader and then cemented a new leadership group around himself, his capacity to keep the U.S. relationship on an even keel became a watermark of his leadership. Deng let everyone know that only he could manage the relationship successfully and thereby secure the increasing flow of economic and security privileges that came with it. The first test came not long after full normalization, when Jimmy Carter lost the U.S. presidential election in 1980 to Ronald Reagan.

Reagan had campaigned against his predecessors' willingness to engage with China. Instead he had insisted that the United States needed to rebuild its relationship with Taiwan. "It is absolutely untrue that I am going to Peking," Reagan had told supporters in 1978. "I have not altered one bit in saying this country must not abandon its friends on Taiwan or weaken our mutual defense treaty with them."[61] As president, under the influence of his advisers Reagan slowly began warming to the policy of building a relationship with China in order to contain the Soviet Union. A key part of convincing the right-wing Republican was supplying him with information that the PRC economy had begun to change toward markets and free enterprise. Some of these accounts were exaggerated, but they did help reduce the distaste Reagan felt for engaging in closer relations with the Communists in Beijing.

The Chinese leaders were understandably concerned with Reagan's rhetoric on the Taiwan issue. They wanted to get clarity on the new administration's plans for weapons deliveries to Taiwan, the need for which Regan had spoken of repeatedly during the election campaign. The talks on this issue between Beijing and Washington lasted up to summer 1982, when, on August 17, the two sides issued a joint communique on Taiwan arms sales. In it, the PRC affirmed "a fundamental policy of striving for a peaceful reunification" with Taiwan, over which the PRC claimed sovereignty. The United States declared that it "understands and appreciates the Chinese policy of striving for a peaceful resolution of the Taiwan question." With those statements "in mind," the United States agreed that it "does not seek to carry out a long-term policy of arms sales to Taiwan, that its arms sales to Taiwan will not exceed, either in qualitative or in quantitative terms, the level of those supplied [since 1979], and that it intends gradually to reduce its sale of arms to Taiwan, leading over a period of time, to a final resolution."[62]

The Taiwan joint communique was a victory for Chinese diplomacy, even if it did not meet Deng Xiaoping's aim of preventing U.S. arms sales to Taiwan. When Reagan, on his own initiative, followed up by issuing assurances to Taiwan of what the United States would *not* do to please Beijing, the reaction in the CCP was strongly negative. The U.S. assurances, made in private to Taibei, stated that Washington had neither agreed to a date for ending arms sales nor agreed to consult with the PRC on such issues. The United States would not mediate between Beijing and Taibei, nor would it pressure Taiwan to negotiate with the PRC. Finally, there would be no change to the U.S. acts of Congress that regulated relations with Taiwan, and there would not be any change to the official U.S. view on the question of sovereignty, meaning the principle of One China.[63] In spite of the progress that had been made, Deng sensed trouble for the future. Already on July 14, when he had agreed to conclude the Taiwan negotiations with the Americans, Deng had told a group of top foreign affairs leaders, meeting at his home, that China should not become too dependent on the United States in foreign relations. The link with the Americans was the most important, but they should attempt to adjust it through contacts with the Europeans, with Japan, with China's southern neighbors, and even with the Soviet Union.[64]

China's foreign policy changed subtly in 1982–1983 toward a more balanced and less shrill approach to world affairs. Deng had many leaders who assisted him on international issues, Party chief Hu Yaobang and Premier Zhao Zi-yang in particular, but also Li Xiannian, who became president of the PRC in 1983, the new foreign minister Wu Xueqian and his main deputies Qian Qichen and Liu Shuqing, and the ambassador to Washington, the experienced diplomat Zhang Wenjin. The team was put together so that it could carry out a more varied foreign policy under new conditions. Having preached the in-evitability of World War III for many years, Deng had begun worrying about the renewed intensity of the Cold War after Reagan became president. China now needed peace for its economic development. The tune changed. "It is possible," Deng announced, "that a large-scale world war can be averted for quite some time, and that there is hope that world peace can be maintained."[65] Even normalization between China and the Soviets was possible, if Moscow dealt with three obstacles: the amassing of Soviet troops on China's borders, the Soviet occupation of Afghanistan, and Soviet support for Vietnam's oc-cupation of Cambodia.[66] Negotiations between the two Communist great pow-ers began in 1983, though little was achieved during the first few years.

As Deng Xiaoping and his new Party leadership group started adjusting China's foreign policy positions in the early 1980s, Deng was feeling the weight of history on his shoulders—and he spoke about it often. He was near-ing age 80 in a country where the life expectancy for men was still below 65. Having been a part of the PRC's great transformation, Deng also yearned to unify the country, which in his signal telling of the tale meant incorporating Hong Kong, Macau, and Taiwan into the PRC state. Though he publicly preached patience on these issues, Deng still hoped to see unification in his lifetime. Hong Kong seemed the best prospect. The lease that the British had signed with the Qing Empire in 1898 for territories across the bay from Hong Kong Island would expire after ninety-nine years. These "new territories" were almost 90 percent of Hong Kong's land, and most Chinese leaders felt that the colony would not be viable without them. If Hong Kong became part of the PRC, then Portuguese Macau, which in many ways was dependent on the British colony next door, would certainly follow suit.

But while wishing for unification, Deng and his associates were careful not to endanger the stability of Hong Kong, since the colony had proven so useful for PRC purposes, not least commercially. Already in 1977, before Deng's latest political ascendance, he had struck a note of caution when visiting Guangdong alongside Ye Jianying and other leaders. Deng said that what was important was not just the PRC's sovereignty over Hong Kong, but also how Hong Kong might assist with modernization on the mainland.[67] Sovereignty, though, was primary. Having invited the British governor of Hong Kong, C. M. MacLehose, to Beijing in March 1979, Deng laid out his policy. When MacLehose inquired whether it might be possible for the PRC to extend the lease for the New Territories to Britain, Deng made it clear that Hong Kong would have to be returned to China in 1997. Meanwhile, he promised: "After China takes back Hong Kong, it can continuously adapt capitalism. Now, some people are worried about the prospect of Hong Kong's future. . . . But one thing is certain: we will respect Hong Kong's special position with the coming of 1997."[68]

Deng, Hua Guofeng, and other Chinese leaders tried to convince the Conservative Party British prime minister Margaret Thatcher that the PRC was a reliable partner on Hong Kong. During Hua's visit to London in the fall of 1979, not long after Thatcher had been elected, he told her that "she should be aware of how highly she was respected in China. . . . The Chinese government," Hua reported to the delighted prime minister, "had long since come to the conclusion that she had grasped the essence of the international situation."[69] The PRC used the same approach for other leaders who could help with Chinese purposes, not least in Southeast Asia. After his visit to that region, Deng acted quickly in cutting China's support for antigovernment Leftists there, advising them to settle their differences with the conservatives who were in charge.[70] Heaping praise on dictators such as Ferdinand Marcos of the Philippines, the Chinese made it clear that they wanted to ally with anyone who was willing to join them in improving the security situation for the PRC.

Some policymakers in Beijing were even thinking about seeking a breakthrough with Guomindang leaders on Taiwan, so that China could be reunified through negotiations. There was much with Taiwan after Chiang Kai-shek's death in 1975 that Deng and the other PRC leaders liked. It had a fast-growing economy and stable economic conditions, linked to exports to Western markets and to Japan. And its dictator, Chiang Ching-kuo, ruled through an efficient and well-educated administration, based on a one-party system and martial law requirements. Taiwan could become a model for some aspects of the mainland's social development as well as a source of capital and new technology for the PRC's modernization drive. Deng and his colleagues began looking for ways to adjust the decades of PRC-ROC enmity and to see if some form of bargain could be entered into.

As in the case of Hong Kong, PRC leaders were keen to reassure the foreign powers involved that it would respect their commercial interests. In an interview with a Japanese newspaper in October 1978, Deng said that "if the reunification of the Motherland is to be realized, our policy in Taiwan will have to be made in accordance with Taiwan's reality. For example, both the United States and Japan have large investments in Taiwan. This is a reality, and we will not ignore this reality."[71] At the end of the Central Committee's Third Plenum in December 1978, Deng told his colleagues that it was essential to have "a new way of thinking" toward resolving the Taiwan issue. He emphasized that in order to achieve China's unification, the CCP should establish the "third united front" with the Guomindang.[72] According to Deng, the CCP should make it clear that after unification, Taiwan would maintain its social and economic system and its way of life, continue to have foreign investments, and continue to have its own armed forces.[73]

These discussions paved the way for the CCP leadership to announce a series of new policies toward the island. In its 1979 New Year's message, Beijing appealed directly to issued "compatriots in Taiwan." People living on both sides of the Taiwan Strait were "descendants of the Yellow Emperor," and Beijing would "take present realities [in Taiwan] into account in accomplishing the great cause of reunifying the motherland, respect the status quo on Taiwan and the opinions of people in all walks of life there, and adopt reasonable policies and measures in settling the question of reunification so as not cause the people of Taiwan any losses." The PLA ceased all military activity directed against Jinmen and Mazu, the Guomindang-held islands close to the Chinese coast.[74] Deng told visiting members of the U.S. Congress that Beijing had formally abandoned the slogan "We Must Liberate Taiwan" and that, if Taiwan returned to the motherland, "we will respect the reality and existing system there."[75]

The CCP's concerns with President Reagan's greater commitment to Taiwan did not lead to more conflict with Chiang Ching-kuo's regime. On the contrary, Deng and others in the Party leadership started pushing for a more open-minded set of policies, reflecting their approach to economic liberalization within the PRC. As with economic reform, Taiwan policy was a matter of testing out what could work. In October 1981, Ye Jianying, in his capacity as chair of the National People's Congress, made new proposals to the Taiwanese. Ye appealed for direct, unconditional negotiations between the CCP and the Guomindang to accomplish national reunification. Meanwhile, the two sides would begin direct trade through restored air and shipping services and allow family reunions, tourism, and academic, cultural, and sports exchanges. The PRC promised that Taiwan should enjoy a high degree of autonomy after unification along the lines of what Deng had proposed earlier. Taiwan's leaders might take up posts in Beijing, Ye suggested, and Taiwanese businesspeople would be free to travel, settle, and invest on the mainland, with PRC financial guarantees.[76]

As in affairs at home, the late 1970s and early 1980s was a heady time in China's foreign relations. Almost everything seemed possible: lasting friendship with the United States; expanding relations with Japan and China's southern neighbors; unification with Hong Kong, Macau, and Taiwan. Even the risk of war with the Soviets seemed to be diminishing. First and foremost, the outside world seemed ready to assist China with its number-one priority: rebuilding the economy after the disasters of the past. All other efforts should serve that purpose. Security and sovereignty were essential, but with war less of an immediate prospect than Mao had thought, Chinese leaders were free to make the foreign serve the domestic to a much higher extent than before.

10

A New China

BY THE END OF THE 1970S, it was clear that something entirely new was happening in China, but it was still unclear what it would consist of. The willingness of the new leaders to dispense with Maoist rectitude was obvious, as were new spaces for discussion and dissent. Both in the cities and in rural areas economic and social change were brewing, some of which came from the top, but even more came from below. In foreign affairs, China had normalized relations with the United States, but also—just as significantly—moved closer to its more market-oriented Asian neighbors. And while anti-Soviet hysteria had lessened, Chinese leaders still obsessed about a possible Soviet encirclement of China, to the point that the country had just fought a mostly purposeless war against its former ally Vietnam for that reason.

In the early 1980s China could still have moved in many different directions, in terms of domestic as well as international affairs. It ended up with market-enhancing reform policies and a close partnership with the United States due to a combination of leadership compromises, security needs, and pressure from below for faster economic growth. It was also because of the leadership skills of Deng Xiaoping; without Deng, there would not have been such a dramatic turn to markets and private enterprise, nor would there have been such a determination to work closely with Washington. Neither, it should be said, would the Communist Party—under such pressure in the late 1970s because of the infelicities it had inflicted on the country—have been able to reinstitute at least a semblance of unity and political legitimacy.

Deng's mix of internal authority, personal popularity, and willingness to compromise with other senior leaders carried the day, time after time, when radical
economic reform plans were in contention. And this achievement was made
even more remarkable by the fact that Deng primarily ruled from behind the
curtain. His own formal position was never higher than that of vice premier,
vice chairman of the Central Committee, and, from 1981, chairman of the
Central Military Commission. Still, he was the man in charge, and everyone
in China knew it.[1]

By mid-1979 it was pretty clear what Deng wanted to do with his new power.
First and foremost, he wanted to speed-charge the Chinese economy, so that
material advantages could be used in order to gain adherents to the continued rule of the Communist Party. The many demonstrations over the past
year of just how unhappy many Chinese were with the dictatorship had really
frightened Deng.[2] After his visits abroad, he was also shocked at how far
behind China was in its economic and technological development, and how
vulnerable the Communist state was because of these deficiencies.[3] More than
most other senior leaders, he feared that the combination of opposition within
and outside the Party could mean the end of the CCP's monopoly on power.
As he moved to eliminate the anti-authoritarian opposition in 1979, Deng also
switched from being one of many economic reform–oriented leaders to getting out ahead of almost all of his senior colleagues at the central level in
terms of his willingness to experiment in order to deliver fast results. Different from some other CCP bosses, Deng had few preconceived notions about
economics, only about politics. And as reform moved along, he was, in his
own mind, able to find political justification for just about any measure that
delivered rapid economic growth.

But Deng had to get ahead on economic reform while not seriously antagonizing his other partners in power within the CCP. His main concern was
not the Cultural Revolution beneficiaries, including Hua Guofeng. While still
retaining their positions, they had lost out in the competition for overall power
in the Party. The ones Deng had to worry about were people such as Ye Jianying, Chen Yun, Li Xiannian, and Peng Zhen—senior leaders who were dedicated to dictatorial Party rule and saw Deng as their leader for that reason, but
who were all more committed to Communist economic orthodoxy than
Deng himself was showing signs of becoming. It was a sliding scale: Chen
Yun and Li Xiannian, who knew much more about economics than Deng did,

were in no way opposed to reform and experimentation in order to improve the economy. But Deng's greater willingness had to be protected by attaching their names to key reforms. And he had to compromise, in word if not always in deed—a skill that Deng had not shown much of in his past political lives.

While Chairman Hua and the other central leaders who had risen to power in the Cultural Revolution were, by now, chastened and humbled, there remained the issue of what to do with them in the longer run. For Deng, it seems that he to some extent linked this issue to the question of how to deal with the consequences of the Cultural Revolution in a broader sense. During the first part of 1979 he decided that Mao's emphasis on class struggle and continuous revolution should be evicted from the CCP vocabulary, to be replaced with slogans about unity, stability, and development.[4] He then agreed with other senior leaders that there would have to be an overall reevaluation of the Cultural Revolution that portrayed the immense damage it had done to China. But the process would have to be gradual, so that it did not unsettle too many people or provide ammunition to those clamoring for democracy and the end to one-party rule. And it would have to be accompanied by further purges of those who had been guilty of crimes, as retroactively defined by the Party.[5] Only after these processes were underway could gradual formal changes in the Party's top leadership take place. Even so, by mid-1979 it was clear to all leaders at the Party Center that Hua Guofeng was a chairman on notice, and that the other Cultural Revolution beneficiaries would not last long in their top positions.

Given the further purges they were planning, by the end of the decade Deng and other leaders understood that they could not just condemn—they also had to promote. They were old; Deng was 76 in 1980, Chen Yun was 75, and Ye Jianying was 83. Even the "new" leaders in charge of the provinces were not young: Huo Shilian in Shanxi was 68, Xi Zhongxun in Guangdong and Liao Zhigao in Fujian only a year younger. All of this in a country where male life expectancy was 65 years. In 1979 and 1980, Deng and the other senior leaders spent a lot of time on finding younger people to promote. Their favorite was Zhao Ziyang, the dynamic party chief of Sichuan, a mere youngster at 61, and known to be dedicated to economic reform. Deng liked to quote a purported Sichuan pun: "要吃粮, 找紫阳" (If you want to eat, look for Ziyang). Zhao was made a member of the Politburo in September 1979.[6] Other favorites were Tian Jiyun, a young economist who was made deputy secretary general of the State Council, and Qiao Shi, a former intelligence official who was put in charge of the Central Committee's International Department. Increasingly, Hu Yaobang—though no spring chicken at 65—was seen as the heir apparent to Deng. Hu had been made chief of the Central Committee secretariat in December 1978, responsible for all the work of the Party administration.

The remarkable speed and seeming ease with which Deng Xiaoping had gone from outcast to supreme Party leader have puzzled historians and contemporary observers alike. That he did so without any major outward changes in the Party hierarchy is even more astonishing. The explanation, it seems, must be sought both in the character of the CCP dictatorship and in cultural norms prevalent in China at the time. In the CCP of the late 1970s, nothing mattered more than meritorious past service. There was significant precedent for this in the history of the Party. Even during the Cultural Revolution, when everything "old" came under attack, past disloyalties or errors—sometimes going back to the 1930s—had to be found or invented to topple Party cadre. By 1978, Deng was lauded not only for his pre–Cultural Revolution achievements but also for his plucky willingness to stand up to the Left as Mao was dying, at a time when so many others fell short. Like people everywhere, many Chinese appreciate an underdog who has made an astonishing comeback. And, similar to Mao Zedong forty years earlier, Deng had now stuck to his guns and triumphed.

But in addition to Deng's merits, there was a commonly perceived need for the Party and for China to have a strong leader. In China in the 1970s, people had never known anything but one-man rule, and Deng seemed to have all the attributes needed for the top position. That he was not designated "Chairman" mattered less. He was portrayed as vigorous, decisive, and feisty, but also comradely and caring. His assistants continuously propagated his willingness to help people in need and to rectify past injustices. They also stressed—somewhat implausibly—that he was not tainted by the past. In terms of CCP history, he linked himself closely with the image of the good premier Zhou Enlai, as the people's champion (even though his real relationship with Zhou had been complicated). His previous ousters simply gave him more credence. Already in the summer of 1977, before Deng had been publicly reinstated, his popularity among common people in Beijing was on

display. While attending a soccer international—soccer was one of Deng's en-
thusiasms—he was not noticed at first, a tiny man with a cap, huddled in an
oversized gray coat. But there were rumors in the stadium that he was attending, and, when Deng reappeared for the second half, most of the 80,000
spectators, uninvited, stood up to applaud him.[7]

While the changes at the top were important for China's future, what really
decided it were changes from below. As we have seen, many of these were
gradual, starting in the early 1970s in ways that were almost unnoticeable except to the people involved. They were liberties that people were taking for
themselves, especially in the countryside, where Communist control was less
strict. Almost all of them were economic, though the circulation of "forbidden" books, the praying at "unauthorized" altars, and the singing of "pro-
scribed" songs were among them. By 1978 some provinces had already seen
market trading, bartering, and production outside the plan. A few People's
Communes had, informally, divided responsibility for production into family
units and allowed these units to keep their surplus. In some places, commune-
operated factories and workshops had taken control of their own production,
and some had introduced incentives for workers. Others were selling or bartering their products, beyond any plan, even at faraway places. Smuggling
was rampant in border areas. Most of the uncertified economic activity was
in counties close to major cities in the east. But, as we have seen, there were
exceptions, such as in Anhui, where destitution forced economic change,
and in Sichuan, where a reformist leader allowed people to find their own
solutions.

What changed after the Third Plenum in 1978 was therefore not so much
the direction things were taking as it was the size, speed, and scope of the
changes. Different from what the Party had intended, the CCP's decisions
(which, of course, most people had not read) were seen as a signal to experiment in economic matters. How these experiments from below ended up
was, at least at first, dependent on who was in charge in the province in question. People could be lauded or arrested entirely according to how Party secretaries interpreted the message from the Center, and, to some extent, their
own predilections. Deng and other reformers at the Center were aware of how
random official policies could be at the local level. Before sending Xi Zhongxun
to head Guangdong Province in 1978, Deng asked him to get rid of petty regulations that stood in the way of economic growth. "I heard," Deng said, "that

in Guangdong raising three ducks is of a socialist nature, whereas raising five ducks is regarded as pursuing capitalism. That is ridiculous."[8]

But in spite of the Center's general willingness to reform, changes from below still outran official policies by a mile. The Third Plenum had decided on higher prices for agricultural products, more credit to rural areas, and low taxes for rural enterprises. It had also opened up for limited contracting of quotas to work groups within the People's Communes. But it staunchly defended collective agriculture, and prohibited the division of land and family farms, except for small plots for private use. But what happened over the next three years changed the Chinese countryside forever and was such a break with Maoist policies that even those who had been at the forefront at clamoring for reform prior to the Third Plenum could barely understand how it was possible. The process began with how the direction of the decisions at the Center was understood in the provinces, where leaders were facing acute rural poverty and increasing pressure from above to increase and diversify food production. Some of these leaders—vaguely, hesitantly—allowed initiatives from below to proceed, providing new models for agricultural production.

Ironically, at the central level, it was Hua Guofeng who had been most preoccupied with solving the issue of rural poverty. His experience in Hunan made him understand agricultural problems in ways other central leaders did not. Hua had been key in improving prices for farm products, providing more loans, and allowing local markets to begin operating again. He also suggested importing more grain from abroad for a limited period, in order to allow greater diversification in Chinese agriculture.[9] The irony was, of course, that serious changes in the countryside only started as Hua's political star was descending. Even so, throughout 1979 Hua Guofeng continued to support change in rural areas, even as other leaders, including Deng Xiaoping and Hu Yaobang, were less engaged or interested. For reformist leaders in the provinces this was important, since it allowed limited experimentation with different kinds of contracting systems to go ahead, even when they came under attack for breaking with socialist orthodoxy. Hua's support was especially important in the spring of 1979, after a much discussed letter was published in the *People's Daily*, exhorting farmers not to give up on their Communist principles.[10]

Even the most reformist provincial leaders, such as Wan Li in Anhui and Zhao Ziyang in Sichuan, were uncertain about how far and how fast to move with agricultural reform. They both presented contract farming, both by work teams and by households, as part of provincial poverty alleviation, authorized by local leaders under extreme circumstances. No provincial leader suggested making a province-wide, never mind a countrywide, experiment out of the new models. Like all other heads of provinces, they tried to understand what might be allowed by the Center and what would be acceptable for their own provincial officials, the vast majority of whom were dedicated to the principles of collective farming and had built their whole careers on it. After all, one of the key issues for the CCP for a generation had been to collectivize Chinese agriculture and make farmers understand that they could achieve more, both in personal and production terms, by thinking of themselves as workers for ever-expanding communal units. Changing such policies, even in limited ways, would touch the very fundament of the Maoist tradition in China.

While CCP leaders hesitated, farmers began to move forward with their own arrangements. More and more grain, meat, oil, and vegetables could be found at local markets, either as collective surplus or produced on private plots. As a result, market towns that had been in decline under socialism began to thrive, as farmers for the first time started joining the money economy. The Party debates over allowing different forms of contracting were not much of a consequence to farmers in most parts of the country, at least not before the end of 1980. In those very small areas where contract farming was introduced, farmers who produced enough to benefit from such arrangements welcomed them, while the very poor—on whose behalf the changes were ostensibly made—preferred government handouts, and rich collectives in provinces such as Jiangsu and Zhejiang saw no reason to change how they produced. In the richer regions, some farmers worried about what would happen to common goods such as health care or education as the collectives were weakened. After all, teachers and healthcare workers were paid by the brigade or the commune in the same work points that farmers received for their part of the collective output. In many areas, such services were *more* important products of the collective income than wages for farmers. Already in 1978, on average, farmers got more in cash from private plots than in wages.[11]

Although the CCP in September 1979 had decided that household contracting could be allowed in all provinces under special circumstances, the Party was far from recommending such policies up to the spring of 1980, when things began to change. The Party head of Anhui Province, Wan Li, had been moved to Beijing to take overall responsibility for agriculture in the Central Committee and the State Council. Wan, who had been a cautious reformer in Anhui, became a much more forceful promoter of rural change as soon as he arrived at the Center. To begin with, he knew that he owed his promotion to reports of successful agricultural experimentation in Anhui. He was a friend of Deng's, who also had other powerful allies in Beijing, such as the former Sichuan Party head Zhao Ziyang, who was promoted to the Politburo at the same time that Wan took over agriculture. But most important of all, Wan sensed that the mood in Beijing was shifting, from piecemeal change to much more radical moves. During April and May 1980, Deng Xiaoping spoke out for implementing household farming as a temporary measure in all poor regions.[12] That Deng seemed more concerned with limiting government handouts than with structural change was of less importance to the reformers. In the summer of 1980, both Zhao Ziyang and Hu Yaobang spoke publicly to say that the Party did not oppose decisions to return to family farming under a household contracting system.[13]

By then the political landscape in Beijing had shifted further. In February 1980 four of the Politburo members who had been promoted during the Cultural Revolution were removed from their top-level positions. Mao's security chief Wang Dongxing, former agricultural head Ji Dengkui, and Beijing mayor Wu De had all been criticized for the roles they had played prior to 1976 and for dragging their feet on reform. In addition, General Chen Xilian, who had been pushed aside on the Central Military Commission after the return of higher-ranked officers, also lost his Politburo seat. Deng had made it clear ever since the Third Plenum that they were out of favor. He even on occasion referred to them as "the little Gang of Four," a highly unfair description, especially since it was Wang Dongxing who had carried out the operation that arrested Jiang Qing and the other leading Leftists back in 1976.[14] Also, there is no evidence of the four being particularly close, except perhaps after they all came under attack in 1978. Ji Dengkui had particular reason to be offended. Having at one point been a serious candidate as successor to Mao Zedong, Ji had worked closely with Zhou Enlai, with Hua Guofeng in 1976, and had supported the post-Mao reform efforts. But none of this helped him in 1980. In Deng's eyes, Ji and the others were tainted by their associations with the Cultural Revolution. He also saw them as potential supporters of Chairman Hua's position, which Deng in 1980 was determined to end sooner rather than later.

At the beginning of the year Deng had laid out his plans for the future in a speech to a Central Committee cadre conference in Beijing. Entitled "The Present Situation and the Tasks before Us," Deng's speech was both a way of taking full possession of the Party and, without being too specific, pointing to a new agenda for the CCP. The Party leader tried to do three different things at the same time: He condemned the past and those responsible for it, while reconstructing the image of Mao as, in the main, a good Communist who in his old age had been betrayed by his associates. He attacked those who no longer believed in the dictatorship of the CCP. And he called for the intensification of reform and the removal of those unwilling or unqualified to lead it. As on many other occasions in the early 1980s, Deng's strategy was to speak in general terms in public, so as not to be blamed if any single initiative went wrong. But he also, much more powerfully than before, wanted to take ownership of the reform agenda and responsibility for leading it.

"The decade of the 'Cultural Revolution' brought catastrophe upon us and caused profound suffering," Deng began. That period was forever over. But the country and the Party still faced acute dangers.

> Even a handful of people could undermine our great undertaking. . . . Although each [opposition] is different in nature, it is entirely possible under certain circumstances for these people to coalesce into a destructive force which can cause us considerable trouble and losses. That is just what happened last year, and it could happen again. . . . A small number of comrades . . . are still soft on such people. In some places, the measures taken against them are far from effective or stern. The people will resent it if we tolerate these remnants of the Gang of Four, counter-revolutionaries, and other criminals. . . . Being soft on criminals only endangers the interests of the vast majority of the people and the overall interests of our modernization drive. . . . When did we ever say that we would tolerate the activities of counter-revolutionaries and saboteurs? When did we ever say that the dictatorship of the proletariat was to be abolished?[15]

But in order to defend the dictatorship, Deng argued, the Party had to combine material progress with good leadership. "We stand for the principle, 'to each according to his work,' and . . . we are also in favor of allowing a part of the population or certain localities to become well-off first through hard work which earns them greater income." But incentives had to be used in conjunction with better government. Today, Deng said, "inside the Party there are too many people who are not professionally competent and too few who are. . . . A number of our Party members do not measure up to standards. Some of the new members who joined the Party during the 'cultural revolution' are not qualified because, never having received Party education, they cannot set an example to the masses. . . . How many of our Party members, and particularly our leading cadres, have mastered professional knowledge? Can we go on in this way?"[16]

By the summer of 1980, Deng and those working closely with him had decided that Chairman Hua would have to follow the other Cultural Revolution beneficiaries out the door.[17] But they agreed that the demolition job had to been done gradually, in stages, the way they had handled the cases of the other former Politburo members. There is no evidence of specific policy differences that produced this outcome. Deng wanted power and legitimacy. He and many of his supporters believed that Hua's position was illegitimate, in the sense that it stemmed from one of the mistakes Mao Zedong had made in his waning years. But they were also afraid that those who were skeptical of more radical economic reforms (and perhaps some of the "democrats," too) could make Hua Guofeng their leader. One of Deng's closest associates, Deng Liqun, told a group of military officers after Hua's fall that "the vestiges of the Gang of Four, the so-called dissidents, all want to wave, or have already waved, the flag of Hua Guofeng. . . . Comrade Hua Guofeng did not participate in these issues, he is not involved in these matters. But people want to save his flag."[18]

In August 1980 Hua lost his position as premier and head of the State Council. At an expanded Politburo meeting, Deng prefaced the decision by saying that the CCP suffered from

> bureaucracy, excessive concentration of power, paternalism, lifetime cadre leadership, and all forms of privilege. . . . Stalin [in his time] seriously damaged the socialist legal system, and Comrade Mao Zedong said that such incidents could not happen in Western countries such as Britain, France and the United States. Although he recognized this, the failure to actually solve

the leadership problem . . . led to the decade-long devastation of the Cultural Revolution. The lesson is profound. . . . The time and conditions are ripe to propose the task of reforming and perfecting the Party and state leadership system to meet the needs of modernization.[19]

Hua accepted the outcome, since he himself had been a main critic of one-man rule within the Party. He also knew that he did not have the votes in the Politburo to shore up his position. And the outcome was contingent on Hua keeping his most important position, that of chairman of the CCP. To the surprise of many, Deng and Chen Yun, the second most powerful leader, had decided on Zhao Ziyang as new premier. The old men would stay in power while leaving management of the state and Party to a younger generation.

Although the August compromise seemed unstable, it was not clear until late October that the senior leaders had also decided to remove Hua as chairman. This time there was opposition. Even some of Deng's closest associates, such as Hu Yaobang, did not think it was right to remove Hua, and certainly not to wage a campaign against him. They feared instability in the Party, since Hua was generally well liked. They also thought it unfair, given the substantial contributions Hua had made since 1976 or even before. But their concerns were overcome by Deng, who had made up his mind. In the weeks before another expanded Politburo meeting in November, Deng met—in a rather conspicuous fashion—with the heads of the military, making it plain where power lay. He got their consent for removing Hua, including that of Ye Jianying, the old marshal who had been seen as Hua's mentor within the Party.[20] At the Politburo sessions in November and early December 1980, Hua was accused of a medley of serious mistakes. The Party Chairman had never, it was said, admitted the disasters of the Cultural Revolution. He had tried to develop a personality cult around himself. He was responsible for "rash advances" in the economy right after he had taken over, all of which had led to setbacks. Worse, he had relied too much on foreign imports to make a new Great Leap (some younger adherents of Deng coined the epithet "Foreign Great Leap Hua"). He was also accused of holding back the rehabilitation of veteran cadres and the righting of Cultural Revolution wrongs.[21]

Hua did not respond to most of these attacks, even though many of them were distorted or outright false. He did admit responsibility for having accepted, during a brief period, the "two whatevers," for economic mistakes, and even for promoting a personality cult, although all of these were decisions of the then Politburo. The one accusation he did not accept was blocking the reinstitution of senior leaders. Even at the pro forma Sixth Plenum of the Central Committee in June 1981, at which the December decision to remove Hua as chairman was validated, he refused to cave in. "You say that I blocked the return of old cadre. But who exactly did I block? I am not going to say any more, say whatever you want!" Deng's retort almost gave the game away: "What was your attitude towards the rehabilitation of old cadre? Did you raise the issue, or did other people raise it? What was your attitude towards old cadre as a whole? You have to look at matters this way, otherwise you will always feel you have been wronged."[22] To Deng, it was accepting the prime position of himself and his generation of leaders that mattered, not what Hua may or may not have done in individual cases. That Hua almost certainly saved Deng's life through the coup against the Left seemed to matter less. Whatever qualities Deng Xiaoping had as a leader, gratitude was not among them.[23]

As in August with the premiership, Deng did not step forward to claim the chairmanship for himself. Instead, he gave the position to Hu Yaobang. This time the choice was more obvious than five months earlier. Hu was perhaps the only CCP leader who was loved among the people he had worked with. He was also respected for his forthrightness and his preoccupation with justice and equity. But it was exactly these qualities that made it difficult for Hu to accept his new post. He first proposed that the chairmanship should rotate among the members of the Politburo Standing Committee. And he repeatedly complained about the treatment of his predecessor. At the concluding meeting in June 1981, Hu argued that if there should be a chairman, it should be Deng. "Even foreigners know that Comrade Deng Xiaoping is the main decision-maker in China's Party today. . . . The old revolutionary generation are still the key figures. . . . Shouldn't the entire Party be informed about this state of affairs?"[24] But Deng hushed him up. "I think that this speech proves that our choice was correct," Deng told the other Party leaders.[25] To be on the safe side, Deng took the position of chairman of the Central Military Committee for himself. From this post he would rule China for the decade to come.

The first big task that Hu Yaobang now had to finish was the question of what, in the end, to do with the imprisoned leaders of the Left. After the coup in October 1976, Jiang Qing and her associates had first been held for sev-

eral months in cells in the vast underground complex below the Zhongnanhai. In a macabre twist, they were kept company by Mao Zedong's body, which
was stored in the same location before his mausoleum in Tiananmen Square
was completed in the summer of 1977.[26] Then Jiang and the others were sent
to Qincheng Prison just north of Beijing. They were repeatedly interrogated
and asked to sign written confessions. Wang Hongwen was singled out for
harsh treatment, perhaps because his jailers thought that he, being the youngest, would break most easily. Meanwhile a CCP case committee, headed by
Wang Dongxing and similar in form to those used during the Cultural Revolution, was traveling the country and scouring the archives to find evidence
to be used against them. Hu Yaobang inherited Wang's investigation reports
after the former head of the security forces fell from power in 1979.[27]

The Party was in a profound dilemma about what to do with Mao's widow
and the other Leftists. The majority of the new leaders wanted a public trial
in which the evil deeds of their prisoners could be exposed and the Party
cleansed of its sins. The problem was how to do this without further damaging the reputation of the CCP and of Mao Zedong, the man under whose rule
they had all joined the Party and whom they had worshipped as a God-like
figure prior to 1976. Deng ordered the trial to be prepared in the most meticulous fashion, leading to it being postponed several times while judges,
prosecutors, and defenders were trained for their purposes and the leaders
deliberated what the verdict should be. Party experts were told to study the
Nuremberg verdicts and other important judicial processes in the West and
instruct the judiciary on the terminologies that should be used, so that both
Chinese and foreigners would see that the trial was conducted according to
international standards.[28]

The trial started in November 1980 and went wrong right from the beginning. At the very last moment, Mao's nephew Mao Yuanxin was removed from
the slate of accused and sent to be court-martialed in Liaoning, away from
the public eye. His replacement in the dock, one of Lin Biao's fallen generals, did not have the star quality a Mao relative would have had. Of the four
main defendants, only Wang Hongwen cooperated with the prosecution, admitting in an almost mechanical fashion to all the accusations leveled against
him, including the more ridiculous ones, such as embezzlement and overin-
dulgence. Yao Wenyuan contested all the charges in a polite piece-by-piece
fashion. Zhang Chunqiao wrote a note saying that he did not recognize the

jurisdiction of the court and then refused to say a word throughout the trial. This left the show to Jiang Qing, and she immediately proceeded to make use of it. Sparring with the prosecutors and judges from the moment she entered the court, she shouted that they were nothing but a bunch of counter-revolutionaries. "You could as well bring me to Tiananmen Square for a public trial and shoot me." "Do not pretend to act," said the former star actress. "Without my props, you would not be able to act in this scene. If you have the courage, please ask your backstage director out. I will confront him. . . . I am without law [and] I am not afraid of you. I have never been afraid of Liu Shaoqi and Lin Biao, [how] can I be afraid of you?"

Hauled out of court on several occasions, Jiang was still allowed to deliver a statement before the judges passed sentence on her. Attacking both Deng and Hua, she pronounced them guilty of using their dictatorship to engage in fascism. "I am implementing the proletarian revolutionary line to defend Chairman Mao," Jiang shouted. "I am doing my best to defend the Great Proletarian Cultural Revolution. . . . Everything in my past was done according to the instructions of the Central Committee. . . . You can convict me whatever way you want. My only challenge now is to be accountable to Chairman Mao. . . . I was Chairman Mao's dog. Because of Chairman Mao, I am not afraid of you. On Chairman Mao's political chessboard, although I am just a pawn, I am now a pawn who has crossed the river." After the court sentenced her to death, with a two-year reprieve, she was carried out of the courtroom, still shouting: "Down with the counter-revolutionary revisionists! It is right to rebel! Long live the victory of Chairman Mao's revolutionary line!"[29]

The spectacle of the trial itself, parts of it shown on Chinese television, left much to be desired for Deng and the Party leadership. But it did serve as a final verdict of sorts not just on the accused but on the Cultural Revolution and what it had entailed. It also gave the new leaders a chance to go after the Left at the local level in a much more thorough fashion than before. Between 1980 and 1985 every single CCP member had to account for their behavior during the Cultural Revolution. Almost one million were sanctioned in one way or another, either through the courts or through Party discipline.[30] Some of the small Leftist groups that survived turned to terrorism. Members of the guards at the Jinan Military Region's headquarters had tried to assassinate Deng Xiaoping during his visit there in March 1980, shouting, "Down with capitalism" and "Revenge for Vice Chairman Jiang [Qing]."[31] But overall the

Jiang Qing is taken out of court after being sentenced
to the death penalty with a two-year probation, 1980.
Source: CPA Media Pte. Ltd./Alamy Stock Photo.

new leaders had the situation well in hand and felt politically safe enough
that they, finally, could issue a resolution that delivered the political verdict
on the past.

After having been discussed at the top level for more than a year, the "Resolution on Certain Questions in the History of Our Party since the Founding
of the People's Republic of China" was passed at the Sixth Plenum in June 1981,
the same meeting at which Hua Guofeng lost his chairmanship. After reviewing the Party's glorious and mostly correct history up to 1966, the resolution
provides a harsh verdict on the decade that followed and on Mao Zedong's
final years in charge. "The chief responsibility for the grave 'Left' error of the
'Cultural Revolution' . . . does indeed lie with Comrade Mao Zedong," the resolution states. "His theoretical and practical mistakes concerning class struggle in a socialist society became increasingly serious, his personal arbitrariness
gradually undermined democratic centralism in Party life, and the personality

cult grew more and more serious." It continues: "The history of the 'Cultural Revolution' has proved that Comrade Mao Zedong's principal theses for initiating this revolution conformed neither to Marxism, Leninism, nor to Chinese reality. They represent an entirely erroneous appraisal of the prevailing class relations and political situation in the Party and state."[32]

Having said what needed to be said about the late Mao's politics—and about the mistakes by Hua Guofeng, whom Mao had put in place—the Party leaders attempted to rescue Mao the historical figure for the CCP. "Comrade Mao Zedong was a great Marxist and a great proletarian revolutionary, strategist and theorist. It is true that he made gross mistakes during the 'Cultural Revolution,' but, if we judge his activities as a whole, his contributions to the Chinese revolution far outweigh his mistakes. His merits are primary and his errors secondary."[33] Deng would not tolerate a Stalin-style hatchet job on the man he had followed for forty years. Instead, in a brave attempt at stating why Mao had been allowed to do so much damage to the Party, the resolution looked at the fundamentals.

> It remains difficult to eliminate the evil ideological and political influence of centuries of feudal autocracy. And, for various historical reasons, we failed to institutionalize and legalize inner-Party democracy and democracy in the political and social life of the country, or we drew up the relevant laws but they lacked due authority. This meant that conditions were present for the over-concentration of Party power in individuals and for the development of arbitrary individual rule and the personality cult in the Party. Thus, it was hard for the Party and state to prevent the initiation of the "Cultural Revolution" or check its development.[34]

This was as far as the Party would ever go, at least publicly, in pondering the deeper causes of what Deng now routinely referred to as "the ten disastrous years." With the end of the trial against its opponents and the publication, finally, of the official pronouncement on the past, the Party leadership could at last concentrate on what Deng Xiaoping insisted was the real issue, namely economic growth in China. Since the Third Plenum in 1978, Deng had moved out ahead of other senior leaders on matters of economic reform. Increasingly, he regarded the country's backwardness as a life-and-death issue for the CCP's rule in China. Stunned by the ongoing economic transformations he had observed elsewhere in the world, Deng believed that China did not have much time to catch up and that forms of shock therapy were in order. But, in reality, the central leadership had not led on economic policy during the past three years. Instead, the CCP had fallen further and further behind the market-driven change from below that was spreading in some parts of the country. Deng was now willing to experiment further. He made his views clear to the State Planning Commission in 1982. "Compared with capitalism," Deng said, "the superiority of socialism is that under socialism the people of the whole country can work as one and concentrate their strength on key projects. A shortcoming of socialism is that the market is not put to best use and the economy is too rigid. How should we handle the relation between planning and the market? If we handle it properly, it will help greatly to promote economic development; if we don't, things will go badly."[35]

Of all the top officials, the new Premier, Zhao Ziyang, was the one who was most in line with Deng's outlook. A consistent economic reformer but cautious on political issues, Zhao was better suited than the new Chairman Hu Yaobang to engage with Deng's partners and rivals in power, such as Chen Yun and the veteran leader Peng Zhen—one of Mao Zedong's bêtes noires— who had been readmitted to the Politburo and put in charge of policing and the judiciary. The old leaders admired Hu's willingness to stand up for what he believed in, but they felt more comfortable with Zhao's patient explana- tions of how to seek economic growth. When Zhao, with Deng's and Hu's support, turned to much more significant rural reform in 1981, the established patterns in the Chinese countryside really started to change.

In late summer that year, after consultations within the top leadership, Pre- mier Zhao publicly stated that household contracting systems may be ap- propriate for the whole country under certain circumstances. All depended on what farmers themselves found to be working best. The point, Zhao said, was to increase production and stimulate specialization, putting better and cheaper food on the table, and securing government quotas and tax income.[36] One of his key arguments in opening up for new methods of production was that agricultural output had improved overall since 1977 and that now was the time to take yields countrywide to a new level. Zhao also argued strongly that groups of farmers were best placed to make these decisions themselves. The result was a rush toward family-based farming, especially in richer areas. Half of all communes had converted most of their land to a household-based system by the end of the year. Seventy-eight percent had done so by the end of 1982, and decollectivization was basically complete by late summer 1983.[37] Collective farming, which had seized the imagination of Chinese Communists in the 1920s and had been the Party's most important policy in the years after it took power, had in the main ceased to exist.

It is clear that decollectivization in the long run secured China's agricultural output much more effectively than collective farming had done, at least under the circumstances produced by the Chinese Communists from 1950 to the late 1970s. But the changes in the early 1980s were not uncontroversial among farmers, even though the vast majority grabbed the opportunity of making their own decisions on what to produce, how to produce, and how to spend the surplus. In the regions where large-scale mechanized farming had been implemented—first and foremost the northeastern provinces of Jilin, Heilongjiang, and Liaoning—household farming would obviously be a step backward in terms of production, and most of the large state-owned farms stayed in place.[38] In places where dire poverty and permanent undernourishment made almost any economic activity beyond subsistence farming impossible, people still clamored for government relief. And in richer areas on the eastern coast, farmers as a rule were not eager to get rid of the collectives until it was clear that household farming would be a countrywide norm. Then farmers rushed to divide up communal property on the principle of devil take the hindmost. Nobody wanted to be left behind in the rush for personal gain.

Deng, Hu Yaobang, and Zhao Ziyang worked closely together to make sure that leadership in the provinces was well-disposed toward radical reform initiatives, at first in agriculture but increasingly in industry as well. By the end of 1980, twenty-five of the twenty-nine provincial CCP first secretaries were rehabilitated cadre. And in some cases their successors had already been agreed upon, too. The successors tended to be slightly younger men (almost all were male), with as good an education as one could get in China at the time—often in engineering—good military contacts, and time spent in training at the Central Party School, Hu Yaobang's "home" institution. Guangdong Province is a case in point. There Xi Zhongxun was appointed Party head in 1978. After Xi was recalled to Beijing in 1981 to join the Politburo, Ren Zhongyi took over his position in Guangdong. Both Xi and Ren were reformers; Xi was a guerrilla leader from the 1930s and an old associate of Deng Xiaoping, and Ren had helped clear up Liaoning, where the Left had substantial support, in the late 1970s. Under Xi and Ren, Guangdong became a showcase for where the new leadership wanted to move in economic terms.

In 1980, Guangdong—the province next to Hong Kong—was almost 80 percent rural. The province was poor overall; it was one of those places in China that remembered better lives for most before the Communist takeover. Until China's war with Japan, parts of Guangdong had been relatively wealthy, with lots of overseas links, both through Hong Kong and through Southeast Asia, where there were many emigrants from the province. The Cantonese used to pride themselves on their business acumen and on their good conditions for agriculture. Much would grow in Guangdong's subtropical climate that would not grow further north—fruit, tea, sugar, and tobacco—and, in addition, it had a good climate for poultry and fish-farming. But during the 1960s the province had been forced to produce more rice, and its commercial agriculture had suffered. With fishermen prevented from going to sea and local trade across borders shut off, much of rural Guangdong fell on hard times.

Things were not so much better in the cities. Guangzhou, the provincial capital, only a hundred miles from Hong Kong, suffered from overcrowded housing, deteriorating transportation and communications, and a chronic lack of investment. The U.S. sinologist Ezra Vogel, who spent a lot of time in the province in the 1980s, used the example of telephones to illustrate the situation.[39] In 1978 the city of Guangzhou had 29,000 phone lines, exactly the same number as when the CCP took over thirty years earlier, even though the population had more than doubled. Worse, they were mainly the same phones, now often in a terrible state of repair. No surprise that many enterprising Cantonese preferred to move to Hong Kong whenever an opportunity to cross the heavily controlled border arose. According to official figures, close to 150,000 had arrived in Hong Kong just in 1979, and, although British authorities had deported more than half of them, others kept trying to make the journey.[40]

When Xi Zhongxun came to Guangdong in 1978 he did not know much about the south. Almost all of his career had been in the northwest, first as a guerrilla leader in Shaanxi, his home province, and then, as a CCP official, even further west, in Gansu, Qinghai, and Xinjiang. Xi had been a member of the Party since he was 15 years old, and he was known for his toughness and his frankness. Mao had purged him before the Cultural Revolution even started, in 1962, and he had been lucky to survive the upheavals that followed. Now, having been rehabilitated by his Party for what he himself claimed was the fourth time, he wanted to make an example out of Guangdong and exploit its unique position to create rapid economic growth. One of the first ideas that came up was to construct export processing zones in areas close to Hong Kong, creating employment and attracting foreign capital and technology, while jump-starting the construction of new industries.[41]

The concept of such regions seems to have been first aired among reformers in Beijing, but Xi Zhongxun and his advisers picked it up in the spring of 1979. Xi proposed to the central leadership that Guangdong would be perfectly suited for such an approach, and it was Deng Xiaoping, in agreeing, who suggested the term Special Economic Zone (SEZ) for the new ventures.[42] When Xi reportedly worried that, as a Communist, he had no experience with overseeing market economics, Deng countered that Xi should think of it as another guerrilla campaign, learning new lessons step by step. And this is indeed what Xi did when he returned to his province, even in the way he spoke about the enterprise: "flexible tactics," "rapid advances," and "showing no mercy" were among his favorite terms. He delighted in shocking provincial officials who had not yet become accustomed to the new priorities in Beijing.[43]

By 1980 four SEZs were up and running, three in Guangdong and one in neighboring Fujian, across from Taiwan. By far the biggest of them was in Shenzhen, on the Hong Kong border. Although in 1980 most of the area consisted of rice paddies and sleepy fishing villages, there were people around who had rich experience in trading with Hong Kong, often in ways that skirted the law. It was the mix of managers, economists and planners from the center, local entrepreneurs, and powerful provincial leaders such as Xi Zhongxun and his successor Ren Zhongyi who laid the foundation for what would become China's biggest experiment with modernity. The first foreign investor was Thailand's Charoen Pokphand Group, set up in Bangkok by emigrants from Guangdong in the 1920s. In 1981 it finished the construction of an animal feed plant in Shenzhen.[44] Through tax exemptions, cheap and disciplined labor provided by the authorities, and easy repatriation of profits, the SEZs started to attract foreign investment, although at first more slowly than the CCP would have liked to see. Right from the beginning, though, foreign companies brought in technology that quickly found its way to other enterprises in the region, helping to set off a boom in industrial development in some areas on the south China coast.

But it was not just its SEZs that Guangdong profited from. Being far away from the center and under control by people Deng trusted, he was happy to make the province a laboratory of economic development, with more leeway to manage its own affairs than was given to other regions. It also helped Guangdong that the new premier, Zhao Ziyang, had spent many years in the province and felt that he knew enough to let reform move ahead while being able to safely evaluate results from afar. The maverick Xi Zhongxun, who had been reading about the U.S. Constitution, wanted to think of his province's relationship with Beijing as akin to that of an American state vis-à-vis the federal government, but that was further than anyone else wanted to go. Still, Guangdong was allowed to set up its own trading companies and find its own export markets. Foreign currency income could be kept in the province, and, uniquely, Guangdong could pay a fixed sum each year to the central government, rather than a percentage of its income. Eventually the province gained the right to carry out its own wage and price reforms, meaning that rationing was abolished and market prices for many products were introduced already in 1980, with wages overall set above national guidelines to compensate.[45]

As Ezra Vogel pointed out, by 1982 Guangdong was ahead in the reform process because of a set of exceptional circumstances. The province's GDP per capita tripled between 1978 and 1985. When he visited Guangzhou in the mid-1980s, Vogel could see the change: "Buses were more widespread, and almost no one traveled standing in a truck bed. The streets were jammed with taxis, vans, cars, and motorbikes, in addition to bicycles. Stores, filled with goods and customers, lined the streets. Open food markets were large and noisy, with a far greater variety of goods for sale than before. New buildings and construction sites could be found in all parts of the city, and dozens of factories had modern production equipment."[46]

Although Guangdong was special, it also reflected what was happening in the wealthier parts of China by 1982. Both in urban areas and within townships (as the former People's Communes had now been renamed), economic output increased rapidly, though unevenly, allowing a small number of people to get rich quickly. Even if China never privatized state-owned enterprises, these companies quickly found themselves in an environment where markets, and not government directives, guided their business decisions. Already in the early 1980s, most of these enterprises produced both for the plan and above the plan, with much of their income coming from what they could sell on the open market. Many of them also quickly established business relationships with collective enterprises, now renamed township and village enterprises (TVEs), quite a number of which were de facto privately run. Transactions between state companies and TVEs were allowed at market prices, and also through an immense variety of joint and cooperative arrangements. These relationships permitted state companies to cut costs by buying from or producing jointly with TVEs that often had considerably lower labor costs and more flexibility in procurements. Crucially, at the latest from 1984 on, projected output according to plan stayed stable, leaving more room for the market to take hold.[47]

The latter decision shows how significant the state was in promoting market breakthroughs in China in the early 1980s. Keeping the planned economy in place probably helped markets develop and certainly prevented more social unrest and macroeconomic instability. The use of planning instruments served to resist inflation and could, at least to some degree, assist with employment or retraining. But the government's role went far beyond the planning regime. State banks provided credit and, at least in some parts of the country, commercial services. The government also allowed people to change jobs and move to where better jobs could be found. All of this was of course new and in no way unproblematic. The concept of finding a better job had been unknown in Maoist China; even the Soviet Union had higher labor mobility than the PRC in the mid-1970s. And migration within the country had been strongly discouraged, except when organized by the state, and would remain contested over the next generation. But by allowing people with experience and training to move between state companies and TVEs, and by allowing what was called "temporary" migration inside and outside of provinces to take place, the state encouraged the economy to slowly outgrow its planning elements.

These changes in the economy of course also created massive social changes, none of them unproblematic. Price increases made life difficult for the poor and for pensioners especially. Workers who joined new forms of enterprises did not have access to what Chinese called "the iron rice bowl," meaning the job security, free housing, health care, schools, and pensions that had been provided through their government-sponsored workplace, in

Chinese called a "work unit" or *danwei*. Some of these functions, such as schools and hospitals, started to move from the work-unit level and be reestablished at the central or provincial level, but this was a slow process. In the meantime, workers in the new kinds of companies had to fend for themselves as best they could, mainly through a massive increase in savings. China's personal savings rate quintupled between 1978 and 1984.[48] And, for some of those who transitioned out of state-owned enterprises, part ownership of their new workplaces could also be a destination for their new and higher wages, not just bank deposits. Many Chinese, especially young people in urban areas or with urban connections, were learning fast how to adapt to new realities.

But while a large number of people benefited from the economic changes, the suggestion that this was reform without losers is false. In addition to those who suffered from inflation and higher prices, women were among the biggest losers, since gender equality in wages declined under reform. There were also fewer work opportunities for women both in the countryside and in the cities. Family farming tended to be more patriarchal than collective farming. And in urban areas women were often outcompeted by young men returning from the provinces both for jobs and for education.[49] The strict family-planning regime—the so-called one child policy—that was introduced in 1980 to limit population growth did little to help women in the workplace and put more pressure on them to produce a male family heir. The policy's very draconian implementation, including mandatory IUDs for women with one child, forced sterilization after two, and abortion for unauthorized conceptions, was an exceptional intrusion into the lives of women. In politics, women's positions and women's concerns were also reduced. In the imagination of men, and of some women, too, part of the problem with the Cultural Revolution was that there had been too many women in positions of influence, taking offices that they did not belong in.[50] Although individual women could do well under reform, especially in the south, the overall level of misogyny and discrimination increased.

Where did the ideas come from for the practices developed within China's early reform era? As we have seen, much of what happened did so from below, and the CCP simply decided not to get in the way, or at least not to get too much in the way. From 1976 on, some CCP leaders had studied the market and incentive-based experiments in socialist countries, mainly Yugoslavia and Hungary, and adapted some of them for use in China.[51] But reform soon broke out of socialist experimentation. By 1982, a few Chinese Communists were increasingly influenced by market doctrines that had emerged in the West. For this, the timing of China's economic reforms is crucial. Just like people in the West, Chinese experts were struck by the sudden turn to market liberalism in the early 1980s—what we know as the Reagan revolution, after Ronald Reagan became U.S. president in 1981, and Thatcherism in Britain. These experts saw advanced capitalist countries as highly successful and other socialist countries as less successful. The socialist countries were also associated with the Soviet Union, which was still China's enemy number one. Put together, this meant that China had more to learn from market liberals than from socialists. Never openly expressed, such views, where they existed, had to be artificially defined within a socialist rhetoric, just like for some cadre, at least, the idea of socialism itself gradually transferred from non- or anti-market practices to simple belief in CCP rule.

But while those who were thinking about principles of liberal markets were usually tucked away in research institutions or advisory groups, those who created facts on the ground were very visible—and sometimes too visible for their own good. As private enterprise flourished, some Party officials tried to hold back the flood, either because of their own political beliefs or because they misinterpreted signals from above. The latter was very easy to do, especially in 1981 and 1982, since the central and provincial leadership said little about what *was* allowed and often hedged on what was not. Zheng Yuanzhong, a farmer from a small town near Wenzhou in Zhejiang, began trading in electrical parts in 1980. He did well, but in 1982 he was arrested as one of the "eight big kings" of illegal trade in Wenzhou. When he was let out, he continued trading, sometimes, in defiance, using the trade name "King of Electrical Appliances." By 1984 he was lauded by the Party as a local hero and went on to set up a garment factory employing more than 1,500 workers.[52] A local official, also in Zhejiang, recounted his struggles with finding out what official policy actually was. Having allowed a small market to be set up in 1980, he found that it expanded very quickly, drawing criticism from county leaders about traffic clogging up the main road. But when he was ordered to close it down, he hesitated. "The masses," he told his associates, "have a very high opinion of this." Instead he moved it away from the road. By the following year, he was handing out licenses to trade in the market, though only for items the traders themselves had produced. Itinerant trading was still not formally allowed, though the official was struck by an old farmer who went from village to village, wanting to exchange homemade candy for duck feathers to be used as fertilizer. "It is an old tradition," said the man, "passed down from our ancestors for hundreds of years, and previous emperors have allowed us to do it. . . . If the Communist Party is for the people, why not allow me to earn a few yuan?"[53]

Chinese economic historians often speak of three basic models of nonstate industrialization outside of urban areas.[54] One was the southern Jiangsu model, which could be said to center on the corporatization of a whole village or a district. Local government had much influence in these cases, and business leaders often subsidized agriculture to make everyone share in their prosperity. The second one was the Wenzhou model, where—as in the aforementioned cases—small private companies produced consumer goods that peddlers tried to sell elsewhere. And finally there was the Pearl River delta model of township and village enterprises with some degree of foreign investment.[55] The latter often grew more rapidly and depended on workers from elsewhere, including from other provinces. In reality, of course, there were many different models of initiatives, control, and ownership beyond these three. Companies were set up by schools and universities, by military units, and by associations and organizations. They often got their capital by borrowing at market rates or from savings, meaning high opportunity costs. In turn this meant a need to maximize profit by finding rewarding business opportunities, especially since local government often demanded a significant percentage of the income. And even if the government share was often reinvested in the companies, for commercial reasons and out of local pride, this still resulted in a high need for rapid returns.

What saved many small enterprises in the first stage of China's reform era was their extreme profitability. With little competition and an enormous market, in addition, of course, to very low labor costs, a 40–50 percent return on capital in the initial years was not uncommon. And that kind of return could keep everyone happy, from managers to workers, investors, and local government. Many of the most successful TVEs also benefited from their location near cities; today we would call them suburban. Not only did they have a huge market next door, but they could also hire expertise from the cities and interact commercially with established state-owned enterprises, which were under increasing pressure to show some profitability. Their location also benefited them politically. Wealthy and influential local governments could protect them, acting as political as well as commercial guarantors for new businesses. If there ever were a Goldilocks zone in business, Chinese suburban entrepreneurs in the early 1980s inhabited it.

When the CCP gathered for its Twelfth Congress in September 1982, the Party already presided over a changed China. Year-on-year economic growth overall was above 9 percent, and in the consumer and export sectors the economy grew with more than twice that figure. On average, rural household income had almost doubled since 1978. The expansion was not just connected to new companies or new farming methods. As of 1982 these had only just started to take hold. With the exception of heavy industry, all of the economy grew, including state-owned companies and long-established collectives. Some of this was due to pent-up demand, innovation, and business skills. But the main cause was simply that the central government interfered less in how people ran their business, how and what they produced, and to which groups they catered. Even if they all applauded economic growth, some Communists gathered at the CCP Congress had begun to worry about the degree to which the economy could be set free under a socialist system. Deng's response, in his opening speech, was to underline the need for the Party to create prosperity. "Economic development," he said, "is the basis for the solution of our external and internal problems." And whatever method that delivered development was one the Party should be in favor of, as long as it did not touch the fundamental principles of CCP rule.[56]

11

To the Point of No Return?

BY THE TIME THE TWELFTH CONGRESS of the CCP was held in September 1982, China was at a turning point. The two main directions that had evolved since 1980, toward more liberalism in economics and more authoritarianism in politics, seemed to be joined in the person of Deng Xiaoping, who was now the country's uncontested leader. Granted, there were senior leaders within the Party who believed that economic liberalization was happening much too fast and, among them, some who queried the overall direction of policy, fearing that it had moved too far from their Party's point of origin. Likewise, there were those inside and outside of the Party who resented the crackdown on the freedom of speech and organization, and who believed that a more economically successful China would also have to be a freer China. But both of these groups were kept in check through a mixture of enticements and suppression.

The main reason Deng was able to stay firmly in the saddle, while keeping a balance between those who believed that he was doing too much and those who believed he was doing too little, was that China's economic reforms already in the early 1980s seemed to deliver economic growth in abundance. While much of the rest of the world was going through a rough patch economically, China registered almost 10 percent year-on-year growth in most sectors of the economy.[1] This growth happened from a very low starting point and had a limited impact, at least to begin with, on people's daily lives—except, perhaps, in high-producing agricultural areas. Even so, it gave hope for the future, and hope was precisely what most Chinese had been short on in the

late Maoist era. Deng's conclusion was that further economic experimentation was needed, as long as it could deliver even more intense economic
growth. The problem, he kept saying to other leaders, was not that China
moved too fast on economic reform, but that it moved too slow.

Deng worried about the drags on economic development. But he was also
troubled by the lack of dedication to the Communist Party shown by many
Chinese, especially among the young. While he believed that they would show
more allegiance as the Party's policies made living standards improve, Deng
did not want to sit around waiting for more unrest of the kind he had encountered in 1979. In order to keep control over schools, news media, and
intellectuals, he made Hu Qiaomu a member of the Politburo and its main
spokesman on ideological issues, while Deng Liqun was in charge of propaganda. Both had been close to Deng Xiaoping since the 1950s, and their con-
servatism on issues of doctrine and freedom of speech was well known to
him. Deng wanted their help in reining in what he saw as Hu Yaobang's enthusiasm for too much democracy and tolerance. Meanwhile, he fired the
two top editors of *Renmin Ribao*, Hu Jiwei and Wang Ruoshui, accusing them
of being too liberal. "The majority of our theorists, writers, and artists are good
or relatively good," Deng instructed in October 1983. "Only a few are guilty of
spreading spiritual pollution. The problem is that the mistakes of those few
have not been severely criticized and that necessary measures have not been
taken to put a stop to their actions and to the dissemination of their wrong
ideas. Spiritual pollution can be so damaging as to bring disaster upon the
country and the people."[2]

At the time of the Twelfth Congress, Hu Yaobang had insisted on giving
up his title as Party chairman. His argument that the CCP had had more than
enough of chairmen and their whims was accepted by the senior leaders, and
Hu was instead designated general secretary of the Party. Hu explained to
others that his new title was also more reflective of his actual position; he was
in charge of the CCP's organization, while Deng and the older bosses made
the overall decisions. Though Deng was undoubtedly in overall command,
Hu may have underrated his own status somewhat. Perceived to be more
liberal than the senior leaders and more sympathetic to the concerns of ordinary people, Hu had strong support both within the Party and among
non-Party members, especially among the youth. But when encouraged by
his supporters to set out his political stall more clearly and build his own im-

age, Hu demurred and said that he worked under the overall leadership of
Deng Xiaoping.[3] Even so, in his March 1983 speech commemorating the one
hundredth anniversary of Karl Marx's death, Hu went out of his way to underline the need for free discussion within the Party and to stress the value
of the CCP's links with scholars and intellectuals. After all, he reminded his
audience, Karl Marx himself had been a controversial intellectual. While the
CCP was "creating a new situation in all fields of socialist modernization,
striving to build a socialist material and spiritual civilization . . . it must be
noted that the grave consequences of the prolonged 'Left' mistakes are far
from being liquidated either in our ideology or public opinion or in various
political, economic and organizational measures adopted."[4] Some of Hu's allies took on the concept of "a socialist spiritual civilization" as a catch-all for
more openness and debates on governance and democracy.

Deng's concerns about people linking the critique of such liberal or hu-
manist values to a criticism of rapid economic change was manifested in the
person of Chen Yun. In terms of seniority, Chen was the only leader, in addition to the now very aged Ye Jianying, who could rival Deng Xiaoping. Chen
Yun was widely admired within the CCP for being an upright, though sometimes very stern, official. Unlike Deng, he had spoken his mind to Mao from
the very beginning of what was now called Leftist deviations, starting with the
Great Leap Forward. As a consequence, he had been sidelined up to 1976,
but after that he had become the main spokesman for the rehabilitation of
old cadre and for a systematic condemnation of the Cultural Revolution, not
least in terms of economics. Chen recognized Deng Xiaoping as the Party's
main leader and had no aspiration to take the number-one position for himself. But by 1982 he believed that some of Deng's main associates—first and
foremost Hu Yaobang—were deviating from Marxism and that an adjustment
of course was necessary to return the Party to its original values. While Chen
supported economic reform overall, he wanted the planned economy to be
in the driver's seat. He also insisted that market forces should help build socialism and solidify the rule of the Communist Party, not the other way
around. Premier Zhao Ziyang, who in many ways admired Chen Yun, even
though they disagreed on important issues, summed up the differences in
the notes he wrote while under house arrest many years later. "Deng," Zhao
said, "believed in expanding the economy with an emphasis on speed and
opening up to the outside world, adopting reforms that moved toward a

market economy. Chen Yun upheld the approach of the first Five-Year Plan in the 1950s; that group insisted on a planned economy and had reservations about the reform program."[5]

While Deng could be annoyed by Hu Yaobang, he had no intention of letting the General Secretary he had picked be done in politically by Chen Yun or anyone else. What Deng wanted to do was facilitate the retirement of the senior leaders, including, eventually, himself, by creating a duopoly of organizational power, with Hu in charge of the Party and Zhao Ziyang in charge of the government. He saw Hu as the conscience of the Party and the person he identified with most in political terms, in spite of their occasional disagreements. Zhao was the perfect technocrat, getting practical results from Party policies.[6] Deng wanted to design a balance between Hu and Zhao. But he also had to give the conservatives something. Chen Yun was in charge of the Party's Central Discipline Inspection Commission, originally set up as an instrument to punish the Left, but now increasingly preoccupied with corruption, economic crimes (as Chen Yun defined them), and smuggling. Chen complained, in particular, about crime and smuggling in Guangdong, and he linked this criticism with his old argument that growth targets were set too high, allowing capitalists and speculators to emerge, especially in and around the SEZs.[7] Echoing Chen Yun, Deng Liqun had started comparing SEZs with the foreign concessions that imperialist powers had carved out of China a hundred years earlier. As a result, the new Guangdong Party chief Ren Zhongyi was called to Beijing twice in early 1982 to face Chen Yun's ire. Given the constellations within the Party leadership, even Hu Yaobang advised Ren to do limited self-criticism of his execution of the new policies, though he did not want Guangdong to change any of its approaches to reform.[8]

With long-time Deng associates Hu Qiaomu and Deng Liqun joining forces with senior leaders Chen Yun and Peng Zhen, the head of the CCP's Central Political and Legal Affairs Commission, in condemning increasing crime as the unacceptable face of reform, Deng had to be seen to take some action against those who went too far. Even though he strongly disliked any championing of Chen Yun from within his own circle, the call for a crackdown on crime coincided to some extent with Deng's own feelings. A disciplinarian at all times, he gave the go-ahead for an anti-crime campaign in early 1982, on the clear condition that it should not in any way be turned against the reform

process. In reality, of course, it provided an opportunity for those Party officials who had always distrusted economic liberalization to go after their favorite targets, entrepreneurs who did not care much about formal rules and
regulations. But officials deemed to be corrupt and ordinary criminals were
also caught in the net, including a number who had been arrested for rape
and murder. The campaign reached a crescendo in May 1983 when a suspected gang leader from northeast China, Zhuo Changren, and some of his
men hijacked a Chinese airliner and forced it to fly to South Korea.[9] Others
tried to escape to Hong Kong and Taiwan, or even across the borders with
Vietnam, Burma, Mongolia, or the Soviet Union. At least 24,000 people were
executed in 1982 and 1983, including many accused of hard-to-define economic crimes.[10]

The anti-crime campaign put a chill into the springtime of economic reform. In many parts of the country, people who had been at the forefront of
change pulled back, afraid of being accused of crimes by competitors, old enemies, or jealous neighbors. Illegal dance parties, listening to Taiwanese or
Hong Kong music, and extramarital sex were among the charges that could
land people in jail for "hooliganism." Having painstakingly tried to put a legal
order together, many Chinese legal experts were wondering whether the arrests and quick trials had any connection to the rule of law, especially when
they found out that provinces, just as in the old days, had quotas of how many
arrests should be made and how many severe sentences should be handed
down. But the campaign was popular among many ordinary people who were
appalled by the corruption and sense of lawlessness that came with the breakthrough for market practices across China. "It is a great thing to crack down
on criminal activities," Deng Xiaoping instructed. "Start in Beijing, then
Shanghai, Tianjin, and other cities. As long as you keep doing this, things
will definitely get better."[11]

Official corruption was everywhere in early reform China, but it was very
hard both to define and get to grips with. When new businesses needed land,
for instance, they would get it from officials who often enriched themselves
in the process. Sons and daughters of senior leaders had better access to know-
how and capital than anyone else in a society in which commerce and trade
had been discouraged—if not always effectively stemmed—for a generation
or more. Many of them "jumped into the sea," as the expression went, meaning that they set up their own company or engaged in "consulting," which at

times was little more than influence peddling or worse. Young princes, as they were often called, did well during China's market revolution, whether they became officials or businesspeople. Everything was easier if you came from a leading "Red" family, and some of China's great fortunes today were created in the 1980s by younger people with close family relations to top CCP leaders. They were expected to keep their heads down and not engage in outrageous behavior or ostentatious displays of wealth. If they sinned against these unwritten rules, sometimes even their lineage could not protect them from anti-crime fervor. A grandson of Marshal Zhu De was executed for rape in 1983, and several "princelings" were detained, at least temporarily, to check their commercial activities.[12]

While the anti-crime campaign was, for the most part, just a temporary chill in the spring of capitalist development, another CCP campaign threatened to have more far-reaching consequences. Jumping onto Deng Xiaoping's repeated warnings against what he at times called "spiritual pollution" and at other times "bourgeois liberalism," ideological conservatives in the Party in late 1983 began preparing a counter-offensive against all kinds of new ideas and debates. They wanted to make sure that the Party, and only the Party, decided what was allowed to discuss, and to bring to heel the universities, academies, and Party schools in which freedom of speech had been encouraged. Led by Deng Liqun and Hu Qiaomu, the "Anti–Spiritual Pollution Campaign" was supported by Chen Yun and other senior leaders, and, somewhat grudgingly, by Deng Xiaoping. Within the Party, there was no doubt that the indirect target for the campaign was Hu Yaobang and his freewheeling style of leadership, alongside his known willingness to let people speak openly and freely. Deng wanted to send the General Secretary a message: reform was necessary, but any political reform would have to be very gradual and agreed to by all the senior leaders. Hu should follow Deng's advice and not rock the boat, thereby giving Chen Yun the chance to become the standard-bearer for political correctness within the Party.[13]

The Anti–Spiritual Pollution Campaign backfired almost from the beginning. Hu Yaobang told provincial leaders that the campaign was not intended to stifle discussions about how best to reform the Party's and the government's policies. Premier Zhao, who at first had been supportive of the campaign, linking "bourgeois liberalism" with increases in crime and hooliganism, retreated and said that the campaign should in no way affect economic reform or changes in the countryside.[14] But it was Wan Li and Xi Zhongxun who went furthest in attacking the way the campaign was conducted. On at least two occasions in November and December 1983 they let fly at Deng Liqun and, to a lesser extent, Hu Qiaomu, personally for having created a Cultural Revolution–type of fear within the Party, undoing what had been achieved since 1978.[15] Even after Deng Xiaoping, again reluctantly, called the whole affair off at the end of the year, they continued to press their charges. On several occasions during 1984 Wan, Xi, and others confronted Deng Liqun, blaming him for undermining General Secretary Hu Yaobang. "In previous years," Wan Li told Deng Liqun to his face in October 1984, "I have had a good impression of you. But now I more and more feel that you are not right [and] it seems that you never broke out of the Leftist box with regard to your thinking."[16]

But even if the campaign lasted less than two months, much damage had been done. Within the top leadership, Hu Yaobang's attempts at dismantling the Anti–Spiritual Pollution Campaign from the beginning had poisoned the personal relationship between him and Deng Xiaoping. Although Deng called the campaign off because he did not like the direction it was taking, he did not easily forgive Hu for undermining him. Even before the campaign was officially launched, Deng had warned Hu, through other leaders, that "in upholding the Four Cardinal Principles and in anti-liberalization efforts, as the party's General Secretary, Yaobang has displayed a weakness that is a fundamental shortcoming."[17] Even Hu Yaobang's energetic defenders, such as Wan Li and Xi Zhongxun, could not stand up against Deng's ire, especially since Deng was joined by Chen Yun and, at times, even by Zhao Ziyang, both of whom thought that Hu did not understand economics and that he promoted the wrong kind of people, those who thought more about political than economic issues. For Deng Liqun and Hu Qiaomu, of course, General Secretary Hu was a lost cause already, with Deng Liqun saying that he no longer considered Hu Yaobang a Communist. Never devoid of humor, the propaganda chief referred to the Central Committee's research office, where both his own adherents and those of the General Secretary worked, as "one office, two systems."[18]

The major damage for the CCP, though, was further down the political food chain. Before the Anti–Spiritual Pollution Campaign, most young Chinese had hoped that their personal aspiration to be richer and freer would mean that they could work both for private gain and for their country through the Communist Party. By 1984 many of them, especially those in schools and universities, no longer believed such a combination to be possible. The CCP had, again, shown that it could turn against their sense of freedom, *any* sense of freedom, with the flick of a switch, exposing those who had spoken out to dire attacks and sanctions. Hu Yaobang remained their hero, and, as long as he stayed in office, not all hope of fundamental political reform was gone. But the campaign, and the CCP slogans against "spiritual pollution," "peaceful change," and "bourgeois liberalization" that long survived it, had created a chasm between Deng's Party and intellectuals, students, and young people that would deepen in the future.

The result of all of this was that many of those who had the opportunity turned away from discussing political reform as "the fifth modernization" and toward "jumping into the sea" to get rich quick. In most cases, there was already a tacit understanding between senior CCP leaders and the emerging business class. Businesspeople would be allowed a great deal of leeway to become rich, as long as they did not touch politics, even in their personal opinions. Most entrepreneurs and business leaders abided by that understanding, at least at the time. As a result, the mid-1980s was when great businesses were formed that would drive China into the future. It was one of the most remarkable aspects of China's transformation: how a country that had had no business but state business suddenly started spawning companies that would become key not just to China's future but to many global developments. The long reach of the state was still felt for every one of them. But the momentum had changed. From then on, business would again be an integral part of Chinese society and life in China.

The starting point, as we have seen already, was a generation's worth of pent-up demand. Chinese, especially urban Chinese, were simply tired of being drab and poor. As terror and restrictions abated, people began to see how others lived in Hong Kong, Taiwan, Singapore, and other places in Asia. These well-dressed people with their own apartments, refrigerators, and sometimes even cars were not wealthy Westerners. They were fellow Asians, and sometimes even Chinese. In the PRC, many aspired to live like them. And the quest to supply consumer goods to this burgeoning market was what drove Chinese businesses, long before export markets came into view. Businesspeople, representing collective, private, or state-owned companies, did their own impromptu market research and found which products were in need or in vogue in different parts of the country. Then they started making those products, often according to foreign models, or importing goods until they could make them themselves. Profits were high for those who succeeded, and taxes and constraints relatively low. By 1984, most officials had got the message that business was good for the country. Quite a few also felt that it was good for them, or at least could be, as they started working closely with local companies rather than attempting to curtail them.

As companies turned toward selling their products to individual consumers, marketing became an increasingly important part of business in China. Although never completely absent during the Maoist era, back then advertisements had a limited range, since they were mostly aimed at collectives or individuals who could get the permission of their work units to buy the goods in question. All of this changed in the 1980s, especially after 1981 when Chinese TV started carrying ads for consumer goods. Along with massive urbanization from the late 1970s on, the demand for new and improved kinds of products grew immensely. Companies, including state-owned companies, began to make new items—deodorant was produced in the PRC for the first time in 1982—and new commercials. In the first few years of increased buying power, people bought more meat, poultry, eggs, and cooking oil. But then many turned to what had previously been considered luxury items: watches, bicycles, TV sets, and fashionable and quality clothing. Branding became more important, as did the standard of commercials.[19] Already by the mid-1980s those Chinese who had access to TVs thought that there were too many commercials on TV, and that their quality was poor, especially for domestic advertising. But in a country where less than 1 percent of rural households owned a TV (and less than 3 percent of the urban population had a refrigerator), the quality of advertising was significantly less important than the availability of the products they touted.[20]

The high savings rate and increasing inflation both served China's budding consumer society well. Although inflation sometimes led to unrest among those who felt hard done by rising prices, it also stimulated consumption, since rising prices meant that buying sooner rather than later seemed a good idea to many. The biggest problem for Chinese companies was therefore not sales or loans, but production, distribution, and, sometimes, imports. Getting machinery delivered and put in place was extremely difficult, as was access to electricity, and many business ventures failed because they could not overcome these challenges. Foreign currency was another bottleneck, since it was strictly controlled by the government, except, to some extent, in Guangdong. Even so, new companies of all sorts were born in massive numbers every day, with applications for registration coming in to the authorities so frequently that they had trouble handling all of them. In some cases businesses began work without any form of official license. It helped, of course, to have contacts within the higher levels of the Party, locally or centrally. In more than one case, businesses were set up right next to Party headquarters, sports stadiums, or public parks, so that power lines could be discreetly thrown over a wall and connected for free to the public network.

The businesses that started in the mid-1980s came in all sizes and shapes. Starting a small café or restaurant was a popular form of enterprise, as was setting up a transportation or cab company. One of the most popular jobs among young people in the cities in 1984 was to be a taxi driver, beating doctors and teachers hands down.[21] A major reason was that cabbies often got in contact with foreigners and so could receive U.S. dollars or the Chinese equivalent, the foreign exchange certificates (FECs) that, unlike ordinary money, could be converted into hard currency. But joining these kinds of services was not easy. Small private outfits were often used as subcontractors by big municipal companies, and the financial conditions were not always great. As a result, an informal economy flourished, in which restaurant visits and cab rides were undertaken wholly on the side of what was reported to the municipal license holders. Such informal income could be used to expand the business, often producing more both for the formal and the informal parts of a small setup, thereby keeping both the official partners and the employees happy. Heads of government-owned companies were often surprised at how well some of their small affiliates were doing, but they did not resent their success, since some of their surplus could count as income for the bigger company, too.

Most of the new companies were not started by young people, but by men and women in their forties, with plenty of contacts and know-how. Quite a few grew out of established institutions: existing state-owned or collective enterprises, of course, but also schools and universities, hospitals, exhibition halls, museums, newspapers, and even military units. Religious communities joined in—in one famous case in Beijing a group of Buddhists had their much-vandalized temple restored to them, only for the group to rent it out to an ice cream company started by monks. In the southwestern province of Guangxi, bordering Vietnam, local border guards set up a chain of restaurants, where tourists could have a meal before "touring" the border in their presence—all for a fixed price paid to their company, named "Watchful." Not all companies originated from an established unit, however. Many street vendors started operating by themselves without any license or link, selling food, clothing, or cheap electronics, always heedful of any official trouble coming their way, but with great rewards if business went well. Quite a few great fortunes took off from street corners in 1980s China.[22]

The year 1984, George Orwell's banner year in his warning against totalitarianism, in China became the year of the new company. A remarkable array of well-known Chinese conglomerates originated, either directly or indirectly, that year. In Qingdao, the former German concession on the Shandong coast, a 35-year-old former Red Guard member named Zhang Ruimin was transferred to the city's failing refrigerator company as manager. For Zhang it was almost a demotion. He had seen great opportunities in the construction industry, where he had worked his way up over the previous twelve years without much attention paid to his past. One perk of his new job was a visit to West Germany, to explore cooperation with the domestic appliances company Liebherr. It was Zhang's first trip abroad, and he was dumbfounded by German industry, wealth, and cleanliness. When he came back, he issued strict new rules for the workers. No long leaves of absence. No gambling. No urinating on the factory floor. He then brought out a load of new factory-built refrigerators he had inspected and found defective, and led the workers in destroying them with sledge-hammers. Zhang decreed that this would be the fate of defective goods hereafter, and that the mistakes each employee had made in production would be read aloud before the wrecking began.[23]

Zhang Ruimin's mixture of German-inspired efficiency, Red Guard ferocity, and appeals to personal responsibility seemed to work. With money borrowed from contacts in the countryside and improved products based on German drawings and advice, the new company became profitable within two years, with output increasing close to 100 percent. Zhang renamed the outfit Haïer, after the last two characters in Liebherr's Chinese name. The municipal government agreed to have it listed as a joint-stock company, in which it shared ownership with the employees at the factory. And the business continued to grow, fed by China's seemingly insatiable appetite for electric goods. Today the Haïer Group is the world's largest white goods producer, with a global market share of more than 10 percent. Besides refrigerators, it produces washing machines, air conditioners, cell phones, computers, microwaves, and televisions. In 2016 it bought GE Appliances for $5.4 billion.[24]

In Shenzhen, the special economic zone that in 1984 had grown into a small city with around 100,000 inhabitants (today it has more than thirteen million), the small trader Wang Shi wanted to do something big. He applied for, and to his surprise got, a job at the new Shenzhen Modern Science and Education Instrument Exhibition and Marketing Center. There he saw opportunities. The center had all kinds of import licenses and, most importantly, a foreign currency license. Wang convinced the others at the Exhibition Center to begin what could, charitably, be seen as currency trading, or else as money laundering. In one of his first operations he persuaded a big Beijing-based state-owned company that had a surplus of U.S. dollars obtained at a favorable rate to allow him to convert the foreign currency to Chinese yuan in Shenzhen at a much higher rate. The Exhibition Center "earned" five million yuan, an absolute fortune in 1984, from the transaction.

Very soon the center had vastly outgrown its exhibition and marketing purposes. It began importing Japanese consumer electronics and started several textile factories, a watch-making company, a bottling plant, and a printing press. "Except for pornography, gambling, drugs, and weapons," Wang said later, "Vanke [as the center was renamed] did almost everything." His use of military transport planes to send goods for sale to the big northern cities led to an investigation, but, as Wang put it later, "over time, the case faded."[25] The investigation teams could not determine whether Wang Shi's behavior was illegal or simply entrepreneurial. A few years later Vanke turned to urban real estate, where the company became a pioneer in China. By the late 2010s it had grown into one of the world's largest residential home developers.

Another Shenzhen company that pioneered capitalist growth in China is Ping An. It had very different origins from the others. When the social safety net for workers began to melt away in the early 1980s, the Shekou Industrial Zone, a set of factories on the Guangdong–Hong Kong border, began setting up its own pension funds, medical insurance, unemployment insurance, and hardship assistance funds. With their close contact across the border, people in Shekou knew how private insurance companies functioned in Hong Kong. And with their own experience in Shekou, they soon wanted to expand the services of their fledgling insurance plans elsewhere. But nobody had set up a private insurance company in the PRC before, and most experts thought it would be illegal. The enterprising Shekou bosses set out to find a solution.

They found it in the legal structure that had set up the Shekou Industrial Zone in the first place. The zone had been established by the China Merchants Group, a state company with a fascinating back history. Privately founded as the China Merchants Steam Navigation Company in 1872, it had been taken over by the government after the revolution but continued to run shipping lines and wharfs. In the nineteenth century, China Merchants had also operated its own insurance company. Why not simply reestablish that company, claim that it was a temporary measure for Guangdong under special circumstances, and promise to merge it with the Chinese People's Insurance Company, the state-owned behemoth that controlled all insurance in China, when it had gained experience and become profitable? The ploy worked. After having attracted capital from some of the Guangdong collective enterprises that had accumulated their profits since the early 1970s, Ping An Insurance was set up in 1988. Today it is the biggest insurance company in Asia and among the twenty largest companies in the world in terms of revenue.

Most of the new companies founded in the mid-1980s had their origin in the south, but not all. Some firms emerged out of institutions in Beijing, such as Legend, later known as Lenovo. Set up by a group of ten scientists at the Chinese Academy of Sciences (CAS) in 1984, the company benefited throughout its infancy from a close association with CAS, which provided money, space, and political backing. Legend's boss, the computer scientist Liu Chuanzhi, first wanted to import TVs and produce digital watches. Both schemes failed. Then Liu began installing and servicing IBM computers that Chinese institutions had bought in the United States.[26] The income gave the new company a chance to strike out on its own. Its first product was a computer expansion card that facilitated the machine's ability to process Chinese text. The card was an immediate success and enabled Legend to begin assembling its own computers, made mostly from imported components. The company also served as IBM's main sales agent in China. Now known as Lenovo, the company is today the world's biggest producer of personal computers, with a global market share of about 25 percent. It bought all of IBM's PC business in 2005. A publicly listed company, Lenovo still has CAS as one of its biggest owners.

Lenovo became the centerpiece of the many new technology companies that grew up around the universities and academies in northeastern Beijing. Zhongguancun, once a sleepy village named after a nearby burial ground for Qing dynasty eunuchs, quickly became where it all happened. Some of the villagers rented land to the new companies, and the local township, which had been a particularly badly run People's Commune, invested money in some of them. Within a few years the village became entirely transformed, and Beijingers began calling it "China's Silicon Valley." More than fifty technology enterprises had been established there by 1985. Liu Chuanzhi's company was not even the biggest of them. Stone, a collective enterprise set up by other academics in Zhongguancun, became China's first software company and tremendously influential until its chairman, Wan Runnan, fled the country after having supported the democracy movement in 1989.[27] Other companies grew by copying the success of the first ones and not dabbling in politics. Foreigners who visited Zhongguancun's "Electronics Street" in the 1980s marveled at what they could find there in terms of Chinese and foreign goods, including sometimes goods with prestigious foreign labels that were really made just down the road in Haidian.

Only a very few companies that started in the early 1980s have had the kind of continuous success of a Lenovo or a Ping An. There were vast opportunities in getting started early, but there were also great dangers. Jianlibao, China's first and most celebrated soft drink company, is a good example. Its founder, Li Jingwei, grew up in an orphanage and had no education. He worked his way up in a local liquor distillery in Sanshui, Guangdong. In 1983 Li visited Guangzhou, drank his first Coca-Cola, and began thinking about producing a Chinese soft drink with the same kind of image as Coke had; sporty, youthful, and energetic. With the first bottles ready, but without any commercial sales, Li offered to sponsor China's Olympics team, just taking off for the 1984 Olympics in Los Angeles, in return for it displaying his bottles at the competitions. It was a huge gamble: Li's offer could have been laughed out of the room, and nobody knew how China's athletes would actually do in the United States. China, after all, had not participated in Olympic competitions since the early 1950s. To Li's surprise the Chinese sports bosses, short of money for their foreign trip, accepted his proposal.

The 1984 Olympics became a great triumph for Chinese sports. In the absence of the Soviets and the East Europeans, who boycotted the games, the PRC won fifteen gold medals and placed fourth in the country rankings. And bottles of Jianlibao were seen everywhere, making the drink a household name in China. The following year Li Jingwei's company produced nearly twenty million bottles, but it could easily have sold many more if production capacity had been available. Only a few years later, though, Li's products began finding it difficult to compete against foreign soft drinks. After a spectacular falling out with the Sanshui local government, which still owned most of the company, Li Jingwei was forced to resign. He was later sentenced to fifteen years in jail for embezzlement and misuse of state funds.[28]

One of Li's problems was the increasing popularity of Coca-Cola in China. Chinese consumers were asking themselves why they should drink lesser-known local brands when they could have "the real thing." Coca-Cola had been produced in China beginning in 1927, and it soon became a preferred drink for the Chinese urban middle class. But since 1949, Coca-Cola had not only been banned but had become the very symbol of the slick seductiveness of American imperialism. During the Cultural Revolution, Red Guards shouted slogans against Coca-Cola colonialism, referencing a product they had never seen (and thereby, presumably, keeping it freshly in mind). Already by 1975 the chairman of the Coca-Cola Company, J. Austin Reed, had begun overtures to PRC representatives in the United States in order to get permission to reenter China. These included sending cases of Coke to the United Nations headquarters in New York for the consumption of the Chinese representatives there. By 1978 Deng Xiaoping had agreed that Coca-Cola could sell its products at hotels and tourist sites in China, in return for the company setting up a joint production plant with U.S. technology in Beijing, working with CerOils, China National Cereals, Oils and Foodstuffs Import and Export Corporation.

But in spite of its many advantages, the breakthrough for Coca-Cola, as for so many other foreign companies in China, was slow in coming. "For quite a number of years Coke was only sold in Friendship stores and foreign hotels," remembers one of the company's first salespeople in China. "Coca-Cola lost a lot of money in the first two to three years shipping Coke from Hong Kong." Guardians of Communist Party orthodoxy accused the officials who worked with Coca-Cola of showing no "national self-respect," and Chen Yun was furious when he first heard about the plans.[29] But young consumers wanted their bottles of Coke. By 1984 the CCP had agreed to two new plants, and by the early 1990s there were ten. Being a Coca-Cola salesperson was the height of prestige. Thousands applied for each position, among them pediatric surgeons as well as former Party officials.[30]

Japanese and European companies were as eager to get in on the action in China as those from the United States. A few smaller Japanese firms with good contacts in China from before the Cultural Revolution had started selling their products through Chinese state-owned companies already in the late 1970s. The bigger companies were holding back, in part because some of the bigger schemes for Sino-Japanese industrial cooperation developed at the same time fell through because the Chinese would not, or could not, fulfill their part of the bargain. The first big company that put a toe forward was Hitachi, which set up a joint-venture production plant for color TVs in Fujian in 1981. Throughout the 1980s, working with Japanese companies was particularly popular among Chinese officials and businesspeople. There was a sense that the Japanese understood the Chinese market better than others and had better long-term business strategies. Also, given the number of Japanese companies that were lining up to do business in China, the Chinese could pick those that were most willing to transfer technology and help train Chinese engineers.

Although businesses from many European countries had begun investing in China by the mid-1980s, it was German firms that were the most popular partners. Like people elsewhere, in the 1980s Chinese leaders equaled West German products with quality and efficiency, and they were eager to bring those kinds of standards to China. And Germany's big industrial companies, flush with capital from foreign exports, were very willing to invest. Giant German firms, such as Volkswagen (VW), Siemens in engineering, and BASF in chemicals, were among the first Western companies to bet big on China. Under pressure from the United States not to do business with the Soviets, the West Germans marveled at a situation where the Americans were actively encouraging investments in a Communist country. Shanghai VW was founded in 1984, only a year after American Jeep agreed to produce vehicles in Beijing. In 1985 Volkswagen made 1,700 of its Santana cars in China. Thirty-five years later it produced close to four million cars there and had a market share of about 20 percent.[31]

The Cold War helped make China's economic transformation easier. The new Reagan administration in the United States put aside its concerns about Taiwan's position and celebrated China's return to the market. President Reagan's notes for a U.S. National Security Council meeting before his visit to China in 1984 underlined the need to build long-range trust and confidence with the Chinese leadership in order to get "more cooperation with U.S. in checking Soviet power and influence." Reagan also told U.S. officials to "do things which encourage Chinese efforts to moderate communist system and expand opening to West."[32] During his visit at the end of April 1984 the president had a set of very friendly meetings with Zhao Ziyang and a more reserved meeting with Deng Xiaoping, the latter possibly because both men at this stage of their careers were hard of hearing and preferred to lecture rather than listen.[33] Deng had also started to worry, again, about American betrayal, fearing that the United States would make a deal with the Soviets.

For Reagan, the highlight of his visit was not the official conversations but in finding a society that he believed was on its way, through markets, to become much like an oriental version of the United States. Reagan had an uncanny ability to put ideologies and even plain facts aside when he wanted to tell a story and make a political point. When he arrived back in the United States, the president told the assembled reporters that "yesterday, before we left, we sat in a Chinese home at one of the now-called townships—they were once called communes—the farm communes where they raise the foodstuffs for all of China, but now there is a difference.

> They owe a portion of what they produce to the government, but then over and above that they can produce on their own and sell in a free marketplace. And in this home, it was most interesting. This young couple, their little son, his mother and father living with them, and he was telling us all the things—and he built that home himself, and a very fine job it was—and then told us of how they're saving and what they're saving to buy next. It could have been in any home in America, talking about the problems of making ends meet and that they were saving for this or that for their future.[34]

The fantasy that China was well underway to becoming another America in Asia was already developing fast.

Even though the CCP leaders were delighted that Reagan's visit had gone well, their attention in 1984 was fixed on Asia. From the moment Deng Xiaoping

President Ronald Reagan walking with Zhao Ziyang
during Zhao's 1984 visit to the White House.
Source: Maidun Collection/Alamy Stock Photo.

came back to power he had made Sino-Japanese relations his foreign policy priority. His colleagues remember him repeating over and over that China could not succeed *against* Japan; it could only succeed *with* Japan.[35] Deng went out of his way to court Japanese politicians and businessmen. He first visited the country right after he returned to power, in October 1978, and again on his way back from the United States in February 1979. On both occasions conversations had gone well and paved the way for Japanese trade and investment. Tokyo and Beijing agreed on many things, Deng found. Both were implacable enemies of the Soviet Union, and both wanted more economic interaction within Asia. Deng was also dumbstruck by Japanese technology, the nation's factories, and Japan's determined approach to have business contribute to national development. It was a model he wanted for China in the future.

When Japanese prime minister Nakasone Yasuhiro visited Beijing in March 1984, Deng did not mince his words. Nakasone was generally regarded as the strongest Japanese leader in decades, a nationalist who had served as an officer during the Asia-Pacific War and who was in favor of Japanese remilitarization. His opponents at home called him a reactionary and a militarist. But Deng welcomed him warmly. "The historical friendly relations between Japan and China must continue onto the 21st century, and then to the 22nd, 23rd, 33rd, and 43rd century," Deng told Nakasone. "Currently, Japan and China do not have urgent problems. The development of Japan-China relations into the 21st century is more important than all other issues."[36] Hu Yaobang concurred. "China will not forget your warm friendship. . . . At this time, the only thing that we can give in return is our declaration that we will develop friendly relations between China and Japan; however, when our economy develops I believe that we will be able to reciprocate your friendship."[37]

"China," Deng told Nakasone, "has an abundance of underground resources, but does not have the funds to develop them. . . . [With enough investment] I believe that the development of energy resources, raw materials, and rare minerals can contribute to Japan." "We must not be caught up with what is immediately in front of us," Deng said. "However, looking even further, longer, and wider is advantageous for the development of Japan-China relations."[38] On foreign affairs, after complaining that Mongolia had been taken from China before the CCP came to power, Deng said that "the stationing of Soviet troops in Mongolia is a threat." Looking at Nakasone, the former officer in the Japanese imperial army, Deng noted laconically that "we all have some understanding of military affairs. Soviet . . . deployment is meant to isolate China with two lines extending eastwards from Vladivostok and westwards from Mongolia. This is the same method used when the Soviets fought the [Japanese] Kwantung Army [in 1945]."[39] For Deng, the Soviet threat could help bring old enemies together as friends.

Another historical issue Deng and his immediate assistants, Hu Yaobang and Zhao Ziyang, had to deal with was Hong Kong. Although Hong Kong Island itself was British territory, most of the Crown colony's land across the bay had been leased from the Qing Empire in 1898 for ninety-nine years. That lease would expire in 1997, and with the PRC claiming sovereignty over all of Hong Kong, authorities in London concluded that it simply was not viable to continue its rule after 1997 over only a rump part of the colony. They thus entered into negotiations with the Chinese with one hand tied behind their backs. But Deng also saw problems with pushing too hard to integrate Hong Kong with the rest of the PRC. Much of the capital China needed for its development came from, or at least through, Hong Kong, and Deng was in no mood to kill the goose that laid the golden eggs. He instructed his assistants to go easy in the negotiations. Deng quite admired Hong Kong's entrepreneurial spirit and wanted to see more of it transfer to China, instead of miring Hong Kong in China's problems. He was also aware that the vast majority of funds flowing into China's new special economic zones came through Hong Kong.[40] He told his diplomats that regaining full sovereignty was non-negotiable. Everything else could be discussed with the British.

China's diplomats used their first informal discussions with the British over the future of Hong Kong, leading up to British prime minister Margaret Thatcher's visit to Beijing in 1982, to make their point about full Chinese sovereignty. British attempts at pushing back on the date for a future handover went nowhere in Beijing. These feeble cracks at gaining time made Deng more convinced that China needed to regain full sovereignty over Hong Kong in 1997. But he also told British emissaries that Hong Kong would be able to keep its own social and economic system in place after the Chinese takeover. When meeting with the British foreign secretary, Lord Carrington, in 1981, Deng said that he himself wanted to use the same policy for Hong Kong as for Taiwan and Tibet, even with regard to politics. "It was not China's intention to change Taiwan's way of life or political system," Deng said. The islanders would "even be allowed their own self-defense force."[41] Deng's policy was what later became known as "one country, two systems." As long as sovereignty was regained, even the character of the political system mattered less.

Thatcher's discussions with Chinese leaders in Beijing the following year showed the formidable British prime minister running on empty, while Deng could sit back, knowing that the 1997 deadline gave him a controlling position on the future of Hong Kong. It was easy for Deng to offer negotiations, as well as cooperation with Britain both in the lead-up to 1997 and thereafter. Although Thatcher knew that the PRC would take over almost all of Hong Kong's territory in fifteen years no matter what she said, Deng knew that Britain would have to negotiate some sort of deal. Thatcher's insistence that she "was simply trying to carry out her duty to the people of Hong Kong" by keeping what she called "the present arrangements" of administration fell on deaf ears. While she spoke about obligations and history, Deng spoke about the end of British colonialism.[42] "In the past," he almost mockingly pointed out to Thatcher,

> Britain had been known as the empire where the sun never set, but Britain had ended her colonial role in very many former colonies. . . . Previous [U.K.] governments had already solved bigger and more difficult issues. If the Hong Kong problem were to be solved during the Prime Minister's period in office, it would mean that Britain's colonial era had been brought to an end. This would redound to British credit. The British Government should therefore support China's policy and decisions on this issue. [Deng] hoped that both sides would co-operate and handle the issue in such a way as to maintain the prosperity of Hong Kong.[43]

With the United States and even Britain's European allies insensitive to Thatcher's Hong Kong predicament, but very alert to the potential for working with the Chinese, the prime minister had no choice but to enter into negotiations on China's conditions. Whenever discussions got stuck, the Chinese issued thinly veiled warnings that Beijing would make a unilateral proclamation about Hong Kong's future without any further negotiations with the British, never mind with the people of Hong Kong. In late 1984 Thatcher agreed to most of the Chinese proposals in a joint declaration about the future of the former Crown colony. The declaration starts by simply stating, "The Government of the People's Republic of China declares that to recover the Hong Kong area (including Hong Kong Island, Kowloon and the New Territories . . .) is the common aspiration of the entire Chinese people, and that it has decided to resume the exercise of sovereignty over Hong Kong with effect from 1 July 1997."[44]

The agreement on Hong Kong was more than a major diplomatic victory for Deng Xiaoping. It also strengthened his plans for expanding social economic zones in the south and along the coast. With Hong Kong as a "special administrative region" of the PRC from 1997 on, Deng was already envisioning an integrated Pearl River delta economic area in which the city joined Macau, Shenzhen, and other fast-developing Guangdong locations as a unified zone. In 1984 this was still in the future, but the significance of Hong Kong for such plans, plus the importance the city still had as a depot for China's trade and investment, meant that Deng was willing to accept wide-ranging special

Hu Yaobang with Queen Elizabeth II at Zhongnanhai
in Beijing during her visit to China, October 1986.
Source: Trinity Mirror/Mirrorpix/Alamy Stock Photo.

rights for the city when sovereignty had been recovered. When receiving
reports on the consultations with prominent Hong Kong business and community leaders about a post-1997 Basic Law for the former colony, Deng
pushed for exceptional concessions. He promised not to introduce socialism
in the city for at least fifty years, and let Hong Kong keep its own laws and
business and property regulations. He also agreed to an independent judiciary and police force, to keep the freedom of speech, organization, and assembly, and to let Hong Kongers choose their own government. Even though
the regulations set out for the latter prevented the direct democracy that most
people in Hong Kong wanted, it was still a major concession by a dictatorial
government. In spite of China's extraordinary leverage, Deng knew better
than to create doubts among local and foreign investors about Hong Kong's
future. He also knew, of course, that the PRC's National People's Congress,
controlled by the Communist Party, could change the Basic Law if needed in
the future.

By 1984, an increasing number of urban Chinese envisaged a future that looked quite a bit like Hong Kong under British rule: a benign but faraway government that kept the peace, built highways, and kept money available and the currency stable. Both authors of this book lived in China that year, and we remember friends at the universities or in business laughing at our concerns that the Communist Party would undermine Hong Kong's freedoms. Instead, they said, in a few years Shanghai, Xiamen, Guangzhou, and Hangzhou—and perhaps even Beijing—would become a lot more like Hong Kong; laissez-faire cities in which people could get rich quick and become consumers of advanced hi-tech products. To our questions as to whether the CCP, with its history, could practice capitalism, most people shrugged their shoulders. They, the leaders, may call it something else, was the usual answer, but the world, and China, was all about markets. Even people close to the leadership started saying that China did not suffer from capitalism, but from a lack of capitalism, and quoted Karl Marx to prove it. Some of them even took the consequences of their belief and jumped into the sea of markets themselves. One started publishing encyclopedias and importing grand pianos, both commodities he claimed that Marx had said that a new bourgeoisie always coveted.[45] Between June 1984 and June 1985, 160,000 goldfish bowls were sold in Shenzhen.[46]

Premier Zhao Ziyang seemed to agree with the overall direction of things. He liked the changes in lifestyle he saw in the cities, with Chinese reinventing themselves as consumers, or at least potential consumers. The premier was no stranger to new entertainments himself. After the first golf course in the People's Republic, designed by legendary golfer Arnold Palmer, opened in 1984, Zhao was often spotted playing a round. He encouraged small businesses—even the ones that were, in fact, private enterprises masquerading as communally owned. When visiting, on the same day, two hotels in Guangzhou, one state-owned and the other a joint venture with a Hong Kong company, Zhao despaired at the differences in quality and service. He announced to his staff that "the gap between these two hotels is the gap between the planned economy and the market economy!"[47] Still, Zhao was keenly attuned to the Marxist verbosity that was needed to promote economic reform among older Party leaders. The premier announced that the next big step in the economic transformation of China would be moving toward what he called a socialist commodity economy. "What is the difference between a socialist commodity economy and a socialist market economy?" he asked his aides. "As far as practical work is concerned, there is no difference."[48] Zhao knew that the economic transformation was not just about production results. Market opportunities provided an outlet for talent and enterprise, a sense of freedom, and a way to break out of the drab dreariness of Maoist China.

Having started to work on a comprehensive new Central Committee document on the economy in 1984, Zhao was surprised about how little opposition there was to his new formulations. Even Chen Yun gave the new reforms his blessing, though the old planner kept emphasizing that state control was primary and the market secondary for China's development. The "Resolution on the Reform of the Economic System" was passed by the Third Plenum on October 20, 1984. In addition to moving toward a socialist commodity economy, the resolution mandated increased autonomy for all enterprises, allowing all products to be traded according to market prices and setting pay according to results and hours worked, and approving a city-centered developmental strategy focusing on the expansion of markets.[49] Even if some of these reforms became stuck in China's Communist bureaucracy and took a long time to implement fully, the resolution was a revolution in the Party's economic outlook. Prior to 1984, Communist reform in China could be compared with reforms in other socialist countries such as Hungary, Poland, or Yugoslavia. The 1984 reform in China took a dramatic step out of the planned economy and toward markets. A structure was set for the Chinese economy that would last up to the late 2010s. After the October 1984 resolution, nobody who watched the Chinese economy was in any doubt that commerce, markets, and money were in the driver's seat for China's development.

But if the economy had an obvious, though sometimes diffuse, direction, politics were much more uncertain. After 1979, Deng Xiaoping had made it clear that there would be no democratization with him in charge, and that the political framework would be strictly regulated by the Party's senior leaders. Even so, it was unclear what that framework was, and where its limits stood. Within the Party, most of the economic reformers had made their peace with authoritarian rule, in part because their fear of Cultural Revolution–style unrest was still very strong. Some of them believed that political freedoms would follow economic freedoms, as had happened in the West. But most stayed away from any immediate connection with political reform, in part because they were too preoccupied with the economy, but also because they did not want to challenge Deng's supremacy. Premier Zhao belonged to this group. His view was that the future would decide on politics, while the task at hand was to build a strong foundation for the Chinese economy, thereby making people wealthier and happier.[50]

In the mid-1980s many people seemed to agree with Zhao. They were too busy making a living to care much about the intricacies of political reform. Having been given the opportunity, for the first time in their lives, to put their families' welfare first, most people concentrated on just that: to get ahead in a society that up to then had offered few opportunities for doing so. There was also a wariness about politics, given the predominance all things political had had during the Cultural Revolution, and a cynical skepticism about the lack of reward for standing up for political principles. Especially in the cities, many people already felt much freer than they ever had before, not just in being able to voice an opinion but also in their choices as consumers. There were exceptions, of course. Writers, students, and scholars longed for the kind of freedom of expression and political participation that they saw people in other countries have, including, increasingly, people in eastern Asia and Eastern Europe. And, perhaps surprisingly, a number of CCP officials and intellectuals disagreed with the view that democracy could wait. Their interpretation of the past was the opposite of Deng's and Zhao's. To them, it was the centralization of power and the feudal instinct for following a leader that had produced the calamities of the Cultural Revolution. And, if not checked, these tendencies in the CCP and in Chinese society could regain the upper hand in the future.

By far the most important of these officials was Hu Yaobang, the CCP's general secretary and the last of the three chairmen of the Party, after Mao and Hua Guofeng. While other leaders had scrambled to conform to Deng's views on politics, and at least pay lip service to the views of Chen Yun and other senior leaders, Hu had refused to do so. On the contrary, the General Secretary often spoke openly about the need for more democracy, more participation, and more freedom of specch.[51] Hu was, in many ways, a contradictory figure. He wanted reform of the Party, not the abolition of one-party rule. He was skeptical of some of the market reforms, fearing that they would lead to more corruption and inequality. And he thought that the economy, at least in some fields, would move ahead faster via campaigns, political motivation, and building "a socialist spiritual civilization" than through the kind of step-by-step macroeconomic measures that Zhao Ziyang and even Chen Yun would support. But his contradictions and somewhat old-fashioned beliefs in the moral and exhorting role of the Party did not prevent Hu from becoming the hero of students and intellectuals and the most beloved leader among large segments of the general public. His public image as the defender of the common man and as the conscience of the CCP only grew in the early 1980s.

By 1984 there were clear signs that Deng Xiaoping was increasingly irritated by Hu's outspokenness. Although they had known each other for more than forty years, and Hu had been among Deng's staunchest supporters whenever the senior leader was in political trouble, Deng now wanted more deference and less disruption. Hu was ordered to conform. While in the coastal resort town of Beidaihe that summer, Deng told other Party leaders that they had to talk about Hu Yaobang's shortcomings. Not only in associating with critical intellectuals, but in being skeptical toward Party dictatorship and in opposing CCP anti-liberalization policies, Hu was seen as weak and wavering.[52] Deng wanted to warn Hu, not to crush him. The senior leader knew that removing Hu Yaobang would be deeply unpopular and would reflect badly on Deng himself. It would also strengthen Party conservatives who disliked at least parts of Deng's economic program. After the summer of 1984, Hu chose a lower profile for a while. But he was the Party's general secretary and could not disappear from the political scene. Soon Hu went back to his more freewheeling ways, saying what he believed was true, that keeping the lid on a society in ferment would ultimately harm both China and the CCP.

By the end of 1984 China had reached a phase in which it would remain for the next generation. It had left the period of revolutionary dislocation and open terror behind and moved into a stage of authoritarianism combined with high economic growth driven by market mechanisms. China's political future still hung in the balance, at least as far as the balance of power within the Party was concerned. But very few Chinese expected rapid democratization, even after—as was expected to happen soon—Deng Xiaoping's generation faded from the scene. Deng was 80 years old in 1984, hard of hearing and at times forgetful but with an iron will and with attention to the two issues he cared most about: Party rule and economic reform. Although Deng often spoke about retiring, he had no plans for doing so. Instead, he exhorted the younger generation to work harder to lift the ideals of a rich and strong China into the future. The CCP championed "personal fulfillment and national strength," said one banner at the PRC's National Day celebrations. But the most-noticed banner at the celebrations in Beijing that day was unauthorized. It was unfurled by a group of students, and said, simply, "Hello Xiaoping!" According to the students, it was meant to celebrate the aged statesman and his achievements.[53] But it could also be taken to mean that young people wanted a voice and that they were watching what was happening around and behind the old men assembled above Tiananmen Square.

Conclusion: The Making and Unmaking of Chinese Reform

CHINA HAS HAD MANY UPS AND DOWNS in its long and tumultuous history, both for ordinary people and for those who want to set up and manage a state. The story told in this book has been, in the main, the story of an "up," the making of a time when many Chinese became richer and freer, and those who ran the state made it less despotic and deadly. But the "long 1970s" is only recognizable as an up if you compare it with what had happened before. Much of China's history since the mid-nineteenth century had been a story of disasters, and some of the worst disasters had been inflicted by the CCP after it came to power in 1949. Compared with these man-made catastrophes, China's road from the Cultural Revolution of the 1960s to the reform and opening era of the 1980s was a definite up, a step on the road to a much better life for most Chinese.

But China's long 1970s is also a story of missed opportunities, for which China has paid a high price. In the midst of so much energy, transformation, and inventiveness at the private and commercial levels, there was so little fundamental reform in administration and especially in the political system. Bureaucrats and senior officials obviously became better qualified and, after our story ends, better at using foreign methods of management and information gathering to improve state services. But China has continued to be ruled as it always has—by an autocratic and self-selecting elite, which, increasingly, consists of the sons and, occasionally, daughters of those who had set up the Communist state. The result has been corruption, mismanagement, and widespread abuses of the rights Chinese citizens have according to the constitution.

Today's China, with its immense internal contradictions, is a product of both these trends. In economic terms, so far it is a glittering success story, with levels of growth that for four decades astonished the world. In 1985 the Chinese economy grew by 13.5 percent. It continued to grow at an average of more than 10 percent up to the mid-2000s. In 1985 the size of the Chinese economy was just 7 percent of the size of the U.S. economy. Today it is about two-thirds in nominal terms, and by purchasing power it is already bigger than that of the United States. Chinese companies, some of which we have shown the feeble origins of, became international giants in their industries, dominating production not only in Asia but globally. Helped by foreign capital and domestic government privileges, these companies acquired levels of technology and skills on par with the best in the world. And the CCP government grew rich in the process, too, allowing for investments in infrastructure and defense to rise at a higher rate than almost anywhere else.

The biggest transformation has been in the lives of ordinary Chinese. When our story begins, in the 1960s, they were poor and often terrified. Large parts of rural China were among the most destitute regions of the world, at the best of times just one step away from starvation. Villages and many towns had no public sanitation system and limited access to clean water. Education and health, though improved in some areas since the CCP came to power, were still lagging behind other countries and struggled to keep up with the increases in population. The literacy rate, according to official figures, was well below 50 percent. And, worse, people suffered under a government that was willing to sacrifice millions of human lives for absurd utopian development schemes. As the regime fragmented under the weight of its own crimes in the 1960s, violence spread, and almost nobody felt safe. For most, it was a miserable, fearful existence.

Economic reform gave the Chinese a possibility for a better life. Farmers could sell what they produced for a profit, getting better equipment, education for their children, and often a growing savings account. Workers could get jobs that paid decent wages, and they could change jobs if they did not like the one they had. Families could own their own dwellings and buy and sell property. The Chinese became consumers, buying appliances for their households, choosing how to dress and what to watch and listen to. It was an almost unimaginable transformation of people's lives, from a drab, gray, rigid form of existence to something that was colorful, exciting, and open, but also risky and frightening. It consumed most people's energy. Their purpose was to get ahead fast, shed the old, envision the new, and the devil take the hindmost.

As in other market revolutions, not everyone benefited, and some public purposes and services suffered. Within two decades, China went from being among the most equal societies on earth to one of the most unequal. During most of the time frame of this book, China had no millionaires; in 2021 there were more than four million of them.[1] This 0.3 percent of the population had got ahead by hard work, but also thanks to official contacts or nepotism. Privatization in China, often held up as an example of how to carry out "structural reform," was no less unjust and chaotic than privatization in Russia or Eastern Europe after socialism. It was just better hidden by a Communist Party that stayed in power and was willing to accept an extreme transfer of wealth to a few individuals, many of whom happened to be relatives or close associates of the men who had founded the People's Republic. About one-third of the population, mainly in inland provinces away from the main commercial hubs, remained distinctly poorer than the two-thirds who generally benefited most from reform. But, overall, the Chinese still saw reform as uplift, as a chance for a better future.

In political terms, the Communist Party suppressed the real possibility for reform that existed after the collapse of the Cultural Revolution. The new Party leadership, which had come to power after the coup in 1976, refused to listen to those voices, inside and outside of the Communist Party, that wanted a more pluralistic political system. Proposals to separate the roles of the state and the Party, provide for an independent judiciary, and respect freedom of organization for workers and intellectuals were consistently undermined by Deng Xiaoping and other senior leaders. Their aim was the opposite—to strengthen the rule of the Party hierarchy by excluding the Left and cracking down on the "chaos" of the Cultural Revolution. And even though freedom of expression and information were gained massively over the repressive, closed-off society that had existed before, Party leaders attempted to restrict such freedoms through campaigns and suppressions, culminating in the violent crushing of the student-led democracy movement in 1989.

At the time when our story ends, the contradictions between increasingly liberal economic policies and ongoing political repression were already clear to see. It was a thin line, as the key leader, Deng Xiaoping, had to be careful not to let the dictatorship go so far that it snuffed out daring and initiative in building a market economy. People were told that as long as they did not meddle in politics, they were free to get ahead in business. Up to 1989, the worst damage from an outdated and shortsighted approach to governance was the sidelining of younger Party leaders who had helped Deng and others save the situation after the Cultural Revolution. Many of them wanted to see more liberal politics as well as a more liberal economy. Hu Yaobang, the last chairman and then general secretary of the CCP, and a hero to many liberals inside and outside of the Party, was forced to resign in early 1987. His successor as top Party leader, Premier Zhao Ziyang, was purged during the 1989 democracy movement because he offered some sympathy to the protesters. Along with them went many other leaders who were dedicated to the Party and to political reform. Those who replaced them were lesser figures, with fewer ideas of their own, who were happy to celebrate the country's economic gains while subscribing to the politics that Deng left behind: the principle that China's economic miracle was a product of Party leadership and of authoritarian government.

What produced this outcome in Chinese history? Since we have written this book in part because we wanted to explain how today's China was created, we need to offer answers to the question. As is often the case in historical studies, we need to understand multiple events in succession that together produced the outcome we are looking at now. Today's situation was certainly not the only possible outcome. It was probably not even the most likely scenario. But still it was an outcome that can be explained historically from the 1960s on. The three main factors to look at are the political bankruptcy of the Left, the alliance between old Party leaders and the military, and economic and social transformation from the ground up.

The Cultural Revolution Left within the CCP had developed gradually since the late 1950s but had deeper roots in groups and forms of thinking that had existed within the Party since its founding. At the heart of the arguments about China's need for a radical, cultural revolution lay moral arguments about inclusion and justice. "Old China" had excluded much of the population—women, youth, the poor—from meaningful participation in society. The purpose of the Chinese Communist revolution was to right this wrong, combating reactionaries, turncoats, and foreign imperialists in the process. The goal was a new society based on collective values, which through a moral, socialist understanding of development would become a more productive community than both "Old China" and foreign countries. Thus an ancient civilization would have found a new purpose, leading the way for the rest of the world toward Communism.

When the CCP broke with the Soviets in the late 1950s, this sense of the need for urgent transformation within the country was a key issue. Mao Zedong, who had played a central role in shaping the CCP Left's interpretation of Chinese society and its ills, now used terms such as "class struggle" and "continuous revolution" to implement most of the Left's views in what became the Great Proletarian Cultural Revolution. By the early 1960s, Mao had consolidated his position as the leader of the Left, assembling around him a coterie of true believers and sycophants, leaders of the CCP who moved to the Left simply because they adhered to the wishes of the chairman. The result was political misery for China and for the CCP. The Cultural Revolution leaders of the Left—Jiang Qing, Zhang Chunqiao, and others—knew a great deal about what they were against but had only abstruse ideas about what they were for. Mao's own thinking was increasingly muddled, caught between his almost paranoid fears of losing power, his distaste for old age, and his awareness that time for a fundamental reordering of Chinese society may have been running out. As a result, between 1966 and 1976 the Left consistently failed to produce policy rather than slogans. Mao's theory and practice of "Continuous Revolution" seemed increasingly out of tune with the everyday experience of most Chinese. The result, especially after Lin Biao's death, was an ever-deeper legitimacy crisis for CCP one-party rule. In addition, the Cultural Revolution Left's leaders were politically entirely dependent on Mao Zedong. As Mao's health failed, they were incapable of translating the at least occasional popularity of Leftist views among parts of the growing working class into real power.

After Mao Zedong died in 1976, the enemies of the Cultural Revolution Left used their much more substantial hard power in a coup that almost immediately incapacitated the most radical factions in the Party. But the coup in itself decided very little about the future. Those who carried out the coup—Hua Guofeng, widely regarded as Mao's hand-picked successor; Wang Dongxing, the head of security; and Ye Jianying, leading the military—believed in continuing Mao's policies, shorn of their Cultural Revolution excesses. But within only a few months it became clear that such continuity was not enough for the majority of the most senior Party leaders. They wanted those who had been purged or sidelined in the Cultural Revolution to come back, as well as the complete political extermination of the Left from the Party. They also wanted the CCP to concentrate on rescuing the Chinese economy, even though such plans at first amounted to little more than a return to 1950s-style planning. It was this void in offering a mixture of competence and bold plans for the future that allowed Deng Xiaoping to establish himself as supreme leader of the Party in late 1978 and early 1979. Supported by the military, Deng pushed Chairman Hua Guofeng aside and took the first spot for himself, in spite of never carrying the title of chairman, premier, or president. From 1982 to 1989 he ruled China as chair of the CCP's Central Military Commission. And from 1989 almost up to his death at age 92 in 1997 he still had the final word on policy without holding any official position at all.

This remarkable outcome was decided both by the coalescing of the most powerful pre–Cultural Revolution military and Party leaders around Deng Xiaoping, and by the willingness of Hua Guofeng and other Mao appointees to step back peacefully. Given the many ups and downs of Deng's political career and the difficult relations he had at times had with a number of his old colleagues, he was to some extent a surprising choice for supreme leader. His longevity within the leadership counted to his advantage. So did the sheer force of his personality. Leaders such as Chen Yun and Li Xiannian regarded Deng's irreverence toward political orthodoxy as outrageous, but they trusted him to lead from within the system. And Deng seemed to have a plan for progress, whereas others did not. His deep support within military ranks instilled an element of fear in potential rivals. And there was, as always in Chinese history, a profound sense that China needed *one* top leader, a ruler who could be a trusted court of last resort on all things that mattered for the state. As the one-time maverick grew old in power, he became increasingly authoritarian and distrustful of anyone outside his inner circle of associates, even as he interfered less and less in day-to-day policy matters.

That Chairman Hua Guofeng would choose to resign without a fight was in many ways even more surprising. No top leader of China had resigned voluntarily since Sun Yat-sen's first departure as president in 1912. There is no doubt that by the time of his resignation Hua had been politically outmaneuvered by Deng Xiaoping, who had run a vicious campaign against him. A few brave Chinese historians have also argued that Hua allowed himself to be bypassed because he was, fundamentally, a decent and comradely leader, who was openminded and pluralistic in his approach to politics. Hua himself said that he could not stomach another internal CCP struggle. He never regretted stepping down, he told the few researchers venturesome enough to attempt to interview him.[2] Hua lived out his life in a compound not far from the Forbidden City in Beijing, where, in his retirement, he became an expert on growing grapes. More than fifty different kinds, it is said, would thrive in his courtyard.[3]

But while the changes at the top were important, much of China's transformation was driven from below. It says a lot about the strength of Chinese society that after spending a generation in the hellish purgatory prepared by the Communist masters, individuals, families, and clans managed to break away and envisage a new future for themselves. They did it without explicit permission from the top, testing and pushing the limits of the permissible, sometimes failing and remaining poor, sometimes failing and ending in jail, but often, in the end, creating a better life for themselves. This is the real content of China's great transformation. In the early 1970s, well before any kind of meaningful reform plans were visible in Beijing, people rebelled against economic and social stagnation in a market revolution from below. Their aim was to get rich, not just "moderately wealthy" as the CCP now sets as its aim for society. Of course, as in all market revolutions, most fell well short of becoming prosperous. And very few realized that in embracing the market, they would have to give up some of the comforts of socialism that most people cherished: free health care, education, and housing, and secure state pensions. But, even so, the striving of the 1970s generation of Chinese prepared the ground for a much better existence for most, of the kind that we see today.

A main argument in this book is that the revolution from below did more to change China than any orders issued by the CCP. China was transformed by the millions of Chinese who took their fate in their own hands, working for a better life. The fact that many did so *before* economic reform was declared at the central level shows where the great transformation originated. Their achievement, and their daring, can be compared with those of emigrants or explorers in times past. The expression often used about them was

下海, "to jump into the sea," to leave safe ground behind and set out on new ventures.[4] In doing so, they transformed not only the Chinese (and the global) economy; they also transformed Chinese society and ways of thinking. The emphasis on material gain and on consumption is today higher in China than in any other society we know, including the United States. The bold entrepreneurs of the 1970s and 1980s have created a thoroughly materialistic society, in which many of the mores, habits, and conventions that we knew in China at the outset of this story have given way to new and harsher values. Elements of the past remain, of course—the centrality of family, the weight of education, the desire for social uplift. But the overall story is one of incredibly rapid change in forms of thinking and patterns of behavior. And this is an ongoing process, of course, that we cannot know where will end.

Along with China's transformation through and of the market came the millions of little and great compromises that ordinary people had to make with the authorities in order to succeed. Although we do not believe that large numbers of Chinese, even in the emerging middle class, have ever aspired to replace China's political system with a democratic one along the lines of the systems in most other countries in the world, there is plenty of evidence that people have wished for a more pluralistic and open China in which the CCP removes dictatorial restrictions imposed on people's daily lives. But at most times, the need for compromises with the authorities in order to get ahead socially or commercially has outweighed the opposition that could come through the annoyances created by authoritarian rule. The result has been a social bargain in which the Party, formally or informally, has allowed people to get ahead financially as long as they do not touch the main levers of power. Gains from the economic roulette can be kept by individuals at all levels if they stay out of politics and conform to whatever slogans the Party chooses to put forward at any time.

Ever since reform began in China, this has been an uneasy balance. Although political and financial power are often separate, especially as private companies have grown, the Party has managed to keep business loyal, mainly through successful macroeconomic policies. However, the big part of the bargain, which often goes unnoticed, is the degree to which the CCP had stood aside and simply let business get on with business. The approach seems to violate everything that the Party has stood for since its inception: anticapitalism, strict central control, and expansion of Party rule to all areas of society.

But it has worked wonders for the Chinese economy. Since the mid-2010s, though, the Party leaders, under General Secretary Xi Jinping, have become increasingly worried about the amount of power that is held outside of their immediate control, and have cracked down on successful companies, influential governors, and any organizations beyond their direct command. They have also severely restricted freedoms in Hong Kong, threatening that city's position as an intermediary between China and the world, and launched draconian campaigns against Uyghurs and Tibetans suspected of lack of loyalty to the Communist regime.

It is hard to say why the Communist Party, after more than a generation of successful economic growth, has turned against some of the bargains that made this growth possible. Xi Jinping himself claims that his predecessors had gone too far in liberalization, resulting in corruption, decadence, immorality, detachment, and outsized foreign influence. His views resonated, at least initially, with many Chinese who were exhausted by forty years of constant struggles to get ahead and especially with those who suspected that they had benefited less from reform than their neighbors or the rich and good-looking people they watched on TV. Some people longed for a strong leader who could set the agenda, as Mao Zedong and Deng Xiaoping had done. Xi and his supporters also cover their authoritarian measures in an increasing degree of pride and nationalism. Chinese people today are understandably proud of the amazing progress their country has made since reform began. Xi tells them that the outside world is envious of China's success, and that only the Party can protect them against foreign-hatched plots to make China weak and poor again.

It is hard not to conclude that at least part of the reason why Xi Jinping has been able to take the country along in his high-risk mix of populism and nostalgia is the lack of accountability with the past. In China—the "People's Republic of Amnesia," as one scholar calls it—very few leaders have ever been held responsible for the crimes that they have committed against their own people.[5] Nobody was ever held responsible for the bloody purges of the 1950s or for the millions who died in the Great Leap Forward. After the Cultural Revolution it was only the leaders of the Left who were cast aside, while most perpetrators continued their lives, often reaching top positions in society. Some observers have seen this as evidence of a Chinese capacity for reconciliation and forgiveness. The reality is that it has set a terrible precedent for impunity among those in power, and challenged the moral foundations of society. The unwillingness to look into the past has also enabled the Communist Party to instill in young people a version of history based on lies and dissimulations, in which the Party is always correct and where all errors come from traitors or foreigners.

Understandably, China's relations with other countries have recently suffered given the new directions the country seems to be moving in. One of the great achievements of the early reform era, as we have shown in this book, was breaking through to a new closeness not only with the United States and Europe but also with China's Asian neighbors, Japan, South Korea, and the Southeast Asian countries. China has benefited enormously from this improvement in relations, to the extent that much of the country's economic progress would have been impossible without it. Since 2010, however, all of these associations have suffered dramatic declines. Not everything in the new conflicts is the CCP's fault. But the fact is that China today is more isolated internationally than at any time since the early 1970s, in spite of its massive economic outreach through the Belt and Road Initiative. CCP leaders tell us that it does not matter, since the PRC's foreign policy is correct. But, for the time being at least, the Party's hubris in foreign affairs seems to mirror the return to megalomania in its domestic position.

China is today, as it always has been, a mass of contradictions. It is so big, so complex and composite, that it defies most easy generalities. The uncertainty this creates has been at the center of our story in this book. Nobody could foresee the reform era emerging from under the wreckage of the Cultural Revolution. Today, it is difficult to imagine a more liberal, pluralistic, and cooperative China emerging from the regime of Xi Jinping. But we believe it could happen, if the Chinese tire of the bombast and empty promises coming from their present leaders. Even so, we must also live with the thought that the country could move in the opposite direction—that China could enter a period of increasing repression at home and discord with rest of the world. Given the global significance China now has, that would be a tragic outcome of all the great transformations we have tried to give an account of in this book.

NOTES

Abbreviations

CCA	中央档案馆 (Chinese Central Archive)
CYNP	Zhu Jiamu (朱佳木) et al., 陈云年谱, *1905–1995* [Chronological Record of Chen Yun, 1905–1995] (Beijing: 中央文献, 2000)
DNP-A	Yang Shengqun (杨胜群) and Yan Jianqi (闫建琪), et al., 邓小平年谱, *1904–1974* [Chronological Record of Deng Xiaoping, 1904–1974] (Beijing: 中央文献, 2009)
DNP-B	Leng Rong (冷溶) and Wang Zuoling (汪作玲), et al., 邓小平年谱, *1975–1997* [Chronological Record of Deng Xiaoping, 1975–1997], 2 vols. (Beijing: 中央文献, 2009)
DWX	Deng Xiaoping (邓小平), 邓小平文选 [Selected Works of Deng Xiaoping], 3 vols. (Beijing: 人民, 1983–1994)
FRUS	*Foreign Relations of the United States* (Washington, DC: U.S. Government Printing Office)
GSPA	Gansu Provincial Archive (甘肃省档案馆)
HBPA	Hubei Provincial Archive (湖北省档案馆)
HPA	Hebei Provincial Archive (河北省档案馆)
LXJ	Liu Shaoqi (刘少奇), 刘少奇选集 [Selected Works of Liu Shaoqi] (Beijing: 人民, 1985)
MNP	Pang Xianzhi et al. (逢先知等), 毛泽东年谱, *1949–1976* [Chronological Record of Mao Zedong, 1949–1976], 6 vols. (Beijing: 中央文献, 2013)
MWG	Mao Zedong (毛泽东), 建国以来毛泽东文稿 [Mao Zedong's Manuscripts since the Founding of the People's Republic], 20 vols. (Beijing: 中央文献, 2023)
MZ	Pang Xianzhi (逢先知等) et al., 毛泽东传, *1949–1976* [Biography of Mao Zedong, 1949–1976] (Beijing: 中央文献, 2003)
RMRB	人民日报 (People's Daily)

UKNA   National Archives of the United Kingdom, London

WGYJZL   Party History Teaching and Research Group at the National Defense University (国防大学党史党建教研室), eds., "文化大革命"研究资料 [A Collection of Cultural Revolution Materials], 3 vols. (Beijing: internal edition, 1988)

ZGWGWK   Song Yongyi (宋永毅), chief comp., "中国文化大革命文库" [The Chinese Cultural Revolution Database]

ZNP   Li Ping (力平) and Ma Zhisun (马芷荪), chief eds., 周恩来年谱, 1949–1976 [Chronological Record of Zhou Enlai, 1949–1976], 3 vols. (Beijing: 中央文献, 1998)

ZZ   Jin Chongji 金冲及 et al., 周恩来传, 1898–1976 [Biography of Zhou Enlai, 1898–1976], vol. 2 (Beijing: 中央文献, 2008)

Introduction

1. Li Zhisui, *The Private Life of Chairman Mao: The Memoirs of Mao's Personal Physician* (New York: Random House, 1994), pp. 3–9; Chen Changjiang (陈长江), 毛泽东最后十年: 警卫队长的回忆 [Mao Zedong's Final Decade: The Reminiscences of His Chief Bodyguard] (Beijing: 中共中央党校, 1998); Zhang Yufeng (张玉凤), "毛泽东晚年生活的片段回忆" [Fragmentary Recollections of Mao Zedong's Later Life], 社会科学论坛 [Social Sciences Forum], no. 12 (2007), pp. 78–83; Qi Li (亓莉), 毛泽东晚年生活琐记 [Incidents from Mao Zedong's Later Life] (Beijing: 中央文献, 1998). We have also interviewed people who were present in Zhongnanhai the night Mao died.

2. For a summary of Mao's medical conditions, see Li, *Private Life of Chairman Mao*, pp. 8–9; and Francois Retief and André Wessels, "Mao Tse-tung (1893–1976)—His Habits and His Health," *South African Medical Journal* 99, no. 5 (May 2009), pp. 302–305. On Mao's health and the circumstances of his death, we have also received information from a number of CCP archivists and historians, who, given the current political situation in China, will have to remain nameless.

3. "Meeting between Mr. Muldoon and Mao Zedong at Chairman Mao's Residence, 30 April 1976," April 30, 1976, Archives New Zealand, item R18227103 ABHS 6943/1 BEI 25/3/3 1, online at the Wilson Center Digital Archive, https://digitalarchive.wilsoncenter.org/document/meeting-between-mr-muldoon-and-mao-zedong-chairman-maos-residence-30-april-1976.

4. "Memorandum of Conversation between Chairman Mao Zedong and President Richard Nixon," February 21, 1972, Wilson Center Digital Archive, Gerald R. Ford Presidential Library, National Security Adviser Trip Briefing Books and Cables for President Ford, 1974–1976 (Box 19), https://digitalarchive.wilsoncenter.org/document/memorandum-conversation-between-chairman-mao-zedong-and-president-richard-nixon. On a later occasion, in the summer of 1975, Mao returned to the issue. "I have not been able to do much," he told visitors to Zhongnanhai. "Only move a few office blocks around in downtown Beijing. That's all." Information from CCP historians, May 2019.

5. See Odd Arne Westad, *Restless Empire: China and the World since 1750* (New York: Basic Books, 2012); and Chen Jian, *Mao's China and the Cold War* (Chapel Hill: University of North Carolina Press, 2001).

6. "关于建国以来党的若干历史问题的决议" [Resolution on Certain Questions in the History of Our Party since the Founding of the People's Republic of China], 人民日报 [*Renmin Ribao* (People's Daily), hereafter *RMRB*], July 1, 1981; for an English text of the document, see the Wilson Center Digital Archive, https://digitalarchive .wilsoncenter.org/document/resolution-certain-questions-history-our-party -founding-peoples-republic-china.

7. This is also the view of Frederick C. Teiwes and Warren Sun, whose *The End of the Maoist Era: Chinese Politics during the Twilight of the Cultural Revolution, 1972–1976* (Armonk, NY: M. E. Sharpe, 2007) is a pathbreaker for the study of the late Maoist period.

8. For an overview of some of these discussions, see Andrew G. Walder, "Bending the Arc of Chinese History: The Cultural Revolution's Paradoxical Legacy," *China Quarterly,* no. 227 (2016), pp. 613–631. For work that sees some of the effects of the Cultural Revolution as less one-dimensional, see, on politics, Guobin Yang, *The Red Guard Generation and Political Activism in China* (New York: Columbia University Press, 2016); on economics, Chris Bramall, "A Late Maoist Industrial Revolution? Economic Growth in Jiangsu Province (1966–1978)," *China Quarterly* 240 (December 2019), pp. 1039–1065; and on production and consumption, Laurence Coderre, *Newborn Socialist Things: Materiality in Maoist China* (Durham, NC: Duke University Press, 2021).

9. See Wang Hui, *The End of the Revolution: China and the Limits of Modernity* (London: Verso, 2011); Mobo Gao, *The Battle for China's Past: Mao and the Cultural Revolution* (London: Pluto Press, 2008); and Chun Lin, *The Transformation of Chinese Socialism* (Durham, NC: Duke University Press, 2006). The two most impressive recent overall accounts of the Cultural Revolution, Andrew G. Walder, *Agents of Disorder: Inside China's Cultural Revolution* (Cambridge, MA: Harvard University Press, 2019), and Frank Dikötter, *The Cultural Revolution: A People's History, 1962–1976* (New York: Bloomsbury, 2016), both see unintended consequences as major aspects of the era. Even so, the majority of historians underline the significance of politics at the central level and Mao's intentions; see Roderick MacFarquhar and Michael Schoenhals, *Mao's Last Revolution* (Cambridge, MA: Belknap Press of Harvard University Press, 2006).

10. For the U.S. role, see Daniel J. Sargent, *A Superpower Transformed: The Remaking of American Foreign Relations in the 1970s* (Oxford: Oxford University Press, 2015); and Fritz Bartel, *The Triumph of Broken Promises: The End of the Cold War and the Rise of Neoliberalism* (Cambridge, MA: Harvard University Press, 2022). For overall perspectives, see Niall Ferguson et al., eds., *The Shock of the Global: The 1970s in Perspective* (Cambridge, MA: Belknap Press of Harvard University Press, 2010).

11. In 2023 U.S. dollars; see "China GDP per Capita 1960–2023," Macrotrends, accessed August 25, 2023, https://www.macrotrends.net/countries/CHN/china/gdp -per-capita.

Chapter 1. To the Cultural Revolution

1. Wuhan Statistics Bureau (武汉市统计局), comp., 武汉市第七次全国人口普查公报 [Report of the Seventh National Census in Wuhan], last modified September 16, 2021, http://tjj.wuhan.gov.cn/ztzl_49/pczl/202109/t20210916_1779157.shtml.

2. For factional struggles among rebel groups in the heyday of the Cultural Revolution, see Roderick MacFarquhar and Michael Schoenhals, *Mao's Last Revolution* (Cambridge, MA: Belknap Press of Harvard University Press, 2006), chaps. 10–11; Wang Nianyi (王年一), 大动乱的年代 [Years of Great Turmoil] (Zhengzhou: 河南人民, 1988), chaps. 4–6.

3. On the revolution in Wuhan up to July 1967, see MacFarquhar and Schoenhals, *Mao's Last Revolution*, pp. 199–205; Bu Weihua (卜偉華), 砸爛舊世界: 文化大革命的動亂與浩劫, *1966–1968* [Smashing the Old World: The Turmoil and Catastrophe of the Cultural Revolution, 1966–1968] (Hong Kong: 中文大學, 2008), pp. 528–531; Xu Hailiang (徐海亮), 武漢七二零事件實錄 [Records of the July Twentieth Incident in Wuhan] (Hong Kong: 中國文化傳播, 2010); Chen Zaidao (陈再道), 浩劫中的一幕: 武汉七二零事件亲历记 [One Episode in the Havoc: Personal Experiences of the July Twentieth Incident in Wuhan] (Beijing: 解放军, 1989). Quotes from Mao Zedong (毛泽东), 毛主席语录 [Quotations from Chairman Mao Zedong] (Beijing: 东方红, 1967), pp. 158, 20; Mao Zedong, "Speech at the Celebration of Stalin's 60th Birthday," December 21, 1939, 人民日报 [*RMRB*], December 20, 1949.

4. Pang Xianzhi et al. (逄先知等), 毛泽东年谱, *1949–1976* [Chronological Record of Mao Zedong, 1949–1976, hereafter *MNP*], 6 vols. (Beijing: 中央文献, 2013), vol. 6, pp. 97–98.

5. *MNP*, vol. 6, pp. 98–103; MacFarquhar and Schoenhals, *Mao's Last Revolution*, pp. 210–212; Shaoguang Wang, *Failure of Charisma: The Cultural Revolution in Wuhan* (Hong Kong: Oxford University Press, 1995), pp. 149–157.

6. Deng Xiaoping (邓小平), "党在组织战线和思想战线上的迫切任务" [The Party's Urgent Tasks on the Organizational and Ideological Fronts], October 12, 1983, in 邓小平文选 [Selected Works of Deng Xiaoping, hereafter *DWX*], 3 vols. (Beijing: 人民, 1983–1994), vol. 3, p. 37.

7. Editorial Committee, 习仲勋传 [A Biography of Xi Zhongxun], vol. 2 (Beijing: 中央文献, 2013), p. 521.

8. Mao Zedong (毛泽东), "中国人从此站起来了" [We the Chinese Have Stood Up], September 21, 1949, in CCP Central Institute of Historical Documents Studies (中共中央文献研究室), ed., 毛泽东文集 [A Collection of Works of Mao Zedong], vol. 5 (Beijing: 人民, 1996), pp. 342–346.

9. For more substantial discussion, see Chen Jian, *Mao's China and the Cold War* (Chapel Hill: University of North Carolina Press, 2001), chap. 3.

10. According to a study by Chinese historian Yang Kuisong (杨奎松) in the "Suppression of Reactionaries" campaign (1950–1951) alone, 712,000 were executed, 1.29 million were arrested, and over 1.2 million were placed under "mass supervision" (管制). The number was provided by Mao himself and was based on a report by Xu Zirong, deputy minister of public safety in January 1954. See Yang Kuisong (杨奎松),

"新中国镇反运动始末" [The Full Story of the Suppression of Reactionaries Campaign in New China], part II, 江淮文史 [Jianghuai History and Literature], no. 2 (2011), p. 19. See also the descriptions in Frank Dikötter, *Tragedy of Liberation: A History of the Chinese Revolution, 1945–1957* (London: Bloomsbury, 2013), chaps. 3 and 9.

11. The Marriage Law of the People's Republic of China (中华人民共和国婚姻法) was passed on April 13, 1950; see 人民日报 [*RMRB*], April 16, 1950, p. 1.

12. Jiang Yongping (蒋永萍), "50年中国城市妇女就业的回顾" [Employment of Chinese Urban Women in the Past Fifty Years], 劳动保障通讯 [Newsletter of Labor Protection], no. 3 (2000), p. 29; Zhu Bing (朱斌), "我国建国初期对女性人力资源的开发" [Development of Female Human Resources in the Early Days of the People's Republic], 唐山师范学院学报 [Journal of Tangshan Teachers College] 29, no. 3 (May 2007), p. 111.

13. Wu Li (武力), ed., 中华人民共和国经济史, 1949–1999 [The Economic History of the People's Republic of China, 1949–1999] (Beijing: 中国经济, 1999), pp. 370–372; see also Nicholas R. Lardy, "Economic Recovery and the First Five-Year Plan," in Roderick MacFarquhar and John K. Fairbank, eds., *Cambridge History of China,* vol. 14: *The People's Republic, Part 1, The Emergence of Revolutionary China, 1949–1965* (Cambridge: Cambridge University Press, 1987), pp. 155–156. Lardy describes that China's "national income grew at an average annual rate of 8.9 percent (measured in constant prices)" during this period.

14. Shen Zhihua and Xia Yafeng, *Mao and the Sino-Soviet Partnership, 1945–1959: A New History* (Lanham, MD: Lexington Books, 2015), chaps. 4–7; Shen Zhihua (沈志华), 苏联专家在中国, 1948–1960 [Soviet Experts in China, 1948–1960] (Beijing: 新华, 2009).

15. Vladislav M. Zubok, *A Failed Empire: The Soviet Union in the Cold War from Stalin to Gorbachev* (Chapel Hill: University of North Carolina Press, 2009), p. 111.

16. 周恩来在成都会议上的讲话 [Zhou Enlai's Speech at the Chengdu Conference], March 1958, in Luo Pinghan (罗平汉), 文革前夜的中国 [China on the Eve of the Cultural Revolution] (Beijing: 人民, 2007), p. 112.

17. Dong Fureng (董辅礽), ed., 中华人民共和国经济史 [The Economic History of the People's Republic of China], vol. 1 (Beijing: 经济科学, 1999), p. 281; Wu, 中华人民共和国经济史, p. 370.

18. On consumption, see Laurence Coderre, "A Necessary Evil: Conceptualizing the Socialist Commodity under Mao," *Comparative Studies in Society and History* 61, no. 1 (January 2019), pp. 23–49.

19. Maurice Meisner, *Mao's China and After: A History of the People's Republic* (New York: Free Press, 1999), p. 84.

20. Anita Chan, Richard Madsen, and Jonathan Unger, *Chen Village: Revolution to Globalization,* 3rd ed. (Berkeley: University of California Press, 2009), pp. 22–24.

21. Chinese Central Archive (中央档案馆) and CCP Central Institute of Historical Documents Studies (中共中央文献研究室), eds., 中共中央文件选集, 1949.10–1966.5 [Selected Documents of the CCP Central Committee, October 1949 to May 1966], vol. 14 (Beijing: 人民, 2013), pp. 129–139.

22. See Wang Fei-Ling, *Organizing through Division and Exclusion: China's Hukou System* (Stanford, CA: Stanford University Press, 2005); see also Cheng Tiejun and Mark Selden, "The Origins and Social Consequences of China's Hukou System," *China Quarterly*, no. 139 (September 1994), pp. 644–668.

23. Hou Yonglu (侯永禄), 农民日记: 一个农民的生存实录 [A Peasant's Diary: A Faithful Record of a Peasant's Struggles for Survival] (Beijing: 中国青年, 2006); see entries for March 9, 14, and 15, 1954.

24. National Bureau of Statistics of China (中国国家统计局), comp., 中国统计年鉴, 1981 [China Statistical Yearbook, 1981] (Beijing: 中国统计, 1981), p. 11.

25. See Bo Yibo (薄一波), 若干重大决策和事件的回顾 [Recollections of Some Important Decisions and Events], 2 vols. (Beijing: 人民, 1999), vol. 1, p. 528; *MNP*, vol. 2, pp. 513–514.

26. Mao Zedong (毛泽东), "增强党的团结, 继承党的传统" [Strengthen Party's Unity and Carry on Party's Traditions], 毛泽东选集 [Selected Works of Mao Zedong], vol. 5 (Beiing: 人民, 1977), p. 296.

27. *MNP*, vol. 2, pp. 574–575.

28. Chu Anping (储安平), "向毛主席和周总理提些意见" [Some Suggestions for Chairman Mao and Premier Zhou], 人民日报 [*RMRB*], June 2, 1957, p. 2.

29. In the early 1980s, an official report by CCP Central United Front Department stated that a total number of over 550,000 were designated "右派" (Rightists) in 1957–1958; see 三中全会以来重要文献选编 [Important Documents since the Third Plenum], vol. 1 (Beijing: 人民, 1982), p. 605. This figure has been generally accepted in official accounts and studies by scholars; see, for example, Shen Zhihua (沈志华), "群众性阶级斗争的必然结果—谈谈反右运动扩大化的问题" [The Necessary Result of Mass Class Struggles: Discussing the Excessive Development of the Anti-Rightist Campaign, Part 2], 江淮文史 [Jianghuai History and Literature], no. 3 (2014), p. 43. However, the figure has been challenged in some studies; see, for example, Luo Bing (罗冰), "反右运动档案解密—实划右派300多万" [Declassifying the Archives of the Anti-Rightist Movement: More than Three Million Were Made Rightists], *Zhengming* (争鸣), no. 1 (2006), p. 1. Jia Ming (贾铭), "对右派总人数的研究" [Research on the Total Number of Rightists], Tian Wen Institute, December 21, 2020, http://www.ustianwen.com/2020/12/blog-post_52.html, sets the number at around four million.

30. The best study of the origins and process of the "Anti-Rightist" campaign in the 1956–1957 Chinese literature is Shen Zhihua (沈志华), 思考與選擇: 從知識分子會議到反右派運動, 1956–1957 [Thinking and Choosing: From the Conference on Intellectuals to the Anti-Rightist Movement, 1956–1957] (Hong Kong: 中文大學, 2008); see also Zhu Zheng (朱正), 一九五七年的夏季: 从百家争鸣到两家争鸣 [Summer 1957: From Competition among Hundred Schools to Competition between Two Schools] (Zhengzhou: 河南人民, 1998); and Chung Yen-lin, "The Witch-Hunting Vanguard: The Central Secretariat's Roles and Activities in the Anti-Rightist Campaign," *China Quarterly*, no. 206 (June 2011), pp. 391–411.

31. Lin Ke (林克), 林克日记 [Lin Ke Diary] (copy of manuscript in authors' possession), November 26, 1956. Mao told Lin, his secretary, that it was wrong for the Soviet Party's Twentieth Congress "to abandon Stalin's sword."

32. Cong Jin (丛进), 曲折发展的岁月 [Years of Tortuous Development] (Zhengzhou: 河南人民, 1989), p. 117; Mao Zedong (毛泽东), "在成都会议上的讲话提纲" [Speech Outlines at the Chengdu Conference], March 10, 1958, in 建国以来毛泽东文稿 [Mao Zedong's Manuscripts since the Founding of the People's Republic, hereafter *MWG*], 20 vols. (Beijing: 中央文献, 2023), vol. 12, p. 254; Zhu Dandan, *1956: Mao's China and the Hungarian Crisis* (Ithaca, NY: Cornell University Press, 2013).

33. Mao Zedong (毛泽东), "在中共中央八届三中全会上的讲话提纲" [Outline of Speech at the Third Plenum of the CCP's Eighth Central Committee], October 9, 1957, *MWG*, vol. 12, p. 46; *MNP*, vol. 3, p. 223.

34. Mao Zedong, "Speech at a Meeting of the Representatives of Sixty-four Communist and Workers' Parties," November 18, 1957, https://digitalarchive.wilsoncenter .org/document/mao-zedong-speech-meeting-representatives-sixty-four-communist -and-workers-parties-edited.

35. Mao Zedong, "在中共中央八届三中全会上的讲话提纲," October 9, 1957, *MWG*, vol. 12, pp. 44–47; 主席讲话 [The Chairman's Speech], October 9, 1957, 1-13-1957, pp. 49–54, Jilin Provincial Archive.

36. Mao Zedong (毛泽东), "工作方法六十条(草案)" [Sixty Articles on Work Methods (Draft)], *MWG*, vol. 7, p. 51.

37. Li Ping (力平), 开国总理周恩来 [The Founding Premier Zhou Enlai] (Beijing: 中央党校, 1994), pp. 360–361; Cong, 曲折发展的岁月, pp. 111–112; Shi Zhongquan (石仲泉), 我观周恩来 [Zhou Enlai in My Eyes] (Beijing: 中央党校, 2008), p. 329.

38. Zhou Enlai (周恩来), 在八大二次会议上的讲话, May 17, 1958, 855-4-1573-3, Hebei Provincial Archive (河北省档案馆, hereafter HPA). In June, Zhou attempted to resign as premier, but the Politburo—with Mao's consent—decided that Zhou should remain in his position. See *MNP*, vol. 3, p. 368; Shi, 我观周恩来, pp. 362–363.

39. For a new, comprehensive Zhou biography, see Chen Jian, *Zhou Enlai: A Life* (Cambridge, MA: Belknap Press of Harvard University Press, 2024).

40. In Mao's own words, "this is mainly about steel"; *MNP*, vol. 3, p. 373.

41. Pang Xianzhi (逄先知等) et al., 毛泽东传, 1949–1976 [Biography of Mao Zedong, 1949–1976, hereafter *MZ*] (Beijing: 中央文献, 2003), pp. 824–825.

42. Mao Zedong (毛泽东), 在北戴河政治局扩大会议上的讲话 [Speech at CCP Politburo Enlarged Meeting at Beidaihe], August 17, 1958, 91-018-0495, 311–333, Gansu Provincial Archive (甘肃省档案馆, hereafter GSPA); see also *MNP*, vol. 3, p. 411–420.

43. *MWG*, vol. 13, p. 53.

44. Mao, 在北戴河政治局扩大会议上的讲话, August 17, 1958, 91-018-0495, 311–333, GSPA; see also *MNP*, vol. 3, pp. 411–420.

45. For a good Liu biography, especially on his experience in the Cultural Revolution, see Lowell Dittmer, *Liu Shaoqi and the Cultural Revolution* (New York: Routledge, 2015).

46. The most comprehensive Deng biographies in English are Ezra Vogel, *Deng Xiaoping and the Transformation of China* (Cambridge, MA: Belknap Press of Harvard University Press, 2011); and Alexander V. Pantsov and Steven I. Levine, *Deng Xiaoping: A Revolutionary Life* (Oxford: Oxford University Press, 2015).

47. Cited from Zhong Yanlin (钟延麟), 文革前的邓小平 [Deng Xiaoping before the Cultural Revolution] (Hong Kong: 中文大學, 2013), p. 272. See also Zhong's "The CEO

of the Utopian Project: Deng Xiaoping's Roles and Activities in the Great Leap Forward," *China Journal,* no. 69 (2013), pp. 154–173; and, on Peng Zhen, "The Unknown Standard-Bearer of the Three Red Banners: Peng Zhen's Roles in the Great Leap Forward," *China Journal,* no. 74 (2015), pp. 129–143.

48. *MWG,* vol. 14, p. 13.

49. Information from authors' interviews with Party historians, January 2014. While it is very difficult to come up with an exact number of people who died as a consequence of the Great Leap, even official statistics indicate a net population loss of about this size. China's official census published by the State Bureau of Statistics in 1981 shows an overall decrease in population between 1959 and 1962. For every year before that, the average increase was about ten million per year; see National Bureau of Statistics of China (中国国家统计局), 中国统计年鉴, 1983 [China Statistical Yearbook, 1983] (Beijing: 中国统计, 1983), pp. 103–105.

50. Shi Xue'ai (时学爱), "我的家人在大饥荒中饿死" [My Family Starved to Death during the Great Famine], 炎黄春秋 [China through the Ages], no. 5 (2013), pp. 51–52. On the links between climate and starvation, see Ying Bai and James Kai-sing Kung, "The Shaping of an Institutional Choice: Weather Shocks, the Great Leap Famine, and Agricultural Decollectivization in China," *Explorations in Economic History* 54 (October 2014), pp. 1–26.

51. 中国共产党八届八中全会关于以彭德怀同志为首的反党集团的错误的决议 [Resolution on the Anti-Party Clique Headed by Comrade Peng Dehuai Passed at the Eighth Plenum of the CCP's Eighth Central Committee], August 16, 1959, in Party History Teaching Group at the PLA Academy of Politics (解放军政治学院党史教研室), eds., 中共党史教学参考资料 [Reference Materials for Teaching CCP History], vol. 23 (Beijing: 国防大学, 1986), pp. 119–122; for a firsthand account of Peng's purge, see Li Rui (李锐), 毛泽东秘书手记: 庐山会议实录, 增订本 [Notes by Mao Zedong's Secretary: A Factual Account of the Lushan Conference, revised and expanded version] (Zhengzhou: 河南人民, 1995).

52. Chen, *Mao's China and the Cold War,* chaps. 2 and 7.

53. When Mao met with Khrushchev on September 30, 1959, he told the Soviet leader that the decision to shell Jinmen was made after Khrushchev concluded his secret visit to Beijing in early August. *MNP,* vol. 4, p. 186.

54. "Discussion between N. S. Khrushchev and Mao Zedong," October 2, 1959, History and Public Policy Program Digital Archive, Archive of the President of the Russian Federation (APRF), f. 52, op. 1, d. 499, ll. 1–33, copy in Volkogonov Collection, Manuscript Division, Library of Congress, Washington, D.C., http://digitalarchive.wilsoncenter.org/document/112088. For Chinese accounts of the meeting, see also Yan Mingfu (阎明复), 亲历中苏关系—中央办公厅翻译组的十年, 1957–1966 [Witnessing Chinese-Soviet Relations: Ten Years at the Group of Interpreters at the Central Administrative Office, 1957–1966] (Beijing: 中国人民大学, 2015), pp. 188–204; and Wu Lengxi (吴冷西), 十年论战: 1956–1966, 中苏关系回忆录 [Ten Year Polemic Debate: A Memoir on Sino-Soviet Relations, 1956–1966], vol. 1 (Beijing: 中央文献, 1999), pp. 221–227.

55. Wu, 十年论战, vol. 1, pp. 340–341.

56. Yan, 亲历中苏关系, pp. 324–359.

57. Liu Shaoqi (刘少奇), "在扩大的中央工作会议上的讲话" [Speech at the Enlarged Central Work Conference], January 27, 1962, in 刘少奇选集 [Selected Works of Liu Shaoqi, hereafter *LXJ*], vol. 2 (Beijing: 人民, 1985), p. 419.

58. Cong, 曲折发展的岁月, chap. 2; Xiao Donglian (萧冬连), 求索中国: "文革"前十年史 [In Search of China's Path Forward: Ten Year History before the Cultural Revolution], vol. 2 (Beijing: 红旗, 1999), pp. 763–770.

59. Xu Zehao (徐泽浩), ed., 王稼祥年谱, 1906–1974 [Chronological Records of Wang Jiaxiang, 1906–1974] (Beijing: 中央文献, 2001), pp. 486–489; Xu Zehao (徐泽浩), ed., 王稼祥传 [A Biography of Wang Jiaxiang] (Beijing: 当代中国, 2006), pp. 554–564.

60. Chairman Mao's speech at the Tenth Plenum of the CCP's Eighth Central Committee, September 24, 1962, 101-12-119, pp. 22–27, Fujian PA; see also *MNP*, vol. 5, pp. 151–153. For a good discussion, see Niu Jun (牛军), "1962: 中国对外政策'左'转的前夜" [1962: Before China's Left Turn in Foreign Policy], 历史研究 [Historical Research], no. 3 (2003), p. 33.

61. Ke Keming (柯克明) et al., 邓子恢传 [A Biography of Deng Zihui] (Beijing: 人民, 1996), chap. 15.

62. For Sun's views overall, see Deng Jiarong (邓加荣), 孙冶方传 [A Biography of Sun Yefang] (Taiyuan: 山西经济, 1998).

63. Chinese Academy of Social Science (中国社会科学院) and Chinese Central Archive (中央档案馆), eds., 中华人民共和国经济档案资料选编 1960–1965 (外贸卷) [Selected Archival Materials about the Economy of People's Republic of China, 1960–1965 (Foreign Trade Volume)] (Beijing: 中国财政经济, 2011), p. 8.

64. On the significance of Hong Kong for China's development, see Peter E. Hamilton, *Made in Hong Kong: Transpacific Networks and a New History of Globalization* (New York: Columbia University Press, 2021).

65. Chinese Academy of Social Science and Chinese Central Archive, eds., 中华人民共和国经济档案资料选编 1960–1965 (外贸卷), p. 9; see also Jason Kelly, *Market Maoists: The Communist Origins of Chinese Capitalist Ascent* (Cambridge, MA: Harvard University Press, 2021), chap. 6.

66. The best source-based study on the lead-up to the war is Anton Harder, "Defining Independence in Cold War Asia: Sino-Indian Relations, 1949–1962" (PhD thesis, London School of Economics and Political Science), 2015; see also Neville Maxwell, *India's China War* (New York: Pantheon Books, 1970); and Lorenz M. Lüthi, ed., *The Sino-Indian War of 1962: New Perspectives* (London: Routledge, 2017). On Tibetan matters, see Sulmaan Wasif Khan, *Muslim, Trader, Nomad, Spy: China's Cold War and the People of the Tibetan Borderlands* (Chapel Hill: University of North Carolina Press, 2015).

67. *MWG*, vol. 16, p. 542; see also *MNP*, vol. 5, p. 198.

68. *MWG*, vol. 17, pp. 129–130.

69. 毛主席和新共总书记威尔科克斯谈话记录 [Records of Chairman Mao's Conversation with General Secretary of the Communist Party of New Zealand Wilcox], May 22, 1963, 中央档案馆 (Chinese Central Archive, hereafter CCA).

70. Editorial Committee, 习仲勋传, vol. 2, chap. 26.

71. 毛主席与日共代表团第二次谈话记录 [Records of Chairman Mao's Second Conversation with a Delegation of the Japanese Communist Party], 1:30–4:00 P.M., October 10, 1964, CCA; see also *MNP*, vol. 5, pp. 337–338, 358.

72. For suspicions in the 1950s that Lin Biao was mentally ill, see Guan Weixun (官伟勋), 我所知道的叶群 [The Ye Qun I Knew] (Beijing: 中国文学, 1993), p. 207; Zhang Yunsheng (张云生), 毛家湾纪实:林彪秘书回忆录 [A True Account of Maojiawan: The Memoirs of Lin Biao's Secretary] (Beijing: 春秋, 1988), pp. 13–14; and Jiao Ye (焦烨), 叶群之谜: 一个秘书眼中的叶群与林彪 [The Riddle of Ye Qun: Ye Qun and Lin Biao in the Eyes of a Secretary] (Beijing: 中国文联, 1993).

73. Zhang Suhua (张素华), 变局: 七千人大会始末 [Changing Scenarios: The Beginning and End of the Seven-Thousand-Cadres Conference] (Beijing: 中国青年, 2006), pp. 141–145.

74. *MWG*, vol. 16, p. 257.

75. Lin Biao (林彪), "在政治局扩大会议上的讲话" [Lin Biao's Speech at the Politburo Enlarged Meeting], May 18, 1966; Party History Teaching and Research Group at the National Defense University (国防大学党史党建教研室), eds., "文化大革命"研究资料 [A Collection of Cultural Revolution Materials, hereafter *WGYJZL*], 3 vols. (Beijing: internal edition, 1988), vol. 1, p. 21.

76. Covell F. Meyskens, *Mao's Third Front: The Militarization of Cold War China* (Cambridge: Cambridge University Press, 2020), p. 202; Barry J. Naughton, "The Third Front: Defense Industrialization in the Chinese Interior," *China Quarterly*, no. 115 (September 1988), pp. 351–386.

77. Hou, 农民日记, pp. 73–74.

78. Liu Huaqing (刘华清) and Ye Jianjun (叶健君), 人民公社化运动纪实 [A Factual Account of the Movement for the People's Communes] (Beijing: 东方, 2014), pp. 117–152; Ji Naiwang (纪乃旺), "人民公社化时期农村公共食堂的兴办: 以江苏为例" [Establishing Public Dining Services in the Countryside during the Time of People's Communes: The Case of Jiangsu], 辽宁行政学院学报 [Liaoning Administrative College Journal], no. 9 (2012), pp. 170–173.

79. Information from Party historians, November 2014; *MNP*, vol. 5, p. 441.

80. *MNP*, vol. 5, pp. 445–446.

81. Yang Shangkun (杨尚昆), 杨尚昆日记 [Yang Shangkun's Diaries], vol. 2 (Beijing: 中央文献, 2001), pp. 478–482; *MZ*, vol. 2, pp. 1372–1375; *MNP*, vol. 5, pp. 457–458.

82. The chairman's customary distrust of intellectuals ran deep, even if in many ways he qualified as one himself. He told one of his secretaries: "Intellectuals . . . are the product of surplus labor. They do not produce things, or direct and assist production. . . . They exploit the surplus labor of workers and peasants. They are equivalent to bandits, but they are civilized bandits." Lin Ke, 林克日记, March 15, 1957.

83. 毛泽东和崔庸健的谈话 [Mao Zedong's Conversation with Ch'oe Yonggŏn], October 7, 1964, CCA.

84. *MNP*, vol. 5, pp. 354–355, 501–502.

85. *MNP*, vol. 5, p. 534; *MZ*, vol. 2, pp. 1394–1395.

86. Huang Yao (黄瑶) and Zhang Mingzhe (张明哲), 罗瑞卿传 [A Biography of Luo Ruiqing] (Beijing: 当代中国, 1996), pp. 512–536.
87. Huang and Zhang, 罗瑞卿传, pp. 540–542.
88. Frank Dikötter, *The Cultural Revolution: A People's History, 1962–1976* (London: Bloomsbury, 2016), p. 45; for Luo's suicide, see also Huang and Zhang, 罗瑞卿传, pp. 569–570.
89. Huang and Zhang, 罗瑞卿传, pp. 569–570; Luo Diandian (罗点点), 我的父亲罗瑞卿 [My Father Luo Ruiqing] (Hohhot: 内蒙古人民, 1994), p. 177.
90. 解放军报 [People's Liberation Army Daily], June 7, 1966.
91. Mao Zedong (毛泽东), "与康生等同志谈话纪要" [Summary of Talk with Comrade Kang Sheng and Others], March 28–30, 1966, in 毛泽东思想万岁 [Long Live Mao Zedong Thought] (Wuhan: n.p., 1968); *MNP*, vol. 5, p. 572.
92. *MNP*, vol. 5, pp. 582–583; Liu Chongwen (刘崇文) and Chen Shaochou (陈绍畴), eds., 刘少奇年谱,下卷 [Chronological Records of Liu Shaoqi], vol. 2 (Beijing: 中央文献, 1996), pp. 637–638.
93. *MNP*, vol. 5, p. 588; 中共中央政治局扩大会议决定 [Decision by the Enlarged Meeting of the CCP Central Committee Politburo], May 23, 1966, *WGYJZL*, vol. 1, p. 24; information from an interview with a leading Party historian, October 2017.
94. 中国共产党中央委员会通知 [CCP Central Committee Notice], May 16, 1966, *WGYJZL*, vol. 1, pp. 1–4.

Chapter 2. Great Disorder under Heaven

1. *RMRB*, June 2, 1966, p. 1.
2. Mao Zedong (毛泽东), "炮打司令部: 我的一张大字报" [Bombard the Headquarters: My Big Character Poster], August 5, 1966, *MWG*, vol. 18, p. 304.
3. *MWG*, vol. 18, p. 262.
4. For practices, see Daniel Leese, *Mao Cult: Rhetoric and Ritual in China's Cultural Revolution* (Cambridge: Cambridge University Press, 2011).
5. Ray Nunes, "Politics and Ideology: Meetings with Kang Sheng 1966–68, Some Observations by Ray Nunes, Chairman, Workers' Party of New Zealand," https://www.marxists.org/history/erol/new-zealand/nunes-kang.pdf, accessed May 24, 2022.
6. "横扫一切牛鬼蛇神" [Sweep Away All Monsters and Demons], *RMRB*, June 1, 1966, p. 1. *Renmin Ribao* (人民日报) is the main official CCP newspaper.
7. Gong Guzhong (龚固忠) et al., 毛泽东回湖南纪实 [Factual Records of Mao Zedong Returning to Hu'nan] (Changsha: 湖南人民, 1993); Ma Shexiang (马社香), "毛泽东在韶山滴水洞" [Mao Zedong at Dishui Cave in Shaoshan], 湖北文史 [Hubei History and Literature] 65, https://www.hbzx.gov.cn/49/2014-09-15/5771.html, accessed May 24, 2022.
8. *MZ*, vol. 2, p. 1419; Gu Baozi (顾保孜) and Qian Sijie (钱嗣杰), 毛泽东正值神州有事时 [Mao Zedong at a Time when Changes Were Taking Place in China] (Beijing: 人民文学, 2013), pp. 149–155.

9. *MNP*, vol. 5, p. 595.

10. The result of Mao's thinking along these lines was most clearly indicated in a letter he wrote to the first group of Red Guards at the Affiliated Middle School of Tsinghua University: "Your two big-character posters of June 24 and July 4 stated that you are against all the landlord class, bourgeoisie, imperialism, revisionism and their lackeys who exploit and oppress workers, peasants, revolutionary intellectuals and revolutionary parties. Expressing [your] deep-seated anger, it shows that the rebellion against the reactionaries is justified, and I express my warm support to you. . . . From here, I want to say that my revolutionary comrades and I all adopt the same attitude. Whether in Beijing or in the whole country, in the Cultural Revolution movement, we will give warm support to all those who adopt the same revolutionary attitude as you." *MWG*, vol. 18, pp. 301–302.

11. "Chairman Mao Swims in the Yangtse," *Peking Review* 31 (July 29, 1966), p. 6.

12. "跟着毛主席在大风大浪中前进" [Follow Chairman Mao and Advance in Great Storms and Waves], *RMRB*, July 26, 1966, p. 1.

13. Huang Zheng (黄峥), 风雨无悔: 对话王光美 [Come Rain or Shine: A Dialogue with Wang Guangmei] (Beijing: 人民文学, 2014), p. 411; Qi Benyu (戚本禹), 戚本禹回憶錄 [Qi Benyu's Memoirs], vol. 2 (Hong Kong: 中國文革歷史, 2016), p. 440.

14. *MNP*, vol. 5, pp. 601–602; Qi, 戚本禹回憶錄, vol. 2, p. 443.

15. CCP History Research Institute (中共中央党史研究室), eds., 中国共产党大事记, *1966* [Record of Important Events for the Chinese Communist Party in 1966], Central People's Government of the People's Republic of China website, August 30, 2007, http://www.gov.cn/test/2007-08/30/content_731993.htm.

16. Mu Xin (穆欣), "关于工作组存废问题" [About the Existence and Abolition of the Work Groups], 当代中国史研究 [Contemporary China History Study], no. 2 (1997), pp. 61–62.

17. Mao Zedong, (毛泽东), "给清华大学附属中学红卫兵的信" [Letter to the Red Guards at Tsinghua University], August 1, 1966, *MWG*, vol. 18, pp. 301–302.

18. *MNP*, vol. 5, p. 606.

19. Mao Zedong (毛泽东), "炮打司令部: 我的一张大字报," August 5, 1966, *MWG*, vol. 12, p. 90.

20. Zhou Jingqing (周敬青), 解读林彪 [Interpreting Lin Biao] (Shanghai: 上海人民, 2015), chap. 3.

21. "毛主席先后检阅一千一百万文化革命大军" [Chairman Mao Inspected 11 Million Soldiers of the Cultural Revolution], *RMRB*, November 27, 1966, p. 1.

22. Zhang Shunqing (张顺清), "谭厚兰曲阜 '讨孔' 纪实" [A Factual Account of Tan Houlan "Attacking Confucius" in Qufu], 炎黄春秋 [China through the Ages], no. 2 (2015), pp. 21–24.

23. Ding Shu (丁抒), "从史学革命到挖祖坟" [From History Revolution to Digging up Ancestral Graves], 华夏文摘 [Huaxia Digest], 1996, 105, http://www.cnd.org/HXWZ/ZK96/zk105.hz8.html#2, accessed March 21, 2023.

24. While destroying the old, revolutionary groups were preoccupied with commemorating the new; see Denise Y. Ho, *Curating Revolution: Politics on Display in Mao's China* (Cambridge: Cambridge University Press, 2017).

25. Li Xun (李逊), 革命造反年代: 上海文革运动史稿 [An Age of Revolutionary Rebellion: A Draft History of the Cultural Revolution in Shanghai], vol. 1 (Hong Kong: Oxford University Press, 2015), p. 289; see also Chen Pixian (陈丕显), 陈丕显回忆录: 在一月风暴的中心 [Memoirs of Chen Pixian: At the Center of the January Storm] (Shanghai: 世纪集团, 2005), pp. 88–89.

26. Qi, 戚本禹回憶錄, p. 536; Wang Li (王力), 王力反思錄 [Reflections by Wang Li] (Hong Kong: 北星, 2001), pp. 595–596.

27. Qi, 戚本禹回憶錄, pp. 541–544; Wang Li (王力), 現場歷史: 文化大革命紀事 [History Created on Site: The Chronicle of the Cultural Revolution] (Hong Kong: Oxford University Press, 1993), pp. 100–104.

28. Zhang Chunqiao (張春橋), 張春橋獄中家書 [Zhang Chunqiao's Letters to Home from Prison] (Hong Kong: 中文大學, 2015), p. 128; Xu Jingxian (徐景賢), 十年一夢 [A Decade Like a Dream] (Hong Kong: 時代國際, 2003), pp. 7–8.

29. *MNP*, vol. 6, p. 30; *MWG*, vol. 18, p. 419.

30. *MNP*, vol. 6, pp. 51–52; Stuart R. Schram, *Mao Tse-tung* (London: Penguin Books, 1967), p. 278; Roderick MacFarquhar and Michael Schoenhals, *Mao's Last Revolution* (Cambridge, MA: Belknap Press of Harvard University Press, 2006), pp. 170–171.

31. Jin Chongji (金冲及) et al., 刘少奇传 [A Biography of Liu Shaoqi] (Beijing: 中央文献, 2008), p. 1055; Liu Chongwen (刘崇文) and Chen Shaochou (陈绍畴), eds., 刘少奇年谱 [Chronological Records of Liu Shaoqi] (Beijing: 中央文献, 1996), p. 654. Julien Offray de La Mettrie (1709–1751) was a French materialist Enlightenment philosopher. Ernst Haeckel (1834–1919) was a German biologist and eugenicist who regarded the social sciences as forms of "applied biology." Apparently Mao picked these names from his reading.

32. Huang Zheng (黄峥), 刘少奇的最后岁月, 1966–1969 [The Last Years of Liu Shaoqi, 1966–1969] (Beijing: 中央文献, 1996), pp. 279–288.

33. Huang Zheng (黄峥), 王光美访谈录 [Records of Interviews with Wang Guangmei] (Beijing: 中央文献, 2006), pp. 427–429.

34. Wang Yan (王焰) et al., eds., 彭德怀传 [A Biography of Peng Dehuai] (Beijing: 当代中国, 1993), pp. 721–722.

35. Michael Schoenhals, "The Central Case Examination Group, 1966–79," *China Quarterly* 145 (March 1996), pp. 101–102.

36. Schoenhals, "Central Case Examination Group," p. 106.

37. Fan Shuo (范硕) et al., 叶剑英传 [A Biography of Ye Jianying] (Beijing: 当代中国, 2006), p. 584.

38. Bu, 砸烂舊世界, p. 444.

39. *MNP*, vol. 6, p. 50.

40. Gao Gao (高皋) and Yan Jiaqi (严家其), 文化大革命十年史 [Ten-Year History of the Cultural Revolution], vol. 1 (Taipei: 遠流, 1990), p.199.

41. Wang, 王力反思錄, pp. 782–784; Qi, 戚本禹回憶錄, vol. 2, pp. 574–579.

42. Wang, 王力反思錄, p. 781.

43. Mao informed Zhou via Zhang Chunqiao: "The Central Cultural Revolution Group should be treated as the Central Secretariat. All important issues concerning the

Party and the State should first be discussed by the Cultural Revolution Group." Li Ping (力平) and Ma Zhisun (马芷荪) et al., 周恩来年谱, 1949–1976 [Chronological Records of Zhou Enlai, 1949–1976, hereafter ZNP], 3 vols. (Beijing: 中央文献, 1998), vol. 3, p. 127; Wang, 王力反思录, pp. 782–783.

44. CCP Central Military Commission (中央军委), "关于集中力量执行支左、支农、支工、军管、军训任务的决定" [Decision to Concentrate on the Tasks of Supporting the Left, the Peasants, the Workers, and Conducting Military Control and Military Training], March 19, 1967, WGYJZL, vol. 1, pp. 361–362.

45. See, for example, Mao Zedong (毛泽东), "接见阿尔巴尼亚卡博、巴卢库谈话纪录" [Record of Conversation with Albania's (Hysni) Kapo and (Beqir) Balluku], February 3, 1967, 17:20–19:00, CCA. The chairman told the Albanian visitors that the fate of the Cultural Revolution would be determined in the three months between February and April, but "settlement of all problems may take until next February, March or April, or even longer."

46. Xiong Jingming (熊景明), Song Yongyi (宋永毅), and Yu Guoliang (余國良), eds., 中外學者談文革 [Chinese and Foreign Scholars on the Cultural Revolution] (Hong Kong: 中文大學, 2018), p. 209. The number of deaths in Guangxi is controversial; some Party historians believe that it is far lower than 40,000, though they do not dispute the ways in which these people died.

47. Qin Hui (秦暉), "親歷當代史: 我的中國研究情懷" [Personally Experienced History of the Recent Past: My Feelings about Studying China], Hongkong Chinese University, interview filmed on November 22, 2011. Video of lecture, 1:51:17, www.youtube.com/watch?v=DmT9KPoeNBk; Song Yongyi (宋永毅), "廣西文革中的吃人狂潮" [Waves of Cannibalism in Guangxi during the Cultural Revolution], 二十一世紀 [The Twenty-First Century], no. 155 (June 2016), pp. 76–90.

48. Wei Se (唯色), 殺劫—不可碰觸的記憶禁區: 鏡頭下的西藏文革, 第一次披露 [Massacre: The Untouchable Forbidden Zone in Memory, Scenes of the Cultural Revolution in Tibet, the First Disclosure] (Taipei: 大塊文化, 2016), p. 73.

49. Most of the Chinese forces stationed in North Vietnam were construction and air artillery units. See Chen Jian, "China's Involvement in the Vietnam War, 1964–69," China Quarterly, no. 142 (June 1995), pp. 356–387.

50. Chen, "China's Involvement in the Vietnam War," pp. 382–385; Shen Zhihua (沈志華), 最後的天朝: 毛澤東, 金日成與中朝關係 [The Last Heavenly Dynasty: Mao Zedong, Kim Il-sung and Chinese-Korean Relations] (Hong Kong: 中文大學, 2017), pp. 595–607.

51. Cheng Yinghong, "Sino-Cuban Relations during the Early Years of the Castro Regime (1959–1966)," Journal of Cold War Studies 9, no. 3 (Summer 2007), pp. 78–114.

52. Julia Lovell, Maoism: A Global History (New York: Knopf, 2019), pp. 306–346.

53. Julia Lovell, "The Cultural Revolution and Its Legacies in International Perspective," China Quarterly, no. 227 (2016), p. 639.

54. For more on perceptions of Maoism, see Jeremy Brown and Matthew D. Johnson, eds., Maoism at the Grassroots: Everyday Life in China's Era of High Socialism (Cambridge, MA: Harvard University Press, 2015).

55. Such a sense of freedom in the midst of terror is of course not exclusive to Chinese Red Guards; the same could be observed in the Nazi Hitler-Jugend or in the Soviet Komsomol.

56. *MNP*, vol. 6, p. 115.

57. Hopson to Brown, "The Burning of the British Office in Peking," confidential, September 8, 1967, FC1/14, FCO 21/34, National Archives of the United Kingdom (hereafter UKNA). See also Ji Chaozhu, *The Man on Mao's Right: From Harvard Yard to Tiananmen Square, My Life inside China's Foreign Ministry* (New York: Random House, 2008), pp. 224–237.

58. *ZNP*, vol. 2, pp. 181–183.

59. *MNP*, vol. 6, p. 89.

60. Bu, 砸爛舊世界, p. 591.

61. *MNP*, vol. 6, pp. 130–131.

62. Wu Li, 中华人民共和国经济史, 1949–1999, pp. 647–648. In some areas, production recovered quite rapidly, but not in ways that produced further growth; see Gene Chang, Shenke Yang, and Kathryn Chang, "The Immiserizing Growth during the Period of China's Cultural Revolution," *Chinese Economy* 51, no. 5 (October 9, 2018), pp. 387–396.

63. Chen Yangyong (陈扬勇), "周恩来与'文化大革命'初期的铁路交通" [Zhou Enlai and the Railway Transportation in the Early Days of the Cultural Revolution], 中共党史研究 [CCP History Study], no. 1 (1996), pp. 75–80.

64. Information provided by local residents, May 2011.

65. Yu Luoke (遇羅克), "出身論" [The Birth Theory], in Song Yongyi (宋永毅) and Sun Dajin (孫大進), eds., 文化大革命和它的異端思潮 [Heterodox Thoughts during the Cultural Revolution] (Hong Kong: 田園書屋, 1997), pp. 120–217.

66. Yilin Dixi (伊林· 滌西), "给林彪同志的一封公开信" [An Open Letter to Comrade Lin Biao], November 15, 1966, in Song and Sun, 文化大革命和它的異端思潮, pp. 233–239.

67. Song and Sun, 文化大革命和它的異端思潮, chap. 6.

68. Song and Sun, 文化大革命和它的異端思潮, chap. 8.

69. Song and Sun, 文化大革命和它的異端思潮, pp. 345–354.

70. Li, 革命造反年代, vol. 2, pp. 913–944.

71. Yu was executed in March 1970. Lu Li'an and Feng Tianan spent twelve years in prison. Other authors or compilers of heterodox literature were removed in different ways. In Shanghai, Chen Jian, still a teenager, was imprisoned twice. He and a group of his friends in a Shanghai high school compiled and printed a two-volume *Sichao ji* (思潮集, Collection of Thought Pieces), which includes almost all the heterodox writings known to them. They were later charged with "serious mistakes and crimes."

72. 中共中央、国务院、中央军委、中央文革布告 [Notice of the CCP Central Committee, the State Council, the Central Military Commission, and the Central Cultural Revolution Group], July 3, 1968, *WGYJZL*, vol. 2, pp. 138–139; *MWG*, vol. 19, pp. 259, 263.

73. *MNP*, vol. 6, pp. 175–177.

74. *RMRB*, December 22, 1968, p. 1.

75. Michel Bonnin (潘鸣啸), "上山下乡运动再评价" [A Reevaluation of the Up to the Mountain and Down to the Countryside Movement], 社会学研究 [Sociology Research], no. 5 (2005), p. 155.

76. Zhou Enlai (周恩来), "在北京市革命群众庆祝大会上的讲话" [Speech at the Revolutionary Masses Celebration in Beijing], September 7, 1968, WGYJZL, vol. 2, pp. 197–199; Song Yongyi (宋永毅), chief comp., "中国文化大革命文库" [The Chinese Cultural Revolution Database, hereafter ZGWGWK].

77. Zhou Enlai (周恩来), "在中共中央八届十二中全会开幕式上的讲话" [Speech at the Opening Session of the Twelfth Plenum of the CCP's Eighth Central Committee], October 13, 1968; see also Wang, 大动乱的年代, p. 311.

78. "中国共产党第八届扩大的第十二次中央委员会全会公报 (1968年10月31日通过)" [Communiqué of the Twelfth Plenary Session of the Enlarged Eighth Central Committee of the Communist Party of China, Passed on October 31, 1968], RMRB, November 2, 1968, p. 1; Central Case Examination Group (中央专案审查小组), "关于叛徒、内奸、工贼刘少奇罪行的审查报告" [Review Report on the Crimes of Traitor, Betrayer, and Backleg Liu Shaoqi], WGYJZL, vol. 2, pp. 224–227.

79. Yang Shengqun (杨胜群) and Yan Jianqi (闫建琪), et al., 邓小平年谱, 1904–1974 [Chronological Records of Deng Xiaoping, 1904–1974, hereafter DNP-A], vol. 3 (Beijing: 中央文献, 2009), pp. 1945–1946; MNP, vol. 6, pp. 205–206, 212.

80. See Wang, 大动乱的年代, pp. 312–313; Bu, 砸烂旧世界, pp. 741–745.

81. Geoff Eley, "Defining Social Imperialism: Use and Abuse of an Idea," Social History 1, no. 3 (1976), pp. 265–290.

82. Xu Yan (徐焰), "1969 年中苏边界的武装冲突" [Chinese-Soviet Border Clash of 1969], 党史研究资料 [Party History Research Materials], no. 5 (1994), pp. 6–9.

83. Wang Taiping (王泰平等) et al., 中华人民共和国外交史, 1957–1969 [The Diplomatic History of the People's Republic of China, 1957–1969] (Beijing: 世界知识, 1994), p. 273; Li Lianqing (李连庆), 大外交家周恩来 [The Great Diplomat Zhou Enlai], vol. 6 (Beijing: 人民, 2017), pp. 137–138.

84. Yang Kuisong (杨奎松), 中华人民共和国建国史 [A History of the Creation of the People's Republic of China], vol. 2 (Nanchang: 江西人民, 2009), p. 278; ZNP, vol. 3, p. 286.

85. MNP, vol.6, pp. 270–271, 273; ZNP, vol. 3, p. 329.

86. Li Dianren (李殿仁) and Xu Xiaoyan (徐小岩), chief eds., 徐向前年谱 [Chronological Records of Xu Xiangqian] (Beijing: 解放军, 2016), p. 250; Chen Xiaolu (陈小鲁), "陈毅和中国外交" [Chen Yi and China's Diplomacy], in Foundation for International Strategy (国际战略基金会) eds., 环球同此凉热:一代领袖们的国际战略思想 [The Globe Sharing the Same Warmth and Cold: The International Strategic Thought of the Leaders of the Mao Generation] (Beijing: 中央文献, 1993), p. 155.

87. 林彪 (Lin Biao), "在中国共产党第九次全国代表大会上的报告" [Report at the Ninth National Congress of the Communist Party of China], WGYJZL, vol. 2, pp. 311–326.

88. Wang Wenyao (王文耀) and Wang Baochun (王保春), 文革前後時期的陳伯達: 秘書的證言 [Chen Boda before and after the Cultural Revolution: The Secretary's Testimonies] (Hong Kong: 天地圖書, 2014), pp. 136–144.

89. MWG, vol. 20, pp. 15–16.

Chapter 3. A Successor Dies

1. Chen Jian, *China's Road to the Korean War: The Making of the Sino-American Confrontation* (New York: Columbia University Press, 1994), p. 153.

2. On Lin's role with regard to the publishing and dissemination of *Quotations from Chairman Mao Zedong*, see Alexander C. Cook, ed., *Mao's Little Red Book: A Global History* (Cambridge: Cambridge University Press, 2014), especially the chapter by Daniel Leese.

3. Xu Yan (徐焰), 北戴河往事追踪报告 [A Summary Report on Past Events at Beidaihe] (Beijing: 中央文献, 2010), pp. 605–618.

4. *MWG*, vol. 19, p. 362; vol. 19, pp. 407–408.

5. 中共中央党史研究室 (CCP History Research Institute), eds., "中国共产党大事记 1970年" [Records of Important Events in 1970], 人民网 [Renmin ribao on-line], http://cpc.people.com.cn/GB/64162/64164/4416088.html, accessed August 8, 2022.

6. *MWG*, vol. 13, p. 4.

7. *MNP*, vol. 6, p. 50.

8. Zhang Songjia (张颂甲), "阎仲川与一号令" [Yan Zhongchuan and Order Number One], 炎黄春秋 [China through the Ages], no. 9 (2015), p. 50; Wang Dongxing (汪东兴), 汪东兴回忆: 毛泽东与林彪反革命集团的斗争 [Wang Dongxing Recalls: Mao's Struggles against Lin Biao's Counter-Revolution Clique] (Beijing: 当代中国, 2010), pp. 14–16; Ding Kaiwen (丁凯文), 重审林彪罪案 [Reexamining Lin Biao's Criminal Case] (Hong Kong: 明镜, 2004), pp. 81–84, 120–122.

9. Wang, 汪东兴回忆, pp. 14–16.

10. Zhang Yunsheng (张云生), 毛家湾纪实: 林彪秘书回忆录 [A True Account of Maojiawan: The Memoirs of Lin Biao's Secretary] (Beijing: 春秋, 1988), p. 372.

11. "中共中央关于传达陈伯达反党问题的指示" [CCP Central Committee's Notice on Relaying Chen Boda's Anti-Party Issue], November 16, 1970, *MNP*, vol. 6, pp. 285, 291–292; *ZNP*, vol. 3, p. 361; *MWG*, vol. 19, p. 516.

12. Lin Biao (林彪), "在中国共产党九届二中全会第一次全体会上的讲话" [Speech at the First Plenary Session of the Second Plenum of the CCP's Ninth Central Committee], August 23, 1970," *ZGWGWK*.

13. Chen Boda (陈伯达), "在中国共产党九届二中全会华北组的发言" [Speech at the North China Group of the Second Plenum of the CCP's Ninth Central Committee], August 24, 1970, *ZGWGWK*.

14. *MNP*, vol. 6, pp. 327–328; *MWG*, vol. 20, pp. 15–16.

15. *WGYJZL*, vol. 2, pp. 491–493; *MWG*, vol. 20, pp. 60–61.

16. Lin Biao (林彪), "在军以上干部会议上的讲话" [Speech at a Meeting of Cadres above the Army Level], March 20, 1967, *ZGWGWK*.

17. Yang Yinlu (杨银禄), 庭院深深钓鱼台—我给江青当秘书 [The Deep Courtyard of Diaoyutai: Serving as Jiang Qing's Secretary] (Beijing: 当代中国, 2015). See also Jung Chang and Jon Halliday, *Mao: The Unknown Story* (New York: Knopf, 2005), esp. pp. 622–633.

18. "中共中央关于清查'五一六'反革命阴谋集团的通知" [The CCP Central Committee's Notice on Cleaning Up the May 16th Counterrevolutionary Clique of Conspiracies], March 27, 1970, *WGYJZL*, vol. 2, pp. 420–421.

19. Information obtained from interviews with Party historians in Hubei Province, August 2014; Wang Nianyi (王年一), 大动乱的年代 [Years of Great Turmoil] (Zhengzhou: 河南人民, 1988), pp. 69–71; Bu Weihua (卜偉華), 砸爛舊世界: 文化大革命的動亂與浩劫, 1966–1968 [Smashing the Old World: The Turmoil and Catastrophe of the Cultural Revolution, 1966–1968] (Hong Kong: 中文大學, 2008), pp. 232–233, 240–248.

20. There is no official figure ever published for these suppression campaigns. Unofficial numbers are given in Ding Shu (丁抒), "风雨如磐的日子: 一九七〇年的"一打三反"运动 [Stormy Days: The "One Attack, Three Antis" Movement in 1970], https://web.archive.org/web/20150923205013/http://www.cnd.org/HXWK/author/DING-Shu/zk0306b-0.gb.html, accessed January 1, 2023; see also the description in Wang, 大动乱的年代, pp. 241–251.

21. 中共中央批转最高人民法院, "关于善始善终地完成复查纠正冤假错案工作几个问题的请示报告" [CCP Central Committee Conveying the Supreme People's Court's "Report for Seeking Instructions on Several Questions Concerning Starting and Completing the Work of Reviewing and Correcting Unjustified, Wrong, and False Cases], December 31, 1979," *ZGWGWK*. The report says that "for the decade from 1967 to 1976, altogether about 241,000 cases have reviewed, which counts for 83% of all cases waiting for review. Among them, about 131,300 cases have been unjust, false or wrongly charged ones, 54% of all cases that have been reviewed." CCP Central Committee Document (中共中央文件) no. 96, 1979.

22. Michael Schoenhals, "Doing PRC Social History: On Research Methods, Sex, and the Decomposition of Paper," working paper, Lund University, 2004, p. 14.

23. Information on Wang is from the Laogai Research Foundation; see "Wang Tongzhu," Laogai Research Foundation, https://laogairesearch.org/prisoner_stories/wang-tongzhu/, accessed August 8, 2022. See also Cong Weixi (從維熙), "四書生四十年祭" [The 40th Memorial Ceremony for the Four Scholars], 民間歷史 [Unofficial History], 香港中文大學中國研究服務中心 (The Universities Service Centre for China Studies), mjlsh.usc.cuhk.edu.hk/Book.aspx?cid=4&tid=5973, accessed August 8, 2022; and Cong Weixi (从维熙), 我的黑白人生 [My Black and White Life] (Beijing: 生活 · 读书 · 新知三联书店, 2014), pp. 126–154.

24. Bai Yintai (白音太), "'内人党'冤案前后" [The Unjust Case of the Inner Mongolian People's Party], 民間歷史 [Unofficial History], 香港中文大學中國研究服務中心 (The Universities Service Centre for China Studies), mjlsh.usc.cuhk.edu.hk/Book.aspx?cid=4&tid=4510, accessed August 8, 2022; 哈斯格尔勒, "'内人党'冤案亲历记" [Experiencing the Unjust Case of the Inner Mongolian People's Party], 炎黄春秋 [China through the Ages], no. 1 (2009), pp. 25–31.

25. See Kerry Brown, *The Purge of the Inner Mongolian People's Party in the Chinese Cultural Revolution, 1967–69* (Kent, CT: Global Oriental, 2006); Uradyn Erden Bulag, "The Cult of Ulanhu in Inner Mongolia: History, Memory, and the Making of National Heroes," *Central Asian Survey* 17, no. 1 (1998), pp. 11–33; and Xu Guanghua and Wu Jianguo, "Social-Ecological Transformations of Inner Mongolia: A Sustainability Perspective," *Ecological Processes* 5, no. 23 (2016), https://doi.org/10.1186/s13717-016-0067-z.

26. The literature in English on China's Laogai system is surprisingly weak. For an overview, see the Laogai Research Foundation, https://laogairesearch.org/.

27. This sentiment was most clearly revealed in the response of many generals who attended the Central Committee's plenum at Lushan in August 1970—they applauded Lin's implicit attack on the Cultural Revolution stars.

28. 周恩来就刘少奇被捕叛变问题致江青的信 [Zhou Enlai's Letter to Jiang Qing about the Issue of Liu Shaoqi Being Arrested and Betraying the Party], September 25, 1968, ZGWGWK.

29. Wu Faxian (吴法宪), 歲月艱難: 吴法憲回憶錄 [Difficult Times: Wu Faxian's Memoir], vol. 2 (Hong Kong: 北星, 2006), p. 733.

30. 吴法宪第一次书面检讨 [Wu Faxian's First Written Self-Criticism], September 30, 1970, ZGWGWK; 叶群第一次书面检讨 [Ye Qun's First Written Self-Criticism], October 12, 1970, ZGWGWK; MWG, vol. 20, pp. 38–48; Wang, 汪东兴回忆, p. 51.

31. ZNP, vol. 3, pp. 395–396, 403, 452.

32. MWG, vol. 20, pp. 38–40, 43–45.

33. ZNP, vol. 3, p. 401.

34. MNP, vol. 6, p. 367; ZNP, vol. 3, pp. 429–430; Qiu Huizuo (邱會作), 邱會作回憶錄 [Qiu Huizuo's Memoir] (Hong Kong: 新世紀, 2011), p. 741.

35. As Lin told his close associates, he had established three principles for himself after Lushan: No matter how much Mao pressured him, he would "say nothing, do nothing, and take no blame." See Qiu, 邱會作回憶錄, p. 775.

36. Qiu, 邱會作回憶錄, p. 778.

37. Du Xiuxian (杜修贤), "林彪对毛泽东的'不辞而别'" [Lin Biao's Departure without Greeting Mao Zedong], in 林彪反革命集团覆灭纪实 [The Collapse of the Lin Biao Counterrevolutionary Clique] (Beijing: 中央文献, 1995), pp. 63–72; Qiu, 邱會作回憶錄, p. 778.

38. Jin Chunming (金春明), 评剑桥中华人民共和国史 [On the Cambridge History of China: The People's Republic] (Wuhan: 湖北人民, 2001), p. 632.

39. "571工程纪要" (一九七一、三月二十二—二十四) [571 Outlines, March 22–24, 1971], WGYJZL, vol. 2, pp. 650–657.

40. "571工程纪要," pp. 650–658.

41. MNP, vol. 6, pp. 389–397, 401–402; MWG, vol. 20, pp. 159–166.

42. Li Haiwen (李海文), "华国锋在'九一三'事件前后(上篇)" [Hua Guofeng before and after the September 13th Incident], 党史博览 [General Review of the Communist Party of China], no. 6 (2014), pp. 14–18.

43. MWG, vol. 20, p. 163.

44. Editorial Group of "History's Judgment" ("历史的审判"编写组), ed., 历史的审判—审判林彪、江青反革命集团纪实 (上) [History's Judgment: The Trial of Lin Biao and Jiang Qing Counter-Revolutionary Clique] (Beijing: 群众, 1981), vol. 1, pp. 38–39; Wang, 汪东兴回忆, pp. 188–190.

45. Wu Zhong (吴忠), "吴忠谈'九一三'事件" [Wu Zhong on the September 13th Incident], 炎黄春秋 [China through the Ages], no. 1 (2012), p. 26.

46. MNP, vol. 6, p. 403; Zhang Yaoci (张耀祠), 回忆毛泽东 [Remembering Mao Zedong] (Beijing: 中共中央党校, 1996), p. 105.

47. MNP, vol. 6, p. 403–404; Wang, 汪东兴回忆, p. 197.

48. Yang Jisheng (楊繼繩), 天地翻覆: 中國文化大革命史 [The World Turned Upside Down: A History of the Chinese Cultural Revolution] (Hong Kong: 天地圖書, 2016), pp. 803–810.

49. *ZNP*, vol. 3, p. 480.

50. Wu, *歲月艱難*, p. 862; Editorial Group of "History's Judgment," *歷史的審判*, p. 40.

51. Wang, *汪东兴回忆*, pp. 205–206.

52. Li Wenpu (李文普), "林彪卫士长李文普不得不说" [Things that Lin Biao's Guard Li Wenpu Has to Say], *中华儿女* [China's Sons and Daughters], no. 2, 1999.

53. *MNP*, vol. 6, p. 405; Wu, *歲月艱難*, pp. 863–864.

54. *ZNP*, vol. 3, p. 483; Ji Dong (纪东), *难忘的八年—周恩来秘书回忆录* [Unforgettable Eight Years: Memoirs of Zhou Enlai's Secretary] (Beijing: 中央文献, 2007), pp. 125, 129.

55. *MNP*, vol. 6, pp. 406–410.

56. Li Zhisui, *The Private Life of Chairman Mao: The Memoirs of Mao's Personal Physician* (New York: Random House, 1994), p. 542.

57. 中共中央关于林彪叛国出逃的通知 (1971年9月18日) [CCP Central Committee's Notice about Lin Biao's Betrayal of the Country and Fleeing Abroad], *WGYJZL*, vol. 2, pp. 557–559.

58. CCP Central Committee's Notice on Conveying and Discussing "The Struggles for Smashing the Lin Biao and Chen Boda Anti-Party Clique" (Materials Group No. 7 [中共中央关于组织传达和讨论 "粉碎林陈反党集团反革命政变的斗争"(材料之一) 的通知], *WGYJZL*, vol. 2, pp. 658–668.

59. Yin Hongbiao (印紅標), *失蹤者的足跡:文化大革命期間的青年思潮* [The Footprints of the Missing: The Trends of Youth Thought during the Cultural Revolution] (Hong Kong: 香港中文大學, 2009), p. 376.

60. Zhou Enlai (周恩来), "给广州军区领导机关干部的报告" [Report to the Leading Cadres of the Guangzhou Military Region], October 1971, in Xue Qingchao (薛庆超), *毛泽东南方决策* [Mao Zedong's Decision Making in the South] (Beijing: 华文, 2013), p. 245; see also *ZNP*, vol. 3, pp. 488–489.

61. *MZ*, vol. 2, p. 1607.

62. *MNP*, vol. 6, pp. 408–409; *ZNP*, vol. 3, p. 486; Liu Jixian (刘继贤) et al., *叶剑英年谱, 1897–1986* [Chronological Records of Ye Jianying, 1897–1986], vol. 2 (Beijing: 中央文献, 2007), p. 1003.

63. Liu et al., *叶剑英年谱*, vol. 2, p. 1090.

64. Li, *Private Life of Chairman Mao*, pp. 547–548; *ZNP*, vol. 3, p. 510.

65. *MNP*, vol. 6, pp. 423–424.

66. Li, *Private Life of Chairman Mao*, pp. 559–560; Zhang Zuoliang (张佐良), *周恩来最后的十年* [The Last Ten Years of Zhou Enlai] (Shanghai: 上海人民, 1997), pp. 245–247.

67. The most profitable production surplus would usually be consumer goods; for consumer demand, see Karl Gerth, *Unending Capitalism: How Consumerism Negated China's Communist Revolution* (Cambridge: Cambridge University Press, 2020).

68. Yang Xiaokai (杨小凯), *百年中国经济史笔记* [Notes on the History of Chinese Economy in the Past One Hundred Years] (Beijing: 东方, 2016), p. 10.

69. Huaiyin Li, "Worker Performance in State-Owned Factories in Maoist China: A Reinterpretation," *Modern China* 42, no. 4 (2016), p. 382.

70. *MNP*, vol. 6, p. 247.

71. Li, "Worker Performance in State-Owned Factories in Maoist China," p. 387.

72. Chen Jianfeng (陈建锋), "1984年前上海青浦社队企业的发展历程及历史作用" [The Development and Historical Significance of Commune Enterprises in Qingpu District of Shanghai before 1984], 上海党史和党建 [Shanghai Party History and Party Construction], no. 4 (2016), pp. 17–19.

73. Shi Cheng, *China's Rural Industrialization Policy Growing under Orders since 1949* (Basingstoke, UK: Palgrave Macmillan, 2006), p. 140.

74. Cheng, *China's Rural Industrialization Policy*, p. 147.

75. Cheng, *China's Rural Industrialization Policy*, p. 143.

76. Chen Run (陈润), 时代的见证者 [Those Who Witnessed Their Times] (Hangzhou: 浙江大学, 2019), chap. 1.

77. Chen Run (陈润), 生活可以更美的—何享健的美的人生 [Life Could Be Better: He Xiangjian's Beautiful Life] (Beijing: 华文, 2010), pp. 21–38.

78. See "Fortune Global 500 List of 2019," https://fortune.com/global500/2019/, accessed June 1, 2022.

79. The head of Dazhai's production brigade, Chen Yonggui, was promoted as a political leader during the Cultural Revolution. He even survived being linked to Chen Boda during the Lushan plenum, claiming (correctly) that being semi-literate had prevented him from reading pro-Chen statements issued in his name. In 1975 he was made a vice premier.

80. Covell F. Meyskens, *Mao's Third Front: The Militarization of Cold War China* (Cambridge: Cambridge University Press, 2020), p. 202.

81. For a general discussion, see Cong Jin (丛进), 曲折发展的岁月 [Years of Tortuous Development] (Zhengzhou: 河南人民, 1989), pp. 467–468; Chen Donglin (陈东林), 三线建设: 备战时期的西部开发 [The Development of the West during the Period of the Third Front Construction] (Beijing: 中共中央党校, 2003); and Ma Quanshan (马泉山), "再谈三线建设的评价问题" [Reexamining the Evaluation of the Third Front Construction], 当代中国史研究 [Contemporary Chinese History Studies], no. 6 (2011), pp. 63–70.

82. The Third Front construction program was a huge and comprehensive effort. The military and civilian personnel involved in railway building under the program reached 5.5 million at its peak. See the Infrastructure Construction Bureau under the Railway Ministry (铁道部基建总局), ed., 铁路修建史料, 1963–1980 [Materials on Railway Construction, 1963–1980], vol. 3, no. 1 (Beijing: 中国铁道, 1991), pp. 22–34, 42, 45, 60–77, 81–97, 101–105, 165–180; and Leading Group for Handling the Aftermath Work of Railway Corps (铁道兵善后工作领导小组), ed., 中国人民解放军铁道兵简史 [A Brief History of the Railway Corps of the Chinese People's Liberation Army] (for internal circulation only, 1986), pp. 138–171, 197–198.

83. Meyskens, *Mao's Third Front*, p. 195.

84. For an overview of Panzhihua, see Liu Lyuhong (刘吕红), 三十年社会变迁与资源型城市发展研究: 以四川攀枝花城市发展为释例 [Thirty Years of Social Change and Development of Resource-Based Cities: A Case Study of the Urban Development of Panzhihua, Sichuan] (Chengdu: 四川大学, 2011).

85. Liu Xiaomeng (刘小萌), 中国知青史—大潮 (1966–1980) [A History of China's Educated Youth: Great Waves (1966–1980)] (Beijing: 中国社会科学, 1998), p. 848; see

also Michel Bonnin, *The Lost Generation: The Rustication of China's Educated Youth (1968–1980)* (Hong Kong: Chinese University Press, 2013).

86. For good overviews, see Zhou Dong, "Understanding the Long Term Impacts of the Critical Historic Event: The Cultural Revolution in China" (PhD diss., University of California, Riverside, 2014); Lin Qianhan, "'Rustication': Punishment or Reward? Study of the Life Trajectories of the Generation of the Cultural Revolution" (PhD diss., University of Oxford, 2012).

87. Jin Dalu (金大陆) and Jin Guangyao (金光耀), "从地方志资料看知识青年上山下乡" [Studying the Down to the Countryside Movement from Local Gazetteers], 当代中国史研究 (Contemporary Chinese History Studies), no. 3 (2015), p. 119.

Chapter 4. Americans

1. For a more detailed discussion, see Chen Jian, "In the Wake of Czechoslovakia, 1968: Reflections on Beijing's Split with Moscow and Rapprochement with Washington," in Chen Jian et al., eds., *The Routledge Handbook of the Global Sixties: Between Protest and Nation-Building* (New York: Routledge, 2018), pp. 289–302.

2. This view was also quite in line with older Chinese strategies of "using a barbarian to check a barbarian [以夷制夷]."

3. Richard Nixon, "Asia after Vietnam," *Foreign Affairs*, 46, no. 1 (October 1967), pp. 442–459.

4. "Memorandum from President Nixon to his Assistant for National Security Affairs (Kissinger) (February 1, 1969)," in *Foreign Relations of the United States* (hereafter *FRUS*), *1969–1972*, vol. XVII (Washington, D.C.: U.S. Government Printing Office, 2006), p. 7.

5. Xiong Xianghui (熊向晖), "打开中美关系的前奏—1969年四位老帅对国际形势研究和建议的前前后后" [Prelude to Opening of U.S.-China Relations: Four Marshals' Study on and Suggestions about the International Situation in 1969], 中共党史资料 [CCP History Materials], no. 42 (1992), pp. 78–79.

6. "Information about A. N. Kosygin's Conversation with Zhou Enlai on 11 September 1969," September 11, 1969, History and Public Policy Program Digital Archive, SAMPO-BArch J IV 2/202/359, translated by Mark H. Doctoroff, National Security Archive, https://digitalarchive.wilsoncenter.org/document/116973, accessed August 24, 2022; "周恩来致柯西金的信" [Zhou Enlai's Letter to A. N. Kosygin], September 18, 1969, in PRC Foreign Ministry (中华人民共和国外交部) and CCP Central Institute of Documentary Studies (中共中央文献研究室), eds., 周恩来外交文选 [Selected Diplomatic Papers of Zhou Enlai] (Beijing: 中央文献, 1990), pp. 462–464; "中共中央转发外交部关于柯西金来京会见周总理的通报" [A Circular from the Foreign Ministry on Kosygin's Meeting with Premier Zhou in Beijing Forwarded by CCP Central Committee], September 22, 1969, 91-011-0009, pp. 25–29, Gansu Provincial Archive.

7. "Further Thoughts by Marshal Chen Yi on Sino-American Relations," *Cold War International History Project Bulletin*, no. 11 (Winter 1998), pp. 170–171.

8. "Editorial Note," in *FRUS*, *1969–1972*, pp. 51–52; *ZNP*, vol. 3, p. 334; Jin Chongji (金冲及) et al., 周恩来传, 1898–1976 [Biography of Zhou Enlai, 1898–1976] [hereafter *ZZ*], vol. 2 (Beijing: 中央文献, 2008), p. 1844.

9. Luo Yishuo (骆以粟), "在波兰的岁月" [My Years in Poland], in Wang Taiping (王泰平) et al., 当代中国使节外交生涯 [Diplomatic Career of Contemporary Chinese Envoys], vol. 4 (Beijing: 世界知识, 1996), pp. 179–180; Stoessel to Secretary of State, 3 December 1969, Record Group 59, Department of State Records, Subject-Numeric Files, 1967–69, POL 23-8 US, National Archives.

10. *ZZ*, vol. 2, p. 1843.

11. *ZNP*, vol. 3, pp. 336–337; *ZZ*, vol. 2, p. 1843. Kissinger immediately noted Beijing's gesture and thought that this must have been Zhou's work; see Henry Kissinger, *White House Years* (New York: Little, Brown, 1978), p. 188.

12. *ZNP*, vol. 3, p. 348; *MNP*, vol. 6, p. 281.

13. *ZNP*, vol. 3, p. 356.

14. See Chen Jian, *Mao's China and the Cold War* (Chapel Hill: University of North Carolina Press, 2001), chaps. 4 and 8.

15. "Meeting between Zhou Enlai and Pham Van Dong," Beijing, April 13, 1968, rpt. in Odd Arne Westad et al., eds., *77 Conversations between Chinese and Foreign Leaders on the Wars in Indochina, 1964–77* (Washington, D.C.: Woodrow Wilson International Center for Scholars, 1998), p. 123.

16. "Meeting between Mao Zedong and Pham Van Dong," Beijing, November 17, 1968, rpt. in Westad et al., *77 Conversations*, p. 143.

17. Philip Short, *Pol Pot: The History of a Nightmare* (London: John Murray, 2004), pp. 188, 197–200.

18. *ZNP*, vol. 3, p. 357; *MWG*, vol. 18, p. 504.

19. "Memorandum from the President's Assistant for National Security Affairs (Kissinger) to President Nixon (May 19, 1970)," in *FRUS, 1969–1972*, p. 210.

20. Mao Zedong (毛泽东), "全世界人民团结起来, 打败美国侵略者及其一切走狗!" [Unite and Defeat the United States Aggressors and All Their Running Dogs!], *RMRB*, May 20, 1970, p. 1; "Text of Mao's Statement Urging World Revolution against U.S.," *New York Times*, May 21, 1970, p. 6.

21. In the meantime, Zhou Enlai tried to make sure that the door to diplomatic contacts was not entirely closed. On July 10, 1970, as a gesture to Washington, he ordered the release of Bishop James Walsh, an American who had been detained since October 1958 on spy charges. See "我专政机关处理外国犯人" [Our Dictatorship Handles Foreign Prisoners], *RMRB*, July 11, 1970, p. 2.

22. *ZNP*, vol. 3, pp. 410–411; *ZZ*, vol. 2, p. 1846; Richard M. Nixon, *Memoirs of Richard Nixon* (New York: Grosset & Dunlap, 1978), pp. 546–547.

23. *MWG*, vol. 20, pp. 63–70.

24. Nixon, *Memoirs of Richard Nixon*, p. 547.

25. Robert B. Semple Jr., "Nixon Eases China Trade Embargo to Allow Nonstrategic Exports," *New York Times*, April 15, 1971, p. 1.

26. *ZNP*, vol. 3, p. 449; Ling Qing (凌青), 从延安到联合国 [From Yanan to the United Nations] (Fuzhou: 福建人民, 2008), pp. 128–129.

27. Lin Ke (林克), Wu Xujun (吴旭君), and Xu Tao (徐涛), 历史的真实 [The Truth of History: Testimonies of Mao's Associates] (Beijing: 中央文献, 1998), pp. 244–248.

28. John Roderick, "Chou Says 'New Page' Has Opened," *New York Times*, April 15, 1971, p. 1; "周恩来同美国乒乓球代表团的谈话" [Zhou Enlai's Conversation with the U.S. Table Tennis Team], April 14, 1971, in PRC Foreign Ministry and CCP Central

Institute of Documentary Studies, 周恩来外交文选, pp. 469–475. In the past, the CCP had been careful to distinguish between "oppressed" people, especially people of color, in the United States and the U.S. government; see Ruodi Duan, "Solidarity in Three Acts: Narrating US Black Freedom Movements in China, 1961–66," *Modern Asian Studies* 53, no. 5 (September 2019), pp. 1351–1380; and, for American perceptions, Robeson Taj Frazier, *The East Is Black: Cold War China in the Black Radical Imagination* (Durham, NC: Duke University Press, 2014).

29. "Message from the Premier of the People's Republic of China Chou En-lai to President Nixon (April 21, 1971)," in *FRUS, 1969–1972,* p. 301; "周恩来总理给尼克松总统的口信" [Premier Zhou Enlai's Message to President Nixon], May 29, 1971, in Chinese Central Archive (中央档案馆), ed., 共和国五十年珍贵档案 [Valuable Archives of People's Republic of China], vol. 2 (Beijing: 中国档案, 1999), pp. 1030–1032.

30. "Record of Nixon-Kissinger Telephone Conversation Discussing Possible Envoys to China, April 27, 1971," https://nsarchive2.gwu.edu/NSAEBB/NSAEBB66, accessed August 23, 2022.

31. Kissinger, *White House Years,* p. 738; Tang Longbin (唐龙彬), "一次神秘的外交使命: 接待基辛格秘密访华" [A Mysterious Diplomatic Mission: Receiving Kissinger during His Secret China Visit], 世界知识 [World Knowledge], no. 6 (1995), pp. 30–31.

32. "Memorandum from the President's Assistant for National Security Affairs (Kissinger) to President Nixon (July 14, 1971)," in *FRUS, 1969–1972,* pp. 454–455.

33. Haig to Eliot, 28 January 1972, enclosing Kissinger to the President, "My Talks with Chou Enlai [Zhou Enlai]," 17 July 1971, Record Group 59, Top Secret Subject-Numeric Files, 1970–1972, POL 7 Kissinger, National Archives; Wei Shiyan (魏史言), "基辛格秘密访华内幕" [The Inside Story of Kissinger's Secret Visit to China], in Editorial Office of Diplomatic History under the Foreign Ministry (外交部外交史编辑室), ed., 新中国外交风云 [Diplomatic Experience of the People's Republic of China], vol. 2 (Beijing: 世界知识, 1990), pp. 40–41.

34. "Memorandum of Conversation, July 9, 1971, 4:35–11:20 P.M.," in *FRUS, 1969–1972,* pp. 375–376.

35. Wei, "基辛格秘密访华内幕," pp. 41–42.

36. *ZNP,* vol. 3, pp. 469–470; Guo Ming (郭明), ed., 中越关系演变四十年 [Forty Years of Evolution of Sino-Vietnamese Relations] (Nanning: 广西人民, 1992), pp. 102–103.

37. Pei Jianzhang (裴坚章) and Feng Yaoyuan (封耀元), eds., 周恩来外交活动大事记, 1949–1975 [Important Events in Zhou Enlai's Diplomatic Activities, 1979–1975] (Beijing: 世界知识, 1993), p. 597; *ZNP,* vol. 3, p. 469; see also excerpt of Zhou's conversations with Kim Il-sung, August 10, 1971, HPA.

38. "The DPRK Attitude toward the So-Called 'Cultural Revolution' in China," March 7, 1967, History and Public Policy Program Digital Archive, original in AVPRF f. 0102, op. 23, p. 112, d. 24, pp. 13–23, obtained by Sergey Radchenko and translated by Gary Goldberg, https://digitalarchive.wilsoncenter.org/document/114570, accessed August 23, 2022.

39. Zhou Bin (周斌), 我為中國領導人當翻譯: 見證中日外交秘辛 [I Interpreted for Chinese Leaders: Witnessing Secret Chinese-Japanese Diplomatic Exchanges] (Hong Kong: 大山文化, 2013), pp. 236–238.

40. "Excerpt of Mao Zedong's Conversation with Japanese Prime Minister Kakuei Tanaka," September 27, 1972, History and Public Policy Program Digital Archive, Chinese Communist Party Central Archives, translated by Caixia Lu, https://digitalarchive.wilsoncenter.org/document/118567.

41. Li Zhisui, *The Private Life of Chairman Mao: The Memoirs of Mao's Personal Physician* (New York: Random House, 1994), p. 563.

42. *MNP*, vol. 6, pp. 427–428; "Memorandum of Conversation, February 21, 1972, 2:50–3:55 P.M.," in *FRUS, 1969–1972*, pp. 677–684.

43. *FRUS, 1969–1972* vol. XVII, pp. 681–682; *MNP*, vol. 6, pp. 427–428.

44. "Joint Communique between the United States and China," February 27, 1972, History and Public Policy Program Digital Archive, Nixon Presidential Library and Museum, Staff Member Office Files (SMOF), President's Personal Files (PPF), Box 73, https://digitalarchive.wilsoncenter.org/document/121325; 中美联合公报 [Joint Communique between the China States and the United States]," *RMRB*, February 28, 1972, p. 1.

45. "Memorandum of Conversation, February 28, 1972, 8:30–9:30 A.M.," in *FRUS, 1969–1972*, pp. 816–824, quotation on 821–823.

46. "中央文献研究室周恩来组访问纪登奎记录" [Zhou Enlai Biography Group of the Central Documents Research Office] (1988) [Record of Interview with Ji Dengkui], cited in Shi Yun (史雲) and Li Danhui (李丹慧), 難以繼續的 "繼續革命" [The Continuous Revolution That Cannot Be Continued] (Hong Kong: 中文大學, 2008), p. 10.

47. Jason Kelly, *Market Maoists: The Communist Origins of China's Capitalist Ascent* (Cambridge, MA: Harvard University Press, 2021), chap. 7.

48. State Planning Revolutionary Committee (国家计划革命委员会), "关于进口成套化纤、化肥技术设备的报告" [Report on Importing Technology and Whole-Set Equipment of Chemical Fiber and Fertilizer], January 16, 1972, 中共党史资料 [CCP History Materials], no. 2 (2004), pp. 4–8; 李先念、华国锋、余秋里致周恩来函 [Letter to Zhou Enlai by Li Xiannian, Hua Guofeng, and Yu Qiuli], January 23, 1972, 中共党史资料 [CCP History Materials], no. 2 (2004), p. 8.

49. State Planning Revolutionary Committee (国家计划革命委员会), "关于进口一米七连续式轧板机问题的报告" [Report on Importing 1.7 Meter Tandem Cold Mills], August 6, 1972, 中共党史资料 [CCP History Materials], no. 2 (2004), pp. 9–10.

50. State Planning Revolutionary Committee (国家计划革命委员会), "关于增加设备进口、扩大经济交流的请示报告" [Report on Increasing Equipment Imports and Expand Economic Exchanges], January 2, 1973, 中共党史资料 [CCP History Materials], no. 2 (2004), pp. 12–19; *ZNP*, vol. 3, pp. 570–571; Chen Jinhua (陈锦华), 国事忆述 [Recollection of My Experience with State Affairs] (Beijing: 中共党史, 2005), pp. 14–15.

51. *ZNP*, vol. 3, pp. 570–571.

52. Zhou Enlai was personally involved in exposing the quality problems of Chinese exports and tried to call utmost attention to this "matter of critical importance." Zhou Enlai (周恩来), "要把质量问题放在议事日程来解决" [To Address Quality Issues on Our Work Agenda], in CCP Central Institute of Historical Documents

Studies (中共中央文献研究室), eds., 周恩来经济文选 [Selected Economic Works of Zhou Enlai] (Beijing: 中央文献, 1993), p. 633.

53. Fujio Mizuoka, "British Colonialism and 'Illegal' Immigration from Mainland China to Hong Kong," in Akio Onjo, ed., *Power Relations, Situated Practices, and the Politics of the Commons: Japanese Contributions to the History of Geographical Thought* (Fukuoka: Kyushu University, 2017), chap. 5. See also Peter E. Hamilton, "Rethinking the Origins of China's Reform Era: Hong Kong and the 1970s Revival of Sino-US Trade," *Twentieth-Century China* 43, no. 1 (January 2018), pp. 67–88.

54. In Hong Kong, Tolo Harbour (Dabuhai 大埔海, or大步海).

55. Stanislaus Lai Ding-kee (黎定基), "A Historical Review of Smuggling in Hong Kong" (doctoral thesis, University of Hong Kong, 1995). For background, see also Philip Thai, *China's War on Smuggling: Law, Economic Life, and the Making of the Modern State, 1842–1965* (New York: Columbia University Press, 2018).

56. "Rediscovering Lost History: Reunification Endeavors in 1975," *Guangming Daily*, October 11, 2002, trans. Shao Da, http://www.china.org.cn/english/2002/Oct/45515.htm.

57. Chih-Jou Jay Chen, "Local Institutions and Transformation of Property Rights in Southern Fujian," in Jean Chun Oi and Andrew Walder, eds., *Property Rights and Economic Reform in China* (Stanford, CA: Stanford University Press, 1999), pp. 55–56. See also Chih-Jou Jay Chen, *Transforming Rural China: How Local Institutions Shape Property Rights in China* (London: Routledge, 2012).

58. Guo Biliang (郭碧良), 石狮:中国民办特区 [Shishi: Private Special Zones of China] (Fuzhou: 福建人民, 1993), chap. 1.

59. Chen, *Transforming Rural China*, chap. 5. Very secretly, there were even attempts at establishing more official contacts with Taiwan. In Mao's conversation with Nixon in February 1972, he called Chiang an "old friend," saying that "our relationship with him is much longer than your relationship." In May 1973, following Mao's instructions, Zhou arranged for Zhang Shizhao (章士钊), who knew several Guomindang leaders well, to visit Hong Kong for "exploring channels of cross-strait talks," but Zhang, who was in his nineties, died before he could complete his mission. In early 1975 Chen Lifu, a senior Guomindang figure, was in touch with CCP leaders to suggest a Chiang meeting with Mao or Zhou. There is evidence that these contacts continued up to when Chiang Kai-shek died in April 1975. Information gained from an interview with two leading CCP historians, October 2017, and discussions with other Party historians.

60. Compiling Committee (编辑委员会), 中国对外经济贸易年鉴 (1984) [China Foreign Economic and Trade Yearbook (1984)] (Beijing: 中国对外经济贸易, 1984), IV-82.

61. 中华人民共和国文化和旅游部 (Ministry of Culture and Tourism of the People's Republic of China), Statistics Section, https://zwgk.mct.gov.cn/zfxxgkml/, accessed January 9, 2023.

62. The literature on the role of foreign contacts and advisers in China in the late 1970s and 1980s is expanding rapidly; see Julian B. Gewirtz, *Unlikely Partners: Chinese Reformers, Western Economists, and the Making of Global China* (Cambridge, MA:

Harvard University Press, 2017); and Pete Millwood, *Improbable Diplomats: How Ping-Pong Players, Musicians, and Scientists Remade US-China Relations* (Cambridge: Cambridge University Press, 2022).

63. The best overviews of early Sino-American trade are Elizabeth O'Brien Ingleson, "The End of Isolation: Rapprochement, Globalisation, and Sino-American Trade, 1972–1978" (PhD thesis, University of Sydney, 2017); and Christian Talley, *Forgotten Vanguard: Informal Diplomacy and the Rise of United States–China Trade, 1972–1980* (Notre Dame, IN: University of Notre Dame Press, 2018).

64. For a good discussion, see Ezra Vogel, *China and Japan: Facing History* (Cambridge, MA: Harvard University Press, 2019), chaps. 9 and 10.

65. Tomoo Marukawa, "Bilateral Trade and Trade Frictions between China and Japan, 1972–2012," *Eurasian Geography and Economics*, no. 4 (2012), pp. 442–456.

66. Shen Jueren (沈觉人) et al., 当代中国对外贸易 [Trade in Contemporary China], vol. 1 (Beijing: 当代中国, 1992), pp. 432–437; Wang Taiping (王泰平), et al. 中华人民共和国外交史, 1970–1978 [The Diplomatic History of the People's Republic of China, 1970–1978] (Beijing: 世界知识, 1999), pp. 305–307.

67. Johnny Erling, "Wie Mao einst Franz Josef Strauß entführte" [How Mao once Seduced Franz Josef Strauss], *Die Welt*, July 1, 2015; *MNP*, vol. 6, pp. 568–569.

68. "Conversation between Federal Chancellor Schmidt and the Chairman of the Central Committee and the Politburo of the Chinese Communist Party, Mao Zedong, in Beijing," October 30, 1975, in History and Public Policy Program Digital Archive, Institut für Zeitgeschichte, ed., *Akten zur auswärtigen Politik der Bundesrepublik Deutschland: 1975. 1. Juli bis 31. Dezember 1975*, trans. Bernd Schaefer (München: Oldenbourg, 2006), 1495–1500, https://digitalarchive.wilsoncenter.org /document/119985; *MNP*, vol. 6, p. 618.

Chapter 5. The Fall and Rise and Fall of Deng Xiaoping

1. Deng Rong, *Deng Xiaoping and the Cultural Revolution: A Daughter Recalls the Critical Years* (Beijing: Foreign Language Press, 2002), pp. 45–46.

2. See Zhong Yanlin (鐘延麟), 文革前的鄧小平 [Deng Xiaoping before the Cultural Revolution] (Hong Kong: 中文大學, 2013), chap. 7.

3. Deng, *Deng Xiaoping and the Cultural Revolution*, p. 44.

4. *DNP-A*, vol. 3, p. 1946.

5. Deng, *Deng Xiaoping and the Cultural Revolution*, p. 187; *DNP-A*, vol. 3, p. 1956.

6. *DNP-A*. vol. 3, p. 1957.

7. Zhou Enlai's letter to Mao, June 7, 1972, quoted in Shi Yun (史雲) and Li Danhui (李丹慧), 難以繼續的"繼續革命" [The Continuous Revolution That Cannot Be Continued] (Hong Kong: 中文大學, 2008), pp. 35–36.

8. *DNP-A*, vol. 3, p. 1958.

9. Deng Xiaoping (邓小平), 给毛泽东的信 [Letter to Mao Zedong], August 3, 1972, *ZGWGWK*.

10. Deng, 给毛泽东的信.

11. *MWG*, vol. 20, p. 255.

12. For Zhou's perspectives, see 周恩来同回国述职大使和外事单位负责同志谈话纪要 [Zhou Enlai's Conversation with Chinese Ambassadors and Foreign Affairs Officials], August 1 and 2, 1972, 1057-8-44, HPA; *ZNP*, vol. 3, pp. 541–542; for Jiang Qing's and Zhang Chunqiao's viewpoints, see *MZ*, vol. 2, p. 1646.

13. *ZNP*, vol. 3, pp. 567–568.

14. *DNP*-A, vol. 3, p. 1969.

15. *MNP*,vol. 6, p. 458; *ZNP*, vol. 3, p. 567.

16. *MNP*, vol. 6, p. 500.

17. *DNP*-A, p. 1972; see also *MWG*, vol. 20, pp. 301–302; and *ZNP*, vol. 3, p. 583.

18. Li Haiwen (李海文), "华国锋奉周恩来之命调查李震事件" [Hua Guofeng Followed Zhou Enlai's Order to Investigate Li Zhen's Death], 党史博览 [General Review of the Communist Party of China], no. 10 (2013), pp. 4–10.

19. *ZNP*, vol. 3, pp. 603–605.

20. Memorandum, Zhou Enlai with Kissinger, November 13, 1973, 10:00 P.M.–12:30 A.M.; and Memorandum, Zhou Enlai with Kissinger, November 14, 1973, 7:35–8:25 A.M., National Security Archive.

21. This is the sequence of events subscribed to by most CCP historians. There is a divergent view, however. Zhang Hanzhi (章含之), the wife of vice foreign minister Qiao Guanhua, a close associate of Zhou, recalls that in her husband's view the premier had actually reported to Mao and received the chairman's approval that evening. 章含之同志谈话 [Interview with Comrade Zhang Hanzhi], April 3, 1998 (copy in authors' possession), p. 4.

22. 章含之同志谈话, April 3, 1998, p. 6; *MNP*, vol. 6, p. 507; Liu Jixian (刘继贤), ed., 叶剑英年谱, *1897–1986* [A Chronological Record of Ye Jianying] (Beijing: 中央文献, 2007), p. 1066.

23. 章含之同志谈话, p. 4.

24. 章含之同志谈话, p. 5.

25. 章含之同志谈话, p. 6; Gao Wenqian (高文谦), 晚年周恩来 [Zhou Enlai in His Late Years] (New York: Mirror, 2003), p. 323. For an account of Deng's presentation by Deng's daughter, see Deng, *Deng Xiaoping and the Cultural Revolution*, pp. 255–256.

26. *ZNP*, vol. 3, pp. 634–635.

27. *ZNP*, vol. 3, p. 636; *MZ*, p. 1672; Wang Nianyi (王年一), 大动乱的年代 [Years of Great Turmoil] (Zhengzhou: 河南人民, 1988), p. 471.

28. Wang Hongwen (王洪文), "在中央读书班上的讲话" [Report to a CCP Central Committee Study Group], January 14, 1974, in John Sisyphus (约翰. 西西弗斯), ed., 群眾暴政與政治投機: 王洪文與"文革" [Mass Tyranny and Political Speculation: Wang Hongwen and the Cultural Revolution], vol. 1 (Taipei: 西西弗斯文化, 2016), p. 95.

29. For overviews, see Li Xun (李遜), 革命造反年代:上海文革運動史稿 [An Age of Revolutionary Rebellion: A Draft History of the Cultural Revolution in Shanghai] (Hong Kong: Oxford University Press, 2015); Elizabeth J. Perry and Li Xun, *Proletarian Power: Shanghai in the Cultural Revolution* (Boulder, CO: Westview Press, 1997); Wang Shaoguang, *Failure of Charisma: The Cultural Revolution in Wuhan* (Oxford: Oxford University Press, 1995); Keith Forster, "The Politics of Destabili-

zation and Confrontation: The Campaign against Lin Biao and Confucius in Zhe-jiang Province, 1974," *China Quarterly*, no. 107 (1986), pp. 433–462; Sebastian Heilmann, "The Social Context of Mobilization in China: Factions, Work Units, and Activists during the 1976 April Fifth Movement," *China Information* 8 (1993), pp. 1–19; and Sebastian Heilmann, *Turning Away from the Cultural Revolution: Political Grass-Roots Activism in the Mid-Seventies*, Occasional Paper 28 (Stock-holm: Center for Pacific Asia Studies, Stockholm University, 1996).

30. Quoted from Perry, *Proletarian Power*, p.177.
31. As a boy, Xu had studied kung-fu as an apprentice monk at the Shaolin Temple for eight years; see Patrick Fuliang Shan, "Becoming Loyal: General Xu Shiyou and Mao-ist Regimentation," *American Journal of Chinese Studies* 18, no. 2 (2011), pp. 133–150.
32. Dong Guoqiang and Andrew G. Walder, "Nanjing's 'Second Cultural Revolution' of 1974," *China Quarterly*, no. 212 (December 2012), p. 903.
33. Hu Angang, *Mao and the Cultural Revolution*, vol. 3 (Singapore: Enrich Profes-sional Publishing, 2017), p. 27.
34. See Dong and Walder, "Nanjing's 'Second Cultural Revolution,'" pp. 903–911.
35. *MWG*, vol. 20, p. 364.
36. *ZNP*, vol. 3, pp. 645–646; Wu Qingtong (吴庆彤), 周恩来在文化大革命中 [Zhou En-lai in the Cultural Revolution] (Beijing: 中共党史, 2002), pp. 254–256.
37. *MZ*, vol. 2, p. 1686.
38. Wu De (吴德), 十年风雨纪事: 我在北京工作的一些经历 [Ten Years of Storms: My Working Experience in Beijing] (Beijing: 当代中国, 2004), pp. 153–154.
39. Mao Zedong (毛泽东), "Mao's Conversation with Zambian President Kenneth Kaunda," February 22, 1974, in *Mao Zedong on Diplomacy* (Beijing: Foreign Lan-guages Press, 1994), p. 454.
40. "中华人民共和国代表团团长邓小平在联大特别会议上的发言" [Speech by Deng Xiao-ping, head of the Delegation of the OK 's Republic of China at the Special Session of the UN Assembly], *RMRB*, April 11, 1974.
41. "中华人民共和国代表团团长邓小平在联大特别会议上的发言."
42. *MNP*, vol. 6, p. 540.
43. *DNP-A*, vol. 3, p. 2056; Yang Shengqun (杨胜群) and Yan Jianqi (闫建琪), et al., 邓小平传, 1904–1974 [A Biography of Deng Xiaoping, 1904–1974], vol. 2 (Beijing: 中央文献, 2009), pp. 1435–1437.
44. *DNP-A*, vol. 3, p. 2058.
45. Cheng Zhongyuan (程中原) and Xia Xingzhen (夏杏珍), 历史转折的前奏: 邓小平在 1975 [Prelude to a Historical Turn: Deng Xiaoping in 1975] (Beijing: 中国青年, 2003), p. 28.
46. *MZ*, vol. 2, p. 1704; *MNP*, vol. 6, p. 552.
47. *MNP*, vol. 6, p. 554.
48. Li, 革命造反年代, vol. 2, p. 1360.
49. *MWG*, vol. 20, pp. 379–380.
50. Zhang Zuoliang (張佐良), 周恩來保健醫生回憶錄 [Memoir of Zhou Enlai's Primary Doctor] (Hong Kong: 三聯, 1998), pp. 151–155; *ZNP*, vol. 3, pp. 686–688; *MZ*, vol. 2, pp. 1713–1714.

51. Zhou Enlai (周恩来), "1975 年国务院政府工作报告" [Report on Government Work], *RMRB,* January 21, 1975, p. 1.

52. Zhang Hua (张化), "邓小平与1975年铁路整顿" [Deng Xiaoping and 1975 Railway Rectification], *百年潮* [One Hundred Year Tide], no. 8 (2014), pp. 33–34; Cheng Zhongyuan (程中原), "邓小平与1975年铁路整顿", *党的文献* [Party Documents], no. 5 (1996), pp. 74–75.

53. *MZ,* vol. 2, p. 1720.

54. Zhang Liqun (张黎群) et al., *胡耀邦传* [A Biography of Hu Yaobang], vol. 1 (Beijing: 人民, 2005), chap. 13; Zheng Zhongbing (鄭仲兵), ed., *胡耀邦年譜資料長編* [Materials for a Chronological Record of Hu Yaobang], vol. 2 (Hong Kong: 時代國際, 2005), pp. 278–284.

55. Yu Guangyuan (于光远), *我忆邓小平* [Deng Xiaoping in My Memory] (Hangzhou: 浙江人民, 2018), pp. 8–11.

56. Zhang, "邓小平与1975年铁路整顿," pp. 35–40; CCP Central Committee (中共中央), "关于加强铁路工作的决定" [Decision on Strengthening Railway Work], March 5, 1975, *WGYJZL,* vol. 3, p. 248.

57. Cheng and Xia, *历史转折的前奏,* pp. 412–415.

58. Cited from Xu Jingxian (徐景賢), *十年一夢* [A Decade Like a Dream] (Hong Kong: 時代國際, 2003), p. 374.

59. Cheng and Xia, *历史转折的前奏,* pp. 525–526.

60. Wu, *十年风雨纪事,* p. 124.

61. Wu, *十年风雨纪事,* pp. 124–125; *MNP,* vol. 6, p. 583.

62. *MNP,* vol. 6, pp. 589, 595–596.

63. *MNP,* vol. 6, p. 603.

64. *MNP,* vol. 6, p. 611; Yu Guangyuan (于光遠), *我憶鄧小平* [Deng Xiaoping in My Memory] (Hong Kong: 時代國際, 2005), pp. 82–83.

65. *ZNP,* vol. 3, p.721.

66. Mao Mao (毛毛), *我的父亲邓小平: 文革岁月* [My Father Deng Xiaoping: Cultural Revolution Years] (Beijing: 中央文献, 2000), pp. 414–415; *MNP,* vol. 6, pp. 619–620.

67. *MNP,* vol. 6, p. 619.

68. *MNP,* vol. 6, p. 619.

69. *MNP,* vol. 6, p. 620; Leng Rong (冷溶) and Wang Zuoling (汪作玲), et al., *邓小平年谱, 1975–1997* [Chronological Record of Deng Xiaoping, 1975–1997, hereafter *DNP-B*], 2 vols. (Beijing: 中央文献, 2009), vol. 1, p. 126.

70. *MNP,* vol. 6, pp. 620–621.

71. Deng Liqun (鄧力群), *鄧力群自述: 十二個春秋, 1975–1987* [Deng Liqun's Autobiography: Twelve Springs and Autumns, 1975–1987] (Hong Kong: 博智, 2006), pp. 40–42.

72. For the view that accounts of Deng's heroic resistance is overblown, see Warren Sun and Frederick C. Teiwes, *Paradoxes of Post-Mao Rural Reform: Initial Steps toward a New Chinese Countryside, 1976–1981* (New York: Routledge, 2016).

73. *MWG,* vol. 13, p. 488.

74. *MWG,* vol. 13, pp. 486–488.

75. Gao, 晚年周恩来, p. 408.
76. *ZNP*, vol. 3, pp. 723–724; Zhang, 周恩來保健醫生回憶錄, p. 370; Gao Zhenpu (高振普), 陪伴病中周恩来的日日夜夜 [The Days and Nights That I Accompanied Zhou Enlai during His Illness] (Beijing: 中国青年, 2016), pp. 264–268.

Chapter 6. 1976

1. Liu Jixian (刘继贤), ed., 叶剑英年谱 1897–1986 [A Chronological Record of Ye Jianying], vol. 2 (Beijing: 中央文献, 2007), p. 1107; *DNP-B*, vol. 1, pp. 142–143; Shi Yun (史雲), ed., 張春橋姚文元實傳: 自傳、日記、供詞 [The Real Stories of Zhang Chunqiao and Yao Wenyuan: Biographies, Diaries, and Testimonies] (Hong Kong: 三聯, 2012), p. 406.
2. *MNP*, vol. 6, p. 634.
3. Information from a roundtable with a group of leading Chinese Party historians, October 2022.
4. *MNP*, vol. 6, p. 634.
5. Gao Wenqian (高文谦), 晚年周恩来 [Zhou Enlai in His Late Years] (New York: Mirror, 2003), p. 414.
6. Shi, 張春橋姚文元實傳, pp. 408–409.
7. Wu De (吴德), 十年风雨纪事: 我在北京工作的一些经历 [Ten Years of Storms: My Working Experience in Beijing] (Beijing: 当代中国, 2004), p. 154; Shi Yun (史雲) and Li Danhui (李丹慧), 難以繼續的"繼續革命" [The Continuous Revolution That Cannot Be Continued] (Hong Kong: 中文大學, 2008), pp. 622–623; Zheng Zhong (郑重), 张春桥: 1949及其后 [Zhang Chunqiao: 1949 and After] (Hong Kong: 中文大学, 2017), pp.712–713.
8. "大辩论带来大变化" [The Great Debate Brought Great Changes], *RMRB*, January 14, 1976, p. 2.
9. *DNP-B*, vol. 1, p. 145; Shi and Li, 難以繼續的"繼續革命," p. 609.
10. *DNP-B*, vol. 1, p. 145.
11. *MNP*, vol. 6, pp. 634–635; *DNP-B*, vol. 1, p. 145.
12. *MNP*, vol. 6, pp. 634–635.
13. "毛远新笔记" [Notes of Mao Yuanxin], January 21, 1976, quoted in *MZ*, vol. 2, pp. 1766–1767; *MNP*, vol. 6, p. 635.
14. Liu Jixian (刘继贤) et al., 叶剑英年谱, 1897–1986 [Chronological Records of Ye Jianying], vol. 2 (Beijing: 中央文献, 2007), pp. 1107–1108; Fan Shuo (范硕) and Ding Jiaqi (丁家琪) et al., 叶剑英传 [A Biography of Ye Jianying] (Beijing: 当代中国, 1997), p. 635.
15. *MWG*, vol. 20, p. 501; *MNP*, vol. 6, p. 635.
16. Li Haiwen (李海文), "周恩来逝世后, 毛泽东为何指定 华国锋为代总理? (下)" [After Zhou Enlai's Passing, Why Did Mao Zedong Make Hua Guofeng Acting Premier? Part 2], 江淮文史 (Jianghuai Literature and History), no. 2 (2016), pp. 27–28.
17. Li, "周恩来逝世后, 毛泽东为何指定华国锋为代总理? (下)," pp. 24–39.
18. CCP Central Committee Doc. 4 (1976), 中央中央1976年第4号文件, "毛主席重要指示" [Chairman Mao's Important Instructions, March 3, 1976], *ZGWGWK*. Mao stated:

"He [Deng Xiaoping] does not understand Marx and Lenin. He represents the bourgeoisie. He promised that he would 'never reverse verdicts.' This cannot be trusted."

19. 中共中央通知 [Notice of the CPC Central Committee], February 2, 1976, *WGYJZL*, vol. 3, 361; *DNP-B*, vol. 1, p. 147; Liu, 叶剑英年谱, vol. 2, pp. 1107–1108.

20. CCP Central Committee (中共中央), "批转军委关于检查1975年军委扩大会议文件的报告" [Conveying the Central Military Commission's Report on Reexamining the Documents of the CMC's Enlarged Meeting in 1975], February 16, 1976, *ZGWGWK*.

21. Xu Jingxian (徐景賢), 十年一夢 [A Decade Like a Dream] (Hong Kong: 時代國際, 2003), p. 373.

22. CCP Central Committee (中共中央), 关于"王洪文、张春桥、江青、姚文元反党集团罪证(材料之一)" 的通知及附件 [Notice on "Evidence of the Crimes of Wang Hongwen, Zhang Chunqiao, Jiang Qing, and Yao Wenyuan Anti-Party Clique (Materials Group No. 1)" and Annexes], December 10, 1976, *ZGWGWK*.

23. Zou Yimin (邹一民), "1975–76 年外交部的批邓、反击右倾翻案风" [Criticizing Deng and Countering the Rightist Reversal Wind in the Ministry of Foreign Affairs in 1975–76], http://w.hybsl.cn/article/13/50826 (胡耀邦史料信息网), accessed September 21, 2023.

24. CCP Central Committee (中共中央), "关于学习毛主席重要指示的通知, 中发[1976]4号" [Notice on Studying Chairman Mao's Instructions], March 3, 1976, Central Committee document, no. 4, 1976, *ZGWGWK*. For an abridged version of the notice, see *MWG*, vol. 13, pp. 486–493.

25. *DNP-B*, vol. 1, 148.

26. Zhou Shaohua (周少华), "回忆父亲周荣鑫: 在文革的政治漩涡中" [Remembering Father Zhou Rongxin: In the Political Vortex of the Cultural Revolution], *Phoenix News*, news.ifeng.com/history/1/jishi/200812/1229_2663_944318.shtml, accessed August 15, 2022.

27. "胡乔木揭发邓小平的言论" [Hu Qiaomu's Exposure of What Deng Xiaoping Has Said], March 2, 1976, *ZGWGWK*.

28. "江青在打招呼会议期间擅自召开的十二省市会议上的讲话记录稿" [Transcript of Jiang Qing's Speech at an Unauthorized Meeting of Twelve Provinces and Cities Held during the Sharing Information Conference], March 2, 1976, *WGYJZL*, vol. 3, pp. 374–384.

29. *MWG*, vol. 13, p. 527.

30. Fu Yi (傅颐), "教育部长周荣鑫的最后岁月" [The Last Years of Education Minister Zhou Rongxin], 百年潮 [One Hundred Year Tide], no. 2 (2022), pp. 29–38.

31. Yuan Min (袁敏), 重返1976: 我所经历的"总理遗言"案 [Returning to 1976: The Case of the "Premier's Last Will" That I Personally Experienced] (Beijing: 人民文学, 2010).

32. For good accounts of the "Nanjing incident of 1976," see Shi and Li, 難以繼續的"繼續革命," pp. 624–628; and Frederick C. Teiwes and Warren Sun, *The End of the Maoist Era: Chinese Politics during the Twilight of the Cultural Revolution, 1972–1976* (Armonk, NY: M. E. Sharpe, 2008), pp. 466–488.

33. Ji Xichen (纪希晨), 史无前例的年代——一位人民日报老记者的笔记 [An Unprecedented Era: Notes by a Senior Reporter from the *People's Daily*]. Beijing: 人民日报, 2001.

34. CCP Central Committee (中共中央), "关于南京大字报问题的电话通知" [Notice on the Big Character Poster Problem in Nanjing], April 1, 1976, *ZGWGWK*.

35. Yao Wenyuan (姚文元), 姚文元日记 [Yao Wenyuan's Diary], April 6, 1976, quoted in Shi, 張春橋姚文元實傳, p. 436.

36. Tong Huaizhou (童怀周), ed., 天安门诗抄 [The Tiananmen Poems] (Beijing: 人民文学, 1978), p. 282.

37. 毛远新笔记 [Mao Yuanxin's Notes], April 4, 1976, quoted in Shi and Li, "難以繼續的"繼續革命," pp. 632–633; Mao Yuanxin (毛远新), "关于中央政治局四月四日讨论天安门事件情况给毛泽东的报告" [Mao Yuanxin's Report to Mao Zedong on the Political Bureau's Discussion of the Tiananmen Incident on April 4], April 5, 1976, *ZGWGWK*.

38. Yao, 姚文元日记, April 3, 1976, quoted in Shi, 張春橋姚文元實傳, p. 429.

39. Zhang Chunqiao (张春桥), 给儿子毛弟的信 [Letter to Son Mao Di], April 18, 1976, quoted in Shi, 張春橋姚文元實傳, p. 434.

40. Wu, 十年风雨纪事, pp. 159–160.

41. Wu, 十年风雨纪事, p. 160.

42. *MNP*, vol. 6, p. 646; *MZ*, vol. 2, p. 1777.

43. "天安门广场事件说明了什么" [What Was Made Clear by the Tiananmen Incident], *RMRB*, April 18, 1976, p. 1.

44. "天安门广场事件说明了什么," p. 1.

45. Deng Rong, *Deng Xiaoping and the Cultural Revolution: A Daughter Recalls the Critical Years* (Beijing: Foreign Language Press, 2002), pp. 399–402.

46. Zhang Yufeng (张玉凤), "回忆毛主席去世前的一些情况" [Recalling Chairman Mao's Situation before His Passing] (unpublished manuscript), quoted in *MZ*, vol. 2, pp. 1778–1779.

47. *MZ*, vol. 2, p. 1782.

48. Zhang Chunqiao (张春桥), 关于批邓反右运动的讲话 [Speech on Criticizing Deng and Opposing the Rightist Movement], June 28, 1976, *ZGWGWK*.

49. This is the figure inscribed at the monument to the victims of the Tangshan earthquake erected in Tianjin on the tenth anniversary of the disaster. For an overview, see Liu Huixian, George W. Housner, Xie Lili, and He Duxin, *The Great Tangshan Earthquake of 1976*, EERL Report, 2002-001 (Pasadena: California Institute of Technology, 2002). See also James Palmer, *Heaven Cracks, Earth Shakes: The Tangshan Earthquake and the Death of Mao's China* (New York: Basic Books, 2011).

50. *MZ*, vol. 2, p. 1782; Ji, 史无前例的年代——一位人民日报老记者的笔记, p. 772.

51. *MNP*, vol. 6, p. 650.

52. *MZ*, vol. 2, pp. 1781–1782.

53. *MZ*, vol. 2, p. 1784.

54. See note 1 in the introduction. In addition to eyewitness accounts, our more detailed narrative is corroborated by several interviews with leading Party historians in January 2014 and October 2017.

55. Ji Xichen (纪希晨), "粉碎'四人帮'全景写真" [A Truthful Overall Account of the Smashing of the Gang of Four], part 1, 炎黄春秋 [China through the Ages], no. 10 (2000), pp. 18–39.

56. *DNP-B*, vol. 1, p. 151; Liu, 叶剑英年谱, vol. 2, p. 1110.

57. Li Zhisui, *The Private Life of Chairman Mao: The Memoirs of Mao's Personal Physician* (New York: Random House, 1994), p. 28.

58. Interview with the local CCP leader, Shandong, March 2012.

59. Wang Weicheng (王维澄) et al., 李先念年谱 [A Chronological Record of Li Xiannian], vol. 5 (Beijing: 中央文献, 2011), p. 448; Zhu Yu (朱玉) et al., 李先念传, 1949–1992 [A Biography of Li Xiannian, 1949–1992], vol. 2 (Beijing: 中央文献, 2009), pp. 899–900; Cheng Zhensheng (程振声) et al., "李先念与粉碎四人帮" [Li Xiannian and Smashing of the Gang of Four], 中共党史研究 (CCP History Study), no. 1 (2002), pp. 47–48; Zhang Gensheng (张根生), "华国锋谈粉碎四人帮" [Hua Guofeng on Smashing the Gang of Four], 炎黄春秋 [China through the Ages], no. 7 (2004), pp. 2–3; Wu, 十年风雨纪事, p. 178.

60. Wang et al., 李先念年谱, vol. 5, pp. 448–449; Zhu et al., 李先念传, 1949–1992, vol. 2, pp. 900–901; Cheng et al, "李先念与粉碎四人帮," p. 48.

61. Wu Jianhua (武健华), "详忆粉碎'四人帮'的前前后后" [Remembering Smashing the Gang of Four, with Details], part 1, 百年潮 [One Hundred Year Tide], no. 10 (2012), pp. 4–5.

62. Wu, 十年风雨纪事, p. 178; Wang et al., 李先念年谱, vol. 5, p. 449; Cheng et al., "李先念与粉碎四人帮," p. 49.

63. *RMRB*, September 19, 1976, p. 1.

64. Shi, 張春橋姚文元實傳, pp. 479–480.

65. Liu, 叶剑英年谱, p. 1111; Wu, 十年风雨纪事, p. 179; Wang et al., 李先念年谱, vol. 5, p. 449.

66. Li Haiwen (李海文), "粉碎'四人帮'前华国锋四次约谈汪东兴" [Hua Guofeng Met with Wang Dongxing Four Times before Smashing the "Gang of Four"], 党史博览 [Broad Survey of Party History], no. 12 (2017), pp. 43–44.

67. Shi and Li, 難以繼續的"繼續革命," p. 687.

68. Ji, "粉碎'四人帮'全景写真," part 1, p. 31.

69. Ji, "粉碎'四人帮'全景写真," part 1, p. 31; see also "徐景贤亲笔记录的肖木向上海市委常委传达的张春桥意见" [Zhang Chunqiao's Opinion Conveyed by Xiao Mu to Party Standing Committee Members in Shanghai CCP in Notes Personally Taken by Xu Jingxian], in CCP Central Committee (中共中央), 关于"王洪文、张春桥、江青、姚文元反党集团罪证 (材料之一)" 的通知及附件 [Notice on "Evidence of the Crimes of Wang Hongwen, Zhang Chunqiao, Jiang Qing, and Yao Wenyuan Anti-Party Clique (Materials Group No. 1) and Annexes"], December 10, 1976, ZGWGWK.

70. Ji, 史无前例的年代, pp. 793–798.

71. Ji, 史无前例的年代, p. 798; Liu, 叶剑英年谱, vol. 3, p. 1112; Wang et al., 李先念年谱, vol. 5, p. 449.

72. 江青在清华大学农村分校的讲话 [Jiang Qing's speech at the Countryside Branch of Tsinghua University], October 1, 1976, ZGWKWK.

73. For overviews of the political situation, see Teiwes and Sun, *End of the Maoist Era*, pp. 536–594; and Joseph Torigian, *Prestige, Manipulation, and Coercion: Elite Power Struggles in the Soviet Union and China after Stalin and Mao* (New Haven, CT: Yale University Press, 2022), pp. 84–135.

74. Liu, 叶剑英年谱, vol. 2, p. 1111.

75. Liu, 叶剑英年谱, vol. 2, pp. 1112–1113; Wu, "详忆粉碎'四人帮'的前前后后," part 1, pp. 6–7.

76. Liu, 叶剑英年谱, vol. 2, p. 1114; Wu, "详忆粉碎'四人帮'的前前后后," part 1, p. 8.

77. Shi and Li, 難以繼續的"繼續革命," pp. 693–694.

78. Shi and Li, 難以繼續的"繼續革命," p. 699.

79. Shi and Li, 難以繼續的"繼續革命," p. 700.

80. Wu Jianhua (武健华), "详忆粉碎'四人帮'的前前后后" [Detailed Recollections of Crushing the Gang of Four], part 2, 百年潮, no. 10 (2012), pp. 21–22; Shi and Li, 難以繼續的"繼續革命," p. 701.

81. Wu, "详忆粉碎'四人帮'的前前后后," part 2, p. 22; Shi and Li, 難以繼續的"繼續革命," p. 701.

82. Wu, "详忆粉碎'四人帮'的前前后后," part 2, p. 26.

83. Wu, "详忆粉碎'四人帮'的前前后后," part 2, pp. 23–24; Zhang Yaoci (张耀祠), "1976: 我负责的'四人帮'抓捕行动" [I Was in Charge of Arresting the Gang of Four in 1976], 同舟共济 [Together], no. 5 (2009), p. 49.

Chapter 7. Succession Struggles

1. Li Haiwen (李海文), "华国锋主持政治局会议解决上海问题" [Hua Guofeng Chaired the Politburo Meeting for Resolving the Shanghai Problem], 党史博览 (Broad Survey of the Communist Party of China), no. 1 (2014), p. 9.

2. Zhang Gensheng (张根生), "华国锋谈粉碎'四人帮'" [Hua Guofeng on Smashing the Gang of Four], 炎黄春秋 [China through the Ages], no. 7 (2004), p. 3; Wu Jianhua (武健华), "详忆粉碎'四人帮'的前前后后" [Remembering Smashing the Gang of Four, with Details], part 3, 百年潮 [One Hundred Year Tide], no. 12 (2012), p. 19.

3. Wu, "详忆粉碎'四人帮'的前前后后," part 3, pp. 19–22; Li, "华国锋主持政治局会议解决上海问题," p. 9.

4. Wu, "详忆粉碎'四人帮'的前前后后," part 3, p. 20.

5. Wu, "详忆粉碎'四人帮'的前前后后," part 3, p. 20.

6. Wu, "详忆粉碎'四人帮'的前前后后," part 3, pp. 20–21.

7. Li Haiwen (李海文) and Wang Shoujia (王守家), "四人帮"上海余党覆灭记, 1976.10–1979.10 [The Demise of Remnants of the "Gang of Four" in Shanghai, October 1976–October 1979] (Beijing: 中国青年, 2015), pp. 16–24; Wang Shaoguang (王绍光), 超凡領袖的挫敗—文化大革命在武漢 [The Failure of a Superior Leader: The Cultural Revolution in Wuhan] (Hong Kong: 中文大學, 2009), p. 240.

8. Li Xun (李逊). 革命造反年代: 上海文革運動史稿 [An Age of Revolutionary Rebellion: A Draft History of the Cultural Revolution in Shanghai], vol. 2 (Hong Kong: Oxford University Press, 2015), pp. 1563–1571.

9. Elizabeth Perry and Li Xun, *Proletarian Power: Shanghai in the Cultural Revolution* (Boulder, CO: Westview Press, 1997), p. 185.

10. 中央领导人关于解决四人帮问题的讲话 [Central Leaders' Speeches on Settlement of the Gang of Four Issue], October 8, 1976, *ZGWGWK*.

11. 中国共产党第十一次全国代表大会新闻公报 [News Release of the Eleventh Congress of the Chinese Communist Party], August 18, 1977, *RMRB*, August 21, 1977, pp. 1–3.

12. Information from interviews with Party historians, August 2014.

13. 中央领导人关于解决四人帮问题的讲话, *ZGWGWK*.

14. 中央领导人关于解决四人帮问题的讲话, *ZGWGWK*.

15. Li, 革命造反年代, vol. 2, p. 1566.

16. Shi Yun (史雲) and Li Danhui (李丹慧), 難以繼續的"繼續革命" [The Continuous Revolution That Cannot Be Continued] (Hong Kong: 中文大學, 2008), p. 712.

17. 华国锋叶剑英等接见上海马天水等人的讲话 [Hua Guofeng and Ye Jianying's Conversation with Ma Tianshui and Others], October 12, 1976, *ZGWGWK*.

18. 华国锋叶剑英等接见上海马天水等人的讲话, *ZGWGWK*.

19. 华国锋叶剑英等接见上海马天水等人的讲话, *ZGWGWK*.

20. Li and Wang, "四人帮"上海余党覆灭记, pp. 41–44.

21. Li, 革命造反年代, vol. 2, pp. 1588–1590.

22. Li, 革命造反年代, vol. 2, p. 1592.

23. Ma ended up in a psychiatric hospital, where he died in 1994. All of the other Shanghai leaders were sentenced to long prison terms, between fourteen and eighteen years in most cases. Later investigations showed that the Left had at least some support in the Nanjing Military Region surrounding Shanghai. General Ding Sheng, who commanded it, was purged in March 1977 for having been hesitant in following orders from Beijing.

24. Foreign new media reported the arrests on October 12, and the first inner-Party announcement was made on October 18. The first public confirmation within China was on October 21, two weeks after the coup.

25. Mang Donghong (莽东鸿), "'四人帮'垮台的消息是怎样传播到民间的" [How Did the News of the Collapse of the "Gang of Four" Spread among Everyday People], 党史博览 [Broad Survey of Party History], no. 9 (2006), pp. 30–35.

26. Li and Wang, "四人帮"上海余党覆灭记, pp. 83–115.

27. Robert Lawrence Kuhn, 他改变了中国—江泽民传 [The Man Who Has Changed China: A Biography of Jiang Zeming] (Shanghai: 上海译文, 2005), pp. 86–87.

28. Li, 革命造反年代, vol. 2, pp. 1594–1596.

29. CCP Liaoning Provincial Committee (中共辽宁省委), 关于辽宁省揭批"四人帮"及其死党毛远新斗争情况的报告 (节选) [Report on the Exposure of and Struggles against the "Gang of Four" and Its Die-Hard Followers such as Mao Yuanxin in Liaoning], July 4, 1977, *ZGWGWK*.

30. Huang Jingyao (黄经耀), "在陕西省委常委 (扩大) 会议上的讲话" [Comrade Huang Jingyao's Speech at the Enlarged Meeting of the Standing Committee of CCP Shaanxi Provincial Committee], May 20, 1977, *ZGWGWK*.

31. CCP Central Committee (中共中央), "云南省委和昆明军区参加中央解决云南问题会议同志向中央的报告" [Report by Comrades of CCP Yunnan Provincial Committee

and PLA Kunming Military Region Who Attended the Conference Summoned by the Party Center on Setting the Yunnan Problem], February 4, 1977, *ZGWGWK*.

32. Even more remarkably, Jia survived the debacle politically, returning a few years later to minor Party positions in Hebei Province. Jia was an old acquaintance of Deng Xiaoping, and even if he had attacked Deng in 1975–1976, he was, in the end, forgiven.

33. Shanghai Municipal Supreme Court (上海市高级人民法院), "关于公判一批现行反革命刑事罪犯的通知" [Notice on Public Trial of a Group of Active Counter-Revolutionary Criminals], January 4, 1977, *ZGWGWK*.

34. "四届人大常委会第三次会议在京隆重举行" [The Third Plenary Session of the Standing Committee of the Fourth National People's Congress Was Held in Beijing], *RMRB*, December 1, 1976, p. 1.

35. For a good description of the Xidan "Democracy Wall," see Xiao Donglian (蕭冬連), 歷史的轉軌: 從撥亂反正到改革開放, 1979–1981 [Historical Shifts: From Setting Things Right to the Reform and Opening, 1979–1981] (Hong Kong: 中文大學, 2008), pp. 42–48, 68–69. See also Helmut Opletal's website Die chinesische Demokratiebewegung 1978 bis 1981—Erinnerungen der damaligen Akteure [The Chinese Democracy Movement 1978 to 1981—Reminiscences of Participants], https://pekinger-fruehling.univie.ac.at/der-pekinger-fruehling, accessed August 2023; Kjeld Erik Brodsgaard, "The Democracy Movement in China, 1978–1979: Opposition Movements, Wall Poster Campaigns, and Underground Journals," *Asian Survey* 21, no. 7 (1981), pp. 747–774; and Andrew J. Nathan, *Chinese Democracy* (New York: Knopf, 1985).

36. 邓小平给华国锋和中共中央的信 [Deng Xiaoping's Letter to Hua Guofeng and the CCP Central Committee], October 10, 1976, *ZGWGWK*.

37. Xiong Lei (熊蕾), "1976年华国锋和叶剑英是怎样联手的" [How Hua Guofeng and Ye Jianying Joined Forces in 1976], 炎黄春秋 [China through the Ages], no. 10 (2008), p. 8.

38. Han Gang (韩钢), "关于华国锋的若干史实" [Some Historical Facts about Hua Guofeng], 炎黄春秋 [China through the Ages], no. 2 (2011), p. 13.

39. Jin Chongji (金冲及) and Chen Qun (陈群) et al., 陈云传 [A Biography of Chen Yun], vol. 4 (Beijing: 中央文献, 2015), p.1459.

40. Cheng Zhongyuan (程中原), Wang Yuxiang (王玉祥), and Li Zhenghua (李正华), 1976–1981 年的中国 [China in 1976–1981] (Beijing: 中央文献, 1998), pp. 44–45.

41. Hua Guofeng (华国锋), "在中央工作会议上的讲话" [Speech at the Working Conference of the CPC Central Committee], March 14, 1977, cited from Han Gang (韩钢), "'两个凡是'的由来及其终结" [The Origins and End of the "Two Whatevers"], 中共党史研究 [CCP History Studies], no. 11 (2009), p. 59.

42. For an excellent discussion of the making of the "two whatevers" notion and its implications, as well as the role played by Wang Dongxing, see Han, "关于华国锋的若干史实," pp. 13–15.

43. Chen Tushou (陈徒手), "出版印刷'毛选'五卷的日子里" [The Day the Fifth Volume of Selected Works of Mao Zedong Was Published and Printed], 随笔 (Essay), no. 3 (2020).

44. The Democratic People's Republic of Korea's reported per capita GDP was three times that of China in the late 1970s.

45. Michel Bonnin, *The Lost Generation: The Rustication of China's Educated Youth (1968–1980)* (Hong Kong: Chinese University Press, 2013), chap. 11.

46. Fan Shuo (范硕), 叶剑英在1976 [Ye Jianying in 1976] (Beijing: 人民, 1995), pp. 315–316. Ye's birthday party was on May 14; see Liu Jixian (刘继贤) et al., 叶剑英年谱, 1897–1986 [Chronological Records of Ye Jianying, 1897–1986], vol. 2 (Beijing: 中央文献, 2007), pp. 1125–1126; see also Editorial Group of Chronological Record of Yang Chengwu (杨成武年谱编写组), 杨成武年谱, 1914–2004 [Chronological Record of Yang Chengwu, 1914–2004] (Beijing: 解放军, 2014), p. 523.

47. Information from Party historians, July 2016.

48. Editorial Group of Wang Zhen Biography (王震传编写组), 王震传 [A Biography of Wang Zhen] (Beijing: 当代中国, 2001), p. 177.

49. 邓小平给华国锋、 叶剑英和中共中央的信 [Deng Xiaoping's Letter to Gua Guofeng, Ye Jianying, and the CCP Central Committee], April 10, 1977, *ZGWGWK*; see also *DNP-B*, vol. 1, p. 157.

50. *DWX*, vol. 2, pp. 38–39.

51. *DNP-B*, vol. 1, pp. 159–160.

52. *RMRB*, July 23, 1977, p. 1; *DNP-B*, vol. 1, p. 162.

53. Han Gang (韩钢), "关于华国锋的若干史实 (续)" [Some Historical Facts about Hua Guofeng, Part 2], 炎黄春秋 [China through the Ages], no. 3 (2011), pp. 10–13.

54. Wen Yong (温勇), "邓小平的时间表和时间观" [Deng Xiaoping's Timetable and Concept of Time], 党的文献 [Party History Documents], no. 4 (2012), p. 117.

55. Deng Xiaoping, "在中央军委全体会议上的讲话" [Speech at a Plenary Meeting of the Central Military Commission], December 28, 1977, *DWX*, vol. 2, pp. 72–84.

56. CCTV (中央广播电视总台), ed., 见证我亲历的改革开放 [The Reform and Opening-up That I Personally Experienced] (Beijing: 中国方正, 2018), pp. 24–30.

57. Yang Xuewei (杨学为) and Fan Kening (樊克宁), "恢复高考: 历史记住这条脉络" [Resuming College Entry Exams: History Remembers This Development], 羊城晚报 [Guangzhou Evening News], June 16, 2007.

58. The Exam Center of the Ministry of Education (教育部考试中心), eds., 难忘1977: 恢复高考的历史实录 [Unforgettable Historical Records of the Resumption of College Entry Exams in 1977] (Tianjin: 天津人民, 2007), pp. 159–163.

59. Wu Qiong (吴琼), "岁月的歌— 数理化自学丛书重版前后" [Song of the Era: The Republication of the "Series on Mathematics, Physics and Chemistry"], 档案春秋 [Memories and Archives], no. 1 (2015), pp. 58–60.

60. "改革招生制度的决策是完全正确的, 教育部负责人就去年高校招生制度改革的有关情况答记者问 [The Decision to Reform the College Entrance Examination System Is Completely Correct: A Leading Person of the Ministry of Education Answers Questions from Reporters about Reforming the College Entrance Examination from the Previous Year], *RMRB*, May 12, 1978, p. 3.

61. Hou Yonglu (侯永禄), 农民家书 [A Peasant's Home Letters] (Beijing: 人民文学, 2011), entry for October 19, 1978, pp. 79–81.

Chapter 8. Visions of China

1. "全面地正确地贯彻执行毛主席的教育方针—高等学校招生进行重大改革" [Comprehensively and Correctly Carry Out Chairman Mao's Education Lines, Make Major Reforms of Universities' Admission Processes], *RMRB*, October 21, 1977, p. 1.

2. CCP History Research Institute (中共中央党史研究室), ed., 中国共产党历史 [A History of the Chinese Communist Party], vol. 2 (Beijing: 中共党史, 2011), p. 969.

3. "千方百计夺取夏季丰收 [Make Every Effort to Guarantee the Summer Harvest], *RMRB*, February 17, 1977, p. 3.

4. Zhu Jiamu (朱佳木) et al., 陈云年谱, 1905–1995 [Chronological Record of Chen Yun, hereafter *CYNP*] (Beijing: 中央文献, 2000), pp. 206–216.

5. Deng Xiaoping (邓小平), 在全国教育工作会议上的讲话 [Speech at National Education Work Conference], April 22, 1978, *DWX*, vol. 2, p. 108.

6. Zhu Jiamu (朱佳木), "改革开放初期的陈云与邓小平" [Chen Yun and Deng Xiaoping in the Early Days of Reform and Opening-Up], 当代中国史研究 (Contemporary Chinese History Studies), no. 3 (2010), pp. 4–15.

7. Hua Guofeng (华国锋), "政府工作报告" [Report on Governmental Work], *RMRB*, March 7, 1978, p. 1.

8. Hua, "政府工作报告," p. 1.

9. Wu Li (武力), ed., 中华人民共和国经济史 1949–1999 [The Economic History of the People's Republic of China, 1949–1999] (Beijing: 中国经济, 1999), pp. 764–767.

10. Cai Wenbin (蔡文彬), ed., 赵紫阳在四川, 1975–1980 [Zhao Ziyang in Sichuan, 1975–1980] (Hong Kong: 新世紀, 2011), p. 41.

11. Editorial Group of Zhao Ziyang's Works (趙紫陽文集編輯組), 趙紫陽文集 (1975–1980), 四川卷 [A Collection of Zhao Ziyang's Works, 1975–1980, Sichuan Volume] (Hong Kong: 中文大學, 2018), pp. 30–42, 152–170.

12. Zhao Wei (赵蔚), 赵紫阳传 [A Biography of Zhao Ziyang] (Beijing: 中国新闻, 1989), p. 209.

13. Chris Bramall, *Chinese Economic Development* (Abingdon, UK: Routledge, 2009), pp. 251–252.

14. Zhang Guangyou (张广友) and Han Gang (韩钢), "万里谈农村改革是怎么搞起来的" [Wan Li Discusses How Reform Began in the Countryside], 百年潮 [One Hundred Year Tide], no. 3 (1998), pp. 1–9.

15. Warren Sun and Frederick C. Teiwes, *Paradoxes of Post-Mao Rural Reform: Initial Steps toward a New Chinese Countryside, 1976–1981* (New York: Routledge, 2016), p. 54.

16. He Honggang, *Governance, Social Organisation and Reform in Rural China: Case Studies from Anhui Province* (New York: Palgrave Macmillan, 2015), p. 64.

17. Wang Guangyu (王光宇), "我所亲历的安徽农村改革" [I Personally Experienced Rural Reform in Anhui], 中共党史研究 [CCP History Studies], no. 5 (2008), pp. 3–4.

18. Wan Li (万里), "尊重生产队的自主权" [Respect the Rights of the Production Team], February 5, 1978, in Wan Li, 万里文选 [Selected Works of Wan Li] (Beijing: 人民, 1995), pp. 103–105.

19. Nie Rongzhen (聂荣臻), "恢复和发扬党的优良作风" [Restore and Promote the Party's Good Style of Work], *RMRB*, September 5, 1977, p. 4.

20. Chen Yun (陈云), "坚持实事求是的革命作风" [Insist on a Revolutionary Style of Seeking Truth from Facts], *RMRB*, September 28, 1977, p. 2; *CYNP*, vol. 3, p. 215.

21. Shi Binhai (施滨海), 历史转折中的华国锋 (1973–1981) [Hua Guafeng in Historical Turning Point] (Beijing: 北京传世家书文化, 2020), pp. 85–91.

22. Yang Zhongmei (杨中美), 胡耀邦传略 [A Short Biography of Hu Yaobang] [Beijing: 新华, 1989], p. 118.

23. Hu Yaobang (胡耀邦), "用马列主义最核心的东西武装干部" [Use the Most Central Part of Marxism-Leninism to Arm Cadres], August 29, 1977, in Hu Yaobang, 胡耀邦文选 [Selected Works of Hu Yaobang] (Beijing: 人民, 2015), pp. 73–77.

24. Hu Deping (胡德平), "耀邦同志在'真理标准'大讨论的前前后后(中篇)" [Comrade Yaobang before and after the Great Debate about the Criterion of the Truth, Part 2], 财经 [Finance and Economics], no. 12 (2008), http://www.hybsl.cn/article/10/102/9769, accessed October 4, 2023.

25. See Yang, 胡耀邦传略, pp. 1–4.

26. Tian Guoliang (田国良) and Sun Daxun (孙大勋), 胡耀邦传 [A Biography of Hu Yaobang] (Beijing: 中央党史资料, 1989), pp. 65–80.

27. Tian and Sun, 胡耀邦传, pp. 71–72.

28. Tian and Sun, 胡耀邦传, pp. 81–82.

29. Hu Yaobang (胡耀邦), "一定要把科研搞上去" [Make Sure to Bring Research in Science to a Higher Level], October 1975, in Hu, 胡耀邦文选, pp. 65–71.

30. Han Gang (韩钢), "关于华国锋的若干史实" [Some Historical Facts about Hua Guofeng], 炎黄春秋 [China through the Ages], no. 2 (2011), pp. 9–18.

31. *DNP*-B, vol. 1, p. 261.

32. Zhen Shi (甄石), "胡耀邦在中央党校" [Hu Yaobang at Central Party School], 党史博览 [Broad Survey of Party History], no. 7 (2010), pp. 4–5; Shen Baoxiang (沈宝祥), "胡耀邦关于支持揭露康生的讲话" [Hu Yaobang's Speech Supporting Exposing Kang Sheng], September 3, 1977, 学习时报 [Study Times], July 8, 2013.

33. Liu Shaoqi, the former president who had been a main target of the Cultural Revolution, was posthumously rehabilitated in May 1980. An exhibition honoring the "glorious life of the great Marxist and proletarian revolutionary Comrade Liu Shaoqi" was opened at the Museum of the Chinese Revolution in Tiananmen Square the same month. See Lowell Dittmer, "Death and Transfiguration: Liu Shaoqi's Rehabilitation and Contemporary Chinese Politics," *Journal of Asian Studies* 40, no. 3 (1981), pp. 455–479.

34. Tian and Sun, 胡耀邦传, pp. 112–113.

35. Hua Guofeng (华国锋), "政府工作报告" [Report on Governmental Work], *RMRB*, February 26, 1978, and March 7, 1978, p. 1.

36. 中华人民共和国宪法 [The Constitution of the People's Republic of China], adopted at the First Meeting of the Fifth National People's Congress on March 5, 1978 (Beijing: 人民, 1978). This paragraph was deleted when the constitution was revised in 1980.

37. Daniel Leese, *Maos Langer Schatten: Chinas Umgang mit der Vergangenheit* [Mao's Long Shadow: China's Treatment of the Past] (Munich: C. H. Beck, 2020), p. 231.

38. Hua, "政府工作报告," *RMRB*, March 7, 1978, p. 1.

39. Hua, "政府工作报告," *RMRB*, March 7, 1978, p. 1.

40. *CYNP*, vol. 3, pp. 223, 228–229.

41. Tian and Sun, 胡耀邦传, pp. 101–106.

42. Zhang Cheng (张成), "标准只有一个" [There Is Only One Criterion], *RMRB*, March 26, 1978, p. 3. Zhang argues in the article: "The criterion of the truth can be one, that is social practice."

43. "实践是检验真理的唯一标准" [Practice Is the Sole Criterion in Judging the Truth], 光明日报 [Guangming Daily], May 11, 1978, p. 1. *RMRB* and 解放军报 [People's Liberation Army Daily] later also published the article.

44. Yu Guangyuan (于光远) et al, 改变中国命运的41天: 中央工作会议、十一届三中全会亲历记 [Forty-One Days That Changed the Fate of China: Personal Experience at the Central Work Conference and the Third Plenary Session of the Eleventh Central Committee] (Shenzhen: 海天, 1998), p. 117.

45. Han Honghong (韩洪洪), 胡耀邦在历史转折关头, 1975–1982 [Hu Yaobang at the Juncture of Historical Turning, 1975–1982] (Beijing: 人民, 2008), p. 104.

46. Zheng Zhongbing (鄭仲兵), ed., 胡耀邦年譜資料長編 [Materials for a Chronological Record of Hu Yaobang's Life] (Hong Kong: 時代國際, 2005), p. 317.

47. Wang Zhongfang (王仲方), "耀邦与我的两次谈话" [Yaobang's Two Conversations with Me], 炎黄春秋 [China through the Ages], no. 7 (2005), p. 17.

48. *DWX*, vol. 2, p. 114.

49. See Frederick C. Teiwes and Warren Sun, "Hua Guofeng, Deng Xiaoping, and Reversing the Verdict on the 1976 'Tiananmen Incident,'" *China Review* 19, no. 4 (2019), p. 97.

50. "落实党的干部政策必须抓紧 (特约评论)" [We Must Step up the Implementation of the Party's Cadre Policy (Special Comment)], *RMRB*, July 28, 1978, p. 1.

51. Joseph Torigian, *Prestige, Manipulation and Coercion: Elite Power Struggles in the Soviet Union and China after Stalin and Mao* (New Haven, CT: Yale University Press, 2022), p. 145.

52. Wu De no longer served as Beijing Party secretary in October 1978. He resigned from the Politburo in February 1980.

53. Michael Schoenhals, "The 1978 Truth Criterion Controversy," *China Quarterly*, no. 126 (1991), pp. 243–268. See also Michael Schoenhals, *Doing Things with Words in Chinese Politics: Five Studies* (Berkeley: Institute of East Asian Studies, University of California, 1992).

54. Yu Guangyuan, "Speech at the Opening Ceremony of the Fourth Symposium on Theory of Distribution According to Work" (October 1978), in Yu Guangyuan, *Chinese Economists on Economic Reform—Collected Works of Yu Guangyuan* (London: Routledge, 2014), pp. 4–5.

55. Zhang Hua (张化), "1978 年中央工作会议若干问题研究" [A Study of Several Questions Concerning the Central Work Conference of 1978], 史学月刊 [Journal of Historical Science], no. 1 (2012), p. 63.

56. Hua Guofeng (华国锋), "在中共中央工作会议开幕会上的讲话" [Speech at the Opening Session of the Central Work Conference], November 11, 1978], SZ 1-4-791, Hubei Provincial Archive (hereafter HBPA).

57. *CYNP*, vol. 3, pp. 226–227.

58. Jin Chongji (金冲及) and Chen Qun (陈群) et al., 陈云传 [A Biography of Chen Yun], vol. 4 (Beijing: 中央文献, 2015), p. 1495.

59. *CYNP*, vol. 3, p. 227.

60. Yu Guangyuan (于光远), 十一届三中全会的台前幕后: 1978我亲历的那次历史大转折 [On the Stage and behind the Scenes of the Third Plenum of the Eleventh Central Committee: The Historical Transition that I Personally Experienced in 1978] (Beijing: 中央编译, 2008), pp. 68–69.

61. Yu, 十一届三中全会的台前幕后, pp. 89–90.

62. Zhu Jiamu (朱佳木), 我所知道的十一届三中全会 [What I Know about the Third Plenum of the Eleventh Party Congress] (Beijing: 当代中国, 2008), p. 99.

63. Zhang Hua, "1978 年中央工作会议若干问题研究," pp. 70–71.

64. Yu, 十一届三中全会的台前幕后, pp. 193–213.

65. Hua Guofeng (华国锋), "在中央工作会议闭幕会上的讲话" [Hua Guofeng's Speech at the Closing Session of the CCP Central Work Conference], December 13, 1978, SZ1-4-791, HBPA.

66. "中国共产党第十一届中央委员会第三次全体会议公报" [Communiqué of the Third Plenary Session of the Eleventh Central Committee of the Communist Party of China], http://cpc.people.com.cn/GB/64162/64168/64563/65371/4441902.html, accessed March 5, 2023.

67. "中国共产党第十一届中央委员会第三次全体会议公报."

68. Wang Huide (王惠德), "重新认识三十年来的理论与实践: 看看毛病究竟出在那里?" [Reinvestigate the Theory and Practice of the Past Thirty Years to See Where the Problems Lie], February 13, 1979, in 理论工作务虚会简报 [Briefing of the Theory Conference], vol. 218, group 3 (48), for internal circulation only (year and place of publication unknown).

69. Zhu Muzhi (朱穆之), "重新认识三十年来的理论与实践: 看看毛病究竟出在那里?" [Reinvestigate the Theory and Practice of the Past Thirty Years to See Where the Problems Lie], February 13, 1979, in 理论工作务虚会简报.

70. Wu Jiang (吴江), "1979 年理论工作务虚会议追忆—真理标准讨论第二阶段" [Recalling the 1979 Theory Conference: The Second Phase of the Truth Criterion Debate], 炎黄春秋 [China through the Ages], no. 9 (2001), p. 5.

71. Wu, "1979 年理论工作务虚会议追忆," p. 6.

72. Information from interview with Party historians, July 2016.

73. Xiao Donglian (蕭冬連), 歷史的轉軌: 從撥亂反正到改革開放, 1979–1981 [Historical Shifts: From Setting Things Right to the Reform and Opening, 1979–1981] (Hong Kong: 中文大學, 2008), p. 46.

74. Xiao, 歷史的轉軌, pp. 43–44.

75. Chen Jian remembers that in the fall of 1978, when he was an undergraduate student of the "Class of 1977" at East China Normal University (华东师范大学) in Shanghai, he and his fellow students went to the People's Square at the center of the city to participate in these activities. At East China Normal University the students printed and distributed their own journal, *Xin Shixue* (新史学, New History), exploring "truthful history and new scholarship breaking up the old orthodoxies." After publishing two issues, the journal was stopped because of pressure from the university authorities.

76. Zheng Zhongbing (郑仲兵), "胡耀邦与胡乔木: 在历史转折的十字路口" [Hu Yaobang and Hu Qiaomu: At the Crossroads of History's Turning], in Zhang Liqun (張黎群), Zhang Ding (張定), Yan Ruping (嚴如平), and Li Gongtian (李公天), eds., 懷念耀邦 [Remembering Yaobang], vol. 4 (Hong Kong: 亞太國際, 2001).

77. Gao Gao (高皋), 後文革史: 中國自由化潮流 [Post–Cultural Revolution History: The Trend of Liberalization in China], vol. 1 (Taipei: 聯經, 1993), pp. 211–226.

78. DNP-B, vol. 1, pp. 436–437.

79. Hu Yaobang's opening speech at the CCP Theoretical Work Conference, January 18, 1979, copy in authors' possession.

80. Zhuo Renzheng (卓人政), "云南知识青年回城事件与全国知青问题的解决" [The Returning to City Incident of Yunnan's Educated Youth and the Settlement of the Educated Youth Problem in the Whole Country], 中共党史资料 [CCP History Materials], no. 1 (2009), pp. 149–154; Liu Xiaomeng (刘小萌), 中国知青史— 大潮 (1966–1980) [A History of Chinese Educated Youth: Great Waves (1966–1980)] (Beijing: 中国社会科学, 1998), pp. 743–748.

81. See Hu Ping (胡平) and Wang Juntao (王軍濤), 開拓—北大學運文獻 [Opening the Path: Documents of Peking University Student Movement] (Hong Kong: 田園, 1990).

82. Xiao, 歷史的轉軌, pp. 48–54.

83. Exploration Magazine Editorial Office (探索杂志编辑部), 探索 [Exploration], vol. 1 (Beijing: self-published January 1979).

84. Yang Jisheng (楊繼繩), 中國改革年代的政治鬥爭 [China's Political Struggles in the Years of Reform and Opening] (Hong Kong: 特區文化, 2004), pp. 111–112.

85. DWX, vol. 2, pp. 167–171.

86. DWX, vol. 2, p. 172.

87. DWX, vol. 2, pp. 176.

88. Zong Fuxian (宗福先), 于无声处 [In a Land of Silence] (Shanghai: 上海文艺, 1978).

89. Lu Xinhua (卢新华), "伤痕" [Scar], 文汇报 [Wenhui Daily], August 11, 1978.

90. Li Xinyu (李新宇), "1978: 我的梦想与期待" [1978: My Dream and Expectation], in Xiang Jidong (向继东), ed., 革命时代的私人记忆 [Private Memories in a Revolutionary Era] (Guangzhou: 花城, 2010), p. 179.

Chapter 9. Imagining the World

1. This now-famous quote was first recounted by Li Shenzhi (李慎之), who had been Zhou Enlai's diplomatic secretary before being purged as a Rightist in 1957. Li was rehabilitated in 1978 and named vice president of the Chinese Academy of Social Science and director of the academy's Institute of American Studies. He accompanied Deng on the 1979 visit to the United States. Information from an interview with a leading Chinese Party historian, August 2008, corroborated verbatim in an interview with a former high-ranking Chinese diplomat, August 2014.

2. For example, in a speech at a CCP Central Military Commission plenary meeting on December 28, 1977, Deng contended that "the global strategy of the United

States has shifted to the defensive after its defeat in Vietnam" and that the Soviet Union, while on the offensive, "has not finished its expansion of global strategic deployment." *DWX*, vol. 2, p. 77.

3. Mao Zedong (毛泽东), "致阿尔巴尼亚劳动党第五次代表大会的贺电" [Congratulatory Message to the Fifth Congress of the Albanian Party of Labor], October 25, 1966, in *MWG*, vol. 12, pp. 151–153.

4. Wang Taiping (王泰平) et al., 中华人民共和国外交史, 1970–1978 [The Diplomatic History of the People's Republic of China, 1970–1978] (Beijing: 世界知識, 1999), pp. 264–273.

5. Report on the Visit of the CC CCP Chairman and Premier of the PRC State Council Hua Guofeng to the Socialist Federative Republic of Yugoslavia, August 21–29, 1978, AJ, 837, I-3-a, Kina. We are grateful to Jovan Cavoski for sharing this document.

6. Yu Guangyuan (于光远), "我从南斯拉夫访问回来" [I Return from Visiting Yugoslavia] and "关于我国实行经济体制改革的若干建议" [Several Suggestions on Reforming Our Country's Economic Structure and System], in Yu Guangyuan, 于光远改革论集 [A Collection of Yu Guangyuan's Essays on Reforms] (Beijing: 中国发展, 2008). Among these East European economists, János Kornai's *Economics of Shortage* was translated into Chinese and published in 1980 [雅诺什·科尔奈: 短缺经济]. It became extremely influential among Chinese economists and policymakers.

7. Chen Jinghua (陈锦华), 国事忆述 [Recollection of My Experience with State Affairs] (Beijing: 中共党史, 2005), chaps. 1 and 3; Compiling Committee (编辑委员会), 中国对外经济贸易年鉴 (1984) [Chinese Foreign Economy and Trade Yearbook] (Beijing: 中国对外经济贸易, 1984), pp. IV18–IV19.

8. *DNP*-B, vol. 1, p. 305; Qian Zhengying (钱正英), "国门初开时的西欧印象: 回忆 1978 年随团出访西欧五国的经历" [Impression of West Europe at the Time of Our Country's Initial Opening: Recalling the Experience of Visiting Five West European Countries with a Delegation], 党的文献, no. 3 (2010), p. 100; Yang Bo (杨波), "开放前夕的一次重要出访" [An Important Foreign Mission on the Eve of Reform and Opening-up], 百年潮 [One Hundred Year Tide], no. 2 (2002), pp. 4–11.

9. Gu Mu (谷牧), 谷牧回忆录 [Gu Mu's Memoirs] (Beijing: 中央文献, 2014), pp. 314–328.

10. Gu, 谷牧回忆录, pp. 316–317.

11. Gu, 谷牧回忆录, pp. 319–326.

12. Hua Guofeng (华国锋), "在中共十一大上的政治报告" [Political Report at the CCP's Eleventh National Congress], August 12, 1977, *RMRB*, August 23, 1977, pp. 1–6.

13. Chen, 国事忆述, pp. 95–96.

14. Chen, 国事忆述, pp. 123–124.

15. Chen, 国事忆述, pp. 149–151.

16. Han Gang (韩钢), "关于华国锋的若干史实 (续)" [Some Historical Facts about Hua Guofeng, Part 2], 炎黄春秋 [China through the Ages], no. 3 (2011), pp. 10–12; Xiao Donglian (萧冬连), "一九七九年至一九八一年的经济调整研究" [A Study of the Economic Adjustment in 1979–1981], 中共党史研究 [CCP History Studies], no. 9 (2015), pp. 65–79.

17. Ezra Vogel, *Deng Xiaoping and the Transformation of China* (Cambridge, MA: Belknap Press of Harvard University Press, 2011), pp. 219–220.

18. "中国经济代表团访日工作报告" [The Chinese Economic Delegation's Work Report on Its Japan Visit], May 31, 1978, cited in Li Haiwen (李海文), "我们所走过的引进道路" [The Path of Importing Technology That We Have Traveled], 经济导报 [Economic Herald], no. 11 (2018), pp. 91–92; Vogel, *Deng Xiaoping and the Transformation of China*, p. 220.

19. Li, "我们所走过的引进道路," pp. 94–96.

20. Li, "我们所走过的引进道路," pp. 94–96.

21. "政治局听取和讨论赴日经济代表团和赴港澳经济贸易考察组的工作报告" [The Politburo Hearing and Discussing the Work Reports of Economy Delegation That Visited Japan and the Study Group on Economy and Trade in Hong Kong and Macao], June 1 and 3, 1978, in Fang Weizhong (房维中), ed., 在风浪中前进: 中国发展与改革编年纪事 (1977–1989) [Marching Forward in Stormy Waves: Chronological Records of China's Development and Reforms, 1977–1989], vol. 1 (printed for internal circulation, 2004), pp. 103–120.

22. Takashi Oka, "Sino-Japanese Ties Stumble over Shanghai Steel Project," *Christian Science Monitor*, June 11, 1981.

23. Li Lanqing (李岚清), 突围: 国门初开的岁月 [Breaking Through: The Birth of China's Opening-up Policy] (Beijing: 中央文献, 2008), p. 54.

24. Li, 突围, pp. 54–55.

25. Wang Weicheng (王维澄) et al., 李先念年谱 [Chronicle Records of Li Xiannian], vol. 5 (Beijing: 中央文献, 2011), pp. 654–656.

26. See also Frederick C. Teiwes and Warren Sun, "China's New Economic Policy under Hua Guofeng: Party Consensus and Party Myths," *China Journal*, no. 66 (July 1, 2011), pp. 1–23. For an overview of Communist China's strategic foreign policymaking, see Sulmaan Wasif Khan, *Haunted by Chaos: China's Grand Strategy from Mao Zedong to Xi Jinping* (Cambridge, MA: Harvard University Press, 2018).

27. Interview with Party historian, August 2014.

28. Vogel, *Deng Xiaoping and the Transformation of China*, pp. 296–297.

29. Vogel, *Deng Xiaoping and the Transformation of China*, p. 300.

30. Vogel, *Deng Xiaoping and the Transformation of China*, pp. 297–298.

31. Deng's discussion of the issue has since been posted by the Japanese National Press Club, http://www.jnpc.or.jp/archive/conferences/19237/report, accessed February 1, 2023.

32. "Record of Meeting between Prime Minister Fukuda and Vice Premier Deng (Second Meeting)," October 25, 1978, History and Public Policy Program Digital Archive, Diplomatic Archives of the Ministry of Foreign Affairs of Japan, 01-935-2, 016-027 (contributed by Robert Hoppens and translated by Stephen Mercado), https://digitalarchive.wilsoncenter.org/document/120019.

33. Vogel, *Deng Xiaoping and the Transformation of China*, p. 304.

34. Jittipat Poonkham, *A Genealogy of Bamboo Diplomacy: The Politics of Thai Détente with Russia and China* (Canberra: Australian National University Press, 2022), p. 258.

35. Poonkham, *Genealogy of Bamboo Diplomacy*, p. 259.

36. Interview with Zhu Liang (朱良), former chief of the CCP Central Liaison Department, January 2011; and Zhu's written memoir on this episode of history (copy in authors' possession).

37. Kean Fan Lim and Niv Horesh, "The 'Singapore Fever' in China: Policy Mobility and Mutation," *China Quarterly* 228 (December 2016), pp. 992–1017.

38. This account of the Lee–Deng meetings is based on conversations with CCP Party historians, January 2011 and August 2014. See also Lee Kuan Yew, *From Third World to First: The Singapore Story, 1965–2000* (New York: HarperCollins, 2000), pp. 599–600; and Liu Yibing (刘一斌), "中国与新加坡建交的漫长历程" [The Long Journey of Establishing Diplomatic Relations between China and Singapore], 党史博览 [Broad Survey of Party of History], no. 10 (2012), pp. 35–36. (Liu was a senior Chinese diplomat deeply engaged in Southeast Asian affairs at the Chinese Foreign Ministry in the 1970s and 1980s.)

39. Lee, *From Third World to First*, p. 599.

40. Lee, *From Third World to First*, pp. 599–600.

41. *Foreign Relations of the United States* (hereafter *FRUS*), *1977–1980*, vol. XIII (Washington, D.C.: U.S. Government Printing Office, 2013), Doc. 50, pp. 191–207; Huang Hua (黄华), 亲历与见闻: 黄华回忆录 [Personal Experiences and Accounts: Memoir of Huang Hua] (Beijing: 世界知识, 2007), p. 247.

42. *FRUS, 1977–1980*, Docs. 109 and 10, pp. 410–431, 433–447; Huang, 亲历与见闻, p. 248.

43. Gong Li (宫力), 邓小平与中美外交风云 [Deng Xiaoping and Chinese-American Diplomatic Encounters] (Beijing: 红旗, 2015), p. 147.

44. Deng had visited New York in 1974, right after his first rehabilitation, to address the UN General Assembly. But on that occasion the text of his speech had been written under Mao's guidance, and the Left was in overall ascendance in Chinese politics. See Deng Xiaoping, "Speech by Chairman of the Delegation of the People's Republic of China, Deng Xiaoping, at the Special Session of the U.N. General Assembly," April 11, 1974, *RMRB*, April 11, 1974, p. 1.

45. Interview with Chinese Party historian, August 2014.

46. Zbigniew Brzezinski, *Power and Principle: Memoirs of the National Security Adviser* (New York: Farrar, Straus, Giroux, 1983), pp. 405–406; Memorandum from Michel Oksenberg of the National Security Council Staff to the President's Assistant for National Security Affairs (Brzezinski), January 29, 1979, in *FRUS, 1977–1980*, Doc. 201, pp. 738–741.

47. Memorandum of Conversations, President Carter and Vice Premier Deng Xiaoping, January 29, 1979, 12:45–2:00 P.M., 3:35–4:59 P.M., in *FRUS, 1977–1980*, Docs. 203 and 204, pp. 748–755, 755–766.

48. Memorandum of Conversation, President Carter and Vice Premier Deng Xiaoping, January 29, 1979, 5:00–5:40 P.M., in *FRUS, 1977–1980*, Doc. 205, pp. 766–770.

49. Note, President J. Carter to Vice Premier Deng Xiaoping, January 30, 1979, Brezinski File, Box 9: China, Folder: China-President's Meeting with Deng Xiaoping, Jimmy Carter Library, Atlanta, GA; Oral Presentation by President Carter to Chi-

nese Vice Premier Deng Xiaoping, January 30, 1979, in *FRUS, 1977–1980*, Doc. 206, pp. 770–771.

50. Jane Perlez and Grace Tatter, "Shared Secrets: How the U.S. and China Worked Together to Spy on the Soviet Union," Part 4 of "The Great Wager," a podcast describing dramatic changes in U.S.-China relations in the "long 1970s," which includes the story of Deng Xiaoping's visit to CIA headquarters during his 1979 visit to the United States: https://www.wbur.org/hereandnow/2022/02/18/great-wager-spy-soviet-union, accessed February 1, 2023.

51. Vogel, *Deng Xiaoping and the Transformation of China*, pp. 344–345.

52. "Memorandum of Conversation, Zhou Enlai and Le Duan, Beijing, 23 March 1966," in Odd Arne Westad et al., eds., *77 Conversations between Chinese and Foreign Leaders on the Wars in Indochina, 1964–1977*, Working Paper 22 (Washington, D.C.: Cold War International History Project, Woodrow Wilson Center, 1998), p. 91.

53. Minutes of Conversation between Deng Xiaoping and Le Duan, September 29, 1975, https://digitalarchive.wilsoncenter.org/document/minutes-conversation-between-deng-xiaoping-and-le-duan, accessed February 1, 2023.

54. Information gained from a renowned Chinese military historian; Zhang Xiaoming, *Deng Xiaoping's Long War: The Military Conflict between China and Vietnam, 1979–1991* (Chapel Hill: University of North Carolina Press, 2015), the author (a military historian), citing one of Ye Jianying's relatives as the source, claims that Ye "opposed Deng's decision to use military force against the SRV (Socialist Republic of Vietnam)" (pp. 53–54).

55. As experienced by both authors, throughout the 1980s popular literature, movies, and music in China extolled PLA soldiers' heroic fighting against the ungrateful Vietnamese in a "war of self-defense." The war against Vietnam joined as a theme in the CCP's campaigns for promoting "love of the socialist motherland," helping its leadership cope with the legitimacy challenge that it faced after the Cultural Revolution.

56. Zhang, *Deng Xiaoping's Long War,* pp. 118–119.

57. Deng Xiaoping (邓小平), "在京党、政、军副部长以上干部大会报告记录" [Report at a Conference Attended by Party, Government and Military Cadres above the Level of Vice Ministers], 91-012-001, GSPA, pp. 19–20.

58. Ni Chuanghui (倪創輝), *十年中越戰爭* [The Ten-Year War between China and Vietnam], vol. 2 (Hong Kong: 天行健, 2009), pp. 574–575.

59. Wang Zhijun (王志軍), *1979 對越戰爭親歷記* [Personal Experience in the Chinese-Vietnamese War of 1979] (Hong Kong: 星克爾, 2000), p. 221.

60. Deng, "在京党、政、军副部长以上干部大会报告记录," p. 16.

61. Frank Van der Linden, *The Real Reagan: What He Believes; What He Has Accomplished; What We Can Expect from Him* (New York: William Morrow, 1981), p. 157.

62. "The U.S.-China Communiqué on Arms Sales to Taiwan, August 17, 1982," https://history.state.gov/milestones/1981-1988/china-communique.

63. "President Ronald Reagan's Six Assurances to Taiwan, July 1982," https://crsreports .congress.gov/product/pdf/IF/IF11665.

64. Dai Bingguo (戴秉国), 战略对话: 戴秉国回忆录 [Strategic Dialogue: Dai Bingguo's Memoirs] (Beijing: 人民, 2016), p. 39; Qian Qichen (钱其琛), 外交十记 [Ten Episodes in Chinese Diplomacy] (Beijing: 世界知识, 2003), pp. 6–7.

65. *DWX*, vol. 3, p. 127.

66. Dai, 战略对话, p. 39.

67. Qi Pengfei (齐鹏飞), 邓小平与香港回归 [Deng Xiaoping and the Return of Hong Kong] (Beijing: 华夏, 2004), p. 56; Vogel, *Deng Xiaoping and the Transformation of China*, p. 488. For an overview, see Chi-Kwan Mark, "Crisis or Opportunity? Britain, China, and the Decolonization of Hong Kong in the Long 1970s," in Priscilla Roberts and Odd Arne Westad, eds., *China, Hong Kong, and the Long 1970s: Global Perspectives* (London: Palgrave Macmillan, 2017), pp. 257–277.

68. *DNP-B*, vol. 1, pp. 500–501.

69. "Record of a discussion between the Prime Minister and Premier Hua Guofeng at 10 Downing Street on 29 October [1979] at 1500 hours," PREM 19/3, UKNA.

70. Interview with Zhu Liang (former head of CCP Central Liaison Department), January 2011; Chin Peng (陈平), *My Side of History: Recollections of the Guerrilla Leader Who Waged a 12-Year Anti-Colonial War against Britain and Commonwealth Forces in the Jungles of Malaya* (Singapore: Media Masters, 2003), pp. 456–459.

71. Deng Xiaoping (鄧小平), "鄧小平等關於'一國兩制'的論述選載" [Selected Essays by Deng Xiaoping on "One Country, Two Systems"], 党的文献 [Party History Documents], no. 1 (1992), p. 15.

72. The first united front between the CCP and the Guomindang existed in 1923–1927; the second existed in 1937–1945.

73. Huang Xiurong (黄修荣), 国共关系七十年 [Seven Decades of Relations between the CCP and the Guomindang] (Guangzhou: 广东教育, 1998), p. 1773.

74. "中华人民共和国全国人大常委会告台湾同胞书" [The Standing Committee of the National People's Congress's Letter to Compatriots in Taiwan], *RMRB*, January 1, 1979, p. 1.

75. "邓小平副总理在华盛顿重申中国希望和平解决台湾问题" [Vice Premier Deng Xiaoping Reiterates in Washington that China Hopes to Peacefully Resolve the Taiwan Question], *RMRB*, February 1, 1979, p. 1.

76. "叶剑英委员长进一步阐明台湾回归祖国实现和平统一的方针政策建议举行两党对等谈判实行第三次合作" [Chairman Ye Jianying Further Clarified the Principles and Policies of Taiwan's Return to the Motherland to Achieve Peaceful Reunification, with the Recommendation to Hold Bipartisan Reciprocal Negotiations to Implement the Third CCP-Guomindang Cooperation], *RMRB*, October 1, 1981, p. 1.

Chapter 10. A New China

1. The best discussion of this period in Chinese history is Julian B. Gewirtz, *Never Turn Back: China and the Forbidden History of the 1980s* (Cambridge, MA: Belknap Press of Harvard University Press, 2022).

2. In 1979 protests and demonstrations happened in many different parts of China, which the CCP leadership called "creating disturbances." In February–August, *Renmin Ribao* published thirty-two articles to criticize such phenomena.

3. For example, on May 4, 1979, Deng Xiaoping told Malaysian prime minister Hussein Onn: "The Chinese economy is underdeveloped, and its technologies are backward." The next day, in meeting a French defense delegation, Deng said: "You are quite advanced in modernization of national defense. . . . and we have lagged behind. There are many things that we should learn from you." See *DNP*-B, vol. 1, pp. 510–511.

4. Deng Xiaoping (邓小平), "坚持四项基本原则" [Adhere to Four Cardinal Principles], March 30, 1979, *DWX*, vol. 2, pp. 168–169, 180.

5. See Deng's discussion about the need to suppress "anti-Party" elements; for examples, see *DWX*, vol. 2, pp. 148, 192–193.

6. One of the sources of inspiration for Zhao's early economic reform in Sichuan was Yugoslavia, which he had visited with Hua Guofeng in August 1978. See "Report on the Visit of the Political Delegation of the League of Communists of Yugoslavia to the PRC on November 12–19, 1979," Архив Југославије [Archives of Yugoslavia], Belgrade, CK SKJ, 507/IX, 60/I-106.

7. "北京国际足球友好邀请赛闭幕" [Conclusion of the Beijing International Football Friendship Tournament], *RMRB*, July 31, 1977, p. 1.

8. Qi Zhang and Mingxing Liu, *Revolutionary Legacy, Power Structure, and Grassroots Capitalism under the Red Flag in China* (Cambridge: Cambridge University Press, 2019), p. 234.

9. Xu Qingquan (徐庆全) and Du Mingming (杜明明), "包产到户提出过程中的高层争论: 访国家农业委员会原副主任杜润生" [Disputes among Top Leaders during the Introduction of Linking Output with Household Incomes: Interview with former Director of State Agricultural Committee du Runsheng], 炎黄春秋 [China through the Ages], no. 11 (2008), p. 1.

10. The dispute was triggered by a letter by Zhang Hao (张浩) that was published in *RMRB*, March 15, 1979, p. 1. For a detailed discussion of the event and its impact, see Yang Jisheng (楊繼繩), 中國改革年代的政治鬥爭 [China's Political Struggles in the Years of Reform and Opening] (Hong Kong: 特區文化, 2004), pp. 180–183.

11. Barry Naughton, *The Chinese Economy: Transitions and Growth* (Cambridge, MA: MIT Press, 2007), pp. 235–236.

12. *DNP*-B, vol. 1, pp. 615–616; *DWX*, vol. 2, pp. 315–317.

13. 赵紫阳给万里的信 [Zhao Ziyang's Letter to Wan Li], June 9, 1980; see Institute of CCP History Research in Inner Mongolian Autonomous Region (中共内蒙古自治区委党史研究室), eds., 中国新时期的农村变革 (中央卷) [Rural Transformation in China's New Era (Central Level Volume)], vol. 1 (Beijing: 中共党史, 2004), p. 93; Wu Xiang (吴象), "胡耀邦与万里在农村改革中" [Hu Yaobang and Wan Li in Rural Reforms], 炎黄春秋 [China through the Ages], no. 7 (2001), p. 15.

14. The term "Little Gang of Four" was never used as an official castigation of these CCP leaders but was widely employed among some CCP cadre. See Su Shaozhi (苏绍智), "超越党文化的思想樊篱—我如何在八十年代由马克思主义信仰者转变为研究者"

[Beyond the Ideological Barriers of Party Culture—How I Transformed from a Marxist Believer to a Researcher of Marxism in the 1980s], 当代中国研究 [Contemporary China Studies], no. 2 (2007), pp. 4–57.

15. Deng Xiaoping (邓小平), "目前的形势和任务" [Current Situation and Tasks], in *DWX*, vol. 2, pp. 252–254.

16. Deng, "目前的形势和任务," pp. 258, 263, 268, 270.

17. By far the best overview of the fall of Hua Guofeng is Joseph Torigian, *Prestige, Manipulation, and Coercion: Elite Power Struggles in the Soviet Union and China after Stalin and Mao* (New Haven, CT: Yale University Press, 2022), pp. 136–192.

18. Deng Liqun (邓力群), "'关于建国以来党的若干历史问题的决议'起草过程和主要内容的介绍: 在驻京部队师以上干部会议上的讲话" ["Resolution on Certain Questions in the History of Our Party since the Founding of the People's Republic of China": Speech at the Meeting of Cadres at the Division Level and above in the Troops Stationed in Beijing], July 1981, 89. Available in the Fairbank Center Collection, H. C. Fung Library, Harvard University, quoted from Torigian, *Prestige, Manipulation, and Coercion*, chap. 5 n129.

19. Deng Xiaoping, "On the Reform of the System of Party and State Leadership, August 18, 1980," in *Selected Works of Deng Xiaoping*, vol. 2 (Beijing: Foreign Language Press, 1994), pp. 319–341.

20. See Liu Jixian (刘继贤), et al., 叶剑英年谱 (1897–1986) [Chronological Records of Ye Jianying, 1897–1986], vol. 2 (Beijing: 中央文献, 2007), pp. 1191, 1195–1196.

21. For an excellent summary of the criticism that Hua had encountered, see Han Gang (韩钢), "关于华国锋的若干史实" [Some Historical Facts about Hua Guofeng], 炎黄春秋 [China through the Ages], no. 2 (2011), pp. 9–18.

22. CCP Central Committee (中共中央), "转发中央常委在十一届六中全会期间召开各组召集人会议上的讲话" [Conveying Speeches of Politburo Standing Committee Members at Meetings of Group Conveners during the Sixth Plenary Session of the Eleventh Central Committee], June 23, 1981, *ZGWGWK*.

23. Hua retired peacefully to the Beijing suburbs, where his main hobby for the remaining almost thirty years of his long life would be to grow grapes on a plot behind his house. "If the party had had another internal struggle," he told a historian many years later, "ordinary people would have suffered. I unwaveringly resigned from all positions. I told Marshal Ye before I did it. Some said that I was a fool. Some said that I was too honest. I do not regret any of it." See Li Haiwen (李海文), "华国锋谈史传写作" [Hua Guofeng Discusses the Writing of History], 炎黄春秋 [China through the Ages], no. 4 (2015), p. 7.

24. Hu Yaobang (胡耀邦), 胡耀邦文选 [Selected Works of Hu Yaobang] (Beijing: 人民, 2015), pp. 261–263.

25. Xiao Donglian (萧冬连), 历史的转轨: 從撥亂反正到改革開放, 1979–1981 [Historical Shifts: From Setting Things Right to the Reform and Opening, 1979–1981] (Hong Kong: 中文大學, 2008), pp. 396–397.

26. Wu Jianhua (武健华), "详忆粉碎'四人帮'的前前后后" [Remembering Smashing the Gang of Four, with Details], part 3, 百年潮 [One Hundred Year Tide], no. 12 (2012), p. 22.

27. Yu Guangyuan (于光远), 十一届三中全会的台前幕后: *1978: 我亲历的那次历史大转折* [On the Stage and behind the Scenes of the Third Plenum of the Eleventh Central Committee: The Historical Transition That I Personally Experienced in 1978] (Beijing: 中央编译, 2008), chap. 8, parts 1 and 2; Editorial Group of Peng Zhen Biography (彭真传编写组), 彭真传 [A Biography of Peng Zhen], vol. 4 (Beijing: 中央文献出版社, 2012), pp. 1367–1368.

28. Fei Xiaotong (费孝通), "一个审判员的感受" [The Feeling of a Judge], in *历史的审判: 审判林彪、江青反革命集团案犯纪实* [The Trial of History: A Factual Record of the Trials of the Criminals of the Lin Biao and Jiang Qing Counter-Revolutionary Cliques] (Beijing: 群众, 2000); Zheng Shanlong (郑善龙), "从东京审判到审判'四人帮'" [From the Tokyo Trial to the Trial of the "Gang of Four"], *世纪* [Century], no. 3 (2007), pp. 56–61.

29. Wang Wenzheng (王文正) and Shen Guofan (沈国凡), *共和国大审判: 审判林彪、江青反革命集团亲历记* [The Great Trial in the Republic: Personal Experiences of the Trials of the Ling Biao and Jiang Qing Counter-Revolutionary Cliques] (Beijing: 当代中国, 2006), pp. 275–278, 308.

30. Bo Yibo (薄一波), "关于整党的基本总结和进一步加强党的建设" [A Basic Summary of the Rectification of the Party and Further Enhancing Party Construction], *RMRB*, June 1, 1987, p. 1.

31. Information from Party historians. Reportedly, there were two other known assassination attempts against Deng in the 1980s. One was in Beijing's Haidian district in September 1982, right after the CCP's Twelfth Congress. The other was at the Xijiao guesthouse (西郊宾馆) in Shanghai in February 1988.

32. "On Questions of Party History: Resolution on Certain Questions in the History of Our Party since the Founding of the People's Republic of China," *Beijing Review*, no. 27 (1981), pp. 20–23.

33. "On Questions of Party History," p. 29.

34. "On Questions of Party History," pp. 25–26.

35. Deng Xiaoping (邓小平), "前十年为后十年做好准备" [Preparing the First Decade for the Next], October 14, 1982, *DWX*, vol. 3, pp. 16–18.

36. Zhao Ziyang (趙紫陽), "從提高經濟效益中找出路, 從挖掘潛力中求速度" [Find a Way out from Improving Economic Benefits, Seek Speed from Tapping Potential] and "千方百計使農業生產有較大發展" [Try Everything Possible to Achieve Greater Development in Agricultural Production], in Editorial Group of Zhao Ziyang's Works (趙紫陽文集編輯組), *趙紫陽文集 (1980–1989)* [A Collection of Zhao Ziyang's Works, 1980–1989], Sichuan Volume (Hong Kong: 中文大學, 2016), pp. 229–232.

37. Du Runsheng (杜润生), "土地家庭承包制的兴起" [The Rise of the Land Household Responsibility System], *中国合作经济* [China's Collective Economy], no. 10 (2008), pp. 45–49.

38. Du, "土地家庭承包制的兴起," pp. 50–51.

39. Ezra F. Vogel, *One Step ahead in China: Guangdong under Reform 1990* (Cambridge, MA: Harvard University Press, 1990).

40. Lu Di (卢荻), "习仲勋与广东反'偷渡外逃" [Xi Zhongxun and Smuggling and Fleeing abroad in Guangdong], *百年潮* [One Hundred Year Tide], no. 10 (2007), pp. 20–27;

see also Wang Shuo (王硕), "逃港潮与相关政策变迁" [The Waves of People Fleeing to Hong Kong and Related Policy Changes], 炎黄春秋, no. 1 (2011), pp. 51–56.

41. Editorial Committee of Xi Zhongxun Biography (习仲勋传编委会), 习仲勋传 [A Biography of Xi Zhongxun] (Beijing: 中央文献, 2013); for Xi's ideas about transforming Guangdong, see Xi Zhongxun (习仲勋), "广东的建设如何大干快上" [How to Substantively and Quickly Construct Guangdong], November 8, 1978, in Xi Zhongxun, 习仲勋文选 [Selected Works of Xi Zhongxun] (Beijing: 中央文献, 1995), pp. 274–285.

42. Teiwes and Sun point out, correctly, that Hua Guofeng chaired the April 1979 meeting when setting up a special zone in Guangdong was first discussed, but party historians insist that it was in a subsequent meeting with Deng that final instructions were given and the term coined. See Frederick C. Teiwes and Warren Sun, "China's New Economic Policy under Hua Guofeng: Party Consensus and Party Myths," *China Journal,* no. 66 (2011), pp. 1–23.

43. See Editorial Committee of Xi Zhongxun in Charge of Guangdong (习仲勋主政广东编委会), 习仲勋主政广东 [Xi Zhongxun in Charge of Guangdong] (Beijing: 中共党史, 2007).

44. Zhang Zehan (张泽晗), "正大集团: 与开放的中国共同成长: 访正大集团农牧食品企业中国区资深副董事长谢毅文" [Charoen Pokphand Group: Growing up along with China's Opening-up: An Interview with Xie Yiwen, Senior Vice Chairman of CP Group's Agriculture, Animal Husbandry and Food Operations in China], 经济 [Economy], no. 8 (2019), pp. 8–11.

45. Guangdong Archive Bureau (广东省档案局), eds., 改革开放三十年重要档案文献·广东(上) [Important Archival Documents in the Thirty Years of Reform and Opening-up (Guangdong)], vol. 1 (Beijing: 中國檔案, 2008), pp. 15–16.

46. Vogel, *One Step ahead in China*, p. 2.

47. Tian Guoqiang (田国强), "中国乡村企业的产权结构及其改革" [Property Rights Structure of China's Township-Village Enterprises and Its Reform], 经济研究 [Economics Studies], no. 3 (1995), pp. 35–39; M. L. Weitzman and C. Xu, "Chinese Township-Village Enterprises as Vaguely Defined Cooperatives," *Journal of Contemporary Economics,* no. 18 (1994), pp. 121–145.

48. Aart Kraay, "Household Saving in China," *World Bank Economic Review,* 14, no. 3 (2000), table A-II, p. 567.

49. For relevant statistics, see Tao Chunfang (陶春芳) and Gao Xiaoxian (高小贤), eds., 中国妇女统计资料 (1949–1989) [Statistical Materials about Chinese Women (1949–1989)] (Beijing: 中国统计, 1991), pp. 318–319.

50. Yong Cai and Feng Wang, "The Social and Sociological Consequences of China's One-Child Policy," *Annual Review of Sociology,* no. 47 (July 2021), pp. 587–606; Sun Yi (孙 伊), "中国女性在家庭中的地位和权利" [The Position and Rights of Chinese Women in the Family] 当代中国研究 [Modern China Studies], no. 4 (2005).

51. Xue Muqiao (薛暮桥), 薛暮桥文集 [A Collection of Xue Muqiao's Works] (Beijing: 中国金融, 2011), p. 58; see also the opinions of Fang Weizhong (房维中), representing the Group on Studying Reform of Economic System (经济体制改革研究小组), about the need of "conducting systematic study of reforms of economic systems

in Yugoslavia, Romania, the Soviet Union, and, especially, Hungary." Economic Group in the Research Office of the CCP Central Secretariat (中共中央书记处研究室经济组), eds., 经济问题研究资料 [Research Materials of Economic Issues, 1979] (Beijing: 中国财政经济, 1984), pp. 34–35.

52. Han Shufang (韩淑芳), 口述: 创业的故事 [Oral Stories of Entrepreneurship] (Beijing: 中国文史, 2018), pp. 9–21.

53. Han Shufang (韩淑芳), 口述: 破冰的故事 [Oral Stories of Icebreakers] (Beijing: 中国文史, 2018), pp. 114–120.

54. For an overview in English, see Naughton, *Chinese Economy*, pp. 282–284.

55. Xin Wang (新望) and Liu Qihong (刘奇洪), "苏南、温州、珠江模式之反思" [Reflection on the Sunan, Wenzhou, and Pear River Models], 中国国情国力 [China's National Situation and National Power], no. 7 (2001), pp. 4–8; Xie Jian (谢健), "区域经济国际化: 珠三角模式、苏南模式、温州模式的比较" [Internationalization of Regional Economies: A Comparison of Pearl Delta Model, the Sunan Model, and the Wenzhou Model], 经济理论与经济管理 [Economic Theory and Economic Management], no. 10 (2006), pp. 47–51; Song Linfei (宋林飞), "中国'三大模式'的创新与未来" [The Innovation and Future of China's "Three Big Models"], 南京社会科学 [Nanjing Social Science], no. 5 (2009), pp. 1–6.

56. Deng Xiaoping (邓小平), "中国共产党第十二次全国代表大会开幕词" [Speech at the Opening Session of the Twelfth National Congress of the Chinese Communist Party], September 1, 1982, in *DWX*, vol. 3, pp. 1–4.

Chapter 11. To the Point of No Return?

1. According to the data provided by the World Bank, China's annual GDP growth rate from the late 1970s to 1988 (the year before the Tiananmen tragedy) was as follows: 1978, 11.3%; 1979, 7.6%; 1980, 7.8%; 1981, 5.1%; 1982, 9%; 1983, 10.8%; 1984, 15.2%; 1985, 13.4%; 1986, 8.9%; 1987, 11.7%; 1988, 11.2%. https://data.worldbank.org.cn/indicator/NY.GDP.MKTP.KD.ZG?locations=CN, accessed April 10, 2023.

2. *DNP*-B, vol. 2, pp. 939–940.

3. Li Rui (李锐), "耀邦去世前的谈话" [Yaobang's Conversation before His Passing], 当代中国研究 [Modern China Studies], no. 4 (2001).

4. Hu Yaobang (胡耀邦), "马克思主义伟大真理的光芒照耀我们前进" [The Light of the Great Truth of Marxism Has Brightened Our March Forward], *RMRB*, March 14, 1983, p. 1.

5. Zhao Ziyang et al., *Prisoner of the State: The Secret Journal of Zhao Ziyang* (New York: Simon & Schuster, 2009), p. 91.

6. Zhao was also fascinated with how foreign knowledge could help China plan for the future; see Julian Gewirtz, "The Futurists of Beijing: Alvin Toffler, Zhao Ziyang, and China's 'New Technological Revolution,' 1979–1991," *Journal of Asian Studies* 78, no. 1 (February 2019), pp. 115–140.

7. Xiao Donglian (萧冬连), 历史的轉軌: 從撥亂反正到改革開放, 1979–1981 [Historical Shifts: From Setting Things Right to the Reform and Opening, 1979–1981] (Hong Kong: 中文大學, 2008), p. 778.

8. Lu Di (卢荻) and Liu Kunyi (刘坤仪), "任仲夷主政广东" [Ren Zhongyi in Charge of Guangdong], 百年潮 [One Hundred Year Tide], no. 4 (2000), pp. 4–10.

9. Zhuo Changren (卓长仁) was eventually given political asylum in Taiwan, where he committed another kidnapping and murder, and was executed in 2001 ("Erstwhile 'Patriots' Put to Death for 1991 Murder," *Taipei Times*, August 11, 2001).

10. Gao Long (高龙) and Han Fudong (韩福东), "1983 年'严打'内幕: 2.4万人被处决" [Inside the "Strike Hard" Campaign of 1983: 24,000 People Executed], 南方都市报 [Southern Metropolis Daily], December 11, 2013, http://w.hybsl.cn/article/13/43590.

11. Deng Xiaoping (邓小平), "严厉打击刑事犯罪活动" [Crack Down on Crime], July 19, 1983, *DWX*, vol. 3, pp. 33–34; see also He Libo (何立波), "1983: 党中央决策'严打'始末" [The Whole Process of the Party Center's Making of the "Strike Hard" Decision in 1983], 检察风云 [Prosecutorial View], no. 17 (2008), pp. 66–68; Cui Min (崔敏), "反思八十年代的'严打'" [Reflection on the "Strike Hard" Campaign of the 1980s], 炎黄春秋 [China through the Ages], no. 5 (2012), pp. 16–22.

12. "案例: 强奸-流氓犯陈小蒙、胡晓阳、葛志文在上海被枪决" [The Case: Convicted Criminals for Raping and Hooliganism Chen Xiaomeng, Hu Xiaoyang, and Ge Zhiwen Were Executed in Shanghai], 中国年鉴 [China Yearbook], 1987, pp. 163–164; Gao Long (高龙), "名门之后朱国华的死刑" [The Death Penalty of Zhu Guohua, Descendant of an Eminent Family], 云南信息报 [Yunnan Information Daily], January 18, 2015.

13. For Deng Liqun's account of the Anti–Spiritual Pollution Campaign, see Deng Liqun (邓力群), 邓力群自述: 十二個春秋, 1975–1987 [Deng Liqun's Autobiography: Twelve Springs and Autumns, 1975–1987] (Hong Kong: 博智, 2006), pp. 261–323.

14. Zhao, *Prisoner of the State*, pp. 162–165.

15. Information from interviews with Party historians, April 2019.

16. Deng, 邓力群自述, p. 338.

17. Zhao, *Prisoner of the State*, p. 164.

18. Deng, 邓力群自述, pp. 322–323; information from a roundtable with a group of leading Party historians, October 2023.

19. Shen Xinshu and Zhao Fuyuan, "Audience Reaction to Commercial Advertising in China in the 1980s," *International Journal of Advertising* 14, no. 4 (1995), pp. 374–390. See also Richard W. Pollay, David K. Tse, and Zheng-yuan Wang, "Advertising, Propaganda, and Value Change in Economic Development: The New Culture Revolution in China and Attitudes toward Advertising," *Journal of Business Research* 20, no. 2 (1990), pp. 83–95.

20. Jeffrey R. Taylor and Karen A. Hardee, *Consumer Demand in China: A Statistical Factbook* (Boulder, CO: Westview Press, 1986), p. 39.

21. Wu Xiaobo (吴晓波), 激荡三十年: 中国企业, 1978–2008 (上) [Thirty Years of Chinese Enterprises, 1978–2008], vol. 1 (Beijing: 中信, 2008), p. 140.

22. It was not only material goods that were in demand. Fortune-telling as a profession flourished again; see Emily Baum, "Enchantment in an Age of Reform: Fortune-Telling Fever in Post-Mao China, 1980s–1990s," *Past & Present* 251, no. 1 (May 1, 2021), pp. 229–261.

23. Mark Landler, "In China, a Management Maverick Builds a Brand," *New York Times,* July 23, 2000, p. BU4.

24. Laurie Burkitt, "China's Haier to Buy GE Appliance Business for $5.4 Billion," *Wall Street Journal,* January 15, 2016.

25. For a brief summary, see the discussion of Wang Shi and Vanke in Jeffrey Alan Towson and Jonathan R. Woetzel, *The 1 Hour China Book: Two Peking University Professors Explain All of China Business in Six Short Stories* (Cayman Islands: Towson Group, 2017).

26. Zeng Zhaohua (曾昭华), 柳传志如是说 [Liu Chuanzhi Tells His Own Story This Way] (Beijing: 中国经济, 2008).

27. Xu Zhiyuan (许知远), "流亡的里程碑" [A Milestone of Exile], *FT中文网* [Financial Times Chinese], February 13, 2014, https://ftchinese.com/story/001054805?full=y&archive.

28. Zhu Wenyi (朱文轶), "李经纬事件调查" [Invesgating the Li Jingwei Case], 三联生活周刊 [Life Weekly], no. 43 (2002), https://www.lifeweek.com.cn/article/46795.

29. Charles Kraus, "More than Just a Soft Drink: Coca-Cola and China's Early Reform and Opening," *Diplomatic History* 43, no. 1 (2019), pp. 107–129.

30. Scott Cendrowski, "Opening Happiness: An Oral History of Coca-Cola in China," September 11, 2014, https://fortune.com/2014/09/11/opening-happiness-an-oral-history-of-coca-cola-in-china/.

31. *The Volkswagen Group Sustainability Report 2022,* https://www.volkswagen-group.com/en/reporting-15808?node=41261, accessed September 15, 2023.

32. Note on President Reagan's meeting with National Security Council, September 20, 1983, https://www.reaganlibrary.gov/public/2020-12/40-315-12026384-R14-059-2020.pdf.

33. Gong Li (宫力), 邓小平与中美外交风云 [Deng Xiaoping and Chinese-American Diplomatic Encounters] (Beijing: 红旗, 2015), pp. 290–297.

34. Ronald Reagan, "Remarks upon Returning from China," May 1, 1984, https://www.reaganlibrary.gov/archives/speech/remarks-upon-returning-china.

35. Information from a roundtable with a group of leading Chinese Party historians, October 2022.

36. "Cable from Ambassador Katori to the Foreign Minister, 'Prime Minister Visit to China (Conversation with Chairman Deng Xiaoping),'" March 25, 1984, History and Public Policy Program Digital Archive, http://digitalarchive.wilsoncenter.org/document/118849; Deng Xiaoping (邓小平), "发展中日关系要看得远些" (We Should Take a Longer-Range View in Developing Sino-Japanese Relations), March 25, 1984, *DWX,* vol. 3, pp. 53–55.

37. "Cable from Ambassador Katori to the Foreign Minister."

38. "Cable from Ambassador Katori to the Foreign Minister."

39. "Cable from Ambassador Katori to the Foreign Minister."

40. Ye Min, "Policy Learning or Diffusion: How China Opened to Foreign Direct Investment," *Journal of East Asian Studies* 9, no. 3 (2009), pp. 399–432.

41. Carrington–Deng conversation, FCO telegram, April 3, 1981, FCO 40/1274/5/6, UKNA.

42. Deng Xiaoping (邓小平), "我们对香港问题的基本立场" [Our Basic Position on the Question of Hong Kong], *DWX*, vol. 3, pp. 12–15; "China: No. 10 Record of Conversation (MT-Vice Chairman Deng Xiaoping of China) [Future of Hong Kong]" [declassified 2013], https://www.margaretthatcher.org/document/128402, accessed April 10, 2023.

43. "China: No. 10 Record of Conversation," pp. 5–6.

44. "Joint Declaration of the Government of the United Kingdom of Great Britain and Northern Ireland and the Government of the People's Republic of China on the Question of Hong Kong," December 19, 1984, https://treaties.un.org/Pages/show Details.aspx?objid=08000002800d4d6e.

45. Though we have never been able to establish the connection to Marx, the idea may come from a footnote in which Marx writes about piano makers as productive workers. See Karl Marx, *The Grundrisse*, ed. and trans. David McLellan (New York: Harper & Row, 1971), p. 79n1.

46. Xu Miaozhong (徐森忠), "深圳特区的居民消费结构及其发展趋势" [The Consumption Structure of Residents in Shenzhen Special Economic Zone and Its Development Trend], 消费经济 [Consumer Economy], no. 1 (1986), pp. 52–57.

47. Chen Yizi (陳一諮), 陳一諮回憶錄 [Memoirs of Chen Yizi: China's Reform in the 1980s] (Hong Kong: 新世紀出版及傳媒有限公司, 2013), p. 318.

48. Chen, 陳一諮回憶錄, pp. 313–314.

49. CCP Central Committee (中共中央), "关于经济体制改革的决定" [Resolution on the Reform of the Economic System], October 20, 1984, *RMRB*, October 21, 1984, p.1.

50. On how to create the necessary growth, Zhao's associates often listened to foreign advisers, such as at the conference of economists held onboard the cruise liner *Bashan* in September 1985; see Julian B. Gewirtz, *Never Turn Back: China and the Forbidden History of the 1980s* (Cambridge, MA: Belknap Press of Harvard University Press, 2022), pp. 95–96.

51. Hu Deping (胡德平), 中國為什麼要改革: 回憶父親胡耀邦 [Why Reforms Are Necessary for China: Remembering My Father Hu Yaobang] (Hong Kong: 中和, 2011).

52. Zhao, *Prisoner of the State*, p. 164.

53. Xu Xiaoping (徐小平) and Wu Miaolin (吴妙琳), "小平您好: 知识分子的心声" [Hello Xiaoping! The Intellectuals' Heartfelt Voice], *RMRB*, October 3, 1984, p. 3.

Conclusion

1. "Number of Millionaires in Mainland China from 2015 to 2022," Statista, https://www.statista.com/statistics/702759/china-number-of-millionaires/, accessed January 22, 2024.

2. Li Haiwen (李海文), "华国锋谈史传写作" [Hua Guofeng Discusses the Writing of History], 炎黄春秋 [China through the Ages], no. 4 (2015), p. 7.

3. 人民网 (People's Daily On-Line), "简单的晚年生活 华国锋远离政治的日子" [A Simple Life in Late Years: Hua Guofeng's Days Away from Politics], https://news.ifeng.com/mainland/200809/0921_17_795678.shtml, accessed July 12, 2023.

4. "To jump into the sea" also had more derogatory connotations, often used in the past about those who sought money illicitly, including prostitutes; for a discussion, see Jos Gamble, *Shanghai in Transition: Changing Perspectives and Social Contours of a Chinese Metropolis* (London: Routledge, 2005), pp. 38–39.

5. Louisa Lim, *The People's Republic of Amnesia: Tiananmen Revisited* (New York: Oxford University Press, 2014).

SOURCES CITED

Archives and Documentary Database

Carter Presidential Library
Chinese Central Archive
中国文化大革命文库 [The Chinese Cultural Revolution Database]
Ford Presidential Library
Gansu Provincial Archive
Hebei Provincial Archive
Hubei Provincial Archive
Japanese National Press Club Archive
National Archives of the United Kingdom
National Security Archive (Washington, DC)
Nixon Presidential Library
Reagan Presidential Library
Shanghai Municipal Archive
Woodrow Wilson Center Digital Archive

Published and Unpublished Documentary Collections

理论工作务虚会简报 [Briefing of the Theory Conference]. Vol. 218 (for international circulation only). Year and place of publication unknown.

CCP Central Institute of Historical Documents Studies (中共中央文献研究室), ed. 毛泽东文集 [A Collection of Works of Mao Zedong]. Beijing: 人民, 1996.

CCP Central Institute of Historical Documents Studies (中共中央文献研究室), ed. 三中全会以来重要文献选编 [Important Documents since the Third Plenum]. Beijing: 人民, 1982.

CCP Central Institute of Historical Documents Studies (中共中央文献研究室), eds. 周恩来经济文选 [Selected Economic Works of Zhou Enlai]. Beijing: 中央文献, 1993.

Chinese Academy of Social Science (中国社会科学院) and Chinese Central Archive (中央档案馆), eds. *中华人民共和国经济档案资料选编 1960–1965 (外贸卷)* [Selected Archival Materials about the Economy of People's Republic of China, 1960–1965 (Foreign Trade Volume)]. Beijing: 中国财政经济, 2011.

Chinese Central Archive (中央档案馆), ed. *共和国五十年珍贵档案* [Valuable Archives of the People's Republic of China]. Vol. 2. Beijing: 中国档案, 1999.

Chinese Central Archive (中央档案馆) and CCP Central Institute of Historical Documents Studies (中共中央文献研究室), eds. *中共中央档选集, 1949.10–1966.5* [Selected Documents of the CCP Central Committee, October 1949 to May 1966]. Vol. 14. Beijing: 人民, 2013.

中国共产党第十一届中央委员会第三次全体会议公报 [Communiqué of the Third Plenary Session of the Eleventh Central Committee of the Communist Party of China]. http://cpc.people.com.cn/GB/64162/64168/64563/65371/4441902.html, accessed March 5, 2023.

Compiling Committee (编辑委员会). *中国对外经济贸易年鉴 (1984)* [China Foreign Economic and Trade Yearbook (1984)]. Beijing: 中国对外经济贸易, 1984.

Deng Xiaoping. "On the Reform of the System of Party and State Leadership, August 18, 1980." In *Selected Works of Deng Xiaoping*, vol. 2. Beijing: Foreign Language Press, 1994, pp. 319–341.

Deng Xiaoping (邓小平). "邓小平等关于 '一国两制' 的论述选载" [Selected Essays by Deng Xiaoping on "One Country, Two Systems"]. 党的文献 [Party History Documents], no. 1 (1992).

Deng Xiaoping (邓小平). *邓小平文选* [Selected Works of Deng Xiaoping]. Beijing: 人民, 1993.

Economic Group in the Research Office of the CCP Central Secretariat (中共中央书记处研究室经济组), eds. *经济问题研究资料* [Research Materials of Economic Issues, 1979]. Beijing: 中国财政经济, 1984.

Editorial Group of Zhao Ziyang's Works (趙紫陽文集編輯組). *趙紫陽文集 (1975–1980), 四川卷* [A Collection of Zhao Ziyang's Works, 1975–1980, Sichuan Volume]. Hong Kong: 中文大學, 2018.

Editorial Group of Zhao Ziyang's Works (趙紫陽文集編輯組). *趙紫陽文集 (1980–1989), 四川卷* [A Collection of Zhao Ziyang's Works, 1980–1989, Sichuan Volume]. Hong Kong: 中文大學, 2016.

Foreign Relations of the United States, 1969–1972. Vol. XVII. Washington, D.C.: United States Government Printing Office, 2006.

Foreign Relations of the United States, 1977–1980. Vol. XIII. Washington, D.C.: United States Government Printing Office, 2013.

Guangdong Archive Bureau (广东省档案局), eds. *改革开放三十年重要档案文献·广东(上)* [Important Archival Documents in the Thirty Years of Reform and Opening-up (Guangdong)]. Vol. 1. Beijing: 中国档案, 2008.

Hu Ping (胡平) and Wang Juntao (王軍濤). *開拓—北大學運文獻* [Opening the Path: Documents of Peking University Student Movement]. Hong Kong: 田園, 1990.

Hu Yaobang (胡耀邦). *胡耀邦文选* [Selected Works of Hu Yaobang]. Beijing: 人民, 2015.

Infrastructure Construction Bureau under the Railway Ministry (铁道部基建总局), ed. 铁路修建史料, 1963–1980 [Materials on Railway Construction, 1963–1980]. Vol. 3. Beijing: 中国铁道, 1991.

Institute of CCP History Research in Inner Mongolian Autonomous Region (中共内蒙古自治区委党史研究室), eds. 中国新时期的农村变革 (中央卷) [Rural Transformation in China's New Era (Central Level Volume)]. Beijing: 中共党史, 2004.

"Joint Declaration of the Government of the United Kingdom of Great Britain and Northern Ireland and the Government of the People's Republic of China on the Question of Hong Kong." December 19, 1984. https://treaties.un.org/Pages/show Details.aspx?objid=0800000280d4d6e, accessed March 26, 2023.

李先念、华国锋、余秋里致周恩来函 [Letter to Zhou Enlai by Li Xiannian, Hua Guofeng, and Yu Qiuli], January 23, 1972. 中共党史资料 [CCP History Materials], no. 2 (2004).

Liu Shaoqi (刘少奇). 刘少奇选集 [Selected Works of Liu Shaoqi]. Beijing: 人民, 1985.

毛泽东思想万岁 [Long Live Mao Zedong Thought]. Wuhan: n.p., 1968.

Mao Zedong (毛泽东). Mao Zedong on Diplomacy. Beijing: Foreign Languages Press, 1994.

Mao Zedong (毛泽东). 建国以来毛泽东文稿 [Mao Zedong's Manuscripts since the Founding of the People's Republic]. 20 vols. Beijing: 中央文献, 2023.

Mao Zedong (毛泽东). 毛主席语录 [Quotations from Chairman Mao Zedong]. Beijing: 东方红, 1967.

Mao Zedong (毛泽东). 毛泽东选集 [Selected Works of Mao Zedong]. Beijing: 人民, 1977.

National Bureau of Statistics of China (中国国家统计局), comp. 中国统计年鉴, 1981 [China Statistical Yearbook, 1981]. Beijing: 中国统计, 1981.

National Bureau of Statistics of China (中国国家统计局), comp. 中国统计年鉴, 1983 [China Statistical Yearbook, 1983]. Beijing: 中国统计, 1983.

Party History Teaching and Research Group at the National Defense University (国防大学党史党建教研室), eds. "文化大革命"研究资料 [A Collection of Cultural Revolution Materials]. Beijing: internal edition, 1988.

Party History Teaching Group at the PLA Academy of Politics (解放军政治学院党史教研室), eds. 中共党史教学参考资料 [Reference Materials for Teaching CCP History]. Beijing: 国防大学, 1986.

PRC Foreign Ministry (中华人民共和国外交部) and CCP Central Institute of Documentary Studies (中共中央文献研究室), eds. 周恩来外交文选 [Selected Diplomatic Papers of Zhou Enlai]. Beijing: 中央文献, 1990.

State Planning Revolutionary Committee (国家计划革命委员会). "关于进口一米七连续式轧板机问题的报告" [Report on Importing 1.7 Meter Tandem Cold Mills], August 6, 1972. 中共党史资料 [CCP History Materials], no. 2 (2004), pp. 9–10.

State Planning Revolutionary Committee (国家计划革命委员会). "关于进口成套化纤、化肥技术设备的报告" [Report on Importing Technology and Whole-Set Equipment of Chemical Fiber and Fertilizer]," January 16, 1972. 中共党史资料 [CCP History Materials], no. 90 (2004), pp. 4–8.

State Planning Revolutionary Committee (国家计划革命委员会). "关于增加设备进口、扩大经济交流的请示报告" [Report on Increasing Equipment Imports and Expand Economic Exchanges], January 2, 1973. 中共党史资料 [CCP History Materials], no. 2 (2004), pp. 12–19.

Tao Chunfang (陶春芳) and Gao Xiaoxian (高小贤), eds. 中国妇女统计资料 (1949–1989) [Statistical Materials about Chinese Women, 1949–1989]. Beijing: 中国统计, 1991.

Wan Li (万里). 万里文选 [Selected Works of Wan Li]. Beijing: 人民, 1995.

Westad, Odd Arne, Chen Jian, Stein Tønnesson, Nguyen Vu Tung, and James G. Hershberg, eds. 77 Conversations between Chinese and Foreign Leaders on the Wars in Indochina, 1964–1977. Working Paper 22. Washington, D.C.: Cold War International History Project, Woodrow Wilson Center, 1998.

Wuhan Statistics Bureau (武汉市统计局), comp. 武汉市第七次全国人口普查公报 [Report of the Seventh National Census in Wuhan]. Last modified September 16, 2021. http://tjj.wuhan.gov.cn/ztzl_49/pczl/202109/t20210916_1779157.shtml.

Xi Zhongxun (习仲勋). 习仲勋文选 [Selected Works of Xi Zhongxun]. Beijing: 中央文献, 1995.

Xue Muqiao (薛暮桥). 薛暮桥文集 [A Collection of Xue Muqiao's Works]. Beijing: 中国金融, 2011.

Yu Guangyuan (于光远). 于光远改革论集 [A Collection of Yu Guangyuan's Essays on Reforms]. Beijing: 中国发展, 2008.

Chronological Records

Editorial Group of Chronological Record of Yang Chengwu (杨成武年谱编写组). 杨成武年谱, 1914–2004 [Chronological Records of Yang Chengwu, 1914–2004]. Beijing: 解放军, 2014.

Leng Rong (冷溶) and Wang Zuoling (汪作玲), et al. 邓小平年谱, 1975–1997 [Chronological Records of Deng Xiaoping, 1975–1997]. Vol. 1. Beijing: 中央文献, 2009.

Li Dianren (李殿仁) and Xu Xiaoyan (徐小岩), chief eds. 徐向前年谱 [Chronological Records of Xu Xiangqian]. Beijing: 解放军, 2016.

Li Ping (力平) and Ma Zhisun (马芷荪) et al. 周恩来年谱, 1949–1976 [Chronological Records of Zhou Enlai, 1949–1976]. Beijing: 中央文献, 1998.

Liu Chongwen (刘崇文) and Chen Shaochou (陈绍畴), eds. 刘少奇年谱 [Chronological Records of Liu Shaoqi]. Beijing: 中央文献, 1996.

Liu Jixian (刘继贤), et al. 叶剑英年谱, 1897–1986 [Chronological Records of Ye Jianying, 1897–1986]. Vol. 2. Beijing: 中央文献, 2007.

Pang Xianzhi (逄先知等) et al. 毛泽东年谱, 1949–1976 [Chronological Records of Mao Zedong]. Beijing: 中央文献, 2013.

Wang Weicheng (王维澄) et al. 李先念年谱 [Chronological Records of Li Xiannian]. Vol. 5. Beijing: 中央文献, 2011.

Xu Zehao (徐泽浩), ed. 王稼祥年谱, 1906–1974 [Chronological Records of Wang Jiaxiang, 1906–1974]. Beijing: 中央文献, 2001.

Yang Shengqun (杨胜群) and Yan Jianqi (阎建琪), et al. 邓小平年谱, 1904–1974 [Chronological Records of Deng Xiaoping, 1904–1974]. Beijing: 中央文献, 2009.

Zheng Zhongbing (鄭仲兵), ed. 胡耀邦年譜資料長編 [Materials for a Chronological Record of Hu Yaobang]. Hong Kong: 時代國際, 2005.

Zhu Jiamu (朱佳木) et al. 陈云年谱, 1905–1995 [Chronological Records of Chen Yun, 1905–1995]. Vol. 3. Beijing: 中央文献, 2000.

Memoirs, Diaries, Interviews, and Oral Histories

Bo Yibo (薄一波). 若干重大决策和事件的回顾 [Recollections of Some Important Decisions and Events]. Beijing: 人民, 1999.

Brzezinski, Zbigniew. *Power and Principle: Memoirs of the National Security Adviser*. New York: Farrar, Straus, Giroux, 1983.

CCTV (中央广播电视总台), ed. 见证我亲历的改革开放 [The Reform and Opening-up That I Personally Experienced]. Beijing: 中国方正, 2018.

Cendrowski, Scott. "Opening Happiness: An Oral History of Coca-Cola in China." September 11, 2014. https://fortune.com/2014/09/11/opening-happiness-an-oral-history-of-coca-cola-in-china/.

Chen Changjiang (陈长江). 毛泽东最后十年: 警卫队长的回忆 [Mao Zedong's Final Decade: The Reminiscences of His Chief Bodyguard]. Beijing: 中共中央党校, 1998.

Chen Jinhua (陈锦华). 国事忆述 [Recollection of My Experience with State Affairs]. Beijing: 中共党史, 2005.

Chen Pixian (陈丕显). 陈丕显回忆录: 在一月风暴的中心 [Memoirs of Chen Pixian: At the Center of the January Storm]. Shanghai: 上海人民, 2005.

Chen Yizi (陳一諮). 陳一諮回憶錄 [Memoirs of Chen Yizi: China's Reform in the 1980s]. Hong Kong: 新世紀, 2013.

Chen Zaidao (陈再道). 浩劫中的一幕: 武汉七二零事件亲历记 [One Episode in the Havoc: Personal Experiences of the July Twentieth Incident in Wuhan]. Beijing: 解放军, 1989.

Cong Weixi (从维熙). 我的黑白人生 [My Black and White Life]. Beijing: 生活·读书·新知三联书店, 2014.

Dai Bingguo (戴秉国). 战略对话: 戴秉国回忆录 [Strategic Dialogue: Dai Bingguo's Memoirs]. Beijing: 人民, 2016.

Deng Liqun (鄧力群). 鄧力群自述: 十二個春秋, 1975–1987 [Deng Liqun's Autobiography: Twelve Springs and Autumns, 1975–1987]. Hong Kong: 博智, 2006.

Deng Rong. *Deng Xiaoping and the Cultural Revolution: A Daughter Recalls the Critical Years*. Beijing: Foreign Language Press, 2002.

Editorial Group of "History's Judgment" ("历史的审判" 编写组), ed. 历史的审判— 审判林彪、江青反革命集团纪实 (上) [History's Judgment: The Trial of Lin Biao and Jiang Qing Counter-Revolutionary Clique]. Vol. 1. Beijing: 群众, 1981.

Exam Center of the Ministry of Education (教育部考试中心), eds. 难忘1977: 恢复高考的历史实录 [Unforgettable Historical Records of the Resumption of College Entry Exams in 1977]. Tianjin: 天津人民, 2007.

Fei Xiaotong (费孝通). "一个审判员的感受" [The Feeling of a Judge]. In 历史的审判: 审判林彪、江青反革命集团案犯纪实 [The Trial of History: A Factual Record of the Trials of the Criminals of the Lin Biao and Jiang Qing Counter-Revolutionary Cliques]. Beijing: 群众, 2000.

Gao Zhenpu (高振普). 陪伴病中周恩来的日日夜夜 [The Days and Nights That I Accompanied Zhou Enlai during His Illness]. Beijing: 中国青年, 2016.

Gu Mu (谷牧). 谷牧回忆录 [Gu Mu's Memoirs]. Beijing: 中央文献, 2009.

Guan Weixun (官伟勋). 我所知道的叶群 [The Ye Qun I Knew]. Beijing: 中国文学, 1993.

Han Shufang (韩淑芳). 口述: 创业的故事 [Oral Stories of Entrepreneurship]. Beijing: 中国文史, 2018.

Han Shufang (韩淑芳). 口述: 破冰的故事 [Oral Stories of Icebreakers]. Beijing: 中国文史, 2018.

Hasigeerle (哈斯格尔勒). "'内人党'冤案亲历记" [Experiencing the Unjust Case of the Inner Mongolian People's Party]. 炎黄春秋 [China through the Ages], no. 1 (2009).

Hou Yonglu (侯永禄). 农民日记: 一个农民的生存实录 [A Peasant's Diary: A Faithful Record of a Peasant's Struggles for Survival]. Beijing: 中国青年, 2006.

Hou Yonglu (侯永禄). 农民家书 [A Peasant's Family Letters]. Beijing: 人民文学, 2011.

Hu Deping (胡德平). 中國為什麼要改革: 回憶父親胡耀邦 [Why Reforms Are Necessary for China: Remembering My Father Hu Yaobang]. Hong Kong: 中和, 2011.

Huang Hua (黄华). 亲历与见闻: 黄华回忆录 [Personal Experience and Accounts: Huang Hua's Memoirs]. Beijing: 世界知识, 2007.

Huang Zheng (黄峥). 风雨无悔: 对话王光美 [Come Rain or Shine: A Dialogue with Wang Guangmei]. Beijing: 人民文学, 2014.

Huang Zheng (黄峥). 王光美访谈录 [Records of Interviews with Wang Guangmei]. Beijing: 中央文献, 2006.

Ji Chaozhu. *The Man on Mao's Right: From Harvard Yard to Tiananmen Square, My Life Inside China's Foreign Ministry*. New York: Random House, 2008.

Ji Dong (纪东). 难忘的八年— 周恩来秘书回忆录 [Unforgettable Eight Years: Memoirs of Zhou Enlai's Secretary]. Beijing: 中央文献, 2007.

Jiao Ye (焦烨). 叶群之谜: 一个秘书眼中的叶群与林彪 [The Riddle of Ye Qun: Ye Qun and Lin Biao in the Eyes of a Secretary]. Beijing: 中国文联, 1993.

Li Lanqing (李岚清). 突围: 国门初开的岁月 [Breaking through: The Birth of China's Opening-up Policy]. Beijing: 中央文献, 2008.

Li Rui (李锐). 毛泽东秘书手记: 庐山会议实录, 增订本 [Notes by Mao Zedong's Secretary: A Factual Account of the Lushan Conference, revised and expanded version]. Zhengzhou: 河南人民, 1995.

Li Rui (李锐). "耀邦去世前的谈话" [Yaobang's Conversation before His Passing]. 当代中国研究 [Modern China Studies], no. 4 (2001). https://www.modernchinastudies.org/cn/issues/past-issues/75-mcs-2001-issue-4/589-2012-01-03-12-11-52.html, accessed March 24, 2023.

Li Wenpu (李文普). "林彪卫士长李文普不得不说" [Things That Lin Biao's Guard Li Wenpu Has to Say]. 中华儿女 [China's Sons and Daughters], no. 2 (1999).

Li Zhisui. *The Private Life of Chairman Mao: The Memoirs of Mao's Personal Physician*. New York: Random House, 1994.

Lin Ke (林克). 林克日记 [Le Ke's Diaries]. Photocopy of manuscript in authors' possession.

Lin Ke (林克), Wu Xujun (吴旭君), and Xu Tao (徐涛). 历史的真实: 毛泽东身边工作人员的证言 [The Truth of History: Testimonies of Mao's Associates]. Beijing: 中央文献, 1998.

Ling Qing (凌青). 从延安到联合国 [From Yanan to the United Nations]. Fuzhou: 福建人民, 2008.

Luo Diandian (罗点点). 我的父亲罗瑞卿 [My Father Luo Ruiqing]. Huhehaote: 内蒙古人民, 1994.

Mao Mao (毛毛). 我的父亲邓小平: 文革岁月 [My Father Deng Xiaoping: Cultural Revolution Years]. Beijing: 中央文献, 2000.

Nunes, Ray. "Politics and Ideology: Meetings with Kang Sheng 1966–68, Some Observations by Ray Nunes, Chairman, Workers' Party of New Zealand." https://www.marxists.org/history/erol/new-zealand/nunes-kang.pdf, accessed May 24, 2022.

Qi Benyu (戚本禹). 戚本禹回憶錄 [Qi Benyu's Memoirs]. Hong Kong: 中國文革歷史, 2016.

Qi Li (亓莉). 毛泽东晚年生活琐记 [Incidents from Mao Zedong's Later Life]. Beijing: 中央文献, 1998.

Qian Qichen (钱其琛). 外交十记 [Ten Episodes in Chinese Diplomacy]. Beijing: 世界知识, 2003.

Qian Zhengying (钱正英). "国门初开时的西欧印象: 回忆 1978年随团出访西欧五国的经历" [Impression of West Europe at the Time of Our Country's Initial Opening: Recalling the Experience of Visiting Five West European Countries with a Delegation]. 党的文献 [Party History Documents], no. 3 (2010).

Qiu Huizuo (邱會作). 邱會作回憶錄 [Qiu Huizuo's Memoirs]. Hong Kong: 新世紀, 2011.

Shi Xue'ai (时学爱). "我的家人在大饥荒中饿死" [My Family Starved to Death during the Great Famine]. 炎黄春秋 [China through the Ages], no. 5 (2013).

Shi Zhongquan (石仲泉). 我观周恩来 [Zhou Enlai in My Eyes]. Beijing: 中央党校, 2008.

Tang Longbin (唐龙彬). "一次神秘的外交使命: 接待基辛格秘密访华" [A Mysterious Diplomatic Mission: Receiving Kissinger during His Secret China Visit]. 世界知识 [World Knowledge], no. 6 (1995).

Wang Dongxing (汪东兴). 汪东兴回忆: 毛泽东与林彪反革命集团的斗争 [Wang Dongxing Recalls: Mao's Struggles against Lin Biao's Counter-Revolution Clique]. Beijing: 当代中国, 2010.

Wang Guangyu (王光宇). "我所亲历的安徽农村改革" [I Personally Experienced Rural Reform in Anhui]. 中共党史研究 [CCP History Studies], no. 5 (2008).

Wang Li (王力). 现场历史: 文化大革命纪事 [History Created on Site: The Chronicle of the Cultural Revolution]. Hong Kong: Oxford University Press, 1993.

Wang Li (王力). 王力反思錄 [Reflections by Wang Li]. Hong Kong: 北星, 2001.

Wang Wenyao (王文耀) and Wang Baochun (王保春). 文革前後時期的陳伯達: 秘書的證言 [Chen Boda before and after the Cultural Revolution: The Secretary's Testimonies]. Hong Kong: 天地圖書, 2014.

Wang Wenzheng (王文正) and Shen Guofan (沈国凡). 共和国大审判: 审判林彪、江青反革命集团亲历记 [The Great Trial in the Republic: Personal Experiences of the Trials of the Ling Biao and Jiang Qing Counter-Revolutionary Cliques]. Beijing: 当代中国, 2006.

Wang Zhijun (王志軍). 1979 對越戰爭親歷記 [Personal Experience in the Chinese-Vietnamese War of 1979]. Hong Kong: 星克爾, 2000.

Wang Zhongfang (王仲方). "耀邦与我的两次谈话" [Yaobang's Two Conversations with Me]. 炎黄春秋 [China through the Ages], no. 7 (2005).

Wu De (吴德). 十年风雨纪事: 我在北京工作的一些经历 [Ten Years of Storms: My Working Experience in Beijing]. Beijing: 当代中国, 2004.

Wu Faxian (吴法宪). 歲月艱難: 吳法憲回憶錄 [Difficult Times: Wu Faxian's Memoirs]. Hong Kong: 北星, 2006.

Wu Jiang (吴江). "1979年理论工作务虚会议追忆—真理标准讨论第二阶段" [Recalling the 1979 Theory Conference: The Second Phase of the Truth Criterion Debate]. 炎黄春秋 [China through the Ages], no. 9 (2001).

Wu Jianhua (武健华). "详忆粉碎'四人帮'的前前后后" [Remembering Smashing the Gang of Four, with Details], part 1. 百年潮 [One Hundred Year Tide], no. 10 (2012).

Wu Jianhua (武健华). "详忆粉碎'四人帮'的前前后后" [Remembering Smashing the Gang of Four, with Details], part 2. 百年潮 [One Hundred Year Tide], no. 11 (2012).

Wu Jianhua (武健华). "详忆粉碎'四人帮'的前前后后" [Remembering Smashing the Gang of Four, with Details], part 3. 百年潮 [One Hundred Year Tide], no. 12 (2012).

Wu Lengxi (吴冷西). 十年论战: 1956–1966, 中苏关系回忆录 [Ten-Year Polemic Debate: A Memoir on Sino-Soviet Relations, 1956–1966]. Beijing: 中央文献, 1999.

Wu Zhong (吴忠). "吴忠谈'九一三'事件" [Wu Zhong on the September 13th Incident]. 炎黄春秋 [China through the Ages], no. 1 (2012).

Xiang Jidong (向继东), ed. 革命时代的私人记忆 [Private Memories in a Revolutionary Era]. Guangzhou: 花城, 2010.

Xu Hailiang (徐海亮). 武漢七二零事件實錄 [Records of the July Twentieth Incident in Wuhan]. Hong Kong: 中國文化傳播, 2010.

Xu Jingxian (徐景賢). 十年一夢 [A Decade Like a Dream]. Hong Kong: 時代國際, 2003.

Yan Mingfu (阎明复). 亲历中苏关系—中央办公厅翻译组的十年, 1957–1966 [Witnessing Chinese-Soviet Relations: Ten Years at the Group of Interpreters at the Central Administrative Office, 1957–1966]. Beijing: 中国人民大学, 2015.

Yang Bo (杨波). "开放前夕的一次重要出访" [An Important Foreign Mission on the Eve of Reform and Opening-up]. 百年潮 [One Hundred Year Tide], no. 2002.

Yang Shangkun (杨尚昆). 杨尚昆日记 [Yang Shangkun's Diaries]. Vol. 2. Beijing: 中央文献, 2001.

Yang Yinlu (杨银禄). 庭院深深钓鱼台—我给江青当秘书 [The Deep Courtyard of Diaoyutai: Serving as Jiang Qing's Secretary]. Beijing: 当代中国, 2015.

Yu Guangyuan. *Chinese Economists on Economic Reform—Collected Works of Yu Guang-yuan*. London: Routledge, 2014.

Yu Guangyuan (于光遠). 我憶鄧小平 [Deng Xiaoping in My Memory]. Hong Kong: 時代國際, 2005.

Yu Guangyuan (于光远). 我忆邓小平 [Deng Xiaoping in My Memory]. Hangzhou: 浙江人民, 2018.

Yu Guangyuan (于光远). 十一届三中全会的台前幕后: 1978我亲历的那次历史大转折 [On the Stage and behind the Scenes of the Third Plenum of the Eleventh Central Committee: The Historical Transition That I Personally Experienced in 1978]. Beijing: 中央编译, 2008.

Yu Guangyuan (于光远) et al. 改变中国命运的41天: 中央工作会议、十一届三中全会亲历记 [Forty-One Days That Changed the Fate of China: Personal Experience at the Central Work Conference and the Third Plenary Session of the Eleventh Central Committee]. Shenzhen: 海天, 1998.

Yuan Min (袁敏). 重返 1976: 我所经历的"总理遗言"案 [Returning to 1976: The Case of the "Premier's Last Will" That I Personally Experienced]. Beijing: 人民文学, 2010.

Zhang Chunqiao (張春橋). 張春橋獄中家书 [Zhang Chunqiao's Letters to Home from Prison]. Hong Kong: 中文大學, 2015.

Zhang Gensheng (张根生). "华国锋谈粉碎'四人帮'" [Hua Guofeng on Smashing the Gang of Four]. 炎黄春秋 [China through the Ages], no. 7 (2004).

Zhang Hanzhi (章含之). 章含之同志谈话 [Interview with Comrade Zhang Hanzhi]. Copy in authors' possession.

Zhang Yaoci (张耀祠). "1976: 我负责的'四人帮'抓捕行动" [I Was in Charge of Arresting the Gang of Four in 1976]. 同舟共进 [Together], no. 5 (2009).

Zhang Yaoci (张耀祠). 回忆毛泽东 [Remembering Mao Zedong]. Beijing: 中共中央党校, 1996.

Zhang Yufeng (张玉凤). "毛泽东晚年生活的片段回忆" [Fragmentary Recollections of Mao Zedong's Later Life]. 社会科学论坛 [Social Sciences Forum], no. 12, 2007.

Zhang Yunsheng (张云生). 毛家湾纪实: 林彪秘书回忆录 [A True Account of Maojiawan: The Memoirs of Lin Biao's Secretary]. Beijing: 春秋, 1988.

Zhang Zehan (张泽晗). "正大集团: 与开放的中国共同成长: 访正大集团农牧食品企业中国区资深副董事长谢毅文" [Charoen Pokphand Group: Growing up along with China's Opening-up: An Interview with Xie Yiwen, Senior Vice Chairman of CP Group's Agriculture, Animal Husbandry and Food Operations in China]. 经济 [Economy], no. 8 (2019).

Zhang Zuoliang (张佐良). 周恩来最后的十年 [The Last Ten Years of Zhou Enlai]. Shanghai: 上海人民出版社, 1997.

Zhang Zuoliang (張佐良). 周恩來保健醫生回憶錄 [Memoir of Zhou Enlai's Primary Doctor]. Hong Kong: 三聯, 1998.

Zhao Ziyang et al. *Prisoner of the State: The Secret Journal of Zhao Ziyang.* New York: Simon & Schuster, 2009.

Zhou Bin (周斌). 我為中國領導人當翻譯: 見證中日外交秘辛 [I Interpreted for Chinese Leaders: Witnessing Secret Chinese-Japanese Diplomatic Exchanges]. Hong Kong: 大山文化, 2013.

Zhu Jiamu (朱佳木). 我所知道的十一届三中全会 [What I Know about the Third Plenum of the Eleventh Party Congress]. Beijing: 当代中国, 2008.

Newspapers and Journals

American Journal of Chinese Studies
党史博览 [Broad Survey of the Communist Party of China]
中共党史资料 [CCP History Materials]
中共党史研究 [CCP History Studies]
世纪 [Century]
China Journal
China Quarterly
China Review
中国合作经济 [China's Collective Economy]
中国国情国力 [China's National Situation and National Power]
中华儿女 [China's Sons and Daughters]
炎黄春秋 [China through the Ages]
Christian Science Monitor
Cold War International History Project Bulletin
消费经济 [Consumer Economy]
当代中国史研究 [Contemporary China History Study]
争鸣 [Debates]
Die Welt
Diplomatic History

经济导报 [Economic Herald]
经济研究 [Economics Studies]
经济理论与经济管理 [Economic Theory and Economic Management]
经济 [Economy]
随笔 [Essays]
探索 [Exploration]
Explorations in Economic History
财经 [Finance and Economics]
光明日报 [Guangming Daily]
羊城晚报 [Guangzhou Evening News]
历史研究 [Historical Research]
华夏文摘 [Huaxia Digest]
湖北文史资料 [Hubei History and Literature Materials]
江淮文史 [Jianghuai Literature and History]
Journal of Asian Studies
Journal of Business Research
Journal of Cold War Studies
史学月刊 [Journal of Historical Science]
解放日报 [Liberation Daily]
三联生活周刊 [Life Weekly]
档案春秋 [Memories and Archives]
Modern China
当代中国研究 [Modern China Studies]
南京社会科学 [Nanjing Social Science]
New York Times
劳动保障通讯 [Newsletter of Labor Protection]
百年潮 [One Hundred Year Tide]
党的文献 [Party History Documents]
Peking Review
解放军报 [People's Liberation Army Daily]
检察风云 [Prosecutorial View]
人民日报 [*Renmin Ribao* (People's Daily)]
上海党史和党建 [Shanghai Party History and Party Construction]
社会科学论坛 [Social Sciences Forum]
南方都市报 [Southern Metropolis Daily]
学习时报 [Study Times]
Taipei Times
同舟共济 [Together]
二十一世纪 [The Twenty-First Century]
民间历史 [Unofficial History]
Wall Street Journal
文汇报 [Wenhui Daily]
世界知识 [World Knowledge]
宣传简报（增刊）[*Xuanchuan jianbao*, Propaganda Briefings] (supplementary issue)
云南资讯报 [Yunnan Information Daily]

Other Sources in Chinese

Bonnin, Michel (潘鸣啸). "上山下乡运动再评价" [A Reevaluation of the Up to the Mountain and Down to the Countryside Movement]. 社会学研究 [Sociology Research], no. 5 (2005).

Bu Weihua (卜偉華). 砸爛舊世界: 文化大革命的動亂與浩劫, 1966–1968 [Smashing the Old World: The Turmoil and Catastrophe of the Cultural Revolution, 1966–1968]. Hong Kong: 中文大學, 2008.

Cai Wenbin (蔡文彬), ed. 趙紫陽在四川, 1975–1980 [Zhao Ziyang in Sichuan, 1975–1980]. Hong Kong: 新世紀, 2011.

CCP History Research Institute (中共中央党史研究室), ed. 中国共产党历史 [A History of the Chinese Communist Party]. Beijing: 中共党史, 2011.

CCP History Research Institute (中共中央党史研究室), ed. "中国共产党大事记, 1966" [Record of Important Events for the Chinese Communist Party in 1966]. Central People's Government of the People's Republic of China website, August 30, 2007. http://www.gov.cn/test/2007-08/30/content_731993.htm.

CCP History Research Institute (中共中央党史研究室), ed. "中国共产党大事记, 1970" [Records of Important Events in 1970]. 人民网. http://cpc.people.com.cn/GB/64162/64164/4416088.html, accessed August 8, 2022.

Chen Donglin (陈东林). 三线建设: 备战时期的西部开发 [The Development of the West during the Period of the Third Front Construction]. Beijing: 中共中央党校, 2003.

Chen Jianfeng (陈建锋). "1984年前上海青浦社队企业的发展历程及历史作用" [The Development and Historical Significance of Commune Enterprises in Qingpu District of Shanghai before 1984]. 上海党史与党建 [Shanghai Party History and Party Construction], no. 4 (2016).

Chen Run (陈润). 生活可以更美的—何享健的美的人生 [Life Could Be Better: He Xiangjian's Beautiful Life]. Beijing: 华文, 2010.

Chen Run (陈润). 时代的见证者 [Those Who Witnessed Their Times]. Hangzhou: 浙江大学, 2019.

Chen Tushou (陈徒手). "出版印刷'毛选'五卷的日子里" [The Day the Fifth Volume of *Selected Works of Mao Zedong* Was Published and Printed]." 随笔 [Essays], no. 3 (2020).

Chen Yangyong (陈扬勇). "周恩来与'文化大革命'初期的铁路交通" [Zhou Enlai and the Railway Transportation in the Early Days of the Cultural Revolution]. 中共党史研究 [CCP History Studies], no. 1 (1996).

Cheng Zhensheng (程振声) et al. "李先念与粉碎四人帮" [Li Xiannian and Smashing of the Gang of Four]. 中共党史研究 [CCP History Studies], no. 1 (2002).

Cheng Zhongyuan (程中原). "邓小平与一九七五年铁路整顿" [Deng Xiaoping and 1975 Railway Rectification]. 党的文献 [Party History Documents], no. 5 (1996).

Cheng Zhongyuan (程中原), Wang Yuxiang (王玉祥), and Li Zhenghua (李正华). 1976–1981 年的中国 [China in 1976–1981]. Beijing: 中央文献, 1998.

Cheng Zhongyuan (程中原) and Xia Xingzhen (夏杏珍). 历史转折的前奏: 邓小平在 1975 [Prelude to a Historical Turn: Deng Xiaoping in 1975]. Beijing: 中国青年, 2004.

Cong Jin (丛进). 曲折发展的岁月 [Years of Tortuous Development]. Zhengzhou: 河南人民, 1989.

Cui Min (崔敏). "反思八十年代的'严打'" [Reflection on the "Strike Hard" Campaign of the 1980s]. 炎黄春秋 [China through the Ages], no. 5 (2012), pp. 16–22.

Deng Jiarong (邓加荣). 孙冶方传 [A Biography of Sun Yefang]. Taiyuan: 山西经济, 1998.

Ding Kaiwen (丁凯文). 重审林彪罪案 [Reexamining Lin Biao's Criminal Case]. Hong Kong: 明镜, 2004.

Ding Shu (丁抒). "从史学革命到挖祖坟" [From History Revolution to Digging up Ancestral Graves]. 华夏文摘 [Huaxia Digest], 1996, p. 105. http://www.cnd.org/HXWZ /ZK96/zk105.hz8.html#2, accessed March 21, 2023.

Ding Shu (丁抒). 风雨如磐的日子: 一九七〇 年的"一打三反"运动 [Stormy Days: The "One Attack, Three Antis" Movement in 1970]. https://post.ea28.com/cankao/haojie.pdf, accessed February 15, 2024.

Dong Fureng (董辅礽), ed. 中华人民共和国经济史 [The Economic History of the People's Republic of China]. Vol. 1. Beijing: 经济科学, 1999.

Dong Guoqiang and Andrew G. Walder. "Nanjing's 'Second Cultural Revolution' of 1974." China Quarterly, no. 212 (December 2012).

Du Runsheng (杜润生). "土地家庭承包制的兴起" [The Rise of Land Household Responsibility System]. 中国合作经济 [China's Collective Economy], no. 10 (2008).

Du Xiuxian (杜修贤). 林彪反革命集团覆灭纪实 [The Collapse of the Lin Biao Counter-Revolutionary Clique]. Beijing: 中央文献, 1995.

Editorial Committee of Xi Zhongxun Biography (习仲勋传编委会). 习仲勋传 [A Biography of Xi Zhongxun]. Beijing: 中央文献, 2013.

Editorial Committee of Xi Zhongxun in Charge of Guangdong (习仲勋主政广东编委会). 习仲勋主政广东 [Xi Zhongxun in Charge of Guangdong]. Beijing: 中共党史, 2007.

Editorial Group of Peng Zhen Biography (彭真传编写组). 彭真传 [A Biography of Peng Zhen]. Vol. 4. Beijing: 中央文献, 2012.

Editorial Group of Wang Zhen Biography (王震传编写组). 王震传 [A Biography of Wang Zhen]. Beijing: 当代中国, 2001.

Editorial Office of Diplomatic History under the Foreign Ministry (外交部外交史编辑室), ed. 新中国外交风云 [Diplomatic Experience of the People's Republic of China]. Beijing: 世界知识, 1990.

Fan Shuo (范硕). 叶剑英在1976 [Ye Jianying in 1976]. Beijing: 人民, 1995.

Fan Shuo (范硕) et al. 叶剑英传 [A Biography of Ye Jianying]. Beijing: 当代中国, 2006.

Fang Weizhong (房维中), ed. 在风浪中前进: 中国发展与改革编年纪事 (1977–1989) [Marching Forward in Stormy Waves: Chronological Records of China's Development and Reforms (1977–1989)]. Printed for internal circulation, 2004.

Foundation for International Strategy (国际战略基金会), ed. 环球同此凉热: 一代领袖们的 国际战略思想 [The Globe Sharing the Same Warmth and Cold: The International Strategic Thought of the Leaders of the Mao Generation]. Beijing: 中央文献, 1993.

Fu Yi (傅颐). "教育部长周荣鑫的最后岁月" [The Last Years of Education Minister Zhou Rongxin]. 百年潮 [One Hundred Year Tide], no. 2 (2022).

Gao, Mobo. The Battle for China's Past: Mao and the Cultural Revolution. London: Pluto Press, 2008.

Gao Gao (高皋). 後文革史: 中國自由化潮流 [Post—Cultural Revolution History: The Trend of Liberalization in China]. Taipei: 聯經, 1993.

Gao Gao (高皋) and Yan Jiaqi (嚴家其). 文化大革命十年史 [Ten-Year History of the Cultural Revolution]. Taipei: 遠流, 1990.

Gao Wenqian (高文谦). 晚年周恩来 [Zhou Enlai in His Late Years]. New York: Mirror, 2003.

Gong Guzhong (龚固忠), Tang Zhennan (唐振南), and Xia Yuansheng (夏远生), eds. 毛泽东回湖南纪实 [Factual Records of Mao Zedong Returning to Hu'nan]. Changsha: 湖南人民, 1993.

Gong Li (宫力). 邓小平与中美外交风云 [Deng Xiaoping and Chinese-American Diplomatic Encounters]. Beijing: 红旗, 2015.

Gu Baozi (顾保孜) and Qian Sijie (钱嗣杰). 毛泽东正值神州有事时 [Mao Zedong at a Time When Changes Were Taking Place in China]. Beijing: 人民文学, 2013.

Guo Biliang (郭碧良). 石狮: 中国民办特区 [Shishi: Private Special Zones of China]. Fuzhou: 福建人民, 1993.

Guo Ming (郭明), ed. 中越关系演变四十年 [Forty Years Evolution of Sino-Vietnamese Relations]. Nanning: 广西人民, 1992.

Han Gang (韩钢). "'两个凡是'的由来及其终结" [The Origins and End of the "Two Whatevers"]. 中共党史研究 [CCP History Studies], no. 11 (2009).

Han Gang (韩钢). "关于华国锋的若干史实" [Some Historical Facts about Hua Guofeng]. 炎黄春秋 [China through the Ages], no. 2 (2011).

Han Gang (韩钢). "关于华国锋的若干史实(续)" [Some Historical Facts about Hua Guofeng, Part 2]. 炎黄春秋 [China through the Ages], no. 3 (2011).

Han Honghong (韩洪洪). 胡耀邦在历史转折关头, 1975–1982 [Hu Yaobang at the Juncture of Historical Turning, 1975–1982]. Beijing: 人民, 2008.

He Libo (何立波). "1983: 党中央决策'严打'始末" [The Whole Process of the Party Center's Making of the "Strike Hard" Decision in 1983]. 检察风云 [Prosecutorial View], no. 17 (2008), pp. 66–68.

Ho, Denise Y. Curating Revolution: Politics on Display in Mao's China. Cambridge: Cambridge University Press, 2018.

Hu Angang. Mao and the Cultural Revolution. Singapore: Enrich Professional Publishing, 2017.

Hu Deping (胡德平). "耀邦同志在'真理标准'大讨论的前前后后 (中篇)" [Comrade Yaobang before and after the Great Debate about the Criterion of the Truth, Part 2]. 财经 [Finance and Economics], no. 12 (2008). http://www.hybsl.cn/article/10/102/9769. Accessed October 4, 2023.

Huang Xiurong (黄修荣). 国共关系七十年 [Seven Decades of Relations between the CCP and the Guomindang]. Guangzhou: 广东教育, 1998.

Huang Yao (黄瑶) and Zhang Mingzhe (张明哲). 罗瑞卿传 [A Biography of Luo Ruiqing]. Beijing: 当代中国, 1996.

Huang Zheng (黄峥). 刘少奇的最后岁月, 1966–1969 [The Last Years of Liu Shaoqi, 1966–1969]. Beijing: 中央文献, 1996.

Ji Naiwang (纪乃旺). "人民公社化时期农村公共食堂的兴办: 以江苏为例" [Establishing Public Dining Services in the Countryside during the time of People's Communes: The Case of Jiangsu]. 辽宁行政学院学报 [Liaoning Administrative College Journal], no. 9 (2012).

Ji Xichen (纪希晨). "粉碎'四人帮'全景写真" [A Truthful Overall Account of the Smashing of the Gang of Four], part 1. 炎黄春秋 [China through the Ages], no. 10 (2000).

Ji Xichen (纪希晨). 史无前例的年代——一位人民日报老记者的笔记 [An Unprecedented Era: Notes by a Senior Reporter from the *People's Daily*]. Beijing: 人民日报, 2001.

Jia Ming (贾铭). "对右派总人数的研究" [Research on the Total Number of Rightists]. Tian Wen Institute, December 21, 2020. http://www.ustianwen.com/2020/12/blog-post_52.html.

Jiang Yongping (蒋永萍). "50年中国城市妇女就业的回顾" [Employment of Chinese Urban Women in the Past Fifty Years]. 劳动保障通讯 [Newsletter of Labor Protection], no. 3 (2000).

Jin Chongji (金冲及) et al. 刘少奇传 [A Biography of Liu Shaoqi]. Beijing: 中央文献, 2008.

Jin Chongji (金冲及) et al. 周恩来传, 1898–1976 [A Biography of Zhou Enlai, 1898–1976]. Vol. 2. Beijing: 中央文献, 2008.

Jin Chongji (金冲及) and Chen Qun (陈群) et al. 陈云传 [A Biography of Chen Yun]. Beijing: 中央文献, 2015.

Jin Chunming (金春明). 评剑桥中华人民共和国史 [On the Cambridge History of China: The People's Republic]. Wuhan: 湖北人民, 2001.

Jin Dalu (金大陆) and Jin Guangyao (金光耀). "从地方志资料看知识青年上山下乡" [Studying the Down to the Countryside Movement from Local Gazetteers]. 当代中国史研究 [Contemporary Chinese History Studies], no. 3 (2015), pp. 112–122.

Ke Keming (柯克明) et al. 邓子恢传 [A Biography of Deng Zihui]. Beijing: 人民, 1996.

Kuhn, Robert Lawrence. 他改变了中国—江泽民传 [The Man Who Has Changed China: A Biography of Jiang Zeming]. Shanghai: 上海译文, 2005.

Leading Group for Handling the Aftermath Work of Railway Corps (铁道兵善后工作领导小组), ed. 中国人民解放军铁道兵简史 [A Brief History of the Railway Corps of the Chinese People's Liberation Army]. For internal circulation only, 1986.

Li Haiwen (李海文). "周恩来逝世后, 毛泽东为何指定华国锋为代总理? (下)" [After Zhou Enlai's Passing, Why Did Mao Zedong Appoint Hua Guofeng as Acting Prime Minister? Part 2]. 江淮文史 [Jianghuai Literature and History], no. 2 (2016).

Li Haiwen (李海文). "华国锋在'九一三'事件前后(上篇)" [Hua Guofeng before and after the September 13th Incident]. 党史博览 (Broad Survey of the Communist Party of China), no. 6 (2014).

Li Haiwen (李海文). "华国锋主持政治局会议解决上海问题" [Hua Guofeng Chaired the Politburo Meeting for Resolving the Shanghai Problem]. 党史博览 (Broad Survey of the Communist Party of China), no. 1 (2014).

Li Haiwen (李海文). "华国锋谈史传写作" [Hua Guofeng Discusses the Writing of History]. 炎黄春秋 [China through the Ages], no. 4 (2015).

Li Haiwen (李海文). "华国锋奉周恩来之命调查李震事件" [Hua Guofeng Followed Zhou Enlai's Order to Investigate Li Zhen's Death]. 党史博览 [Broad Survey of Party History], no. 10 (2013).

Li Haiwen (李海文). "粉碎'四人帮'前华国锋四次约谈汪东兴" [Hua Guofeng Met with Wang Dongxing Four Times before Smashing the "Gang of Four"]. 党史博览 [Broad Survey of Party History], no. 12 (2017).

Li Haiwen (李海文). "我们所走过的引进道路" [The Path of Importing Technology That We Have Traveled]. 经济导报 [Economic Herald], no. 11 (2018).

Li Haiwen (李海文) and Wang Shoujia (王守家). "四人帮"上海余党覆灭记, 1976.10–1979.10 [The Demise of Remnants of the "Gang of Four" in Shanghai, October 1976– October 1979]. Beijing: 中国青年, 2015.

Li Lianqing (李连庆). 大外交家周恩来 [The Great Diplomat Zhou Enlai]. Beijing: 人民, 2017.

Li Ping (力平). 开国总理周恩来 [The Founding Premier Zhou Enlai]. Beijing: 中央党校, 1994.

Li Xun (李逊). 革命造反年代: 上海文革運動史稿 [An Age of Revolutionary Rebellion: A Draft History of the Cultural Revolution in Shanghai]. Hong Kong: Oxford University Press, 2015.

Liu Huaqing (刘华清) and Ye Jianjun (叶健君). 人民公社化运动纪实 [A Factual Account of the Movement for the People's Communes]. Beijing: 東方, 2014.

Liu Lyuhong (刘吕红). 三十年社会变迁与资源型城市发展研究: 以四川攀枝花城市发展为释例 [Thirty Years of Social Change and Development of Resource-Based Cities: A Case Study of the Urban Development of Panzhihua, Sichuan]. Chengdu: 四川大学, 2011.

Liu Xiaomeng (刘小萌). 中国知青史— 大潮 (1966–1980) [A History of China's Educated Youth: Great Waves (1966–1980)]. Beijing: 中国社会科学, 1998.

Liu Yibing (刘一斌). "中国与新加坡建交的漫长历程" [The Long Journey of Establishing Diplomatic Relations between China and Singapore]. 党史博览 [Broad Survey of Party of History], no. 10 (2012).

Lu Di (卢荻). "习仲勋与广东反'偷渡外逃'" [Xi Zhongxun and Smuggling and Fleeing abroad in Guangdong]. 百年潮 [One Hundred Year Tide], no. 10 (2007).

Lu Di (卢荻) and Liu Kunyi (刘坤仪). "任仲夷主政广东" [Ren Zhongyi in Charge of Guangdong]. 百年潮 [One Hundred Year Tide], no. 4 (2000).

Luo Bing (罗冰). "反右运动档案解密—划右派300多万" [Declassifying the Archives of the Anti-Rightist Movement: More Than Three Million Were Made Rightists]. 争鸣 [Debates], no. 1, 2006.

Luo Pinghan (罗平汉). 文革前夜的中国 [China on the Eve of the Cultural Revolution]. Beijing: 人民, 2007.

Ma Quanshan (马泉山). "再谈三线建设的评价问题" [Re-examining the Evaluation of the Third Front Construction]. 当代中国史研究 [Contemporary Chinese History Studies], no. 6 (2011).

Ma Shexiang (马社香). "毛泽东在韶山滴水洞" [Mao Zedong at Dishui Cave in Shaoshan]. 湖北文史资料 [Hubei History and Literature Materials]. Vol. 65. https://www.hbzx .gov.cn/49/2014-09-15/5771.html, accessed May 24, 2022.

Mang Donghong (莽东鸿). "'四人帮'垮台的消息是怎样传播到民间的" [How Did the News of the Collapse of the "Gang of Four" Spread among Everyday People]. 党史博览 [Broad Survey of Party History], no. 9 (2006).

Ministry of Culture and Tourism of the People's Republic of China (中华人民共和国文 化和旅游部). Statistics Section. https://zwgk.mct.gov.cn/zfxxgkml/, accessed January 9, 2023.

Mu Xin (穆欣). "关于工作组存废问题" [About the Existence and Abolition of the Work Groups]. 当代中国史研究 [Contemporary China History Studies], no. 2 (1997).

Ni Chuanghui (倪創輝). 十年中越戰爭 [The Ten-Year War between China and Vietnam]. Hong Kong: 天行健, 2009.

Niu Jun (牛军). "1962: 中国对外政策'左边'转的前夜" [1962: Before China's Left Turn in Foreign Policy]. 历史研究 [Historical Research], no. 3 (2003).

Pang Xianzhi (逄先知) et al. 毛泽东传, 1949–1976 [A Biography of Mao Zedong, 1949–1976]. Beijing: 中央文献, 1993.

Pei Jianzhang (裴坚章) and Feng Yaoyuan (封耀元), eds. 周恩来外交活动大事记, 1949–1975 [Important Events in Zhou Enlai's Diplomatic Activities, 1949–1975]. Beijing: 世界知识, 1993.

People's Daily Online (人民网). "简单的晚年生活: 华国锋远离政治的日子" [A Simple Life in Late Years: Hua Guofeng's Days Away from Politics]. https://news.ifeng.com /mainland/200809/0921_17_795678.shtml, accessed July 12, 2023.

Qin Hui (秦晖). "亲历当代史: 我的中国研究情怀" [Personally Experienced History of the Recent Past: My Feelings about Studying China]. Hongkong Chinese University, interview filmed on November 22, 2011. Video of lecture, 1:51:17. www.youtube.com /watch?v=DmT9KPoeNBk.

Shen Jueren (沈觉人) et al. 当代中国对外贸易 [Trade in Contemporary China]. Beijing: 当代中国, 1992.

Shen Zhihua (沈志華). 最後的天朝: 毛澤東, 金日成與中朝關係 [The Last Heavenly Dynasty: Mao Zedong, Kim Il-sung and Chinese-Korean Relations]. Hong Kong: 中文 大學, 2017.

Shen Zhihua (沈志华). "群众性阶级斗争的必然结果—谈谈反右运动扩大化的问题" [The Necessary Result of Mass Class Struggles: Discussing the Excessive Development of the Anti-Rightist Campaign, Part 2]. 江淮文史 [Jianghuai History and Literature], no. 3 (2014).

Shen Zhihua (沈志华). 苏联专家在中国, 1948–1960 [Soviet Experts in China, 1948–1960]. Beijing: 新华, 2009.

Shen Zhihua (沈志華). 思考與選擇: 從知識分子會議到反右派運動, 1956–1957 [Thinking and Choosing: From the Conference on Intellectuals to the Anti-Rightist Movement, 1956–1957]. Hong Kong: 中文大學, 2008.

Shi Binhai (施滨海). 历史转折中的华国锋 (1973–1981) [Hua Guafeng in Historical Turning Point (1973–1981)]. Beijing: 北京传世家书文化, 2020.

Shi Yun (史雲), ed. 張春橋姚文元實傳: 自傳, 日記, 供詞 [The Real Stories of Zhang Chunqiao and Yao Wenyuan: Biographies, Diaries, and Testimonies]. Hong Kong: 三聯, 2012.

Shi Yun (史雲) and Li Danhui (李丹慧). 難以繼續的"繼續革命" [The Continuous Revolution That Cannot Be Continued]. Hong Kong: 中文大學, 2008.

Sisyphus, John (約翰. 西西弗斯), ed. 群眾暴政與政治投機: 王洪文與"文革" [Mass Tyranny and Political Speculation: Wang Hongwen and the Cultural Revolution]. Vol. 1. Taipei: 西西弗斯文化, 2016.

Song Linfei (宋林飞). "中国'三大模式'的创新与未来" [The Innovation and Future of China's "Three Big Models"]. 南京社会科学 [Nanjing Social Science], no. 5 (2009).

Song Yongyi (宋永毅). "广西文革中的吃人狂潮" [Waves of Cannibalism in Guangxi during the Cultural Revolution]. 二十一世纪 [The Twenty-First Century], no. 155 (June 2016).

Song Yongyi (宋永毅) and Sun Dajin (孫大進), eds. 文化大革命和它的異端思潮 [Heterodox Thoughts during the Cultural Revolution]. Hong Kong: 田園書屋, 1997.

Su Shaozhi (苏绍智). "超越党文化的思想樊篱—我如何在八十年代由马克思主义信仰者转变为研究者" [Beyond the Ideological Barriers of Party Culture—How I Transformed from a Marxist Believer to a Researcher of Marxism in the 1980s]. 当代中国研究 [Modern China Studies], no. 2 (2007), pp. 4–57. https://www.modernchinastudies.org/cn/issues/past-issues/96-mcs-07-issue-2/1004-2012-01-05-15-35-22.html.

Sun Yi (孙伊). "中国女性在家庭中的地位和权利" [The Position and Rights of Chinese Women in the Family]. 当代中国研究 [Modern China Studies], no. 4 (2005). https://www.modernchinastudies.org/cn/issues/past-issues/90-mcs-2005-issue-4/936-2012-01-05-15-34-56.html.

Tian Guoliang (田国良) and Sun Daxun (孙大勋). 胡耀邦传 [A Biography of Hu Yaobang]. Beijing: 中央党史资料, 1989.

Tian Guoqiang (田国强). "中国乡村企业的产权结构及其改革" [Property Rights Structure of China's Township-Village Enterprises and Its Reform]. 经济研究 [Economics Studies], no. 3 (1995), pp. 35–39.

Tong Huaizhou (童怀周), ed. 天安门诗抄 [The Tiananmen Poems]. Beijing: 人民文学, 1978.

Wang Nianyi (王年一). 大动乱的年代 [Years of Great Turmoil]. Zhengzhou: 河南人民, 1988.

Wang Shaoguang (王紹光). 超凡領袖的挫敗: 文化大革命在武漢 [The Failure of a Superior Leader: The Cultural Revolution in Wuhan]. Hong Kong: 中文大學, 2009.

Wang Shuo (王硕). "逃港潮与相关政策变迁" [The Waves of People Fleeing to Hong Kong and Related Policy Changes]. 炎黄春秋 [China through the Ages], no. 1 (2011).

Wang Taiping (王泰平) et al. 中华人民共和国外交史, 1970–1978 [The Diplomatic History of the People's Republic of China, 1970–1978]. Beijing: 世界知识, 1999.

Wang Taiping (王泰平) et al. 当代中国使节外交生涯 [The Diplomatic Career of Contemporary Chinese Envoys]. Beijing: 世界知识, 1996.

Wang Taiping (王泰平) et al. 中华人民共和国外交史, 1957–1969 [The Diplomatic History of the People's Republic of China, 1957–1969]. Beijing: 世界知识, 1994.

Wang Yan (王焰) et al., eds. 彭德怀传 [A Biography of Peng Dehuai]. Beijing: 当代中国, 1993.

Wei Se (唯色). 殺劫—不可碰觸的記憶禁區: 鏡頭下的西藏文革,第一次披露 [Massacre: The Untouchable Forbidden Zone in Memory, Scenes of the Cultural Revolution in Tibet, The First Disclosure]. Taipei: 大塊文化, 2016.

Wen Yong (温勇). "邓小平的时间表与时间观" [Deng Xiaoping's Timetable and Concept of Time]. 党的文献 [Party History Documents], no. 4 (2012).

Wu Li (武力), ed. 中华人民共和国经济史, 1949–1999 [The Economic History of the People's Republic of China, 1949–1999]. Beijing: 中国经济, 1999.

Wu Qingtong (吴庆彤). 周恩来在文化大革命中 [Zhou Enlai in the Cultural Revolution]. Beijing: 中共党史, 2002.

Wu Qiong (吴琼). "岁月的歌—数理化自学丛书重版前后" [Song of the Era: The Republication of the "Series on Mathematics, Physics and Chemistry"]. 档案春秋 [Memories and Archives], no. 1 (2015).

Wu Xiang (吴象). "胡耀邦与万里在农村改革中" [Hu Yaobang and Wan Li in Rural Reforms]. 炎黄春秋 [China through the Ages], no. 7 (2001).

Wu Xiaobo (吴晓波). 激荡三十年: 中国企业, *1978–2008 (上)* [Thirty Years of Chinese Enterprises, 1978–2008]. Vol. 1. Beijing: 中信, 2008.

Xiao Donglian (蕭冬連). *歷史的轉軌: 從撥亂反正到改革開放, 1979–1981* [Historical Shifts: From Setting Things Right to the Reform and Opening, 1979–1981]. Hong Kong: 中文大學, 2008.

Xiao Donglian (萧冬连). *求索中国: "文革"前10年的历史* [In Search of China's Path Forward: Ten Year History before the Cultural Revolution]. Vol. 2. Beijing: 红旗, 1999.

Xiao Donglian (萧冬连). "一九七九年至一九八一年的经济调整研究" [A Study of the Economic Adjustment in 1979–1981]. 中共党史研究 [CCP History Studies], no. 9 (2015).

Xie Jian (谢健). "区域经济国际化: 珠三角模式、苏南模式、温州模式的比" [Internationalization of Regional Economies: A Comparison of Pearl Delta Model, the Sunan Model, and the Wenzhou Model]. 经济理论与经济管理 [Economic Theory and Economic Management], no. 10 (2006).

Xin Wang (新望) and Liu Qihong (刘奇洪). "苏南、温州、珠江模式之反思" [Reflection on the Sunan, Wenzhou, and Pear River Models]. 中国国情国力 [China's National Situation and National Power], no. 7 (2001).

Xiong Jingming (熊景明), Song Yongyi (宋永毅), and Yu Guoliang (余國良), eds. 中外學者談文革 [Chinese and Foreign Scholars on the Cultural Revolution]. Hong Kong: 中文大學, 2018.

Xiong Lei (熊蕾). "1976年华国锋和叶剑英怎样联手的" [How Hua Guofeng and Ye Jianying Joined Force in 1976]. 炎黄春秋 [China through the Ages], no. 10 (2008).

Xiong Xianghui (熊向晖). "打开中美关系的前奏—1969年四位老帅对国际形势研究和建议的前前后后" [Prelude to Opening of U.S.-China Relations: Four Marshals' Study on and Suggestions about the International Situation in 1969]. 中共党史资料 [CCP History Materials], no. 42 (1992).

Xu Miaozhong (徐淼忠). "深圳特区的居民消费结构及其发展趋势" [The Consumption Structure of Residents in Shenzhen Special Economic Zone and Its Development Trend]. 消费经济 [Consumer Economy], no. 1 (1986).

Xu Qingquan (徐庆全) and Du Mingming (杜明明). "包产到户提出过程中的高层争论: 访国家农业委员会原副主任杜润生" [Disputes among Top Leaders during the Introduction of Linking Output with Household Incomes: Interview with former Director of State Agricultural Committee du Runsheng]. 炎黄春秋 [China through the Ages], no. 11 (2008).

Xu Yan (徐焰). "1969 年中苏边界的武装冲突" [Chinese-Soviet Border Clash of 1969]. 党史研究资料 [Party History Research Materials], no. 5 (1994), pp. 6–9.

Xu Yan (徐焰). 北戴河往事追踪报告 [A Summary Report on Past Events at Beidaihe]. Beijing: 中央文献, 2010.

Xu Zehao (徐泽浩), ed. 王稼祥传 [A Biography of Wang Jiaxiang]. Beijing: 当代中国, 2006.

Xu Zhiyuan (许知远). "流亡的里程碑" [A Milestone of Exile]. *FT中文网* [Financial Times Chinese], February 13, 2014. https://ftchinese.com/story/001054805?full=y&archive.

Xue Qingchao (薛庆超). 毛泽东南方决策 [Mao Zedong's Decision Making in the South]. Beijing: 华文, 2013.

Yang Jisheng (楊繼繩). 中國改革年代的政治鬥爭 [China's Political Struggles in the Years of Reform and Opening]. Hong Kong: 特區文化, 2004.

Yang Jisheng (楊繼繩). 天地翻覆: 中國文化大革命史 [The World Turned Upside Down: A History of the Chinese Cultural Revolution]. Hong Kong: 天地圖書, 2016.

Yang Kuisong (杨奎松). "新中国镇反运动始末" [The Full Story of the Suppression of Reactionaries Campaign in New China], part II. 江淮文史 [Jianghuai History and Literature], no. 2 (2011).

Yang Kuisong (杨奎松). 中华人民共和国建国史 [A History of the Creation of the People's Republic of China]. Nanchang: 江西人民, 2009.

Yang Shengqun (杨胜群) et al. 邓小平传, 1904–1974 [A Biography of Deng Xiaoping, 1904–1974]. Beijing: 中央文献, 2014.

Yang Xiaokai (杨小凯). 百年中国经济史笔记 [Notes on the History of Chinese Economy in the Past One Hundred Years]. Beijing: 东方, 2016.

Yang Xuewei (杨学为) and Fan Kening (樊克宁). "恢复高考: 历史记住这条脉络" [Resuming College Entry Exams: History Remembers This Development]. 羊城晚报 [Guangzhou Evening News], June 16, 2007.

Yang Zhongmei (杨中美). 胡耀邦传略 [A Short Biography of Hu Yaobang]. Beijing: 新华, 1989.

Yin Hongbiao (印紅標). 失蹤者的足跡: 文化大革命期間的青年思潮 [The Footprints of the Missing: The Trends of Youth Thought during the Cultural Revolution]. Hong Kong: 中文大學, 2009.

Zeng Zhaohua (曾昭华). 柳传志如是说 [Liu Chuanzhi Tells His Own Story This Way]. Beijing: 中国经济, 2008.

Zhang Guangyou (张广友) and Han Gang (韩钢) "万里谈农村改革是怎么搞起来的" [Wan Li Discusses How Reform Began in the Countryside]. 百年潮 [One Hundred Year Tide], no. 3 (1998).

Zhang Hua (张化). "邓小平与1975年铁路整顿" [Deng Xiaoping and 1975 Railway Rectification]. 百年潮 [One Hundred Year Tide], no. 8 (2014).

Zhang Hua (张化). "1978年中央工作会议若干问题研究" [A Study on Several Questions Concerning the Central Work Conference of 1978]. 史学月刊 [Journal of Historical Science], no. 1 (2012).

Zhang Liqun (张黎群), Zhang Ding (张定), Yan Ruping (严如平), and Li Gongtian (李公天). 胡耀邦 (1915–1989) [Hu Yaobang, 1915–1989]. Beijing: 北京联合出版公司, 2015.

Zhang Liqun (张黎群), Zhang Ding (張定), Yan Ruping (嚴如平), and Li Gongtian (李公天), eds. 懷念耀邦 [Remembering Yaobang]. Hong Kong: 亞太國際, 2001.

Zhang Shunqing (张顺清). "谭厚兰曲阜'讨孔'纪实" [A Factual Account of Tan Houlan "Attacking Confucius" in Qufu]. 炎黄春秋 [China through the Ages], no. 2 (2015).

Zhang Songjia (张颂甲). "阎仲川与一号令" [Yan Zhongchuan and Order Number One]. 炎黄春秋 [China through the Ages], no. 9 (2015).

Zhang Suhua (张素华). 变局: 七千人大会始末 [Changing Scenarios: The Beginning and End of the Seven-Thousand-Cadres Conference]. Beijing: 中国青年, 2006.

Zhao Wei (赵蔚). 赵紫阳传 [A Biography of Zhao Ziyang]. Beijing: 中国新闻, 1989.

Zhen Shi (甄石). "胡耀邦在中央党校" [Hu Yaobang at Central Party School]. 党史博览 [Broad Survey of Party History], no. 7 (2010).

Zheng Shanlong (郑善龙). "从东京审判到审判'四人帮'" [From the Tokyo Trial to the Trial of the "Gang of Four"]. 世纪 [Century], no. 3 (2007).

Zheng Zhong (鄭重). 張春橋: 1949及其後 [Zhang Chunqiao: 1949 and After]. Hong Kong: 中文大學, 2017.

Zhong Yanlin (鐘延麟). 文革前的鄧小平 [Deng Xiaoping before the Cultural Revolution]. Hong Kong: 中文大學, 2013.

Zhou Jingqing (周敬青). 解读林彪 [Interpreting Lin Biao]. Shanghai: 上海人民, 2015.

Zhu Bing (朱斌). "我国建国初期对女性人力资源的开发" [Development of Female Human Resources in the Early Days of the People's Republic]. 唐山师范学院学报 [Journal of Tangshan Teachers College] 29, no. 3 (May 2007).

Zhu Jiamu (朱佳木). "改革开放初期的陈云与邓小平" [Chen Yun and Deng Xiaoping in the Early Days of Reform and Opening-up]. 当代中国史研究 [Contemporary Chinese History Studies], no. 3 (2010), pp. 4–15.

Zhu Wenyi (朱文轶). "李经纬事件调查" [Invesgating the Li Jingwei Case]. 三联生活周刊 [Life Weekly], no. 43 (2002). https://www.lifeweek.com.cn/article/46795.

Zhu Yu (朱玉) et al. 李先念传, 1949–1992 [A Biography of Li Xiannian, 1949–1992]. Vol. 2. Beijing: 中央文献, 2009.

Zhu Zheng (朱正). 一九五七年的夏季: 从百家争鸣到两家争鸣 [Summer 1957: From Competition among Hundred Schools to Competition between Two Schools]. Zhengzhou: 河南人民, 1998.

Zhuo Renzheng (卓人政). "云南知识青年回城事件与全国知青问题的解决" [The Returning to City Incident of Yunnan's Educated Youth and the Settlement of the Educated Youth Problem in the Whole Country]. 中共党史资料 [CCP History Materials], no. 1 (2009), pp. 149–154.

Zong Fuxian (宗福先). 于无声处 [In a Land of Silence]. Shanghai: 上海文艺, 1978.

Zou Yimin (邹一民). "1975–76年外交部的批邓、反击右倾翻案风" [Criticizing Deng and Countering the Rightist Reversal Wind in the Ministry of Foreign Affairs in 1975–76]. www.hybsl.cn/beijingcankao/beijingfenxi/2016-05-10/58760.html (胡耀邦史料资讯网), accessed August 15, 2022.

Other Sources in Western Languages

Bartel, Fritz. *The Triumph of Broken Promises: The End of the Cold War and the Rise of Neoliberalism*. Cambridge, MA: Harvard University Press, 2022.

Baum, Emily. "Enchantment in an Age of Reform: Fortune-Telling Fever in Post-Mao China, 1980s–1990s." *Past & Present* 251, no. 1 (May 1, 2021), pp. 229–261.

Bonnin, Michel. *The Lost Generation: The Rustication of China's Educated Youth (1968–1980)*. Hong Kong: Chinese University Press, 2013.

Bramall, Chris. *Chinese Economic Development*. Abingdon, UK: Routledge, 2009.

Bramall, Chris. "A Late Maoist Industrial Revolution? Economic Growth in Jiangsu Province (1966–1978)." *China Quarterly*, no. 240 (December 2019), pp. 1039–1065.

Brodsgaard, Kjeld Erik. "The Democracy Movement in China, 1978–1979: Opposition Movements, Wall Poster Campaigns, and Underground Journals." *Asian Survey* 21, no. 7 (1981), pp. 747–774.

Brown, Jeremy, and Matthew D. Johnson, eds. *Maoism at the Grassroots: Everyday Life in China's Era of High Socialism.* Cambridge, MA: Harvard University Press, 2015.

Brown, Kerry. *The Purge of the Inner Mongolian People's Party in the Chinese Cultural Revolution, 1967–69.* Kent, CT: Global Oriental, 2006.

Bulag, Uradyn Erden. "The Cult of Ulanhu in Inner Mongolia: History, Memory, and the Making of National Heroes." *Central Asian Survey* 17, no. 1 (1998), pp. 11–33.

Cai, Yong, and Feng Wang. "The Social and Sociological Consequences of China's One-Child Policy." *Annual Review of Sociology* 47 (July 2021), pp. 587–606.

Chan, Anita, Richard Madsen, and Jonathan Unger. *Chen Village: Revolution to Globalization.* 3rd ed. Berkeley: University of California Press, 2009.

Chang, Gene, Shenke Yang, and Kathryn Chang. "The Immiserizing Growth during the Period of China's Cultural Revolution." *Chinese Economy* 51, no. 5 (October 9, 2018), pp. 387–396.

Chang, Jung, and Jon Halliday. *Mao: The Unknown Story.* New York: Knopf, 2005.

Chen, Chih-Jou Jay. *Transforming Rural China: How Local Institutions Shape Property Rights in China.* London: Routledge, 2012.

Chen Jian. "China's Involvement in the Vietnam War, 1964–69." *China Quarterly,* no. 142 (June 1995), pp. 356–387.

Chen Jian. *China's Road to the Korean War: The Making of the Sino-American Confrontation.* New York: Columbia University Press, 1994.

Chen Jian. *Mao's China and the Cold War.* Chapel Hill: University of North Carolina Press, 2001.

Chen Jian. *Zhou Enlai: A Life.* Cambridge, MA: Belknap Press of Harvard University Press, 2024.

Chen Jian et al., eds. *The Routledge Handbook of the Global Sixties: Between Protest and Nation-Building.* New York: Routledge, 2018.

Cheng, Shi. *China's Rural Industrialization Policy Growing under Orders since 1949.* Basingstoke, UK: Palgrave Macmillan, 2006.

Cheng, Tiejun, and Mark Selden. "The Origins and Social Consequences of China's Hukou System." *China Quarterly,* no. 139 (September 1994), pp. 644–668.

Cheng, Yinghong. "Sino-Cuban Relations during the Early Years of the Castro Regime (1959–1966)." *Journal of Cold War Studies* 9, no. 3 (Summer 2007), pp. 78–114.

Chin Peng (陳平). *My Side of History: Recollections of the Guerrilla Leader Who Waged a 12-Year Anti-Colonial War against Britain and Commonwealth Forces in the Jungles of Malaya.* Singapore: Media Masters, 2003.

Coderre, Laurence. "A Necessary Evil: Conceptualizing the Socialist Commodity under Mao." *Comparative Studies in Society and History* 61, no. 1 (January 2019).

Coderre, Laurence. *Newborn Socialist Things: Materiality in Maoist China.* Durham, NC: Duke University Press, 2021.

Cook, Alexander C., ed. *Mao's Little Red Book: A Global History.* Cambridge: Cambridge University Press, 2014.

Dikötter, Frank. *The Cultural Revolution: A People's History, 1962–1976.* New York: Bloomsbury, 2016.

Dikötter, Frank. *Tragedy of Liberation: A History of the Chinese Revolution, 1945–1957.* London: Bloomsbury, 2013.

Dittmer, Lowell. *Liu Shaoqi and the Cultural Revolution.* New York: Routledge, 2015.

Duan Ruodi. "Solidarity in Three Acts: Narrating US Black Freedom Movements in China, 1961–66." *Modern Asian Studies* 53, no. 5 (September 2019), pp. 1351–1380.

Eley, Geoff. "Defining Social Imperialism: Use and Abuse of an Idea." *Social History* 1, no. 3 (1976), pp. 265–290.

Ferguson, Niall, et al., eds. *The Shock of the Global: The 1970s in Perspective.* Cambridge, MA: Belknap Press of Harvard University Press, 2010.

Forster, Keith. "The Politics of Destabilization and Confrontation: The Campaign against Lin Biao and Confucius in Zhejiang Province, 1974." *China Quarterly,* no. 107 (1986), pp. 433–462.

"Fortune Global 500 List of 2019." https://fortune.com/global500/2019/, accessed June 1, 2022.

Frazier, Robeson Taj. *The East Is Black: Cold War China in the Black Radical Imagination.* Durham, NC: Duke University Press, 2014.

Gamble, Jos. *Shanghai in Transition: Changing Perspectives and Social Contours of a Chinese Metropolis.* London: Routledge, 2005.

Gerth, Karl. *Unending Capitalism: How Consumerism Negated China's Communist Revolution.* Cambridge: Cambridge University Press, 2020.

Gewirtz, Julian. "The Futurists of Beijing: Alvin Toffler, Zhao Ziyang, and China's 'New Technological Revolution,' 1979–1991." *Journal of Asian Studies* 78, no. 1 (February 2019), pp. 115–140.

Gewirtz, Julian B. *Never Turn Back: China and the Forbidden History of the 1980s.* Cambridge, MA: Belknap Press of Harvard University Press, 2022.

Gewirtz, Julian B. *Unlikely Partners: Chinese Reformers, Western Economists, and the Making of Global China.* Cambridge, MA: Harvard University Press, 2017.

Hamilton, Peter E. *Made in Hong Kong: Transpacific Networks and a New History of Globalization.* New York: Columbia University Press, 2021.

Hamilton, Peter E. "Rethinking the Origins of China's Reform Era: Hong Kong and the 1970s Revival of Sino-US Trade." *Twentieth-Century China* 43, no. 1 (January 2018), pp. 67–88.

Harder, Anton. "Defining Independence in Cold War Asia: Sino-Indian Relations, 1949–1962." PhD thesis, London School of Economics and Political Science, 2015.

He Honggang. *Governance, Social Organisation and Reform in Rural China: Case Studies from Anhui Provice.* New York: Palgrave Macmillan, 2015.

Heilmann, Sebastian. "The Social Context of Mobilization in China: Factions, Work Units, and Activists during the 1976 April Fifth Movement." *China Information* 8 (1993), pp. 1–19.

Heilmann, Sebastian. *Turning Away from the Cultural Revolution: Political Grass-Roots Activism in the Mid-Seventies.* Occasional Paper 28. Stockholm: Center for Pacific Asia Studies, Stockholm University, 1996.

Ingleson, Elizabeth O'Brien. "The End of Isolation: Rapprochement, Globalisation, and Sino-American Trade, 1972–1978." PhD thesis, University of Sydney, 2017.

Kelly, Jason M. *Market Maoists: The Communist Origins of Chinese Capitalist Ascent.* Cambridge, MA: Harvard University Press, 2021.

Khan, Sulmaan Wasif. *Haunted by Chaos: China's Grand Strategy from Mao Zedong to Xi Jinping.* Cambridge, MA: Harvard University Press, 2018.

Khan, Sulmaan Wasif. *Muslim, Trader, Nomad, Spy: China's Cold War and the People of the Tibetan Borderlands.* Chapel Hill: University of North Carolina Press, 2015.

Kissinger, Henry. *White House Years.* New York: Little, Brown, 1978.

Kraay, Aart. "Household Saving in China." *World Bank Economic Review*, 2000, table A-II.

Kraus, Charles. "More than Just a Soft Drink: Coca-Cola and China's Early Reform and Opening." *Diplomatic History* 43, no. 1 (2019), pp. 107–129.

Lai, Stanislaus Ding-kee. "A Historical Review of Smuggling in Hong Kong." Doctoral thesis, University of Hong Kong, 1995.

Lee, Kuan Yew. *From Third World to First: The Singapore Story, 1965–2000.* New York: HarperCollins, 2000.

Leese, Daniel. *Mao Cult: Rhetoric and Ritual in China's Cultural Revolution.* Cambridge: Cambridge University Press, 2011.

Leese, Daniel. *Maos Langer Schatten: Chinas Umgang mit der Vergangenheit* [Mao's Long Shadow: China's Treatment of the Past]. Munich: C. H. Beck, 2020.

Li, Huaiyin. "Worker Performance in State-Owned Factories in Maoist China: A Reinterpretation." *Modern China* 42, no. 4 (2016), pp. 377–414.

Lim, Kean Fan, and Niv Horesh. "The 'Singapore Fever' in China: Policy Mobility and Mutation." *China Quarterly*, no. 228 (December 2016), pp. 992–1017.

Lim, Louisa. *The People's Republic of Amnesia: Tiananmen Revisited.* New York: Oxford University Press, 2014.

Lin, Chun (林春). *The Transformation of Chinese Socialism.* Durham, NC: Duke University Press, 2006.

Lin Qianhan. "'Rustication': Punishment or Reward? Study of the Life Trajectories of the Generation of the Cultural Revolution." PhD diss., University of Oxford, 2012.

Liu Huixian, George W. Housner, Xie Lili, and He Duxin. "The Great Tangshan Earthquake of 1976." EARL Report 2002-001. Pasadena: California Institute of Technology, 2002.

Lovell, Julia. "The Cultural Revolution and Its Legacies in International Perspective." *China Quarterly*, no. 227 (2016), pp. 632–652.

Lovell, Julia. *Maoism: A Global History.* New York: Knopf, 2019.

Lowell, Dittmer. "Death and Transfiguration: Liu Shaoqi's Rehabilitation and Contemporary Chinese Politics." *Journal of Asian Studies*, no. 3 (1981), pp. 455–479.

Lüthi, Lorenz M., ed. *The Sino-Indian War of 1962: New Perspectives.* London: Routledge, 2017.

MacFarquhar, Roderick, and John K. Fairbank, eds. *Cambridge History of China.* Vol. 14: *The People's Republic, Part 1, The Emergence of Revolutionary China, 1949–1965.* Cambridge: Cambridge University Press, 1987.

MacFarquhar, Roderick, and Michael Schoenhals. *Mao's Last Revolution*. Cambridge, MA: Belknap Press of Harvard University Press, 2006.

Marukawa, Tomoo. "Bilateral Trade and Trade Frictions between China and Japan, 1972–2012." *Eurasian Geography and Economics* 53, no. 4 (2012), pp. 442–456.

Marx, Karl. *The Grundrisse*. Edited and translated by David McLellan. New York: Harper & Row, 1971.

Maxwell, Neville. *India's China War*. New York: Pantheon Books, 1970.

Meisner, Maurice. *Mao's China and After: A History of the People's Republic*. New York: Free Press, 1999.

Meyskens, Covell F. *Mao's Third Front: The Militarization of Cold War China*. Cambridge: Cambridge University Press, 2020.

Millwood, Pete. *Improbable Diplomats: How Ping-Pong Players, Musicians, and Scientists Remade US-China Relations*. Cambridge: Cambridge University Press, 2022.

Nathan, Andrew J. *Chinese Democracy*, New York: Knopf, 1985.

Naughton, Barry. *The Chinese Economy: Transitions and Growth*. Cambridge, MA: MIT Press, 2007.

Naughton, Barry J. "The Third Front: Defence Industrialization in the Chinese Interior." *China Quarterly*, no. 115 (September 1988), pp. 351–386.

Nixon, Richard M. *Memoirs of Richard Nixon*. New York: Grosset & Dunlap, 1978.

Oi, Jean Chun, and Andrew Walder, eds. *Property Rights and Economic Reform in China*. Stanford, CA: Stanford University Press, 1999.

Onjo, Akio, ed. *Power Relations, Situated Practices, and the Politics of the Commons: Japanese Contributions to the History of Geographical Thought*. Fukuoka: Kyushu University, 2017.

Palmer, James. *Heaven Cracks, Earth Shakes: The Tangshan Earthquake and the Death of Mao's China*. New York: Basic Books, 2011.

Pantsov, Alexander V., and Steven I. Levine. *Deng Xiaoping: A Revolutionary Life*. Oxford: Oxford University Press, 2015.

Perlez, Jane, and Grace Tatter. "The Great Wager." https://www.wbur.org/hereandnow/2022/02/18/great-wager-spy-soviet-union, accessed February 1, 2023.

Perry, Elizabeth J., and Li Xun. *Proletarian Power: Shanghai in the Cultural Revolution*. Boulder, CO: Westview Press, 1997.

Pollay, Richard W., David K. Tse, and Zheng-yuan Wang. "Advertising, Propaganda, and Value Change in Economic Development: The New Culture Revolution in China and Attitudes toward Advertising." *Journal of Business Research* 20, no. 2 (1990), pp. 83–95.

Poonkham, Jittipat. *A Genealogy of Bamboo Diplomacy: The Politics of Thai Détente with Russia and China*. Canberra: Australian National University Press, 2022.

Retief, Francois, and André Wessels. "Mao Tse-tung (1893–1976)—His Habits and His Health." *South African Medical Journal* 99, no. 5 (May 2009), pp. 302–305.

Roberts, Priscilla, and Odd Arne Westad, eds. *China, Hong Kong, and the Long 1970s: Global Perspectives*. London: Palgrave Macmillan, 2017.

Sargent, Daniel J. *A Superpower Transformed: The Remaking of American Foreign Relations in the 1970s*. Oxford: Oxford University Press, 2015.

Schoenhals, Michael. "The Central Case Examination Group, 1966–79." *China Quarterly*, no. 145 (March 1996), pp. 101–102.

Schoenhals, Michael. "Doing PRC Social History: On Research Methods, Sex, and the Decomposition of Paper." Working paper, Lund University, 2004.

Schoenhals, Michael. *Doing Things with Words in Chinese Politics: Five Studies*. Berkeley: Institute of East Asian Studies, University of California, 1992.

Schoenhals, Michael. "The 1978 Truth Criterion Controversy." *China Quarterly*, no. 126 (1991), pp. 243–268.

Schram, Stuart R. *Mao Tse-tung*. London: Penguin Books, 1967.

Shan, Patrick Fuliang. "Becoming Loyal: General Xu Shiyou and Maoist Regimentation." *American Journal of Chinese Studies* 18, no. 2 (2011), pp. 133–150.

Shen Zhihua and Xia Yafeng. *Mao and the Sino-Soviet Partnership, 1945–1959: A New History*. Lanham, MD: Lexington Books, 2015.

Shen Xinshu and Zhao Fuyuan. "Audience Reaction to Commercial Advertising in China in the 1980s." *International Journal of Advertising* 14, no. 4 (1995), pp. 374–390.

Short, Philip. *Pol Pot: The History of a Nightmare*. London: John Murray, 2004.

Sun, Warren, and Frederick C. Teiwes. *Paradoxes of Post-Mao Rural Reform: Initial Steps toward a New Chinese Countryside, 1976–1981*. New York: Routledge, 2016.

Talley, Christian. *Forgotten Vanguard: Informal Diplomacy and the Rise of United States–China Trade, 1972–1980*. Notre Dame, IN: University of Notre Dame Press, 2018.

Taylor, Jeffrey R., and Karen A. Hardee. *Consumer Demand in China: A Statistical Factbook*. Boulder, CO: Westview Press, 1986.

Teiwes, Frederick C., and Warren Sun. "China's New Economic Policy under Hua Guofeng: Party Consensus and Party Myths." *China Journal*, no. 66 (July 1, 2011), pp. 1–24.

Teiwes, Frederick C., and Warren Sun. *The End of the Maoist Era: Chinese Politics during the Twilight of the Cultural Revolution, 1972–1976*. Armonk, NY: M. E. Sharpe, 2008.

Teiwes, Frederick C., and Warren Sun. "Hua Guofeng, Deng Xiaoping, and Reversing the Verdict on the 1976 'Tiananmen Incident.'" *China Review* 19, no. 4 (2019), pp. 85–124.

Thai, Philip. *China's War on Smuggling: Law, Economic Life, and the Making of the Modern State, 1842–1965*. New York: Columbia University Press, 2018.

Torigian, Joseph. *Prestige, Manipulation, and Coercion: Elite Power Struggles in the Soviet Union and China after Stalin and Mao*. New Haven, CT: Yale University Press, 2022.

Towson, Jeffrey Alan, and Jonathan R. Woetzel. *The 1 Hour China Book: Two Peking University Professors Explain All of China Business in Six Short Stories*. Cayman Islands: Towson Group, 2017.

Van der Linden, Frank. *The Real Reagan: What He Believes; What He Has Accomplished; What We Can Expect from Him*. New York: William Morrow, 1981.

Vogel, Ezra. *China and Japan: Facing History*. Cambridge, MA: Harvard University Press, 2019.

Vogel, Ezra. *Deng Xiaoping and the Transformation of China*. Cambridge, MA: Belknap Press of Harvard University Press, 2011.

Vogel, Ezra F. *One Step ahead in China: Guangdong under Reform 1990*. Cambridge, MA: Harvard University Press, 1990.

Walder, Andrew G. *Agents of Disorder: Inside China's Cultural Revolution.* Cambridge, MA: Harvard University Press, 2019.

Walder, Andrew G. "Bending the Arc of Chinese History: The Cultural Revolution's Paradoxical Legacy." *China Quarterly,* no. 227 (September 2016), pp. 613–631.

Wang Fei-Ling. *Organizing through Division and Exclusion: China's Hukou System.* Stanford, CA: Stanford University Press, 2005.

Wang Hui. *The End of the Revolution: China and the Limits of Modernity.* London: Verso, 2011.

Wang Shaoguang. *Failure of Charisma: The Cultural Revolution in Wuhan.* Hong Kong: Oxford University Press, 1995.

Weitzman, M. L., and C. Xu. "Chinese Township-Village Enterprises as Vaguely Defined Cooperatives." *Journal of Contemporary Economics* 18, no. 2 (1994), pp. 121–145.

Westad, Odd Arne. *Restless Empire: China and the World since 1750.* New York: Basic Books, 2012.

World Bank. "China's Annual GDP Growth Rate." https://data.worldbank.org.cn/indicator/NY.GDP.MKTP.KD.ZG?locations=CN, accessed April 10, 2023.

Xu Guanghua and Wu Jianguo. "Social-Ecological Transformations of Inner Mongolia: A Sustainability Perspective." *Ecological Processes* 5, no. 23 (2016). https://doi.org/10.1186/s13717-016-0067-z.

Yan Jiaqi and Gao Gao. *Turbulent Decade: A History of the Cultural Revolution.* Honolulu: University of Hawai'i Press, 1996.

Yang, Guobin. *The Red Guard Generation and Political Activism in China.* New York: Columbia University Press, 2016.

Ye Min. "Policy Learning or Diffusion: How China Opened to Foreign Direct Investment." *Journal of East Asian Studies* 9, no. 3 (2009): 399–432.

Ying Bai and James Kai-sing Kung. "The Shaping of an Institutional Choice: Weather Shocks, the Great Leap Famine, and Agricultural Decollectivization in China." *Explorations in Economic History* 54 (October 2014), pp. 1–26.

Zhang Qi and Liu Mingxing. *Revolutionary Legacy, Power Structure, and Grassroots Capitalism under the Red Flag in China.* Cambridge: Cambridge University Press, 2019.

Zhang Xiaoming. *Deng Xiaoping's Long War: The Military Conflict between China and Vietnam, 1979–1991.* Chapel Hill: University of North Carolina Press, 2015.

Zhong Yanlin. "The CEO of the Utopian Project: Deng Xiaoping's Roles and Activities in the Great Leap Forward." *China Journal,* no. 69 (2013), pp. 154–173.

Zhong Yanlin. "The Unknown Standard-Bearer of the Three Red Banners: Peng Zhen's Roles in the Great Leap Forward." *China Journal,* no. 74 (2015): 129–143.

Zhong Yanlin. "The Witch-Hunting Vanguard: The Central Secretariat's Roles and Activities in the Anti-Rightist Campaign." *China Quarterly,* no. 206 (June 2011), pp. 391–411.

Zhou Dong. "Understanding the Long Term Impacts of the Critical Historic Event: The Cultural Revolution in China." PhD diss., University of California, Riverside, 2014.

Zhu Dandan. *1956: Mao's China and the Hungarian Crisis.* Ithaca, NY: Cornell University Press, 2013.

Zubok, Vladislav M. *A Failed Empire: The Soviet Union in the Cold War from Stalin to Gorbachev.* Chapel Hill: University of North Carolina Press, 2009.

INDEX

Page numbers in italics indicate figures.

Afghanistan, 229, 243
Africa, 229, 231
agriculture, 77–78, 190, 205, 253; collectivization of, 13, 14, 253; decollectivization of, 193–194, 263–264; diversification in, 252; family agriculture, 30; grain purchasing regulations, 13–14; mechanization of, 79, 80; modernization of, 126; reform under Hua Guofeng, 191–194, 252; rise of household responsibility system, 264. *See also* grain production
Ai Qing, 16
Ai Weiwei, 16
Albania, 50, 217, 324n45
An Ziwen, 203
Anting Incident, 43–44
Anti-Rightist Campaign, 16, 20, 110, 316n29
Anti–"spiritual pollution" campaign, 278–279, 280
ASEAN (Association of Southeast Asian Nations), 226, 229, 241
August 17, 1982, communique between China and the United States, 242

Baoshan Steel plant (Shanghai), 222–223, *223*
Beidaihe, 69, 71, 72, 298
Beijing, 118, 295
Belt and Road Initiative, 309
"big character posters," 36–37, 41, 209, 210, 322n10
Bo Yibo, 75, 203
Brandt, Willy, 92, 106, 107
Brezhnev, Leonid, 92, 95
Britain, 19, 256, 270; burning of British consulate offices in Beijing, 52; diplomatic relations with PRC, 100; Hong Kong handover negotiations and, 244, 292–293; trade with PRC, 106
Brus, Włodzimierz, 218
Brzezinski, Zbigniew, 231–232, 234, 235
Burma, 181, 197, 276
Bush, George H. W., 93

Cambodia: Khmer Rouge regime, 90, 227, 237–238; U.S. invasion of, 236; Vietnamese invasion/occupation of, 227, 234–235, 241, 243

(1930s), 27, 146; trial of, 259, 260, *261*; Zhou criticized by, 113, 115. *See also* Cultural Revolution; Gang of Four; Politburo Left

Jiang Zemin, 174

Jianlibao (Chinese soft drink), 286, 287

Johnson, Lyndon B., 89

Kang Sheng, 29, 34, 36, 115, 197, 203; in Central Cultural Revolution Group, 34; Cultural Revolution and, 38, 40, 47–48, 51, 56; death of, 133–134; at Ninth Party Congress (1969), *60*

Ke Qingshi, 18

Khmer Rouge, 90, 227, 237–238

Khrushchev, Nikita, 15, 18, 24, 25, 168, 174, 207; Castro compared to, 50; identified with revisionism, 35

Kim Il-sung, 95

King, Martin Luther, Jr., 89

Kissinger, Henry, 87–88, 91, 116, 333n11; first (secret) visit to China, 93–94; Sino-American trade and, 105; trip to China with Nixon, 97, 99

Korea, North (DPRK), 50, 94, 95, 181, 348n44

Korea, South, 98, 309

Korean War, 10–11, 12, 16, 23, 61, 240

Kornai, János, 218, 354n6

Kosygin, Aleksei, 57, 88

labor camps (Laogai), 11, 37, 66, 82, 182, 195; number of inmates in, 67; "re-education through labor," 66

Le Duan, 237, 238

Lee Kuan Yew, 226, 227–229, *228*

Legend (later, Lenovo), 285–286

Lenin, Vladimir, 17, 18, 38, 125, 133, 156

Li Dongmin, 177

Li Fuchun, 26, 76

Li Jingwei, 286–287

Li Shenzhi, 353n1

Li Xiannian, 26, 70, 75, 113, 121, 124, 199, 217, 305; coup against Politburo Left

and, 169; economic reform and, 248–249; at economic theory forum (1978), 223, 224; at Eleventh CCP Congress (1977), *185*, 185; foreign policy issues and, 243; "Gang of Four problem" and, 159, 160; on pace of Deng's reforms, 132; power struggle after Mao's death and, 158

Li Xin, 158–159, 162

Li Zhen, 115

Li Zuopeng, 62, 63

Liao Zhigao, 249

Lin Biao, 33, 100, 110, 119, 133, 213; "conspiracy" of, 168; Cultural Revolution and, *42*, 48, 51, 52–53, 56, 62; death in plane crash, 72–74, 96, 111, 304; emotional instability of, 62, 65; escape plans of, 71–72; glorification of Mao, 64; Great Leap Forward and, 29, 61; as Mao's designated successor, 41, 61; at Ninth Party Congress (1969), 58–59, *60*; and Order Number One (October 1969), 63; "People's War" concept and, 50; PLA and, 68; pressure building against, 68–69, 329n35; suspicion of past links to, 120, 121; as traditional Stalinist, 62

Lin Hujia, 221, 222

Lin Liguo, 52, 62, 70, 71–72, 114

literacy, 11, 14, 46, 301

"little Gang of Four," 254, 359n14

"Little Red Book" (*Quotations from Chairman Mao*), 9, 29, 50

Liu Chuanzhi, 285, 286

Liu Qingtang, 146

Liu Shaoqi, 33, 64, 109, 110, 128, 133; accused of revisionism, 25; as "capitalist roader," 46; "conspiracy" of, 168; Cultural Revolution and, 38, 45; death of, 57; expelled from CCP, 56; Great Leap Forward and, 21–22, 24; posthumous rehabilitation of, 350n33; purge of, 160

Liu Shuqing, 243

Zhou Enlai, 15, 19–20, 58, 125–126, 254; as chief diplomat of PRC, 100; Cultural Revolution and, 40, 42, 48, 52, 56; death of, 123, 134, 135, 158; Deng linked with memory of, 250; forged will of, 145; Four Modernizations and, 26, 219; funeral of, 135–137; Great Leap Forward and, 21; illnesses of, 112, 116, 121, 123, 131; Lin Biao's plane crash and, 72–74; at Ninth Party Congress (1969), 60; Nixon's visit to Beijing and, 97, 97–99; political survival of, 116; popular adu-lation of, 135, 145, 147–148, 148, 176, 203; in Premier position, 20, 317n38; Sino-American rapprochement and, 88–89, 93, 96–97, 111, 333n11; student protest in defense of, 146; Taiwan issue and, 103; Vietnam conflict and, 89, 236

Zhou Quanying, 54
Zhou Rongxin, 143
Zhu De, 56, 278
Zhu Yongjia, 169
Zhuang Zedong, 146
Zong Fuxian, 214